7089
32

Changing Horizons

LUTON SIXTH FORM COLLEGE

-7. APR. 1987	-9. OCT. 1995	
-7. MAY 1987	25. APR. 1997	
	-3. OCT. 1997	
25. JUN. 1987	20. APR. 1998	
10. OCT. 1988	3 0 JAN 2013	
-6. NOV 1989		
-5. NOV 1990		
20 MAR 1995		
SHOULD THIS BE 3 DAY		
25. SEP. 1995		
28. SEP. 1995		

This book is due for return on or before the last date shown above.

3123

Changing Horizons

Britain 1914–80

W. O. Simpson

Stanley Thornes (Publishers) Ltd

©Text W. O. Simpson 1986
©Diagrams ST(P) Ltd. 1986

First published in 1986 by
Stanley Thornes (Publishers) Ltd,
Old Station Drive,
Leckhampton,
CHELTENHAM GL53 0DN

British Library Cataloguing in Publication Data

Simpson, W.
    Britain 1914-80.
    1. Great Britain—History—20th century
    I. Title
    941.082   DA566

    ISBN 0-85950-226-0

Typeset by Grafikon pvba, Oostkamp, Belgium in 11/12 pt Garamond.
Printed and bound in Great Britain at The Bath Press, Avon.

Preface

This book would not have been written without the help of many people. My first debt is to the pupils who presented the challenge to explain and clarify Britain's complex history in the twentieth century. They have been a constant stimulus. I would like to thank in particular my colleague, Dr Martin Jones, for his guidance through the maze of Middle East history, and for allowing me to consult his forthcoming book, *Failure in Palestine;* Mrs Gillian Deadman, for typing the manuscript so promptly and impeccably; and the staff at Stanley Thornes, for their advice, encouragement and scrupulous editing. Above all I would like to thank my wife; not only has she supplied the title and compiled the index, she has cheerfully, if not uncritically, supported me over an apparently endless succession of holidays in which *Changing Horizons* has claimed priority. It is to her and to our three children that this book is dedicated.

William O. Simpson

Acknowledgements

The author and publishers are grateful to the following for permission to reproduce previously published material:

George Allen & Unwin, for extracts from *European Armies and the Conduct of War* by H Strachan, *Realities Behind Deplomacy* by R Kennedy and *Rise of the Anglo-German Antagonism* by P Kennedy;

Edward Arnold, for extracts from *British Appeasement in the 1930s* by W R Rock, *The Development of the British Economy 1914–67* by S Pollard and *The Lost Peace: International Relations in Europe 1918–1939* by A Adamthwaite;

Batsford, for an extract from *The 1945–51 Labour Governments* by R Eatwell;

Basil Blackwell, for an extract from *The Making of Modern Britain* by M Pugh;

Jonathan Cape Ltd, for extracts from *Suez 1956: A Personal Account* by Selwyn Lloyd and *Hugh Gaitskell: A Political Biography* by Philip M Williams;

Chatto and Windus, for an extract from *Germany's Aims in the First World War* by Fritz Fisher;

Collins, for extracts from *The Downfall of the Liberal Party* by T Wilson and *Aneurin Bevan* by M Foot;

Cambridge University Press, for extracts from *British Monetary Policy 1924–31* by Moggridge and *Essays on John Maynard Keynes* edited by Keynes;

Constable Publishers, for an extract from *The Damnable Question* by George Dangerfield;

Andre Deutsch, for an extract from *Politics In An Industrial Society* by Keith Middlemas;

Eyre & Spottiswoode Ltd, for an extract from *The Unknown Prime Minister, Bonar Law* by R Blake;

Victor Gollancz Ltd, for an extract from *The Chamberlain Cabinet* by Ian Colvin;

Hamish Hamilton Ltd, for an extract from *The Origins of The Second World War* by A J P Taylor;

A M Heath & Co Ltd, the estate of the late Sonia Brownwell Orwell and Martin, Secker & Warburg Ltd, for an extract from *The Road to Wigan Pier* by George Orwell;

William Heinemann Ltd, for extracts from *Ernest Bevin, Foreign Secretary* by A Bullock and *As It Happened* by C R Attlee;

David Higham Associates Ltd and Jonathan Cape Ltd, for an extract from *Ramsay MacDonald* by David Marquand;

Lawrence & Wishart Ltd, for an extract from *The Labour Government, 1945–51* by D N Pritt;

Longman, for an extract from *Unemployment in Britain Between the Wars* by S Constantine;

Macmillan, for extracts from *The Life of Neville Chamberlain* by K Feiling, *The Middle Way* by H Macmillan and *The Economic Consequences of Peace* by J M Keynes;

Macmillan Publishing Company, for an extract from *Full Circle* by Sir Anthony Eden;

Martin, Secker & Warburg Ltd, for an extract from *The Tragedy of Ramsay MacDonald* by L MacNeill Weir;

Methuen & Co Ltd, for an extract from *Peacemaking 1919* by H Nicholson;

Oxford University Press, for extracts from *History of Germany* by G A Craig, *English History, 1914–45* by A J P Taylor, *The Letters of H H Asquith to Venetia Stanley* edited by M & E Brock, and *Labour in Power* by K O Morgan;

Weidenfeld & Nicholson, for extracts from *Baldwin* by Middlemas & Barnes, *The Appeasers* by Gilbert & Gott, *Ireland Since the Famine* by F S L Lyons and *The Edwardians* by Thompson.

We also wish to thank the following who provided photographs and gave permission for reproduction:

BBC Hulton Picture Library (pp. 6, 7, 10, 11, 50 (both), 51, 69, 75, 76, 82, 114, 115, 121, 146, 161, 173, 186, 187, 194, 236, 237, 239, 241, 251, 253, 264, 265, 268, 289, 296, 311, 313, 325, 328, 344, 351, 359, 360, 361, 380, 386, 396, 397, 399, 409, 410, 426, 439, 452, 465, 466, 480, 481, 488 and 493)

Bridgeman Art Library (p. 437)
Imperial War Museum (p. 67)
Mansell Collection (pp. 125, 129, 130, 132, 133, 174, 212, 225 and 496)
Popperfoto (p. 389)
Punch (pp. 27, 43, 88, 103, 118, 131, 152, 179, 224, 276, 279 and 290)

Every attempt has been made to contact copyright holders, but we apologise if any have been overlooked.

Contents

Preface   v
Acknowledgements   vii
List of Maps   xiii
List of Time Charts   xiv
Organisation of the Book   xv

Period	CHAPTER CONTENTS	Page
From 1900 to 1918	**Chapter 1: Britain in 1914**	1
	The British Economy	1
	The Political System	8
	The British Empire in 1914	19
	Points at Issue: How Stable was England in 1914?	25
	Further Reading	30
	Chapter 2: Britain and Europe: The Causes of the First World War	32
	The European Background	32
	British Diplomacy 1900–14	40
	The Outbreak of War	46
	Points at Issue: The Nature of German Ambitions	56
	The Reasons for Anglo-German Hostility	57
	British Responsibility for the Outbreak of War in 1914	59
	Further Reading	62
	Chapter 3: Britain and the First World War	63
	Introduction	63
	Military Operations	68
	Naval Operations	82
	The War at Home	86
	Points at Issue: The Western Front	97
	The Effects of War on British Society and Politics	99
	Further Reading	104
	Local Research Project: The Effects of the First World War	104
	Time Chart 1900–18	106

Period	CHAPTER CONTENTS	Page

**From 1918
to 1929**

Chapter 4: Economic and Political Developments 1918–29 108

The Economy 108
Political Developments 113
Points at Issue: The Return to the Gold Standard in 1925 137
Further Reading 139
Local Research Project: The General Strike, 1926 139

Chapter 5: Britain and Europe, 1918–29 141

Peacemaking 141
Anglo-Soviet Relations 155
British Diplomacy 1924–29 159
Points at Issue: The Treaty of Versailles 164
Further Reading 168

Chapter 6: The Problems of Empire, 1914–39 169

The Legacy of War 169
The Irish Tangle 171
Britain and India 184
Britain and The Middle East 192
Empire to Commonwealth 198
Points at Issue: Ulster and the Irish Treaty 201
Further Reading 204

Time Chart 1919–29 205

**From 1929
to 1945**

Chapter 7: The Years of Crisis 1929–31 208

The Economic Background 208
The Political Background 212
Domestic Politics and Policies, June 1929–July 1931 214
The 1931 Crisis and the Fall of the Labour Government 218
Points at Issue: Ramsay MacDonald and the Formation of
the National Government 228
Further Reading 233

**Chapter 8: The British Economy and the National
Government** 234

Introduction 234
The Conditions of the British Economy, 1931–39 234

Living Standards   238
Politics and Policies   241
Opponents and Critics   248
Points at Issue: Public Spending and Unemployment   257
Further Reading   261
Local Research Project: Conditions during the Slump   261

Chapter 9: Britain and the World, 1929–39: The Outbreak of the Second World War   263

The International Background   263
Policy Makers and Policies   269
The MacDonald-Baldwin Era, 1929–37   273
The Chamberlain Years, 1937–39: Austria, Czechoslovakia and Poland   283
The Ending of Appeasement   289
Points at Issue: Appeasement and the Munich Settlement   298
Further Reading   303

Chapter 10: Britain and the Second World War   304

Main Features of the War   304
The European War, 1939–41   310
Britain and the Grand Alliance   317
The British Contribution to Allied Victory, 1941–45   321
Britain and the War against Japan   331
Points at Issue: The Strategic Air Offensive   335
Further Reading   338

British Military, Naval and Air Operations, 1939–45   339

Chapter 11: The War at Home   341

Wartime Politics   341
The War Economy   348
Reconstruction   354
The War and Social Change   360
Further Reading   369
Local Research Project: The Effects of the Second World War   369

Time Chart 1930–45   371

Period	CHAPTER CONTENTS	Page
From 1945 to 1980	**Chapter 12: Conflict and Consensus 1945–79**	375
	Problems and Politics	375
	The Work of the Labour Governments, 1945–51	379
	The Years of Consensus, 1951–70	395
	The Years of Division, 1970–79	408
	Points at Issue: Socialism and the Labour Governments, 1945–51	412
	Further Reading	417
	Local Research Project: 1945–80 Parliamentary Elections, the Welfare State	418
	Chapter 13: Britain and the World, 1945–79	419
	Britain and the Changing Balance of Power	419
	Britain and the Cold War	423
	Britain and Europe	442
	Points at Issue: Marshall Aid and the Cold War	456
	Further Reading	460
	Chapter 14: The Retreat From Empire	461
	The British Empire in 1945	461
	Britain and India	463
	Britain and the Middle East	470
	Decolonisation	483
	The Survival of the Commonwealth	493
	Retrospect and Prospect	498
	Points at Issue: The Suez Crisis, 1956	500
	Further Reading	506
	Time Chart 1945–80	507

List of Maps

	Page
Europe in 1914: Triple Alliance and Triple Entente	37
The Balkans in 1912–13	48
The Western Front: British Zone, June 1916	73
The War in France and Belgium, 1914–18	74
The Gallipoli Campaign, 1915	78
The Mesopotamian Campaigns	80
Germany after the Treaty of Versailles	149
Ireland, 1912–20	181
Ulster's Boundaries, 1925	182
The British Mandate in Palestine	196
Territorial Changes in Western Europe, 1935–39	292
The Mediterranean and the North African Theatre, 1941–43	315
The Site of the Invasion, 1944	329
East Europe in 1945: the Polish Frontier	427
East Europe in 1955: the Warsaw Pact	438
The EEC and EFTA, 1957–61	447
India at Independence, 15 August 1947	469
British or British-protected Territories, showing Dates of Independence or British Departure (inset showing the central part of America)	497

List of Time Charts

1900–18   106
1919–29   205
British Military Naval and Air Operations, 1939–45   339
1930–45   371
1945–80   507

Organisation of the Book

MAIN THEMES

This book attempts to keep in focus four separate themes which can be seen to run through Britain's history in the last seventy years. First are the *changes in the British economy* reflected, for instance, in the disappearance of traditional industries and the emergence of new ones based on different technologies. Despite a rate of growth that was high by historic standards, Britain has also had to accept the loss of the dominant position she once occupied as other countries have reached economic maturity. This change in her economic status has made Britain increasingly vulnerable to fluctuations in the world economy. Her varying economic fortunes are described at different points in the story and they form the background to the political and social changes which make up the second theme, the *progress towards a more egalitarian society*. This is to be seen in the emergence of the Labour party as a party of government; in the steady growth of the welfare state; in the widening of educational opportunities; and in the changes, limited though they may have been, in the distribution of wealth.

Throughout the twentieth century Britain has been closely concerned with Europe. Since the negotiation of the Anglo-French *entente* in 1904 Britain has been inexorably drawn into European affairs. She participated in the First World War, and played an active role in inter-war diplomacy. Britain was the only European country to be at war with Germany throughout the Second World War. At its end she took the lead in building up a system of collective security to meet the threat of Soviet expansion. Though having little to do with the creation of the European Economic Community, Britain applied for membership three times, finally being admitted in January 1973. *Britain's relationship to Europe* is our third theme.

Finally, there is the *dramatic change in Britain's imperial responsibilities*. The British Empire reached its zenith in 1920, when nearly a quarter of the world's population recognised British overlordship in some form or other. By 1965 only a handful of colonies remained and the Empire had been transformed into a Commonwealth. This process forms the fourth theme. The retreat from Empire required a series of adjustments, not always easily accomplished, and it left behind an important legacy in the immigrant communities that grew up in Britain as the imperial flags came down.

While these themes are pursued in separate chapters, it needs always to be remembered that history, in the words of the cliché, is 'a seamless web'. It is all too easy to forget the coincidences that make the work of statesmen so difficult. In 1919, for instance, Lloyd George was grappling with protest movements in Ireland, India and Egypt. He was negotiating the Treaty of Versailles in Paris; and he was having to cope with the problems of demobilisation and industrial unrest in Britain. As a reminder of such complications Time Charts based on the four themes have been included at regular intervals.

CHRONOLOGICAL DIVISIONS

The period is dominated by two traumatic events, the First and Second World Wars. So wide ranging were they in their effects that they have inevitably determined the chronological structure of the book, which is divided into the following periods:

1900–18
1918–29
1929–45
1945–80

1929 has been chosen as a further dividing line for a number of reasons. 1929 was the year of the Wall Street Crash which sparked off the world depression. In Britain this led in turn to the fall of the second Labour government in 1931, a watershed in British political life. Similarly, the Japanese invasion of Manchuria in 1931 marked the first stage in the process of aggression that culminated in the Second World War.

The final part of the book demands a word of explanation. Two limitations need to be born in mind when dealing with the post-war period. In the first place, the thirty-year rule requires all confidential government records to be kept under wraps until thirty years have elapsed. Information from such records, cabinet minutes for example, takes time to filter through. It was only in 1984 that an authoritative account of Ernest Bevin as Foreign Secretary appeared. [Bullock, *Ernest Bevin, Foreign Secretary*] In the second place, the true significance of an event can only be gauged when it is seen in perspective. The Suez Crisis of 1956 is a case in point. Thus much of what is said in the final three chapters may stand in need of revision as more evidence becomes available, and events which loom so large to the contemporary observer may recede into the background with the passage of time.

POINTS AT ISSUE

It is a truism that historians disagree, and this is no less the case when they are confronted with too much evidence rather than too little. While the paucity of evidence about King Arthur allows a wide variety of views to be held on who he was and when he lived, Neville Chamberlain's foreign policy, while fully documented, is just as much a matter of controversy. 'Points at Issue' have been included at the end of most chapters in order to ventilate such disagreements.

The issues in question have been selected on two grounds: for their intrinsic importance, and because they demonstrate how both participants and later commentators can draw opposite conclusions from the same set of facts. It would be wrong to infer, however, that one man's view of the past is as good as the next man's. History should be based on a judicious interpretation of all the evidence available. It is hoped that readers will weigh for themselves the force of the arguments presented, and draw their own conclusions.

SOURCES AND FURTHER READING

The source of quotations will be found in the marginal notes alongside the main text, where author and title are cited (with the publication date for the first reference of each book in every chapter). Full publication details are giving in the reading lists at the end of each chapter. Books for further reading have been divided into two categories: *essential* and *recommended*. The distinction is bound to be an arbitrary one, and is made for the sake of convenience and economy. Books placed in the *essential* category are there either because they reflect recent research or because, in the author's judgment, they are the best and most reliable guides to the subject in question.

Some books, however, are mentioned in the text but are not included in the reading lists; their full publication details are cited in the marginal notes.

The Points at Issue are treated differently: at the end of each one, a complete list of books cited is given.

LOCAL RESEARCH

In recent years there has been a growing emphasis on local history, and in some senses a nation is only the sum of the local communities of which it is made up. Local history may be conceived of in two ways. It may be study of a particular community, town or village studied as a social entity in its own right. An example of such a study would be Le Roy Ladurie's celebrated book, *Montaillou*, an account of a small town in South West France as it was shortly after the Albigensian Crusade. Alternatively, it may be national history 'localised'. There have been many recent studies of English Counties before and during the English Civil War (J. S. Morrill's study of Cheshire, for instance), which fall into the second category. A community is studied for the light which it can shed on national events.

It is local history in the second sense that is our concern here. The purpose of the local research projects suggested is that they should illuminate, amplify and in some cases modify general accounts of national events such as the General Strike. If properly carried through, such projects should also have the benefit of providing opportunities for serious historical research.

Possible areas for investigation have been listed at the end of chapters 3, 4, 8, 11 and 12, together with suggestions for background reading and possible lines of enquiry.

THE BOOK'S PERSPECTIVE

There is an undeniable temptation to think of Britain's history in the twentieth century in terms of decline. As the first country in history to experience an industrial revolution Britain enjoyed a pre-eminent position in the world economy until the final quarter of the nineteenth century. As late as 1889 Britain could still aim to have a navy larger than the combined navies of her two closest rivals. The combination of industrial wealth and maritime supremacy enabled Britain to acquire a huge, if unwieldy Empire.

But power is no indicator of national virtue, or indeed of national greatness. It was Winston Churchill, on reading Seebohm Rowntree's *Poverty*, who remarked: 'For my part, I see little glory in an Empire which can rule the waves and is unable to flush its sewers.' [R. S. Churchill, p. 32] The years of Britain's industrial leadership, armed might and imperial expansion were also years of grim hardship for much of the population. Conversely, as Britain lost her industrial pre-eminence and shed her Empire, living standards improved and opportunities expanded.

The humbler station which Britain came to occupy owed nothing to the loss of Victorian values. It was simply the consequence of changes in the world around her. But if the changes in her horizons were beyond control, Britain's response to them was not. It may be that a quicker and more realistic appreciation of her reduced circumstances would have yielded better results, and that is one of the questions this book raises. It is easy, however, to be wise after the event. After examining the problems facing Britain in the twentieth century the author is more disposed to sympathise with than to criticise those whose responsibility it was to tackle them.

CHAPTER 1

Britain in 1914

A ▬▬▬▬▬▬▬▬▬▬▬ THE BRITISH ECONOMY

In the first half of the nineteenth century Britain could reasonably claim to be the workshop of the world. In 1830, for instance, she produced over three-quarters of Europe's mined coal, half of Europe's cotton and iron, and most of Europe's steam engines. But such a situation could not be expected to last. The industrial revolution in Britain, which gave her such predominance, was followed by similar economic developments in Belgium, France, Germany, Russia and the United States. In 1914 Britain still held more than half the world's trade in cotton goods; British shipbuilders were still producing over half the world's new tonnage; and Britain still had the largest share (31%) of world trade in manufactures. [Thompson, p. 185] But though she produced 287 million tons of coal in 1913, more than she would ever do again, the United States produced 500 million tons in the same year. As early as the 1890s both Germany and the United States exceeded Britain's steel production, which was the basis of most manufacturing industry. Although Britain's rate of economic growth of 2.2% per annum on average between 1870 and 1914 was a faster rate than had been achieved at any period in the industrial revolution it could not prevent her being overtaken by countries with greater natural resources.

There were other worrying signs: in the chemical and electrical industries German technology was by now superior to Britain's; in the production of machinery, Britain's share of world output had fallen to 11.8% by 1913, Germany's had risen to 20.6%; the *Census of Production* for 1907 appeared to show that the American worker was five times as productive as his British counterpart; in 1912 a leader in *The Times* complained of 'obsolete' engineering works in Britain. [Read, p. 119] By 1914 not only had Britain lost her overall lead in the traditional industries but there was also a danger of being overtaken in the newer industries such as chemicals, vehicle manufacture and electrical engineering, in which she had no inherent advantages and no head start. Indeed, it might be argued that precisely because Britain was the first country to experience an industrial revolution she would find it harder to adapt to the changing technologies of the twentieth century. The old staple industries of coal mining, textiles, iron and steel and shipbuilding had been the basis of Britain's prosperity in the past. It would be difficult to accept that they might no longer be so important in the future. One thing was certain. After 1914 Britain faced a world

The Ending of Dominance

P. Thompson, *The Edwardians* (1975)

D. Read, *Edwardian England* (1972)

of intense industrial competition for which her earlier pre-eminence did little to prepare her.

The Pattern of Output and Employment

It was not until the birth of the Central Statistical Office in 1941 that national income, and therefore output, was properly measured. All national income statistics prior to that date have therefore to be treated with a certain degree of caution. In addition, as new products come on to the market and techniques of industrial production change, problems of industrial classification abound. With these *caveats* in mind, it is still possible to make an approximate estimate of Britain's national output in the years before 1914. According to the Census of Industrial Production in 1907 Britain was still heavily dependent on the industries which had grown up during the industrial revolution. In that year mining and manufacturing contributed £750 million towards a total National Income estimated at £2000 million. In order of magnitude, the shares of the largest industries were as follows:

Coal Mining	£106 m
Engineering	£ 50 m
Cotton	£ 45 m
Building and Contracting	£ 43 m
Iron and Steel	£ 31 m
Brewing and Malting	£ 28 m
Clothing	£ 27 m
Shipbuilding	£ 21 m

Of the other main components of National Output, agriculture provided 6.7%, while the service industries made up the remaining 56.8%.

We can be more precise about employment because from 1911 onwards the decennial population census listed the occupations of all British subjects. Of Britain's population of 45 million, 18 million (40%) were in full-time employment; this proportion is not significantly different from that in 1980 when the working population was 25 million (45%) out of a total population of 55 million. However, there have been important changes in the composition of the working population. In 1914 most children left school at 14, and retirement, for those who survived to enjoy it, began at 70. Women made up only 29% of the working population, the majority of them being in domestic service. Today women constitute between 40% and 45% of those employed, more than counter-balancing the effects of raising the school-leaving age to 16, the increase in the student population and the fall in the age of retirement.

Employment is conventionally classified into three groups: primary industry (agriculture, fishing, mining and quarrying); secondary industry (manufacturing and construction) and tertiary industry (banking, retailing, central and local government and domestic service). In 1914 the primary sector accounted for 15% of total employment; a further 38% were employed in the secondary sector; and the tertiary sector accounted for the remaining 47%. The next 60 years were to see a significant fall in the primary sector. Numbers employed in agriculture fell from 1 250 000 in 1911 to 250 000 in 1975; the number of miners, which rose to over 1 million in 1921, fell also to 250 000 by 1975. In the secondary sector there were increases in employment overall up to 1966, but shipbuilding and textiles saw a big reduction in employment. While the tertiary sector also expanded, domestic service, Britain's largest single occupation with 2.6 million employees in 1914, would virtually disappear by 1951. Its place was taken by an increase in public and professional services growing from 1.5 million in 1914, to 3.3 million in 1951.

These changes in occupation were also linked to changes in the location of industry. The first British industrial revolution had been concentrated round Britain's coal fields and iron ore deposits. Industry grew up in the North East and North West of England, in the central lowlands of Scotland and in South Wales. But with the development of 'footloose' manufacturing industry powered by electricity, employment tended to move away from these areas to the Midlands and the South East. Thus changes in the occupational structure of the population were exacerbated by changes in the location of industry. Such changes were the inevitable price of technological progress. But the process of adjustment to the new patterns of employment that took place in Britain after 1914 was bound to impose strains on those affected, and much of the industrial unrest endured by Britain in the inter-war period can be traced to it.

Overseas Trade and Finance

Since the industrial revolution, if not before, Britain has been heavily dependent on foreign trade. The growth in population began to outstrip the increase in food production in about 1800, and since then Britain has been a net importer of foodstuffs. As industrial processes became more complex there was a corresponding increase in the demand for raw materials. By 1914 food and raw materials accounted for about 75% of Britain's total import bill. Imports were largely financed by the export of manufactures, cotton goods alone accounting for 57% of British exports in 1914. There were only three years between 1800 and 1914 when British visible exports exceeded her visible imports, but the difference was made good by the growth in 'invisible' exports. These were provided in two ways: first by the sale of services such as insurance, shipping and tourism; second by the interest payments received on overseas loans and investments. Between 1870 and 1914 a huge amount of British capital went overseas, reaching a total of £4000 million, which exceeded the amount invested at home over the same period. It yielded, on average, £200 million per annum in interest payments, nearly half as much as the £430 million received from visible exports. It may well be that British industry suffered in consequence, but in the meantime Britain's overseas investments enabled her to bridge the gap between exports and imports and insulated British governments from the balance of payments problems that were to be so serious later on.

Another very important feature of the British economy in 1914 was the dominant role of London as a financial centre. Most of the trading countries of the world at this time were on the gold standard, i.e. their currencies had a fixed value in terms of gold. The British sovereign, for instance, was valued at 123.277 47 grains of gold, the United States dollar at 25.8 grains. Thus the pound was worth nearly five times as much as the dollar. Any debts between countries could be settled in gold and it was useful to keep large gold reserves in banks where such transactions could be carried out. As so much of the world's trade was conducted in pounds, London became the world's leading money market. It was here that foreigners came to deposit their surplus funds. Gold imports into Britain amounted to £154 million between

1889 and 1914. It was here, too, that many of the loans needed to float new companies were raised, that the world's ships were insured (through Lloyds) and that commodities such as rubber, wheat and copper were traded. In the long term Britain clearly benefited from all this financial business and it was to be one of the strongest arguments used for keeping the country on the gold standard. But should there be a loss of confidence in the financial health of the British economy or in the country's political stability, the gold reserves would flow out as easily as they had floated in. Britain became increasingly vulnerable to such speculative pressures after the First World War.

The Role of the State

The proper role of the state in relation to the economy was as contentious an issue in 1914 as it is today. One school of thought looked back to Adam Smith, author of the first really systematic book on economics, *The Wealth of Nations*, published in 1776. Smith argued that the economy would function best if left to itself. He visualised society as a network of competing producers and consumers, each pursuing their own best interests. The producers would endeavour to sell as much as they could by making their products as cheaply and as efficiently as possible; the consumers would seek the best value for their money. Prices would reflect consumers' demands and producers' costs, drawing resources to where they could be most usefully employed. The invisible hand of the market would ensure that all wants were satisfied. It followed from Smith's reasoning that the State should confine its activities to the maintenance of law and order, and to external defence. It should interfere neither with prices nor with wages. Smith was equally opposed to any other restraints on the market. He was against tariffs, monopolies, trade unions and employers' organisations.

A. Smith,
The Wealth of Nations (Penguin, 1970)

His views continued to command the support of many writers and politicians, as they still do. But they came under attack from two sources. On the one hand, Tory philanthropists such as Lord Shaftesbury protested at the evils of unfettered competition which led to the employment of children in factories and mines. The tradition of the good landlord, responsible for the welfare of his tenants, became part of the Conservative creed which, under Disraeli, admitted the need for the State to protect all workers against exploitation. On the other hand, radicals of various kinds, ranging from the Lloyd George wing of the Liberal party to fully committed Socialists, attacked the inequalities which resulted from an economy based on the free operation of market forces. Faced with the evidence produced by their own investigations, most Victorian governments in practice adopted a pragmatic rather than a doctrinaire approach to State intervention. Step by step, the State was brought into the regulation of the economy as fresh abuses were discovered and new needs identified. The first effective Factory Act, regulating the hours worked by children in textile mills, was passed in 1833 following the report on the employment of children that Parliament itself commissioned. By 1875 the principle of controlling hours and conditions of work extended to most industries. The urban conditions resulting from rapid industrialisation were ameliorated by Public Health legislation. Between 1851 and 1909, 28 measures relating to housing alone were passed. Primary education was made available to all in 1870, compulsory in 1880 and free in 1891. Under the Balfour Education Act of 1902, local authorities were made responsible for all maintained schools and brought under the overall direction of the Board of Education. The Liberal government that took office in 1905 greatly added to these responsibilities. In 1908 an act was passed to provide Old Age Pensions for all over 70 (5/- for a single person, 7/6d. for a married couple). In 1909 Trades Boards were set up to ensure that adequate wages were paid in the so-called 'sweated' industries, the first to be covered being tailoring, box making, lace making and chain making. These industries accounted for 200 000 workers. In 1911 Lloyd George's National Insurance Act broke new ground. The first part of the Act provided unemployment insurance in certain industries where there was a fluctuating demand for labour, notably shipbuilding, mechanical engineering and iron founding. The second part provided sickness benefit and free medical treatment for a much larger number of workers. The principle underlying both schemes was that they should be self-financing. Benefits would be paid out of a fund to which employees, employers and the State all contributed at rates of 4d. per week, 3d. per week and 2d. per week respectively.

By 1914 it had become generally accepted that the State had a duty to educate its citizens, to ensure that they enjoyed proper working conditions and, in some cases, to see that they were properly paid. Once entered upon, these commitments were bound to expand the role of the State, for no government could afford to undo the work of its predecessors and each new generation of voters would come to expect an improvement in the level of welfare provided.

The Class Structure: Rich and Poor

'Social class is a grouping of people into categories on the basis of occupation.' [Reid, p. 15] In 1911, for the first time, the national census attempted such a classification. Its categories were as follows: Higher Professional, Lower Professional, Skilled Manual, Semi-skilled Manual and Unskilled Manual. Under this system of classification, 80% of the working population belonged to the final three categories and might broadly be defined as working-class. The occupations to which they belonged would have included coal miners, bricklayers, postmen, bus conductors, office cleaners and railway porters. Above them in the Lower Professional Class might have been found the clerks such as Mr Pooter, immortalised in that Victorian classic *The Diary of a Nobody*, published in 1892, or the schoolteachers, Gudrun and Ursula, of D. H. Lawrence's novel *Women in Love*, published in 1921. Those in the Higher Professional Class included lawyers, doctors, accountants and all those who did not need to earn a living at all because of their possession of landed estates or stocks and shares. If the economic rewards enjoyed by each group had been less unevenly distributed the class structure need not have been so significant a feature of British society. As it was, an enormous gulf separated those at either end of the social scale and class divisions were still acute.

I. Reid, *Social Class Differences in Britain* (1981)

G.W. Grossmith, *The Diary of a Nobody* (Collins, 1955)

D.H. Lawrence, *Women in Love* (Heinemann, 1954)

In calculating the distribution of wealth it is necessary to distinguish between the ownership of property and annual income. Wealth in the form of property (land and houses, industrial shares and investments) was very unevenly divided. It has been calculated that in 1914, 170 000 people (0.4% of the population) owned 65% of the country's wealth. At the other end of the spectrum, 87.4% of the population could lay claim to a mere 8.5%. The Duke of Portland enjoyed an income of several million pounds a year, mainly derived from the coal mines on his estates. At the other end of the social scale millions of the population had little beyond their personal possessions. Incomes were less unevenly divided – 1.25 million people belonged to families with incomes of over £700 a year, and a further 3.75 million to families with between £160 and £700 per year. People in these categories would all have enjoyed a comfortable standard of living. But the annual average wage was only £80 per year and a survey completed in 1914 indicated that 2 million workers in full-time employment earned less than £65 per year, the minimum sum reckoned necessary to keep a family adequately fed, clothed and housed. Charles Booth in his *Life and Labour of the People of London*, published in 1902, estimated that one in three of London's population lived in conditions that did not permit them to achieve 'physical efficiency'. Seebohm Rowntree, who investigated every household in York, reached much the same conclusions in his book *Poverty, a Study of Town Life*, published in 1901.

Rich and poor: Park Lane 1910

C. Booth, *Life and Labour of the People of London* (Macmillan, 1902)

S. Rowntree, *Poverty, A Study of Town Life* (Macmillan, 1901)

Poverty was not only a matter of income. The affluent could afford comfortable houses; they could send their children to private schools and universities; they could pay for medical treatment and hospital bills. Unemployment was no hazard to the man with a private fortune. The starkest evidence of inequality is to be found in the medical statistics. Life expectancy in the middle-class suburb of Hampstead was 50 years. In working-class Southwark it was 36. Infant mortality rates varied from 4 per 1000 in the most prosperous parts of Britain to 33 per 1000 in the worst of the slums. When conscription was introduced in 1916, only one-third of the recruits were classified as fully fit.

Rich and poor: Slum children 1910

In the face of such inequalities it is not surprising that attempts should from time to time have been made to redress the balance. The years 1911 to 1914 saw an upsurge in trade union militancy to which the closest parallel was the Chartist agitation of 1837–42. The industries most affected were coal mining, the transport industries and the docks. In 1911 there was the first national rail strike and there were serious disputes with dockers and seamen in the ports of London, Liverpool and Hull. South Wales miners went on strike for ten months in 1910–11, and there was a national coal strike lasting for three months in 1912. In that year 41 million working days were lost, the highest total then recorded. In 1914 the Triple Alliance was formed between unions representing miners, railwaymen and dockers. They were planning concerted industrial action in September 1914 when the First World War intervened.

This outbreak of trade union militancy has been variously explained. One interpretation is that the British worker was simply seeking to defend his living standards. After 1908 price increases rose faster than money wages, so workers were experiencing a fall in real wages at a time of reasonably full employment. Trade unions were also gaining in confidence. Membership numbers increased from 2 million to 4 million between 1900 and 1914. The Taff Vale case had ruled that unions were liable for damages caused to employers by strike action in 1901, but this judgment was over-ruled by the Trades Disputes Act of 1906, which gave legal immunity to trade unions from civil actions for damages arising out of trades disputes. Unions in consequence were readier to seek recognition by employers, and this was the issue at stake in the 1911 rail strike.

Class Conflict and Industrial Relations

A more alarming possibility lay in the spread of Syndicalist ideas from the continent. Syndicalists favoured industrial action as a prelude to revolutionary change and the direct seizure of power by the workers. Tom Mann and Ben Tillett used syndicalist rhetoric at times, and they were both prominent in the dockers' union. In 1912 the South Wales miners produced a pamphlet called *The Miners' Next Step* in which they advocated workers' control of industry to be achieved by 'extremely drastic and militant action!'

Anon, *The Miners' Next Step*, R. Davies (Tonypandy, 1912)

The Government reacted to the strikes with a mixture of firmness and conciliation. Troops were sent to South Wales and to the ports in 1911. But the Conciliation Act providing for mediation in industrial disputes was invoked over 300 times between 1911 and 1913. Lloyd George brought the 1911 railway strike to a halt by his personal intervention; and the miners' strike in 1912 was ended after the passage of a Minimum Wage Bill. The level of actual violence was not very great. A miner was killed in Tonypandy, and rioters were shot in Llanelli and Liverpool. Nevertheless, there was considerable apprehension in the upper classes; Austen Chamberlain reported that a Birmingham gunsmith had sold out of revolvers in 1912. Churchill warned that had the rail strike not been ended in 1911 'it would have hurled the whole of that great community into an abyss of horror which no man can dare to contemplate'. [Benning, p. 50]

K. Benning, *Edwardian England, Society in Transition* (1980)

Whether the dangers of revolution were exaggerated or not, it is clear that Britain in 1914 was still a very divided country. We must now examine the political system to see how well it was adapted to contain those divisions.

THE POLITICAL SYSTEM ▬▬▬▬▬▬▬▬▬▬ B

The British Constitution

Among those countries which could claim to be democracies in 1914 Britain was almost unique in having no written constitution in the shape of a single formal document, a characteristic which she shared only with New Zealand. Her system of government had evolved over centuries and was defined by habit and custom rather than by law. Such habits and customs gradually acquired the status of constitutional conventions, unwritten rules of political behaviour, whose binding force was just as powerful as the terms of any written constitution.

Thus, while there is no law to prevent the Queen from refusing her assent to an Act of Parliament the fact that no monarch has done this since Queen Anne vetoed the Scottish Militia Bill in 1707 is a virtual guarantee that the royal veto will never be exercised again. Similarly, there is no written obligation on a Prime Minister who is defeated on a vote of confidence in the House of Commons to resign; when Lord Melbourne did so in 1841 he set a precedent which Ramsay MacDonald in 1924 and James Callaghan in 1979 felt bound to follow. To understand the British political system in 1914 one must look not only at the political institutions out of which it was constructed but also at the unwritten rules which defined their powers.

The Monarchy

In his famous book *The English Constitution*, published in 1867, Walter Bagehot wrote: 'The Sovereign has, under a constitutional monarchy such as ours, three rights – the right to be consulted, the right to encourage, the right to warn.' He added some words which are often forgotten: 'And a king of sense and sagacity would want no others.' Queen Victoria might have agreed with the first part of the statement. She would not have accepted the second. In the latter part of her reign she frequently attempted to influence policy and bewailed her inability to do so. She attacked Home Rule for Ireland; she opposed the military reforms introduced by Edward Cardwell; she deplored Gladstone's handling of the Khartoum affair which led to the death of General Gordon. In 1880 she did her utmost to prevent Gladstone becoming Prime Minister and she refused to accept into his cabinet two men of whom she strongly disapproved, Henry Labouchere and Sir Charles Dilke. In a draft letter to Gladstone, never sent, she revealed her true sentiments: 'She will not be the Sovereign of a Democratic Monarchy.' [Hardie, p. 35] Gladstone remarked ruefully on one occasion: 'The Queen alone is enough to kill any man.' [Hardie, p. 69]

W. Bagehot, *The English Constitution* (1967)

F. Hardie, *The Political Influence of the British Monarchy* (1970)

By 1914 things had changed. Under Edward VII and George V the monarchy became less intrusive, but more popular. Edward VII might dislike the policies of his governments, but he accepted that there was little he could do to change them, and he made no attempt to interfere with appointments. George V took his constitutional role extremely seriously and while always ready to help in a crisis, never stood in the way of his elected governments. In the Parliament Act crisis of 1910–11, he gave his promise to Asquith that he would if necessary create enough peers to force through the Parliament Bill should the Liberals win another majority in the election of December 1910. In 1924 when the first Labour government took office, he went out of his way to ease their path. In the crisis of 1931 he used all his influence to persuade Ramsay MacDonald, the Labour Prime Minister, to remain in office at the head of a National government.

On the other hand, both Edward VII and George V deliberately made themselves more visible to their subjects. Edward VII, admittedly, preferred to be seen at the racecourse or the theatre; but he was the first monarch to make a point of visiting the dominions and his visit to Paris in 1903 was used to improve Anglo-French relations. George V resolutely embarked on a programme of industrial tours and he was the first monarch to broadcast to the Nation, which he did with consummate success in 1935. Thus what the monarchy lost in political influence it gained in public esteem. Because it was above politics it could not be blamed for unpopular decisions or unsuccessful policies. But as the monarchy became more exposed to the public gaze it had a new role thrust upon it. It had to live up to the image of the country's model family. The monarch was still the official head of the Church of England and the coinage of the realm continued to display the words *Fidei Defensor* (Defender of the Faith) which Henry VIII had undeservedly earned from the Papacy. This link with the Church of England was still important, and it was the main reason for Edward VIII's abdication in 1937 when he announced his determination to marry the twice-divorced Mrs Simpson.

By 1914 it was accepted that the powers still enjoyed by the monarchy could only be exercised on the advice of a minister supported by a majority in the House of Commons. But the choice of Prime Minister still lay with the monarchy. In most cases this was usually a formality, the King inviting the leader of the largest single party in the House of Commons to form a government. But circumstances could, and did, arise when either the majority party had no leader, or when no party had a clear-cut majority. In each case this gave a certain discretion to the Crown. In 1923 when Bonar Law retired from the premiership for reasons of ill health, George V was confronted with the task of choosing his successor. Bonar Law declined to give his advice as to who this should be and instead the King consulted A. J. Balfour, the previous Conservative party leader; he recommended Baldwin rather than the heir apparent, Lord Curzon, on the grounds that the Prime Minister ought to be in the House of Commons.

In the subsequent General Election no party emerged with a clear majority, the Conservatives gaining 258 seats, the Liberals 158 and the Labour party 191. Baldwin did not resign until he was defeated in a vote on the King's speech by a combination of Liberal and Labour votes. George V again took advice, but he acted in accordance with his own convictions as well as constitutionally in sending for Ramsay MacDonald, the leader of Labour, the next largest party. He recorded his views in a letter to his mother: 'They have different ideas to ours as they are all socialists, but they ought to be given a chance and ought to be treated fairly.' [Nicolson, p. 389].

H. Nicolson, *George V* (1952)

The Premiership

The position of Prime Minister was only officially recognised in 1905 when Edward VII drew up a Table of Precedence in which the Prime Minister ranked fourth, after the two Archbishops of Canterbury and York, and the Lord Chancellor. But Britain had certainly had a recognisable first minister since the Younger Pitt became First Lord of the Treasury in 1784. The holder of this office generally assumed the responsibility for appointing other members of the cabinet and so became the King's Prime Minister. To achieve this office it was necessary first to become leader of your party and then to secure the support of a majority in the House of Commons. Each

H.H. Asquith, Prime Minister 1908–16

of the major parties had their own methods of choosing their leaders. The Liberals elected Sir Henry Campbell-Bannerman in 1899; on his resignation in 1908, Asquith had established such a strong claim to the leadership that, though not formally elected, his succession was seen as inevitable. The Liberal party split in 1916 but Asquith remained its formal leader until his retirement in 1926. Because of the continued divisions in the party the leadership remained in abeyance until 1931 when Samuel emerged as leader.

Until 1965 the Conservative party had no formal mechanism for electing their leader. They relied instead on what Harold Macmillan once called 'the customary processes of consultation'. In some cases this meant that the outgoing Prime Minister nominated his successor, as Lord Salisbury nominated his nephew, Balfour, in 1902 and Churchill nominated Eden in 1955. At other times there might be a polite struggle for the leadership, as occurred in 1911 when Bonar Law was 'elected'. His rivals all withdrew before the vote was taken.

A.J. Balfour,
Prime Minister
1903–5,
Cabinet Minister
1915–22

The Labour party alone had a clear-cut procedure for electing their leader. At the beginning of each parliamentary session, the Labour MPs elected their leader, though it was not until the re-election of Ramsay MacDonald in 1921 that the position became a more or less permanent one.

The Prime Minister has been variously described. Nominally he was only *primus inter pares* (first among equals). But John Morley, the Liberal politician who was in the cabinet from 1892–95 and from 1905–14, described the Prime Minister as 'the keystone of the cabinet'. Sir Ivor Jennings, an authority on constitutional law, elevates the Prime Minister to 'the keystone of the Constitution'. In practice he enjoyed much more authority than his colleagues. He appointed, and could therefore dismiss, his ministers; he took the chair at meetings of the cabinet; he alone had the power to request a dissolution of Parliament; he could be his own Foreign Secretary, as were both Lord Salisbury and Ramsay MacDonald. He presided over meetings of Colonial Prime Ministers and of the Committee of Imperial Defence. When he chose to use them his powers were thus very considerable. But as Asquith once remarked, 'The office of Prime Minister is what its holder chooses to make it' [cited in Harvey and Bather, p. 228] and in order to survive he needed both the support of his cabinet and of his party. When Asquith lost the confidence of his colleagues in 1916 he was himself ousted from office. When Chamberlain lost the backing of about 100 of his supporters in 1940, despite still commanding a majority in the House of Commons, he too was impelled to resign.

J. Harvey and L.C. Bather, *The British Constitution and Politics* (1984)

The Cabinet

The cabinet is the focal point of the British system of government. Its members are all chosen by the Prime Minister but they have to be drawn from members of his own party in Parliament, with very few exceptions. Thus the cabinet provides the link between Parliament and government and is, as Bagehot puts it, 'a hyphen which joins, a buckle which fastens the legislative part of the State to the executive part of the State'. [Bagehot, p.68] Up to 1914 the size of the cabinet varied between 15 and 20 members. It always included the heads of the major departments: the Foreign Secretary, the Home Secretary, the Lord Chancellor, the Secretary of State for War and the First Lord of the Admiralty. Britain's imperial responsibilities required the inclusion of the Colonial Secretary, the Secretary of State for India, and the Chief Secretary for Ireland. Two offices without departmental responsibilities, the Chancellor of the Duchy of Lancaster and the Lord President of the Council, were there for largely historic reasons, the other departments such as the Board of Education, the Board of Agriculture and Fisheries and the Local Government Board might or might not be represented in the cabinet, depending on the whim of the Prime Minister.

Bagehot, *The English Constitution*

Until 1916 cabinet meetings were conducted very informally. No minutes were kept, there was no secretariat, and the only record of the decisions made was the Prime Minister's account of the proceedings made for his weekly audience with the Sovereign. But certain conventions were already established. Only the Prime Minister could summon a cabinet meeting, and he would take the chair, unless he deputed someone else to do so in his absence. Votes were rarely taken, but when a serious disagreement arose, as it did over the declaration of war in 1914 for instance, it was necessary to secure a clear majority before action could be taken. Once a decision had been reached all members of the cabinet were bound to support it, both inside and outside Parliament; if unable to do so, they were expected to resign. This became known as the principle of collective responsibility, and it ensured that the cabinet spoke with a united voice. Exceptions to the principle were occasionally made. In 1932 four Liberal members of the National Government claimed the right to vote against tariff increases, while remaining in the cabinet; and in 1975 eight members of the Labour cabinet gained the right to campaign against the cabinet's official recommendation that Britain should remain in the EEC prior to the referendum that was held on this issue. Neither proved to be a very happy precedent.

The cabinet performed four essential functions: first it had to approve all future legislation; the initiative would usually come from an individual minister or department but nothing could be presented to Parliament which had not been previously accepted by the cabinet. Secondly, the cabinet had to agree on the particular policies to be pursued in a crisis, as in the General Strike in 1926 or the run on the pound in 1931; thirdly, the cabinet had to co-ordinate the policies of the departments concerned where these overlapped, for instance in making cuts in public expenditure, or mobilising the country's manpower; finally, it was the task of the cabinet to make long-term plans for the future both on the domestic and the international fronts. To categorise the cabinet's functions in this way is, however, to mislead. Until Lloyd George introduced the cabinet secretariat in 1916, meetings were conducted haphazardly, and the return to peace in 1918 brought about a relaxation in procedure, if not quite a return to the old informalities.

Much ink has been spilt over the respective powers of the Prime Minister and the cabinet. In the long run, neither could function effectively without the other. A cabinet depended for its successful operation upon strong leadership. But equally, no Prime Minister who ignored or attempted to over-ride his cabinet colleagues was likely to get his way for long.

Parliament: The House of Lords

In 1914, as now, Parliament consisted of the House of Lords and the House of Commons. The House of Lords was still largely hereditary in composition. In 1910 it was made up of 548 English peers, 16 Scottish peers and 28 Irish peers (all of whom had hereditary titles); 26 bishops; and 4 Law Lords (senior judges). The attractions of an hereditary peerage were still considerable, and the sale of peerages was one of the accepted ways in which party funds might be replenished. There were 139 new peerages between 1895 and 1915, while Lloyd George created no fewer than 90 peers between 1916 and 1922, many of whom paid handsomely for the honour. Not surprisingly, the House of Lords was overwhelmingly Conservative in its allegiance. No Conservative government was in danger of having its measures refused in the House of Lords. After the Liberal landslide victory in 1906 (the party gained 400 seats to the Conservatives' 157), Balfour deliberately encouraged the House of Lords to defeat Liberal measures. It did so, rejecting in succession an Education Bill, a Licensing Bill, a bill to end plural voting and in 1909 the Budget itself. With some justice, Lloyd George contemptuously christened the House of Lords as 'Mr Balfour's Poodle'. The rejection of the Budget led to a serious constitutional crisis. Though the budget was finally passed in 1910, the Lords refused to accept the Parliament Bill limiting their powers until, as we have seen, George V threatened to create enough new peers to force its passage. In its final form the Parliament Act, passed in 1911, provided that no money bill could be rejected by the Lords; that any other bill passed by the House of Commons in three successive sessions would automatically become law, even if rejected by the Lords; and that elections would now have to be held at intervals of not more than five rather than seven years. The Act also recommended that there should be changes in the composition of the Lords, but no action was taken in this respect until the introduction of Life Peerages in 1958.

The Parliament Act finally tilted the balance of power to the elected chamber. From 1911 onwards, the Lords could only delay legislation for two years (reduced to one in 1949); Lord Salisbury, who retired in 1902, was the last Prime Minister to sit in the House of Lords. Lord Home had to resign his peerage when he became Prime Minister in 1963. But the Upper House continued to play an important part in the revision of legislation, and its delaying powers could still have an important effect, as they did over Asquith's Home Rule Bill for Ireland in 1912–14.

Parliament: The House of Commons

Britain's claims to be a democracy rested upon the House of Commons, the elected chamber. In 1914 the formula of 'one man, one vote' was still some way from being achieved. Only 58% of adult males over 21 had the right to vote, while 500 000 enjoyed two or more votes through the ownership of business premises which also entitled them to a vote. University graduates of Oxford and Cambridge and the Scottish universities were also able to elect university members. All property qualifications were finally brought to an end in the Representation of the People Act in 1918. Business votes and the university vote lasted until 1948.

The struggle for women's suffrage was at its height in 1914. In 1897 the National Union of Women's Suffrage Societies was formed, to be followed in 1903 by the foundation of the Women's Social and Political Union by Mrs Emmeline Pankhurst. The activities of the National Union were peaceful and persuasive. The WSPU used more aggressive tactics, blowing up letter boxes, assaulting cabinet ministers and breaking windows, among other things, as ways of publicising the cause. The suffragettes deliberately courted arrest and then went on hunger strike. Their most dramatic gesture was performed by Emily Davison who flung herself under the hooves of the King's horse in the Derby in 1913. Though the majority of MPs were in favour of granting women the vote, Asquith refused to give government support to the various private members' bills that were introduced with this purpose. In this, as in so much else, the First World War wrought a complete change in public attitudes, and there was little opposition on a free vote in the House of Commons to the amendment to the Representation of the People Act which gave votes to women over 30 in 1918. In 1928, women finally gained the vote on the same terms as men.

At last the House of Commons could reasonably claim to represent the whole nation, and it was through Parliament that the electorate's wishes could be given effect. In the first place, Parliament provided the country's rulers. The route to office lay generally through the House of Commons and future ministers won their spurs in the debating chamber at Westminster – Winston Churchill realised very early in life that if he was to achieve anything he must get elected to Parliament. The House of Commons was the nursery of future statesmen and in voting for MPs the electorate were genuinely choosing their own rulers. Parliament also sustained the Government of the day. With a commanding majority behind him, a Prime Minister could generally rely on having his policies approved and his legislation carried. Conversely, in exceptional circumstances Parliament could bring the life of a Government to an end, as it did in 1924 and 1940.

Strictly speaking, Parliament did not make law. With 670 MPs in the House of Commons and over 600 Peers in the House of Lords it was hardly fitted for the technicalities of initiating and drafting legislation. Rather, Parliament gave its approval to and in some cases amended the measures laid before it by the cabinet. The same could be said of parliamentary control over finance. Though all adjustments to taxation and all financial expenditure had to be approved by the House of Commons, in practice it was the Chancellor of the Exchequer and the Treasury who between them determined the volume of taxation and how it was to be raised, and the departmental ministers and the cabinet as a whole who decided where money was to be spent. The major battles over spending came not between the cabinet and the House of Commons but between the Chancellor of the Exchequer and the big spending departments. There was just such a controversy between Lloyd George and Churchill in 1912 over Churchill's plan to increase the naval building programme.

It would not be accurate to say that Parliament had no control over legislation or finance. In the case of minority governments such as the Labour administrations of 1924 and 1929–31 not a single measure was safe from rejection, which explains the meagre harvest of legislation during those years. But with an assured majority any government was generally able to get its way.

On the other hand, the House of Commons did subject ministers to fairly searching scrutiny. Ministers were answerable to Parliament for the efficient running of their departments and could be challenged daily at Question Time. The government's actions were always liable to exposure through public debate. A system of committees – of which the most important was the Public Accounts Committee, founded by Gladstone in 1861 – evolved to interrogate ministers and civil servants. Most important of all, the presence on the other side of the House of Commons of an organised opposition to the government's supporters guaranteed that the process of scrutiny would be effective and that the House of Commons would never become a rubber stamp. The party battle continued after every election in preparation for the next one, and while this may have led to a great deal of barren controversy it also ensured that no government could escape unscathed when its policies failed or its ministers blundered.

Organised political parties developed in Britain during the nineteenth century and by 1914 the independent MP had virtually disappeared from the House of Commons, with the exception of the few who sat for university seats. Each of the main parties, Conservative, Liberal, Labour and Irish Nationalist had originated at a different time and in different circumstances but they had certain features in common. Each party appealed to certain identifiable interest groups, the Conservative party to the landed aristocracy, the Labour party to the manual workers, for instance; each party pursued specific policy objectives and each party existed to win elections and secure office. As the size of the electorate increased party organisation improved to ensure that potential supporters were made to register and to use their votes to best advantage in two-member constituencies. In 1867 the Conservative party set up the Central Office and founded the National Union of Conservative and Constituency Associations. The Liberal party followed suit, establishing the National Liberal Federation in 1877. Within Parliament each party had a Chief Whip and a number of Assistant Whips, whose task was to ensure that members voted according to their leaders' wishes, as the 'whipper in' on the hunting field kept his hounds on the scent of the fox. In the constituencies, local enthusiasts came together to form local branches of each party, and it was these groups who selected the candidates, subject to the approval of the central party organisation. By 1914 every General Election took the form of a contest between rival organisations, each with its core of committed supporters, and to a greater or lesser extent, its own set of policies. Political parties also served two other functions: they encouraged a greater

Political Parties

political awareness and a high level of voter participation in elections (70% on average); and they presented the voters with competing alternatives from which to make a choice. To see what those alternatives were we must examine what each party stood for.

The Conservative Party

The term 'Conservative' was first used in 1830 and was officially adopted in 1867. As the term implies, Conservatives were generally in favour of the status quo. They had little faith in the power of the State to bring about improvements. Conservatives could be relied on to support the monarchy, the House of Lords and the Church of England. They were also committed to the maintenance of the United Kingdom. When Gladstone first proposed Home Rule for Ireland in 1886, it was Conservatives who opposed him and who attracted the Liberal Unionists such as Joseph Chamberlain (hence the label Conservative and Unionist party which was adopted thereafter). The Conservatives were also the party of empire. It was Disraeli who bought shares in the Suez Canal and who, under royal prompting, made Queen Victoria Empress of India. Imperialism, as we shall see, was a movement with many facets and it was never the exclusive preserve of the Conservative party. But it is safe to say that the Conservatives were always readiest to leap to the defence of imperial interests and most reluctant to shed imperial responsibilities. There was another strand in Conservative thinking, however; it runs through the careers of men like Lord Shaftesbury, Disraeli, Neville Chamberlain and Harold Macmillan. This was the belief that the State did have a duty to look after its citizens, which was reflected in the Factory Acts sponsored by Shaftesbury, the social reforms supported by Disraeli between 1874 and 1880, Chamberlain's activities at the Ministry of Health between 1924 and 1929 and in Macmillan's attempts to promote a more active assault on unemployment in his book *The Middle Way*, published in the 1930s.

H. Macmillan, *The Middle Way*, C. Macmillan, 1966)

The Conservative party drew its support initially from the landed aristocracy and country gentry who voted Conservative by instinct. By 1914 many of the middle classes in the professions, in commerce and in industry had been won over, too. Bonar Law, elected leader in 1911, was very much a middle-class figure, as was Stanley Baldwin, his successor. However, no Conservative government could have been elected on these sources of support alone. Disraeli clearly realised this when he declared in a speech made in 1872: 'The Tory party, unless it is a national party, is nothing ....' [McKenzie, p. 155] As a leader in *The Times* pointed out, Disraeli discerned the Conservative working man 'in the inarticulate mass of the English populace' as 'the sculptor perceives the angel imprisoned in a block of marble.' Despite the fact that after 1884 the working classes made up the majority of the electorate, the Conservative party won more elections than any other party in the next hundred or so years. How it did so is one of the conundrums of British politics that will be explored in subsequent chapters.

R.T. McKenzie, *British Political Parties (1963)*

The Liberal Party

The Liberal party really dated from the General Election of 1868 when Gladstone became Prime Minister for the first time, though its antecedents could be traced back a good deal earlier. It was never as cohesive a party as the Conservative. It split over Home Rule for Ireland in 1886 and its supporters were bitterly divided over the Boer War between 1899 and 1902. Some Liberals were committed to social reform, others were opposed to any policy that would increase the power of the State. About the only principles on which all Liberals were agreed in 1914 were Free Trade and Home Rule for Ireland. The Liberal party could usually count on the support of Non-Conformists (members of the Methodist, Baptist and Unitarian Churches) if only because the Conservatives were so strongly attached to Anglicanism. The party had strong roots in Scotland, Wales and the West of England. It attracted as many of the middle classes as the Conservative party. But it failed, in the long run, to hold on to its working-class supporters. This may have been partly due to the refusal of all but a handful of Liberal constituencies to adopt working-class candidates. Ramsay MacDonald even went so far as to say: 'We didn't leave the Liberals. They kicked us out and slammed the door in our faces.' [Pelling, p. 224] This is too simple an explanation. The eclipse of the Liberal party owed at least as much to the positive attractions of a party which developed outside Parliament to defend the interests of the working class.

H. Pelling, *The Origins of the Labour Party* (1966)

The Labour Party

Whereas Conservatives and Liberals, with a few exceptions such as Charles Masterman and Walter Wedgwood-Benn, accepted the working of the capitalist system with all its faults, another tradition which rejected the whole basis on which the British economy was organised developed in the nineteenth century. The most powerful critic of capitalism was, of course, Karl Marx. Marx spent the years from 1849 until his death in 1883 in England. His two best-known works had strong links with England – *The Communist Manifesto* was drafted in 1847 for the League of the Just, a radical English working-class organisation and *Das Kapital*, the first volume of which appeared in 1867, owed much to Marx's researches in the British Museum and to his reading of English economists – and in these two works Marx demonstrated the evils of the capitalist system and predicted its inevitable destruction. Marx provided the ideological framework on which a socialist party might base itself; but while some English socialists accepted Marx's diagnosis, very few of them believed, as he did, in the need for violent revolution. If revolutionary action was rejected, two alternative courses of action presented themselves. One was to make socialist ideas respectable until public opinion came to accept them. The other was to create a separate Socialist party which would come to power through the ballot box. The complex early history of the Labour party shows both processes at work.

K. Marx, *Communist Manifesto* (Penguin, 1969) *Das Kapital* (Penguin, 1976)

The first Socialist party grew out of the Democratic Federation, a loose association of radicals founded in 1881. Under the influence of H. M. Hyndman, an ex-Etonian stockbroker and a convert to Marxism, it adopted Socialist policies in 1883, and was renamed the Social Democratic Federation in 1884. The Fabian Society also emerged in 1884. The early Fabians were agreed on the need to reconstitute Society 'in such a manner as to secure the general welfare and happiness', but it was necessary to wait for the right moment as Fabius had done when warring against Hannibal. The Fabians included George Bernard Shaw, Sydney and Beatrice Webb and H. G. Wells. They formed a middle-class pressure group who hoped to win converts to socialist ideas by publishing tracts, holding conferences and establishing contacts with leading politicians in the two major parties.

More important in the long run than either of these two groups was the Independent Labour party (ILP), founded in 1893 by Keir Hardie. Hardie had been elected to Parliament the previous year without the official backing from the Liberal party, and had asserted his independence from the political establishment by arriving at Westminster in a cloth cap and tweed jacket. At the Bradford Conference which inaugurated the new party, its objectives were defined in socialist terms: 'to secure the collective ownership of the means of production, distribution and exchange'. But the title Labour was preferred to Socialist because of the need to appeal to an electorate still suspicious of the new creed.

The fledgling party had no chance of gaining widespread support without the backing of the trade unions. In the 1895 General Election it failed to gain a single seat and it did little better in 1900. But gradually the Trades Union Congress (TUC) was won round to the idea that working-class interests might best be served through a separate Labour party. In 1900 the Labour Representation Committee was created. At a conference attended by representatives from the SDF, the ILP, the Fabian Society and the Parliamentary Committee of the TUC it was agreed to establish 'a distinct Labour group in Parliament'. An executive committee was set up with two members each from the ILP and the SDF, one from the Fabian Society and seven from the TUC. A contemporary journalist described the event as 'a little cloud, no bigger than a man's hand'. But while Labour candidates polled only 1.8% of the total vote in 1900, their share rose to 5.9% in 1906, to 7.1% in 1910 and to 22% in 1918. There was as yet no clear-cut programme and the party had to wait until 1918 before adopting a clearly socialist set of policies, and until 1945 for the opportunity to translate them into action.

The Irish Nationalist Party

By an Act of Union in 1801, the Irish lost their own Parliament, gaining the right to send 100 MPs and 28 peers to Westminster instead. Until 1829 no Catholic was allowed to sit in the House of Commons and it was not until the passage of the 1867 Reform Act and the introduction of the secret ballot in 1872 that Irish MPs could truly be said to represent the Catholic peasantry who made up the bulk of the population. But with the 1874 election, Home Rule became a live political issue. Isaac Butt founded the Irish Home Rule party and this won 59 seats in the 1874 election. In 1878 Charles Stuart Parnell took over the leadership and swiftly organised his followers into a tightly knit organisation capable of exploiting their bargaining power to great effect. In return for their support, Gladstone introduced the first Irish Home Rule Bill in 1886, splitting his party in the process. Unfortunately for the Irish Nationalist party Parnell was cited as co-respondent in a divorce case in 1890. He forfeited the support of the Catholic hierarchy in Ireland and the Non-Conformists in England. Despite urgings from Gladstone, Parnell refused to resign the leadership and the momentum for Home Rule was lost in mutual recriminations. However by 1900 the split was over and the party recovered to win 83 seats in the 1906 election. The Liberals had such a massive victory in this election that they had no need to depend on Irish votes; but after the two elections that took place in 1910 the Liberal vote in the House of Commons was reduced to 272, exactly the same number as the Conservatives, and the Irish Nationalists, with 84 seats, held the balance. This guaranteed that Ireland's affairs, not for the first or last time, would come top on the political agenda.

The British constitution was under considerable strain in 1914. Trade unions threatened concerted industrial action; suffragette militancy was at its height; civil war loomed in Ireland. It seemed that the political system was incapable of containing the pressures for and against change within constitutional channels. But the First World War intervened, the British people came together in face of the common foe and internal conflicts were postponed, if not resolved.

C ▬▬▬▬▬▬▬ THE BRITISH EMPIRE IN 1914

'No Caesar or Charlemagne ever presided over a dominion so peculiar.' [Disraeli, cited in Morris, p. 177] Britain in 1914 was the centre of a web whose threads extended across the globe; since the sixteenth century when she surrendered Calais, the last of her continental possessions, Englishmen had turned their attentions to other continents. As a result of their activities the British Empire included possessions in every part of the world. In his book *The Expansion of England* (1888), Sir John Seeley denied any explicit purpose to the process: 'We seem,' he wrote 'as it were to have conquered and peopled half the world in a fit of absence of mind.' In fact British expansion was not as lacking in deliberate intent as the remark suggests, but Seeley was certainly right to stress the generally accidental way in which the Empire has grown. In most cases the acquisition of colonies was the consequence of individual initiatives given subsequent formal recognition by the British government. For this reason Britain's imperial possessions were of an astonishing variety and their relations with the mother country showed a corresponding complexity.

The Nature of the Empire

J. Morris, *Pax Britannica* (1980)

Sir J. Seeley, *The Expansion of England* (University of Chicago Press, 1972)

The most dependable and least troubled parts of the Empire were the white dominions of Canada, Australia and New Zealand. In each of these a nucleus of British settlers had emerged as the dominant elite, anxious to maintain their human and emotional ties with the mother country while being free to pursue their separate identities.

The White Dominions

In 1914 Canada was a country of some 8 million people, about a quarter of whom were of French-Canadian stock. Under the British North America Act 1867, Canada enjoyed 'responsible' government and 'dominion' status. In simple terms this meant that while the Governor General was appointed by the British government his role was that of a constitutional monarch who acted on the advice of the elected Prime Minister. The Canadian government assumed responsibility for all matters except defence and foreign policy. The constitutional relationship worked out for Canada became a prototype for all the other white dominions.

Australia, with a population of about 6 million, became a united country in 1901 when the six separate colonies of Victoria, Tasmania, New South Wales, Queensland, South Australia and Western Australia agreed to adopt a federal constitution. There was a significant difference from Canada in that Australia retained the right to amend its new constitution without reference to the British government, but in other respects the imperial relationship was similar to Canada's.

New Zealand, with a population of 1.2 million in 1914, had contemplated merging with Australia, but the 1000 miles of sea separating the two countries proved too wide a gap and New Zealand opted for self-government. Of all the dominions she was the most closely linked to Britain and, despite the bitterness of the Maori wars in the nineteenth century, the least troubled by ethnic minorities.

The last of the white dominions, South Africa, was in a different category from the others and was dominated by two racial conflicts. The first, that between Boer and Briton, had been temporarily resolved by the first and second Boer wars, ending with the Treaty of Vereeniging in 1902. Under the terms of this treaty the two Boer republics of the Transvaal and the Orange Free State lost their independence. In 1909 they were merged with the two British provinces of Cape Colony and Natal to form the Union of South Africa on which the British government conferred dominion status. On the face of it, this was a remarkable transformation so soon after the bitterness generated by the second Boer War in which 20 000 Boer women and children lost their lives. But the agreement between the two white races was only skin deep; furthermore it rested on a tacit understanding to exclude the large black majority and a substantial Indian minority from any share in political power. In 1914 the injustice of this arrangement was barely recognised; it lay at the root of the second conflict, that between the white and coloured races. South Africa, of all the dominions the most richly endowed in mineral wealth and climatic conditions, would prove to be the most troublesome to the British conscience.

India

More important than any of the white dominions in terms of its influence on British policy was India. Beginning with the East India Company's settlements in the seventeenth century, British influence had gradually extended over the whole sub-continent until by 1914 about one half of it was ruled directly from Westminster while the remaining 600 native states were usually controlled indirectly through British Political Advisers. This meant that the Indian population of about 300 million was effectively the responsibility of a tiny British elite – the Indian Civil Service – supported by the British army in India of 50 000 men, and by the Indian army, a force of 200 000 Indian soldiers commanded by 3000 British soldiers.

India was valued as a market for British goods, especially cotton, as a source of manpower for the army (the Indian army played an important role in both World Wars), and for the prestige conferred by possession. It also provided Englishmen with the satisfaction of being engaged, as Lord Mayo, Viceroy from 1869–72, put it in 'the magnificent work of governing an inferior race.' [Beloff, vol I, p. 35] Lord Rosebery claimed that British foreign policy was mainly 'guided by consideration of what was best for our Indian Empire'. It is certainly suspicion of Russian intentions towards India that provides the best explanation for the bad relations between Britain and Russia throughout most of the nineteenth century.

M. Beloff, *Imperial Sunset* (1970)

Few in 1914 envisaged that India would go her own way. Some tentative steps towards self-government were taken in 1909 in the Morley-Minto reforms. These provided for majorities of elected members on Indian Provincial Councils, and for Indian representation on the Council of India and on the Viceroy's Executive Council. At the time, these concessions were not seen by the British as a staging post on the journey to dominion status but the Indian Congress party already regarded them as inadequate. The gap between Indian aspirations and British assumptions was already dangerously wide.

Britain's remaining colonial possessions were of such bewildering variety that they defy categorisation. They were to be found in every continent. In Asia, the British flag flew over Hong Kong, the Malay States, Singapore, Ceylon, Wei-hei-wei, Burma and Sarawak. In Australasia, British colonies included Fiji, the Gilbert and Ellis Islands, the British Solomon Islands and the New Hebrides, to mention only the most obvious. In North Africa, Britain exercised a protective authority over Egypt and the Sudan; in East Africa, she had acquired British Somaliland, Zanzibar, Kenya, Uganda and Nyasaland. Further south, she ruled a network of territories adjoining the Union of South Africa: Bechuanaland, Basutoland, Swaziland, Southern Rhodesia and Northern Rhodesia. Her West African possessions included Nigeria, the Gold Coast, Sierra Leone, Gambia and the Cameroons. In the Western hemisphere, she had numerous islands in the Caribbean, notably the Bahamas, Jamaica, Barbados, Trinidad, the Windward and the Leeward Islands; on the mainland of South America, she ruled British Honduras and British Guiana. In the South Atlantic, she had acquired St Helena, Ascension Island and the Falkland Islands; in the Mediterranean, Gibraltar, Malta and Cyprus provided useful outposts.

The Colonies and Other Possessions

Ireland

It might at first sight seem misleading to place Ireland in the Empire rather than the United Kingdom but there are good reasons for doing so. During most of its unhappy history the relationship between Britain and Ireland was an imperial one. British settlers effectively colonised Ireland in the sixteenth and seventeenth centuries, much as they did parts of the New World. The Irish legislature, until its demise in 1801, was treated as a colonial assembly. After the Act of Union in 1801, despite the presence of 100 Irish MPs and 16 peers at Westminster, Ireland was still ruled by a Viceroy based in Dublin Castle and a Chief Secretary with a seat in the British cabinet. Britain provided an imperial police force in the shape of the Royal Irish Constabulary; and when trouble threatened, as it did in 1916 and again between 1919 and 1921, an occupying army was sent to maintain imperial authority. On the credit side, the more enlightened of British politicians who had dealings with Ireland accepted the obligations that went with imperial responsibilities. Beginning with the Land Commission set up in 1881, the British government embarked on a wide range of policies designed to improve living conditions for the Irish peasantry, while they ignored the plight of the English agricultural labourer. A final proof that Ireland is best thought of as an imperial possession is to be found in the arguments that arose over Home Rule. The Conservatives opposed Home Rule for Ireland at least in part because they feared it would be the prelude to the dismemberment of the Empire. Leonard Courtney, a Liberal Unionist, wrote in a letter to a friend in India in 1887: 'I see the contagion of Home Rule is extending to India, as we know it must.' [cited in Beloff, vol. I, p. 28] Conversely, there was a persistent strand of anti-imperialism in Irish nationalism. Irish nationalists frequently expressed their sympathy for the other oppressed peoples of the Empire. Two volunteer Irish brigades even fought on the Boer side in the Boer War.

Beloff, *Imperial Sunset*

But if the South sought liberation, the North East of Ireland was peculiarly linked to the United Kingdom. In Ulster two-thirds of the population were the Protestant descendants of those Scots and English who had settled there in the seventeenth century. As the prospect of Home Rule approached so their commitment to the British connection grew stronger. By 1914, in consequence, Ireland was in a state of crisis. A Home Rule Bill had been introduced in 1912; though twice rejected by the House of Lords, it was due to become law under the terms of the Parliament Act of 1911 in the summer of 1914. In order to prevent this outcome the Ulster Volunteers, a para-military organisation, was formed under the active patronage of the Conservative party. Bonar Law, Leader of the Opposition, even stated that he could imagine 'no length of resistance to which Ulster can go in which I should not be ready to support them ....' [Blake, p. 130] As good as his word, Bonar Law was in close touch with Field Marshal Earl Roberts and Sir Henry Wilson, Director of Military Operations. He secured their approval for a plan to amend the Annual Army Act in the House of Lords in such a way that the use of the army in Ulster would have been prevented until given approval after a General Election. The plan was dropped but was rendered unnecessary by the so-called Curragh Mutiny. This episode occurred in March 1914, though it was more like a strike than a mutiny. The Commander-in-Chief in Ireland, Sir Arthur Paget, fearing that those of his fellow officers who lived in Ulster might reasonably object to acting against the Ulster Volunteers, won a highly damaging concession from the War Office. Any officer domiciled in Ulster was to be allowed to 'disappear' for the period of operations, to be reinstated without penalty when they were over. Any other officer who for conscientious reasons was not prepared to carry out his duty as ordered might choose to be dismissed. Brigadier Gough and 57 out of 70 officers in the 3rd Cavalry Brigade decided to choose dismissal rather than undertake operations in Ulster. The Government took fright and persuaded Gough and the others to withdraw the threat of resignation, but only after giving an assurance that the Government would not use their right to 'crush political opposition to the policy or the principles of the Home Rule Bill'. Clearly, the army could no longer be relied on to support the Government's own policies. Worse was to follow. In April 1914 the Ulster Volunteers succeeded in smuggling into Ireland 20 000 rifles and 3 million rounds of ammunition. In the South a comparable organisation, the Irish Volunteers, was set up to meet the threat from the North. Their efforts at gun-running were less successful. A convoy of vehicles was intercepted at Howth in July 1914 and three lives were lost when British troops fired on a hostile but unarmed mob. Of all Britain's imperial responsibilities it was the one closest to home that caused her most difficulty, and in the summer of 1914 Ireland dominated the political scene.

R. Blake, *The Unknown Prime Minister: The Life and Times of Andrew Bonar Law* (Eyre & Spottiswoode, 1955)

Imperial Machinery

As the United Kingdom lacked a written constitution, so did the British Empire. All the territories mentioned owed an allegiance to the British Crown, but the tightness with which the bonds of authority were drawn varied enormously. Administrative arrangements were equally confused. The white dominions were largely self-governing so far as internal affairs were concerned, but Britain retained responsibility for defence and external affairs. From 1887 onwards at regular intervals, Colonial Conferences were held at which defence issues were discussed, and in 1904 Balfour set up the Committee of Imperial Defence with the aim of co-ordinating defence policies. When war broke out in 1914 all the dominions, including South Africa, pledged their support within a matter of days.

But the Committee of Imperial Defence was the only body to assume responsibility for the Empire as a whole. In other respects responsibility was divided between four different departments: the Foreign Office, the India Office, the Colonial Office, and the Chief Secretary's Irish Department. The Foreign Office normally took initial charge of newly acquired territories such as Cyprus and the East African Protectorate.

Egypt remained a Foreign Office responsibility throughout the years of the British connection. The post of Secretary of State for India was created in 1858 following the assumption by the British government of the powers previously exercised by the East India Company. In India itself the Viceroy's authority was virtually unchallenged, except by the Commander-in-Chief of the Indian army. In 1905 there was an historic clash over their respective spheres of authority between the Viceroy, Lord Curzon and the Commander-in-Chief, Lord Kitchener, as a result of which Curzon was obliged to resign. But the Indian army was the only part of the British Raj not under the Viceroy's direct control.

The Colonial Office emerged as a separate department in its own right in 1854 and achieved real political status when Joseph Chamberlain chose to become Colonial Secretary in 1895, a post he continued to occupy until his resignation in 1903. The Colonial Office exercised a general supervision over Britain's other dependencies. Where there was a sizeable white minority, as in some of the Caribbean Islands and Southern Rhodesia, for instance, locally elected assemblies had considerable influence, though their legislation still needed the approval of British appointed governors. In other cases, as in Nigeria, a system of indirect rule prevailed, with tribal chieftains continuing to enjoy their traditional authority under the supervision of British advisers.

Elsewhere every conceivable permutation of local autonomy and imperial control was to be found. In Egypt, British influence was maintained through the British Agent and Consul General, though all laws required the official sanction of the hereditary Khedive of Egypt. In Gibraltar, on the other hand, the Governor's rule was absolute. Cyprus still remained officially part of the Turkish Empire, though Britain had gained the right to occupy and administer the island in 1878. It was finally annexed only on the outbreak of war with Turkey in 1914. The untidiness of Britain's imperial administration only serves to underline the haphazard way in which the Empire had been acquired. We must now try to see what held it together.

Imperial Attitudes

Support for the British Empire reached its zenith in 1897 when the attention of rulers and ruled was focused on the extraordinary spectacle of Queen Victoria's Diamond Jubilee. The extravagant outburst of patriotism this evoked demonstrated the essence of the British Empire; it was an empire held together by sentiment. Britain might have had the largest navy in the world, but ships could not police a continent or subdue a rebellion. The British army in 1897, a force of 212 000 men, had only 32 000 stationed in the colonies, with a further 72 000 in India.

The Boer War might appear to contradict this image of a peace-loving empire, founded on mutual goodwill. But while the Boer War made Britain very unpopular in Europe, there was little sympathy for the Boer cause elsewhere in the Empire, except among French Canadians and Irishmen. Between them, Canada, Australia and New Zealand contributed 30 000 men to the British forces in South Africa, and contingents from the Indian army were among the first to arrive there. It is arguable that the Boer War actually strengthened the sense of imperial partnership.

Within Britain, the war had a much more divisive effect. There were serious doubts about the justice of Britain's cause, and the Liberal leader, Campbell-Bannerman attacked 'the methods of barbarism' used by Kitchener to bring Boer resistance to an end. But the pro-Boers were not hostile to the Empire as an entity. It is true to say that the majority of British people in 1914 believed in the Empire. There were differences in the strength of their enthusiasm but hardly anyone questioned Britain's right to keep what she had gained, even if at the time there had been protests about how the gains had been made.

At one end of the spectrum were the committed imperialists such as Joseph Chamberlain, Lord Milner and Lord Curzon. Curzon found in the Empire 'not only the key to glory and wealth but the call to duty and the means of service to mankind.' [Morris, p. 122] As Viceroy of India from 1898–1905, and as Foreign Secretary from 1919–24, Curzon did his best to live up to these obligations. Milner, British High Commissioner in South Africa from 1896–1905, and subsequently a member of Lloyd George's War Cabinet and Colonial Secretary from 1919–21, was an equally ardent supporter of the Empire. His imperialism was based on a conviction that Britain needed her Empire to resist the challenges of Germany and the United States. If Milner lacked the romantic idealism of Curzon, he was severely practical in pursuing his objectives. As High Commissioner in South Africa, Milner did much to bring about the Boer War, but he also played an important part in the reconstruction of South Africa after it was over. In the process he gathered round him a school of disciples known as his 'kindergarten' (Milner was of German origins), and their influence continued to be significant in the 1920s through an informal organisation, *The Round Table*, of which he was a founder member.

J. Morris, *Farewell the Trumpets* (1980)

Joseph Chamberlain retired from active politics after suffering a stroke in 1906, and he died in 1914. But his influence on colonial policy persisted through his supporters such as Leo Amery. His greatest ambition was to weld the Empire into a closer union, largely through the device of imperial preference, and this remained a goal for an important element in the Conservative party. Conservatives as a whole were uncritical supporters of the Empire and could be guaranteed to resist any moves to reduce it. The party had been divided over imperial preference between 1903 and 1905, and echoes of that struggle continued to reverberate from time to time. There would also be divisions over India, but these lay far over the horizon in 1914. The Liberal party, too, had its imperialist wing. They had supported the Boer War and included Asquith, Grey, Haldane and Lord Rosebery. More surprising, on the face of it, was the support given to the Empire by the Fabian Society. Some of its members, Sydney Webb and Bernard Shaw in particular, wanted to see the Empire developed 'as a powerful and self-conscious force' [*Cambridge History of the British Empire*, vol. III, p. 349], so that the world's economic resources might be efficiently exploited and British standards of justice prevail.

Cambridge History of the British Empire, vol. III (1969)

Critics of the Empire were to be found among the inheritors of the Gladstonian faith in free trade. John Morley, for instance, deplored what he called 'All this Empire-building, why, the whole thing is tainted with the spirit of the hunt for gold ....' [Morris, p. 102] A more trenchant critic was the Liberal economist and journalist, J. A. Hobson, who described imperialism as 'a depraved choice of national life imposed by self-seeking interests which appeal to the lusts of quantitative acquisitiveness and of forceful domination' [*Cambridge History of the British Empire*, vol. III, p. 350] The Independent Labour party took an equally hostile view of imperialism, seeing it as a form of capitalism 'in its most predatory and militant phase.' [*Cambridge History of the British Empire.*, vol. III, p. 349). But neither Hobson nor Keir Hardie wished to see the British Empire liquidated. They even

Morris, *Farewell the Trumpets*

shared with Curzon his belief in its civilising mission. Britain would best fulfil her role not by divesting herself of her imperial possessions but by promoting their economic development and preparing them for self-government. This unlikely alliance explains why the Empire, as a going concern, had so few serious opponents. Once territories had been acquired, Britain exchanged the role of conqueror for that of trustee, in which even its severest critics saw the British Empire, potentially at least, as a force for good.

The Empire had of course a much more popular appeal. In 1900 the *Daily Express* was launched with this declaration: 'Our policy is Patriotism; our policy is the British Empire.' To its readers, the linking of the two ideas was self-evident. Empire Day, Queen Victoria's Birthday, became a national holiday. Movements such as the Boy Scouts and the Girl Guides, the Navy League and the National Service League were all founded in the decade before 1914, and helped to spread popular awareness of the Empire. The novels of G. A. Henty and the poetry of Henry Newbolt bathed the Empire in a not wholly spurious glamour. Less justifiable was the boast of Cecil Rhodes: 'We happen to be the best people in the world with the highest standards of decency and justice, liberty and peace, and the more of the world we inherit, the better it is for humanity.' [Morris, p. 124]

Morris, *Farewell the Trumpets*

POINTS AT ISSUE
POINTS AT ISSUE POINTS AT ISSUE POINTS AT ISSUE
POINTS AT ISSUE

How Stable was England in 1914?

All contemporary observers of Britain in 1914 were agreed that the country's political stability was under threat. The Triple Alliance between miners, transport workers and railwaymen raised the spectre of concerted industrial action. Suffragette militancy was reaching a peak. Two rival armies faced each other in Northern Ireland, while the loyalty of the forces of the Crown was not to be guaranteed. The Government's legitimacy was being challenged by the Conservative opposition, itself prepared to condone the use of force to oppose measures that had been approved by Parliament.

In these circumstances, the outbreak of the First World War might be seen as a safety valve, relieving pressures that might otherwise have exploded into civil war in Ireland and economic chaos in England. Alternatively, it may be argued that with the passage of the Parliament Act in 1911 the country's political institutions were basically healthy; that the social reforms passed by the Liberal government between 1906 and 1911 had dulled the edge of class conflict; that the Government's shrewd handling of industrial disputes between 1911 and 1914 had mollified the trade unions; and that the passage of the Home Rule Bill in an amended form, giving Ulster the right to delay joining the South for six years, would have provided an acceptable compromise. From this view, the outbreak of the First World War was not so much a deliverance from impending internal strife but rather a devastating intrusion upon a society that was basically secure, and capable of resolving its problems without resort to violence. Both arguments are presented here.

POINTS AT ISSUE
POINTS AT ISSUE
POINTS AT ISSUE
POINTS AT ISSUE

The Threat of Industrial Conflict

Lloyd George's Speech at the Mansion House on the occasion of the Lord Mayor's Banquet, 17 July 1914

'If more industrial action should coincide with civil strife over Ulster, "The situation will be the gravest which any government in this country has had to deal with for centuries."' [quoted in Hazlehurst, *Politicians and the War*, p. 28] This view is supported by G. D. H. Cole and R. Postgate in *The Common People* (1938), a left wing view which stresses the strength of trade union militancy:

> Everything, now, was interpreted in terms of class war; there were very few who knew the words, but a great many who believed that *La Lutte Finale* of the "*Internationale*" was really at hand. Trade union membership in 1914 nearly reached four million; but something better encouraged the rebels. One million, three hundred and fifty thousand of these millions had been united in a powerful industrial alliance to wage war upon the capitalists in the most vital trades. The great model union, the N.U.R., the fighting Transport Workers' Federation and the Miners' Federation of Great Britain agreed in principle in April (1914) upon a Triple Industrial Alliance, whose object was plainly and simply to arrange for concerted strikes, and from whose counsels the despised craft unions were effectively barred ....
>
> In many circles, with either hope or fear, it was believed that all that remained to be settled was the date when this formidable force would deliver its straight left to the chin of fat. [Cole and Postgate, p. 494]

K. Middlemas, *Politics in an Industrial Society* (1979) and P. Thompson, *The Edwardians* (1971), on the other hand argue that the fundamental moderation of the governing classes and the Labour movement made industrial conflict unlikely:

> At this period unions and employers did not possess a clear, comprehensive understanding of their collective power, nor of how it could be directed into the political field to guarantee industrial advantage. On the union side that deficiency might have been made good by the Triple Alliance (born in 1914, but untried before 1919) with its aims of workers' control of self governing industries. But although the Alliance with its anarcho-syndicalist overtones constituted a terrible warning to the political parties its existence only increased the tendency for government to intervene to safeguard the parliamentary system by promoting industrial and class harmony.' [Middlemas, p. 64]
>
> A revolutionary situation was not approached because it required a combination of structural stresses in the working classes – stresses which certainly existed – with an inflexible response, and ultimately collapse, by authority. The historical experience of neither side predisposed it to such a course .... The Conservative leaders could draw on a long tradition of social paternalism and the Liberals of democratic radicalism ....
>
> There was a complementary disposition in the labour movement, again founded upon historical experience, to work for change within rather than against the social system. Had labour unrest been met by unbending coercion and resistance, it could well have proved a revolutionary movement .... But the potential revolutionary leaders remained unheeded, or at least confined to the industrial struggle, because the rank and file were never driven to the point where they might have called on them. The governing classes neither proved intransigent nor collapsed. [Thompson, pp. 272–3]

A NATION OF FIRE-EATERS

PEACEFUL TEUTON: "HIMMEL! THEY HAVE ALL THOSE ARMIES! AND THE FATHERLAND HAS ONLY ONE!"

Punch 1914

The Threat of Civil War in Ireland

The danger from Ireland appeared much more acute, compounded as it was by the willingness of the Conservative party to condone the use of force by Ulster. This had been made quite clear in a speech given by Bonar Law to a Conservative rally at Blenheim on 29 July 1912:

> In our opposition to them (the Liberal government) we shall not be guided by the consideration or bound by the restraints which would influence us in an ordinary Constitutional struggle. We shall take the means, whatever means seem to us most effective, to deprive them of the despotic power which they have usurped and compel them to appeal to the people whom they have deceived. They may, perhaps they will, carry their Home Rule Bill through the House of Commons but what then? I said the other day in the House of Commons and I repeat here that there are things stronger than Parliamentary majorities.

He continued:

> Before I occupied the position which I now fill in the party I said that, in my belief, if an attempt were made to deprive these men of their birthright – as part of a corrupt Parliamentary bargain – they would be justified in resisting such an attempt by all means in their power including force. I said it then, and I repeat it now with a full sense of the responsibility which attaches to my position, that if such an attempt is made, I can imagine no length of resistance to which Ulster can go in which I should not be prepared to support them, and in which, in my belief, they would not be supported by the overwhelming majority of the British people. [cited in Blake, *The Unknown Prime Minister: The Life and Times of Andrew Bonar Law*, p. 130]

Bonar Law is defended by his biographer: 'Bonar Law at an early stage saw that the problem of Ulster was a genuine problem of frontier nationalism. As he repeatedly declared, it was ultimately a question of civil war; and in civil war the constitutional conventions do not apply.' [Blake, pp. 207–8]

In his authoritative book on recent Irish history, *Ireland Since the Famine* (1973), F. S. L. Lyons sees no constitutional path out of the Irish impasse:

> The breakdown of the Conference (between Conservatives and Liberals) was announced on 24 July 1914. Two days later the Irish Volunteers carried out their gun-running on the Ulster model, but improved the occasion by doing it in broad daylight. This too was a decisive event, more decisive than was realised at the time, even in Ireland .... The immediate political effect of this tragedy (3 killed and 38 injured) was to make it more impossible than ever before for the Nationalist leaders to compromise. Since Carson was equally adamant there seemed no way out short of the civil war which had been threatening for so long. But quite suddenly the domestic quarrel was submerged in the vaster European crisis .... [Lyons, p. 309]

The General Outlook

The view that Britain was on the point of political collapse was most forcibly expressed by George Dangerfield in his book *The Strange Death of Liberal England*. Dangerfield's thesis 'is not a record of personalities but of events; and not of great events but of little ones which, working with the pointless industry of termites, slowly undermined England's parliamentary structure until, but for the providential intervention of a world war, it would certainly have collapsed'. [cited in Benning, *Edwardian Britain, Society in Transition*, p. 100] Published in 1936, Dangerfield's book has recently enjoyed a revival. In its most recent edition, published in 1970, Dangerfield's thesis was supported in the preface by Paul Johnson:

> Writing in the mid-thirties, when the scars of the Great War were still unhealed, and the shadow of a new one already visible, Dangerfield set himself the task of demolishing the myth that the 1914–18 war had destroyed the world which Asquith ruled and personified, and which otherwise would have remained secure and permanent. On the contrary, he argued, Liberal England in 1914 was a society in process of decomposition; its values and attitudes were already being pulverised under the impact of new social, political and economic forces. England, on the eve of war, was in a state approaching revolution – only our submersion in a general European catastrophe averted a crisis in our national fortunes. Our parliamentary democracy itself, was, perhaps, saved in the mud of Flanders.' [Johnson, Preface to *The Strange Death of Liberal England*, p. 10]

A more optimistic view was taken by one of the main participants in the events of 1914, Winston Churchill:

> These shocking events [the Curragh mutiny] caused an explosion of unparalleled fury in Parliament and shook the State to its foundations. ... Was it astonishing that German agents reported and German statesmen believed, that England was paralysed by faction and drifting into Civil War, and need not be taken into account as a factor in the European situation? How could they discern the deep unspoken understanding which lay far beneath the froth and foam and fury of the storm?
>
> In all these scenes I played a prominent and vehement part, but I never doubted for a moment the strength of the foundations on which we rested. [Churchill, *The World Crisis*, vol. I, pp. 184–5]

Churchill's view has received support from Trevor Wilson, author of *The Downfall of the Liberal Party*, published in 1966.

> The whole notion that "Liberal England" died "strangely" between 1910 and 1914 is based on the assumption that during these years the Nation experienced a cataclysm of internal violence to which the war provided a fitting climax. The elements in this cataclysm of internal violence were the intransigence of the House of Lords, widescale industrial unrest, the excesses of the suffragettes, and the imminence of bloodshed in Ireland. But did these add up to a "pattern" of violence, rather than an accidental convergence of unrelated events? Some of the problems were passing: the Upper House had been put in its place and the strike wave seemed to be receding. The suffragette question, and perhaps even Ireland, might have been settled before this with a firmer lead from the government; and even now they were not past redemption. [Wilson, *The Downfall of the Liberal Party*, p. 20]

Books cited

C. Hazlehurst, *Politicians at War* (Cape, 1971)
G. D. H. Cole and R. Postgate, *The Common People* (Methuen, 1938)
K. Middlemas, *Politics in an Industrial Society* (A. Deutsch, 1979)
P. Thompson, *The Edwardians* (Weidenfeld & Nicolson, 1971)

R. Blake, *The Unknown Prime Minister: The Life and Times of Andrew Bonar Law* (Eyre & Spottiswoode, 1955)

F. S. Lyons, *Ireland since the Famine* (Weidenfeld & Nicolson, 1973)

G. Dangerfield, *The Strange Death of Liberal England* (Paladin Books, 1983)

K. Benning, *Edwardian Britain, Society in Transition (Evidence in History)* (Blackie, 1980)

W. S. Churchill, *The World Crisis* (Thornton-Butterworth, 1923)

T. Wilson, *The Downfall of the Liberal Party* (Fontana, 1966)

CHAPTER 1
FURTHER READING

General

Essential

K. W. Aikin, *The Last Years of Liberal England* (Collins, 1972)

C. Cook and J. Stevenson, *The Longman Handbook of British History* (Longman, 1983)

D. Read, *Edwardian England* (Historical Association, 1972) *Edwardian Reassessments* (Croom Helm, 1982)

Recommended

G. Dangerfield, *The Strange Death of Liberal England* (Paladin, 1983)

The Economy and Society

Essential

S. Pollard, *The Development of the British Economy, 1914–80* (Arnold, 1983)

P. Thompson, *The Edwardians* (Weidenfeld & Nicolson, 1975)

Recommended

K. Benning, *Edwardian Britain, Society in Transition (Evidence in History)* (Blackie, 1980)

I. Reid, Social Class Differences in Britain (Grant Macintosh, 1981)

The Constitution

Essential

J. Harvey and L. C. Bather, *The British Constitution and Politics* (Macmillan, 1984)

Recommended

W. Bagehot, *The English Constitution* (Fontana, 1963)

The Monarchy

Essential

F. Hardie, *The Political Influence of the British Monarchy* (Batsford, 1970)

Recommended

P. Magnus, *Edward VII* (John Murray, 1964)

H. Nicolson, *George V* (Constable, 1952)

K. Rose, *George V* (Weidenfeld & Nicolson, 1983)

The Prime Minister

Essential

Lord Blake, *The Office of Prime Minister* (British Academy, 1975)

Recommended

R. H. S. Crossman, *Introduction to W. Bagehot, The English Constitution* (Fontana, 1963)

The Cabinet

Essential

J. P. Macintosh, *The British Cabinet* (Methuen, 1981)

Recommended

Sir I. Jennings, *Cabinet Government* (CUP, 1969)

Parliament

Essential

P. Norton, *The Commons in Perspective* (Martin Robertson, 1981)

Recommended

R. Butt, *The Power of Parliament* (Constable, 1967)
Sir I. Jennings, *Parliament* (CUP, 1969)

Political Parties

Essential

Lord Blake, *The Conservative Party from Peel to Churchill* (Fontana, 1972)
H. Pelling, *The Origins of the Labour Party* (OUP, 1966)
T. Wilson, *The Downfall of the Liberal Party* (Fontana, 1966)

Recommended

S. Beer, *Modern British Politics* (Faber, 1965)
P. F. Clarke, *Lancashire and the New Liberalism* (CUP, 1971)
R. T. McKenzie, *British Political Parties* (Heinemann, 1963)
R. McKibbin, *The Evolution of the Labour Party, 1910–1924* (Clarendon Press, 1973)

The Empire

Essential

M. Beloff, *Imperial Sunset* (Methuen, 1970)
Cambridge History of the British Empire, Vol. III (CUP, 1969)

Recommended

J. Morris, *An Imperial Trilogy:*
    Pax Britannica
    Heaven's Command
    Farewell the Trumpets (Penguin, 1980)
B. Porter, *The Lion's Share: A Short History of British Imperialism* (Longman, 1976)
A. P. Thornton, *The Imperial Idea and its Enemies* (Macmillan, 1959)

CHAPTER 2

Britain and Europe: The Causes of the First World War

THE EUROPEAN BACKGROUND ▬▬▬▬▬▬▬ A

Nation States and Multi-National Empires

The Europe to which Britain belonged in 1900 can be broadly divided into nation states and multi-national empires, though it is a distinction which cannot be pressed too far. The nation states were those countries whose frontiers coincided with ethnic, linguistic and cultural divisions. Their inhabitants shared a common sense of national identity, a corresponding attachment to the soil from which they sprang and a more or less instinctive loyalty to the sovereign institutions which ruled over them. Under this definition might be included the countries of France, Britain, Italy and Germany.

Multi-national empires, on the other hand, contained within their borders substantial ethnic minorities who did not share the same linguistic and cultural background. Their inhabitants were frequently unwilling citizens of the empires to which they belonged, and they owed their first loyalty not to their official rulers but to the minority groups of which they were members. The Habsburg Empire, the Russian Empire and the Ottoman Empire, which still had a foothold in Europe each included such minorities.

The distinction cannot be pressed too far, partly because the nation states also possessed overseas empires, and in the case of Britain, an ethnic minority in Ireland. National sentiment, too, might be as powerful in a country like Russia as it was in any of the nation states. But one difference is of crucial importance. In the nation states patriotism was always a source of strength and unity. Rupert Brooke spoke for his whole generation when he wrote:

> If I should die, think only this of me,
> That there's some corner of a foreign field
> That is for ever England.

32   *BRITAIN AND EUROPE: THE CAUSES OF THE FIRST WORLD WAR*

The Good Soldier Schweik, the story of an Austrian officer's Czech servant, displays no such affection for the Austrian Empire; indeed, those Czech soldiers who were conscripted into the Austrian army in 1914 and captured on the Eastern Front, volunteered to continue the fight on the side of France and Britain. National sentiment was as likely to be a source of disruption as it was to be a force for unity in the multi-national empires. In the mood of heightened patriotism that characterised Europe in 1900, Austria-Hungary, Russia and Turkey were all riven with nationalist divisions. It made them wary and defensive. In the newly arrived nation states of Germany and Italy, on the other hand, national sentiment encouraged governments to adopt aggressive policies as a way of cementing their peoples more closely together.

J. Hasek, *The Good Soldier Schweik* (1930) (Penguin, 1951)

The Habsburg Empire

The Habsburg Empire was peculiarly vulnerable to disruption. According to the Census of 1910 it contained no fewer than twelve distinct ethnic groups: Germans, Magyars, Czechs, Poles, Ruthenians, Rumanians, Croats, Serbs, Slovaks, Slovenes, Italians and Moslems. Out of a population of about 50 million, the Germans made up 12 million, the Magyars 11 million and the Czechs 6 million, but there were at least half a million in each of the other minorities. A workable compromise had been reached with the Magyars in the *Ausgleich* (Compromise) of 1867, when the Dual Monarchy was established. This arrangement provided for a common army and a customs union, but in other respects Hungary enjoyed autonomy with its own parliament and administration.

But no such accommodation was available to the Czechs or Poles in the northern part of the Empire or to the Serbs, Slovenes and Croats in the South. A further source of difficulty was the area of Bosnia-Herzegovina, acquired by Austria as a Protectorate at the Congress of Berlin in 1878.

Nominally a constitutional monarchy, in practice the Habsburg Emperor Franz Joseph, who had come to power in the wake of the 1848 revolutions, was responsible for all appointments and the conduct of foreign policy, though this was usually delegated to his ministers. Legislation required the approval of the two parliaments in Austria and in Hungary. The vote was limited to 25% of adult males in Hungary, while in Austria the system of representation was heavily weighted in favour of the wealthier classes.

With the advantage of hindsight it is easy to claim that the Austro-Hungarian Empire was doomed to disintegrate. Its defenders [see Edward Crankshaw, *The Fall of the House of Habsburg*] argue that serious though the divisions were, they did not prevent the state from functioning and 'they showed no signs of doing so.' [Crankshaw, p. 306] But consciousness of her weakness tempted Austria's politicians into unwise initiatives and reflexes that were ultimately more damaging.

E. Crankshaw, *The Fall of the House of Habsburg* (Longmans, 1963)

Russia

Russia too was an empire ringed by minorities: Finns, Latvians, Esthonians, Lithuanians, Poles, Ukrainians on her western borders; Tatars, Armenians and Georgians in the South; and Moslems of various racial groups in the East. But with the possible exception of the Poles and Ukrainians these minorities were either too small or lacked the political consciousness to be a serious threat to the stability of the empire in 1900.

The political structure of the State, on the other hand, was much less secure. Until 1905 Russia was a Tsarist autocracy unmitigated by any form of national representative assembly. The revolutionary violence which broke out in 1905, partly as a consequence of Russia's defeat in the Russo-Japanese War, led to the inauguration of the Duma (Parliament) in 1906. But this proved to be little more than a constitutional facade. The first two Dumas were dissolved in acrimony. Changes in the electoral law in 1907 greatly restricted the franchise, resulting in the victory of right-wing parties at subsequent elections. The third and fourth Dumas were thus readier to co-operate with the Tsar, but in any case, thanks to French loans, the government could get its way whether the Duma co-operated or not. The workers and peasants were still effectively excluded from a real share in political power, and revolutionary movements continued to lurk below the surface.

The Ottoman Empire

Christened 'the sick man of Europe' by Tsar Nicholas I, the Ottoman Empire nonetheless showed remarkable powers of survival. At its zenith in the sixteenth century it extended throughout the Balkan peninsula, up to Budapest. Vienna twice came under siege, in 1529 and 1683. By 1900 the Ottoman Empire had retreated a long way. Greece, Montenegro, Serbia, Rumania and Bulgaria had all achieved independence. Bosnia-Herzegovina was under Austrian rule. This left only a relatively small stretch of territory between Greece and Serbia still in Turkish hands. On the other hand, Turkish rule still extended over the Arabian Peninsula, much of the Middle East, and over Tripoli in North Africa. Arab nationalism was also beginning to ferment in these areas and they were to go the way of Turkey's European territories before very long. The multi-national Empires of Austria-Hungary, Russia and Turkey were all vulnerable to change and their statesmen were motivated by fear rather than ambition.

It would be wrong to draw too sharp a contrast with the nation states of Britain, France, Italy and Germany. They, too, were plagued by internal divisions; but in the case of these countries, nationalism was a source of strength and more was to be gained by encouraging than trying to suppress it.

France

France had been a united country since the sixteenth century. Her frontiers, except on the East, had effectively been established since 1648. The 20 years of warfare between 1792 and 1815, while they made Napoleon the temporary ruler of Europe, did little in the long run to alter France's permanent boundaries. In the course of the nineteenth century she acquired a substantial overseas empire, mainly in Indo-China, North Africa and Equatorial Africa. But in 1871, as a result of her defeat in the Franco-Prussian War, France lost the two border provinces of Alsace and Lorraine. This was a bitter blow for which all her colonial gains were no consolation. From 1871 onwards the cardinal goal of French foreign policy was the recovery of her lost provinces.

Since 1789 France had experienced a variety of different regimes and had endured further revolutions in 1830, 1848, 1851 and 1871:

1789–92	Constitutional Monarchy
1792–99	The First Republic
1799–1804	The Consulate

1804–14	The First Empire (Napoleon I)
1814–48	Constitutional Monarchy
1848–51	The Second Republic
1851–70	The Second Empire (Napoleon III)
1871–1940	The Third Republic.

By 1900 most Frenchmen had come to accept the Third Republic as the form of government which divided them least, but it had few enthusiastic supporters. Its politicians came and went with remarkable frequency, partly because every ministry depended for its survival on the support of a majority in the Chamber of Deputies, and partly because the party system itself was so fragmented. Thus France in 1900 combined short-lived governments with a strong sense of nationhood and a deep sense of grievance.

Italy

Italy, dismissed by the Austrian Chancellor Metternich in 1815 as a 'mere geographical expression', achieved statehood in three successive stages. The first Italian Parliament met at Turin in 1861; the province of Venetia was added in 1866; and finally, with the withdrawal of French troops from Rome in 1870 (where they had been defending the Papal enclave) Rome became the national capital. Italy sought great power status without the national wealth and resources such a position required. She entered the race for colonies, suffering a humiliating defeat at the battle of Adowa in Abyssinia in 1896. She laid claim to the Italian-speaking parts of the Austrian Empire, notably the Trentino, the South Tyrol and Dalmatia. Her frontiers with France and Austria-Hungary gave her a strategic importance that made her friendship worth having, but in other respects Italy was a passive rather than an active influence in Europe.

Italy was a constitutional monarchy under the House of Savoy. Political power rested with the wealthy middle classes of the North. Universal suffrage was not introduced until 1912, and the divisions between the relatively prosperous and industrialised North and the largely agrarian South were a serious source of weakness.

Germany

Of all the countries of Europe in 1900 it was Germany that dominated the scene. The German Empire came into existence, as Bismarck had prophesied it must, through 'Eisen und Blut' (iron and blood). The three wars Prussia fought against Denmark in 1864, Austria in 1866 and France in 1870–71 removed the obstacles to unification, but they imparted a militaristic character to the new nation, symbolically represented by the military ceremonies with which the Empire was proclaimed in the Hall of Mirrors at Versailles. Windhorst, future leader of the German Catholic Centre party commented: 'Versailles is the birth place of a military absolutism like that brought to bloom by Louis XIV.' [Craig, p. 50]

G. A. Craig,
Germany 1866–1945,
(1978)

In fact the constitution of the new German Empire as designed by Bismarck was rather more complicated than the absolute monarchy of Louis XIV. The king of Prussia became hereditary emperor and enjoyed an unrestricted power of appointment and effective control over foreign policy, usually exercised through his ministers. But the Reichstag was elected by secret ballot under universal manhood suffrage.

Its assent was required for all legislation and for the military budget. Bismarck, Chancellor from 1871 to 1890, and his successors could certainly not ignore the Reichstag. But they could, to some extent, manipulate it; whereas no French or British prime minister could survive against a hostile majority in the National Assembly or the House of Commons, German Chancellors were irremovable so long as they had the Emperor's backing.

What was perhaps more disturbing about the new German Empire was the sense of destiny that attended its birth. This was characteristically expressed in a speech delivered to commemorate the hundredth anniversary of the birth of Hegel, the German philosopher, at Tübingen in 1871:

Craig, *Germany 1866–1945*

> Before our astonished eyes, this year has become one of the great landmarks, one of the guiding lights of humanity, which in a trice illumines the dark and twisted pathways of the past and opens before our eyes a broad highway leading clearly into the distant future. [Craig, p. 35]

Though Bismarck recognised that Germany was a satiated power in 1871 not all his contemporaries did so, and a later generation of politicians would demand that she become a world as well as a European power.

Diplomatic Alignments

The conflicting fears and ambitions of the European powers led inevitably to the creation of rival power blocs. Bismarck summed up the situation in a conversation he had with the Russian ambassador, Saburov, in 1880: 'All politics reduce themselves to this formula: to try to be one of three as long as the world is governed by an unstable equilibrium of five powers.' [Craig, p. 102] The three powers Bismarck had in mind were Germany, Austria and Russia. He temporarily achieved his ambition with the formations of the Three Emperors' League, signed in 1873 and renewed in 1881. But the rival interests of Russia and Austria in the Balkan peninsula were always likely to undermine this grouping. Bismarck himself took the first step in this process when he negotiated the Dual Alliance with Austria in 1879. Unlike the Three Emperors' League, which was no more than an informal agreement to co-operate, the Dual Alliance pledged each signatory to come to the aid of the other in the event of an attack by Russia, and benevolent neutrality if either Germany or Austria were attacked by another European power. Bismarck did his best to reassure the Russians, who did not know the exact terms of the Dual Alliance, by signing the Reinsurance Treaty in 1887. This bound each country to remain neutral in a war waged by the other, except in two cases: the treaty would not apply in a war caused by a German attack on France, or a Russian attack on Austria.

Craig, *Germany 1866–1945*

But in 1888 Wilhelm II succeeded the more conciliatory Frederick as German emperor. He had little appreciation of Bismarck, or of the subtlety of his diplomacy. Bismarck was dismissed in 1890. Wilhelm allowed himself to be persuaded by the influential Friedrich von Holstein, an official in the foreign ministry, that the Reinsurance Treaty offered more to Russia than it did to Germany, and it was allowed to lapse. Meanwhile in 1882 the Dual Alliance had been strengthened by the accession of Italy. Under the terms of what now became the Triple Alliance, Germany and Austria were committed to come to Italy's assistance should she be attacked by France, and a parallel obligation rested on Italy in the case of a French attack on Germany or Austria.

But the promise of Italian assistance (which in the event was not forthcoming in 1914) was a poor exchange for the loss of Russian neutrality. The fear that had always haunted Bismarck, an alliance between France and Russia, now materialised. Their shared suspicion of German intentions and France's anxiety for an ally to assist her in the recovery of Alsace-Lorraine proved stronger than the ideological gulf separating the two countries. In 1891 the French fleet visited Kronstadt, and the Russian Tsar stood bareheaded while the band played that hymn to revolution, the *Marseillaise*. In 1892 military conversations were opened, and the terms of the alliance were finally agreed in 1894. Each power would come to the other's assistance if attacked by Germany, while France promised to mobilise in the event of an Austrian attack on Russia. The alliance was to last as long as the Triple Alliance. This final provision underlined the purpose of the alliance and confirmed the division of Europe into two power blocs. By 1907, Britain had also entered into informal agreements with France and Russia, and the Franco–Russian Alliance developed into the Triple Entente. All military plans and dispositions were henceforth based on the supposition that any future war would be between Germany, Austria and possibly Italy on one side, France, Russia and possibly Britain on the other.

EUROPE IN 1914, TRIPLE ALLIANCE AND TRIPLE ENTENTE

Armanents and War Plans

It is something of an irony that one of the longest periods of uninterrupted peace in Europe (1871–1914) should also have witnessed an unparalleled increase in armaments. All the European powers took to heart the advice offered to Roman emperors: *Si pacem vis para bellum* (if you wish for peace, prepare for war). The kind of war for which they prepared was determined by the economic and technical advances brought by the industrial revolution, and by changes in the technology of war itself. The industrial revolution made possible the recruitment of mass armies and their equipment. Labour could now be spared from the fields and the rise of the metallurgy industries made possible the mass production of weapons and ammunition. The development of railways enormously accelerated the speed with which armies could be deployed. The German General Staff calculated that an army corps of 30 000 men could be transported 900 km in 117 trains in 9 days, a distance it would have taken two months to march. Improvements in rifling and explosives increased the range of small arms from about 640 m in 1815 to 3650 m in 1890. By that year, artillery had an effective range of 10 km.

The experience of the Austro-Prussian war (1866) which lasted only six weeks, and the Franco-Prussian war (1870–71) whose decisive battles were fought in the first two months indicated that victory would go to the side which could mobilise the largest number of men in the shortest possible time. Consequently every European power, with the exception of Britain, which was protected by the Channel, embarked on a system of conscription to provide huge reserves of trained manpower and developed its railway system so that its armies could be rapidly deployed. By 1914 the peacetime strength of the German army was 800 000, with a further 5 million trained reservists. The French army was expanded in 1913 by the introduction of a three year service law to a peacetime strength of 790 000. French reserves, too, were 5 million. The Russian army was increased to a peacetime strength of 1.5 million in 1913 with another 3 million in reserve.

To mobilise and deploy these huge forces effectively each country devised its own war plans. Of these, the one which did most to determine the course of events was the Schlieffen Plan. Count von Schlieffen was Chief of the German General Staff from 1892 to 1905. After the conclusion of the Franco-Russian alliance Germany was faced with the prospect of a war on two fronts and the Schlieffen Plan was designed specifically to deal with this eventuality. The first version of the Plan in 1899 was based on the premise that Russia would mobilise much more slowly than France. It would therefore be necessary to defeat the French army quickly before facing the larger threat from the East. Schlieffen based his tactics on those employed by Hannibal at the battle of Cannae. German armies would sweep round the northern end of the French defensive lines through Belgium and Holland, taking the French armies on the flank and in the rear. The whole operation was to be completed within six weeks. Von Moltke, Schlieffen's successor, modified the Plan to exclude Holland whose neutrality he thought it vital to preserve as an outlet for Germany's overseas trade: 'She must be the windpipe that enables us to breathe.' [Turner, p. 62] This alteration made it necessary for all German troops to be funnelled through Belgium and made the rapid capture of Liège essential. Should war break out, there would be no time for diplomatic niceties before the breach of Belgian neutrality. More seriously, the Schlieffen Plan committed the German armies to a single strategic response in the event of war. It dangerously narrowed the freedom of manoeuvre of German politicians in the crisis of 1914.

Although an early version of the Schlieffen Plan had been secretly betrayed to French Intelligence in 1904, the French General Staff refused to believe what they were shown. They could not accept that Germany would deliberately invite British intervention by invading Belgium. They therefore made no preparations to meet a strong German envelopment of their left wing. Under Plan 17, which was adopted in 1913, French armies would launch their major offensive in Lorraine in the hope of breaking through to the Rhine and recovering their lost provinces. But the French realised that the bulk of the German army was also likely to be turned against them in the opening stages of any war, which made it all the more necessary for Russia to relieve the pressure by invading East Prussia. With this in mind, France lent vast sums of money to Russia to be spent on improving railway communications in Poland so as to permit a rapid deployment of Russian forces on Germany's eastern frontier. The Russians accepted this obligation. Under Plan 19, as finally amended in 1913, they agreed to launch offensives against Austria in Galicia and against Germany in East Prussia. Mobilisation was to be completed within 30 days. [Stone, p. 41]

N. Stone, *The Eastern Front* (1975)

Austria had two war plans prepared. Plan R (Russia) presupposed a defensive war with Serbia and allocated 13 army corps to the Russian front. Plan B (Balkans) allowed for an offensive war against Serbia and allocated only nine corps to the Russian front. It was Plan B that General Conrad von Hötzendorff decided, much to Moltke's alarm, to adopt in 1914.

War Psychology

The armaments race was both a product and an encouragement of an atmosphere in which war was anticipated, if not positively welcomed. The professional warriors who had spent their careers preparing for it greeted the prospect of war with equanimity, sometimes with relish. Few had experienced the horrors of trench warfare and most believed that with such vast forces on either side a decision would be reached within weeks rather than months. Among politicians there was a much greater reluctance to risk the arbitrament of war, but to most of the statesmen of the time war was a lesser evil than national humiliation or loss of prestige. Every country had its own fire-eaters who urged war either for precautionary reasons or in the pursuit of national objectives.

In Germany, for instance, General von Bernhardi's book *Deutschland und der nächste Krieg*, published in 1912, prophesied world power or destruction for Germany and stressed that expansion could only be achieved through war. [Turner, p. 28–9] In Austria General Conrad von Hötzendorf pressed for a preventive war against Serbia from 1906 onwards. In France there was always a militant faction seeking revenge for the loss of Alsace-Lorraine. Jules Cambon, the French ambassador to Berlin, commented in 1914: 'Since the Dreyfus affair we have had a militant and nationalist party which will not brook a *rapprochement* with Germany at any price and excites the aggressive tone of a great number of newspapers.' [Turner, p. 67] One of them, *La France Militaire*, went so far as to predict that 'it will be a beautiful war which will deliver all the captives of Germanism'.

L.C.F. Turner, *Origins of the First World War* (1970)

In Britain equally bellicose spirits were to be found. Admiral Sir John Fisher, First Sea Lord from 1904–10, seriously contemplated a preventive raid on Kiel as early as 1904 [Steiner, p. 48]; while the *Army and Navy Gazette* called for the German navy to be 'Copenhagen-ed'. [Kennedy, p. 272] Sir Henry Wilson, Director of

Z. Steiner, *Britain and the Origins of the First World War* (1977)

Military Operations from 1910–14 spent his summer holidays reconnoitring possible deployment areas for the British Expeditionary Force in Belgium and Northern France. Two best-selling books, Erskine Childers's *The Riddle of the Sands* and Le Quex's *Invasion of 1910* lent a certain credibility to German ambitions in the popular mind, and in the case of Childers's book led the Naval Intelligence Department to consider the feasibility of the fictional invasion it described.

P. M. Kennedy, *The Rise of the Anglo-German Antagonism* (1980)

In all the countries of Europe in the two decades before the First World War patriotism was encouraged both officially by governments and unofficially by the popular press and voluntary organisations. A few illustrations will have to suffice: in 1898 the German Navy League was founded. By 1914 it had 331 000 individual members and another 776 000 in affiliated groups. It was used by Tirpitz specifically to win support for his naval building programme. Its British equivalent, founded in 1894, had less official connection with the governments of the day, but its activities were generally welcomed by the Admiralty. Similarly, the youth of both countries were encouraged by organisations such as the Boy Scouts, the Boys' Brigade, the Officers' Training Corps in Britain and by the Ministry for education and religious affairs in Prussia to imbibe the virtues of patriotism. In *Scouting for Boys*, young readers were asked to remember 'whether rich or poor, from castle or from slum, you are all Britons in the first place, and you've got to keep Britain up against outside enemies.' In Prussia, school history books were to 'have a definite pedagogical purpose'. The Ministry stated that 'it would be a sin against the coming generation if we were to delay familiarising it with the blessings which accrue to it by virtue of its connection with the Prussian state. It would be an equally great injustice to the state itself if an unpatriotic generation were reared.' [Kennedy, p. 376] Michael Howard, the well-known military historian, has commented pertinently: 'If the youth of rival countries howled for war in 1914, it was because for a generation or more they had been taught to howl.' [cited in Steiner, p. 157]

E. Childers, *The Riddle of the Sands* (1903) (Penguin, 1952)

W. Le Quex, *Invasion of 1910* (Eveleigh Nash, 1906)

R. Baden Powell, *Scouting for Boys* (1908) (C. Arthur Pearson, 1954)

BRITISH DIPLOMACY, 1900–14 ▬▬▬▬ B

The Making of Policy

While Britain shared in the war mentality that became so apparent in the years before 1914, she was a reluctant participant in the developing power struggle. There was, as there continues to be, a fundamental ambiguity in her relationship with Europe. On the one hand Britain's insularity and her overseas empire disposed her to stay aloof from continental entanglements. On the other, her concern for the balance of power, her dependence on overseas trade for imports and export markets, and the challenges mounted by other European powers to her imperial interests required that she involve herself in Europe's affairs.

Responsibility for British foreign policy between 1901 and 1914 rested primarily with the two Foreign Secretaries, Lord Lansdowne, 1901–5, and Sir Edward Grey, 1905–16. To a quite unusual degree, each man was the architect of the policies pursued. Lord Salisbury retired from the premiership in 1903, and his successors, A. J. Balfour, Campbell-Bannerman and Asquith, were generally prepared to extend a much freer hand to their Foreign Secretaries.

The cabinet would be consulted at times of crisis, but was otherwise only brought in when domestic considerations, increases in defence spending for instance, made this necessary. Another influence on foreign policy, the Committee for Imperial Defence, founded by Balfour in 1904, met on an *ad hoc* basis, and was more likely to underwrite decisions already reached than to produce policies of its own.

Finally, there were the permanent officials at the Foreign Office. Three of these men may be said to have had a significant influence. They were Sir Arthur Hardinge, Permanent under-secretary, 1905–10; Sir Arthur Nicolson, British ambassador to St Petersburg, 1906–10, and Permanent under-secretary, 1910–14; and Sir Eyre Crowe, Senior Clerk, 1905–12 and Assistant under-secretary, 1912–15. All these men held strong anti-German views, and while they did not actually make policy, they certainly helped to influence it.

The Making of the Ententes

After the collapse of the Quadruple Alliance that defeated Napoleon in 1815 in the 1820s, Britain made no permanent attachments. Lord Salisbury, the major influence on foreign policy between 1886 and 1903, shared with Bismarck the view that no parliamentary-based system of government could enter into a permanent alliance, because one government might very well repudiate the obligations assumed by its predecessor. Britain took no part in the formation of either the Triple Alliance between Germany, Austria and Italy, or the Dual Alliance between Russia and France. But her isolation was exposed in a series of imperial crises at the end of the century.

In 1895, the Jameson Raid on the Transvaal prompted a congratulatory telegram from Kaiser Wilhelm II to President Kruger after the Raid's dismal failure. From 1895 to 1897, a boundary dispute between Britain and Venezuela over British Guiana led to serious friction with the United States. In 1898 a collision with France was narrowly averted when French and British troops met at Fashoda on the head waters of the Nile; and when the Boer War broke out in 1899 Britain found herself without any friends on the continent of Europe.

One of the main concerns that shaped British policy was the need to conserve her naval superiority, for as Lord Selborne, First Lord of the Admiralty 1900–05, put it in a memorandum in 1901: 'Our stakes are out of all proportion to those of any other power. To us defeat in a maritime war would mean a disaster of almost unparalleled magnitude.' [Kennedy, p. 416] Since the Naval Defence Act of 1889 it had been British policy to adopt the 'two power standard'. The British navy was to be at least as large as the combined strength of its two closest rivals. But even this preponderance might not suffice if her naval forces were too widely dispersed. It was this apprehension which led to the first departure from isolation. In 1902 Britain signed a defensive alliance with Japan, which would operate should either country be attacked by two other powers. This would enable Britain to meet what was seen as a growing threat from Franco-Russian naval strength in the Far East without having to reduce the size of the British home fleet. But while this alliance was unprecedented, the fact that it was directed against Russia indicates that the real change in British policy had yet to come.

Kennedy, *The Rise of the Anglo-German Antagonism*

Throughout the nineteenth century war with France was always a possibility. There were war scares in 1830, 1841 and 1898. Relations with Russia were even worse. Britain went to war in the Crimea in 1853–55, and threatened to do so in the Near East crisis 1875–78. There was continual suspicion of Russian ambitions in Afghanistan and Persia, and of her bid to control the Dardanelles. What brought about a change in British attitudes to both these countries was a growing hostility towards Germany.

The emergence of the German Empire in 1871 was a challenge to Britain in many ways. Germany's growing industrial output made her a rival in the search for export markets, especially in the Far East and Latin America. The German bid for colonies, beginning in 1884, was deliberately undertaken by Bismarck, if A. J. P. Taylor is to be believed, to reduce Anglophile sentiment in Berlin; this is how it was seen by Bismarck's son, Herbert: 'When we entered upon a colonial policy, we had to reckon with a long reign of the Crown Prince [Frederick, married to Queen Victoria's daughter]. During this reign, English influence would have been dominant. To prevent this we had to embark on a colonial policy, because it was popular and conveniently adapted to bring us into conflict with England at any given moment.' [Taylor, p. 293–4; Kennedy, p. 171] Whatever the motives, Germany thwarted Rhodes's dream of a belt of British territory stretching from the Cape to Cairo. By themselves these sources of friction might not have tilted the scales decisively. As well as being her trading rival, Germany was also Britain's largest customer and both powers were prepared to sign colonial agreements in anticipation of the partition of the Portuguese Empire in 1898 and 1914. But economic and colonial rivalries undoubtedly compounded the impact made by German naval policy, and strengthened the impression that Germany was aiming at world domination.

A. J. P. Taylor, *The Struggle for Mastery in Modern Europe* (1952)

The third, and by far the most powerful source of friction was the German decision to build a High Seas Fleet specifically designed to challenge the British navy. The new policy was inaugurated in the Navy Laws of 1898 and 1900 and was due largely to the influence of Admiral von Tirpitz. In a memorandum to Wilhelm II, dated 1897, Tirpitz argued: 'For Germany, the most dangerous enemy at the present time is England. It is also the enemy against which we most urgently require a certain measure of naval force as a political power factor.' He added: 'Our fleet must be constructed so that it can unfold its greatest military potential between Heligoland and the Thames.' [Craig, p. 308] The British ambassador in Berlin commented, reasonably enough, in 1902 that he had no doubt that 'the German navy is professedly aimed at that of the greatest naval power—us.' [Hayes, p. 110] Sir Edward Grey went so far as to describe Germany as 'our worst enemy and our greatest danger' even before he went to the Foreign Office. [Steiner, p. 40] Lord Curzon, Viceroy of India, expressed what was to become the view of the Conservative establishment in Britain when he wrote in 1901: 'In my opinion the most marked feature in the international developments of the next quarter century will be the aggrandisement of the German Empire at the expense of the British.' [Hayes, p. 109]

G. A. Craig, *Germany, 1866–1945* (1978)

P. Hayes, *Modern British Foreign Policy* (1981)

Steiner, *Britain and the Origins of the First World War*

Such growing anti-German sentiment in governing circles made Britain naturally sympathetic to overtures from France which came in 1903. The Anglo-French *entente* was sealed in 1904. It consisted of a set of agreements over points in dispute in Newfoundland, Siam, West Africa and North Africa. The most important of them covered French recognition of Britain's claims to Egypt and the Sudan in return for British recognition of French interests in Morocco. The *entente* was strengthened and tested the following year. In April 1905, the Kaiser announced that the German

Empire had 'a great and growing interest in Morocco', and proved his point by paying a ceremonial visit to Tangier. Such a challenge to French pretensions was not to be ignored. It led eventually to the Algeçiras Conference which convened in 1906. Britain supported France's exclusive claims to Morocco and Germany sustained an unexpected diplomatic rebuff.

SOLID

GERMANY: "DONNERWETTER! IT'S ROCK. I THOUGHT IT WAS GOING TO BE PAPER." *Punch 1911*

Britain pursued a similar line when a second Moroccan crisis occurred in 1911. On this occasion disorders broke out in the capital city of Fez and French troops seized this as an opportunity to occupy the city. Germany protested at this supposed breach of the Algeçiras agreement and sent a gunboat, the *Panther*, to Agadir. She claimed to be protecting German nationals, the nearest of whom were 70 miles from Agadir; her real aim was to secure compensation in West Africa in return for the extension of French influence in Morocco. Opinions on how to react to Germany's action were divided in the British cabinet. But the speech that caught the headlines was that delivered by Lloyd George on 21 July at the Mansion House. Since Germany had failed to respond to a message that Britain expected to be consulted over any changes in Morocco, Lloyd George delivered a magisterial warning that if Britain were treated 'where her interests are vitally affected, as if she were of no account in the Cabinet of nations: then I say emphatically that peace at that price would be intolerable for a great country like ours to endure.' [Hayes, p. 159] Though Germany in the end was compensated by a 'large but worthless tract in central Africa' [Craig, p. 329] she again felt that she had been humiliated. Moltke commented ominously: 'If we creep out of this affair with our tail between our legs, if we cannot be aroused to an energetic set of demands which we are prepared to enforce by the sword, then I am doubtful about the future of the German Empire.' [Craig, p. 329]

Hayes, *Modern British Foreign Policy*

Craig, *Germany, 1866–1945*

The two Moroccan crises made clear Britain's diplomatic support for France. The Anglo-Russian *entente* was a logical sequel, though never as popular. The way to it was cleared by the Russo-Japanese War. Britain was able to remain neutral when the war broke out under the terms of the Anglo-Japanese alliance, because Japan had only one opponent. There was an awkward moment when the Russian Baltic Fleet, en route to the Pacific, encountered a British fishing fleet in the North Sea and sank two Hull trawlers under the misapprehension that they were Japanese torpedo boats. But Russia willingly accepted an international investigation of the incident and the subsequent loss of the Russian fleet at the battle of Tsushima in 1905 removed any fears of Russian naval power. In 1906 conversations were opened between the British ambassador, Sir Arthur Nicolson, and the Russian Foreign Minister, Isvolski. They bore fruit the following year in the Anglo-Russian Convention. Agreements were reached over Afghanistan, Tibet and Persia. Friction continued, especially over Persia, but the final link joining the Entente powers together was now in place.

Military and Naval Conversations

How strong was the chain? The answer is to be found in the military and naval conversations with France and Russia that took place between 1905 and 1914. Talks with France began, with Grey's approval, in December 1905 and continued until the following May. As a result, Haldane, British Minister for War, agreed that a British Expeditionary Force (BEF), consisting of four infantry divisions and one cavalry division, should be sent to France in the event of war with Germany. In 1911 Sir Henry Wilson strengthened this commitment. At the height of the Agadir crisis he made plans to land 150000 men in the Rouen-Le Havre area. When Wilson outlined these arrangements to the Committee of Imperial Defence on 23 August 1911, there were loud protests from the Admiralty whose members had not been consulted and who opposed the whole idea of British participation in a land war. Similarly, there were strong objections from certain members of the cabinet when they were finally made aware of the military conversations, of which they had known nothing in October 1912. As a result, Asquith assured both the cabinet and

Parliament that no communications between the General Staff here and the Staffs of other countries could commit Britain to military or naval intervention, and that no further communications relating to concerted action by land or sea should be entered into without cabinet approval. Asquith may have been strictly correct, but Wilson continued to make plans. The Committee of Imperial Defence, strange to say, did not consider the nature of Britain's military obligations to France again before 1914. When war finally came, no one in Britain or France knew what was likely to happen. Asquith was reluctant to send an Expeditionary Force at all. Its commander, Sir John French, favoured a landing in Belgium. In the end, Wilson's plans were dusted down and the British Expeditionary Force was concentrated on the left of the French line, even though the most recently revised French War Plan, 17, had made no allowance for it.

There was equal confusion over the role of the navy. The Admiralty were much less anxious to co-operate with the French than were the War Office, but circumstances compelled a measure of consultation. In 1912 Winston Churchill, the newly appointed First Lord of the Admiralty, decided in the interests of economy to withdraw part of the Mediterranean fleet to home waters. The cabinet insisted that Britain's Mediterranean interests must be safeguarded and this gave the French the opportunity they had been seeking. They agreed to move the bulk of the French fleet from Brest to Toulon in return for some positive evidence of co-operation from the British navy in the event of war. A formal exchange of letters between Grey and Paul Cambon, the French ambassador, committed both powers to discuss joint action in the event of a threat to peace from a third power. But the cabinet insisted on a preamble which ran: 'Consultation between experts is not, and ought not to be regarded as an engagement that commits either government to action in a contingency that has not arisen and may not arise.' [Taylor, p. 480] Churchill put his finger on the weakness of this arrangement: 'Everyone must feel who knows the facts that we have all the obligations of an alliance without its precise definitions.' [Steiner, p. 103] When the radical journalist C. E. Montagu read the documents in question in August 1914, after the declaration of war, he commented to C. P. Scott, editor of the neutralist-inclined *Manchester Guardian*: 'The Mediterranean naval arrangement with France made years ago was a deadly piece of self-committal.' [Hazlehurst, p. 51]

Taylor, *The Struggle for Mastery in Modern Europe*

Steiner, *Britain and the Origins of the First World War*

C. Hazlehurst, *Politicians at War* (1971)

The final attempt to concert naval strategy occurred in May 1914, when Grey, under pressure from France and Germany, embarked reluctantly on naval staff talks with Russia. They proved utterly abortive because news of them was leaked by a German spy in the Russian embassy. Grey issued a wholly misleading denial in the House of Commons: 'No such negotiations are in progress and none are likely to be entered upon as far as I can judge.' [Steiner, p. 123] He later admitted privately to the German ambassador, Prince Lichknowsky, that the talks had indeed begun, but assured him that Britain's freedom of actions was unimpaired.

By 1914, nonetheless, Britain had made her choice. The initial agreements with France had been strengthened and confirmed by the Moroccan crises of 1905 and 1911. The British army's role in the event of war would be determined by French military strategy, while her naval dispositions required French co-operation. But there was no comparable agreement with Russia for whose government there was little sympathy in Liberal circles. This raised the whole question of how Britain would react in a crisis in which Russian but not French interests were at stake. So long as they could be kept separate, Britain could play the role of honest broker. But because of the Schlieffen Plan it was all too likely that a threat to Russia would become a threat to France. In that case, Britain would find it almost impossible to stand aside.

THE OUTBREAK OF WAR ▒▒▒▒▒▒ C

The Balkan Tangle

The First World War began in the Balkan peninsula. It was an inherently unstable area in which two disruptive forces were at work. Pan-Slav sentiment united the existing states of Serbia, Bulgaria, Montenegro and Greece in a common resentment of the Ottoman Empire and a common resolve to expel the Turks from the areas of Europe which they still occupied. But each Balkan state was fiercely jealous of its neighbours, and Balkan nationalism made it certain that there would be divisions over the spoils. Russia, Austria and Germany also had vested interests in the Balkans. Russia never abandoned her long-standing ambition to control the Dardanelles which linked the Black Sea to the Mediterranean. Nor could the Russian government ignore the claims of their fellow Slavs to Russian support. Pan-Slavism was one of the few popular cards the Tsarist regime had to play and a vital source of distraction from the internal tensions that threatened it. For precisely opposite reasons, Austria could not tolerate the spread of nationalist sentiment in the Balkans. The expulsion of the Turks from Europe was only too likely to be followed by demands for self-determination from the minorities within her borders. Furthermore, Serbia exerted a magnetic attraction for the provinces of Bosnia and Herzegovina which had become an Austrian protectorate in 1878. Any gain in Serbia's power was certain to be strongly resisted in Vienna.

Despite Bismarck's dictum that the whole of the Near East was not worth the bones of a Pomeranian Grenadier, Wilhelm II was very anxious to increase German influence in the Ottoman Empire. On a visit to the Sultan, Abdul Habid, in 1898 he declared that the 300 million Moslems in the Empire could count on Germany's friendship. A German firm had begun building railways in Turkey in 1893 and in 1899 Germany secured a valuable concession to build a railway from the Sea of Marmora to the Persian Gulf. Russian suspicions were immediately aroused, and though the railway had made only limited progress by 1914, it proved to be a constant source of friction and a constant reminder of German interference in an area where Russia claimed a proprietorial interest. With so many conflicting interests at work, it was hardly surprising that a succession of crises in the Balkans should have preceded the outbreak of war in 1914.

The Annexation Crisis, 1908

In 1908 the recently appointed Austrian Foreign Secretary, Aehrenthal, determined to transform the shadowy authority Austria had exercised over Bosnia and Herzegovina since 1878 into full sovereignty. Anxious to secure Russian acquiescence in advance, he had a private meeting with the Russian Foreign Minister, Isvolski, at a country house in Buchlau on 15 September. In return for Russia's consent to the annexation of the two provinces, Aehrenthal promised to support Russia's claim to the right of passage for her warships through the Dardanelles. No record was kept of the six hours of conversation which led to this agreement and each partner interpreted it to suit himself. When, three weeks later, on 5 October Aehrenthal announced the annexation as a *fait accompli*, having done nothing in the meantime to secure European support for the Russian position over the Straits, Isvolski considered himself to have been grossly deceived. There was an immediate outcry in Russia, fuelled by Pan-Slav sentiment. Though Germany had received no notice of Austria's intentions, she pledged her immediate support, Von Bülow, the German Chancellor, writing to Aehrenthal on 30 October: 'I shall regard whatever decision you come to as the appropriate one.' [Taylor, p. 453] As the crisis deepened, Moltke, Chief of the German General Staff, promised that as soon as Russia mobilised Germany would do likewise 'with her whole army'. This threat was enough to persuade Russia to accept the annexation, without receiving any compensation over the Dardanelles. After the Russo-Japanese war she was in no position to risk another conflict. But after one humiliation it would be more difficult to accept another and the crisis had shown Germany's willingness to underwrite Austrian policy in the Balkans. Von Bülow noted at the time: 'In eastern questions above all, we cannot place ourselves in opposition to Austria who has nearer and greater interests in the Balkan peninsula than ourselves.' [Craig, p. 322]

Taylor, *The Struggle for Mastery in Modern Europe*

Craig, *Germany, 1866–1945*

The Balkan Wars, 1912–13

The next crisis owed more to Russian initiatives. Hartwig, the Russian minister in Belgrade and a passionate opponent of Austria, helped to promote a secret alliance between Serbia and Bulgaria providing for joint action against Turkey. This agreement was extended to Greece and Montenegro and resulted in the formation of the Balkan League under Russian patronage. In October 1912 the League declared war on the Turks, and within a month its armies had driven them out of most of Europe. The powers stood by until the fighting was over. Then Grey convened an Ambassadors' Conference in London. The one matter of concern that had to be negotiated was Austria's determination to deny Serbia an outlet on the Adriatic, whatever other gains she might make. A satisfactory outcome to this problem was achieved by the creation of the new state of Albania, formally recognised in the Treaty of London which was signed in May 1913. This was the last time that the European powers co-operated in the settlement of an international dispute, but the results were very short-lived.

In June a second Balkan war broke out, this time between Bulgaria on one side, and Greece, Montenegro, Rumania and a revived Turkey on the other. Bulgaria was speedily defeated and the Treaty of Bucharest, signed in August 1913, led to her surrender of Macedonia to Serbia. This provoked a further war scare. In September Serbian troops invaded Albania, supposedly in pursuit of Macedonian rebels who found Serbian rule no more to their taste than that of the Turks. Austria protested loudly at this breach of the Treaty of London, and was again strongly supported by Germany, the Kaiser promising Berchtold, Aehrenthal's successor, 'You can be certain I stand behind you and am ready to draw the sword whenever your action makes it necessary ... whatever comes from Vienna is for me a command.' [Taylor, p. 500]

The final episode in this troubled year occurred in November when Liman von Sanders, head of the German military mission to Turkey, was appointed to the command of the first Ottoman army corps at Constantinople. This led to angry

Russian protests. The French, through their ambassador, Delcassé, promised that 'France will go as far as Russia wishes' [Turner, p. 59] and the Russian Imperial Council even considered occupying Trebizond on the Black Sea until Sanders's appointment was revoked. Instead, a compromise was reached under which Sanders was promoted to Field Marshal, and to the less sensitive post of Inspector-General of the Turkish army. Events in the Balkans between 1908 and 1913 reflected the febrile international atmosphere. On the one hand, there was a fearsome readiness to reach for the sword for what would seem to a later generation the most trivial of reasons; on the other, an equal determination on the part of some European statesmen at least to use all the resources of diplomacy to avert conflict. But when the next crisis came, those resources finally proved inadequate.

Turner, *The Origins of the First World War*

THE BALKANS IN 1912–13

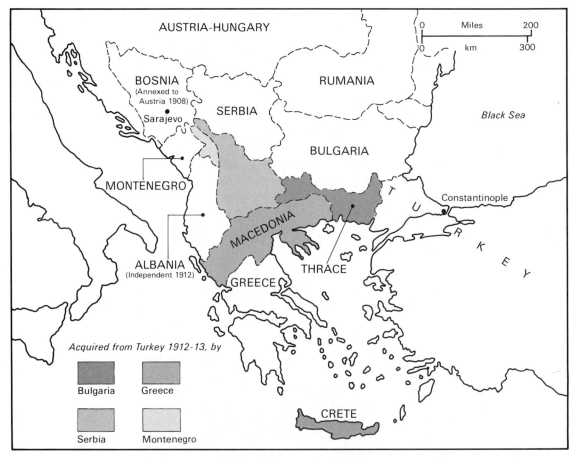

Sarajevo and its Consequences

'The spring and summer of 1914 were marked in Europe by an exceptional tranquillity.' [Churchill, vol. I, p. 178] 'The situation is extraordinary. It is militarism run staring mad and unless someone acting for you can bring about a different understanding there is some day to be an awful cataclysm.' (Colonel House to President Wilson, 29 May 1914, [quoted in Turner, p. 69] 'In the matter of external affairs the sky has never been more perfectly blue.' (Lloyd George, in a speech delivered at the Guildhall on 9 July 1914) These contradictory impressions of the international climate in 1914 bring out the paradoxes that mark the events that led to war in 1914. It was a war which no one, strictly speaking, wanted and yet it had been long expected. Its outbreak was feverishly welcomed in the capital cities of Europe, and bitterly regretted by the statesmen on whom the onus fell of declaring war. Every previous crisis had somehow or other been resolved peacefully. Yet an event in an obscure Balkan town on this occasion proved to be fatal in its consequences. To explain this outcome, it is necessary to see how the drama unfolded; so many figures played key roles that a cast list may be helpful.

W. S. Churchill,
The World Crisis,
vol. I (1923)

Central Powers (Germany and Austria)

Austria
Emperor Franz Joseph
Archduke Franz Ferdinand (nephew and heir to the throne)
Count Leopold von Berchtold (Foreign Minister)
Count Tisza (Prime Minister of Hungary)
General Conrad von Hötzendorff (Chief of Staff)
Germany
Kaiser Wilhelm II
Theobald Bethmann Hollweg (Chancellor)
Gottlieb von Jagow (Foreign Minister)
Helmuth von Moltke (Chief of the General Staff)
Prince Lichknowsky (Ambassador to Britain)

Entente Powers (Russia, France and Britain)

Russia
Tsar Nicholas II
Sergei Sazonoff (Foreign Minister)
General V. Sukhomlinov (Minister for War)
General N. Janushkevich (Chief of Staff)
France
Raymond Poincaré (President)
René Viviani (Prime Minister and Foreign Minister)
Paul Cambon (Ambassador to Britain)
Maurice Paléologue (Ambassador to Russia)
General J. J. C. Joffre (Chief of Staff)
Britain
Herbert Asquith (Prime Minister)
Sir Edward Grey (Foreign Minister)
Winston Churchill (First Lord of the Admiralty)

Of those listed above, none actually wanted war, though if it had to come, some took the view that the sooner it happened the better. Poincaré, Paléologue and Joffre were optimistic about the prospects of victory for the Entente powers and certainly did nothing to discourage Russian mobilisation. Moltke and Conrad, on the other hand, feared that the longer war was delayed the worse the chances for the central powers. Against these men must be set the views of Sazonoff who rightly feared the irreparable harm that war would do to the Russian economy and the Tsarist regime;

Sir Edward Grey, whose final words when the deluge broke were: 'I hate war: I hate war!' [Steiner, p. 240]; and, with some reservations, the Kaiser and Bethmann Hollweg. Both of these men began by urging Austria to take a tough line with Serbia,

Dr Theobald von Bethmann-Hallweg Chancellor of Germany

Sir Edward Grey, British Foreign Secretary

but as war approached they each made desperate efforts to stave it off. When Bethmann Hollweg was asked by Von Bülow how the war had come about, 'He raised his long thin arms to heaven and answered in a dull exhausted voice: "Oh – if only I knew!" ' [Turner, p. 112]

Steiner, *Britain and the Origins of the First World War*

Turner, *The Origins of the First World War*

The fuse was lit by the murder of the Archduke Franz Ferdinand and his wife on 28 June at Sarajevo by Gabriel Princip, a Serb from Bosnia. The assassination had been planned by Colonel Dimitrievitch, Chief of the Intelligence Section of the Serbian General Staff and head of the terrorist organisation, the Black Hand; how much the Serbian Prime Minister, Pasic, knew of the plot is uncertain. A vague warning was sent to the Archduke of possible trouble, particularly as he had tactlessly chosen to visit Sarajevo on the anniversary of the battle of Kossovo, a day held sacred in Serbian folk memory, even though it commemorated what had been a notable defeat.

The victims of Sarajevo: the Archduke Franz Ferdinand and his wife, one hour before their assassination

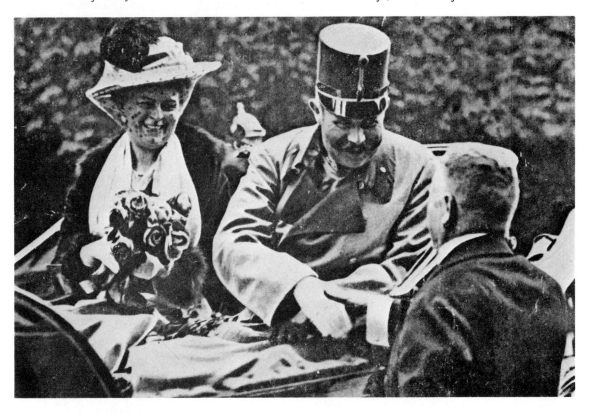

Between the pistol shots fired by Princip on 28 June and the outbreak of a general European war at the beginning of August several critical decisions were made, none of them necessarily preordained. First was the Austrian decision to use the assassination as an excuse to crush Serbia. This decision was taken as soon as Austria could be sure of German support, promised by the Kaiser and Bethmann Hollweg on 5 July: 'Germany advises us to strike at once .... Germany will support us unreservedly even if our march into Serbia lets loose a great war.' [Berchtold to Conrad, 7 July, Turner, p. 83]

Turner, *The Origins of the First World War*

CHART OF EVENTS, JUNE–AUGUST, 1914

	Europe	Britain
Sunday, 28 June	Assassination of Franz Ferdinand.	
Sunday, 5 July	German promise of support to Austria.	
Thursday, 23 July	Austrian ultimatum delivered to Serbia.	
Friday, 24 July	Russian Council of Ministers requested partial mobilisation.	Cabinet discussed Balkan crisis for the first time.
Saturday, 25 July	Russia introduced 'The Period preparatory to War'.	Grey suggested extending time limit to Vienna.
Sunday, 26 July	Grey's suggestion of four-power conference rejected by Germany.	Grey suggested four-power conference.
Monday, 27 July	Austrian decision to declare war on Serbia. Kaiser returned to Berlin.	Cabinet considered intervention. Five members threatened resignation.
Tuesday, 28 July	Austria declared war on Serbia.	
Wednesday, 29 July	Tsar ordered general mobilisation, later amended to partial mobilisation.	Cabinet refused to make pledges to Germany or France.
Thursday, 30 July	Tsar ordered general mobilisation.	Labour party vote to stay out of war.
Friday, 31 July	Germany ordered mobilisation. Ultimatum to Russia.	
Saturday, 1 August	German declaration of war on Russia.	Cambon requested British support. Asquith non-committal.
Sunday, 2 August	Ultimatum presented to Belgium.	Cabinet agreed to defend French coasts if attacked by Germany.
Monday, 3 August	German declaration of war on France. Invasion of Luxemburg.	Cabinet agreed to defend Belgium. Grey's speech to House of Commons.
Tuesday, 4 August	German invasion of Belgium.	11.00 am British ultimatum to Germany. 11.00 pm British declaration of war on Germany.
Thursday, 6 August	Austrian declaration of war on Russia.	

52

BRITAIN AND EUROPE: THE CAUSES OF THE FIRST WORLD WAR

The Austrian ultimatum, delivered on 23 July, was deliberately framed to be unacceptable. When Sazonoff saw it he exclaimed: 'C'est la guerre européenne!' [Turner, p. 91] Grey described it as 'the most formidable document I have ever seen addressed by one state to another that was independent.' [Steiner, p. 222] The reaction of Eyre Crowe, Assistant under-secretary at the Foreign Office, to the ultimatum was to conclude that the struggle between the Triple Alliance and the Triple Entente had now been joined: 'Our interests are tied up with those of France and Russia in this struggle, which is not for the possession of Serbia, but one between Germany aiming at a political dictatorship in Europe and the Powers who desire to retain individual freedom.' [Steiner, p. 222] Delivery of the ultimatum had been held up for nearly a month to enable Austria to make her military preparations, and also to enable Poincaré and Viviani, both of whom were on a state visit to Russia, to make their departure before the blow fell. Having waited so long before making their demands, however, the Austrian government allowed the Serbs only 48 hours to make their reply.

Steiner, *Britain and the Origins of the First World War*

All now hinged on the Russian reaction. If Russia came to Serbia's assistance both the Dual and the Triple Alliances would begin to operate, or so it was feared. Military plans and staffs now began to influence diplomacy. The Schlieffen Plan required Germany to remain on the defensive in the East until the rapid strike against France had been completed. But if Russia were to mobilise first, it would be imperative for Germany to precipitate war in the West before the Russian steam-roller was ready to trundle into action. The French were equally apprehensive that were Russia not to mobilise in time they would have to bear the full brunt of the German offensive. It was this combination of pressures that brought about the next critical decision. On 24 July the Russian Council of Ministers agreed to request the Tsar to order partial mobilisation. But no plans for partial mobilisation existed so that they had to be content with the introduction of 'The Period Preparatory to War', a preliminary to mobilisation which involved the manning of frontier posts, the mining of harbours and the imposition of censorship, but not the calling up of reserves.

Austria refused to accept the conciliatory Serbian reply to their ultimatum and when this expired on 26 July Bethmann Hollweg pursued a suicidal course, urging Austria to declare war on Serbia as soon as possible, evidently on the doubtful assumption made by the Foreign Minister, Jagow, that 'the more boldness Austria displays, the more strongly we support her, the more likely is Russia to keep quiet'. [Turner, p. 98] Grey, on the contrary, did all he could to avert the conflict. On 25 July he saw Lichknowsky and suggested mediation by France, Britain, Italy and Germany, a suggestion which Lichknowsky endorsed, without success. On 26 July Grey suggested re-convening the Ambassadors' Conference which had settled the first Balkan war. The suggestion was rebuffed by Germany: 'We could not take part in such a conference as we cannot drag Austria in her conflict with Serbia before a European tribunal.' [Turner, p. 100] Finally, on 27 July, in desperation, Grey suggested that Berlin should induce Austria to accept the Serbian reply at least as a basis for negotiation. This proposal was belatedly passed on to Vienna. But before it arrived, Jagow emphasised to Szogény, the Austrian ambassador in Berlin, that:

Turner, *The Origins of the First World War*

the German government assured Austria in the most binding fashion that it in no way identifies itself with the proposals which may shortly be brought to Your Excellency's notice by the German government; it is, on the contrary, decidedly opposed to consideration of them, and it is only passing them on out of deference to the British request. [Fischer, p. 70]

F. Fischer, *Germany's Aims in the First World War* (1967)

THE OUTBREAK OF WAR

The remaining four days before the outbreak of war were taken up by last-minute efforts to draw back from the brink, while those who accepted the inevitability of conflict sought to gain the initiative. As soon as military considerations came into play all negotiations took place within an ever narrowing time limit, and the views of generals took precedence over those of the diplomats.

When the Kaiser saw the terms of the conciliatory Serbian reply to the ultimatum on the morning of 28 July, he commented: 'A brilliant achievement in a time limit of only 48 hours. It is more than one could have expected! A great moral success for Vienna; but with it all reason for war disappears ....'. [Turner, p. 103] But he was too late to stop Austria declaring war on Serbia, even had he wished to do so. Similarly, when Bethmann Hollweg heard on 29 July from Lichknowsky that Britain could not stand aside indefinitely in the event of France and Russia getting involved in the Austro-Russia conflict, he too made desperate efforts to persuade the Austrian government to continue negotiations with Russia. But by that time the Russians had decided to mobilise. The Tsar ordered general mobilisation on the evening of 29 July; in response to an agonised telegram from the Kaiser, he changed this to partial mobilisation, but under pressure from Sazonoff and the generals, Sukhomlinov and Janushkevich, he finally allowed the order for general mobilisation to go out.

Moltke, who up to this point had not pressed for German mobilisation, now swung to the opposite extreme. Learning that Conrad intended to put Plan B into operation, remaining on the defensive in Galicia, Moltke feared that the whole weight of the Russian army would be directed against East Prussia, thus jeopardising the Schlieffen Plan. It made a rapid German response even more imperative. At Moltke's insistence German mobilisation was ordered on 31 July, and an ultimatum was delivered to Russia requiring her to cease all military measures against Germany and Austria within 12 hours. Wilhelm II, still hoping for Britain's neutrality, seized on an offer from Britain to guarantee France's neutrality and after the mobilisation order had been signed, ordered Moltke to 'hold up the advance westward'. Moltke and the German General Staff were in despair. The rigidity of the Schlieffen Plan did not allow for a war against Russia alone. When this was pointed out, the Kaiser reluctantly withdrew his objections. Meanwhile, as no reply was forthcoming from Russia, Germany declared war at 6.00 pm on 1 August. French mobilisation was also ordered on 1 August, but as a last-minute gesture, her troops had been withdrawn to a distance of 10 km behind Franco-German frontiers. It made no difference. On 3 August, after making false allegations of French air raids on Nuremburg, Germany declared war on France. On 4 August, in fulfilment of the Schlieffen Plan, German troops entered Belgium.

British entry into the war was by no means a foregone conclusion and it has been argued that the uncertain course Britain pursued in the final weeks of crisis actually helped to bring the war about. In June and July of 1914 the Ulster crisis attracted far more attention than events in the Balkans, and the cabinet did not even consider them until Friday 24 July, nearly a month after the assassination of Franz Ferdinand. There was no dissent from Grey's suggestion of British mediation, but over the weekend divisions within the cabinet, the Liberal party and in the country became apparent. When on Monday 27 July, Grey mooted the possibility of British intervention on the side of France, five members of the cabinet, Burns, Morley, Simon, Beauchamp and Harcourt threatened to resign. At a subsequent meeting on

Wednesday 29 July, the cabinet refused to give any pledge to France or Germany 'either under all conditions to stand aside, or in any conditions to go in'. [Steiner, p. 225] On the same day a group of radical Liberals sent a letter to Grey urging British neutrality. At a meeting of the Liberal Foreign Affairs Group, the letter reported,

Steiner, *Britain and the Origins of the First World War*

> It was decided that everything possible should be done to counteract the influences which already seem to be working for our participation in what may prove to be a European conflict. On this point very strong views were expressed and it was the feeling of the meeting that we could not support the Government in any military or naval operations that would carry this country beyond its existing treaty obligations. [Hazlehurst, p. 35]

Hazlehurst, *Politicians at War*

In the country opposition to intervention came from the *Manchester Guardian*. One leader contained the message: 'We care as little for Belgrade as Belgrade for Manchester.' Two organisations were created to press for a policy of non-intervention, the British Neutrality Committee formed by Graham Wallas, and the Neutrality League formed by Norman Angell. The Parliamentary Labour party also declared unanimously on 30 July that Britain should stay out of the war. As late as 2 August, Asquith wrote to Venetia Stanley, his private confidante: 'I suppose a good three-quarters of our party are for non-intervention at any price.'

Two things brought about a change of heart. On Saturday 1 August, Cambon, the French ambassador, raised the question of Britain's likely response to German naval activity in the Channel. Asquith, much to Cambon's dismay, could give him no definite answer but agreed to raise the matter at cabinet the following day. After two lengthy and acrimonious meetings on 2 August, the cabinet finally agreed that Britain could not tolerate a German naval presence in the Channel and would defend France against any naval bombardment. Only John Burns and John Morley demurred. Nothing was said about British military intervention. Later that night, Grey heard news of Germany's ultimatum to Belgium demanding unopposed passage for her armies. Those members of the Liberal party who were not prepared to go to war in defence of the Entente now had an excuse to come off the fence. Belgian neutrality had been guaranteed by a treaty in 1839 to which Britain was a signatory. What Bethmann Hollweg, in an unguarded moment, referred to as a 'scrap of paper' provided the moral argument needed to justify British intervention, and it strengthened the hand of those in the cabinet and the Foreign Office who had long been urging the need to oppose German pretensions. Grey described the impact of the Belgian issue on his colleagues in these terms: 'As it became more and more certain that the German army was going to invade Belgium, the cabinet began all to face the same way, for we had our backs to the same wall.' [Grey, vol. II, p. 9] On 3 August the cabinet met again. Grey evidently outlined the terms of the speech he intended to make that afternoon. Four members of the cabinet, Simon, Beauchamp, Morley and Burns, offered their resignations. By the end of the day, Simon and Beauchamp had been prevailed on to stay. Grey's speech to the House of Commons tilted the scales in Parliament. He stressed Britain's obligations to France, arising out of the naval arrangements made in 1912: 'We could not stand aside with our arms folded if a foreign fleet battered and bombarded these undefended coasts.' He admitted that he understood the German government 'to be prepared, if we would pledge ourselves to neutrality, to agree that its fleet would not attack the

Lord Grey, *Twenty Five Years*, vol. II (1925)

northern coast of France, but it is far too narrow an engagement for us'. He then moved on to 'the more serious consideration – becoming more serious every hour' of Belgian neutrality. Grey cited the precedents of 1870 when at the time of the Franco-Prussian war Britain had promised to stand by Belgium, and he voiced what was probably that which the majority of his hearers believed when he said: 'If, in a crisis like this, we run away from those obligations of honour and interest as regards the Belgian treaty, I doubt whether, whatever material force we might have at the end, it would be of very much value in face of the respect that we should have lost.' [Grey, pp. 295–309] The opponents of intervention in the subsequent debate, F. D. Morel, Ramsay MacDonald and Arthur Ponsonby, were given an unsympathetic hearing.

Lord Grey, *Twenty Five Years*, vol. II

News of the invasion of Belgium reached London on 4 August. In conformity with a cabinet decision reached the previous day, Grey addressed an ultimatum to Germany requesting the withdrawal of German troops from Belgium. A reply was required by midnight. German clocks were one hour ahead of British ones, so that at 11.00 pm Britain found herself involved in a war that was not of her making and which her Foreign Secretary had done his best to avert. But Britain cannot escape all responsibility for the outbreak of the First World War. With hindsight it can be seen that the German naval threat was exaggerated. Fisher's readiness to contemplate a pre-emptive strike on the German fleet in 1904; Lloyd George's Mansion House speech in 1911; the anti-German tone of much of the popular press; all these helped to worsen Anglo-German relations. Uncertainty about the strength of Britain's commitments to France and Russia contributed to the willingness in some quarters in Germany to gamble on British neutrality in the event of war. When the crisis came in 1914 it found a cabinet badly divided on what steps to take. In consequence, Grey was neither able to play a restraining influence in St Petersburg nor to convince Berlin, until very late in the day, that Britain's weight would be thrown onto the side of France and Russia. Finally, as a result of the military and naval conversations with France, Britain had in fact, if not in writing, committed herself to a continental war on a scale she had never contemplated and for which she was quite unprepared.

POINTS AT ISSUE POINTS AT ISSUE **POINTS AT ISSUE** POINTS AT ISSUE
POINTS AT ISSUE POINTS AT ISSUE **POINTS AT ISSUE** POINTS AT ISSUE

The Nature of German Ambitions

Germany's aims and policies in the years prior to 1914 have been the object of acute controversy. The debate has essentially gone through three stages. Under Article 231 of the Treaty of Versailles, Germany was clearly held responsible for the outbreak of the First World War, and was saddled with the obligation of paying reparations for the damages caused by it. In the inter-war years there was a growing tendency to spread the blame more evenly. R. H. Lutz, for instance, wrote in 1930: 'All the powers in 1914 put their own interest, true or supposed, and their own ambitions before the peace of the world .... No belligerent except Belgium was blameless and

none was the sole culprit.' [cited in Morgan, *Foreign Affairs, 1886–1914*, p. 121] S. B. Fay, in *The Origins of the World War* was similarly disposed to allocate responsibilities for the war between the central and the Entente powers fairly evenly.

But a new twist to the debate was given in 1961 by the publication in Germany of Fritz Fischer's *Griff nach der Weltmacht*, translated into English in 1967 under the title *Germany's Aims in the First World War*. Fischer produced a wealth of evidence to illustrate the aggressive objectives of German foreign policy, both before and during the war. He summarises German policy up to 1914 as follows: 'Economic expansion was the basis of Germany's political world diplomacy, which vacillated in its methods between *rapprochement* and conciliation at one moment, aggressive insistence on German claims the next, but never wavered in its ultimate objective, the expansion of German power.'

A more recent history of Germany by G. A. Craig, *Germany, 1866–1945*, published in 1978, endorses much of the Fischer thesis and emphasises the internal stresses in German society which encouraged German politicians to embark on an adventurous foreign policy as a way of diverting attention from the attractions of socialism. He says of Von Bülow, Chancellor from 1900–09, that his programme for defeating the left,

> had two components. First he hoped to promote a union of the agrarian and industrial interests, based on the recognition and satisfaction of their economic desiderata, that would be strong enough to dominate the parliamentary situation in the Reichstag .... To complement it and to provide an element of excitement and accomplishment that would impress the masses and fill them with a new love and joy in the state, he embarked upon a spirited foreign policy on a global scale, a grandiose Welt-und Flottenpolitik. 'I am putting the main emphasis on foreign policy', he wrote in December, 1897. 'Only a successful foreign policy can help to reconcile, pacify, unite. [Craig, p. 275]

Tirpitz, the driving force behind the creation of the German navy, similarly felt that 'In the national purpose and economic gains consequent upon it lies a strong palliative against trained and potential Social Democrats.'

Books cited

M. C. Morgan, *Foreign Affairs, 1886–1914* (Collins, 1973) (for a brief analysis)
S. B. Fay, *The Origins of the World War* (MacMillan, 1929) (British ed.)
F. Fischer, *Germany's Aims in the First World War* (Chatto and Windus, 1967), (see especially pages 3–92)
G. A. Craig, *Germany, 1866–1945* (OUP, 1978), (see especially pages 302–38)

The Reasons for Anglo-German Hostility

The deterioration in Anglo-German relations that took place between 1890 and 1914 has had various explanations. The rivalries over commerce, colonies and naval power were perhaps the inevitable consequence of the emergence of the new German Empire in 1871, a natural challenger to the established might of the British Empire.

The most recent contribution to this debate has come from Paul Kennedy's book, *The Rise of the Anglo-German Antagonism*, published in 1980. Kennedy concludes his exhaustive survey of Anglo-German relations by arguing that the most profound cause of estrangement was economic. He points out that whereas German steel production was half that of Britain in 1860, by 1914 it was twice that of Britain. Germany's lead in this vital commodity epitomised the challenge to Britain's economic predominance. Two additional factors stressed by Kennedy were the proximity of the German threat to Britain posed by the Schlieffen Plan, and the ideological differences between British liberty loving radicals and the Prussian Junker class. Social tensions in each country also contributed to growing antagonism:

> What also emerges from the analysis in the preceding chapters is that fundamental social trends, especially in the growth of an industrial working class, made significant contributions to the changing Anglo-German relationship. The most obvious consequence was that it tempted beleagured elites in Germany to seek a solution in overseas expansion and, when later frustrated by their failure to gain 'a place in the sun', to repeat the Bismarckian tactic of solving domestic problems by a foreign war: which, given the operational efficiency planning of the army, meant a westward military drive and a probable clash with the British .... In Britain the effects of the rise of labour were more complex; but it seems fair to argue that this domestic trend, coinciding as it did with gloomy external developments, produced a ferment of discontent with the Unionist party which pulled it further to the right and thereby not only enhanced the party's anti-German stance but also enhanced the tactical position of the imperialist and 'interventionist' wing of the Liberal party. The harsher, more nervous political tone of Edwardian Britain also meant that the appearance of an external challenger would be greeted with more suspicion than in an earlier age. [Kennedy, p. 466]

Kennedy does not acquit Britain of all responsibility:

> It is scarcely the case, of course, that the British themselves can be given a clean sheet in their handling of Germany. There was far too much disdain at the failure to imitate British practices .... There was, in the debates upon commercial rivalry, far too much stress upon 'underhand' or 'unfair' competition, rather than an open recognition of superior quality and efficiency. There was an all too evident niggardliness in the treatment of German colonial claims .... There was, on occasion, an excessive suspicion of Germany's aggressive intentions ... and, with rare exceptions, (for example Balfour) a lack of comprehension of German *fears* for its own security.

Even so, Kennedy doubts whether a more conciliatory attitude on the part of Britain would have made very much difference in altering 'the elemental German push to change the existing distribution of power - which, unless the British were willing to accept a substantial diminution in national influence and safety, was bound to provoke a reaction on their part.' [Kennedy, p. 469]

A. J. Marder in his monumental history of the British Navy, *From the Dreadnought to Scapa Flow*, stresses the importance of naval rivalry. He cites with approval a memorandum delivered by the German Naval Attaché in London, in 1907: 'The steadily increasing sea power of Germany constitutes the greatest obstacle to England's freedom of political action. This is the central point of the unsatisfactory relations of the two countries to one another. All other frequently advanced grounds – competition in commerce, industry and shipping, partisanship during the Boer

War, etc. – are side issues.' Marder concludes: 'Now, the naval rivalry did not cause the war; but it ensured that when war did break out, Great Britain would be on the side of Germany's enemies.' [Marder, p. 432]

Books cited

P. M. Kennedy, *The Rise of the Anglo-German Antagonism* (Allen and Unwin, 1980), (see especially pages 441–70)
A. J. Marder, *From the Dreadnought to Scapa Flow, vol. I, The Road to War* (OUP, 1961)

British Responsibility for the Outbreak of War in 1914

The main charge against Britain in the crisis of 1914 rests upon her refusal to commit herself to the obligations of an alliance either with France or Russia, and hence the uncertainty about her intentions should these countries be drawn into a war. It has been argued that had Germany's politicians known that Britain would definitely intervene on the side of France and Russia they would not have been tempted to gamble on British neutrality. Conversely, had Britain made it clear to France and Russia that she would not come to their support in a war in which her interests were not directly threatened, Russia might not have mobilised when she did, thus avoiding the need for German mobilisation.

From the start, Grey always refused to consider turning the *entente* with France into an alliance. He told the French ambassador to London, Paul Cambon, in 1906: 'Should such a defensive alliance be formed, it was too serious a matter to be kept secret from Parliament. The Government could conclude it without the assent of Parliament, but it would have to be published afterwards. No British government could commit the country to such a serious thing and keep the engagement secret.' [Morgan, *Foreign Affairs 1886–1914*, p. 79] Grey did not believe then, or later, that the country would have accepted such a commitment. If so, this makes the military and naval conversations entered into in 1905 harder to justify, particularly when they were kept secret from the rest of the cabinet until 1911. There can be little doubt that there was a dangerous ambiguity about Britain's diplomatic position in 1914. Her admirals and generals fully expected to be drawn into a war between France and Germany; but many politicians and public opinion as a whole were unaware of the obligations Britain had assumed. It was hardly surprising in the circumstances that Germany misinterpreted Britain's likely reactions.

When the crisis broke in July 1914, while Grey and Asquith were clear that in the event of an attack on France by Germany, Britain was in honour bound to come to France's assistance, they could not speak for the rest of the cabinet. In his letters to Venetia Stanley, Asquith makes the confusion of British policy all too clear. He wrote on 26 July, on hearing the terms of the Serbian reply to the Austrian ultimatum: 'The news this morning is that Serbia has capitulated on the main points, but it is very doubtful if any reservations will be accepted by Austria, who is resolved upon a complete and final humiliation.' He did not anticipate that Britain would get involved, although Russia, as patron of Slav interests, 'is trying to drag us in'. He concluded somewhat lamely: 'It is the most dangerous situation of the last forty years, and may have incidentally the good effect of throwing into the background the lurid pictures of "civil war" in Ulster.' [Koss, *Asquith*, p. 155]

On 29 July Asquith summed up the dilemma facing Britain:

> It is one of the ironies of the case that we being the only Power who has made so much as a constructive suggestion in the direction of peace, are blamed by both Germany and Russia for causing the outbreak of war. Germany says: 'if you say you will be neutral, France and Russia won't dare to fight.' And Russia says: 'if you boldly declare that you will side with us, Germany and Austria will at once draw in their horns.' *Neither of course is true.*' (author's italics) [Koss, p. 156]

Was Asquith's final assumption justified? In fact, Grey, on his own initiative, had informed the German ambassador, Lichknowsky that the moment France was drawn into war, Britain would not be able to stand aside. This, according to Fischer, threw German policy into complete disarray:

> This upset the calculation on the basis of which Germany had urged Austria to take military action against Serbia and believed herself capable of regarding the prospect of European war 'with equanimity' in the confident hope that Britain would after all remain neutral if the responsibility for the war were laid on Russia. Now the situation suddenly became threatening. Only three days before Jagow had confidently told Jules Cambon, the French ambassador, who thought that Britain would intervene: 'You have your information, we have ours; we are certain of British neutrality.' The Germans, Bethmann Hollweg most of all, were surprised, even shattered, by Lichknowsky's report, and they grew unsure of themselves. [Fischer, p. 79]

Bethmann Hollweg's immediate reaction was to urge restraint on Austria, which he did in the early hours of 30 July. But it was already too late. Austria had declared war on Serbia on 28 July, and as Fischer says:

> although the premises of Bethmann Hollweg's policy, his conditions for undertaking war as laid down by him on July 5 and 6, had collapsed, he could not steel himself to change his policy, to talk unambiguously to Vienna and to force it to obey him. A declaration to this effect, combined with a threat to leave Austria alone if she disregarded it, could have saved the Reich from the catastrophe of a war waged under conditions which had become so unfavourable. But nothing was done.

If Fischer's reading of the situation is correct, an unambiguous declaration by Britain of her support for France much earlier in the crisis might have made a difference to German policy. But such an undertaking no British politician was in a position to give.

This is made abundantly clear in the summary of Britain's position which Asquith obligingly provided for Venetia Stanley in the letter he wrote to her on 30 July:

> Happily I am quite clear in my own mind as to what is right and wrong. I put it down for you in a few sentences:
> (1) We have no obligation of any kind to France or Russia to give them military or naval help.
> (2) The despatch of the Expeditionary Force to help France at this moment is out of the question and wd serve no object.
> (3) We mustn't forget the tie created by our long-standing and intimate friendship with France.
> (4) It is against British interests that France should be wiped out as a great power.

(5) We cannot allow Germany to use the Channel as a hostile base.
(6) We have obligations to Belgium to prevent her being utilised and absorbed by Germany.

The implicit contradiction between the first two and the remaining four principles does much to explain the uncertainty of Britain's response to the 1914 crisis.

Books cited

M. C. Morgan, *Foreign Affairs, 1886–1914* (Collins, 1973)
S. Koss, *Asquith* (Allen Lane, 1976)
F. Fischer, *Germany's Aims in the First World War* (Chatto & Windus, 1967)

BIBLIOGRAPHY BIBLIOGRAPHY BIBLIOGRAPHY BIBLIOGRAPHY BIBLIOGRAPHY BIBLIOGRAPHY
BIBLIOGRAPHY BIBLIOGRAPHY BIBLIOGRAPHY BIBLIOGRAPHY BIBLIOGRAPHY BIBLIOGRAPHY
BIBLIOGRAPHY BIBLIOGRAPHY BIBLIOGRAPHY BIBLIOGRAPHY BIBLIOGRAPHY BIBLIOGRAPHY
BIBLIOGRAPHY BIBLIOGRAPHY BIBLIOGRAPHY BIBLIOGRAPHY BIBLIOGRAPHY BIBLIOGRAPHY
BIBLIOGRAPHY BIBLIOGRAPHY BIBLIOGRAPHY BIBLIOGRAPHY BIBLIOGRAPHY BIBLIOGRAPHY
BIBLIOGRAPHY BIBLIOGRAPHY BIBLIOGRAPHY BIBLIOGRAPHY BIBLIOGRAPHY BIBLIOGRAPHY

CHAPTER 2
FURTHER READING

General European Background

Essential

N. Stone, *Europe Transformed, 1878–1919* (Fontana, 1983)

Recommended

E. J. Knapton and T. K. Derry, *Europe, 1815–1914* (J. Murray, 1965)
D. Thompson, *Europe since Napoleon* (Longman, 1957)

Individual Countries

Essential

Austria-Hungary
F. R. Bridge, *From Sadowa to Sarajevo: the Foreign Policy of Austria-Hungary* (Routledge & Kegan Paul, 1972)

Russia
H. Seton-Watson, *The Russian Empire* (OUP, 1967)
N. Stone, *The Eastern Front* (Hodder & Stoughton, 1975)

Italy
D. Mack Smith, *Italy, a Modern History* (University of Michigan Press, 1959)

France
D. W. Brogan, *The Development of Modern France, 1870–1939* (Hamish Hamilton, 1940)

Germany
G. A. Craig, *Germany, 1866–1945* (OUP, 1978)
F. Fischer, *Germany's Aims in the First World War* (Chatto & Windus, 1967)

European Diplomacy up to 1914

Essential

F. R. Bridge, *1914 The Coming of the First World War* (Historical Association, 1983)
A. J. P. Taylor, *The Struggle for Mastery in Modern Europe* (OUP, 1952)
L. C. F. Turner, *The Origins of the First World War* (Arnold, 1970)

Recommended

L. Albertini, *The Origins of the War of 1914* (OUP, 1952–57)

War Plans

Essential

P. M. Kennedy (ed.), *The War Plans of the Great Powers, 1880–1914* (Allen & Unwin, 1979)

British Diplomacy

Essential

P. M. Kennedy, *The Rise of the Anglo-German Antagonism* (Allen & Unwin, 1980)
C. J. Lowe and M. L. Dockrill, *The Mirage of Power, British Foreign Policy, 1902–1922* (Routledge & Kegan Paul, 1972)
M. C. Morgan, *Foreign Affairs, 1886–1914* (Collins, 1973)
Z. Steiner, *Britain and the Origins of the First World War* (Macmillan, 1977)

Recommended

M. & E. Brock (eds), *The Letters of H. H. Asquith to Venetia Stanley* (Macmillan, 1982)
W. S. Churchill, *The World Crisis*, Vol. I (Thornton–Butterworth, 1923)
Lord Grey, *Twenty-Five Years* (Hodder & Stoughton, 1925)
P. Hayes, *Modern British Foreign Policy* (A. & C. Black, 1981)
C. Hazlehurst, *Politicians at War*, Vol. I (Cape, 1971)
F. H. Hinsley, *The Foreign Policy of Sir Edward Grey* (CUP, 1977)
S. Koss, *Asquith* (Allen Lane, 1976)
G. Monger, *The End of Isolation, British Foreign Policy, 1900–1907* (Nelson, 1963)
K. S. Robbins, *Sir Edward Grey* (Cassell, 1971)

The Crisis of July 1914

Essential

I. Geiss, *July, 1914: Selected Documents* (Batsford, 1967)
B. W. Tuchman, *August, 1914* (Constable, 1962)

Britain and the First World War

Aims of the Combatants

None of the countries that entered the war in 1914 did so with clearly defined objectives. Austria-Hungary wanted to 'crush Serbia'; France welcomed the opportunity to recover Alsace-Lorraine. But, at the outset, neither Germany nor Russia made any specific territorial demands. *Punch* summed up what was perhaps the view of the average Englishman:

> I shall be asked to a general scrap
> All over the European Map,
> Dragged into somebody else's war
> For that's what a double entente is for.

However, within a month the fierce fighting that took place on the frontiers had brought about a stark change in national attitudes. Following Germany's initial successes in Belgium and northern France, her war aims took on a more aggressive character. In a memorandum presented on 2 September to the German government by Mathias Erzberger, Bethmann Hollweg's close assistant, Germany claimed the right to control Belgium and the French coast from Dunkirk to Boulogne; the cession to Germany of the Briey-Longwy iron basin and the fortress of Belfort; and the handing over of French and Belgian colonies in Africa. Europe was to accept German hegemony. By the Pact of London, signed by Britain, France and Russia, on 4 September the three Entente powers pledged that they would not 'conclude peace separately during the present war'. In a conversation with the French ambassador, Paléologue, on 20 August, the Russian foreign minister, Sazonoff had already agreed upon a substantial territorial adjustment, to follow the destruction of German imperialism. It was to include the restoration of an independent Poland, the recovery of Alsace-Lorraine by France and of Schleswig-Holstein by Denmark, the liberation of Bohemia from Austria-Hungary, and the confiscation of all Germany's colonies. Britain's war aims were not formally defined until January, 1918. But when they were, Lloyd George also pledged British support for the return of Alsace-Lorraine, the creation of an independent Poland and the surrender of Germany's colonies. Thus what had begun as a war to settle a dispute in the Balkans became a struggle for power and possession which extended across the globe.

German atrocities committed during the invasion of Belgium added a further dimension to the war. Faced with the prospect of civilian resistance which might delay the smooth operation of the Schlieffen Plan, the German High Command countenanced brutal counter measures. On August 21–23 84 civilians were shot in the market square at Tamine. The cathedral city of Louvain was given up to six days of looting and burning between 24 and 30 August. News of these events spread rapidly through the world's press. Atrocity stories were magnified in the telling. No babies were bayoneted, no nuns raped, as the popular press alleged. But there was enough substance in some of the accusations to convince many on the side of the Entente that they were engaged in a crusade against German barbarism.

Finally, while the battle for the frontiers that took place in August 1914 dispelled one myth, that the war would be over by Christmas, it created another: the myth of the 'knock out blow'. The initial success of the Schlieffen Plan appeared to indicate that with enough men and artillery support a breakthrough was always possible.

Both the central powers and the Entente powers clung to the belief that total victory was always within reach. Any chance of a negotiated settlement disappeared as each side stepped up its claims and deployed more and more resources in pursuit of victory, whatever the cost.

Strategy

THE SIDES

Central Powers	Entente Powers
1914 Germany Austria-Hungary Turkey (Nov.)	1914 Serbia Russia France Britain
1915 Bulgaria (Oct.)	1915 Italy (May) v. Austria
	1916 Italy (May) v. Germany Rumania (Aug.–Dec.)
	1917 United States (Apr.) Greece (Jun.)
	1918 Russian withdrawal (Mar.) after Treaty of Brest Litovsk

As can be seen from the above analysis, in terms of manpower and resources the Entente powers enjoyed a considerable advantage, particularly after the entry of the United States. The Central Powers faced the prospect of a war on two, or more, fronts simultaneously. On the other hand they had the benefit of interior lines. It was much easier to move German divisions from the Western to the Eastern or Italian Fronts than to do the same with British or French divisions. Indeed, after Turkey came into the war all direct communication with Russia, except through Archangel, was severed, a matter that came to have increasing importance as the Russian war machine began to seize up.

It would be misleading to assume that either side had a clearly thought out strategy. In war, more than in most areas, policy is made in reaction to the pressure of events. Here, too, the fighting that took place in August 1914 did much to shape the subsequent course of the war. Though the ultimate objective of the Schlieffen Plan was not achieved, its implementation was still sufficiently successful to leave Germany in occupation of Belgium and much of northern France. In the East, the battles of Tannenburg and the Masurian Lakes blunted the first Russian offensive in August 1914. To win the war the Germans could afford to remain on the defensive in the West, while with the outbreak of the Russian Revolution in 1917, they had the opportunity to make sweeping gains in the East.

The strategy of the Entente powers was determined by these unpalatable facts. Granted that the Russian steamroller was incapable of crushing German armies in the East, the only way to dislodge Germany from her unacceptable gains in the West was to defeat her there, or to starve her into surrender.

Weapons

Every war is conditioned by the current state of technology. By 1914 all the European armies had at their disposal, in varying quantities and qualities, the following weapons:

Rifles

Accurate to a range of 915 metres with a rate of fire of thirty rounds a minute in the hands of a good marksman.

Machine Guns

Based on the principle of the Maxim gun, they had a rate of fire of up to 600 rounds a minute.

Artillery

Guns varied in size from the enormous siege guns employed by the Germans to reduce the forts at Liège in 1914, which threw shells weighing 2 tons, to the light field guns with which British batteries were mainly equipped whose shells weighed 18 pounds. What was novel about artillery in the First World War was the scale of its deployment. In the week before the battle of the Somme in 1916, 1437 British guns fired off over 1.5 million shells into the German lines. Improvements in methods of observation and fire control permitted developments such as the creeping barrage, with shells falling just in front of the advancing infantry. Every offensive would be preceded by a bombardment.

To these weapons were added trench mortars, gas shells, mines, Mills bombs and grenades of various kinds, and above all, in 1916, the tank. Aeroplanes came to be used extensively for artillery spotting and reconnaissance. But perhaps the most used weapon of the First World War was an agricultural implement, thousands of years old: the spade. The only forms of protection against an artillery barrage were the trench and the dug-out. They became essential features of every battlefield.

Tactics

Wars are won by capturing ground, or by sapping the enemy's will to go on fighting. In the First World War the two became inextricably linked. But whether the objective was to capture a particular feature, or merely to commit enemy troops to battle, the pattern of an offensive was always the same. After the bombardment, lines of men would have to advance on foot, laden by up to 60 pounds of equipment, towards enemy trenches and fortifications that were usually well defended.

The most common form of defence was barbed wire, designed to delay the attacker while machine guns were brought to bear. The combination was lethal. Despite a ferocious artillery bombardment much of the German wire was still uncut on the first day of the Somme offensive: 'On the worst sector, frantic men ran along the wire searching for gaps, but if they did discover one, often found themselves in a death trap. The German machine gunners were covering every gap.' [Middlebrook, p. 131] Where the defenders had time to prepare for an assault, as the Germans did by retiring to the Hindenburg Line in 1917, trenches were supplemented by strong points, dug-outs and fortifications of all kinds, each one supporting its neighbours.

M. Middlebrook, *The First Day on the Somme* (1971)

Sir L. Woodward, *Great Britain and the War of 1914–18* (1967)

The problem that was never satisfactorily solved was how to protect the advancing troops as they crossed 'No-man's land'. This gave a decided advantage to the defenders and on the Western Front in particular led to a condition of stalemate that could be broken, if at all, only at the cost of enormous casualties. Faced with this problem, Kitchener, British minister for war from 1914–1916, once remarked to Grey (the foreign secretary): 'I don't know what is to be done. This isn't war'. [Woodward, p. 39] Unfortunately it was.

Two solutions were eventually adopted which went some way to overcome the advantage held by the defender. The British developed the Tank, an armoured fighting vehicle capable of going across country and sufficiently well armoured to withstand small arms fire. It could be used with other tanks in an old-style cavalry charge, or, more profitably, in conjunction with infantry to wipe out enemy positions. Unfortunately it was some time before a mechanically reliable tank was available. At the battle of the Somme over half of them broke down before crossing the start line. Tanks were employed with much greater success at the battle of Cambrai in November 1917; but the initial breakthrough did not have sufficient infantry support and the Germans soon recovered all the ground that had been won. It was only in the summer of 1918 that the tank can be said to have had a decisive effect on the battlefield.

The Germans tried in a different tactic. Instead of sending their infantry into an advance in carefully spaced ranks of extended lines, which proved so disastrous in the Somme offensive, they trained their infantry to move in small self-contained groups, each under the orders of an NCO. They also varied the pattern of the preliminary bombardment, thus recovering to some extent the weapon of surprise. These tactics were employed with some success in the March 1918 offensive, though it has to be said that the German attacks were directed at the weakest point in the British line.

These developments brought back a degree of mobility to the battlefield. The front line on the Western Front moved further, in both directions, in the final six months of the war than it had done in the previous three years. But the basic characteristics of trench warfare lasted to the bitter end. Every advance was still costly in terms of casualties. Britain lost almost as many soldiers in the successful offensives of 1918 as she had done in the previous ones of 1916 and 1917, which had failed.

BRITONS

"WANTS

YOU"

JOIN YOUR COUNTRY'S ARMY!

GOD SAVE THE KING

Reproduced by permission of LONDON OPINION

The mass slaughter that characterised the fighting in the First World War resulted from a series of unhappy coincidences. Advances in technology made possible the mass production of armaments and ammunition; the increasing reach of the State extended to the whole of the working population and enabled it to recruit conscript armies and the workers to man the munitions factories. The advent of the popular press encouraged the growth of patriotic sentiment. In every European capital the outbreak of war was greeted with enthusiastic demonstrations. Socialist parties in France, Germany and Britain all put their patriotic duty before their class interests. There was no need to introduce conscription in Britain until 1916, such was the willing response to Kitchener's accusing finger and his famous appeal: 'Your country needs you'. It made an all too apposite epitaph for the millions who flocked to the colours in 1914.

MILITARY OPERATIONS ▬▬▬▬▬▬▬▬▬ B

No attempt will be made here to recount the history of the First World War. Within the limits available all that can be done is to concentrate on the experiences of the British forces involved, and on their contribution by land and sea to the victory of the Entente.

Resources

At the outset of the war the British army consisted of about 250 000 men stationed in various parts of the Empire. In addition there were 200 000 in the Army and Special Reserve, and a further 250 000 in the Territorial Army. Britain could also call upon her forces in India, and on the volunteers recruited in the White Dominions (Australia, Canada, South Africa and New Zealand).

The only troops immediately available to go to France were the five infantry divisions and one cavalry division that had been earmarked for the British Expeditionary Force since 1911. A tremendous increase in the size of the British army took place in the next two years. By 1916 there were no fewer than 48 divisions on the Western Front, with 20 000 men to each division. In 1918 total numbers in the British army were as follows:

Western Front :	1 949 100
Other theatres :	888 315
In Britain :	1 460 862
Total :	4 298 277

J. Douglas Terraine,
Haig, The Educated Soldier (1962)

[Terraine, pp. 392–3]

This expansion was achieved by grafting new battalions on to the regular and Territorial battalions created under the Haldane army reforms, and by the creation of entirely new formations, as with the 30 new divisions that made up Kitchener's New Army. The Indian army provided 800 000 troops, 50 000 of whom fought in Western Europe. The White Dominions contributed a further 857 000 in all, many of whom proved to be the best fighting soldiers on the side of the Entente.

The majority of these soldiers served in the infantry. Though some British generals, Haig among them, cherished a belief that the cavalry could play a decisive role on the battlefield once an initial breakthrough had been achieved, in practice the cavalry only formed a small proportion of the forces involved – as little as 1% in 1918. Only in the Syrian campaign in 1918 did cavalry operate successfully. Far more significant was the part played by the artillery. Each division had its own quota of guns, but for set-piece battles all the guns in the army would be co-ordinated. At the battle of Passchendaele in 1917, there was one gun for every five yards of front line. British tanks were first used at the battle of Flers on 15 September 1916, but of the 49

An early tank as used in Cambrai

supposedly available only 18 saw action. They were first used decisively at the battle of Cambrai on 20 November 1917, when 381 tanks went into action. Their first real success was achieved on 8 August 1918 when 534 tanks took part in a combined offensive.

These fighting arms all needed to be co-ordinated and serviced. The problems are well summarised by Colonel Charteris, Haig's Chief Intelligence Officer:

Terraine, *Haig*

> Can you imagine what it is to feed, administer, move about, look after the medical and spiritual requirements of a million men, even when they are not engaged in fighting, and not in a foreign country? Add to that the purely military side of the concern. That we have to concentrate great accumulations of this mass of humanity quickly into some particular restricted area, have to deal with enormous casualties, and have to keep a constant flow of men backwards and forwards for hours .... [Terraine, p. 178]

The staff have not enjoyed a good reputation, and it is true that they did not face the same rigours as the front line soldier. But it needs to be remembered what an astonishing feat of organisation it was to create out of such small beginnings an army of over 4 million men, and to deploy it all over the globe.

Deployment

The British army between 1914 and 1918 fought in three continents: Europe, Asia and Africa. It was in Europe that it made much its greatest contribution. Out of a total of 2.75 million casualties (killed and wounded) the British Empire sustained 2.5 million on the Western Front. In these terms, the other fronts were indeed 'sideshows'.

But while the Western Front was where German resistance was finally broken the other fronts were important in other respects. Firstly, it was by no means obvious to contemporaries that the war would be decided in France and Belgium. A continuous argument went on between generals and politicians as to whether British troops might not be better employed elsewhere. Churchill and Lloyd George each hankered after ways of breaking the brutal deadlock on the Western Front and canvassed various alternatives: landings on the north German coast, strengthening the Italian Front, forcing the Dardanelles, invading the Austro-Hungarian Empire through the Balkans. Some of these alternatives were in fact tried and the primacy of the Western Front could never be assured. The conduct of operations there, was at times seriously affected by these alternative possible strategies.

Secondly, it needs to be remembered that for Britain, the First World War was also an imperial war. She benefited enormously from the assistance she received from India and the Dominions. But conversely she had imperial possessions to defend. The Suez Canal required a constant British presence, British colonies in Africa needed defending and in the furtherance of her imperial interests, Britain played a major role in the defeat of Germany's ally, Turkey, through her campaigns in Mesopotamia, Egypt and Syria. This gave Britain a preponderant voice in the Middle East settlement at the end of the war. The Western Front may have claimed far more lives, but the fruits of victory were secured elsewhere.

BRITISH MILITARY OPERATIONS

Date	Western Front	Date	Gallipoli and Salonika
1914 August 9–17	BEF landed at Boulogne	*1914* November 3	Outer forts guarding Dardanelles bombarded
August 24	Mons		
August 26	Le Cateau		
October– November	First Ypres		
1915 March 10–13	Neuve Chapelle	*1915* February 19	Naval attacks on forts
May 9	Aubers Ridge	March 18	Serious naval losses
May 12–15	Festubert	April 25	Gallipoli landings
September 15– October 16	Loos	August 6–7 October	Landings at Suvla Bay British forces land at Salonika
		December 8– January 9	Evacuation of Gallipoli Peninsula
1916 July 1– November 18	The Somme		
1917 April 9–16	Arras		
June 17	Messines		
July 15– November 12	Passchendaele		
1918 March 27– July 15	German offensive	*1918* September 15	Salonika offensive
August 8 September 29	British offensive Hindenburg Line breached		
November 11	Armistice signed		

Date	Mesopotamia	Date	Egypt, Arabia, Palestine and Syria
1914 November	Occupation of Basra	*1914* August	British Protectorate declared over Egypt
1915 September November 22	Capture of Kut Ctesiphon	*1915* February	Turkish attack on Suez Canal
1916 April 29	Surrender of Kut	*1916* June December	Outbreak of Arab Re- volt Capture of El Arish

Date	Mesopotamia	Date	Egypt, Arabia, Palestine and Syria
1917 March 11	Capture of Baghdad	*1917* March– April July October November December	Unsuccessful attacks on Gaza Capture of Aqaba Capture of Beersheba Capture of Gaza Capture of Jerusalem
1918		*1918* September 19 October 1 October 20	Megiddo Capture of Damascus Turks requested an armistice

The Western Front

Britain's commitment to the Western Front arose out of the military conversations held in 1906 between British and French general staffs, but the ambiguity of Britain's position remained, and as John Terraine puts it: 'Britain went to war on a French Plan, not a British one; and as the French lost the initiative to the Germans, the British effort was, in fact, dictated by the enemy.' [Terraine, p. 62] British troops were thus deployed in the first instance on the left of the French Line, and here they remained throughout the war, under whose command it was not always clear. While Kitchener's instructions to the commander of the BEF, Sir John French, required him 'to support and co-operate with the French army ...' he was distinctly to understand 'that your command is an entirely independent one, and that you will in no case come in any sense under the orders of any allied general.' [Tuchman, p. 202] This did not make for easy relations with the French. Further efforts were made to solve the problem of divided commands in the course of the war. At the Calais Conference held in March 1917 Haig reluctantly agreed to place his forces at the disposal of the French Commander-in-Chief, General Nivelle. But the catastrophic failure of the ensuing offensive brought an abrupt end to that experiment. In November 1917, a Supreme War Council was established at Versailles with the aim of centralising control of the reserves. But this solution did not work very satisfactorily either. It was not until the German offensive of March 1918 that it was finally agreed to make Marshal Foch Supreme Commander of all the Allied armies on the Western Front. Thus, for most of the war British armies on the Western Front worked in uneasy partnership with the French, never directly under French command, but never free to act independently either.

Terraine, *Haig*

B. Tuchman, *August 1914* (1962)

British military operations on the Western Front can be divided into five distinct phases:

1. the response to the Schlieffen Plan (August–November 1914)
2. the offensives launched under Sir John French (March–October 1915)
3. the battle of the Somme (July–November 1916)
4. the Flanders campaign, known as Passchendaele (July–November 1917)
5. the British response to the final German offensive and the British counter offensive (March–November 1918).

During the first phase the crack divisions of the British army came up against von Kluck's greatly superior numbers and fought two successful delaying actions at Mons and Le Cateau. South of Antwerp they succeeded in holding off the German drive for the Channel ports in a series of actions round Ypres, but only at tremendous cost. By November, of the original 160 000 members of the BEF, 90 000 were casualties. The flower of the regular British army had perished. The French army, meanwhile, had defeated the Schlieffen Plan at the battle of the Marne and the war of movement ground to a halt. Before the next phase of war opened, each side dug itself in. A line of trenches extended all the way from the Belgian coast to the Swiss frontier. The British share of this line covered 85 miles, by comparison with 15 miles held by the Belgians and 300 miles held by the French.

THE WESTERN FRONT: BRITISH ZONE, JUNE 1916

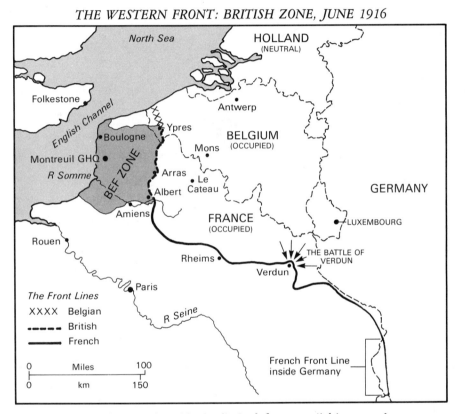

In 1915 Sir John French, with the limited forces available, agreed to support French offensives south of British positions by launching a series of diversionary attacks from the British front. These duly took place at Neuve Chapelle, Aubers Ridge and Festubert. In no case did they achieve their objectives and heavy casualties were sustained. In September, following reverses on the Eastern Front, a further offensive was ordered at Loos. There were 15 000 casualties on the first day, and by the time the battle was called off on 16 October the total had reached 50 000. When French was appointed to the command of the BEF in 1914, one of his corps commanders, Haig, had recorded his reservations: 'In my own heart I know that French is quite unfit for this great command in a time of crisis in our Nation's history.' [Terraine, p. 79] The events of 1915 bore out only too clearly French's incapacity. In December he was asked to resign and was replaced by his critical subordinate, Haig himself.

Terraine, *Haig*

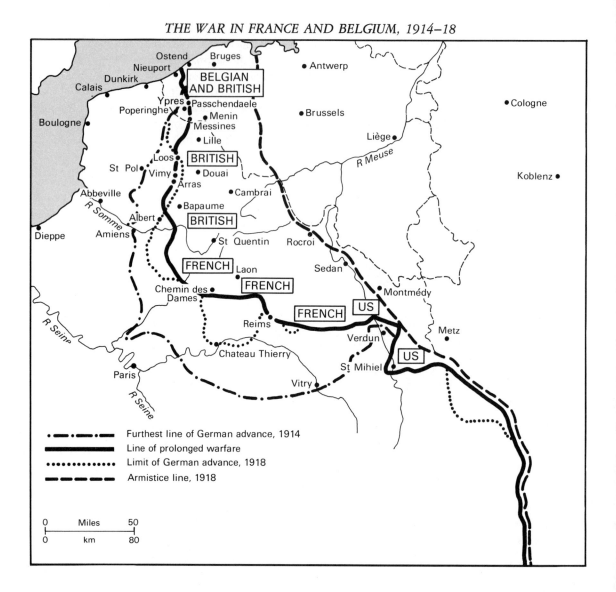

THE WAR IN FRANCE AND BELGIUM, 1914–18

Ostend · Bruges
Nieuport · Antwerp
Dunkirk
Calais
BELGIAN
AND BRITISH
Boulogne
· Cologne
Ypres · Passchendaele
Poperinghe · Brussels
· Menin
Messines · Liège
· Lille
St Pol Loos BRITISH
· Vimy · Douai
Abbeville Arras
R Somme · Cambrai
Albert Bapaume
BRITISH
Dieppe Amiens
· St Quentin
Rocroi
FRENCH
Laon
FRENCH Sedan
Chemin des
Dames FRENCH US
· Reims Montmédy
R Seine Verdun Metz
Chateau Thierry St Mihiel
US
Paris
R Seine Vitry

·–·–·–· Furthest line of German advance, 1914
———— Line of prolonged warfare
········ Limit of German advance, 1918
– – – – Armistice line, 1918

0   Miles   50
0   km   80

The Battle of the Somme

The third phase of the war was dominated by the battle of the Somme. Though the request for a major British offensive came from the French, who had to withstand the German onslaught on Verdun, Haig gave it his unqualified support. He was firmly convinced that with adequate preparation a decisive breakthrough could be achieved. Most of the troops engaged in the battle would come from Kitchener's New Army, all volunteers, and certainly making up in enthusiasm and spirit what they lacked in training and experience. It has been argued that the battle of the Somme was lost by three minutes, the length of time it took for German machine-gunners to emerge from their dug-outs after the bombardment had lifted, in time to mow down the steadily advancing lines of infantry. Despite the weight of the five-day bombardment which preceded the attack, much of the German wire remained uncut, and the defenders, though certainly shaken by the battering they

had received, were quite capable of manning their positions. Because of their inexperience, the attacking troops were instructed to advance in regular formation, at a slow pace, in successive waves, each man carrying at least 66 pounds of equipment. The advance was timed for 7.30 am in perfect visibility. By the end of the first day, nearly 20 000 British soldiers had been killed and a further 40 000 wounded, a casualty rate of nearly 50%. It was 75% for junior officers. Terraine has argued that proportionately this was no worse than the battle of Waterloo, but in this case the first day of the Somme was only the prelude to a series of bloody battles which went on until 18 November. When the offensive was finally called off the British had advanced some 6 to 7 miles over a 30-mile front at a cost of 400 000 casualties.

The full horror of the Western Front was not reached, however, until the fourth phase, the Flanders campaign of 1917. In December 1916, Lloyd George replaced Asquith as Prime Minister, and it looked as if no further expensive offensives would be allowed, Lloyd George avowing that 'he was not prepared to accept the position of a butcher's boy driving cattle to the market and that he would not do it.' But Lloyd George showed more faith in French than in British generals. He was taken in by General Nivelle's supreme self-confidence, and duly permitted British troops to support a French offensive by a diversionary attack at Arras on 4 April. It achieved very little, while the French offensive was even more disastrous.

Haig, in the meantime, had been drawing up his own plans for a British offensive north of Ypres, with the aim of clearing the Belgian coastline of German troops. The cabinet expressed their doubts about the feasibility of Haig's plans. But two new factors strengthened his case. Partly in consequence of the failure of Nivelle's offensive there were 55 mutinies in French units between 29 April and 10 June 1917.

According to the French Prime Minister, Painlevé, there were only two reliable divisions in the whole of the French army. Then, at a meeting of the War Committee on 20 June, Jellicoe, the First Sea Lord, stated that 'owing to the general shortage of shipping due to German submarines, it would be impossible to continue the war in 1918.' He continued: 'There is no point discussing plans for next spring – we cannot go on.' [Marder, vol. VI, p. 203–4] Though Jellicoe's pessimism was not shared by his colleagues his view that it was imperative to deny Belgian bases to German submarines, combined with the fragile state of the French army, secured Lloyd George's reluctant acquiescence to the Flanders offensive.

A. Marder, *From the Dreadnought to Scapa Flow*, vol. VI (1978)

The Western Front: A British machinegun post in July 1916 at the battle of the Somme

The Battle of Passchendaele

It opened on 15 July with two distinct objectives: first to advance up the Belgian coast, if possible with amphibious support, secondly to break out of the Ypres salient, now surrounded on three sides by German troops and a constant drain on British manpower for that reason. The amphibious support never materialised and Ypres proved to be a disastrous base from which to launch an attack. The offensive lasted for three and a half months. There were isolated successes where the artillery preparation had been thorough enough and where well led and seasoned troops were employed, for example the capture of the Menin Road Ridge on 20 September and the battle of Polygon Wood on 26 September. But when the rains came in October the attacks literally bogged down. All the drainage ditches had been destroyed by shellfire and the battlefield became a sea of mud, making all movement virtually impossible. When a halt was finally called on 6 November the British had sustained 250 000 casualties without achieving any of Haig's initial objectives. German losses remain a matter of conjecture and have been hotly disputed. Haig's apologist, John Terraine, concludes: 'But that they at least equalled those of the Allies, and probably exceeded them, seems a safe assumption.' [Terraine, p. 372] Even if that were the case it hardly justifies the unnecessary losses suffered by the British army in launching offensives in such unfavourable conditions.

Terraine, *Haig*

The final stage of fighting on the Western Front was perhaps the most critical of all. With the collapse of the last Russian offensive, ordered by Kerensky in June 1917, it became clear that Germany could now concentrate all her energies on the Western Front. The entry of the United States into the war in April 1917, did something to redress the balance, but there would be a brief interval before the build-up of American troops could take place to compensate for the withdrawal of Russia from the fighting line.

Ludendorff, now Chief of the German General Staff, determined to seize this opportunity. At a war conference held at Mons on 11 November 1917 he summed up the position as follows: 'Our general situation requires that we should strike at the earliest moment, if possible before the end of February or the beginning of March, before the Americans can throw strong forces into the scale. We must beat the British.' [Barnett, p. 284] In December it was decided to direct a series of attacks on the British sector, in the hope of dividing the British and French armies and cutting the British off from the Channel ports. The offensive began on 21 March, after a five-hour bombardment from 6000 guns. Its main weight fell on General Gough's weakened and depleted army which had borne the brunt of the Passchendaele battles. Within three days the Germans had broken through the British defences and were advancing on a 30-mile front. In desperation Haig appealed to Pétain for 20 French divisions to plug the gap. On 26 March a conference was held at Doullens at which Foch was made Supreme Commander to co-ordinate the allied defences.

C. Barnett, *The Swordbearers* (1963)

The Germans launched a further attack on the Ypres sector on 9 April, which provoked Haig's most celebrated order of the day: 'There is no other course open to us but to fight it out. Every position must be held to the last man. There must be no retirement. With our backs to the wall and believing in the justice of our cause each one must fight to the end.' But instead of concentrating on the British sector Ludendorff now ordered secondary offensives against the French, which opened on 27 May at Chemin des Dames and on 15 July west of Reims. Though the German armies in 1918 made more extensive gains than any of the British or French offensives their efforts were to no avail. The allied fronts finally held. By June there were 1.4 million American soldiers in France. Ludendorff's resources were stretched to the limit, while Haig and Foch had enough reserves of fresh troops to launch their counter offensives. The first of these, the French offensive, began on 18 July. On 8 August the British army attacked in strength from Amiens with 534 tanks. Ludendorff described it as 'the blackest day of the German army'. The Germans suffered 27 000 casualties, two-thirds being taken prisoner. On 29 September the Hindenburg Line was pierced. This provoked Ludendorff into calling for 'an immediate armistice in order to save a catastrophe'. Negotiations were opened with President Wilson on 4 October, and though fighting continued throughout October (the British suffering a further 120 000 casualties in the final month of the war) German resistance finally crumbled. Armistice terms were agreed on 11 November.

Gallipoli

Of the alternatives to the Western Front, the one which attracted most support was the Gallipoli campaign. The Turkish Empire was drawn into the war partly out of natural hostility to its age-old rival, the Russian Empire, partly through German influence. In August 1914, two powerful cruisers, the *Goeben* and the *Breslau*, managed to escape the attentions of the British Mediterranean Fleet and arrived at Constantinople. Officially sold to the Turks, the British having refused to deliver two battleships that had just been completed for the Turkish navy in British shipyards, the *Goeben* and *Breslau* were re-named *Jawus* and *Midilli*, and under their enterprising commander, Admiral Souchon, proceeded to bombard the Russian ports of Odessa, Sebastopol and Feodorian on 28 October. This action, for which the Turks were held responsible, brought declarations of war by Russia on 4 November and by Britain and France on 5 November. But the Dardanelles were in consequence closed to all Russian shipping. Now dependent on the ice-bound ports of Archangel and Vladivostok, Russian exports and imports fell disastrously. The Russian

THE GALLIPOLLI CAMPAIGN, 1915

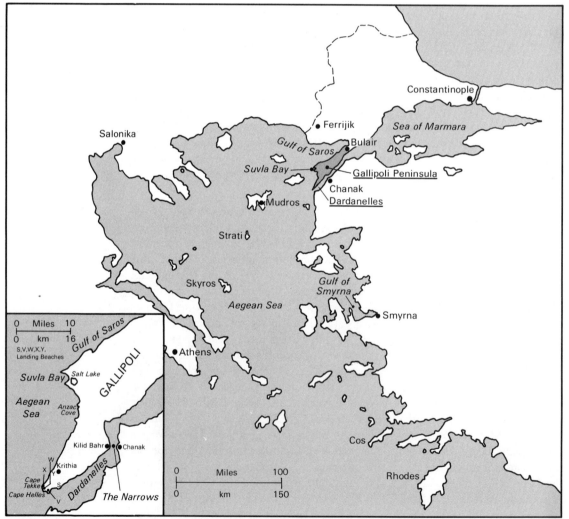

armaments industry was quite incapable of supplying the needs of her 15 million-strong armies. If the Allies were to make use of Russia's huge advantage in manpower it was essential to restore the vital artery that linked the Mediterranean to the Black Sea. A successful attack on Constantinople might bring Bulgaria and Greece into the war on the side of the Entente. Finally, if the Turkish troops could be diverted from attacking the Russians in the Caucasus, this would free more Russian forces for the Eastern Front. It was in such hopes that the Gallipoli campaign was conceived.

If the objectives of the campaign were confused, so were its methods. At the outset a purely naval assault was envisaged. On 5 January 1915, Winston Churchill, First Lord of the Admiralty, was assured by Vice Admiral Carden, the local squadron commander in the eastern Mediterranean, that the Straits might be forced with a large fleet of battleships. Such a fleet could easily be assembled, as it happened, from the obsolescent ships in the British and French navies. On 13 January the War Council gave its approval to the preparation of 'a naval expedition in February to bombard and take the Gallipoli peninsula, with Constantinople as its objective.' How ships were to conquer the land was not at this stage discussed. But by 16 February doubts had surfaced on this score, and it was agreed to send the 29th Division to Mudros on the island of Lemnos. With reinforcements from Egypt troops would then be available 'in case of necessity to support the naval attack on the Dardanelles'.

Thus from its inception the Gallipoli campaign was doomed by the failure of those responsible to make up their minds as to whether they were hoping to force a passage through the Straits, or whether to capture the peninsula which overlooked them. The naval assault came to an abrupt halt on 15 March after two British battleships and one French one had been sunk by mines. On 22 March Admiral de Robeck, who had replaced Carden, decided that he could not hope to get through the Sea of Marmora without military assistance. General Sir Ian Hamilton, appointed to the command of the military forces now being assembled, concurred. But by now the Turks were thoroughly prepared, and all hope of an unopposed landing had gone.

On 25 April the first landing took place on five different beaches. At only one of them, Y beach, was surprise achieved, and here it was not exploited. Bridgeheads were established at great cost. Offensives were launched on 6–8 May on a three-mile front, but they made little progress and a similar stalemate to that on the Western Front set in, with vastly greater problems of supply to contend with. Hamilton and Churchill nonetheless remained confident of success. Three further divisions were released from the Western Front and arrived in August under the command of the elderly and inexperienced Lieutenant General Stopford. They were landed at Suvla Bay on the north side of the Gallipoli peninsula where the Turks were not expecting a landing. But once again, failure to exploit an initial surprise prevented them from capturing the dominant geographical features and the last hope of success was missed. The campaign lingered on with mounting casualties, as much from the climate as the enemy. Two things brought it to an end. On 25 September a German attack on Serbia resulted in the decision to send three divisions to Salonika to buttress Serbian opposition. The Entente powers could not hope to reinforce both the Gallipoli landings and the Serbs. Secondly, General Sir Charles Monro, sent out to relieve Hamilton on 31 October, after no more than two days at Gallipoli, concluded that evacuation was the only sensible course of action. Had the same care and thought been given to the preparation of the landings as went into the evacuation, the Gallipoli campaign might have met with more success. Not a single life was lost in the series of carefully planned withdrawals that took place between 8 December 1915 and 9 January 1916. But of the 410 000 troops who took part in all the Gallipoli operations 205 000 became casualties.

Salonika

Described by the Germans as 'their largest internment camp', it is doubtful whether the Salonika enterprise could ever have had a decisive effect on the war. It was originally intended to provide assistance to Serbia, but when Bulgaria entered the war on the German side in October 1915, all communications with Serbia were effectively blocked. Despite British objections, an increasing entente contingent gradually concentrated on Salonika. Its only apparent purpose was to dissuade the Greeks from joining the German side. The first British troops, the 10th Division, arrived from Gallipoli on 5 October 1915. By March 1917 there were 234 000 British troops stationed there. Their only positive contribution to the war effort was their part in a combined offensive against Bulgaria in September 1918. This admittedly brought about Bulgaria's withdrawal from the war, and this in turn helped to weaken Ludendorff's resolve at a critical moment. But in other respects the allied presence in Salonika achieved very little.

THE MESOPOTAMIAN CAMPAIGNS

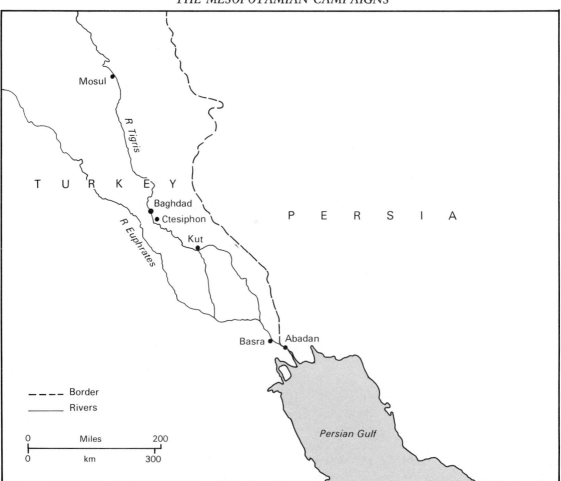

Mesopotamia

The Mesopotamian expedition was dispatched initially to protect Britain's oil supplies, in particular the oil pipe-line and refinery at Abadan. It was the responsibility of the Indian army to begin with, and was controlled from the India Office. But what began as a purely defensive operation developed into an ambitious series of campaigns, with their attendant disasters and triumphs. In November 1914 Basra was occupied without serious opposition. In August 1915 General Townshend led his forces up the valleys of the Tigris and Euphrates. He reached the town of Kut, but an indecisive battle at Ctesiphon on 22 November left his army dangerously exposed and isolated. Townshend retired to Kut, which was then surrounded. The relief expedition failed to get through and food ran out. On 27 April 1916 the British garrison surrendered and 12 000 men were taken into captivity, most of them to die in Turkish prison camps.

A new British general, F. S. Maude, was appointed, and with better supply lines achieved greater success. In February 1917 Kut was recaptured. Baghdad fell to British troops on 11 March. From then on a policy of 'active defence' was pursued, the British eventually reaching north as far as Tigris. Maude's successes helped to erase the humiliation of Kut, and meant that when the war ended Britain's influence would be paramount in the new state of Iraq which emerged in the river valleys of Mesopotamia.

Egypt, Arabia, Palestine and Syria

Britain's primary military commitment in this area was the defence of the Suez Canal. At one time this task occupied a garrison of no fewer than 250 000 men, far more than was strictly necessary. A Turkish attack on the Canal in February 1915 was easily repulsed but no offensive action could be undertaken until the ending of the Gallipoli campaign. In June 1916 the Arab Revolt against Turkish rule broke out, led by Hussein, the Sherif of Mecca. It was given support and direction by T. E. Lawrence, and while its importance may have been exaggerated by Lawrence's literary masterpiece, *The Seven Pillars of Wisdom* (his account of the revolt) it put the Turkish army under considerable pressure. In December 1916 a British army under the command of General Murray, who had been appointed the previous year, advanced eastwards from Cairo and captured the port of El Arish. The advance was thwarted at Gaza in March but this failure was counterbalanced by Lawrence's capture of the port of Aqaba at the head of the Red Sea in July. General Allenby, who replaced Murray in June 1917, outflanked Gaza and captured Beersheba in October. Gaza fell in November, and on 9 December British troops entered Jerusalem. Allenby had to release 60 000 of his best troops for the Western Front in March 1918 to meet the German offensive, but in September he was able to renew his attack and won a notable victory over a demoralised Turkish army at Megiddo. On 1 October Damascus fell to the British. In the space of 38 days they had advanced 350 miles and captured 75 000 prisoners at a cost of 5 000 casualties. The contrast with the fighting on the Western Front could hardly have been greater. On 20 October the Turks requested an armistice.

T. E. Lawrence, *The Seven Pillars of Wisdom* (1926) (Penguin, 1962)

Thus the war ended with the cities of Baghdad, Jerusalem and Damascus in British hands. Among the unsought consequences of the First World War was the collapse of the Turkish Empire and a corresponding extension of British responsibilities in the Middle East.

NAVAL OPERATIONS

There were two ways in which the war at sea could decide the final outcome. Had the German High Seas Fleet defeated the British Grand Fleet the Channel would no longer have been the moat on which Britain's security rested, or as Churchill put it: 'The destruction of the British Battle Fleet was final. Jellicoe [its Commander-in-Chief] was the only man on either side who could lose the war in an afternoon.' [Churchill, part I, p. 112] But the war could also be won by whichever side managed to stifle its opponent's overseas trade. Britain imported two-thirds of her food (18.1 million tons) in 1914. Germany, while her imports were equivalent to only 20% of her Gross National Product, was heavily dependent on imported cotton, saltpetre, non-ferrous metals and artificial fertilisers. Both countries made determined efforts to strangle each other's trade during the war, and certainly in the case of Britain the threat to her survival was a very real one.

W. S. Churchill, *The World Crisis, 1916–1918*, part I (Thornton Butterworth, 1927)

Admiral of the fleet John Jellicoe

Battleship Encounters

Despite Germany's efforts, Britain was still well ahead in the naval arms race in 1914. The German High Seas Fleet could thus only hope to inflict a decisive defeat on the Royal Navy by achieving temporary local superiority or by luring British ships to destruction by minefield or torpedo. The battleship war was one of skirmishes designed to tempt the British Grand Fleet into vulnerable situations. The one major encounter, the battle of Jutland, was a direct result of such tactics.

First, however, the ships Germany had at sea in 1914 remained to be dealt with. In August 1914, as we have seen, the *Goeben* and the *Breslau* escaped from the

Mediterranean to Constantinople, with dire consequences. On 1 November Admiral Cradock, commanding a British task force in the Pacific, made contact with Admiral von Spee's powerful squadron off Coronel, on the Chilean coast. Cradock unwisely gave battle before the guns of the battleship *Canopus* could be brought to bear. The British cruisers *Good Hope* and *Monmouth* were quickly sunk by von Spee's weightier and better directed salvoes. However, the tables were quickly turned at the battle of the Falkland Islands, a month later. On 8 December two British battle cruisers out-gunned von Spee, sinking four of his ships including the *Gneisenau* and the *Scharnhorst*. That left only the cruisers *Dresden*, *Königsberg* and *Emden* to be rounded up. All were eventually dispatched, but only after they had accounted for about 70 British merchant ships.

In the North Sea each side suffered casualties. On 28 August 1914, at the battle of Heligoland Bight, three German light cruisers were sunk, while on 22 September three British cruisers, *Aboukir*, *Hogue* and *Cressy* were torpedoed by a German submarine. The German navy then undertook the first of its 'hit and run' raids on the British coast, bombarding Yarmouth on 3 November and Scarborough and Whitby on 15–16 December. On 23–24 January 1915, Admiral Hipper carried out another raid but was intercepted off the Dogger Bank by a superior British force, and lost the battleship *Blucher* in the ensuing battle. This brought the policy of raids to a halt.

The battle of Jutland began with an attempt by Admiral Scheer to bring Beatty's battle cruiser squadron, based at Rosyth, into the path of German U-boats and the German High Seas Fleet before the main British Fleet at Scapa Flow could come to Beatty's support. The battle has been re-fought many times, both by the participants and by later historians. Perhaps the most appropriate comment is Jellicoe's: 'The whole situation was so difficult to grasp, as I had no real idea of what was going on and we could hardly see anything except flashes of guns, shells falling, ships blowing up, and an occasional glimpse of an enemy vessel.' [Marder, vol. III, p. 95] In brief, on 31 May 1916, Scheer and Hipper set sail from the Jade and Elbe estuaries. British naval intelligence passed on the information that German naval units had entered the North Sea, and Beatty and Jellicoe set out to meet them. Beatty blundered into Hipper's battle cruiser squadron; each then drew the other towards their respective main fleets. In the ensuing manoeuvres Scheer managed to extricate his out-gunned fleet from Jellicoe's 28 dreadnoughts (Scheer had only 16), and reached the sanctuary of the Jade estuary in the early hours of 1 June. During the course of the battle the superiority of German gunnery and ship design was clearly demonstrated, as the total losses on each side indicate:

A. Marder, *From the Dreadnought to Scapa Flow*, vol. III (1978)

	British	German
Battleships	–	1
Battle Cruisers	3	1
Cruisers	3	–
Light Cruisers	–	4
Destroyers	8	5
Killed	6097 (8.84%)	2551 (6.97%)

But whereas the Grand Fleet had 24 undamaged Dreadnoughts (up-to-date battleships) at the end of the battle, the Germans had only 10. Marder rightly comments: 'Not only was the British sea command unimpaired, but the results of the battle ensured that it would remain unimpaired.' [Marder, vol. III, p. 205] It is not correct to say that the German High Seas Fleet remained locked up in harbour for the rest of the war. It emerged three times, in August and October 1916 and again in April 1918. But each time it retired quickly rather than risk another battle. When finally ordered to sea in October 1918 in a desperate bid either to go down fighting or to improve the armistice terms, and sow the seed of a new German fleet in the future, the German sailors mutinied rather than face 'death with honour'. Merely by existing unscathed, the British Grand Fleet achieved its purpose.

U-Boat Warfare

Germany came much closer to success in her efforts to strangle Britain's trade, though it was not until 1917 that the policy was adopted in its uncompromising form. Both Britain and Germany had to tread carefully in their interference with neutral shipping for fear of antagonising the United States. Attempts had been made to define the rights of neutrals under the Declaration of London 1909, partially ratified by Britain in 1914. The legal niceties need not concern us. Suffice it to say that a full-scale blockade took some time to be implemented. In February 1915 Germany declared all waters round Britain to be a war zone within which 'every merchant vessel would be destroyed'. Britain responded by claiming the right to detain and take into port ships containing goods 'of presumed enemy destination, ownership or origin'. In May 1915 the *Lusitania*, a passenger liner, was sunk off the coast of Ireland by a German U-boat. 1200 lives were lost, 128 Americans among them. As a result of American protests Germany called off submarine warfare in the Channel and the Western Approaches. But in February 1916 she claimed the right to sink armed merchant ships on sight, and on 24 March a cross-Channel steamer, the *Sussex*, was torpedoed with the loss of 24 lives. The decision to embark on unrestricted boat warfare was made in January 1917, following the presentation to the Kaiser of a memorandum by the Chief of the Naval Staff, Admiral von Höltzendorff. In it he calculated that if 600 000 tons of shipping belonging to the Entente powers could be sunk each month, within five months Britain would be forced to surrender. His reasoning was accepted, despite the risk of American entry into the war.

For a time it looked as though his predictions were to be proved correct. In the worst month of the war, April 1917, U-boats sank 869 103 tons of allied shipping (373 ships), a rate of sinking that if sustained would certainly have forced Britain to the negotiating table. Furthermore, at the outset the Admiralty had no successful counter-measures. In the first three years of the war, in 142 actions between British destroyers and German submarines only seven had been sunk. Balfour, First Lord of the Admiralty from May 1915 to December 1916, when warned of the submarine menace told the War Committee that 'we must be content for the present with palliation'. To a list of sinkings read out to him his only comment was: 'It is very tiresome. These Germans are intolerable.' [Marder, vol. III, p. 280] The one solution that was suggested, the convoy system, was continually resisted both by the Admiralty and by the merchant seamen themselves. Curzon, a member of Lloyd George's War Cabinet, replied to a request that convoys should be looked at again by saying that 'The question of convoys has been considered. You know the drawbacks. (1) The pace of the convoy is that of the lamest duck. (2) We have not enough destroyers.' [Marder, vol. IV, p. 137] Another reason for the Admiralty's refusal to adopt convoys was their gross exaggeration of the size of the problem. Until April 1917 their estimate of the numbers of ships needing protection was based on the totals of ships entering and leaving British ports, some 5000 a week. But Commander R. C. H. Henderson pointed out that this number included ships of as little as 100 tons, cross-Channel steamers and coastal shipping. The figures for ocean-going ships were between 120 and 140 a week. This information made the task of assembling and protecting convoys look much more feasible. Lloyd George had been pressing the Admiralty to adopt a convoy system since February 1917 without success. On 27 April, however, it was finally decided to run a trial convoy from Gibraltar. On 30 April Lloyd George paid a personal visit to the Admiralty, in his own words 'to take peremptory action on the question of convoys'. [Lloyd George, vol. III, p. 1162–3] But by now he was preaching to the converted. His visit passed off very amicably. It was only in retrospect that he claimed responsibility for the conversion.

Marder, *From the Dreadnought to Scapa Flow* vols III and IV

I. D. Lloyd George, *War Memoirs*, vol. III (Ivor Nicholson & Watson, 1933)

The first convoy sailed from Gibraltar on 10 May. By August both outward- and home-bound convoys were in operation across the Atlantic. There can be no question as to their success. By September the tide of battle had turned. Of 26 604 vessels convoyed in 1917, a mere 147 (0.55%) were sunk. During the same period 65 out of 139 U-boats that were operational were lost. Marder concluded: 'A military decision in the war was unquestionably dependent in the first instance upon the submarine campaign. And here the high hopes of the German government and naval staff had been shattered.' [Marder, vol. IV, p. 287]

Marder, *From the Dreadnought to Scapa Flow*, vol. IV

While the German effort to blockade Britain failed, the British progressively tightened their grip on German trade. During the war the volume of imports fell to 40% of the pre-war total, and exports by much more. All German merchant shipping was driven from the seas. For a time imports into Germany via the neighbouring neutral states of Holland, Denmark and Sweden made up the differ-ence. The British government negotiated agreements with the Netherlands, Norway, Denmark and Switzerland which guaranteed that imports into those countries would not be re-exported to Germany. In return their ships were issued with certificates ('navicerts') which exempted them from having to go to allied ports to have their cargoes examined. Sweden, which refused to make any such undertaking, had supplies of copper and oil cut off in May 1916 in order to prevent large-scale imports of those commodities into Germany. It was reported to the War Cabinet in January 1917 that 'with some minor exceptions, no goods from overseas are getting through to Germany.' [Bell, p. 605] The overall consequences of the blockade on the German economy are hard to assess. The shortage of raw materials could be circumvented in some cases by the development of 'ersatz' industries, for example the production of artificial nitrogen. But German agriculture suffered severely from shortages of fertilisers. Goods like tea and coffee became unobtainable. Living standards fell. Among the reasons given for the failure of the final German offensive in 1918 is the discovery by the advancing German troops that their privations were not being endured by their opponents. Thus, in keeping open their own supply-lines and in closing those of Germany and Austria-Hungary the British navy created the conditions in which victory could be won.

A. C. Bell, *A History of the Blockade* (London, 1961)

THE WAR AT HOME === D

Party Politics and the Direction of the War

T. Wilson, *The Downfall of the Liberal Party, 1914–1935* (1966)

In a parliamentary system the fate of governments was indissolubly linked to the fortunes of war. Had Asquith been able to provide a coherent strategy and an effective government machine to direct it he might have remained Prime Minister of a Liberal government. As it was, as Trevor Wilson puts it: 'The outbreak of the First World War initiated a process of disintegration in the Liberal party which by 1918 had reduced it to ruins.' [Wilson, p. 23]

At the outset, once doubts about the justice of the cause of the entente powers had been dispelled by the aggressiveness of German policy, all the political parties were committed to the support of the government. The Conservatives had offered their support as early as 2 August 1914. John Redmond volunteered the support of the Irish Nationalists on 4 August. On 5 August the Parliamentary Labour party rejected Ramsay MacDonald's proposal to oppose war credits, and on 29 August voted to support recruitment. There were a few dissentients. John Morley and John Burns resigned from the cabinet rather than support the British declaration of war. A handful of Liberal MPs such as Philip Morrell, P. A. Molteno and Joseph King continued to oppose the war. Ramsay MacDonald and some members of the Independent Labour party opposed British participation in what they saw as 'an appalling crime'. But there was overwhelming support for Asquith, both in Parliament and in the country once Belgium had been invaded. Much of that support was forfeited as a result of the ineptitude of his government.

We have already seen the damaging disagreements over policy. They were compounded by the lack of any effective body to direct the war effort: 'The cabinet of some twenty members was far too big to provide clear direction and rapid decision on the multitude of diverse but important issues that arose immediately war broke out. Decisions were actually taken by a few ministers hastily called together to deal with any emergency; and no proper record of what they had decided was kept.' [Roskill, vol. I, p. 144] In so far as there was any central direction of policy, this was in the hands of Kitchener, appointed Minister for War on the strength of his record in Egypt and the Boer War, but painfully unprepared for the problems of trench warfare.

S. W. Roskill, *Hankey, Man of Secrets* (1970)

The first effective challenge to Asquith's authority materialised in May 1915. There had already been sniping from the Harmsworth Press (Harmsworth owned both *The Times* and the *Daily Mail*) when two issues combined to force a change in the Government. First, the shell shortage was publicly exposed. After the battle of Aubers Ridge, Colonel Repington, the military correspondent of *The Times*, despatched a telegram that was printed on 15 May. It stated that 'the want of an unlimited supply of high explosive shells was a fatal bar to our success'. Sir John French had previously assured Kitchener on 14 April that he had all the ammunition he needed, but this information was concealed until 1919. A second blow was delivered by Admiral Fisher, the First Sea Lord, who also chose 15 May to hand in his resignation. He gave as his reason Churchill's determination to increase the naval forces at Gallipoli at the expense of the Home Fleet. Faced with the certainty of opposition from the Conservatives, Asquith sought to deflect it by sharing responsibility with them. But Bonar Law insisted on his own terms. These included

86   BRITAIN AND THE FIRST WORLD WAR the removal of Churchill from the Admiralty and Haldane (wrongly suspected of pro-German sympathies) from the government. In the subsequent reshuffle, announced on 19 May, Bonar Law became Colonial Secretary, Balfour went to the Admiralty and Lloyd George took over a new department, the Ministry of Munitions. Thus the last Liberal government came to an end.

It is doubtful whether these changes did much to improve the calibre of the Government. Perhaps more important was the setting up of the Dardanelles Committee in June with Captain Hankey, previously of the Royal Marines and Secretary of the Committee of Imperial Defence from 1912 onwards, as its secretary. Though supposedly limited to consideration of the Gallipoli campaign, in fact the Dardanelles Committee acted as an unofficial War Committee and was officially constituted as such on 5 November 1915. It had a membership of nine, still too many for Hankey's liking, but at least proper records were now kept. Final responsibility still rested with the cabinet, however; after a meeting with this body on 7 December, Hankey was prompted to comment: 'This delay in decision is absolutely fatal ... the Government are really dreadfully to blame. They put off decisions, squabble (and) have no plan of action or operation. I see only one solution – to suspend the Constitution and appoint a dictator.' [Roskill, vol. I, p. 237]

Roskill, *Hankey*

The Government's weaknesses were further highlighted in 1916 by the inept handling of conscription, the Easter Rebellion in Dublin, the failure of the Somme offensive, the shortcomings of the navy, made apparent at Jutland, and in the failure to meet the German submarine threat. Two Commissions – one on the Dardanelles, the other on Mesopotamia – were set up, much against Hankey's advice, in July to investigate the Government's failures. Also in July, Kitchener, whose inadequacy was by now generally recognised, was dispatched to Russia. His ship, the *Hampshire*, was sunk by a mine off Scapa Flow. His death created a critical vacancy. Lloyd George became his successor as Minister for War, the opportunity he had been waiting for. But he found he had responsibility without power. The War Committee was evidently no improvement on the cabinet. Hankey again commented on 10 November: 'Yet another War Committee. These have been really dreadful (meetings). Yesterday the P.M. was writing answers to Parliamentary Questions all the time, with the result that discussions never kept to the point ....' [Roskill, vol. I, p. 317] Faced with such frustrations, Lloyd George felt impelled to act. On 1 December he suggested the formation of a small War Cabinet with himself as chairman and Law and Carson as members. Asquith would remain Prime Minister but would not take part in the War Cabinet. Lloyd George had already taken the precaution of securing Bonar Law's approval for this suggestion in advance. Asquith, initially hostile to the arrangement, was induced to accept it on 3 December by the threat of Conservative resignations. But the publication of an article in *The Times* on 4 December, commenting on the proposed changes in terms adverse to Asquith, caused him to change his mind. He would not 'be relegated to a position of an irresponsible spectator of the War'. Asquith's final rejection of Lloyd George's proposal led to the resignations first of Lloyd George, then of the Conservative Ministers and finally of Asquith himself on 5 December.

Roskill, *Hankey*

A conference of party leaders, attended by Asquith, Bonar Law, Lloyd George, Henderson and Balfour took place at Buckingham Palace on 6 December. The premiership was offered to Bonar Law, who would only accept it if Asquith would agree to serve under him. This Asquith refused to do. But despite earlier disclaimers,

A NON-PARTY MANDATE

JOHN BULL: "I DON'T CARE WHO LEADS THE COUNTRY SO LONG AS HE LEADS IT TO VICTORY."

Punch 1916

Conservative ministers were prepared to serve under Lloyd George. On 7 December George V reluctantly offered him the premiership. With perhaps equal misgivings, Lloyd George accepted it. Grey and the other Liberal ministers resigned with Asquith, but while Liberal MPs continued to recognise Asquith as the leader of the Liberal party, they also pledged their determination 'to give support to the King's Government engaged in the prosecution of the war.' [Wilson, p. 106] The subsequent split in the Liberal party was already implicit in this division of loyalties.

Wilson, *Downfall of the Liberal Party*

So far as the direction of the war was concerned, however, Lloyd George's premiership brought about a substantial improvement. He immediately appointed a War Cabinet consisting of himself, Bonar Law, Lord Curzon, Lord Milner and Arthur Henderson. Balfour went to the Foreign Office, Carson replacing him at the Admiralty.

The War Cabinet, freed from departmental responsibilities, met nearly every day, and under Hankey's watchful eye a cabinet secretariat drafted agendas, kept minutes and circulated decisions for action. At last there was an effective governmental machine, even if it did not always work as well as has been claimed. It comes as something of a surprise to discover that when it was decided that Carson must be replaced at the Admiralty he was 'booted up' to the War Cabinet in July 1917. There were complaints from Curzon and others about Lloyd George's high handedness. Friction between the politicians and the generals continued right up to the end of the war. But at least the Government was now headed by a man of energy and determination, ready to try anything.

The final episode of political importance occurred in May 1918. This arose during the final German offensive that had begun in March. Lloyd George, sensitive to the criticism that he had deliberately kept troops in England where they could not be squandered in useless offensives, stated on 9 April that there were more British troops in France in January 1918 than there had been in January 1917. Strictly speaking this was correct, but only if one included labour battalions and lines of communication troops. On 7 May General F. D. Maurice, the recently retired Director of Military Operations, wrote to the press accusing the Government of 'a series of misstatements'. Asquith called for a select committee of enquiry, the only serious challenge he mounted to Lloyd George. In a debate on 9 May the Prime Minister dismissed the charge, pointing out that the figures he cited came from Maurice's own department. He failed to state, however, that he had received a corrected version on 7 May. Lloyd George won his point, but 108 Liberals voted with Asquith. Some of them were subsequently forgiven, but Lloyd George did not forget the slur on his integrity. Thus when the war ended, Lloyd George was in thrall to his Conservative supporters, while Liberals were torn between a residual loyalty to Asquith and an unwilling admiration for the man who had won the war.

The Role of the State

The First World War brought a marked extension in the responsibilities of government. For the most part this was achieved through pragmatic responses to the demands of war. There were several groups who positively welcomed the advances made, for instance the Labour party, the Trades Union Congress (TUC), the radical wing of the Liberal party, a handful of civil servants and a few social imperialists such as Lord Milner, who favoured an active role for government in the promotion of empire. Conversely, many of the departures from a market-based economy were undertaken reluctantly and unwillingly. The business community as a whole resented government interference, except where it was positively helpful; conventional economic thinking still remained faithful to the virtues of free enterprise and the unfettered operation of the price mechanism. Thus while it is incontestable that, in the words of the War Cabinet's Report for 1918 that the war had brought 'a transformation of the social and administrative structure of the State' [Marwick, p. 254], it is a moot point whether the transformation was permanent. The short-term effects of the war on the operations of government are clearly visible, the long-term consequences much less so.

A. Marwick, *The Deluge, British Society and the First World War* (1967)

Methods of Control

The doctrine of parliamentary sovereignty removed any potential barriers to state intervention. In the absence of a written constitution or a bill of rights there were, for instance, no constitutional guarantees to protect the rights of conscientious objectors. Conscription, the requisition of property, the control of working conditions, all could be imposed by Act of Parliament, and were. Furthermore, Parliament itself surrendered some of its powers through successive Defence of the Realm Acts (DORA). The first of these was passed on 8 August 1914 and conferred on 'His Majesty in Council', i.e. the cabinet, powers 'to issue regulations as to the powers and duties of the Admiralty and Army Council, and other persons acting on their behalf, for securing the public safety and defence of the realm'. This Act and its successors gave government departments a very wide discretion, as well as opening the door to censorship and the detention of suspected persons. Parliament largely acquiesced, though the right to trial by jury for breaches of DORA was restored in March 1915. Two qualifications need to be made. The government could not always be sure of passing its legislation. A conscription bill was defeated in April 1916. Organised labour benefited from its increased bargaining power to the point that the active co-operation of trade unions had positively to be sought.

The Mobilisation of Manpower

Total war required the mobilisation of the whole working population and its deployment in the most efficient way. Successive governments fumbled their way towards this goal without ever quite achieving it. The first requirement was more soldiers. It was hoped initially to rely on the voluntary principle. Kitchener's famous appeal met with an immediate response – 750 000 had volunteered by the end of September 1914 and in all 2.5 million men enlisted voluntarily before conscription was introduced. But as losses mounted on the Western Front it became clear that the supply of volunteers would run out before the enemy's resolve. A war of attrition needed more victims. In October 1915 Lord Derby was made Director General of Recruiting. His plan was to invite all men between the ages of 18 and 41 to attest their willingness to serve. If enough bachelors were forthcoming, married men could be spared. But the scheme failed to produce enough volunteers. Nor did it discriminate between those in essential occupations and those whose jobs could be done by others. In January 1916 the first Conscription Act made military service compulsory for all unmarried men between the ages of 18 and 41. An amendment, threatening to extend conscription to married men unless enough of them attested voluntarily, was rejected by the House of Commons in April. In May, the Government took the logical step of extending conscription to all men, married or not. Hankey commented: 'The only real military case for the bill was the coming offensive [the Somme] .... But the army want a regular orgy of slaughter, and it is for this that they demand the extra men.' [Roskill, vol. I, p. 266] The only exceptions permitted were to those in reserved occupations. Conscientious objection on religious grounds was allowed, but only on condition that those who refused to shed blood would contribute to the war effort in other ways. Of those who refused to join up approximately 7000 served as noncombatants, 3000 worked in labour camps, and a further 6000 were imprisoned for their refusal to contribute to the war effort.

Roskill, *Hankey*

The provision of troops was only part of the much wider problem of how to use the nation's man – and woman – power most effectively. The first government initiative in this direction was the Treasury Agreement reached with trade union delegates in March 1915. Under this Agreement unions engaged in war work would forego the right to strike and would abandon restrictive trade practices in return for the restraint of profits and the Government's guarantee to assist in the restoration of pre-war conditions. The Agreement was given legal authority in the Munitions Act, passed in May. The Ministry of Munitions was also set up and by 1918 it had a staff of 65 000, employing over 3 million workers in some 20 000 factories.

In August 1915 a National Register of all males and females between the ages of 15 and 65 was drawn up. Its purpose, Lord Lansdowne stated, was to ensure 'that every member of the community should bear not only a part in the national task but the part he is best qualified to take.' [Marwick, p. 62] In practice the draconian powers implied by the compiling of the Register were never fully exercised. The huge increase in the employment of women in the munitions industry, offices and on the land was achieved by exhortation rather than compulsion. When the Ministry of National Service was set up in March 1917, its first director, Neville Chamberlain 'found himself doing little more than running an appeal for National Service Volunteers, who were to take on civilian jobs and release men for the forces.' [Marwick, p. 253] Under Chamberlain's successor, Sir Auckland Geddes, the Ministry confined its activities to military recruitment. Britain thus escaped full direction of labour. Even so, one man in three was conscripted into the armed forces; in human terms this was the most striking example of the enhanced authority of the State.

Marwick, *The Deluge*

The Control of the Resources

The *ad hoc* methods used to mobilise the population were also employed in the efforts made to control production and distribution, action usually being taken when shortages appeared. Some essential raw materials were in short supply from the start of the war, sugar and wheat in particular. In both cases the Government made arrangements for bulk purchases of these commodities from 1914 onwards. The War Office made special arrangements to safeguard the supply of jute (needed for sandbags) from India and of flax (needed for tent canvas) from Russia.

Food shortages only became really serious with the increase in sinkings by German submarines in the autumn of 1916. At their worst in April 1917, Britain was reduced to four days' supply of sugar and nine weeks' supply of wheat. Lloyd George tackled the problem in two ways. He appointed Lord Devonport, a successful grocer, to be Food Controller to take care of distribution, and Sir George Prothero to be President of the Board of Agriculture, with the specific task of increasing domestic food production. Prothero, acting through a network of local agricultural committees, was remarkably successful. By 1918 an additional 3 million acres of arable land had been brought into cultivation. Wheat production rose by 1 million tons, the potato crop by 1.5 million tons. Lord Devonport proved a broken reed. Appointed in December

1916, he resigned the following May; but his successor, Lord Rhondda, managed to establish an effective system of rationing of essential foodstuffs: meat, bacon, tea, sugar and butter, among others. Bread was never rationed and its price was kept down through the payment of a subsidy. Despite the fact that at the outset of the war Britain produced only one-third of the food consumed, her population never went hungry.

There was no shortage of home-produced coal, providing the industry kept going. But labour shortages developed as miners volunteered in huge numbers for Kitchener's army; there was also a serious coal strike in July 1915. It was the threat of further industrial unrest that prompted Lloyd George to appoint a Coal Controller in February 1917. The mines remained under private ownership and management but their profits were fixed and guaranteed at pre-war levels. Surpluses went to the Treasury and to a pool from which guaranteed profits might be made up in individual cases. This arrangement permitted national wage agreements to be reached in 1917 and 1918, and it encouraged hopes of full-scale nationalisation after the war.

The Control of Transport

The war imposed great strains on the nation's transport system and both railways and shipping were brought under government control. Railways had so dominated military thinking in the decades before 1914 that in this area, at least, problems had been anticipated. Under the Regulation of Forces Act 1871, it was provided that in time of war the railways would be put at the government's disposal. In 1896 a Railway War Council was established. Thus when war was declared on 4 August 1914, the railways passed into the hands of a Railway Executive Committee presided over by the President of the Board of Trade, but actually run by the General Managers of the largest companies. Profits were to be held at 1913 levels and receipts pooled, with the Government making up the deficits where necessary in return for the free passage of its troops. These arrangements worked very smoothly and led the TUC to recommend full-scale nationalisation at their annual conference in 1915.

There was a shortage of shipping space throughout the war. The British mercantile marine had to meet allied needs as well as Britain's. In June 1916, a Shipping Control Committee was set up to advise on the allocation of shipping. It calculated that a cut of 4 million tons in Britain's imports would be needed to ensure the arrival of essential goods. Lloyd George's response to this problem was to appoint Sir John Maclay, a Scottish ship-owner, as Shipping Controller. He was joined shortly after by Sir Eric Geddes, who was made Controller of the Navy with responsibility for all shipbuilding, in the merchant fleet as well as the Royal Navy. By 1918 virtually all merchant shipping had been requisitioned by the Ministry of Shipping. Profits were limited to pre-war levels. The introduction of convoys and the improvement in the rate of production of British shipyards meant that by September 1917 total British mercantile shipping construction at last exceeded monthly losses. [Marder, vol. V, p. 80]

Marder, *From the Dreadnought to Scapa Flow*, vol. V

Paying for the War

In 1916 it was calculated that the war was costing £3.85 million a day, or £1405 million per annum. This compared with a peacetime expenditure of £29 million on the army and £51.5 million on the navy. Astonishingly enough, this huge increase was absorbed without causing serious economic dislocation. Seventy per cent of the costs of the war was met by increases in the National Debt which rose from £625 million in 1914 to approximately £7980 million in 1918. Increases in taxation were needed to make up the remaining 30% and to service the interest payments on the increased National Debt. Successive Chancellors of the Exchequer 'tightened the screw'. Lloyd George (1914–15) contented himself with increasing the standard rate of income tax from 9d. in the pound to 1/6d., and with increasing the excise duties. McKenna (1915–16) raised income tax to 3/6d. in the pound, and introduced an excess profits tax. Bonar Law (1916–18) raised income tax to 6/- in the pound (30%) and excess profits tax to 80%. The tax burden rose from £3/11/4d. per head of population to £22 per head, and the number of tax payers from about 1.5 million to 7.75 million. There were also corresponding increases in death duties, rising to 40% on estates of over £2 million.

Much of the money raised in loans came from the banking system, with consequential increases in the money supply. Prices were also pushed up by increasing demand in relation to the falling supply of consumer goods. Over the four years of war the cost of living rose by about 75%. But in most industries and occupations money wages at least doubled so that real wages (i.e. the purchasing power of wages and salaries) actually improved.

The economic policies of the wartime governments may have been piecemeal and hand-to-mouth; but they were more successful than those of any other combatant country in harnessing the nation's resources to the chariot of war. The experiments in state control also proved that a collectivist approach to the provision of goods and services could work, a lesson that was to be too easily forgotten when the war ended.

The Labour Party and the Trade Unions

The most significant political developments during the First World War were the advances in the fortunes of the Labour party and in the strength and status of the trade unions. Both were closely linked. With only 42 members in the House of Commons in 1914, the Labour party had little claim to a share in government. But, as the War Cabinet somewhat sententiously put it, 'For the vigorous prosecution of the war a contented working class was indispensable.' [Middlemas, p. 130] Trade unions had a vital role to play in winning working-class co-operation, and the Labour party was, in some senses at least, the political wing of the trade union movement.

In the first Coalition government constructed by Asquith in May 1915, Arthur Henderson, who had succeeded Ramsay MacDonald as leader of the Labour party in 1914, was appointed President of the Board of Education, an acknowledgement that the Labour party had come of age. Lloyd George went a good deal further in his bid to secure Labour party support. He raised Henderson to the War Cabinet and appointed eight Labour members to other posts. G. N. Barnes headed the newly created Ministry of Pensions, J. Hodge the newly created Ministry of Labour. J. R. Clynes succeeded Lord Rhondda as Food Controller. Arthur Henderson was obliged to resign from the War Cabinet in August 1917 for supporting Labour representation at the projected peace conference at Stockholm; but he was immediately replaced by Barnes, so that Labour representation continued at the highest level until the end of the war. But while the Labour party clearly benefited from the experience of office it avoided Lloyd George's embrace. After his resignation Henderson devoted

Political and Social Changes

K. Middlemas, *Politics in Industrial Society* (Deutsch, 1979)

his energies to revising the Labour party Constitution and to devising a new party programme. This was published under the title *Labour and the New Social Order* in time for the 1918 General Election. For the first time the Labour party was committed to public ownership of the means of production, distribution and exchange. A delegate conference held on 14 November 1918, decided that the party should withdraw from the Coalition and fight the election independently. Though the party only gained 59 seats, its share of the total vote increased from 7.2% to 22% and it became the main opposition party. It emerged from the war with its organisation improved, its policies better defined and its credibility as a party of government enhanced.

The war naturally strengthened the bargaining power of trade unions, partly because it brought an increased demand for labour, partly because any hold up in war production could have devastating results on the war effort. All the ministers concerned with industry sought to win trade union co-operation over a whole range of issues: strikes, restrictive practices, dilution (the replacement of skilled by unskilled and women workers), conscription. The Treasury Agreement of 1915 and the Munitions of War Act later in the year were both approved by trade union leaders, subject to amendment. Middlemas comments: 'By the middle of 1916 a new conception of trade unionism was becoming current in England in which responsibility and representative leadership was seen to merit a role in the country's political life.' [Middlemas, p. 40] Lloyd George even chose an audience of trade union leaders to hear his first considered statement of British war aims on 5 January 1918. Indeed, so close were the bonds established between government and the Trades Union Congress (TUC) that workers in many industries came to feel that their interests were no longer being adequately protected. In many parts of the country locally elected shop stewards took over the role of the full-time officials, sometimes in defiance of them. One such area was Red Clydeside where angry protests were staged against the surrender of the strike weapon in the Munitions Act. Lloyd George was given a very hostile reception when he addressed an audience of Scottish shop stewards in Glasgow on Christmas Day 1915. Seven of their leaders were subsequently imprisoned. Shop stewards also played an important part in the strikes which hit the engineering industry in May 1917. In fact, despite the presence of Labour ministers in the Government, the level of industrial discontent increased after 1916. The number of disputes rose from 532 in that year to 1165 in 1918, and the number of days lost in strikes went up from 2 446 000 to 5 875 000. So worried did the Government become that Lloyd George appointed eight commissions in 1917 to investigate the causes of industrial unrest. They concluded that the main grievances were the cost of living, war profiteering, dilution of labour, conscription and administrative incompetence. Thus while the official leadership of the trade union movement moved closer to the seat of power, by doing so (perhaps inevitably) it forfeited the support of many of the rank and file.

K. Middlemas, *Politics in Industrial Society* (Deutsch, 1979)

Votes for Women

One of the most striking features of the women's suffrage movement was the zeal which some of its leaders showed for the war effort. The *Suffragette* was re-christened *Britannia*. Mrs Emmeline Pankhurst led a demonstration demanding 'The Right to Serve'. Her wishes were granted. Under the pressure of necessity women's employment went up rapidly as may be seen in the following figures:

Women employed in:	1914	1918
Industry	2 179 000	2 971 000
Transport	18 000	63 700
Commerce	505 000	934 000
Central and local government	262 000	460 000

It is a truism that it was the war which won the vote for women. Asquith, one of the main opponents of women's suffrage before the war, admitted that they had earned the vote by their own efforts, and actually took the lead in urging implementation of proposals to give it to them. The growth in anti-suffragist sentiment, clearly visible in 1914, was effectively reversed by the spectacle of women munitions workers, bus conductresses, landgirls, police constables and nurses all making their contribution to the war effort. The examples of Nurse Edith Cavell, who helped British prisoners of war to escape and was executed for doing so, and of Dr Else Inglis who ran hospitals in Serbia, were widely publicised.

If women had earned the right to vote, so had the two out of five male adults who were still disenfranchised under Britain's complicated electoral laws. In 1917 a Speaker's Conference recommended a simple six months' residential qualification for all male voters, and this proposal was adopted in the Representation of the People Act passed in February 1918. An amendment, giving the vote to all women over 30 on the same terms as men, was passed during the committee stage by 385 votes to 55.

At the time it seemed a notable landmark. In retrospect it made little difference to the roles women were still expected to play. The only woman elected to Parliament in 1918 was Countess Marciewicz (Constance Gore-Booth), a member of the Sinn Fein Party – and she declined to take up her seat. In the area of women's rights, as elsewhere, the immediate impact of the war was more noticeable than its long-term effects.

Changes in the Class Structure and in Living Standards

The same could be said for the effects of war on the class structure. Increases in taxation, especially the rise in death duties and the high incidence of war casualties in the ranks of the aristocracy, had some effects on landed wealth. The Conservative party also changed its character as it fell more and more under the influence of businessmen. But the distribution of wealth was not seriously altered. In 1911 8% of the National Income went to those earning £5000 a year and over. In 1929 those earning £9500 and over (an equivalent figure, allowing for inflation) still received 5.5% of the National Income. Whereas 0.4% of the population owned two-thirds of the country's wealth in 1914, only 2.5% owned a similar share in 1929.

More significant was the rise in numbers of the class of salary earners, from 1.7 million in 1911 to 2.7 million in 1921, from 12% to 22% of the working population. The increase was made up from the expansion of the professions, the civil service and local government, and the managerial class. Many of the new salary earners were women who stayed on, particularly in office jobs, at the end of the war. There was a corresponding decline in the number of domestic servants which fell by about 30% over the country as a whole, though with marked regional variations.

Marwick, *The Deluge*

For those at the bottom of the social scale, the skilled and unskilled manual workers, the war brought marginal improvements. Wage increases generally kept ahead of price increases, but by no means everywhere or all the time. Marwick puts it succinctly: 'The working class in 1914 was large and it was poor. In the early twenties it was not quite so large, and it was not quite so poor.' [Marwick, p. 304]

More important for the future than the limited rise in real wages were the plans made for improvements in social welfare. As the casualty lists mounted, so did the pressure to justify them. Not only was this to be 'the war to end wars' (the phrase was coined by H. G. Wells), it was to be the prelude to a better and fairer society. Reconstruction became the shorthand term for all the changes that would be set in train. Asquith created a Standing Reconstruction Committee of the cabinet in 1915, and Lloyd George set up a Ministry of Reconstruction under the active Dr Christopher Addison in 1917. Addison produced far reaching-plans for improvements in health and housing, some of which came to fruition in the post-war government. In 1916 Lloyd George also appointed H. A. L. Fisher to the Board of Education, the first academic (he was Vice Chancellor of Sheffield University) to hold the position. Fisher produced an ambitious Education Act in 1918 which had the immediate effect of raising the school-leaving age to 14 and giving teachers a uniform salary structure and pension scheme. Most of its other provisions were not implemented. The terms of the National Insurance Act of 1911 were extended to cover all those engaged in war work, and the Ministry of Pensions, created in 1916, took on the task of looking after all those widowed or disabled by the war. While in some ways these measures could all be seen as logical extensions of pre-war legislation, the war added a new dimension to the State's responsibilities. Those who had served and suffered on the nation's behalf had an extra claim to support. 'Heroes' were entitled to 'homes'. Though the coming of peace brought a retreat from the high hopes of Reconstruction, not all the ground was lost. Politicians in all parties showed a greater sense of obligation to the casualties of society, even if the provisions made for them were often woefully inadequate.

The Costs of the War

None of the social gains brought about during the war could possibly outweigh the losses in human terms. The war cost Britain 650 000 lives, and a further 1.6 million permanently disabled. Whereas in 1911 there were 155 men per 1000 of population between the ages of 20 and 40, the figure for 1921 was 141. Casualties were particularly severe among junior officers who were mainly recruited from the middle and upper classes. Out of 14 560 Oxford graduates who served, 2680 lost their lives. While statisticians may discount the notion of 'a lost generation' – the figures of human dead per head of population were 1 : 57 in Britain's case – they cannot remove the countless human tragedies that affected millions of individuals. Asquith lost one son on the Western Front, Bonar Law two. Both men, according to their contemporaries, never really recovered from the loss. In their various ways the poets and authors who experienced the full horrors of trench warfare dispelled, at least for one generation, the myth that war was ennobling. In 1914 Julian Grenfell caught the mood of innocent adventure with which young men volunteered:

The naked earth is warm with spring,
And with green grass and bursting trees
Leans to the sun's gaze glorying
And quivers in the sunny breeze;
And life is colour and warmth and light,
And a striving evermore for these;
And he is dead who will not fight;
And who dies fighting has increase.

Siegfried Sassoon, Isaac Rosenberg, Edmund Blunden, Ivor Gurney, Herbert Read and many others had a different tale to tell. Let Wilfred Owen, who was killed in the last month of the war speak for them all:

What passing-bells for those who die as cattle?
– Only the monstrous anger of the guns
Only the stuttering rifles' rapid rattle
Can patter out their hasty orisons.

POINTS AT ISSUE POINTS AT ISSUE **POINTS AT ISSUE** POINTS AT ISSUE
POINTS AT ISSUE POINTS AT ISSUE

The Western Front

Fierce debate continued throughout the war as to where British troops would best be deployed. The Generals, Kitchener, French, Haig and Robertson (Chief of the Imperial General Staff from December 1915 onwards) took the view that the Western Front was the decisive one, because it was only there that Germany could be defeated. As the German flank could not be turned, there was no alternative to a war of attrition. In the following excerpts, Haig makes the case for concentrating on the Western Front:

Diary, 28 March 1915:

> We cannot hope to win until we have defeated the German army. The easiest place to do this is in France, because our lines of communication are the shortest to this theatre of war. [Terraine, *Douglas Haig, the Educated Soldier*, p. 135]

Letter to Francis Wigram (George V's Private Secretary), July 1915:

> In spite of what you write to me and the decision of the Cabinet, I still think it is fatal to pour more troops and ammunition down the Dardanelles sink. [Terraine, p. 146]

Memorandum to War Cabinet, October 1917:

> One more indispensable condition of decisive success on the Western Front is that the War Cabinet should have a firm faith in its possibility and resolve finally and unreservedly to concentrate our resources on seeking it, and to do so at once .... To ensure this we must take risks elsewhere and cut down our commitments in all other theatres to the minimum necessary to protect really vital interests.

POINTS AT ISSUE
POINTS AT ISSUE
POINTS AT ISSUE
POINTS AT ISSUE

But Haig's views were not shared by all the politicians. Churchill and Lloyd George, in particular, refused to accept the logic of Haig's arguments, and advocated using Britain's command of the sea to break the deadlock on the Western Front. Churchill suggested landings on Jutland in 1914 and on Gallipoli in 1915; Lloyd George favoured Salonika.

Letter to Asquith from Churchill, 29 December 1914:

> I think it quite possible that neither side will have the strength to penetrate the other's lines in the Western theatre .... On the assumption that these views are correct, the question arises, how ought we to apply our growing military power. Are there not other alternatives than sending our armies to chew barbed wire in Flanders?' [Churchill goes on to suggest the invasion of Schleswig-Holstein, to which the essential preliminary would be the capture of the island of Borkum.] [Bettey, *English Historical Documents, 1906–1939*, pp. 53–4]

Memorandum on War Strategy written by Lloyd George and circulated to Members of the War Council 1 January 1915

> 1. *Stalemate on the Western Front*
> I cannot pretend to have any military knowledge, but the little I saw and gathered in France as to the military position, coupled with such reading on the subjects as I have been able to indulge in, convinced me that any attempt to force the carefully prepared German lines in the West would end in failure and in appalling loss of life ... [Lloyd George proceeded to give three further reasons for abandoning a Western Front strategy before putting forward his own alternative.]
>
> 5. *An Alternative Suggestion*
> I suggest that our new forces should be employed in an attack upon Austria, in conjunction with the Serbians, the Rumanians and the Greeks. The assistance of the two latter countries would be assured if they knew that a great English force would be there to support them. [Lloyd George, *War Memoirs*, vol. I, pp. 369–80]

In view of the fates of the Gallipoli expedition and the Salonika enterprise it may reasonably be doubted whether the other alternatives to the Western Front suggested would have been any more successful.

The adoption of a Western Front strategy did not necessarily justify the bloody and expensive offensives launched in 1915, 1916 and 1917. The battles of the Somme and Passchendaele in particular have aroused a great deal of controversy. John Terraine, Haig's most sympathetic biographer, does his best to defend Haig's conduct of these battles on the grounds that in both cases the casualties inflicted on the Germans exceeded those suffered by the British: 'From now on the Battle of the Somme took on its true character – a long swaying struggle, flaring into furious intensity, now on the left, now in the centre, but never silent, never still anywhere. It was, without comparison, the supreme ordeal of the British army during the war. As the summer wore away and the weather deteriorated, conditions became indescribable; that neither the army nor its chief faltered in this terrible task is hardly less than a miracle. The German army suffered irreparable harm.' [Terraine, p. 214]

Terraine conceded that mistakes were made in the battle of Passchendaele, particularly in the appointment of General Gough to command the 5th army – 'his gravest and most fatal error' – and in Haig's over-optimistic assessment of the decline in German morale. But again he argues that German casualties probably 'considerably exceeded' British casualties [Terraine, p. 372] and concludes: 'In fact, if Flanders had not inflicted the decisive defeat on the enemy that Haig had aimed at, there can be no doubt whatever that it carried forward very substantially that wearing-out of the German army without which he never supposed victory could be won.'

Naturally enough, those who did the fighting took a somewhat different view. Here are three views of the battle of the Somme as seen from different levels.

1. *The Australian official history, describing a series of attacks made by the Anzac Corps*:

> 'Even if the need for maintaining pressure be granted, the student will have difficulty in reconciling his intelligence to the actual tactics. To throw the several parts of an army corps, brigade after brigade ... twenty times in succession against one of the strongest points in an enemy's defence may certainly be described as 'methodical', but the claim that it was economic is entirely unjustified. [Liddell Hart, *History of the First World War*, p. 326]

2. *An infantry subaltern serving with a New Zealand division, describing a battalion level attack on 27 September 1916*:

> Of the thirty-two in my platoon, five were killed outright, twenty-five were wounded, two remained unwounded. A like proportion held in each of the twelve attacking platoons, and all those casualties must have been sustained in the first ten minutes. The communiqué, I remember, was terse, suggesting a successful advance .... This might pass for home consumption; I should rather have put it that unimaginative staff work at some level had extinguished three companies. [Aitken, *Gallipoli to the Somme, Recollections of a New Zealand Infantryman*, p. 170]

3. *Private P. Smith 1st Border Regiment, on 1 July 1916*:

> It was pure bloody murder. Douglas Haig should have been hung drawn and quartered for what he did on the Somme. The cream of British manhood was shattered in less than six hours. [Middlebrook, *The First Day on the Somme*, p. 316]

Books cited

J. Terraine, *Douglas Haig, the Educated Soldier* (Hutchinson, 1962)
J. H. Bettey, *English Historical Documents, 1906–1939* (Routledge & Kegan Paul, 1967)
D. Lloyd George, *War Memoirs* (Ivor Nicholson & Watson, 1933)
B. H. Liddell Hart, *A History of the First World War* (Cassell, 1930)
A. Aitken, *Gallipoli to the Somme, Recollections of a New Zealand Infantryman* (OUP, 1967)
M. Middlebrook, *The First Day on the Somme* (Allen Lane, 1971)

The Effects of War on British Society and Politics

One of the major controversies now surrounding the First World War concerns the nature and strength of its impact on British society and politics. It can be argued that the war brought about dramatic changes in the role of the state; the economic and political strength of organised labour; and the position of women; and that it caused the demise of the Liberal party and brought about a critical change in the character of the Labour party. There are two problems in assessing the validity of these claims: first, all the changes referred to were already under way in 1914;

secondly, in some areas the impact of war was short-lived, and the gains apparently achieved disappeared with the return of peacetime conditions.

In terms of its effect on society, Arthur Marwick presents the strongest case for the liberating effects of the war. Among its consequences he lists:

> the huge physical demand of the war for manpower and machines, which, given, of course, the deeper pressure of the will to survival, created an irresistible pressure for the reorganisation and reorientation of society; what forms the reorganisation took, what lessons were learned from it depended on other circumstances, but the immediate and eventual ramifications were immense. [Marwick, *The Deluge, British Society and the First World War*, p. 312]

He argues first that the experiment in state control, while its lessons were lost on the immediate post-war generation of politicians, had two vital consequences:

> In the first place the precedents had been set, establishing in fact a new measure of tolerance for state intervention .... In the second place ideas which could in pre-war years be laughed off as Utopian fantasies, denounced as contrary to economic law, or displayed as evidence of the sinister intentions of socialism, had been put to work and had been seen to work. [Marwick, p. 315]

The position of the working class was also improved: 'The working class as a social class, though suffering many hardships and grievances, derived a number of permanent advantages from their favourable market position – wage rates were doubled, the average working week was reduced from 55 hours to 48 – and, more important still, they got a taste of the better material comforts of modern civilisation.' [Marwick, p. 316]

The emancipation of women, both in political and economic terms, owed much to the war because of the demand it created for women's jobs:

> The manner in which the situation was exploited owed much to the experience the women's leaders had derived from the pre-war suffrage movements; it is also true that before the war the doors to a number of professions were already opening. Yet it is difficult to see how women could have achieved so much in anything like a similar time span without the unique circumstances arising from the war. [Marwick, p. 317]

The sense of insecurity engendered by the war also helped to promote the extension of unemployment insurance, Addison's Housing Act and the Fisher Education Act. Finally, 'Many of the other wartime developments – the growth of women's spending power, for example, fit into the chain reaction; by accelerating pre-war trends, they create still further acceleration.' [Marwick, p. 317]

Other historians are more concerned to stress the continuities with pre-1914 England. In his book *The Making of Modern British Politics*, Martin Pugh queries the novelty which Marwick ascribes to collectivist ideas:

> The truth is that every political school found interventionist ideas acceptable in certain respects but repugnant in others; sections of every party had already moved towards the modern conception of the state; and the collectivist policies practised in the 50 years after 1918 were essentially extensions of those principles established before 1914. Liberals had characteristically come to see the state as a humanitarian agency of social welfare and a redistributor of surpluses for the benefit of society, but drew the line at protectionism and confiscation, and sought to make free enterprise work effectively rather than to

POINTS AT ISSUE
POINTS AT ISSUE
POINTS AT ISSUE
POINTS AT ISSUE

100

BRITAIN AND THE FIRST WORLD WAR

eliminate it. The Labour party shared these attitudes; it espoused state ownership of one or two special industries, but shrank from a state that threatened freedom of labour or freedom of trade, and was innocent of the role of a sophisticated modern bureaucracy. Socialists, while being clear about the superiority of the common good, ranged all the way from Fabian confidence in a benevolent state to the Guild Socialist and syndicalist suspicion of it. Conservatives were willing enough to bow to state control in the civil and military spheres when pressing national interests required it, but in economic affairs they accepted the paraphernalia of control on a strictly temporary basis and retained intact their belief in minimal government and minimal taxation; while the bulk of the party had shifted closer to *laissez faire* they had made trade a special exception, and one school of imperialists had embraced a Bismarckian concept of the state. The First World War did not so much modify any of these attitudes as rearrange the places of those who held them. [Pugh, pp. 202–3]

Pugh also suggests that the position of women was much less affected by the war in the long term than has been accepted:

> It is significant that where women who undertook male tasks during the war have left a record of their feelings they seem to have taken for granted that they were stepping in on a purely temporary basis, and they vacated their jobs at the end of the war without protest. This is not surprising in view of the relatively conservative, middle-class nature of the pre-1914 women's movement which had largely confined itself to the narrow question of the franchise and neglected the wider social objectives that the vote might help them to attain. In this light the grant of the franchise in 1918 to women over 30 years who were either local government electors themselves or the wives of local government electors is explicable. Both the Speaker's Conference and Parliament were determined to keep women in a minority among voters, and to enfranchise only those who as relatively mature, family women seemed likely to constitute a stable, loyal section of the community. [Pugh, p. 188]

The effect of the war on the comparative fortunes of the Liberal and Labour parties has also been a matter for debate. Marwick likens the two parties to two cars on a funicular railway: 'It was during the war that the Liberal party, going down, met the Labour party coming up.' [Marwick, p. 336] He concedes that the image is not very apt, implying as it does that the demise of the Liberal party was inevitable. But the image brings home the interdependence of the two parties. They were both competing for what might be called the 'progressive' as well as the working-class vote. Loss of support for one party would necessarily mean a gain in support for the other. What is in question is the effect of the war on this shift in allegiances.

The 'point of no return' for the Liberal party has been variously dated. In his book *The Strange Death of Liberal England*, George Dangerfield is quite specific: 'The year 1910 is not just a convenient starting point. It is actually a landmark in English history, which stands out against a peculiar background of flame. For it was in 1910 that fires long smouldering in the English spirit suddenly flared up, so that by the end of 1913 Liberal England was reduced to ashes. From these ashes, a new England seems to have emerged.

I realise, of course, that the word 'Liberal' will always have a meaning so long as there is one democracy left in the world, or any remnant of a middle class; but the true pre-war Liberal – supported as it still was in 1910, by Free Trade and the illusion of Progress – can never return. It was killed, or it killed itself, in 1913. And a very good thing too.' [Dangerfield, p. 14] On this interpretation, the First World War was irrelevant to the fortunes of the Liberal party. Its fate had already been sealed by 1913.

Trevor Wilson sees the prospects for Liberalism in 1914 in much more auspicious terms in his account of *The Downfall of the Liberal Party*, published in 1966. He points out that the Liberals were doing better than the Labour party in by-elections between 1911 and 1914; that the social reforming wing of the Liberal party was 'making the running', and that the Labour party had put forward no proposals which the Liberal party was unable to implement. He likens the Liberal party to 'an individual who, after a period of robust health and great exertion, experienced symptoms of illness (Ireland, labour unrest, the suffragettes). Before a thorough diagnosis could be made, he was involved in an encounter with a rampant omnibus (the First World War), which mounted the pavement and ran him over.' Wilson concludes: 'If it is guesswork to say that the bus was mainly responsible for his demise, it is the most warrantable guess that can be made.' [Wilson, pp. 20–21]

Similar differences can be detected in relation to the effect of the war on the growth of the Labour party. In *The Evolution of the Labour Party 1910–24*, Ross McKibbin plays down the impact of the war. He argues that 'The rise of the Labour Party and the slow attrition of the Liberal Party, I have suggested both came from an acutely developed working-class consciousness.' [McKibbin, p. XIV] This process was well under way by 1914 and would have continued with or without the war. Where the war did have a significant effect was in bringing about the 1918 Representation of the People Act which

> gave Britain for the first time an electorate in which the industrial working class was now unquestionably predominant. The Liberal vote may even have survived more or less intact, but after 1918 was overwhelmed by voters who could not be enrolled by official Liberalism. Much of this new electorate voted Labour in 1918; but had it been enfranchised it probably would have done so in 1914 as well. [McKibbin, p. XV]

Against this view, M. Pugh argues that the First World War had other substantial influences on the growth of the Labour party. He cites the increase in trade union membership, which rose from 4.1 million to 6.5 million, with TUC affiliated unions rising from 2.6 to 5.2 million. This brought a considerable increase in party resources, enabling the party to put 388 candidates into the field in the 1918 elections. He also stresses the breakdown of the Liberal–Labour electoral alliance 'more by Liberal ineptitude than through Labour's intention'. While also acknowledging the importance of the Representation of the People Act, he concludes finally: 'The potential for a government party based on the working class had existed unrealised for decades, but there are no good grounds for thinking that Labour would have attained this status in the 1920s but for the decisions and blunders of 1914–18.' [Pugh, p. 181]

Books cited

A. Marwick, *The Deluge, British Society and the First World War* (Bodley Head, 1967)

M. Pugh, *The Making of Modern British Politics, 1867–1939* (Blackwell, 1982)

G. Dangerfield, *The Strange Death of Liberal England* (Paladin, 1983)

T. Wilson, *The Downfall of the Liberal Party, 1914–1935* (Fontana, 1966)

R. McKibbin, *The Evolution of the Labour Party, 1910–1924* (Clarendon Press, 1973)

AT LAST!

Punch 1918

The women's movement ... largely confined itself to the narrow question of the franchise and neglected the wider social objectives that the vote might help them to obtain. [Pugh, p. 188]

BIBLIOGRAPHY BIBLIOGRAPHY BIBLIOGRAPHY BIBLIOGRAPHY BIBLIOGRAPHY BIBLIOGRAPHY
BIBLIOGRAPHY BIBLIOGRAPHY BIBLIOGRAPHY BIBLIOGRAPHY BIBLIOGRAPHY BIBLIOGRAPHY
BIBLIOGRAPHY BIBLIOGRAPHY BIBLIOGRAPHY BIBLIOGRAPHY BIBLIOGRAPHY BIBLIOGRAPHY
BIBLIOGRAPHY BIBLIOGRAPHY BIBLIOGRAPHY BIBLIOGRAPHY BIBLIOGRAPHY BIBLIOGRAPHY
BIBLIOGRAPHY BIBLIOGRAPHY BIBLIOGRAPHY BIBLIOGRAPHY BIBLIOGRAPHY BIBLIOGRAPHY
BIBLIOGRAPHY BIBLIOGRAPHY BIBLIOGRAPHY BIBLIOGRAPHY BIBLIOGRAPHY BIBLIOGRAPHY

CHAPTER 3
FURTHER READING

General Surveys

Essential

Sir L. Woodward, *Great Britain and the War of 1914–18* (Methuen, 1967)

Recommended

C. R. M. F. Cruttwell, *A History of the Great War* (OUP, 1940)

B. H. Liddell Hart, *A History of the First World War* (Cassell, 1930)

J. Terraine, *The Great War of 1914–18* (Secker & Warburg, 1983)

Individual Campaigns

Essential

The Western Front
J. Keegan, *The Face of Battle* (Penguin, 1976)
J. Terraine, *Douglas Haig, the Educated Soldier* (Hutchinson, 1962)
B. Tuchman, *August, 1914* (Constable, 1962)

Gallipoli
R. Rhodes James, *Gallipoli* (Batsford, 1965)

The War at Sea
R. Hough, *The Great War at Sea* (OUP, 1983)

Recommended

M. Middlebrook, *The First Day on the Somme* (Allen Lane, 1971)

R. Blake, *The Private Papers of Douglas Haig* (Eyre & Spottiswoode, 1952)

C. Barnett, *The Swordbearers* (Eyre & Spottiswoode, 1963)

A. Marder, *From the Dreadnought to Scapa Flow*, 5 vols (OUP, 1978)

The Direction of the War

Essential

Lord Hankey, *The Supreme Command* (Allen & Unwin, 1961)

S.W. Roskill, *Hankey, Man of Secrets*, 3 vols (Collins, 1970–74)

The War at Home

Essential

A. Marwick, *The Deluge, British Society and the First World War* (Bodley Head, 1967)

A. S. Milward, *The Economic Effects of Two World Wars on Britain* (Macmillan, 1972)

M. Pugh, *The Making of Modern British Politics* (Blackwell, 1982)

T. Wilson, *The Downfall of the Liberal Party, 1914–1935* (Fontana, 1966)

Recommended

Lord Beaverbrook, *Politicians and the War* (Hutchinson, 1928)

C. Hazlehurst, *Politicians at War* (Cape, 1971)

R. McKibbin, *The Evolution of the Labour Party, 1910–24* (Clarendon Press, 1973)

M. Pugh, *Women's Suffrage in Britain, 1867–1928* (Historical Association, 1980)

LOCAL RESEARCH PROJECT

The Effects of the First World War

The First World War can be studied both for its effects on the lives of individuals, and for its impact on the local community. Possible areas for investigation might be the experience of trench warfare as reflected in autobiographies and letters, or through the history of individual regiments. Many British infantry regiments were based on parent counties (the Gloucestershire Regiment, the Durham Light Infantry, or the Argyll and Sutherland Highlanders, for instance). Kitchener's New Army was expanded by grafting new battalions on to the original ones, or by raising new locally based regiments like the Leeds Rifles. Such regiments were then grouped together in territorially linked divisions such as the Wessex or Highland Divisions. The fortunes of local regiments or divisions could have devastating consequences on the areas from which they were recruited. Belfast suffered very badly from the appalling casualties sustained by the Ulster Division at the battle of the Somme. The experiences of such a unit could throw an interesting light on the parent community.

The war can also be studied for its effects on the home front. The introduction of Personal Identity Cards; rationing; the increased employment of women; the incidence of local industrial disputes and the effect of conscription could all be investigated, and there are plenty of other possibilities.

Suggested sources of information

Introductory

Autobiographies (Where recent editions are available, these have been cited.) Among the best are:

E. Blunden, *Undertones of War* (1930, Penguin, 1984)

V. Brittain, *Testament of Youth* (1936, Gollancz, 1978)

R. Graves, *Goodbye to All That* (1929, Penguin, 1969)

S. Sassoon, *Memoirs of an Infantry Officer* (1930, Faber, 1965)

H. Williamson, *A Soldier's Diary of the Great War* (Faber & Gwyer, 1928)

Two accounts of battles give a good description of the experiences of particular units:

M. Middlebrook, *The First Day on the Somme* (Allen Lane, 1971)

L. MacDonald, *They Called it Passchendaele* (Papermac, 1983)

The best book on the home front is A. Marwick, *The Deluge, British Society and the First World War* (Bodley Head, 1967), which also has an excellent bibliography.

Further sources

Individual regimental and divisional histories should be accessible in local libraries. The Imperial War Museum should be able to provide guidance on those which are available.

The County Record Office may well have collections of letters and diaries relating to the First World War, though these will not be open to inspection until fifty years after the deaths of those concerned. Municipal Records and possibly Trade Union Records should also to available in County Record Offices.

Local Reference Libraries provide the easiest means of access to local newspapers. When consulting these it is as well to have a specific date in mind as they are not likely to be indexed.

TIME CHART 1900–18

Date	Social and Economic	Political	Foreign Affairs	The Empire and Ireland
1900		*Feb.* Labour Represen-tation Committee formed.		
1901	*Jan.* Taff Vale Case.			
1902	*Dec.* Balfour Education Act.	*Jul.* Salisbury resigned in favour of Balfour.	*Jan.* Anglo-Japanese alliance.	Treaty of Vereeniging.
1903	*Oct.* Woman's Social and Political Union formed.	Split in Tory party over Tariff Reform	*Mar.* Edward VII's visit to Paris.	
1904			*Apr.* Anglo-French *en-tente*	
1905		*Dec.* Balfour resigned, Campbell Banner-man made premier.	*Mar.* First Moroccan Crisis. *Dec.* Anglo-French Military Conver-sations.	
1906	*Dec.* Trades Disputes Act passed.	*Jan.* General Election, Liberals gained overall majority. 29 Labour MPs elected.	*Jan.–Apr.* Algeçiras Conference. *May.* Anglo-Russian talks begun.	Irish Nationalist Party gained 84 seats at Westminster.
1907	Boy scout movement founded by Baden–Powell.		*Aug.* Anglo-Russian *entente.*	
1908		*Apr.* Asquith became premier.	*Oct.* Bosnia annexed by Austria.	
1909	*Jan.* Old Age Pensions first paid. *Apr.* Trade Boards Act passed.	*Nov.* Lloyd George's budget defeated in House of Lords.		*May.* Morley-Minto Re-forms in India. *Oct.* Union of South Africa Act.
1910	Start of Suffragette militancy.	*Jan.* General Election, Liberals lose over-all majority. *Dec.* General Election, no change.		
1911	National Health and Unemployment Insurance Act introduced.	*Aug.* Parliament Act passed House of Lords. *Nov.* Bonar Law replaced Balfour.	*Jul.–Aug.* Agadir Crisis.	

Date	Social and Economic	Political	Foreign Affairs	The Empire and Ireland
1912	National Insurance implemented. 41 million days lost in strikes. Minimum Wage Act in the coal industry.		*Oct.* Outbreak of first Balkan War. *Nov.* Anglo-French Naval Agreement.	*Jan.* Ulster Volunteers formed. *Apr.* First Home Rule Bill.
1913	Coal production reached 287 million tons. Osborne Judgment reversed.		*May* Treaty of London. *Jun.* Second Balkan War. *Aug.* Treaty of Bucharest.	*Jan.* Home Rule Bill rejected in House of Lords.
1914	TU membership up to 4 million. Attempts to form Triple Alliance of miners, dockers and transport workers.	*Aug.* All parties supported war. *Aug.* Burns and Morley resigned from cabinet; Macdonald from Labour leadership.	*May* Anglo-Russian naval talks. *Jun.* Assassination of Archduke Franz Ferdinand. (See chart p. 53 for detailed events.)	*Mar.* Curragh Mutiny. *Apr.* Larne Gun Running. *Jul.* Bachelor's Walk Massacre. *Aug.* All Dominions declare war.
1915	*Mar.* Treasury Agreement. *May* Munitions Act passed. *Aug.* National Register drawn up.	*May* Coalition Government, Henderson first Labour Minister.	*Apr.–Dec.* Gallipoli offensive. Battle of Loos.	
1916	*Jan.* Conscription for unmarried men. *May* Conscription for all.	*Dec.* Asquith forced to resign. Lloyd George formed War Cabinet, Cabinet Secretariat.	*May* Jutland. *Jul.–Nov.* Somme. *Sep.* British surrender at Kut.	*Apr.* Easter Rising in Dublin. *May* Sykes-Picot Agreement. *Dec.* Lucknow Pact (Hindu/Muslim).
1917	*Jan.* Shipping Controller appointed. *Jun.* Rationing introduced.	*Aug.* Henderson resigned from War Cabinet.	*Feb.* Outbreak of Russian Revolution. *Apr.* Entry of United States into War. *Apr.* Worst month for sinkings by U-boats. *Jul.–Nov.* Passchendaele offensive.	*Jul.* Irish Convention. *Nov.* Balfour Declaration.
1918	Fisher Education Act. Representation of the People Act. Votes for women over 30. TU membership up to 6.5 million.	*May* Maurice Debate. *May* New Labour Party Constitution. *Nov.* Labour leaders left Coalition. *Nov.* Coupon Election, victory for Lloyd George Coalition.	*Mar.* Treaty of Brest Litovsk. *Mar.* Final German offensive. *May–Nov.* Final, Allied offensive.	*Jul.* Montagu-Chelmsford Report. *Nov.* Victory for Sinn Fein in 1918 election.

CHAPTER 4

Economic and Political Developments, 1918–29

THE ECONOMY ▬▬▬▬▬▬▬▬▬▬▬▬▬▬▬▬▬▬▬▬▬▬ A

The Effects of War

There can be little doubt that the British economy was affected more adversely by what the First World War did to the world economy in general rather than by what it did to the British economy itself in particular. The war brought about the collapse of four empires: the Habsburg, the German, the Russian and the Ottoman. In all these areas it took several years before political stability was restored, and political stability was the pre-requisite on which international trade depended.

The war also completely destroyed the delicate mechanism of international finance which had sustained the world's commerce. The gold standard which had worked at least tolerably well before 1914 had gone for good in its old form, and though attempts were made to restore it Europe never again enjoyed the financial stability it had experienced before the war. The problem of international finance was made worse by the legacy of indebtedness. Britain and France each had incurred substantial debts with the United States in order to maintain their war efforts. They in turn had been forced to lend money to their allies, notably Russia and Italy. These debts strengthened the case for obtaining reparations from Germany. The final consequence of all these unwelcome obligations was that Germany was saddled with a reparations bill of £6600 million, mainly owed to Britain and France; Britain owed £1000 million to the United States; and the United States found herself lending huge sums of money to Germany to enable reparations payments to be met. The hyperinflation endured by Germany in 1922–3 was at least partly caused by reparations. Just as damaging was the harm done to international confidence and co-operation by the constant bickering over war debts that persisted until 1924. It was thus several years before the world economy settled down and normal trading relations were restored. By the time they were, Britain's export industries had missed the boat.

The direct effects of the war on the British economy are not easy to gauge. Some things, however, can be quantified. Total loss of life for Great Britain alone, according to the most recent estimates, was 616382, with a further 1656755 wounded. [Milward, p. 12] But with unemployment standing at over a million for most of the inter-war period, it would be hard to argue that the war caused a shortage of labour, callous though such a calculation must seem. In terms of physical destruction Britain escaped much more lightly than France and Belgium. She lost 7.75 million tons of merchant shipping, 38% of the total tonnage available in 1914. But much of this loss had been made good by 1918, and by 1921 there was already a surplus of shipbuilding capacity in British shipyards.

A. S. Milward, *The Economic Effects of the Two World Wars on Britain* (Economic History Review, 1970)

More serious was the loss of export markets. Exports of cotton goods to India, for instance, fell by 53% between 1913 and 1923. Over the same period there was a fall of 33% in exports to South America. Countries which had previously relied on Britain for the supply of coal, cotton, iron and steel, and ships developed their own industries, or found other suppliers such as the United States. While the war cannot be held entirely responsible for these developments, by disrupting old trading patterns it undoubtedly helped to worsen Britain's economic position.

It had been hoped initially that Britain would be able to meet all the costs of imports without resorting to foreign borrowing, if necessary by the sale of overseas investments. In fact, as the war progressed, the trade balance with the United States inevitably deteriorated, and even after the sale of £265 million of foreign investments Britain had incurred debts of £1365 million, mainly with the United States. She herself was owed £1741 million, but had little prospect of recovering much of this, notably the £565 million lent to Russia. Agreement on the American debt was eventually reached in January 1923, when Britain pledged to repay the total over 61 years, paying 3% interest for the first 10 years, and 3.5% for the remaining 52.

As well as adding to foreign debts, the war had caused a huge increase in the National Debt which reached a peak of £7830 million in March 1920. Interest payments absorbed 40% of the budget, equivalent to 7% of the National Income. How serious a burden this was has been much debated. In one sense all that was entailed was the transfer of money from the pockets of taxpayers to those of *rentiers*, the holders of government securities. But there were two more damaging consequences. First, at a time when all governments believed as an article of faith in the need to balance budgets, the share of revenue pre-empted by interest payments meant that there was less money to spend on more desirable projects, housing subsidies or school building for instance. Secondly, the need to re-cycle the Debt required further government borrowing which in turn kept interest rates higher than they might have been. Many business men had made huge profits during the war, Baldwin among them. In what is sometimes dismissed as a quixotic gesture, Baldwin purchased £150000 of War Loan and presented it to the government for cancellation as his contribution to the reduction of the National Debt. If enough others had followed his example, the British economy would have stood to benefit. As it was, the size of the Debt continued to exercise a malign influence over economic policy, even if in itself it was of no great significance.

The war had some more positive effects. It accelerated the pace of technological development. In 1916 the Department of Scientific and Industrial Research was created. There were major advances in the motor car industry, and the aircraft industry owed its inception to the demand for military aircraft, of which no fewer than 52057 were produced. There were significant advances in radio communications and in medical science. The munitions industry encouraged the much wider use of machine tools and assembly-line techniques. Many of the jobs in manufacturing industry that could only have been tackled by skilled craftsmen before the war were now within the capacity of semi-skilled labour. Labour productivity generally improved. The losses and shortages caused by the war led, initially at least, to a post-war boom. Between 1918 and April 1920, 2.9 million extra workers found jobs, though it is true that 500 000 women also left the labour market over the same period. But when the boom collapsed, as it did in 1921, Britain's dependence on the old staple industries became all too apparent, and bears out the view of A. S. Milward that 'it would surely be an exaggeration to suggest that the war produced any profound change in the British economic system, despite the strong pressure for change.' [Milward, p. 40]

Milward, *The Economic Effects of the Two World Wars on Britain*

Growth and Decline

The British economy in the inter-war years faced the problems of adjusting to a world of new technologies and changing markets. In some respects the adaptation was remarkably successful, in others much less so. Between 1919 and 1929 Britain experienced the fastest rate of technological innovation so far achieved in her history. By 1924 manufacturing output had recovered to its 1913 level and continued to grow until 1929. The annual rate of economic growth averaged 1.9% for manufacturing industry as a whole, and was much higher in some sectors: for electrical goods it was 10.2%, for cars 10.1% for instance. The electrical supply industry established itself as a main source of energy. In 1920 it supplied 730 000 consumers, in 1938 it supplied 8 920 000. The setting up of the Central Electricity Generating Board in 1926 made possible the development of the National Grid, providing relatively cheap sources of power in all the populated areas of Great Britain.

The car industry which produced 33 000 cars in 1913, increased this figure to 95 000 in 1923 and 511 000 in 1937. By 1930 the aircraft industry was employing 30 000. Other industries that showed a more or less continuous growth both in output and employment in the 1920s were chemicals, aluminium, rubber, the boot and shoe industry, artificial fibres, food canning and scientific instruments. After being run down during the war the construction industry expanded rapidly and in the early 1930s was responsible for the most rapid rate of house building in British history. Even so, the growth in employment in these industries was not sufficient to absorb more than a fraction of those who lost their jobs in other sectors of the economy. For while employment in the electrical, automobile, aircraft, rayon, hosiery, chemical and scientific instrument industries rose from 370 500 in 1907 to 745 000 in 1924 and 914 000 in 1930, there were much bigger losses in the staple industries of coal, iron and steel, shipbuilding and textiles, as the following figures indicate:

TOTAL EMPLOYEES

	1924	*1930*
Coal	1 259 000	1 069 000
Iron and steel	313 000	287 000
Shipbuilding	254 000	205 000
Cotton	572 000	564 000
Wool	262 000	240 000

PERCENTAGE UNEMPLOYED

	1924	1930
Coal	6.9	28.3
Iron and steel	20.4	32.6
Shipbuilding	28.3	31.7
Cotton	15.9	44.7

[Mowat, pp. 273–4]

C. L. Mowat, *Britain
between the Wars*
(1955)

The reasons for the decline in these industries were both general and specific. First was the loss of export markets. It has been calculated that the numbers made redundant by the fall in exports in the six leading staple export trades amounted to between 700 000 and 800 000. These job losses accounted for virtually the whole of the intractable core of the unemployment of the 1920s. [Pollard, p. 117] This in turn can be partly explained by lack of competitiveness which showed itself in the use of antiquated machinery, restrictive practices, low profitability and low investment. These industries were not growth industries in the same way that the car or electricity industries were. It has also been argued that when Britain returned to the gold standard in 1925 she did so at an overvalued rate of $4.86 to the pound, which made British exports unnecessarily expensive.

S. F. Pollard, *The
Development of the
British Economy,
1914–1980* (1983)

Each industry also had its specific problems. The coal industry was plagued by bad management, under-investment and appalling industrial relations. Though domestic demand held up well, export markets fell from an average of 100 million tons per year to 50 million tons at best. The iron and steel industry was weakened by a flood of cheap imports and devastated by the world depression which began in 1929, production of pig iron falling in that year by 53% while steel production fell by 45%.

Shipbuilding experienced a brief boom in 1919–20, and Britain even managed to retain a 40% share in world output in the 1920s. But world capacity soon outstripped world demand and the onset of the depression brought about a catastrophic collapse. Launches from British shipyards in 1933 were only 7% of their pre-war figures.

The cotton industry was peculiarly vulnerable to overseas competition. Between 1909 and 1911 Britain had a 65% share in the trade in cotton piece goods and cotton yarn; 75% of British output was exported; and cotton goods accounted for 25% of the value of British exports. After 1914 Britain failed to compete with lower cost producers in the Far East, India and the United States. The real challenge came in the 1930s, and by 1936–38 Britain's share of cotton exports had fallen to 28%; the labour force fell from 621 500 in 1912 to 393 000 in 1938.

The impact of the decline of these industries was made much worse because of their geographical concentration in certain parts of the country, notably the Central Lowlands of Scotland, West Cumberland, Lancashire, the North East and South Wales. Unfortunately the new industries tended to be located in the Midlands or the South East. This meant that any increases in employment took place outside the old industrial areas, and the familiar pattern of widely differing regional rates of unemployment began to appear:

PERCENTAGE UNEMPLOYED

	1924	1930
London	9.0	9.8
Midlands	9.4	18.6
North East	11.7	24.5
North West	12.7	29.3
Scotland	13.5	23.5
Wales	5.6	31.2
Great Britain	11.2	19.9

Mowat, *Britain between the Wars*

C. L. Mowat sums up Britain's economic position in these terms: 'Hence the two Englands, or rather the two Britains of the inter-war years: chronic depression in the North and in the Celtic fringe, moderate prosperity in the South.' [Mowat, p. 274]

Government Policies and the Problems of Adjustment

The failure of the new industries in the Midlands and the South East to absorb those who had lost their jobs in the old staple industries presented successive governments with two problems. The first was the inexorable rise in unemployment. By March 1921, 15% of the insured population were without jobs. The figure was never below 9–11%, about 1 million, for the remainder of the decade. Unemployment reached its peak in August 1932, when it totalled 3 million, 25% of the insured population. Some recovery took place in the 1930s, but even with the spur of rearmament there were still over 1 million unemployed when war broke out in 1939.

The second problem, closely related to it, was also caused by falling demand in the staple industries. Faced with the need to compete in shrinking markets employers inevitably tried to cut costs by reducing wages. This in turn provoked industrial unrest as workers sought to maintain their living standards which were low enough as it was. The correlation between falling demand and industrial unrest is most marked in the coal industry. While it only accounted for 6.2% of the working population, the coal industry provided 41.8% of all strikers between 1911 and 1945, and the most serious industrial dispute between the wars, the General Strike, was the direct consequence of the attempt to cut miners' wages. Miners were not the only group of workers to go on strike. Railwaymen, foundry workers, engineers, even the police, were all on strike in 1919–20. It is still the case that industrial unrest, not surprisingly, was most common where jobs and wages were under threat.

Faced with these problems, the inter-war governments had little to offer except the tried doctrines of free-market economics. They sought economic security, if not salvation, in free trade, a return to the Gold Standard and balanced budgets. The belief in free trade ran deep. There were minor infractions of the principle, admittedly, in the McKenna duties which imposed a 33.33% *ad valorem* duty on luxury articles in 1915; and in the Safeguarding of Industries Act 1921, which extended the same protection to certain 'key' industries. But the Balfour Committee, appointed to consider Industry and Trade in 1924, came down strongly against tariffs in 1927, and when Baldwin advocated Protection in 1923, his party was decisively defeated.

By 1929 only 17% of the total value of British imports were subject to any import duties, and of these only 2--3% were imposed for the purpose of protection rather than revenue. It needed the onset of the world depression to change government thinking towards the abandonment of free trade.

Britain had left the Gold Standard for all practical purposes in 1914 when the Bank of England refused to continue exchanging holdings of pounds for gold at a fixed parity. In March 1919 the position was formalised by the passing of the Gold (Export Control) Act. But already the Cunliffe Committee on Currency and Foreign Exchanges had urged the 're-establishment of the currency upon a sound basis' in their first report which came out in August 1918. Their final report, in December 1919, reaffirmed their original recommendations. From April 1920 onwards a return to the Gold Standard became a prime objective of economic policy. If this were to happen it implied that there would have to be tight control of the domestic money supply and an improvement in the value of the pound in relation to other currencies. In fact, it was not until 1925 that these conditions were felt to be met, and when Britain did return to the Gold Standard it was in a modified form. But the objective had been constantly pursued and was therefore a significant influence on the government's other economic policies.

The third premise on which economic policy rested was the belief in balanced budgets, i.e. that total government expenditure should not be allowed to exceed total revenue. This belief was held by all those concerned with the making of economic policy; no one held it more firmly than Philip Snowden, the Labour Chancellor of the Exchequer in 1924 and from 1929 to 1931. In a speech delivered to the House of Commons in 1929, Winston Churchill, also Chancellor of the Exchequer at the time, expounded the orthodox Treasury doctrine 'which has steadfastly held that, whatever might be the political or social advantages, very little additional employment and no permanent additional employment can, in fact, and as a general rule, be created by State borrowing and State expenditure.' [Pollard, p. 209] In practice, not only were budgets generally balanced throughout the 1920s; on several occasions surpluses were achieved which were used to redeem part of the National Debt. But this was only at the expense of severe cuts in public expenditure and their deflationary consequences. It is an ironical comment, not without contemporary significance, on government policies that the Public Works Unemployment Grants Committee spent a mere £69.5 million between 1920 and 1932, while during the same period of time £600 million had to be spent on unemployment benefit and relief.

Pollard, *The Development of the British Economy, 1914–1980*

Thus governments of all persuasions, while facing problems that were not of their making, were also shackled by the economic doctrines of an earlier era.

B ▬▬▬▬▬▬▬▬▬▬▬▬▬▬▬ POLITICAL DEVELOPMENTS

The Formation of the Coalition

The political situation at the end of the war was extremely fluid. Lloyd George was firmly in the saddle at the head of a victorious Government, but his party was acutely divided. The Conservatives, brought into Asquith's Government in 1915, while

The Experiment in Non-Party Government

ready to back Lloyd George as a war-time Prime Minister, were hardly his natural allies in peacetime. The Labour party, having tasted the fruits of office, had to decide whether to continue the electoral arrangement they had had with the Liberal party since 1903, whether to campaign under Lloyd George's banner, or whether to strike out on their own. Only one thing was certain; after eight years without an election the people would expect an opportunity to go to the polls as soon as the war ended.

Lloyd George as Prime Minister, 1916–22

As the war drew to a close a number of these doubts were resolved. The first move occurred on 17 May 1918, shortly after the Maurice debate (see p. 89), when a group of Lloyd George's Liberal supporters held a meeting to plan their futures. The Chief Whip, F. E. Guest, then wrote to Lloyd George on 13 July urging among other things that 'a form of agreement with the Conservatives should be prepared and signed without delay.' [Wilson, p. 151] On 29 October he was able to inform Lloyd George that 'I have come to an agreement with Mr. Bonar Law that we should receive their support where necessary for 150 Lloyd George candidates, 100 of them are our Old Guard.' [Wilson, p. 152] This agreement was the basis of the notorious 'coupons', as Asquith termed them, under which approved candidates would not be opposed by Conservatives in the constituencies concerned. The favoured 150 were carefully selected on the basis of their voting records over the previous 18 months, not just on the Maurice debate, as has sometimes been alleged.

T. Wilson, *The Downfall of the Liberal Party, 1911–1935* (Fontana, 1966)

By making this agreement the Conservatives had committed themselves to the continuation of Lloyd George's premiership. This was partly an act of political calculation, but partly also because of genuine admiration for Lloyd George's leadership and a belief that he was the only man who could unite the forces of the right against the threat of Bolshevism. The Labour party chose differently. Henderson's dismissal from the War Cabinet in September 1917; growth in the party's financial resources through the increase in trade union membership; the prospect of support from the greatly increased electorate; and the disintegration of the Liberal party; all these factors encouraged the Labour party to leave the Coalition and to fight the election outside its embrace. Two Labour ministers, Barnes and Roberts, preferred to stay with Lloyd George. They retained their seats but were expelled from the party.

Bonar Law as Prime Minister 1922–23

The result of the election was a triumph for the Coalition whose supporters gained 526 seats out of 707. Contrary to popular belief the election was not particularly hotly contested. The total poll was only 57% of the electorate; though calls were made to 'hang the Kaiser' by George Barnes and to 'squeeze Germany until the pips squeak' by Sir Eric Geddes, Lloyd George did not indulge in anti-German rhetoric. K. O. Morgan, the most recent historian of the Coalition government, argues that if the Coupon Election 'embodied anything, it was a mandate for peace, reconstruction and reform.' [Morgan, p. 42]

K. O Morgan, Consensus and Disunity, the Lloyd George Coalition (1979)

The Policy of Reconstruction

In a speech delivered to the Liberal party MPs on 12 November 1918, Lloyd George spelled out his hopes for the future. They included plans to raise standards in health and housing; a minimum wage; shorter working hours; the acquisition and purchase of land to ensure reasonable access; and he concluded by explaining the watchword of his government would be 'progress, wise progress'. Lloyd George did not inform his hearers of the deal he had just concluded with Bonar Law. How genuine were his reforming intentions?

If economic circumstances had permitted him an easier ride, it is likely that the Coalition government would have left behind it a reputation for constructive social reform, even though it never posed a serious threat to the existing distribution of wealth. There were significant initiatives in the fields of housing, unemployment insurance and agriculture. Addison's Housing Act of 1919 placed on all local authorities the obligation to see that all citizens were decently housed. To that end the Government offered to meet the costs of all municipal housing that exceeded the proceeds of a penny rate. Private house builders were also offered a subsidy of £260 per house under certain circumstances. The Act ran into much opposition for its extravagance, but 210 237 new houses were built with its aid between 1919 and 1923.

In 1920 the Unemployment Act extended unemployment insurance to another 12 million workers, covering the majority of the wage-earning population. Agricultural workers, domestic servants and civil servants were still excluded and benefit was only payable for the first 15 weeks of unemployment. The Act had been framed on the assumption that unemployment was unlikely to rise beyond 5.32%. When it did so in 1921, and for every succeeding year, the scheme ceased to be self-financing and required constant modification. But at least the principle of comprehensive protection against unemployment had been explicitly recognised, and without this Act the plight of the unemployed would have been very much worse.

The Government also provided continuing support to agriculture. The Agriculture Act of 1920 maintained the system of price guarantees for wheat and oats that had been introduced in the Corn Production Act of 1917. Tenant farmers were given greater security of tenure and agricultural wages were to be protected.

But all these initiatives were blunted or curtailed when the slump began in April 1921. By the end of the year exports had fallen by 47.9% on 1920 figures and unemployment had risen to over 2 million. Lloyd George's response was to appoint a committee of business men under the chairmanship of Sir Eric Geddes. Its sittings began in August 1921 and its first report came out in February 1922. It recommended sweeping cuts in public expenditure, ranging from cuts of £46.5 million from the armed services to £18.2 million from education. The latter cuts, if implemented, would have implied school class sizes of 60–70, a prospect that Lloyd George evidently faced with equanimity. In the end the spending departments managed to reduce the total cuts recommended from £75 million to £64 million, and the cuts in educational spending were reduced to £6.5 million. But the Geddes axe, as it came to be called, was hardly the most appropriate weapon to wield at a time when jobs were disappearing.

The cabinet also imposed cuts on Addison's housing programme, precipitating his resignation and subsequent departure to the Labour party. The Agriculture Act of 1920 was hastily repealed in 1921 as world wheat prices fell and the cost of subsidising English farmers rose. Agricultural wages were again left to be determined by market forces and agricultural workers lost all the gains they had made during the war. The provisions of the Unemployment Act of 1920 were altered in 1921 and 1922, first by extending the period for which benefit was payable from 15 to 32 weeks, secondly by allowing the Unemployment Fund to borrow up to £30 million from the Treasury to finance what was called 'uncovenanted' benefit, i.e. the benefit that might be claimed after the 32 weeks had expired; thirdly by the introduction of allowances of 5/- a week for the wives and 1/- a week for the children of those unemployed; and finally by requiring that all claimants of benefit must prove that they were 'genuinely seeking' work. This last provision, necessary though it might seem, led to the proliferation of a vast network of committees to ensure that aid went only to the deserving, and it led to great resentment.

Industrial Relations

In its handling of industrial relations the Coalition government showed the same shift from reforming intentions to reactionary policies. In the wave of strikes that took place in 1919 Lloyd George showed all his negotiating skills. He brought the nine days' rail strike that occurred in September to an end; he averted the threat of a coal strike by appointing the Sankey Commission to investigate the conditions of the coal industry. New machinery was created for the negotiation of wage rates, hours, training and production methods. This took the form of Joint Industrial Councils, as recommended by the Whitley Report in 1917. By 1920 there were 56 such councils, covering 3.25 million workers. In February 1919, a National Industrial Conference was held attended by leaders of all the main trade unions and 300 employers. Its unanimous report recommended a 48-hour week, policies to stabilise employment, more generous pensions and other benefits, and a permanent National Industrial Conference made up of 400 members, half to be elected by trade unions, half by employers. But the scheme was allowed to die in July 1921.

Confrontation rather than co-operation became the keynote of industrial relations as the economic climate deteriorated and as Lloyd George found himself more dependent on the Conservative members of the Coalition. The Sankey Commission recommended nationalisation of the mines by seven votes to six, the mine owners predictably voting against, the trade union representatives for. Lord Justice Sankey, the chairman, voted with the majority. But only five members of the cabinet, Barnes, Roberts, Addison, Montagu and Milner, were prepared to back the majority report. Lloyd George sought a compromise, offering nationalisation of royalties and a scheme which would have involved some amalgamation of collieries. In the event, neither suggestion was taken up. A seven-hour day was authorised for the industry in 1920, and government control of the industry was extended until 1921. But falling coal prices, which caused losses of £5 million a month at the beginning of 1921, led the government to bring forward the date when the mines would be returned to private control from 31 August to 31 March. Mine owners reacted at once by imposing a 50% cut in wages. Once again a coal strike threatened, this time supported by the revived Triple Alliance of miners, railwaymen and transport workers. At the last moment, the railwaymen and transport workers backed down because the miners' leaders refused to resume negotiations, a retreat that came to be known as Black Friday. The miners stayed out on strike until July, when they were forced to go back to work on the owners' terms. The coal industry indeed remained 'the supreme indictment of an unreconstructed capitalism' [Morgan, p. 66] and the Coalition government had missed an opportunity to do something about it.

Morgan, *Consensus and Disunity*

The Coalition showed an increasing tendency to rely on strong-arm tactics in the face of industrial unrest. In 1920 an Emergency Powers Act was passed, giving the government powers to declare a state of emergency whenever action threatened to deprive the community of the essentials of life. In such a state of emergency the government would have power to make regulations by Order in Council and to set up summary courts to deal with offenders. Fifty-six battalions of troops were held in readiness to deal with the threatened Triple Alliance strike in 1921, though they never had to be used. It is hard to know whether the government's apprehensions were justified. Left-wing rhetoric always tended to outstrip organisation. But there can be no doubt that Lloyd George's hopes of creating a national consensus that would unite the classes had failed. He could no longer be seen as the bringer of unity.

The Fall of the Coalition

Despite the huge majority which the Coalition enjoyed in the House of Commons after 1918, Lloyd George's position was always more vulnerable than it seemed. Though he enjoyed the support of many Conservatives, including Bonar Law, Austen Chamberlain, Balfour, Milner and Lord Birkenhead, he was equally distrusted by others for various reasons. Lord Robert Cecil disliked him for his conduct of the peace negotiations. A group of right-wingers, known as the Die Hards, had always opposed his leadership and resented his policy towards Ireland; other more moderate Conservatives were suspicious of his style of government, his reliance on personal advisers rather than the cabinet, and his dubious trafficking in honours. While Austen Chamberlain insisted that Lloyd George's continuing leadership was essential to keep the Labour party out of office, his brother Neville did not have the same confidence in the Prime Minister. In January 1922 Neville Chamberlain wrote: 'This dirty little Welsh attorney and his Coalition Liberal sycophants think they can dictate a policy to the whole Unionist Party.' [Cowling, p. 131] Such was the hostility Lloyd George aroused in some quarters.

M. Cowling, *The Impact of Labour 1920–24* (1971)

THE SCAPEGOAT THAT TURNED

["IF I AM DRIVEN ALONE INTO THE WILDERNESS . . ."— *Mr. Lloyd George at Manchester*

"MY HUSBAND THOROUGHLY ENJOYS A FIGHT."— *Mrs. Lloyd George at East Ham.*]

Punch 1922

Aware of his vulnerability, Lloyd George sought to fuse the Coalition Liberals with the Conservative party. In February 1920, he urged Liberal ministers that 'Liberal labels lead nowhere: we must be prepared to burn them.' [Morgan, 'Lloyd George's Stage Army', in *Lloyd George, Twelve Essays*, Taylor, ed., p. 246] But the Coalition Liberals refused to shed their identity and in a meeting with Lloyd George in March 1920, they made this very clear to him. As a result he was forced into even greater dependence upon his Conservative supporters. He suffered a further setback when Bonar Law resigned on grounds of ill health in March 1921. His successor as leader of the Conservative party, Austen Chamberlain, did not carry the same weight and it meant that should Bonar Law be prevailed on to return to political life, an alternative Prime Minister would be available.

A. J. P. Taylor (ed.), *Lloyd George, Twelve Essays* (1971)

When Lloyd George floated the idea of an early election in January 1922, he was publicly humiliated by the chairman of the Conservative party, George Younger, who gave four interviews to the press opposing the idea. A month later, Younger called for 'a bill of divorcement' to end the 'matrimonial alliance' of Conservatives and Coalition Liberals. Throughout the summer Lloyd George and his Conservative allies, notably Austen Chamberlain and Birkenhead, did their best to hold the Coalition together. But when the Chanak crisis (see p. 154) threatened to cause a rebellion on the Conservative back benches, Chamberlain decided to force the issue. On 9 October he proposed to his fellow Conservatives in the cabinet that they should reaffirm their decision to go to the country as a Coalition under Lloyd George's leadership. This provoked the resignations of Baldwin and Boscawen. There followed a week of intense intrigues. Bonar Law was eventually prevailed on by Baldwin and others to return to political life. Austen Chamberlain conceded the need to hold a meeting with all Conservative back benchers to decide on whether or not the Coalition should continue. The meeting was held on 19 October at the Carlton Club. It coincided with news of Conservative gain in a by-election at Newport, previously held by a Coalition Liberal. Chamberlain spoke for half an hour in defence of the Coalition but Baldwin in a brief but effective speech had a much more attentive hearing. He warned his audience that Lloyd George was 'a dynamic force'; 'It is owing to that dynamic force', Baldwin continued, 'and that remarkable personality, that the Liberal Party, to which he formerly belonged, has been smashed to pieces; and it is my firm conviction that, in time the same thing will happen to our party.' [Middlemas and Barnes, p. 123] Bonar Law also spoke in favour of ending the Coalition. These two speeches put the issue beyond doubt. By 187 votes to 87 the Conservative members of Parliament brought the Coalition to an end. Austen Chamberlain resigned from the leadership of the Conservative party, and Lloyd George resigned from the premiership. The experiment in non-party government was over.

K. Middlemas and J. Barnes, *Baldwin* (1969)

The Working of the Electoral System and Changes in Party Leadership

Three Party Politics, 1922–24

The instability of British politics between 1922 and 1924 which witnessed three elections in three years was brought about by the vagaries of the electoral system and the peculiar division of support in the electorate between the four competing parties, Conservatives, Labour, National Liberals and Asquithian Liberals. This can best be illustrated by the table on the following page.

ELECTIONS

	15 November 1922	6 December 1923	29 October 1924
Conservative			
Seats	345	258	419
% Vote	38.2	38.1	47.3
Liberal (Asquith)			
Seats	62	159	40
% Vote	19	29.6	17.6
Liberal (Lloyd George)			
Seats	54		
% Vote	10		
Labour			
Seats	142	191	151
% Vote	29.5	30.5	33.0

(In 1923 and 1924 the differences between Lloyd George and Asquith were temporarily resolved.)

[Pugh, p. 242]

M. Pugh, *The Making of Modern British Politics* (1982)

Pugh, *The making of Modern British Politics*

From the above figures several important if obvious conclusions may be drawn. In the first place, the division within the Liberal party and the ending of the electoral pact with the Labour party clearly benefited the Conservatives. It has been pointed out that whereas in the Liberal 'landslide' election of 1906 the Conservatives only gained 157 seats out of 670, with 44% of the vote, in 1922 with 38.2%, a smaller share by 5%, they gained 345 seats out of 615 [Pugh, p. 243] Secondly, it is worth noting the consistency of popular support for the Labour party, which went up from 29.5% to 33%. Finally, it can be seen that what determined the fortunes of the parties in terms of seats was what happened to the Liberal vote. In 1923 a swing of 0.1% from the Conservatives resulted in the loss of 87 seats, mainly to Liberal candidates. In 1924 a drop of 12% in the Liberal vote resulted in the Labour party losing 40 seats, even though their share of the total vote went up by 2%. There was not much justice about the way the system worked; various proposals for reforming it were made, both in 1918 and in 1931, but came to nothing because the parties in power at the time could see no electoral advantage to be gained from the changes suggested.

These years were also marked by arguments over the leadership of the three main parties. Bonar Law's replacement of Austen Chamberlain as Leader of the Conservative party in 1922 proved to be short-lived. Bonar Law was suffering from cancer of the throat, though this was not officially diagnosed until May 1923 when he announced his determination to resign. Bonar Law was greatly exercised about the problem of his successor. On past precedents he could be expected to make a recommendation to the King, but this he shrank from doing. There were two obvious candidates: Lord Curzon, ex-Viceroy of India, member of Lloyd George's War Cabinet, and Foreign Secretary from 1918 onwards; and Stanley Baldwin, who had played such an important part in the downfall of Lloyd George. Baldwin had entered

Parliament at the age of 40, as member for Bewdley, the 'family' seat, in 1908. In his first six years as an MP he made only six speeches. His ministerial career began in 1916 when he became Bonar Law's Parliamentary Private Secretary. In 1917 he took on the post of Financial Secretary to the Treasury, where he remained until 1921. He then moved to the Board of Trade, and when Bonar Law became Prime Minister he offered Baldwin the Chancellorship of the Exchequer, after Reginald McKenna had turned it down.

Stanley Baldwin,
Prime Minister
1923–24, 1924–29,
1935–37

Unlike Curzon, whose sights had been set on the premiership all his political life, Baldwin had no such ambitions. When J. C. Davidson, Bonar Law's Parliamentary Private Secretary, mooted the possibility, Baldwin evidently averred that he would rather take a single ticket to Siberia than become Prime Minister. [Middlemas and Barnes, p. 162] The choice finally rested with George V. The King received conflicting advice. At the request of Lord Stamfordham, J. C. Davidson submitted a memorandum on the two men. He favoured Baldwin, partly on the grounds of Curzon's temperamental unsuitability, and because Curzon represented 'that section of privileged Conservatives which has its value but which in this democratic age cannot be too assiduously exploited', but mainly because the premiership should be held by someone in the House of Commons. Stamfordham nonetheless backed Curzon, as did Lord Salisbury whose advice was also canvassed. A. J. Balfour, who had never liked Curzon, advised George V to send for Baldwin. The King concluded privately that the monarchy would lay itself open to criticism should he appoint a peer and had no doubt that Baldwin should be offered the succession. Both men were summoned to Buckingham Palace on 22 May. Curzon's journey from Montacute House was a triumphal progress ending in a humiliating interview with Stamfordham who had the difficult task of breaking the news. Baldwin set off inconspicuously from Chequers, lent to him by Bonar Law, and left Buckingham Palace as Premier. He remained leader of the Conservative party for 14 years, and served as Prime Minister for 8 of them.

The Labour leadership was complicated by the war. Ramsay MacDonald had been elected chairman of the Parliamentary Labour party in February 1911. He felt impelled to resign his position when the party, against his advice, voted to support British entry into the war in August 1914. His opposition to the war led to his defeat by a Coalition candidate in his Leicester constituency in the Coupon Election. He was also defeated at a by-election in Woolwich in February 1921. At the 1922 election he was finally nominated to the safe working-class constituency of Aberavon and was returned with a comfortable majority. The Parliamentary Labour party now had 142 seats, many of them held by middle and upper class supporters such as Sir Charles Trevelyan, Arthur Ponsonby, Sidney Webb and Clement Attlee. It was felt that the time had come to replace J. R. Clynes as leader by a more charismatic character. MacDonald, whatever his other weaknesses, had the appearance, the oratorical ability and the experience to be the obvious candidate. The election was nonetheless a close one, MacDonald winning by 61 votes to Clynes's 56. As with Baldwin, MacDonald was destined to remain at the forefront of the nation's affairs until he too retired in 1937.

The leadership of the Liberal party was never satisfactorily resolved. Asquith remained the nominal leader until his retirement in 1926 but he showed little stomach for political life after 1916. Lord Gladstone commented in 1918: 'Our stroke neither sets the time nor rows his weight', while McKenna described Asquith's conduct after the Coupon Election as 'stoical to the point of indifference'.

The problem was complicated by the fact that Asquith lost his seat in 1918 and did not get back into Parliament until 1920. He was again defeated in 1924 and moved to the House of Lords from where his leadership was if anything even more tenuous. Lloyd George was never prepared to acknowledge his former leader's authority but his political fund was vital to the Liberal party's straitened finances. There was an uneasy *rapprochement* between the two wings of the party in 1923, as a result of which Lloyd George agreed to provide £90 000 to election expenses. Though Lloyd George secured the chairmanship of the Liberal party in Parliament in 1924, he continued to be opposed by a group of irreconcilables. A further dispute occurred between Asquith and Lloyd George over the attitude the party should take to the General Strike in 1926, and even though Asquith finally retired the same year the problem of the leadership was not over. Lloyd George remained in command at Westminster but Herbert Samuel took over control of the party machine.

One of the enigmas of the politics of the 1920s is the influence exerted by Lloyd George. A possibly apocryphal story is told of a meeting between MacDonald and Baldwin on Crewe Station in 1929, at which MacDonald is reputed to have said: 'Well, whatever happens, we shall keep the Welshman out.' Whether true or not, it indicates the suspicion Lloyd George aroused; it also underlines the community of interest that joined Baldwin and MacDonald. Each sought to squeeze the Liberal party and aided by the ineptitude of the Liberal leadership they were able to do so.

Bonar Law and Baldwin, 1922–24

The Conservative administration which lasted from October 1922 to January 1924 had an effective majority in Parliament but brought about its own defeat. On assuming the premiership following Lloyd George's resignation Bonar Law immediately requested a dissolution of Parliament. The Conservative manifesto contained an anodyne promise of 'Tranquillity and freedom from adventures both at home and abroad', but also a specific pledge from Bonar Law that 'this Parliament will not make any fundamental changes in the fiscal system of this country.' Despite Churchill's gibe that Bonar Law's cabinet was a Second XI, and Lloyd George's description of Bonar Law as 'honest to the point of simplicity', the Conservatives won a comfortable victory, thanks to the division of the opposition.

The new Government had little to offer by way of new policies. The only legislation of any significance was Neville Chamberlain's Housing Act. This replaced the Addison Act and encouraged the building of cheap houses by local authorities through the grant of a £6 subsidy, payable for 20 years, for all houses below certain specified dimensions.

Baldwin, as we have seen, replaced Bonar Law in May 1923, and it was his political inexperience which brought the Government to its premature end. On 23 October he persuaded the cabinet to adopt a policy of wholesale protection, a decision he announced to the Conservative Party Conference at Plymouth on 25 October. On 13 November he obtained George V's consent for a dissolution of Parliament. On 6 December a General Election was held in which the Conservatives suffered a net loss of 87 seats.

There has been much speculation as to why Baldwin should have decided to urge Protection on his party, and then to submit this change in policy to the electorate. Baldwin has not made the task of explaining his conduct any easier by different versions he gave at the time and subsequently for acting as he did. There seems little doubt that in the summer of 1923 he became genuinely convinced that a policy of Protection was essential to safeguard British industry against the threat of cheap European imports, aided as they were by low exchange rates. He also felt that Bonar Law's pledge not to alter the fiscal system barred him from introducing such a policy without putting it to the voters. But when reminiscing with the Cabinet Secretary, Tom Jones, in 1925, he gave a rather different explanation:

> Rightly or wrongly I was convinced that you could not deal with unemployment without a tariff. After the war, opinion was more fluid and open. On political grounds the tariff issue had been dead for years and I felt it was the one issue which would pull the Party together including the Lloyd George malcontents. The Goat (Lloyd George) was in America. He was on the water when I made the speech and the Liberals did not know what to say. I had information that he was going protectionist, and I had to get in quick. No truth that I was pushed by Amery and the cabal. I was loosely in the saddle and got them into line in the cabinet. Dished the Goat, as otherwise he would have got the Party with F.E. (Birkenhead) and there would have been an end to the Tory Party as we know it. I shall not forget the surprise and delight of Amery. It was a long calculated and not a sudden dissolution. Bonar had no programme and the only thing was to bring the tariff issue forward. [Middlemas and Barnes, p. 212]

Baldwin may here have been indulging in the politician's tendency to give his actions a rationality which they did not at the time possess. But whatever his motives, the consequences were disastrous. So far from coming out in favour of Protection, Lloyd George reaffirmed his commitment to Free Trade, the only issue which could unite the Liberal party, as it did. When the election results were announced the Conservatives had dropped to 258 seats, while the Labour party gained 191 and the Liberals 159.

Baldwin's immediate reaction was to resign, but news reached him of a Conservative plot to urge the King to send for another Conservative leader rather than MacDonald or Asquith. For a man who had shown so much reluctance to assume the leadership, Baldwin's determination to hang on to it was remarkable. It stiffened his resolve to stay on as Prime Minister unless and until he was defeated in the House of Commons. Neither he nor Asquith, however, were prepared to enter into any arrangement to keep the Labour party out. Baldwin felt that the Labour party had earned the right to office while Asquith argued that if a Labour government were to be tried 'it could hardly be under safer conditions; it is we, if we really understand our business, who really control the situation.' [Marquand, p. 299] Asquith evidently hoped to come to office 'whenever Labour incompetence made MacDonald's overthrow convenient to the Liberal party.' [Cowling, p. 348] It proved to be a serious miscalculation for which Asquith has been much criticised. The arrival of the first Labour government was thus the consequence of a mistake by Baldwin and a gamble by Asquith. The circumstances in which the Labour government took office did much to determine its future.

D. Marquand, *Ramsay MacDonald* (1977)

Cowling, *The Impact of Labour, 1920–24*

The First Labour Government, 1924

The results of the 1923 election also posed a problem for the Labour party. By taking office they would have an opportunity to demonstrate that Labour was 'fit to govern'; but dependence on Liberal support would prevent them from implementing socialist policies. Left-wingers even urged MacDonald to press ahead with a full socialist programme, get defeated and then go to the country again. The argument that weighed most strongly with MacDonald was that should he decline to take office the Liberals would do so instead, and on their subsequent defeat would replace the Labour party as the official opposition. In a series of meetings in December 1923, the National Executive Committee (NEC), the TUC and the Parliamentary Labour party all agreed that should the opportunity arise to form a government the Labour party should take it.

Thus it was that when Parliament met in January 1924, Baldwin's government was defeated by 72 votes and Ramsay MacDonald was summoned to Buckingham Palace. MacDonald noted after his meeting with George V: 'King plays the game straight; though I feel he is apprehensive. It wd be a miracle if he were not.' [Marquand, p. 305] George V was similarly impressed. His *Diary* entry reads: 'I held a council at which Mr. Ramsay MacDonald was sworn a member. I then asked him to form a Government which he accepted to do. I had an hour's talk with him, he impressed me very much; he wishes to do the right thing.' [H. Nicolson, p. 382]

Marquand, *Ramsay MacDonald*

H. Nicolson, *George V* (Constable, 1952)

In forming his cabinet MacDonald inevitably found himself short of members with ministerial experience. At the same time he had to satisfy those colleagues who felt entitled to office by virtue of long service to the party. He did not find the task of constructing his government either easy or congenial, remarking at one stage: 'I feel like an executioner. I knock so many ambitious heads into my basket.' MacDonald took the Foreign Office himself, Snowden went to the Treasury,

MR. SIDNEY WEBB, M.P.   MR. F.W. JOWETT, M.P.

MR. CHARLES PHILIPS TREVELYAN, M.P.   MR. JOHN WHEATLEY, M.P.   COL. JOSIAH WEDGWOOD, M.P.   MR. THOMAS SHAW, M.P.

MR. STEPHEN WALSH, M.P.   LORD THOMSON   LORD OLIVIER   MR. NOEL BUXTON, M.P.   MR. VERNON HARTSHORN, M.P.

THE RT. HON. WILLIAM ADAMSON, M.P.   VISCOUNT CHELMSFORD   THE RT. HON. JAMES RAMSAY MACDONALD   THE RT. HON. JAMES HENRY THOMAS, M.P.

LORD PARMOOR   MR. PHILIP SNOWDEN, M.P.   MR. JOHN R. CLYNES, M.P.   THE RT. HON. ARTHUR HENDERSON.

VISCOUNT HALDANE, KT., O.M.

Henderson to the Home Office and J. H. Thomas became Colonial Secretary. J. R. Clynes became Leader of the House and Lord Privy Seal. But for many of his other appointments McDonald had to look beyond the regular stalwarts of the party. Haldane became Lord Chancellor, Lord Chelmsford – an ex-Viceroy of India – became First Lord of the Admiralty, and Lord Parmoor – an ex-Conservative MP who had joined the Labour party in 1919 – became Lord President of the Council. In his *Memoirs* J. R. Clynes recalled the cabinet's first meeting with George V: 'I could not help marvelling at the strange turn of Fortune's wheel, which had brought MacDonald, the starveling clerk, Thomas the engine driver, Henderson the foundry labourer and Clynes the millhand to this pinnacle beside the man whose forbears had been Kings for so many generations. We were making history.' [quoted in Nicolson, p. 386]. Truth to tell there were only five trade unionists in a cabinet of twenty, and the advent of a Labour government brought with it no dramatic changes in policy.

H. Nicolson, *George V*

Not surprisingly, the Labour government achieved very little in its nine months in office. The Wheatley Housing Act sponsored by John Wheatley, a genuine socialist from Glasgow, was its most radical measure. It advanced beyond the Chamberlain Act by offering a subsidy of £9 per house, payable for 40 years, for houses to let at controlled rents. Under its terms 521 200 houses were built in the next 10 years. Snowden's only budget managed to reduce direct taxes by £29 million and indirect taxes by £14 million but it was still designed to produce a net surplus. A special Committee on Unemployment reviewed a variety of schemes for creating jobs, including electrification of the railways, a Severn Barrage, the Channel Tunnel and the setting up of a National Grid. But the Government fell before any of these could be realised and it is doubtful whether they would have received Treasury sanction. Though MacDonald succeeded in getting work on a naval base at Singapore suspended, he bowed to the views of the Committee of Imperial Defence that a Channel Tunnel would endanger national security.

It was the Government's foreign policy which aroused suspicion. In August 1924 diplomatic relations were officially resumed with the Soviet Union. Two treaties were in the process of negotiation: one would have enabled holders of pre-war Russian Bonds to receive some compensation from the Soviet government, the other – dependent on the first – would have extended a loan to Russia for the purchase of British exports. The Conservatives were certain to oppose the two treaties, the Liberals were likely to. It was under these circumstances that the Campbell Case burst upon the political scene.

In July 1924, J. R. Campbell, temporary editor of the *Workers' Weekly*, allowed an article to appear calling on British soldiers not to fire on their fellow workers in a class war. Sir Patrick Hastings, the Attorney General, authorised the Director of Public Prosecutions to prosecute Campbell for incitement to mutiny. What followed next is far from clear. MacDonald's initial reaction was to express his annoyance at the decision to prosecute, but also his belief that the prosecution must go ahead. But at a subsequent cabinet meeting, chaired by MacDonald, it was agreed to accept a suggestion by Hastings that if Campbell wrote a letter of apology proceedings against him would be halted. Though such a letter was never in fact written, on 13 August proceedings were dropped. When Parliament reassembled on 30 September questions were naturally asked as to whether improper pressure had been brought to bear on Hastings. In his answer MacDonald, in Hankey's words, told 'a bloody lie': 'I was not consulted regarding either the institution or the subsequent withdrawal of these proceedings.' [Marquand, p. 371] Whatever the extenuating circumstances, it was an appalling blunder and made MacDonald's position increasingly embarrassing. The Conservative opposition moved a motion of censure, subsequently withdrawn in favour of a Liberal amendment which called for a Select Parliamentary Committee to investigate the whole affair. MacDonald felt bound to resist such an investigation and turned the matter into a vote of confidence. When the Liberals and Conservatives pressed the matter to a division the government was defeated by 364 votes to 198.

Marquand, *Ramsay MacDonald*

The subsequent election took place in a mood of angry suspicion. The Labour party's policies towards the Soviet Union aroused even greater opposition with the publication on 25 October, the weekend before polling day, of the *Zinoviev Letter*. This purported to come from Zinoviev, President of the Communist International, and was addressed to the Central Committee of the British Communist party. Among other things, the letter called for 'the revolutionizing of the international and British proletariat'. The Foreign Office had received a copy of the letter nine days earlier and MacDonald had drafted a strong protest to the Soviet Union on the assumption that the letter was genuine. But this did not emerge until the letter was printed in the press, and very unfairly MacDonald was held responsible for trying to suppress the whole thing. It now seems that the letter was a forgery. [see Chester, Fox and Young, pp. 48–64] Those responsible were a group of White Russian *Emigrés* in Berlin, presumably anxious to prevent the resumption of good relations between Britain and the Soviet Union. It is also possible that officials in the Conservative Central Office and members of the Intelligence Service had a hand in it.

L. Chester, S. Fox and H. Young, *The Zinoviev Letter* (Heinemann, 1967)

What effect it had on the election is hard to say. Not only did the Labour vote go up from 4.4 to 5.4 million but there was a loss of 1.3 million Liberal votes to the Conservatives which also has to be explained. It may well be that the Labour government would have fallen over the Russian treaties and been defeated even without the Zinoviev Letter. Either way, the first Labour government came to an inglorious end; it could still claim that its defeat was due not to its own shortcomings but to an unhappy combination of circumstances.

Baldwin's Leadership

Baldwin's second term of office lasted its full five-year term and he had the largest Conservative majority since 1895. The internal divisions which had threatened the Party in 1922–23 had largely been overcome. Austen Chamberlain and Birkenhead were now reconciled to Baldwin's leadership and Churchill – whose erratic political career had so far taken him from the Conservative party to the Liberal party and into and out of Asquith's and Lloyd George's cabinets – had returned to the fold.

The Baldwin Administration, 1924–29

In choosing his cabinet Baldwin recognised these claimants. Chamberlain was made Foreign Secretary while his brother Neville returned to the Ministry of Health. Birkenhead became Secretary of State for India while Churchill to his own and others' surprise was made Chancellor of the Exchequer. Two other significant appointments were the right-winger, Sir W. Joynson Hicks, as Home Secretary and the more conciliatory Arthur Steel-Maitland as Minister of Labour.

Baldwin's disposition was to preside over his cabinet rather than to direct it. He has been accused of idleness; it would be truer to say that he had few firm convictions about specific policies. His general outlook was perhaps most typically expressed in the speech he delivered to Parliament on 6 March 1926 in connection with the Macquisten Bill. This Private Members' Bill was intended to change the law relating to the Political Levy paid by members of trade unions to the Labour party. As the law stood, members of trade unions might, if they wished, 'contract out' of paying the levy. About 25% did so. Macquisten's Bill would have required members of trade unions to 'contract in', thus depriving Labour party funds of the advantages they gained from the force of inertia. The Political Levy was the Labour party's main source of finance and any attack on it was certain to be strongly resented. Baldwin argued against the Bill in cabinet and in the House of Commons. While conceding the justice of the Bill he urged his party to make a gesture of peace; he wanted, he said, 'to create a new atmosphere in a new Parliament for a new age in which the people can come together'. He concluded with these words: 'Although I know that there are those who work for different ends from most of us, in this House, yet there are many in all ranks and parties who will re-echo my prayer: "Give peace in our time, O Lord".' Baldwin was always seeking to conciliate; he got on better with many members of the Labour party than with some of his own. Ironically, it was under his premiership that Britain experienced the most serious industrial dispute of the inter-war period, but it is, perhaps, also the case that under any other Conservative premier it might have taken an uglier course than it did.

The General Strike

Any government would have faced a crisis in the coal industry between the wars. Its only years of prosperity were in 1923–24 when German exports were halted because of French occupation of the Ruhr. In 1924 the miners gained a substantial pay increase in consequence. But the Dawes Plan (p. 153) brought a settlement of the reparations dispute between France and Germany and the consequent withdrawal of French troops. German coal exports resumed. In 1925 Britain also returned to the Gold Standard at a parity which had the effect of raising British export prices by about 10%. As a result, coal exports fell off alarmingly. In the first six months of 1925 the coal industry made a loss of £2.1 million.

The mine owners responded by attempting to cut costs. On 30 June 1925 the miners were given a month's notice of the ending of the 1924 wage agreement and the option of returning to an eight-hour day or wage reductions ranging from 13%–38%. Despite recent increases miners' wages were still very low. The Macmillan Committee appointed to investigate them in 1925 reported that in real terms they were lower than they had been in 1914. Not surprisingly, the Miners Federation of Great Britain (the MFGB) rejected the terms out of hand; nor did it ever change its bargaining stance, summed up by A. J. Cook, its Secretary, in the epigram:

> Not a penny off the pay,
> Not a minute on the day.

The General Council of the TUC backed the miners' case, partly out of sympathy for those doing a hard and dangerous job – between 1922 and 1924, 3603 miners were killed and 597 158 injured – and also because they feared that an attack on

miners' wages would be followed by wage reductions elsewhere. Thus the TUC endorsed the miners' refusal of the owners' terms. On 25 July 1925 the executives of the railwaymen's, transport workers' and seamen's unions agreed to place an embargo on the movement of coal. The government played for time, partly because they were not ready to handle the dispute and partly because Baldwin genuinely hoped to secure a settlement. On 31 July – Red Friday, as it came to be known – a subsidy was offered to the mine owners (eventually totalling £23 million) to enable them to continue paying existing wages. In September the Samuel Commission was appointed to investigate the problems of the coal industry and to make appropriate recommendations. The Government also set in motion its preparations for dealing with a general strike, dividing the country up into 10 areas each under the control of a Civil Commissioner. Local authorities were informed of these steps in November 1925 and conferences were held in December and January to co-ordinate the work of national and local officials. Trade union preparations, by comparison, were minimal.

When the Samuel Commission Report came out in March 1926 it made several recommendations favourable to the miners, including nationalisation of coal royalties, reorganisation of the industry to eliminate inefficient pits, better industrial relations through the introduction of pit head committees, profit sharing, and 'holidays with pay when prosperity returns to the industry'. But in the meantime miners would have to accept some reduction in pay, though not an increase in hours which the Commission rightly pointed out would only add to the existing surplus of coal.

A miner's family

The MFGB met the Miners Association (the owners) on three occasions, 20 March, 31 March and 1 April 1926, without making any headway. The owners' final offer was for a return to an eight-hour day and a national minimum wage 20% above the 1914 level, as against the 33% which had operated since 1924. The recommendations of the Samuel Commission were irrelevant, except in so far as reorganisation might improve the efficiency of the pits to the point where the owners could maintain existing wage rates. This was a straw at which the moderates continued to cling. The Government had agreed to implement the terms of the Samuel Commission if miners and owners would accept them. The General Council did its best to persuade the MFGB to consider reorganisation as a *quid pro quo* for temporary wage reductions but Herbert Smith, the President, was not prepared to accept vague promises: 'I want to see the horse I am going to mount.'

As the possibility of compromise waned the battle-lines began to form. On Friday 30 April the miners, having refused the owners' terms, were locked out. Union executives, meeting in London, voted on behalf of their members in favour of 'co-ordinated action' by 3 653 527 to 49 911. Midnight on Monday 3 May was fixed as the time for this to begin. Even at this late stage the government and the TUC cast about for a solution. A negotiating committee representing the General Council and consisting of Arthur Pugh, J. H. Thomas and A. B. Swales met with a cabinet sub-committee consisting of Baldwin, Birkenhead and Steel-Maitland at 8.00 pm on

Saturday 1 May. After five hours of talks they agreed on a procedural formula: 'The Prime Minister has satisfied himself, as a result of the conversations ... that if negotiations are continued, it being understood that the notices cease to operate, the representatives of the TUC are confident that a settlement can be reached on the lines of the [Samuel] Report within a fortnight.' [Middlemas and Barnes, p. 406] The General Council met at 9.00 am the following morning to consider the formula. But the miners' representatives had not been consulted and many of their Executive had gone home. A. J. Cook angrily refused to accept the formula. For their part the other members of the cabinet, who met at noon, were equally sceptical, especially when they heard from the Post Master General that strike notices had already been sent out by telegram. At 9.00 pm a final meeting took place between the two groups who had met the previous day. At 11.00 pm Birkenhead drew up another formula which read: 'We will urge the miners to authorise us to enter upon a discussion with the understanding that they and we accept the Report as a basis of settlement, and we approach it with the knowledge that it may involve some reduction in wages.' The two groups then separated.

Middlemas and Barnes, *Baldwin*

THE LEVER BREAKS

Punch 1926

Shortly after midnight news came through to the cabinet that *Daily Mail* printers had refused to print an editorial condemning the strike. This clinched it. The hard-liners in the cabinet now had the majority on their side. In his own account to the trade union representatives who were now summoned, Baldwin announced that he had been instructed by the cabinet to break off negotiations because of the overt acts that had already taken place, 'including gross interference with the freedom of the Press'. The trade union representatives were taken aback. They framed a reply repudiating the printers' action, but when they returned to the cabinet room it was to find it deserted. Baldwin had retired to bed and other members of the cabinet had gone home.

To be strictly accurate, therefore, the General Strike began with the miners being locked out and the TUC's efforts to continue negotiations being rejected. This is surely sufficient proof of the defensive nature of the strike and the unwillingness of the TUC to embark on it.

When the strike came, however, the response was whole-hearted. At first only front-line unions were called out: railwaymen, dockers, workers in the iron and steel trades, metals, heavy chemicals, building trades, electricity and gas industries – about 1.5 million altogether. Virtually all the workers in these industries obeyed the strike call but unlike the Government the TUC had made no plans beyond arranging a stoppage of work. Their offers to assist the government in the distribution of food and essential supplies were ignored. The local strike committees and councils-of-action that sprang up had little to do except ensure that the strike was effective

'Our reply to Jix' (Johnson-Hicks, Known as 'Jix' was Home Secretary in 1926

OUR REPLY TO "JIX"

The General Council urges the men and women of Great Britain not to be stampeded into panic by the provocative utterances of the Home Secretary.

The inference contained in his broadcast appeal for special constables on Wednesday evening, to the effect that the Trade Union Movement was violating law and order, is quite unjustifiable.

Only on that same afternoon, in fact, the General Council of the Trades Union Congress had officially urged every member taking part in the dispute to be exemplary in his conduct and not to give any opportunity for police disturbances.

The General Council had also asked pickets to avoid obstruction and to confine themselves strictly to their legitimate duties.

There is no need for the panic which the Home Secretary seems intent on provoking. The strikers are standing firm, and they mean to conduct themselves in a disciplined, quiet and orderly manner.

The unnecessary and unwise action of the Home Secretary is more likely to imperil good order than to preserve it.

without causing damage to life or property. This, to a remarkable degree, they achieved. The Government, on the other hand, invoked the Emergency Powers Act and put into operation the plans they had drawn up the previous winter. Volunteers were recruited through the Organisation for the Maintenance of Supplies and middle-class amateurs enjoyed the chance to drive trains and buses on a limited scale. The services were employed to keep the power stations going and to escort food convoys where necessary, and 226 000 Special Constables were recruited, though their services were hardly necessary. Churchill was given responsibility for producing the *British Gazette*, a government newspaper – an appointment designed as Baldwin put it, 'to keep him busy and stop him doing worse things'.

The Government claimed that the General Strike was a challenge to the Constitution, a view that was endorsed by the Liberal lawyer, Sir John Simon. Simon claimed that as the strike was directed against the State, trade union leaders were not protected by the 1906 Trades Disputes Act and were therefore liable for damages caused 'to the last farthing' of their personal possessions. His view was subsequently challenged by expert legal opinion but at the time it was given wide publicity and met with general approval. In one of its more intemperate communiqués the *British Gazette* even claimed that 'An organised attempt is being made to starve the people and to wreck the State.' This was clearly a gross exaggeration; the TUC had, after all, offered to assist in the distribution of food. Even so it is hardly possible to dismiss the General Strike as just a sympathetic strike on behalf of the miners. It was, after all, intended to bring pressure to bear on the Government. Equally, the picture of general amity which is conveyed by some accounts of the strike is misleading. In some areas the level of co-operation between police and strike committees was remarkable, as at Plymouth and Lincoln, for instance, but trams were overturned in Bradford, and in the East End of London there was a good deal of anger as armoured convoys brought food from the docks. The *Flying Scotsman* express to London was de-railed in Northumberland, if only because the volunteer driver refused to heed the warning given to him that the track had been raised. There were no serious casualties but

The de-railing of the Flying Scotsman

the miners responsible received prison sentences of up to eight years. Altogether there were about 3000 arrests for various offences, and 1041 of these resulted in prison sentences.

Local evidence suggests that as the strike went on tempers on both sides were becoming frayed. On Tuesday 11 May, the second-line unions, engineers and ship-builders were called out. Yet the strike never looked like becoming the revolution which some Conservative leaders feared. It was the last thing the moderate trade union leadership wanted, as J. H. Thomas clearly stated in a debate on the strike: 'I have never disguised that in a challenge to the Constitution, God help us unless the Government won.' [Mowat, p. 319] Negotiations to end the strike were going on behind the scenes more or less continuously. Samuel returned from Italy to offer his services. Though the cabinet would not authorise him to negotiate on their behalf, the General Council were quite ready to talk to him. On Monday 10 May he produced the Samuel Memorandum proposing that 'negotiations in the coal industry should be resumed and the subsidy renewed for the time being; that present and future disputes should be referred to a National Wages Board', and that there should be no revision of wages until the Board was convinced that the Samuel Report's reorganisation proposals would be 'effectively adopted'. The General Council were prepared to accept the Samuel Memorandum as a basis for calling off the strike. The miners were not; nor did the cabinet ever commit itself to the Samuel Memorandum. But the intransigence of the miners gave the General Council the excuse they needed to call off a strike they had never wanted. Baldwin, aware of what was happening, invited the General Council to see him on the evening of 11 May. It was agreed to send a delegation to 10 Downing Street the following day. When it arrived Baldwin made it clear that he had no terms to offer, while pledging that he would 'lose no time in using every endeavour to get the two contending parties together and to do all I can to ensure a just and lasting settlement'. The TUC had surrendered unconditionally and the miners were left to continue the fight on their own.

Mowat, *Britain between the Wars* (1955)

Still the miners stayed out. Baldwin's efforts to get negotiations going again came to nothing, as much because of the intransigence of the mine owners as of the MFGB. In the end the Government's sole contribution to ending the dispute was to pass the Eight Hours Bill, on the grounds, as Neville Chamberlain put it that 'if you substitute a longer working day for wage reductions, the women and children come out of the picture altogether'. [Middlemas and Barnes, p. 428] The lock-out dragged on officially until November, but the drift back to work began in the more prosperous collieries in August and on 17 November a delegate conference authorised a return to district wage settlements. Conditions varied from area to area; in most cases they involved an eight-hour day and wage reductions that averaged 15%.

Middlemas and Barnes, *Baldwin*

In practice many returning strikers found that they were being victimised in various ways and refused the call to return to work. There were actually more men on strike on 13 May, the day after the strike was officially over, than on 12 May. In his speech to the House of Commons that night Baldwin did his best to justify the pledge he had made: 'I will not countenance any attack on the part of employers to use the present occasion for trying in any way to get reductions in wages.' His words may have had some effect. Within the next few days most men returned to their jobs, though as late as October 45000 members of the National Union of Railwaymen (NUR) were still unemployed and there were other isolated cases of victimisation.

The General Strike was the single most traumatic event in Britain's domestic history between 1918 and 1939, and it had lasting results. It caused the loss of 162 million working days, much the highest total ever recorded. Coal exports fell from 54.5 million tons in 1925 to 20.5 million tons in 1926. Total losses, including wages, have been put at £175 million to £270 million.

The trade union movement suffered a severe setback. Union membership, which had been dropping from a peak of 8.3 million in 1920 fell from 5.3 million in 1926 to 4.3 million in 1933. Though the government resisted demands for repeal of the 1906 Trades Disputes Act, which granted immunity for losses resulting from strike action, it passed the Trades Disputes Act of 1927. This Act (i) banned all sympathetic strikes, or those designed to coerce the government; (ii) defined intimidation and made it illegal; (iii) changed the position over the Political Levy from contracting out to contracting in; and (iv) forbade members of the Civil Service from belonging to unions affiliated to the TUC. Needless to say, the Act was bitterly opposed by the Labour party who promised to repeal it at the first available opportunity. This they did in 1946.

It was on the coal industry that the General Strike had its most lasting effects. For the miners it was another episode in the long saga of industrial conflict, and one they had lost. The General Strike underlined all the arguments for nationalisation for, while this would not solve all the problems of a declining industry, it was the only way to ensure decent treatment for those who worked in it. Despite good intentions Baldwin's Government had shown its inability to achieve that objective.

Tory Reforms

The stereotypes of politicians are often misleading. While Churchill and Neville Chamberlain were numbered among the hawks in their approaches to the General Strike, they were individually and jointly responsible for significant social and administrative reforms. Baldwin, too, gave his support to measures of vital importance in relation to the supply of electricity and broadcasting. Finally, it was owing to Baldwin's Government that women achieved political equality.

As Chancellor of the Exchequer, Churchill has had to bear responsibility for Britain's return to the Gold Standard in 1925. It was a move urged on him by Montagu Norman, the influential Governor of the Bank of England, and by the Treasury. Despite his own misgivings he finally accepted their advice and has been much criticised for doing so (see Points at Issue). Two other measures have met with more approval. In his 1925 Budget he introduced pensions for widows, orphans and for those over 65. The scheme was linked to National Health Insurance and applied only to those insured under the scheme. Rates were 10/- for widows, 7/6d. for orphans and 10/- for the over-65s. Non-contributory pensions for those over 70 were not affected. Because the benefits were paid out of increased contributions the new scheme was self-financing, but it brought under the umbrella of the Welfare State a wide range of deserving cases.

In his 1928 Budget, Churchill also made significant changes. As a stimulus to agriculture and industry he abolished all rates on agricultural land and buildings, and reduced those payable on industrial buildings and on railways by 75%. Local authorities who lost £24 million in rates as a result were compensated by 'block grants', adjusted to take account of the social and economic needs of the areas they represented.

Neville Chamberlain, unfairly labelled by Lloyd George as 'a good Lord Mayor of Birmingham in a lean year', turned his municipal experience to good effect as Minister of Health. He sponsored 25 bills, of which 21 were enacted between 1924 and 1929. Of these, much the most important was the Local Government Act, 1929. This completely re-shaped the responsibilities of local authorities and deserves to be placed with the Elizabethan Poor Law of 1598 or the Poor Law Amendment Act of 1834 in terms of its scope. The 635 Poor Law Unions created under the 1834 Act were ended, and their responsibilities transferred to Public Assistance Committees working under County Councils and County Boroughs. These authorities were also given extra responsibility for roads, public health, maternal and child welfare, and town and country planning. The rationalisation of the structure of local government, carried out in the nineteenth century, had at last been amplified by a rationalisation of its functions. Chamberlain's Local Government Act remained largely unaltered until the Reorganisation of Local Government Act of 1973.

Perhaps the most important measures passed by the Baldwin Government were the ones which at the time attracted least attention. In 1925 Baldwin appointed Lord Weir, one-time President of the Employers' Federation, to make recommendations for the proper organisation of the electricity industry. Weir's suggestions were adopted and incorporated in the Electricity Supply Act of 1926. A Central Electricity Board was set up, which would buy current from selected generating stations and arrange for its sale and distribution. This system worked very well. By 1933 Britain had 4000 miles of transmission lines and the national grid had come into existence. It would be hard to exaggerate the economic and strategic importance of that achievement.

Equally significant was the creation of the BBC. The *Daily Mail* sponsored the first commercial broadcast in this country in 1920, a recital by Nelly Melba, the Australian soprano. In 1922 the Post Office granted to the British Broadcasting Company an exclusive licence to send out wireless programmes. The Company was headed by John Reith, a fiercely independent Scotsman with a strong moral conscience. He set his stamp on the Company's approach and when its licence expired in 1926, he was a natural choice to head the British Broadcasting Corporation set up in its stead. The BBC was to be financed from the sale of licence fees and to be under the overall direction of a Board of Governors appointed by the Prime Minister. In this way Britain acquired a national broadcasting system that was both independent of commercial pressures and of government.

The final achievement of the Baldwin Government was to give women political equality with men. This had been promised by the Conservative election manifesto in 1924. Churchill and Birkenhead were still opposed to lowering the voting age for women from thirty to twenty-one, but a cabinet committee recommended the change and it was finally accomplished in 1928.

By 1929 Britain appeared to have settled down. The country had returned to the Gold Standard; unemployment had levelled off at about 10% of the working population; the scars left by the General Strike were healing; living standards were rising. Few anticipated the crises that were just around the corner.

POINTS AT ISSUE
POINTS AT ISSUE **POINTS AT ISSUE** POINTS AT ISSUE
POINTS AT ISSUE

POINTS AT ISSUE
POINTS AT ISSUE
POINTS AT ISSUE
POINTS AT ISSUE

The Return to the Gold Standard in 1925

The advisability of Britain's returning to the Gold Standard was hotly disputed in 1925, and has been ever since. Defenders of the decision to return to gold argued that Britain's economic interests would best be served by a return to international financial stability, and that this in turn depended on the resumption of fixed exchange rates based on the Gold Standard. Such a view is well represented by Sir Otto Niemeyer's Memorandum to Churchill in February 1925. Niemeyer was a senior Treasury official.

> The most serious argument against the return to the Gold Standard is the feared effect on trade and employment. No one would advocate such a return if he believed that in the long run the effect on trade would be adverse.
>
> In fact everyone upholds the Gold Standard because they believe it to be proved by experience to be best for trade ... No one believes that unemployment can be cured by the dole, and palliatives like road digging. Every party – not least Labour – has preached that unemployment can only be dealt with by radical measures directed to the restoration of trade, whether with Europe or with the Dominions. What could be worse for trade than for us to have a different standard of value to South Africa or Australia ... or to Germany and the United States – fluctuating while they are stable *per se*? On a long view – and it is only such views that can produce fundamental cures – the Gold Standard is in direct succession to the main steps towards economic reconstruction and is likely to do more for British trade than all the efforts of the Unemployment (Grants) Committee. [quoted in Moggridge, *British Monetary Policy 1924–31*, pp. 68–9]

Critics of the policy of returning to the Gold Standard have used three main arguments: first, that it was done at the wrong parity; secondly, that in order to defend that parity, Britain had to impose unnecessarily high interest rates in order to attract foreign deposits; and thirdly, that Britain's weakened economic position did not really entitle her to play the central financial role which a return to the Gold Standard implied.

In his pamphlet, *The Economic Consequences of Mr. Churchill*, Keynes used all three arguments. They have been largely accepted by Sidney Pollard in his book *The Development of the British Economy, 1914–1980* (1983).

> Keynes's criticism ran along two lines. The first was concerned to show that at the old parity the pound would be overvalued to the extent of about 10%. This was borne out not only by the exchange rates of 1923–24, but also by the internal price levels: with pre-war at 100, British internal prices even in the favourable month of April 1925 stood at 176 compared with 165 in the USA ... world prices fell after 1925 and several other countries, including France, Belgium and Germany, returned to gold at lower parities, thus making the competitive disability of British prices greater still. It was unlikely that a government less responsive to the demands of the City would have taken such appalling risks with British industry.
>
> A price differential of 10%, or somewhat less (the exact figure has been disputed), while encouraging imports, formed a most severe handicap to the export industries in their most difficult period, when Britain was falling most calamitously behind other industrial countries.

The ill effects of the high interest rates which the Bank of England was forced to maintain to prevent the loss of gold as a result of the weaker trade balance were more pervasive still. They kept up the burdens of the national debt charge, and thus of taxation. They burdened enterprise with many fixed payments at an unnecessarily high rate. They attracted foreign and British speculative funds of dangerous instability into London. Above all, dear money was designed to depress enterprise directly, and to preserve the foreign exchanges by creating deflation and unemployment at home. This high structure of interest rates in a period of depression was to be described later as 'putting on the brake when going uphill' ...

The Gold Standard, re-established with great *éclat* by Britain, would have been difficult to work at the best of times, in view of the permanent structural changes; as it happened, it set on its course in the most unfavourable circumstances. ... In the pre-war days the Bank of England had held sufficient short-term claims by London on foreign centres to balance roughly the foreign short-term claims on London, and to make the effects of a change in bank rate felt quickly in all parts of the globe; but in the 1920s, foreign short-term holdings in London greatly exceeded the sterling bills on foreign account and other similar assets by a margin estimated by the Macmillan Committee at £250–300 million. [Pollard, pp. 219–23]

In his *English History 1914–45*, A. J. P. Taylor, not surprisingly, takes a different view:

In his [Keynes's] view there was a 10% discrepancy between British and American prices. Most judges put it much lower: 2 $\frac{1}{2}$% or none at all. It was hardly worth while to quibble at so little. Things were different with countries like France and Italy which returned to gold at a low rate, after really savage depreciation. Neither of these countries was a serious competitor against British exports. Germany and the United States – the other great exporters – were not gravely out of line. Industrialists often complained that the old parity made British prices too high and therefore hampered exports. The real obstacle was that Great Britain was offering old-style products which the rest of the world did not want more of even at lower prices. There was a compensating gain: Great Britain got her foodstuffs and raw materials even more cheaply than before. [Taylor, p. 286]

The arguments about Britain's return to the Gold Standard are echoed today in the differences between economists and politicians over whether Britain should join the European Monetary System or whether the British economy would benefit from a higher, or lower, exchange rate. Where the experts disagree about the present, it is unlikely that historians will agree about the past.

Books cited

D. E. Moggridge, *British Monetary Policy, 1924–31* (CUP, 1972)
S. F. Pollard, *The Development of the British Economy, 1914–1980* (Arnold, 1983)
A. J. P. Taylor, *English History, 1914–45* (Pelican, 1970)

BIBLIOGRAPHY BIBLIOGRAPHY BIBLIOGRAPHY BIBLIOGRAPHY BIBLIOGRAPHY BIBLIOGRAPHY
BIBLIOGRAPHY BIBLIOGRAPHY BIBLIOGRAPHY BIBLIOGRAPHY BIBLIOGRAPHY BIBLIOGRAPHY
BIBLIOGRAPHY BIBLIOGRAPHY BIBLIOGRAPHY BIBLIOGRAPHY BIBLIOGRAPHY BIBLIOGRAPHY
BIBLIOGRAPHY BIBLIOGRAPHY BIBLIOGRAPHY BIBLIOGRAPHY BIBLIOGRAPHY BIBLIOGRAPHY
BIBLIOGRAPHY BIBLIOGRAPHY BIBLIOGRAPHY BIBLIOGRAPHY BIBLIOGRAPHY BIBLIOGRAPHY
BIBLIOGRAPHY BIBLIOGRAPHY BIBLIOGRAPHY BIBLIOGRAPHY BIBLIOGRAPHY BIBLIOGRAPHY

CHAPTER 4
FURTHER READING

General

Essential
C. L. Mowat, *Britain between the Wars* (Methuen, 1955)
A. J. P. Taylor, *English History, 1914–1945* (Pelican, 1970)

The Economy

Essential
S. Constantine, *Unemployment between the Wars* (Longman, Seminar Series, 1980)
D. E. Moggridge, *British Monetary Policy, 1924–1931* (CUP, 1972)
S. F. Pollard, *The Development of the British Economy, 1914–1980* (Arnold, 1983)

Recommended
W. Ashworth, *An Economic History of England, 1870–1939* (Methuen, 1960)
S. Glynn and J. Oxborrow, *Interwar Britain: A Social and Economic History* (Allen & Unwin, 1976)

Political Developments

Essential
D. Marquand, *Ramsay MacDonald* (Cape, 1977)
K. Middlemas and J. Barnes, *Baldwin* (Weidenfeld & Nicolson, 1969)

K. O. Morgan, *Consensus and Disunity: the Lloyd George Coalition, 1918–22* (OUP, 1980)
M. Pugh, *The Making of Modern British Politics* (Blackwell, 1982)
A. J. P. Taylor (ed.), *Lloyd George, Twelve Essays* (Hamish Hamilton, 1971)

Recommended
M. Cowling, *The Impact of Labour 1920–24* (CUP, 1971)
R. D. Dilks, *Neville Chamberlain*, vol. I, 1869–1929 (CUP, 1984)
M. Gilbert, *Winston Churchill*, vols IV and V (Heinemann, 1975)
H. Nicolson, *George V* (Constable, 1952)

The General Strike

Essential
M. Morris, *The British General Strike* (Historical Association, 1975)
    The General Strike (Pelican, 1976)

Recommended
A. Bullock, *The Life and Times of Ernest Bevin*, vol. I (Heinemann, 1960)
P. Renshaw, *The General Strike* (Eyre Methuen, 1975)
J. Symons, *The General Strike* (Cresset Press, 1957)

LOCAL RESEARCH PROJECT

The regional history of the General Strike is still being investigated. Possible questions to be asked at the local level might be: How extensive was support for the strike? How was it organised? What action did the local authorities take to deal with it? How good were relations between the police and the strikers? What was the attitude of the strikers to the dispute? What were the effects of the strike on local employment?

The General Strike, 1926

Introductory
The best short account of the General Strike is M. Morris's *The General Strike* (Historical Association, 1975), which also has a useful bibliography. The fullest account of the strike is by W. H. Crook, *The General Strike* (Chapel Hill, 1931).

Suggested sources of information

Information on the strike in the regions is to be found in E. Burns, *The General Strike, May 1926: Trades Councils in Action* (London, 1926), and in M. Morris, *The General Strike* (Pelican, 1973). This book has regional studies of the strike in Battersea, Glasgow, Pontypridd and Sheffield, which provide good examples of the kind of study that might be attempted.

Further sources

Municipal Records should provide some information on how local authorities reacted to the strike. The work of the Organisation for the Management of Supplies and of the Regional Commissioners is likely to be covered by documents in the Public Record Office. Correspondence between the Central Strike Co-ordinating Committee of the TUC and the local trade union leadership is to be found in the General Correspondence File in the TUC Library.

Local newspapers, where they continued to be printed (in itself worth investigating), should provide useful information. A facsimile edition of the Government's *The British Gazette* and the TUC's *The British Worker* was published by David and Charles in 1971.

Britain and Europe, 1918–29

A PEACEMAKING

The Secret Treaties

The allied statesmen who met at Versailles in 1919 arrived there encumbered with obligations assumed and promises made under the stress of war. The first such promise had been made to Russia in March 1915. Though it had been a cardinal principle of British foreign policy throughout the nineteenth century to keep Russia well away from the Dardanelles and the route to India, under the pressure of the Gallipoli campaign Russia was promised Constantinople should she fight the war to a successful end.

The following month Italy was wooed from the Triple Alliance. By the Secret Treaty of London, signed on 26 April 1915, Italy was offered the Trentino, South Tyrol, Dalmatia, Istria and Trieste in return for her participation on the side of the Entente.

A critical shortage of destroyers in 1917 at the height of the German U-boat campaign won a reward for Japan. In return for the supply of a flotilla of Japanese torpedo boats for use in the Mediterranean, Japan's claims to all German Pacific islands north of the Equator and to Germany's commercial concessions in the Shantung province of China were conceded.

In the Middle East the situation was even more complicated, in that several contradictory promises had been made as to the future of the Ottoman Empire's non-Turkish provinces. The first of these promises was made to Hussein, Sherif of Mecca, in October and November of 1915. Anxious to recruit Hussein's support for an Arab Revolt against the Turks, Sir Henry MacMahon, British High Commissioner in Egypt, promised British recognition of and support for the independence of the Arabs in all areas specified by Hussein, with the exception of an area east of Damascus and 'saving the interests of our ally, France'. [Lawrence, p. 282] Hussein did not concede these qualifications, but actively promoted the Arab Revolt which broke out in June 1916, nonetheless.

The Legacy of Wartime Diplomacy

T.E. Lawrence,
The Seven Pillars of Wisdom (Penguin, 1962)

In the meantime, the British government entered negotiations with the French government over the Middle East. They lasted from December 1915 to May 1916. The negotiations were handled on the British side by Sir Mark Sykes, a Conservative MP who had acquired an extensive knowledge of the Ottoman Empire through his travels there before the war. His French counterpart was George Picot, formerly Consul General in Syria. The Sykes-Picot Agreement, as it finally came to be known, was signed in May 1916. It provided for the division of the area, stretching from Lebanon and Syria in the North to the Persian Gulf in the South, between France and Britain; the French would control the northern half, the British the southern. Russia also gave her approval to this arrangement, subject to her gaining Turkish Armenia, and the Italians were also brought into the deal in 1917, being promised territory in Asia Minor. Though there was no explicit contradiction between the MacMahon correspondence and the Sykes-Picot agreement, much was left in dispute, especially the area to be excluded from Arab rule.

A further complication was added by the Balfour Declaration of 2 November 1917. Balfour, Foreign Secretary at the time, had been converted to Zionism by Chaim Weizmann, and it was one of the few causes for which he showed real enthusiasm. Weizmann, a prominent Zionist, was also a professor of Chemistry at Manchester University. He had met Balfour in 1908 and again in 1914, and his influence in the British cabinet was greatly strengthened by his contribution to the war effort. He discovered ways of increasing the production of acetone, a vital constituent in the manufacture of explosives, and was employed by the Ministry of Munitions, where he met Lloyd George, and in the Admiralty between 1915 and 1917. Though opposed by the only Jew in the cabinet, Edwin Montagu, Balfour gained majority support for the declaration which bore his name: it read 'His Majesty's Government view with favour the establishment in Palestine of a national home for the Jewish people, and will use their utmost endeavours to facilitate the achievement of this object. ...' Weizmann would have preferred *the* national home to *a* national home; even so Britain was now committed to a course of action that was bound to bring her into conflict with Arab sentiment.

After the Bolshevik Revolution in November 1917, Trotsky instigated the publication in *Isvestia* of the details of all the secret treaties to which Imperial Russia had been a signatory. This proved a serious source of embarrassment to the other powers of the Entente, and though it did not lead them to surrender any of their claims, it helped to provoke the announcement of a very different set of objectives from the territorial claims represented by the secret treaties.

The Fourteen Points and the Armistice

With the entry of the United States into the war in April 1917, the cause of the Entente took on a new complexion. Woodrow Wilson, President of the United States from 1913 to 1921, had campaigned in the 1916 presidential election on the slogan 'He kept America out of the War'. Pushed into it by German adoption of unrestricted U-boat warfare and German intrigues in Mexico, Wilson still felt the need to justify American participation by presenting the war as a crusade; in his War Message to Congress he stated America's intention: 'The world must be made safe for democracy.' Yet safety lay not only in victory over German militarism; it also required a just and lasting peace. In another speech to Congress, Wilson laid down what seemed to him the necessary conditions of that peace. They have become known as the Fourteen Points. Impossible to paraphrase, they are reproduced here in abbreviated form.

1 'Open covenants of peace openly arrived at, after which there shall be no private understandings of any kind ...'
2 'Absolute freedom of navigation upon the seas outside territorial waters alike in peace and war ...'
3 'The removal, as far as possible, of all economic barriers ...'
4 'Adequate guarantees given and taken that national armaments will be reduced to the lowest point consistent with domestic safety.'
5 'A free, open-minded and absolutely impartial adjustment of colonial claims based upon a strict observance of the principle that in determining all such questions of sovereignty the interests of the populations concerned must have equal weight with the equitable claims of the Government whose title is to be determined.'
6 'The evacuation of all Russian territory ... Russia to be given unhampered and unembarrassed opportunity for the independent determination of her own political development and national policy ...'
7 Belgium to be evacuated and restored.
8 France to be evacuated, the invaded portions 'restored' and Alsace-Lorraine returned to her.
9 'A readjustment of the frontiers of Italy should be effected along clearly recognisable lines of nationality.'
10 'The peoples of Austria Hungary ... to be accorded the freest opportunity for autonomous development.' [Later modified to provide for complete independence.]
11 Rumania, Serbia and Montenegro to be evacuated, occupied territories to be 'restored'. Serbia to be given free access to the sea.
12 Turkish portions of the Ottoman Empire to be assured 'a secure sovereignty'. Subject nationalities to be assured security and 'absolutely unmolested opportunity of autonomous development'. Freedom of the Straits to be guaranteed.
13 Independent Polish State to be erected 'which should include territories inhabited by indisputably Polish populations, which should be assured a free and secure access to the sea.'
14 A general association of nations to be formed under specific covenants 'for the purpose of affording mutual guarantees of political independence and territorial integrity to great and small states alike'.

[Nicolson, pp. 39–40]

H. Nicolson,
Peacemaking, 1919
(1964)

The Fourteen Points were amplified by Four Principles and Five Particulars, spelled out in subsequent speeches. They deal only in generalities of unexceptionable intention, for instance 'Each part of the final settlement must be based upon the essential justice of that particular case' or 'Peoples and provinces must not be bartered about from sovereignty to sovereignty as if they were chattels or pawns in a game.' The Principles were also prefaced by a statement that the eventual Peace should contain 'no annexations, no contributions, no punitive damages'. Harold Nicolson has pointed out that 'Of President Wilson's twenty-three conditions, only four can, with any accuracy be said to have been incorporated in the Treaties of Peace.' [Nicolson, p. 44] There was indeed an enormous gulf between the idealistic generalities of the President and the hard-headed realism of his contemporaries. The Fourteen Points were nonetheless very important. Wilson may have abandoned some of them, but his commitment to the League of Nations, envisaged in the last of the Points, was absolute and this had a very significant effect on the negotiations. Secondly, the Fourteen Points provided the formula through which Germany was brought to the point of surrender.

Nicolson, *Peacemaking* 1919

The sequence of events is important. On 3 October the liberal-minded Prince Max of Baden became Chancellor in Germany. On 7 October he transmitted through the Swiss embassy in Washington a request for President Wilson to intervene, and announced the willingness of the German Government to accept 'as the basis for its negotiations, the programme laid down by the President of the United States...' [Watt, p. 36]. An exchange of notes followed, but Wilson declared on 23 October that neither he nor the Allies would deal with 'the military masters and autocrats of Germany'. [Watt, p. 172] On 26 October General Ludendorff was dismissed. Wilson also received an assurance that Germany would evacuate Belgium and France as soon as an armistice was signed. Wilson then agreed to transmit Germany's official request for an armistice based on the Fourteen Points to the Allied War Council in Paris.

R. M. Watt, *The Kings Depart* (1973)

On 29 October Lloyd George and Clemenceau (the French Prime Minister) met Colonel House, Wilson's special envoy. Both men expressed serious reservations about the Fourteen Points; Clemenceau objected to the abandonment of secret diplomacy, Lloyd George to the clause on Freedom of the Seas which would deprive Britain of the weapon of blockade. Both men insisted on the right to impose punitive damages. But Colonel House threatened, first that the United States might consider a separate peace, and secondly publication of the Allied reservations to a war-weary public. At this point Lloyd George and Clemenceau gave way and agreed to make peace with Germany 'on the terms of peace laid down in the President's address to Congress, and the principles of settlement enunciated in his subsequent address'. [Watt, p. 41] Colonel House allowed two reservations: 'Freedom of the Seas' was admitted to be open to various interpretations; Germany would make compensation 'for all damage done to the civilian population of the Allies'.

Watt, *The Kings Depart*

The Allies' note of acceptance was forwarded to Wilson on 5 November. He passed it on straight away, and on 8 November a German delegation arrived at Compiègne. On 11 November Armistice terms were signed. Germany agreed to evacuate all occupied territory, including Alsace-Lorraine, within 14 days and the Left Bank of the Rhine within 31 days. All prisoners of war and a large quantity of military equipment were to be handed over. All submarines, and the bulk of the German navy were to be interned in a neutral or Allied port; and in the meantime the blockade of German ports would continue.

The legacy of wartime diplomacy had very damaging effects upon the peace-making process. In the first place the secret treaties made it certain that there would be serious clashes with the disinterested principles enunciated by Wilson; in the second, the gap between German and Allied perception of the Fourteen Points ensured that Germany would feel betrayed by any departure from them.

Organisation

Delegates to the Paris Peace Conference assembled on 12 January 1919 and proceedings were formally opened on 19 January. They continued in some form or another for the next 18 months. Treaties were signed with Germany (Versailles) in June 1919; with Austria (St Germain, September 1919); with Hungary (Trianon, June 1920); with Bulgaria (Neuilly, November 1919) and with Turkey (Sèvres, August 1920). While a good deal of preparatory work had been done by some delegations, no agreement had been reached on the programme to be followed or how the Conference was to be organised. In practice procedures were improvised as the occasion required, and as it became clear where the real power of decision rested. Initially, the Conference was to be directed by a Council of Ten, consisting of two representatives from each of the major Allied powers: France, Britain, the United States, Italy and Japan. The Japanese soon retired to the back of the stage, except where their particular interests were involved. It also became clear that the Allied leaders preferred not to be joined by their foreign ministers. Thus what had begun as a Council of Ten became a Council of Four, consisting of Clemenceau (France), Lloyd George (Britain), Wilson (United States) and Orlando (Italy). On 24 April 1919, Orlando left Paris in a huff because Wilson opposed the inclusion of Fiume in the territory claimed by Italy under the Treaty of London. Thus in its final weeks before the Treaty of Versailles was agreed, all the vital decisions were taken by a Council of Three, very often in the privacy of Wilson's study.

Other delegations were allowed to make submissions from time to time, though without much effect. A network of committees, 58 in all, was also set up. Some of these dealt with topics such as Reparations, War Guilt and the League of Nations. Others, known as the Territorial Committees, were concerned with the changes in frontiers that became such an important feature of the settlements. Many criticisms have been made of the way the Conference was conducted: the choice of Paris as its venue where the echoes of war were still all too audible; the decision of the Allied leaders personally to participate in the work of detailed negotiation; the domination of the small powers by the larger ones; the dilatory way in which the Conference began and the precipitate haste in which it ended. But these were all comparatively unimportant. More serious was the lack of a prepared set of priorities which meant that a great deal of time was wasted on minor issues, and the uncertainty as to whether the Conference was to produce terms that were to be a basis for subsequent negotiation, or terms that were to be unilaterally imposed. What really determined the outcome of the Conference were the policies of the main protagonists, which in turn reflected the popular pressures to which they were subjected.

The Big Three

Two memorable portraits of the three leading statesmen at the Conference have survived, both penned by members of the British delegation. Keynes likened the leaders to 'An old man of the world (Clemenceau), a *femme fatale* (Lloyd George), and a non-conformist clergyman (Woodrow Wilson)'. [Keynes, p. 34] Balfour, British Foreign Secretary at the time, was even less flattering. In a letter to Victoria Sackville-West he referred bitingly to 'These three all-powerful, all-ignorant men, sitting there and carving up continents ....' [cited in Roskill, p. 89] In fact they deserve sympathy rather than condemnation.

J. M. Keynes, *Essays in Biography* (1933)

S. Roskill, *Hankey, Man of Secrets*, vol. II (Collins, 1972)

Clemenceau was justly concerned with the problem of France's security. His country had twice been invaded without justification in 1870 and 1914. In 1871

France suffered the loss of Alsace-Lorraine and was made to pay reparations which exceeded Germany's war costs. French casualties between 1914 and 1918 were proportionately the highest sustained by any of the Entente powers. In demanding a secure Eastern frontier and compensation for the losses France had endured, Clemenceau was asking no more than every Frenchman expected.

The big four. (From left to right, Lloyd George, Orlando, Clemenceau and Wilson)

Lloyd George, while announcing in the election campaign of 1918 that he expected Germany to pay 'to the limit of her capacity' for the damage she inflicted, was in practice much more concerned to see that Germany was not left embittered; he did what he could to ease some of the harsher terms that were proposed.

Woodrow Wilson suffered the fate of all those who try to bring morality into the conduct of international politics. He was accused of woolly idealism on the one hand and of betraying his principles to gain a political point on the other. But Wilson was genuinely disinterested in his search for European security. He suffered a physical collapse through overwork at the Conference itself, and a stroke in 1920 when campaigning on behalf of the League of Nations. Though he can be blamed for taking too much upon his own shoulders and for his failure to take his political opponents in the United States sufficiently into his confidence, no one can dispute the sincerity of his intentions or the zeal with which he pursued them. The peace treaties that finally emerged from the Peace Conference reflected the differing views of these men and the strength with which they argued their cases. It also needs to be remembered how narrow were the parameters within which they had to work. Germany's aggressive conduct, both in 1914 and during the course of the war, made it inevitable that she would be treated as the guilty party. Similarly, the collapse of the Austrian and Ottoman Empires had created power vacuums in central Europe and the Middle East. The force of national sentiment would have compelled the creation of successor states of doubtful political stability and viability, whatever Wilson's views on national self-determination. No one could have re-drawn the map of Europe in such a way that the problem of racial minorities could have been avoided. Let us now examine the terms eventually agreed, with these considerations in mind.

Versailles

Territorial Changes

On her western boundaries Germany was to return Alsace-Lorraine to France and Eupen and Malmédy to Belgium. In the North, Schleswig was restored to Denmark after a plebiscite. Though the Rhineland was not divorced from Germany, as Clemenceau had wished, it was to be occupied by Allied troops for 15 years and was to remain permanently demilitarised for 50 km east of the Rhine. The Saar region was placed under League of Nations control, while the coal mines there were handed to France 'in full and absolute possession'. A plebiscite would be held after 15 years, following which Germany might repurchase the mines.

On her eastern boundary Germany had to cede to Poland a strip of territory that included most of Posen and Upper Silesia; Danzig was made into a free city under League of Nations control; a Polish corridor thus separated East Prussia from the rest of Germany.

Germany's colonies were divided up among Britain and the Dominions. Lip-service was paid to the fifth Article of the Fourteen Points calling for the recognition of the interests of the populations concerned by adopting a system of mandates. The mandatory powers would be required to prepare the local inhabitants for self-government, and would be supervised by the League of Nations. On these conditions Britain gained German East Africa and the German Cameroons; Australia took over New Guinea; and New Zealand acquired Samoa. Japan was permitted the gains in the Pacific that had been promised to her in 1917.

Armaments

The Allies were all agreed that German naval and military power must be severely limited. The German army was reduced to a total of 100 000 men; no artillery, tanks or aeroplanes were permitted. The General Staff was dissolved and the navy reduced to a token force of 15 000 men, with no ships over 10 000 tons and no submarines. An Allied Control Commission was set up to police these arrangements.

The Peace Treaties

Reparations and War Guilt

There was a close association between Reparations and the War Guilt Clause. If Germany was to be expected to pay for the costs of the war, she had to be branded as the aggressor. Article 231 of the Treaty made this clear: 'The Allied and Associated Governments affirm and Germany accepts the responsibility of Germany and her allies for all the loss to which the Allied and Associated Governments and their nationals have been subjected as a consequence of the War imposed upon them by the aggression of Germany and her Allies.'

It will be remembered that Britain and France had insisted and Wilson had agreed, prior to the Armistice, that Germany should make compensation for 'all damage done to the civilian population of the Allies'. This was a very elastic definition. The French sought to stretch it to include the loss of wages and production caused by the diversion of manpower into the army. Britain expected 'damage' to include the loss of merchant shipping and the cost of pensions to those disabled, widowed or orphaned by the war. Astronomical figures were bandied about. The French suggested a total of £40 000 million; Lord Cunliffe, for Britain, suggested first £24 000 million, but then reduced it to £12 000 million. Keynes, on the other hand, argued that £2000 million was as much as Germany could reasonably be expected to pay. In the end, at Lloyd George's suggestion, the amount was left to be determined by the Reparations Commission, which finally recommended a sum of £6600 million in 1921.

The League of Nations

The final article of the Treaty of Versailles provided for the creation of a League of Nations, as envisaged in the last of Wilson's Fourteen Points. The constitution of the League was defined in the Covenant, which also prescribed the procedures to be followed in the settlement of disputes. Wilson insisted on the inclusion of the League of Nations within the Treaty of Versailles because he hoped that it would prove the mechanism through which defects in the Treaty might be remedied, and also because he thought that the American Senate, which had already expressed its reservations about the League, would not go to the lengths of rejecting the whole Treaty. This, in fact, is what did happen in 1920. The League of Nations was to be handicapped from the start by the absence of the country whose President had done most to bring it into being.

The terms of the Treaty were first presented to the German delegation on 7 May 1919, Clemenceau introducing them ominously with the words: 'The hour has struck for the weighty settlement of our account.' The Germans were shocked by the harshness of the terms, and refused to admit sole responsibility for starting the war. They were allowed 15 days, later extended to 3 weeks, to make written observations. A series of notes and queries passed between Germany and the Allies in the next few days, but German counter-proposals were formally presented on 29 May. Nearly every provision in the Treaty came under attack, but the most serious objections were made over the territorial clauses relating to Poland and the Saar, Reparations and War Guilt.

On 16 June the Allies made their considered response. The only concession they were prepared to make was to allow a Plebiscite in Upper Silesia. On the question of War Guilt, Germany was put further in the dock, the Allies asserting that the War 'was the greatest crime against humanity and the freedom of peoples that any nation calling itself civilised has ever consciously committed'. [Watt, p. 493]. The allies gave Germany until 21 June to sign the Treaty, under threat of invasion. On 21 June the Weimar assembly voted to accept all the terms except those relating to War Guilt and Reparations [Articles 227–31]. This still did not suffice, and 39 divisions stood ready to march into Germany. On 23 June the German government finally declared its readiness to sign 'yielding to overwhelming force, but without on that account abandoning its view in regard to the unheard of injustice of the conditions of peace'. It was not a good augury.

Watt, *The Kings Depart*

GERMANY AFTER THE TREATY OF VERSAILLES

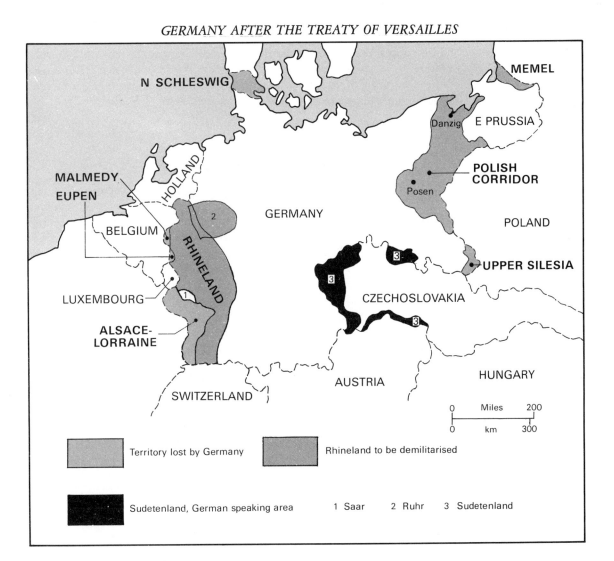

Britain gained what it wanted from the Treaty of Versailles: the destruction of German naval power (the German fleet scuttled itself in Scapa Flow on 21 June 1919); the acquisition of German colonies; and reparations. But in his more prescient moments Lloyd George realised the dangers of humiliating Germany. At a meeting with the British delegation at Fontainebleau in March 1919 a memorandum was drawn up which made the point: 'You may strip Germany of her colonies, reduce her armaments to a mere police force and her navy to that of a fifth rate power; all the same in the end if she feels that she has been unjustly treated in the peace of 1919 she will find means of exacting retribution.' After reading the German response of 29 May to the Treaty terms Lloyd George was so perturbed that he summoned a full meeting of the cabinet in Paris, and on 2 June presented a series of proposed revisions to the Council of Four. They included reducing the period of occupation of the Rhineland to two years; a plebiscite for Upper Silesia; and the early admission of Germany to the League of Nations. It was too late. Even Wilson was not prepared to make any significant changes in the Treaty at this stage: 'The time to consider all these questions was when we were writing the treaty, and it makes me a little tired for people to come and say now that they are afraid the Germans won't sign, and their fear is based upon things that they insisted on at the time of the writing of the treaty ....' [Watt, p. 501] It was a fair point. But Lloyd George's doubts were to be echoed by many other British politicians in the years to come and they further helped to undermine belief in the sanctity of the Treaty of Versailles.

Watt, *The Kings Depart*

The Treaties of St Germain, Trianon and Neuilly

Britain had much less direct concern in the settlement of central Europe, her chief interest being a desire not to get committed to the defence of any patent injustices. In brief, under the Treaty of St Germain the non-German spreaking parts of Austria were transferred to the new succession states of Czechoslovakia, Poland and Yugoslavia. Three million German-speaking inhabitants of the Sudetenland were also placed under Czechoslovakia. Any future junction of Austria and Germany (*Anschluss*) was also forbidden. Austria's population was reduced from 28 million to less than 8 million.

Under the Treaty of Trianon, Hungary similarly lost 13 million of her citizens, many of them to Rumania. Thus the Austro-Hungarian Empire was replaced by two old but severely truncated states (Austria and Hungary), two revived ones (Poland and Czechoslovakia), and a greatly enlarged Serbia (Yugoslavia). Attempts were made to apply the principle of national self-determination, but not with any great success, and the presence of substantial numbers of Germans in Poland and Czechoslovakia would be bound to create problems in the future. Bulgaria paid the penalty of joining the wrong side by having to cede Western Thrace to Greece. The Treaty of Neuilly also required her to pay reparations and limited her armaments.

The Treaty of Sèvres

Britain took a much greater part in deciding the fate of the Ottoman Empire, and had already declared her interest through the Sykes-Picot Agreement of 1916 and the Balfour Declaration. There were three distinct problems to be dealt with: the control of the Dardanelles; the disposal of the non-Turkish parts of the Ottoman Empire; and the claims made by Venizelos, the Greek Prime Minister, to areas where there was a substantial Greek population.

So far as the first was concerned, it was perhaps just as well that the Soviet Union repudiated the promise of Constantinople made to Imperial Russia in March 1915. Initially, it was hoped that the Straits would be internationalised under the supervision of the United States acting as the mandatory power. Wilson favoured this suggestion but it was rejected by the Senate in March 1920. The final arrangement agreed under the Treaty of Sèvres was that the Straits should be de-militarised and placed under international supervision.

The terms of the Sykes-Picot Agreement were broadly applied to the second problem, the French acquiring what is present-day Syria and Lebanon, the British what is present-day Israel, Jordan and Iraq. In each case these territories were to be treated as Mandates, but there was considerable opposition from the local inhabitants both in Syria and in Iraq to the arrival of the mandatory powers.

The third problem proved the most contentious. The Treaty of Sèvres awarded Eastern Thrace, the Gallipoli peninsula and several islands in the Aegean to Greece. The Greeks also gained the right to occupy Smyrna for five years, at the end of which a plebiscite would be held. All these terms were agreed on by the Allies at the San Remo Conference held in April 1920, and were incorporated in the Treaty of Sèvres that was signed in September of that year. Yet the Treaty was barely signed before its provisions became inoperable.

Reparations

While they bitterly resented the terms of the Treaty of Versailles, the Germans had little option but to comply with most of them. But Reparations were a different matter in that they required a positive effort on the part of the German government. Nor had the Allies worked out how payments were to be made. If in the form of goods, such as coal, this would amount to Germany 'dumping' her exports on to an already saturated market; if in the form of gold, this could only be secured through foreign loans or by Germany's running a favourable trade balance which she was in no position to do in 1919. Inevitably, the Reparations question bedevilled international trade and delayed the establishment of good relations between Germany and the victorious powers. It also led to a growing division between Britain and France.

For France, Reparations were a way of keeping Germany economically weak and were to be ensured, if necessary, by the use of force. For Britain, they proved an increasing source of embarrassment. By 1920 Britain was anxious to promote Germany's economic recovery in the belief that this would assist Britain's export markets. France might have been ready to take a more conciliatory line had Britain been prepared to sign a security treaty with France. But this no British politician was prepared to do. Thus every attempt to reach a settlement of the Reparations question came to grief because of French intransigence on the one hand and British reluctance to extend her commitments on the other.

The first of a series of conferences at which Reparations were discussed took place at Spa in July 1920. This settled the division of the spoils. France was to have 52%, Britain 22%, Italy 10%, Belgium 8% and the rest 8%. In April 1921 the Reparations Commission agreed on a total figure of £6600 million. In January 1922 a further conference was held at Cannes. This came nearer to success, Briand, the French

Unfinished Business

THE TRIUMPH OF "CULTURE"

. THE PRUSSIAN BULLY DECLARES HIMSELF TO BE THE APOSTLE OF CULTURE.

Punch

THIS ALLIED IMAGE OF GERMANY PERSISTED IN HER DEFEAT

representative, establishing a rapport with Lloyd George. But Briand was replaced by Poincaré who was strongly anti-German. Lloyd George, undeterred, arranged another conference at Genoa which met in April 1922. It was attended by 15 countries, including the Soviet Union, but had no positive results. It did provide, however, an opportunity for the two 'outcasts', Germany and Russia, to sign a Trade Agreement known as the Treaty of Rapallo. This did little to increase sympathy for the German case.

The replacement of Lloyd George by Bonar Law in October 1922 and by Baldwin in May 1923, brought no change in British policy. Bonar Law suggested a reduction in German obligations to 'a figure which the world would say that Germany could pay', but Poincaré was unwilling to make any concessions. When Germany fell behind in timber deliveries Poincaré used this as an excuse to occupy the Ruhr. French occupation began in January 1923 and lasted until August 1924. During that time Germany adopted a policy of passive resistance which reduced the Ruhr area to an industrial desert. To make matters worse it was also in 1923 that Germany experienced hyper-inflation. By September the exchange value of the mark in relation to the pound had fallen to 15 000 000. Economic chaos threatened. When Baldwin met Poincaré in September 1923 he urged the French premier to end the military occupation of the Ruhr and he also used his influence to help secure the appointment of two committees, under the auspices of the Reparations Commission, to report on Germany's financial problems.

The first of these committees, known as the Dawes Committee after its American Chairman, sat from January to April 1924. It produced what came to be known as the Dawes Plan. Under this Plan, Reparations payments were to be phased over a longer period and annual payments would consequently be reduced to £50 million a year, rising to £125 million a year. In the meantime Germany would be given a loan of £40 million to tide her over her immediate problems. Payments would be made in a new currency, the Rentenmark, which would then be turned into foreign currencies under American superintendence. By the time the Plan came out MacDonald had replaced Baldwin. Acting as his own Foreign Secretary, MacDonald devoted a great deal of time to the Reparations issue. He noted in his Diary: 'France must have another chance. I offer co-operation but she must be reasonable and cease her policy of selfish vanity .... The "weather"must be improved.' [Marquand, p. 333] The replacement of Poincaré by Herriot and the elevation of Stresemann to the Chancellorship in Germany improved the 'weather' of their own accord. But MacDonald worked hard to secure French and German acceptance of the Dawes Plan. He presided over a conference in London in July 1924, and when agreement was finally reached on 16 August it owed something to MacDonald's persistence. Marquand comments: 'It was the high point of his Government – perhaps of his career.'

D. Marquand, *Ramsay MacDonald* (1977)

This was not quite the end of the Reparations story. In 1929 a further conference was held under the chairmanship of Owen D. Young, an American financier. The conference produced the Young Plan which extended the period of Reparations payments by 60 years, thus easing the annual burden on Germany. The Reparations Commission was abolished and responsibility for dealing with any default in payments was given to the Permanent Court of Justice at the Hague. But the onset of the Depression and Hitler's advent to power brought payments to an end in 1932. Altogether Germany paid about one-tenth of the total due and most of this was borrowed from abroad. For all the trouble that Reparations caused, the Allies would have been well advised to forego their claims to compensation for the costs of the war.

The Near East

The Treaty of Sèvres failed to bring peace to the Near East for two reasons. In the first place, it was rejected by the nationalist leader, Mustafa Kemal, who put himself at the head of a Government of National Defence in opposition to the Sultan in 1919. Kemal, who had played an important part in the Gallipoli Campaign, established his headquarters at Ankara in Anatolia and by 1920 had won the support of a majority of his countrymen. The Sultan, Fuad I, meanwhile, retained his nominal authority only by courtesy of the Allied troops who occupied Constantinople and its vicinity. The second reason for the failure of the Treaty was Greek intransigence. Having gained Eastern Thrace and Smyrna, the Greeks refused any suggestion of compromise and, given the opportunity, would have seized Constantinople as well.

A. J. P. Taylor (ed.)
Lloyd George: Twelve Essays (1971)

British policy towards the Treaty was largely determined by Lloyd George's sympathy for the Greeks, partly inspired by his friendship with the Greek Prime Minister, Venizelos, and by his antipathy towards the Turks. He encouraged Greece's aspirations 'in the hope that she will become a powerful, liberalising factor in the Eastern Mediterranean'. [A. E. Montgomery, 'Lloyd George and the Greek Question, 1918–22', A. J. P. Taylor (ed.), p. 259]

His view of the Turks he confided to Lord Riddell:

> The Turks nearly brought about our defeat in the War. It was a near thing. You cannot trust them and they are a decadent race. The Greeks, on the other hand, are our friends, and a rising people ... We must secure Constantinople and the Dardanelles. You cannot do this effectively without crushing Turkish power. [Taylor, pp. 265–6]

Thus Lloyd George supported Greek claims to Eastern Thrace and Smyrna, even after the return of the pro-German King Constantine to the Greek throne and the removal of Venizelos in November 1920. He described Mustafa Kemal as 'a bandit' and, unlike the French, saw no reason to recognise his authority.

In March 1921, with Lloyd George's tacit approval if not his active encouragement, Greece declared war on Kemal's government which by then was receiving military aid from Russia. The war brought no decisive result in its first year and Britain confined her aid to rhetorical support of the Greek case. However, on 4 August 1922, Lloyd George made an impassioned speech, condemning Turkish atrocities and hinting at British intervention. This evidently provoked Kemal into launching an offensive in Asia Minor. Smyrna fell to the Turks on 9 September. Kemal now threatened the British forces occupying the southern shores of the Dardanelles. On 15 September the cabinet decided to act. A warning delivered to Kemal asked him to respect the zone of the Straits and telegrams were sent to the Dominions requesting help in a possible clash with the Turks. These requests met with a very lukewarm response, only New Zealand offering any assistance. On 23 September the Turkish armies reached Chanak, the British base. On 29 September the cabinet authorised the local Commander, General Harington, to deliver an ultimatum demanding Turkish withdrawal. Harington wisely delayed the delivery of the ultimatum and instead, at a conference with the local Turkish Commander at Mudania, secured Turkish agreement to respect the neutral zone.

The Chanak crisis has been hailed as a victory for Lloyd George and an example of firmness in the face of aggression. But to some of his colleagues it seemed more like unnecessary sabre rattling and it contributed to his downfall a month later at the Carlton Club meeting. In the long term the British stand at Chanak had little effect. Negotiations were opened with Kemal's government in the two Lausanne Conferences which took place between November 1922 and July 1923. At the first of these, presided over by Lord Curzon, the Treaty of Lausanne was negotiated, though it was not signed until July, 1923. Turkey retained Eastern Thrace and Smyrna; de-militarised zones were established on either side of the Bosphorus and the Dardanelles; navigation of the Straits was opened to ships of commerce of all nations in time of peace, and to warships of all nations in certain conditions.

The Treaty of Lausanne was the first significant revision of the Peace settlement and its signature marked the ending of the hostilities that had lingered on after 1918. Peace-making had proved a laborious and difficult process but by 1924, with the French out of the Ruhr and the Greek-Turkish boundary finally settled, Europe could at last look forward to a period of stability.

B ANGLO-SOVIET RELATIONS

The Russian Revolutions

In February 1917 the Tsarist government of Nicholas II collapsed. It was replaced by a Provisional government, headed initially by Prince Lvov and subsequently by Alexander Kerensky. But in April Lenin arrived in Russia, smuggled there through the efforts of the German Foreign Office in a sealed train which took him from Zurich to Stockholm and then to the Finland Station in Petrograd. As leader of the Bolshevik party Lenin had long argued the need for an élite group of committed revolutionaries to seize power if the 'dictatorship of the proletariat', prophesied by Marx, was to be realised. In the summer and autumn of 1917 his ambitions were achieved. Kerensky, vainly trying to abide by Russia's obligations to her Entente partners, launched a disastrous offensive in July 1917 which led to a wave of mutinies. A right-wing coup, inspired by General Kornilov in September 1917, was thwarted with Bolshevik help; and in November 1917 the Bolsheviks won control of Moscow and Petrograd, the seats of government. Negotiations were soon opened with the Imperial German government and in March 1918 Russia signed the Treaty of Brest Litovsk, at great sacrifice to herself but also leaving the Allies to continue the war against Germany on their own.

British Reactions

British reactions to the abdication of the Tsar had been guardedly optimistic. At last, it seemed, Russia might join the ranks of genuine parliamentary democracies and, so long as she stayed in the War, the change of regime would be beneficial. But the triumph of the Bolsheviks aroused a much more mixed reaction, ranging from fierce disapproval to sympathetic enthusiasm. At one extreme, Winston Churchill was implacably opposed to Lenin and all he stood for. In a speech to the House of

Commons in 1919 he described Bolshevism as a disease: 'Lenin was sent into Russia by the Germans in the same way that you might send a phial containing a culture of typhoid or cholera to be poured into the water supply of a great city, and it worked with great accuracy'. [Gilbert, p. 355] In an article, written in 1920, he said of Lenin: 'He has a conscious purpose. He has pursued it all his life, and it is plainly diabolical.' [Gilbert, p. 375]

M. Gilbert, *Winston S. Churchill, vol. IV 1917–22* (1975)

Lloyd George was no more enthusiastic than Churchill about the Bolsheviks but he was not willing to go to the lengths of intervening in Russia's internal affairs to bring them down. Furthermore, he believed that wooing Russia back into a commercial relationship with Europe would have far more effect in ameliorating the Bolshevik regime than a policy of armed intervention. In a Commons debate in 1920 he went so far as to say that the moment trade was established 'Communism would go.' [White, p. 3]

S. White, *Britain and the Bolsheviks, 1920–24* (1979)

Ramsay MacDonald and the right-wing members of the Labour party, believing as they did in the processes of parliamentary democracy, were highly suspicious of the Bolshevik reliance on violence and conspiracy. The Labour party as a whole always drew a clear distinction between Socialism and Communism. The 1918 election manifesto promised a new order but it was to be achieved by constitutional means. The 1922 manifesto declared that Labour's proposal to bring about a more equitable distribution of wealth 'was neither Bolshevism nor Communism, but commonsense and justice'. It represented 'the best bulwark against violent upheaval and class war'. At the 1924 Party Conference a resolution was passed stating that no member of the Communist party should be eligible for endorsement as a Labour candidate for Parliament or for a local council.

In some quarters of the Labour party there was more support for the Bolsheviks. Many of the Fabians such as H. G. Wells, Beatrice and Sydney Webb and George Bernard Shaw were prepared to applaud what they saw as a new experiment in social organisation. Wells, after visiting the Soviet Union in 1920, published an article in the *Daily Express*, in which he described the Bolsheviks as the only government that could prevent the final collapse of Russia. In the 1930s there was to be much more sympathy for the Soviet Union in intellectual circles with the rise of Fascism and the apparent inability of capitalist economies to cope with the problem of large-scale unemployment.

The British Communist party was the only political grouping actively to identify their aims with those of the Bolsheviks. Founded in 1920 the party had an official membership of only 4000, dropping to 3000 by 1924. Its influence was much less important, at least so far as its official activities were concerned, than those groups within the Labour party and in the intellectual establishment who were prepared to take a sympathetic view of what the Bolsheviks were trying to achieve.

The Bolshevik attitude to the outside world remained consistent in its belief that capitalism was doomed. But there were important differences of opinion about the tactics that would best assist in producing that outcome. Until 1921 it was hoped that other European countries would follow Russia's example. The Comintern – 'the general staff of world revolution' as Lenin dubbed it – was founded in 1919 precisely with that objective in mind. The Spartacist risings in Germany, the establishment of Communist regimes in Hungary and Bavaria in 1919 and the attempts to impose a Communist government on Poland in 1920 lent some credibility to Lenin's hopes and Churchill's fears. But the Communist experiments in Germany and Hungary proved very short-lived. The Poles defeated the Bolsheviks in 1920. Russia herself suffered an appalling famine in 1921. This in turn provoked Lenin's adoption of the New Economic Policy which depended in part on the import of Western technology. Clearly a more conciliatory approach was called for. Soviet foreign policy began to speak with two voices: the first, that of the Comintern, preached World Revolution; the second, that of the Soviet government, urged the need for good relations with those countries – including Britain – whose economic co-operation they valued.

Thus British policy towards the Bolsheviks reflected not only the attitudes of those in power in Britain; it also shifted in response to changes in Soviet objectives. One can distinguish three main phases. During the first, lasting from 1918 to 1920, British policy was one of outright hostility to the Bolshevik regime, manifested in the open support given to the anti-Bolshevik forces that surfaced during the Russian Civil War. The second phase, coinciding roughly with the adoption of the New Economic Policy in 1921, saw Britain moving from grudging recognition of the Bolshevik regime to normalisation of diplomatic relations and economic co-operation under Ramsay MacDonald's premiership. The Zinoviev Letter, the return of a Conservative government in 1924, the General Strike in 1926 and finally the Arcos affair (p. 159) in 1927 brought a cooling of relations and the severing of diplomatic relations once again.

During the first phase, Britain's initial reaction to the Bolsheviks was a sense of betrayal as the Peace of Brest Litovsk closed the Eastern Front and enabled Germany to concentrate all her forces on the Western Front in the last critical offensive of 1918. Churchill expressed, in typically exaggerated language, what was a common view in a speech he delivered in April 1919: 'Every British soldier done to death last year was really done to death by Lenin and Trotsky, not in fair war, but by the treacherous desertion of an ally without parallel in the history of the world.' [Gilbert, p. 278]

Gilbert, *Winston S. Churchill*, vol. IV

British intervention began with the dispatch of troops to Murmansk and Archangel in March 1918 to guard supplies sent there, and to ensure that they did not fall into Bolshevik hands. Almost imperceptibly British policy changed from one of neutrality to active support of the White Russian forces opposed to the Bolsheviks, a policy that was strenuously advocated by Churchill who became Minister for War in January 1919. By the spring of 1919 there were White Russian armies operating under Yudenitch in Estonia, under Admiral Kolchak in Siberia and under Denikin in the Caucasus. There were British contingents at Archangel and Murmansk, at Batum and in Siberia. The Royal Navy also had 200 ships blockading the Baltic, of which 17 were sunk. Total numbers of British troops involved were relatively small, about 30 000 in all, of whom 329 were killed. But economic assistance was much more substantial. Lloyd George claimed that by October 1919 Churchill's policy of support had cost £100 million, though admittedly much of this was in the form of war surplus equipment already available. At one point, after Denikin's capture of Kiev in August 1919, it looked as though the White Russian forces might succeed. But by October these hopes were dashed, and by the end of 1919 all British forces had been withdrawn.

Though it was clear from this point that the Bolsheviks had established control in Russia itself, this was not the end of the story of British intervention. In 1920 the Poles launched an offensive against the Bolsheviks for which they needed British arms and ammunition. An indication of working-class sympathy for the **Bolsheviks** was given when in May British dockers refused to load the *Jolly George* with arms already purchased by the Polish government. In August, when Warsaw itself came under threat of Russian occupation, Lloyd George delivered an ultimatum threatening that the British fleet would sail for the Baltic unless the Russian advance was halted. This move provoked a flurry of action in Britain. The Parliamentary Labour party, the Executive of the Labour party and the Parliamentary Committee of the TUC met on 9 August and agreed to set up a National Council of Action to bring pressure on the British government to prevent British involvement. Another 300–400 local Councils of Action also emerged in response to the encouragement given by the National Council. Fortunately for Lloyd George he was saved by the Poles themselves from having to implement his ultimatum. The Russian advance was halted and an armistice was signed between the Russian and Polish governments on 12 October. The Treaty of Riga, fixing the Russian-Polish frontier some 250 km east of the Curzon line (the ethnic frontier), was finally agreed in March 1921. Though Churchill's policy of intervention had failed to topple the Bolsheviks, British, and more particularly French, support for Poland had some success in creating a barrier to further Russian expansion.

Phase Two began with an Anglo-Soviet Trade Agreement, negotiations for which were finally completed in March 1921. Under its terms each side agreed to refrain from hostile propaganda, while the Soviet government recognised 'in principle' its obligation to private citizens in Britain who had not yet been paid for goods supplied to Russia during the War. There can be little doubt that the main reason for the timing of the Agreement was the rising level of unemployment in Britain, coupled with the knowledge that if Britain did not find export markets in Russia, other countries in Europe were ready to do so.

In 1922 Lloyd George sought to widen the scope of the Agreement at the Genoa Conference. But the Conference only served to highlight the differences between two economic systems. The Western countries insisted on the settlement of individual debts and the recognition of private property rights, the Soviet Union demanded compensation for damage inflicted by Allied intervention during the Civil War and indicated the impossibility of returning factories which had been nationalised to private ownership.

With the fall of Lloyd George in October 1922 Lord Curzon emerged from the shadows to play a much more dominant role as Foreign Secretary. He was much less committed to economic co-operation, and as a life-long imperialist highly sensitive to the dangers of Bolshevik propaganda in stimulating Indian nationalism. On 8 May 1923 he delivered a severe attack on the Soviet government for infractions of the undertaking to refrain from hostile propaganda, and threatened to terminate the Trade Agreement. The Russian government replied in a conciliatory vein, and the Agreement survived, but it was clear that Curzon would take no further steps towards recognising the legitimacy of the Bolshevik regime.

In its 1923 election manifesto the Labour party pledged itself to the resumption of full economic and diplomatic relations with Russia. This pledge MacDonald fulfilled on taking office on 4 February 1924. MacDonald also held out hopes of a Trade Treaty which would provide an increased market for British exports. Negotiations were opened on 14 April. The main obstacle was the old question of debts to British creditors. Talks nearly broke down on this issue but by August agreement had been reached and two treaties were signed, though not ratified by Parliament. They provided that in the event of a satisfactory arrangement over the settlement of British debts the British government would guarantee a loan of £30 million, two-thirds of which would be spent in this country, but Lloyd George, the erstwhile champion of economic co-operation, reversed his stance, describing the treaties as 'a thoroughly grotesque agreement'. Asquith and the Conservatives joined him in their denunciation. Even had MacDonald's government not fallen, it is highly likely that the Treaties would not have been ratified, and they naturally lapsed with Baldwin's victory.

After 1924 relations with the Soviet Union entered their third phase. Conservative politicians never doubted the veracity of the Zinoviev Letter which had contributed to their victory in the 1924 General Election. The Soviet trade unions donated £250 000 to the Miners Federation of Great Britain during the General Strike, which led to angry protests by the British cabinet. Finally, the Arcos affair in 1927 appeared to prove that the Soviet Union was exploiting the diplomatic facilities extended to it for the purpose of espionage. Arcos – the name stands for the All Russian Co-operative Society – had been established in London since 1920. It became the main organisation through which Anglo-Soviet trade was conducted, but its operations also provided a useful cover for less acceptable activities. On 12 May 1927 the Home Secretary organised a raid on the Arcos premises, shared with the Soviet Trade Delegation. What exactly was discovered in the raid has never been made public but, according to one recent authority, a list of named contacts and secret 'post boxes' used by the Soviet Secret Service in North and South America, Australia, New Zealand and South Africa was found on one of the staff. Baldwin stated to the House of Commons that 'Both military espionage and subversive activities throughout the British Empire and North and South America were directed and carried out from the ARCOS and Soviet Delegation offices.' [Boyle, pp. 98–9] Three tons of documents were removed by the police. Whether Baldwin's indictment was justified depends on what those documents contained. The cabinet had no doubts. On 23 May it was agreed to put an end to the trade agreement and to demand the withdrawal of the Soviet Diplomatic Mission from London. Anglo-Soviet relations were soured once again and suspicion of Soviet intentions remained a powerful barrier in the way of an anti-Fascist alliance in the 1930s.

A. Boyle, *The Climate of Treason* (Hodder & Stoughton, 1979)

C ▬▬▬▬▬▬▬▬ BRITISH DIPLOMACY, 1924–29

The Return to Stability (?)

With the ending of the Russo-Polish War in 1921, the Middle East Settlement reached at Lausanne in 1923 and the French evacuation of the Ruhr in 1924, it began to look as though Europe was at last settling down to a period of peace. As it transpired the stability achieved was illusory. But the rise of the dictators in Italy, Germany and Japan and the breakdown of the world economy in 1929 could not have been anticipated. The main problem raised by the diplomacy of the 1920s is to determine why, in an improving international climate, so little was done to remove the causes of future conflict.

Britain's objectives during these years were perfectly clear. She had gained all she wanted from the peace settlements, as a Foreign Office memorandum put it in 1926:

'We have no territorial ambition, nor desire for aggrandisement. We have got all we want, perhaps more.' [Kennedy, p. 256] Britain had a vested interest in the preservation of peace and her policies were directed towards that objective. At the same time there was a natural reluctance to assume any commitments that might involve her in another European war. On the one hand, therefore, Britain would support any moves to reduce Franco-German hostility; but on the other she would not risk any agreement that would tie her hands too firmly. This ambivalent approach was reflected in British attitudes to the League of Nations, to the problem of Germany's frontiers and to disarmament. Britain's uncertain course in these respects did nothing to promote the stability she so desired.

P.M. Kennedy,
The Realities Behind Diplomacy (1981)

Britain and the League of Nations

Though the League of Nations owed its inception chiefly to Woodrow Wilson, it evoked enthusiastic support in Britain. The Union of Democratic Control and the Parliamentary Labour party had both advocated the setting up of an international organisation during the course of the War. In right-wing circles Lord Robert Cecil became a passionate advocate of the League, and General Smuts not only gave the League his active support, he produced a pamphlet on 'The League of Nations – A Practical Suggestion' many of whose ideas were incorporated in the Constitution of the League. As one of the victorious powers Britain was naturally represented on the Council of the League, its executive body, and Ernest Drummond, its first General Secretary, was British. The League of Nations Union proved a popular and effective pressure group. Its Chairman, Professor Gilbert Murray, claimed in 1928: 'All parties are pledged to the League ... all Prime Ministers and ex-Prime Ministers support it ....' [Kennedy, p. 244]

Kennedy, *The Realities Behind Diplomacy*

But while they might support the League in principle, few British politicians really believed in its efficacy as an instrument for solving international disputes in practice. Nor was Britain prepared to see the League's authority increased at the expense of the autonomy of the British Empire. This can best be illustrated by the history of the Geneva Protocol. In 1923 the Assembly of the League accepted a draft treaty of mutual assistance designed to outlaw 'aggressive war'. Signatories to the treaty were to bind themselves to come to the assistance of any fellow signatory deemed by the Council of the League to be a victim of aggression. Though the proposal emanated from the British representative, Lord Robert Cecil, it was strongly opposed by the Admiralty and by the Dominion governments. In April 1924 the Committee of Imperial Defence advised against Britain's adherence to the treaty and MacDonald heeded their advice.

But MacDonald was not prepared to leave the matter there. In September, in a speech to the Assembly, he urged the principle of compulsory arbitration. The French seized on the suggestion and in October it was embodied in what came to be known as the Geneva Protocol. Any state refusing to submit a dispute to arbitration or rejecting the decision of an arbitrator would be regarded as an aggressor and liable to the penalties provided for under Article 16 of the Covenant, which included sanctions, and in the last resort, force. The Protocol was to come into force following the successful conclusion of a disarmament conference due to be held in June 1925. Several members of MacDonald's cabinet expressed their reservations. The service departments were again strongly opposed to the Protocol, as were the Dominion governments. France and 18 smaller countries did sign it, however. When Baldwin took office in November 1924 he submitted the Protocol to a sub-committee of the Committee of Imperial Defence chaired by Hankey. Hankey was an inveterate opponent of the Protocol, disliking its 'vague, unlimited commitments'. In February 1925, after the receipt of Hankey's hostile report, the cabinet agreed not to support it. Thus passed the last chance to strengthen the League's authority, though it may be doubted whether the Protocol would in practice have made very much difference.

Britain and Germany

Britain's failure to sign the Geneva Protocol did nothing to allay France's fears of a resurgent Germany. Austen Chamberlain, who became Foreign Secretary in November 1924, was ready to do what he could in this respect. When Stresemann, the German Foreign Minister, suggested a mutual security pact in January 1925, Chamberlain responded enthusiastically to the idea. Despite the disapproval of his cabinet colleagues who feared any commitment to France, Chamberlain helped to bring about the Locarno Conference which assembled on 5 October. It included representatives from Britain, France, Germany, Italy, Poland, Czechoslovakia and Belgium. The three main participants, Chamberlain, Stresemann and Briand were all anxious to see an improvement in Franco-German relations. On 16 October the Locarno Pact was finally agreed. It consisted of several different treaties. Germany's western frontiers with France and Belgium were accepted as final and were guaranteed by Britain and Italy. Germany would not accord the same recognition to her eastern boundaries; instead she signed arbitration treaties with Poland and Czechoslovakia, and Germany also recognised the treaties of mutual military assistance signed between France, Poland and Czechoslovakia. Finally, Germany was to be welcomed into the League of Nations.

The signing of the Treaties of Locarno, 1925. (Left to right Gustav Streseman, Austen Chamberlain, Aristide Briand, J. von Schubert)

At the time the Locarno Pact was seen as a great landmark, signifying the real transition between war and peace. Austen Chamberlain was awarded the Nobel Peace Prize for his efforts. But several reservations need to be made. In the first place, Germany did not abandon any of her ambitions in the East. The recovery of Danzig, the Sudetenland and the Polish Corridor remained very much on the agenda. Britain had also indicated her unwillingness to underwrite the Versailles settlement so far as Germany's eastern frontier was concerned. In a letter to the British ambassador in Paris, Lord Crewe, Chamberlain made this quite plain. Echoing Bismarck in a different context, he wrote: 'No British government ever will, or ever can, risk the bones of a British grenadier ... for the Polish corridor.' [cited in Hayes, p. 227]

P. M. Hayes, *Modern British Foreign Policy* (A. and C. Black, 1978)

K. Middlemas and J. Barnes, *Baldwin* (1969)

A. J. P. Taylor, *English History, 1914–1945* (1970)

Subsequently he defended the Locarno Pact in the House of Commons on the grounds that the obligations assumed under it 'could not be more narrowly circumscribed to the conditions under which we have a vital national interest'. [Middlemas and Barnes, p. 359] A. J. P. Taylor goes so far as to say that the Locarno Pact 'marked the moment when Britain regarded the European responsibilities which she had taken up in August, 1914 as fully discharged. The British, by pledging themselves on the Rhine, turned their backs on Europe – or so they thought. Splendid isolation had come again.' [Taylor, p. 285] The Locarno Pact certainly improved the international atmosphere. Germany did enter the League of Nations in 1926 but the problem of her eastern frontiers was no nearer solution, and the gap between British and French policies in this respect was as wide as ever.

Defence Policy and Disarmament

British policy towards defence and disarmament had two distinct but related aspects. British governments had to assess Britain's defence requirements in the light of the current international situation and in terms of what the country could afford. But this calculation would in turn be affected by the level of armaments adopted by Britain's potential opponents. It was the policy of successive British governments to keep defence spending as low as possible, and to promote disarmament whenever they could.

Britain ended the war with an army of 5.5 million, a navy of 458 000 and an airforce of 290 000. The navy had 58 capital ships and 103 cruisers, not to mention all the lesser craft. The RAF had over 20 000 aeroplanes. The burden of defence spending was enormous and could only be met, as we have seen, by extensive borrowing. No one had any doubts that it must be reduced as soon as the war was over. What could not have been anticipated was the extraordinary change in the premiss on which defence spending was to be based. This was the so-called Ten Year Rule. It arose out of a suggestion of Hankey's that the Committee of Imperial Defence should 'draw up a basis of policy on which the Royal Navy, the Army and the Royal Air Force should work out their estimates'. [Taylor, p. 201] At a cabinet meeting on 15 August 1919 such a basis was agreed. Service departments were to assume 'for framing revised Estimates, that the British Empire will not be engaged in any great war for the next ten years; and that no Expeditionary Force is required for this purpose'. [Taylor, p. 212] In 1928 Churchill, then Chancellor of the Exchequer, and bent on economies, induced the Committee of Imperial Defence to accept the Ten Year Rule as permanent and self-perpetuating, subject to the safeguard that any department might raise it at any time. Until the Ten Year Rule was finally dropped in 1933 it remained the basis on which all defence spending was fixed. Not surprisingly the total fell from £760 million between 1919 and 1920

Taylor (ed.), *Lloyd George:*

to £102 million in 1932. So far as the individual services are concerned the army reverted to its pre-war role of imperial police force; the RAF preserved its separate identity thanks to the determination of Lord Trenchard, but remained small in numbers and limited in capacity. The Navy fared better, because in this connection Britain's defence needs and disarmament initiatives coincided.

Though the war had brought about the destruction of Britain's main naval rival, Germany, it also witnessed the rise of American and Japanese naval power. Britain had to decide whether to compete with the United States. In November 1921 President Harding summoned a conference of naval powers at Washington. It was attended by the United States, Britain, France, Italy and Japan. The conference led to the conclusion of the Washington Naval Agreement under which capital ships allowed to the countries concerned would be in the following ratios:

United States	5
Britain	5
France	3
Italy	1.75
Japan	1.75

No new capital ships were to be constructed. Britain's alliance with Japan was to end, instead it was replaced by a Four Power Treaty signed by Britain, the United States, France and Japan, guaranteeing the status quo in the Far East. For Britain the Washington Naval Agreement marked the formal end of the two power standard. In return she avoided a wasteful and unnecessary naval race with the United States, which she could not have afforded.

There was, however, an unhappy sequel to the Agreement. In 1927 the United States convened another naval conference at Geneva, this time to extend the limitations on armaments to cruisers. The Admiralty insisted that Britain needed a minimum of 70 cruisers to meet her imperial commitments. The United States regarded 40 as the maximum number they were prepared to allow. The conference broke down in disarray and damaged Anglo-American relations unnecessarily.

Other disarmament initiatives were no more successful. The Preparatory Commission on Disarmament which met in 1927 failed to make headway, initially because of differences between France and Britain, then because Italy and the United States feared a private deal had been struck by France and Britain.

It was against this background that the Kellogg-Briand Pact came into existence. It stemmed from a suggestion by Kellogg, the American Secretary of State, to Briand, his French counterpart, that the two countries might agree to renounce war between each other. As much for domestic reasons as anything else, in an election year, Kellogg widened his suggestion to include any country that would be willing to sign. Chamberlain had distinct reservations, but Britain signed the Pact on 27 August 1928. By 1929, 54 countries had agreed to renounce war. Apart from paving the way for the reconvening of the disarmament conference in 1929, the Pact had no other effects.

At a superficial glance, the international scene in 1929 looked relatively hopeful. The Locarno Treaties, German entry into the League of Nations and the Kellogg-Briand Pact all seemed to indicate a readiness to settle disputes by negotiation rather than by force. But under the surface German rearmament was proceeding secretly with Russian connivance. Her territorial grievances in the East were felt as strongly as ever. The forces of militarism were beginning to stir in Italy and Japan. Friction between Britain, France and the United States prevented a common approach to disarmament and the problem of Germany. When the economic blizzard struck, as it did in 1929, it was to find a Europe still all too vulnerable to old antipathies.

POINTS AT ISSUE

The Treaty of Versailles

The instability of Europe between the wars has often been attributed to the Treaty of Versailles. Criticism has been chiefly directed at the punitive clauses imposed on Germany, and on the selective application of the principle of national self-determination which was applied mainly to Germany's disadvantage. The main authors of the Treaty have been blamed for its shortcomings. Clemenceau has been attacked for his vindictiveness, Wilson for his naiveté and Lloyd George for his duplicity. Curiously, on this issue, contemporaries were harsher in their criticism than later historians have been. Distance has lent charity, if not enchantment, to the view. With hindsight it is possible to see more clearly the difficulties which faced the statesmen who met at Paris in 1919 and the pressures to which they were subjected. But it remains an open question as to whether the faults of the Treaty of Versailles were inevitable in the context of 1919, or whether more resolute and enlightened statesmanship might have produced a more acceptable settlement.

Two of the most outspoken critics of the Treaty of Versailles were members of the British delegation: Harold Nicolson, who was employed by the Foreign Office, mainly on frontier rectification; and J. M. Keynes, who was there to advise the Treasury on Reparations. Nicolson kept a diary in which he recorded his immediate impressions; in 1933 he produced a measured account of the Paris Peace Conference, *Peacemaking, 1919*, in which he tried to explain its failures. The following excerpts come first from the diary, secondly from *Peacemaking, 1919*.

1. *June 8, Sunday, 1919*
   (Letter to my father):

   > I have every hope that Lloyd George, who is fighting like a Welsh terrier, will succeed in the face of everybody in introducing some modification in the terms imposed upon Germany. Now that we see them as a whole we realise that they are much too stiff. They are not stern merely but actually *punitive*, and they abound with what Smuts calls 'pinpricks' as well as dagger thrusts .... Yet the real crime is the reparation and indemnity chapter, which is immoral and senseless. There is not a single person among the younger people here who is not unhappy and disappointed at its terms .... [Nicolson, *Peacemaking, 1919*, p. 359]

2.

   We came to Paris confident that the new order was about to be established; we left it convinced that the new order had merely fouled the old. We arrived as fervent apprentices in the school of Wilson: we left as renegades. I wish to suggest, in this chapter (and without bitterness), that this unhappy diminution of standard was very largely the fault (or one might say with greater fairness 'the misfortune') of democratic diplomacy. [Nicolson, *Peacemaking, 1919*, p. 187]

J. M. Keynes attacked the Treaty of Versailles first in his book *The Economic Consequences of the Peace*, written at the suggestion of General Smuts after Keynes had resigned in disgust from the British delegation. It was written in the heat of the moment and in the hopes of influencing opinion towards changing the Treaty. Even so it is a savage indictment as the following passages indicate:

> The policy of reducing Germany to servitude for a generation, of degrading the lives of millions of human beings, and of depriving a whole nation of happiness should be abhorrent and detestable, – abhorrent and detestable, even if it were possible, even if it enriched ourselves, even if it did not sow the decay of the whole civilised life of Europe. Some preach it in the name of Justice. In the great events of man's history, in the unwinding of the complex fates of nations Justice is not so simple. And if it were, nations are not authorised, by religion or by natural morals, to visit on the children of their enemies the misdoings of parents or of rulers. [Keynes, *The Economic Consequences of the Peace*, pp. 209–10]

The German Report on the Treaty's likely effects on the German population concluded with the words: 'Those who sign this Treaty will sign the death sentence of many millions of German men, women and children.' Keynes, quoting this passage went on to say: 'I know of no adequate answer to these words.'

In 1933 Keynes also published *Essays in Biography*, which included his sketches of Clemenceau, Wilson and Lloyd George. It was to their defects that he attributed all the faults of the Treaty of Versailles. Of Clemenceau, Keynes wrote:

> He felt about France what Pericles felt of Athens – unique value in her, nothing else mattering; but his theory of politics was Bismarck's. He had one illusion – France; and one disillusion – mankind, including Frenchmen and his colleagues not least. His principles for the Peace can be expressed simply. In the first place, he was a foremost believer in the view of German psychology that the German understands and can understand nothing but intimidation, that he is without generosity or remorse in negotiation, that there is no advantage he will not take of you, and no extent to which he will not demean himself for profit, that he is without honour, pride or mercy.

It must be France's object to set the clock back and undo what Germany had accomplished since 1870:

> If France could seize, even in part, what Germany was compelled to drop, the inequality of strength between the two rivals for European hegemony might be remedied for many generations. Hence sprang those cumulative provisions of the Treaty for the destruction of highly organised economic life.

> This is the policy of an old man, whose most vivid impressions and most lively imaginations are of the past and not of the future ...
> [Keynes, *Essays in Biography*, pp. 13–16]

What, Keynes asked, induced Wilson to accept Clemenceau's Carthaginian peace? The answer was very simple:

> Yet the causes were very ordinary and human. The President was not a hero or a prophet; he was not even a philosopher; but a generously intentioned man, with many of the weaknesses of other human beings, and lacking that dominating intellectual equipment which would have been necessary to cope with the subtle and dangerous spell-binders whom a tremendous clash of forces and personalities had brought to the top as triumphant masters in the swift game of give and take, face to face in Council – a game of which he had no experience at all.

Wilson came ill-prepared to the Conference: 'He had no plan, no scheme, no constructive ideas whatever for clothing with the flesh of life the commandments which he had thundered from the White House.' His mind 'was slow and unadaptable'; he was a poor negotiator: 'There can seldom have been a statesman of the first rank more incompetent than the President in the agilities of the council chamber.' He failed to take advice. Finally, Keynes argued, Wilson's theological or Presbyterian temperament prevented him from admitting that he had compromised the Fourteen Points, and thus all departures from them had to be disguised with sophistries, which, to the Germans, looked like hypocrisy.

Lloyd George might still have saved the day had he been willing to support Wilson. But Lloyd George had to side with Clemenceau on the question of Reparations and the Secret Treaties.

> If the President's morale was maintained intact, Mr. Lloyd George could not hope to get his way in these issues; he was, therefore, almost equally interested with Clemenceau in gradually breaking down this morale. But besides, he had Lord Northcliffe and the British Jingoes on his heels, and complaints in the French Press were certain to find their echo in a certain section of the British also.
>
> If, therefore, he were to take his stand firmly and effectively on the side of the President, there was needed an act of courage and faith which could only be based on fundamental beliefs and principles. But Mr. Lloyd George has none such, and political considerations pointed to a middle path.

Keynes concludes his portraits with this accusation:

> These were the personalities of Paris – I forbear to mention other nations or lesser men: Clemenceau, aesthetically the noblest; the President, morally the most admirable; Lloyd George, intellectually the subtlest. Out of their disparities and weaknesses the Treaty was borne, child of the least worthy attributes of each of its parents, without nobility, without morality, without intellect. [Keynes, *Essays in Biography*, pp. 32–39]

Historians, while admitting the defects of the Treaty, have been much less inclined to attribute the blame to individuals. A. J. P. Taylor in *English History, 1914–45* exonerates Lloyd George. He is described as 'an adroit conciliator'; 'the man who had tried to moderate the treaty was soon saddled with the blame for its supposed faults.' Taylor also points out that Keynes 'thought £2 000 million a practical figure for reparations. Germany paid in all £1000 million, and this only with money borrowed from the United States'. [Taylor, pp. 184–5]

In *The Realities Behind Diplomacy* Paul Kennedy argues that:

> So far as Lloyd George was concerned, however, Britain and its Empire could be happy with the overall result.
> [Kennedy, p. 213]

There were deficiencies in the Treaty, Kennedy admits. But:

> The settlement of so many complicated and contentious issues in such a relatively short time could not possibly satisfy everyone. Even at the time, British radicals were beginning to complain that it deviated from Wilson's Fourteen Points, an argument put even more forcibly by German nationalists. Vast numbers of ethnic minorities were placed on the wrong side of new borders. A patchwork quilt of small unstable states had been established throughout East-Central Europe in place of the old empires, but these new units were only likely to survive so long as German and Russian power remained weak. The reparations question was fobbed off, not settled. Imperialist annexations, disguised by the fig-leaf of the mandates system, had occurred on a wide scale. Above all, it was later said, the 1919 peace settlement had failed to solve the Franco-German antagonism and was in fact the worst of both worlds, being too severe to be permanently acceptable to most Germans yet too lenient to check a resurgence of German power.
>
> All this was true; but it was equally true that there were few simple solutions to these problems which all sides would happily accept. The 'Big Three', jumping from question to question and often under severe domestic pressures which made a 'fair' settlement impossible, were not unaware of the deficiencies in their handiwork. But this was precisely why, so far as Lloyd George was concerned, the League of Nations was created ...' [Kennedy, pp. 219–20]

Perhaps the strongest defence of the Peace Settlements as a whole is to be found in Anthony Adamthwaite's book, *The Lost Peace: International Relations in Europe 1919–1939*. Adamthwaite points out that 'No peace settlement could have fulfilled the millenial hopes of a new heaven and a new earth. It was the destruction of these Utopian hopes that provoked the denunciation of the settlement.' In fact, he argues,

> Much more can be said for the peace settlement than was conceded at the time. Versailles was a brave attempt to deal with intractable, perhaps insoluble, problems. Peace making went on for five years after the armistice of 1918, but after 1945 the process went on in Europe for nine years, with Japan for eleven years, and no peace treaty has been concluded with Germany. The Paris Peace Conference has been compared unfavourably with the Congress of Vienna. The comparison is not a fair one. The collapse of four empires in Europe and the Near East confronted the Paris statesmen with problems on a scale which no previous peace congress had encountered. The pressures were enormous. The conference met against a background of revolution, famine and economic chaos which had not been experienced since 1848. The Vienna statesmen safely ignored the incipient nationalism of their world, allied leaders in 1919 were presented with a *fait accompli* – self determination in Central and Eastern Europe was a reality. The Europe of 1815 was a self-contained system; in 1919 the old balance of power had gone for ever. Russia, a central link in the old balance, was torn by civil war and absent from the conference. The United States disavowed Wilson's work and withdrew from political commitments in Europe. [Adamthwaite, pp. 2–3]

Books cited

H. Nicolson, *Peacemaking, 1919* (Methuen, 1964)

J. M. Keynes, *The Economic Consequences of the Peace* (Macmillan, 1919)
   Essays in Biography (Hart-Davis, 1933)

A. J. P. Taylor, *English History, 1914–45* (Pelican, 1970)

P. M. Kennedy, *The Realities Behind Diplomacy* (Allen & Unwin, 1981)

A. Adamthwaite, *The Lost Peace: International Relations in Europe 1919–1939* (Arnold, 1980)

CHAPTER 5
FURTHER READING

General

Essential

A. Adamthwaite, *The Lost Peace: International Relations in Europe 1919–1939* (Arnold, 1980)

P. M. Kennedy, *The Realities Behind Diplomacy* (Allen & Unwin, 1981)

Peacemaking

Essential

H. Nicolson, *Peacemaking, 1919* (Methuen, 1964)

A. J. P. Taylor (ed.), *Lloyd George: Twelve Essays* (Hamish Hamilton, 1971)

R. M. Watt, *The Kings Depart* (Penguin 1973)

Recommended

Lord Hankey, *The Supreme Control. At the Paris Peace Conference, 1919* (Allen & Unwin, 1963)

J. M. Keynes, *Essays in Biography* (Hart-Davis, 1933)
        The Economic Consequences of the Peace (Macmillan, 1919)

Anglo-Russian Relations

Essential

M. Gilbert, *Winston S. Churchill, vol. IV, 1917–22* (Heinemann, 1975)

S. White, *Britain and the Bolsheviks, 1920–1924* (Macmillan, 1979)

Recommended

L. Chester, S. Fay and H. Young, *The Zinoviev Letter* (Heinemann, 1967)

Diplomacy in the 1920s

Essential

D. Marquand, *Ramsay MacDonald* (Cape, 1977)

K. Middlemas and J. Barnes, *Baldwin* (Weidenfeld & Nicolson, 1969)

W. N. Medlicott, *British Foreign Policy since Versailles* (Methuen, 1968)

The Problems of Empire, 1914–39

A ▬▬▬▬▬▬▬▬▬▬▬▬▬▬▬ THE LEGACY OF WAR

The British Empire reached its zenith in 1920. The peace settlements with Germany and Turkey resulted in Britain and the Dominions acquiring all Germany's colonies, while in the Middle East, Britain assumed control of Palestine, Transjordan and Iraq. Of her erstwhile rivals, Germany was shattered by defeat, her fleet scuttled; France, though also on the winning side, had suffered grievous casualties, and though seen as a potential rival in the Middle East, posed no real challenge; Russia was in the throes of civil war. The links of empire had also been strengthened in the furnace of war. Each of the Dominions had contributed more than its fair share of manpower to the British cause. Their premiers had taken part in the direction of the war through meetings of the imperial War Cabinet; Jan Christian Smuts of South Africa was a regular member of Lloyd George's war cabinet. The Dominions were separately represented at the Paris Peace Conference and one of them was given a seat on a rotating basis on the British delegation. It seemed indeed that the war had forged a new sense of imperial unity and that the British empire had triumphed over all its rivals.

Yet, as Max Beloff has put it, 'despite the illusion conveyed by maps and tables, the meridian had passed; the final liquidation of Britain's world power – the imperial sunset – lay only fifty years ahead.' [Beloff, p. 361] That *dénouement* could not have been anticipated in 1920. But behind the facade of imperial unity and strength the cracks were already beginning to appear. The ramshackle structure that was the Empire was subject to various strains, both internal and external, that would cause its disintegration.

M. Beloff, *Imperial Sunset* (1969)

The ending of the Anglo-Japanese alliance in 1922 and the emergence of an aggressive and expansionist-minded clique in Japan made the defence of Britain's Far Eastern possessions increasingly difficult. This was to be made devastatingly apparent in 1941 and 1942. The growing power of the United States was no recompense for the loss of Britain's naval superiority, for in the isolationist mood of American foreign policy in the 1920s and 1930s, coupled with innate American suspicion of Britain's imperial pretensions, the United States could not be expected to protect British imperial interests.

A much more direct threat to the Empire was the spread of nationalism. With hindsight it can be seen that to resist the force of this sentiment was to adopt a stance like that of Canute's to the incoming tide. But, to do the British justice, the problems caused by nationalism in her dependent territories were never simple. Too rapid a surrender to the demands for British withdrawal might mean handing over power to hands not yet ready to exercise it. Alternatively, and more insoluble still, were the problems of religious and racial divisions within the territories for which Britain was responsible. The rivalries of Catholic and Protestant in Ireland, of Hindu and Muslim in India, of Arab and Jew in Palestine made the task of imperial rule much more difficult. They also made withdrawal harder to accomplish honourably.

The growing force of nationalism, reflected in episodes such as the Easter Rising in Dublin, the disturbances in India in 1919 and 1920 and the anti-British riots in Egypt in 1919, was accompanied by growing doubts in British intellectual circles about the legitimacy of empire. At first it was only a few isolated voices who raised them. In 1913 Leonard Woolf resigned from the Ceylon Civil Service and expressed his rejection of the imperial ethic in his book *A Village in the Jungle*. In 1924 E. M. Forster published his profound study of Anglo-Indian relations, *A Passage to India*. It concluded with one of the main characters, the Muslim Doctor Aziz, prophesying to his English friend, Fielding: ' "If I don't make you go, Ahmed will, Karim will, if it's fifty or five hundred years we shall get rid of you, yes we shall drive every blasted Englishman into the sea, and then" – he rode against him furiously – "and then," he concluded, half kissing him, "you and I shall be friends." '

L. Woolf, *A Village in the Jungle* (Chatto & Windus, 1951)

E. M. Forster, *A Passage to India* (Penguin, 1984)

George Orwell, who served in the Burma Police, expressed the doubts which assailed all who sought to exercise disinterested authority in the face of resistance: 'I perceived that when the white man turns tyrant it is his own freedom that he destroys.' [Crick, p. 96] Englishmen raised to believe in the virtues of parliamentary democracy and in the duty to uphold the white man's burden found it increasingly difficult to reconcile the two concepts. When Gandhi was put on trial for encouraging civil disobedience in India in 1922, the magistrate trying the case sentenced him to six years imprisonment. But he concluded by saying that 'if the course of events in India should make it possible for the Government to reduce the period and release you no one would be better pleased than I'. [Woodcock, p. 284] The confident, not to say brash, defence of imperialism sounded by such men as Joseph Chamberlain, Cecil Rhodes, Curzon and Milner was not generally echoed after the First World War. The moral basis for imperialism if such could be found, rested on the belief that the imperial power used its authority benevolently. As Gandhi discovered, when forced by nationalist opposition to act violently, the British government did so without conviction.

B. Crick, *George Orwell* (Secker & Warburg, 1980)

G. Woodcock, *Who Killed the British Empire?* (1974)

There was, finally, the sheer cost of administering and defending such a heterogeneous collection of territories. Throughout the inter-war years, as we have seen, governments were under continual pressure to reduce their defence budgets. Wherever possible imperial garrisons were reduced. The RAF was employed to maintain order in Iraq because bombing recalcitrant villages was cheaper than mounting infantry expeditions. In 1925 the British garrison in Palestine was reduced to one squadron of armoured cars. The Washington Naval Treaty in 1922 marked the ending of Britain's naval superiority. Total defence-spending on the Empire amounted to £154 million in 1930 [Woodcock, p. 328], by current standards, no doubt, a relatively small sum. But at that time it seemed more than the country could afford and every increase was likely to be resisted.

Woodcock, *Who Killed the British Empire?*

Thus, while the British Empire emerged in 1918 from the First World War with its territories extended and its rivals weakened, its dissolution was inevitable. The British people lacked both the resources and the conviction to hold down growing resistance to imperial rule indefinitely. The real test of statesmanship was whether the imperial retreat could be managed without bloodshed and without plunging into chaos the areas freed from the British yoke. It must be admitted that in both respects Britain's record was mixed.

The process of decolonisation lasted 50 years, beginning with the Irish Treaty in 1921, and ending, to all intents and purposes, with the creation of Zimbabwe in 1980. The Second World War provides a natural dividing line so that the rest of this chapter will be confined to the period up to 1939, and attention will be focused on the particular problems of Ireland, India and the Middle East.

B   THE IRISH TANGLE

'This most perplexing and damnable country' [Asquith, 1916]

As we saw earlier, Ireland was poised on the brink of Civil War in 1914, and was only saved from it by the larger conflict that broke out in Europe. In the North most of the Ulster Volunteers joined the British army, many of them to die in the Ulster Division which suffered severely in the battle of the Somme. In the South the moderate nationalist leader, John Redmond, urged his countrymen to support the British cause, which was also that of Belgium, a small, defenceless and Catholic country. Many of them did so. Until the end of 1915 there were more Irish Catholics than Irish Protestants in the British army.

Ireland during the War

But within the Irish nationalist movement there were more extreme factions who took the view that Britain's predicament was Ireland's opportunity. The Irish Volunteer movement split in two, the militants appropriating the original title while Redmond's supporters became known as the National Volunteers. Within the Irish Volunteers there developed a splinter group, the Irish Republican Brotherhood, who planned armed rebellion. The IRB was an eclectic organisation. It included among its supporters men such as Sir Roger Casement, formerly a member of the British Consular Service but now a passionate supporter of Irish nationalism; Padraic Pearse, a school teacher whose nationalism was based on a romantic vision of Irish history and culture; James Connolly, born in Edinburgh of Irish parentage, who combined a powerful belief in socialism with a strong sense of Ireland's claim to nationhood; and Eamonn de Valera, born in New York to a Spanish father and an Irish mother but brought up in rural Ireland, and by 1914 a keen member of the Gaelic League and teacher of mathematics.

Whatever their different backgrounds and different objectives, they were united in the belief that Ireland's freedom could only be won through bloodshed. For Pearse the gesture was more important than the prospect of success. In the funeral oration he delivered at the graveside of another patriot, O'Donovan Rossa, in 1915 he proclaimed that 'Life springs from death, and from the graves of patriot men and

P. Pearse, *Peace and the Gael* (Political Writings and Speeches, Dublin, 1966)

and women spring living nations.' Pearse had an unhealthy belief in the cleansing quality of warfare. In a passage in *'Peace and the Gael'* (published in December 1915), he wrote:

G. Dangerfield, *The Damnable Question* (1977)

> On whichever side the men who rule the peoples have marshalled them, whether with England to uphold the tyranny of the seas, or with Germany to break that tyranny, the people themselves have gone into battle because the old voice that speaks out of the soil of a nation has spoken anew .... It is good for the world that such things should be done. The old heart of the earth needed to be warmed with the red wine of the battlefields. Such august homage was never before offered to God, the homage of millions of lives given gladly for love of country.
> [Dangerfield, p. 282]

When other countries were shedding blood with such profligacy it behoved Ireland to do so too: 'What peace (Ireland) has known these latter days has been the devil's peace, peace with dishonour.'

Others took a more realistic view. Connolly had little time for Pearse's call for blood sacrifice and created his Citizens' Army with a view to making it an effective fighting force. But the history of the Easter Rising makes it clear that when it finally took place the odds against success were impossibly high, as the leaders realised; ironically, it was this which gave the Rising its mythical character and endowed its martyrs with their heroic reputations.

The Easter Rising was originally planned to take place on Easter Sunday 1916, a day with symbolic overtones. It was planned to coincide with the arrival of a ship-load of arms, provided by Germany, to be landed in Tralee Bay. But from the start there was appalling confusion. Eoin MacNeill, Chief of Staff of the Irish Volunteers, had always taken the line that armed rebellion would only be justified if there were reasonable prospects of its succeeding. In 1916 these prospects looked remote. For this reason he was deliberately deceived by the Military Council of the IRB who had planned the Rising. He was not informed that any insurrection was planned until the Thursday before Easter; his immediate opposition to the scheme was overcome by a forged letter purporting to come from the British authorities in Dublin Castle and threatening to disarm the Volunteers, and by the news that a German ship, the *Aud*, was about to land arms and ammunition. But on Good Friday the *Aud* was intercepted by the British navy; she was scuttled by her captain on the way into Queenstown harbour. When news of this reached MacNeill, together with proof that the letter from Dublin Castle had been forged, MacNeill was rightly incensed. On Easter Saturday he sent out orders countermanding the Rising: 'Volunteers have been completely deceived. All orders for action are hereby cancelled, and on no account will action now be taken.' [Dangerfield, p. 172]

Dangerfield, *The Damnable Question*

In the meantime, Sir Roger Casement, whose efforts to recruit Irish prisoners-of-war to fight against the British had met with little success, was landed by German submarine on the Kerry coast. Casement was disillusioned by the lack of support he had received and came ashore intending to advise against the Rising. But he was arrested on the beach. Thus by Easter Sunday plans were in complete disarray. MacNeill had ordered the Volunteers to take no part in the Rising. The German arms shipment was at the bottom of Queenstown harbour, Casement was in custody.

But the intransigent members of the IRB were not to be put off. They deceived MacNeill again by apparently going along with his instructions, cancelling the orders for parades in Dublin on Easter Sunday, while at the same time making preparations for the Rising to begin on Easter Monday. The amended orders involved the seizure of a number of key posts in Dublin: the General Post Office, the Four Courts, the South Dublin Union, the Mendicity Institution, Jacob's Biscuit Factory, Boland's Mills and St Stephen's Green. These were to be garrisoned in the hope that this venture would fire resistance elsewhere in Ireland, hardly a likely prospect after MacNeill's instructions. Connolly evidently had few illusions. 'We are going to be slaughtered', he said to his friend William O'Brien.

In the street fighting that followed about 1600 rebels faced up to 12 000 British troops equipped with artillery and aided by the gunboat *Helga*. Contrary to expectation, the British showed no reluctance to destroy valuable property with shell fire. Despite heroic resistance the final outcome was never in doubt. The last fighting came to an end on Sunday 30 April. At that point Connolly and Pearse gave orders for unconditional surrender of the posts still held. The Rising cost the lives of 450, with a further 2614 wounded. Included in these figures were 116 British soldiers killed and 368 wounded. It is impossible to distinguish between the insurgents and innocent civilians caught in the cross-fire so far as the other casualties are concerned.

Eamonn de Valera, Easter Rebel and future Prime Minister of Ireland

Up to this point the Rising could be seen as a futile enterprise, causing needless loss of life and destruction. This is how it evidently appeared to the citizens of Dublin when the rebels were escorted to gaol. But the British Commander, General Maxwell, was determined to exact fierce punishment and 3430 men and 79 women were taken into custody. Many were subsequently released after interrogation, but 1841 were interned in England. Much more serious were the death sentences carried out on 15 of the leaders. Among them James Connolly was so badly wounded that he had to be propped on a chair; Joseph Plunkett was dying of tuberculosis; and William Pearse, Padraic's brother, could not by any stretch of the imagination be described as a ring-leader. De Valera escaped the death penalty partly because representations were made on his behalf by the American Consul in Dublin, partly because by the time his turn came, the British government realised the damage they were doing by treating their prisoners as traitors. Pearse and his fellows thus achieved more by their deaths than they could possibly have accomplished had they been allowed to survive. Their heroism exposed the vindictiveness of British rule; it also invested the cause of militant Irish nationalism with a false lustre.

Sackville Street, Dublin after the Rising

Until the Easter Rising, British policy in Ireland after 1914 had been a matter of letting sleeping dogs lie. Augustine Birrell, the moderate and conciliatory Chief Secretary, had turned a blind eye to the activities of the Irish Volunteers. He got on well with John Redmond and, left to themselves, these two men would have readily postponed the settlement of Ireland's problems until the end of the war. But the Rising changed everything. Birrell resigned, to be replaced by H. E. Duke. Real power remained, however, with the military authorities – General Maxwell until November 1916 and Lord French, who became Lord Lieutenant of Ireland in May 1918.

On the Irish side Redmond's authority diminished with every by-election as Sinn Fein candidates began to win seats from the Irish Nationalists. In January 1917, Count Plunkett, father of Joseph Plunkett who had been put to death after the Rising, was elected for North Roscommon. In July, De Valera, released from gaol a month earlier, won East Clare in a campaign in which he had voiced the wish 'that the British Empire will be blown in ruins'.

In the face of such opposition, British policy was an inept mixture of conciliation and threat. In May 1916 Lloyd George was dispatched to Dublin in the hope that his negotiating skills might provide a formula for Home Rule on which Redmond and Carson could agree. The critical issue, as always, was Ulster. For a brief moment it looked as though a compromise was near. By promising Redmond that the exclusion of Ulster from a united Ireland would only be temporary, and by guaranteeing to Carson that it would be permanent, Lloyd George papered over the cracks. But when it became clear that Conservative members of the government such as Walter Long and Lord Lansdowne would never tolerate a settlement which did not protect the right of Ulstermen to withdraw from the rest of Ireland for the foreseeable future, the negotiations came to an abrupt end. Redmond felt betrayed and was unfairly discredited by his countrymen.

A final attempt at a negotiated settlement was made in July 1917 when an Irish Convention was summoned. But Sinn Fein refused to participate and the Ulster Unionists proved as intransigent as ever. Though the Convention lingered on until April 1918, it had no real prospect of success.

The greatest blunder in British policy was to raise, unnecessarily as it transpired, the issue of conscription. Faced with the final desperate German onslaught on the Western Front in March 1918, the War Cabinet decided to extend the Military Service Act to Ireland. Lloyd George defended this decision to his colleagues on 6 April in these words:

> I do not believe it possible in this country to tear up single businesses, to take fathers of 45 and upwards to fight the battle of Catholic nationality on the Continent without deep resentment at the spectacle of sturdy young Catholics in Ireland spending their time in increasing the difficulties of this country by drilling and compelling us to keep troops in Ireland ...
> [Dangerfield, p. 275]

Dangerfield, *The Damnable Question*

Under the terms of the Act, conscription would be extended to Ireland by Order in Council when the government deemed it appropriate to do so. Lloyd George intended to sweeten the pill by coupling with it the granting of Home Rule. But so long as the Ulster question was not settled, that offer could not be made.

In fact, conscription never came into operation, but while the threat remained it united the opposition in Ireland as nothing else could have done. The Irish Nationalist party withdrew from the House of Commons and joined with Sinn Fein in urging all Irishmen to take a pledge 'solemnly to one another to resist conscription by the most effective means at our disposal'. The Catholic bishops, who had previously condemned the use of force, issued a manifesto urging the Irish people to resist conscription 'by every means consonant with the law of God'. Ironically, not only did the threat of conscription have no effect on recruitment, it increased the security problem in Ireland to the point that by October 1918 there were 87 500 British troops stationed there.

In a final error of judgment Lord French ordered the arrest of Sinn Fein leaders in May 1918 and 73 were deported to England, including De Valera, Arthur Griffith and William Cosgrave. They were suspected of having dealings with Germany but the government offered no evidence. In June, Griffith turned his arrest to good account, winning a by-election at East Cavan. It was an indication of growing support for Sinn Fein.

When the General Election came in December 1918 it revealed how far opinion had shifted. Sinn Fein candidates stood on a platform which called for the establishment of an Irish Republic, to be achieved by withdrawal from the Westminster Parliament and the formation of a constituent assembly in Ireland. Many of the candidates had to campaign from prison and the election manifesto was heavily censored. Even so, the verdict of the polls was decisively in favour of Sinn Fein.

Irish MP's	prior to the 1918 election	after the 1918 election
Irish Nationalist	68	6
Independent	10	–
Unionist	18	26
Sinn Fein	7	73

It is true that nearly a third of the electorate failed to vote and that Sinn Fein's share of the popular vote was still only 47%. It was still enough to change the face of Irish politics and to make the task of reaching agreement even harder than it had been in 1914.

Ireland 1918–23

The hopes aroused in Nationalist circles by the success of the Sinn Fein party were only to be partially realised, and then only after years of bitter struggle. In the election manifesto put forward by the Lloyd George Coalition in November 1918, the position of the British government towards the Irish problem was clearly spelt out: 'But there are two paths that are closed – the one leading to a complete severance of Ireland from the British Empire, and the other to the forcible submission of Ulster to a Home Rule Parliament against their will.' It was precisely down these roads that the supporters of Sinn Fein wished to travel. Painful progress was made down the first; the second still remains closed.

Between January 1919 and July 1921, Ireland experienced what have come to be known euphemistically as 'The Troubles'. True to their election promises, the Sinn Fein members refused to take their seats at Westminster and assembled in their own Parliament, known as the Dail, in Dublin. For the next two years Southern Ireland was ruled by two competing authorities. On 3 February De Valera escaped from Lincoln gaol and on 1 April he was elected President of the new Irish Republic. At first, the British government tolerated its existence, but as attacks on the Royal Irish Constabulary mounted, and the Dail appeared to be making its authority felt, tension increased. In September 1919 Sinn Fein was banned in several counties and the Dail forbidden to meet. From this point on repression became official British policy.

The myopia of British policy was revealed in the Government of Ireland Act, 1920 which indicated how little the British government understood Irish aspirations. It provided for separate parliaments in Dublin and Belfast with 128 and 52 seats respectively; 42 Irish members would continue to sit at Westminster and the British government would retain control over war and peace, the conduct of foreign affairs, customs and excise, the army and navy, land and agricultural policy, and the maintenance of law and order. Almost the only encouraging feature was the provision for a Council of Ireland on which 20 members of each parliament would sit as a step towards eventual unification. The Act was dismissed derisively by Sinn Fein as 'a scheme for the plunder and partition of Ireland'. In Ulster it was grudgingly accepted as a second best alternative to the maintenance of the Union.

Having rejected the Government of Ireland Act, the Sinn Fein party now adopted a policy of violence. The Irish Republican Brotherhood and the Irish Volunteers emerged as the Irish Republican Army (IRA). Their numbers have been estimated at about 3000 activists with a further 12 000 supporters. Against them were ranged about 40 000 British troops, 14 000 police and some 7000 additional recruits to the Royal Irish Constabulary (RIC). These were divided into two groups: the Auxiliaries, recruited from ex-British army officers, and the so-called Black and Tans, mainly recruited from non-commissioned ranks. Both groups acquired an unsavoury and justified reputation for brutality and violence.

Granted the disparity in numbers the IRA could only make their presence felt by pursuing a war of raids and ambushes. Frequently disguised as civilians they were hard to detect. This inevitably provoked reprisals, very often upon innocent bystanders, and the conflict became increasingly ugly. A typical episode occurred in November 1920 when 14 British officers were killed in their hotel bedrooms in Dublin. British troops retaliated by opening fire on a crowd at a football match the following day, killing nine spectators. The ambushing of a group of Black and Tans in December in Cork led to a savage attack on the city in which 300 buildings were destroyed and £300 million worth of damage inflicted.

As news of these atrocities filtered through to the British public there were growing demands for a truce. On 23 June 1921, on his visit to open the Northern Ireland Parliament in Belfast, George V appealed to all Irishmen 'to pause, to stretch out the hand of forbearance and conciliation, to forgive and to forget, and to join in making for the land they love a new era of peace, contentment and goodwill.' On 11 July a truce was called and negotiations began.

There were four main points at issue: the status of the new Irish state, partition, the right of Britain to the use of Irish ports for purposes of defence, and the Oath of Allegiance to the Crown. On the Irish side the chief negotiators were Michael Collins and Arthur Griffith, on the English side they were Lloyd George, Churchill and Lord Birkenhead. De Valera remained in Dublin on the understanding that any terms would have to be approved by the Dail before they would be accepted. Lloyd George wooed Arthur Griffith with the promise of a Boundary Commission to determine the frontier between Northern and Southern Ireland, and a strong hint that the Ulster thus defined would be so reduced as not to be viable. The British government were prepared to extend dominion status to Ireland, while the Irish delegation accepted the right of British warships to use the ports of Berehaven, Cork, Lough Swilly and Belfast. But negotiations nearly came to a halt over the Oath of Allegiance. De Valera was strongly opposed to the inclusion of Ireland within the British Empire. Lloyd George was equally insistent that Ireland must remain in it. De Valera was prepared to recognise the King as head of the Associated States but that was as far as he would go. On the final day of the negotiations, 5 December, the British offered a new formula:

> I ... do solemnly swear true faith and allegiance to the Constitution of the Irish Free State as by law established and that I will be faithful to HM King George V, his heirs and successors at law in virtue of the common citizenship of Ireland with Great Britain and her adherence and membership of the group of nations known as the British Commonwealth.
> [Lyons, pp. 435–6]

F. S. L. Lyons, *Ireland since the Famine* (1971)

Griffith was prepared to sign the Treaty on these terms but the other members of the Irish delegation had serious reservations. Lloyd George insisted that all must sign and threatened that should they fail to do so 'it is war, and war within three days'. Faced with this ultimatum they signed, Collins reputedly remarking as he did so that he was signing his own death warrant. (See Points at Issue, pp. 201–3)

The Treaty did not solve the Irish problem. On 8 December when the Irish cabinet saw it there was an angry debate and it was accepted by only four votes to three, the dissentients being De Valera, Cathal Brugha and Austin Stack. On 7 January 1922 the Dail approved the Treaty by an equally slender majority, 64 votes to 57. De Valera was voted out of the Presidency on the same day by 60 votes to 58.

With the signing of the Irish Treaty, direct British involvement in Ireland's affairs might be thought to have come to an end. But Britain's continuing responsibility for Ulster and continuing pressure to redefine the imperial relationship between Britain and the Irish Free State meant that British politicians were still caught in the Irish tangle.

So strong was opposition to the Treaty in some quarters that before long the anti-Treaty forces were adopting the same tactics towards the new Irish government that they had used against the British. On 15 March 1922 De Valera founded a new party, *Cumann na Poblachta* (League of the Republic), and declared in a series of speeches that if the Treaty were accepted another civil war would have to be fought. In one of them he went so far as to say that if the Irish Volunteers were to continue the work of the last four years 'They would have to wade through Irish blood, through the blood of the soldiers of the Irish Government, and through, perhaps, the blood of some of the members of the Government in order to get Irish freedom ...' [Lyons, p. 452] It was not long before his words were taken at face value. On 13 April Rory O'Connor and a group of anti-Treaty Republicans seized the Four Courts in Dublin, posing a visible threat to the legitimacy of the existing Irish government. Desperate efforts were made to avert civil war. On 20 May Collins and De Valera signed an electoral pact under which constituencies in the forthcoming election would be shared between pro and anti-Treaty candidates on the basis of their existing strengths in the Dail. This would have ensured a small majority for the pro-Treaty forces but would also have guaranteed places in the new government to the opponents of the Treaty. The British government objected strongly to this arrangement and Collins repudiated the pact just before the election was held.

Lyons, *Ireland since the Famine*

Polling took place on 16 June and the results were announced on 24 June. The pro-Treaty forces gained a decisive majority, winning 58 seats against the 36 gained by the anti-Treaty party. It has been calculated that in terms of popular votes 486 419 were cast for pro-Treaty candidates and 133 864 for those opposed to the Treaty. [Coogan, p. 41] It is possible that this verdict might have been accepted but

T. P. Coogan, *Ireland since the Rising* (1966)

THE MAD BULL

FARMER CRAIG: "IF YOU CAN'T KEEP THAT BRUTE ON YOUR SIDE OF THE FENCE I SHALL DEAL WITH HIM AS I THINK FIT."

FARMER COLLINS: "WELL, BETWEEN YOU AND ME, I WISH TO GOD YE WOULD."

Punch 1922

once again violence intervened. On 22 June Field Marshal Sir Henry Wilson, former CIGS and since his retirement Northern Ireland's military adviser, was shot dead on the steps of his London home. His assassins were both members of the IRA but refused to divulge on whose orders they had acted. The British government assumed, wrongly as it transpired, that the orders must have emanated from the Four Courts. They insisted that Rory O'Connor and his garrison must be expelled and provided the Irish government with the weapons to carry out the operation. On 24 June the shelling of the Four Courts began. It led to the outbreak of the Irish Civil War.

The war was fought with brutality on both sides. Liam Lynch, Chief of Staff on the anti-Treaty side, ordered the killing of all members of the Dail who had voted for the Treaty, a threat that was speedily met by reprisals on the government side. Altogether, it has been calculated that between September 1922 and July 1923, 665 lives were lost and a further 3000 were wounded. Among the victims were Arthur Griffith who died of a heart attack, and Michael Collins, killed in an ambush. Among opponents of the Treaty, Cathal Brugha was killed in the fighting over the Four Courts; Erskine Childers and Rory O'Connor were among the 77 executed, in Childers's case, for possessing a firearm. Probably the last of the war's victims was Kevin O'Higgins, Minister for Home Affairs, who was assassinated after attending Mass in 1927.

Thus the Treaty brought no peace to the South. In the North the Government of Ireland Act of 1920 was little more successful. IRA attacks across the border provoked reprisals on the Catholic community in Northern Ireland. Lloyd George complained in 1922 that 400 Catholics had been killed and a further 1200 injured without a single person being brought to justice. The security problem led to the passage of the Special Powers Act in 1922 which, among other things, enabled the Minister for Home Affairs to detain suspects without trial and order searches without warrant. The Catholic minority, one-third of the population of Northern Ireland, owed their allegiance to the Irish Free State and for the first few years refused to take part in any political activity in the North.

The fundamental problem left unsolved was, of course, the division between North and South. Partition was not so much a cause as a sympton of that division. As one historian of Ulster has put it, partition 'is like a tourniquet applied to stop bleeding at a particular time and in particular circumstances .... It might be said to have only one positive advantage, but this one is paramount. Partition is preferable to civil war.' [Stewart, p. 157] Between 1919 and 1923 Ireland had experienced civil war. The solutions provided by the Government of Ireland Act and the Irish Treaty were at best temporary. But they provided a respite.

A. T. Q. Stewart, *The Narrow Ground, Aspects of Ulster, 1609–1969* (1977)

Anglo-Irish Relations, 1923–39: the Dismantling of the Treaty

Between 1923 and 1939 two distinct trends can be discerned in Anglo-Irish relations. On the one hand, the divisions between North and South became more sharply defined and the prospects of reunification receded; on the other, the remaining links binding Southern Ireland to the Empire were gradually snapped.

The Boundary Commission envisaged in the Treaty was appointed in 1924 under a South African Chairman, Judge Feetham. It had an unhappy history. The Unionist party in the North refused to nominate a representative and the British government had to do so instead; their choice fell on J. R. Fisher, a former newspaper editor.

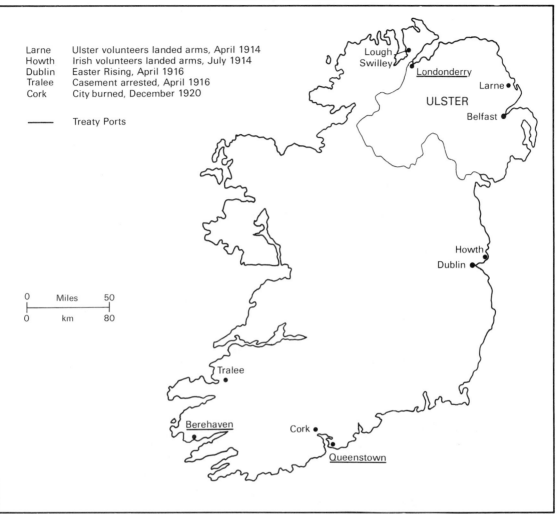

Larne   Ulster volunteers landed arms, April 1914
Howth   Irish volunteers landed arms, July 1914
Dublin Easter Rising, April 1916
Tralee Casement arrested, April 1916
Cork   City burned, December 1920

——— Treaty Ports

The Irish government nominated Eoin MacNeill, former head of the Irish Volunteers. The Commission sat throughout most of 1925; its report was leaked to the *Morning Post* in November, whereupon MacNeill resigned rather than accept its recommendations which would have involved the transfer of part of East Donegal to Northern Ireland. The Irish government were equally reluctant to accept the Commission's findings and immediately sent a delegation to London. Here a Tripartite Agreement was reached between the British, Dublin and Belfast based governments. The existing frontier was left unaltered, to include the Six Counties of Antrim, Armagh, Down, Fermanagh, Londonderry and Tyrone; the Irish government would be released from certain financial obligations (its share of the British public debt and war pensions); and the Northern Ireland government would assume responsibility for those matters relating to Northern Ireland which would previously have been given to the Council of Ireland. Thus the only forum where North and South might have met came to an inglorious and abortive end. The effect of the Agreement was to strengthen the Boundary without altering any of its anomalies or reducing the size of the irreconcilable Catholic minority in Ulster.

THE IRISH TANGLE

ULSTER'S BOUNDARIES, 1925

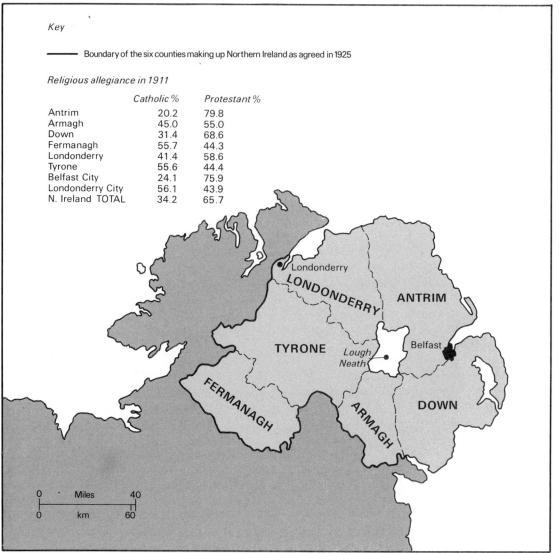

Key

——— Boundary of the six counties making up Northern Ireland as agreed in 1925

Religious allegiance in 1911

	Catholic %	Protestant %
Antrim	20.2	79.8
Armagh	45.0	55.0
Down	31.4	68.6
Fermanagh	55.7	44.3
Londonderry	41.4	58.6
Tyrone	55.6	44.4
Belfast City	24.1	75.9
Londonderry City	56.1	43.9
N. Ireland TOTAL	34.2	65.7

The first change in the relationship between Britain and the Irish Free State arose out of the Imperial Conference held in London in 1926. Pressure was brought by South Africa and Canada, as well as the Irish government, to redefine dominion status. Arthur Balfour, Lord President of the Council, was pressed into service as Secretary of the Inter-Imperial Relations Committee. It was reputedly Balfour who welded the various suggestions made to him into an artfully worded formula that retained the semblance of imperial authority while conceding the substance. The Dominions were henceforth to be recognised as 'Autonomous communities within the British Empire, equal in status, in no way subordinate one to another in any aspect of their domestic or external affairs, though united by a common allegiance to the Crown, and freely associated as members of the British Commonwealth of Nations.' In 1931 this definition was incorporated into the Statute of Westminster.

The significance of this step was only realised when De Valera became Prime Minister in 1932. De Valera had forfeited the allegiance of the IRA in 1925; he founded his own party, Fianna Fail, in 1926, and entered the Dail in 1927, overcoming his scruples about the Oath of Allegiance, which all members had to take, by dismissing it as an empty formula. In 1932 Fianna Fail campaigned on a programme of ending the Oath and won 72 seats. For the next 16 years De Valera was to be Prime Minister. He soon proceeded to use the powers attributed to him under the Statute of Westminster. In 1932 the Oath of Allegiance was duly abolished. The Governor-General, a distinguished ex-member of the Indian Civil Service, was dismissed and replaced by a country shop-keeper.

In 1935 the Irish Nationality and Citizenship Act gave Irishmen their distinct identity, while the Aliens Act defined as Aliens British citizens who were not citizens of the Irish Free State. In 1936 the External Relations Act permitted the monarchy to remain 'for the purpose of the appointment of diplomatic and consular representatives', but all references to the King were eliminated in the new Constitution that was produced in 1937. The office of Governor-General was abolished. The new Constitution laid claim to all 32 counties of Ireland which was described as 'a sovereign, independent, democratic state'. All that remained was to remove the last vestiges of royal authority and proclaim Ireland a republic, a step that was finally taken in 1948.

The British government could do nothing to prevent these moves. Indeed, the Judicial Committee of the Privy Council reported in 1935 that the Irish government were fully entitled to abrogate the terms of the Irish Treaty under the Statute of Westminster. On one issue, however, retaliation was possible. Under financial agreements signed in 1923 and 1926 the Irish government had undertaken to hand over the interest payments due on loans the British government had made to the Irish peasantry, enabling them to buy their own holdings under the various Land Purchase Acts passed between 1891 and 1909. These payments were known as Land Annuities and amounted to £3 million a year. As he had promised in his election campaign, De Valera withheld these payments from 1932 onwards. Britain retaliated by imposing tariffs on Irish imports in order to recoup the sums lost. This in turn gave De Valera the opportunity he had been seeking to embark on a policy of economic self-sufficiency, and tariffs were placed on British exports to Ireland. The tariff war continued for the next six years, with damaging effects on both countries. British coal exports fell off considerably and Irish cattle prices dropped catastrophically.

An improvement in Anglo-Irish relations began, however, with the appointment of Malcolm MacDonald, Ramsay's son, to be Dominions Secretary in 1936. MacDonald made it clear that he would like to settle the issue. As the international climate darkened it became imperative to ensure that Britain would have a friendly Ireland on her doorstep. For his part, De Valera was worried that Britain's right to use of the Treaty ports might compromise Irish neutrality in the event of a war. Neville Chamberlain, who became Prime Minister in 1937, supported MacDonald's initiative and serious negotiations opened in January 1938. They were concluded in April and three issues were resolved. Britain gave up her rights to the three Treaty ports in the Irish Free State (Cork, Lough Swilly and Berehaven); De Valera undertook to pay £10 million in final settlement of British claims to the Land Annuities; and each side withdrew the tariffs they had imposed on the other's exports. Churchill strongly attacked the handing back of the Treaty ports as 'an improvident example of appeasement', and their loss did indeed have serious consequences in the battle of the Atlantic in the Second World War. But the Chiefs of Staff, while they would have preferred Ireland as an active ally, advised the surrender of the ports if that was the necessary price for a well-disposed Ireland. Remembering what had happened in the First World War they may well have been right.

As a result of the London Agreement, relations between the British and Irish governments reached a new degree of amity. But the IRA delivered an unhappy reminder that there were still extremists to whom a divided Ireland was an affront which justified any atrocity. In a bombing campaign launched in 1939 there were 120 separate incidents in Britain which cost 6 lives and 125 serious injuries. On this occasion, however, De Valera's response was very different from what it might have been in 1916 or 1922. The IRA was declared to be an illegal organisation and the Offences Against the State Bill was passed, enabling suspects to be imprisoned without trial. Though Ulster remained a continuing bone of contention, the British and Irish governments had learned to live with each other.

BRITAIN AND INDIA ═══════════════════════════════ C

The Effects of War

The problems faced by British governments in India were those of Ireland writ large. In both cases arguments developed not so much over the direction of constitutional change as over its pace and its destination. In India, too, there was the problem of how to protect the interests of a large religious minority, in this case the Muslims, when power passed into the hands of a majority belonging to a different religious persuasion, the Hindus. As with Ireland, the First World War had the effect of raising the political temperature and bringing forward the demands for independence.

In 1914 Indians volunteered in huge numbers to serve the King-Emperor. Altogether, 1 200 000 were recruited. Of these, 138 000 combatants fought in France, 675 000 in Mesopotamia and 144 000 in Egypt and Syria. Throughout the war they served with exemplary courage, often in conditions of appalling hardship, as on the Western Front in 1914 and in the campaign which led to the surrender of the garrison at Kut in 1916. The British garrison in India was reduced to 15 000 men. Indians took over the posts of many British administrators. An initial grant of £100 million was made to the British Government in 1914, and a further £20–£30 million was contributed annually thereafter. But as the war dragged on, imperial fervour waned. War against the Turks put a strain on Muslim troops who still recognised the Turkish Sultan as Kalifa. In 1916 the nationalist Congress Party and the Muslim League signed the Lucknow Pact, agreeing to join forces in the cause of Indian independence. Faced with this evidence of a united opposition the Secretary of State for India, Edwin Montagu, persuaded the cabinet to promise a measure of constitutional advance.

In a speech to the Commons on 26 April 1917 Montagu announced that 'The policy of H.M. Government, with which the Government of India are in complete accord, is that of the increasing association of Indians in every branch of the administration, and the gradual development of self-governing institutions, with a view to the progressive realisation of responsible government in India as an integral part of the Empire.' [Spear, p. 336] Montagu visited India in 1917–18 to see for himself how far it would be safe to go. He and the Viceroy, Lord Chelmsford, produced a report in July 1918 and this formed the basis of the so-called Montford Reforms which came into effect in 1921. They were framed very much with a view to implementing Montagu's declaration of policy. At the provincial level 'transferred subjects', including industry, education, public health and agriculture, were to be the responsibility of Indian ministers answerable to provincial legislatures. 'Reserved subjects', revenue, law, justice and police, would still be looked after by provincial governors and their councils. This was the system known as Dyarchy. At the centre there was to be a bi-cameral legislature made up of a legislative assembly with 106 elected and 40 nominated members and a Council of State with 61 members. The franchise was carefully tailored to each institution. Three million would have the right to vote for provincial legislatures, 1 million for the legislative assembly and 17 000 for the Council of State.

P. Spear, *The Oxford History of Modern India* (1978)

Further safeguards were built into the system in that while the Viceroy's Council would now contain three Indian members out of seven, the Viceroy was given power to legislate by ordinance for six months in the case of an emergency; he could pass laws if certified as necessary to the safety and tranquillity of India; and certain major items of expenditure, notably defence, were outside the control of the assemblies.

The Indian opposition

It was characteristic of Anglo-Indian relations that Indian demands would always be one step, if not two, in advance of the concessions Britain was prepared to make. The Nationalists can be broadly divided into those who were prepared to work within the existing constitutional framework, and to participate in the new political structures that Britain devised, and those for whom the pace of change was so slow that they rejected the means by which it might be achieved. This group can be further divided into those, like Gandhi and Nehru, who were prepared to adopt a policy of passive resistance to the Raj as a way of bringing pressure to bear, and those such as Subhas Chandra Bose for whom the use of violence was seen as a legitimate tactic. Organised opposition was largely in the hands of the Indian National Congress. This body was founded in 1885 with the blessing of the then Viceroy, Lord Dufferin. Its creator was an ex-member of the Indian Civil Service, Allan Octavian Hume. At its first session, its 70 members were all self-chosen. But there were 450 members at the second session in 1888. By 1920 it had developed all the apparatus of a political party: local branches, annual conferences, a working committee and an elected president. At first it had links with the British administration, members of the legislative council being selected from its ranks. But these links were severed as it adopted a more hostile stance to British rule.

During the war the moderate leadership of G. K. Gokhale, who was a constitutionalist, gave place to the more radical leadership of B. Tilak who committed Congress to a policy of immediate home rule. But the man who came to exert the greatest influence on Congress was Mahatma Gandhi. Gandhi began his adult life as a loyal servant of the Raj. He studied law and qualified as a barrister at Lincoln's Inn. He organised a field ambulance to serve with the British forces in the Boer

War and did the same in 1914. But his experiences as a lawyer defending Indians in South Africa exposed him to racism in its most blatant and uncompromising form. His years there convinced him that the rule of the white man in India must be brought to an end. When he finally returned to India from South Africa in 1915 he joined the Congress party and soon became its most effective spokesman. But while Gandhi never wavered in his devotion to the cause of Indian independence, he was equally committed to non-violence. In 1920 he urged on Congress a policy of 'swaraj', freedom; but this was to be gained by exercising what he called 'soul force'. This derived from the Hindu concept of satyagraha, the vow to hold to the truth and convince one's opponent of the rightness of one's aim; and ahimsa, the avoiding of harm. Soul force might be exercised through a hartal, a day of fast and suspension of normal business (the equivalent of a one-day strike); the refusal to pay taxes; or the deliberate flouting of the law to court imprisonment. British opponents of Gandhi argued that there was a strong element of coercion in such tactics and they could easily spill over into violence, as they sometimes did. But Gandhi remained faithful to his principles and on several occasions called off his civil disobedience campaigns – to the consternation of his supporters – when they looked like getting out of hand. If he did a great deal to stimulate a sense of nationalism, particularly among the Indian peasantry, Gandhi was also invaluable to the British in helping to contain the forces he encouraged within peaceful channels.

Indian Nationalists: Mohandas Ghandi, seen at the Round Table Conference, 1931

Sabhas Chandra Bose with George Landsbury, in 1928. (Bose later founded the Indian National Liberation Army)

Limited as they were in Indian eyes, the Montford reforms were at least evidence of Britain's good intentions. But they did not come into effect until 1921. By that time it was already too late. In 1919, faced with the threat of disorder, the Indian government passed the Rowlatt Bills giving provincial governors the power to intern without trial, and providing for trials without juries in political cases. The Indian members of the Viceroy's Council all advised against the bills and they were met with a wave of protests.

In the city of Amritsar in the Punjab a hartal was proclaimed which passed off peacefully, but was followed by the arrest and deportation of two of the nationalist leaders. This provoked serious rioting in which five Europeans were killed, two banks were burned to the ground and a European missionary, Miss Sherwood, was attacked and left for dead. She was subsequently taken in and looked after by an Indian family. The governor of the Punjab, Sir Michael O'Dwyer, sent General Dyer to restore order. Dyer banned all public meetings but despite this, on 13 April, a crowd assembled in the Jallianwalla Bagh, a large enclosed space with only one exit. Dyer arrived with 2 armoured cars, 90 riflemen and 40 Gurkhas armed with Kukris. Without warning he ordered his soldiers to open fire on the densely packed and unarmed crowd. Escape was impossible; 1605 rounds were fired, killing 379 and wounding a further 1200. Martial law was proclaimed in the city and the notorious 'crawling order' imposed, requiring all Indians to crawl past the site of the attack on Miss Sherwood when using the passage where it had occurred. News of Dyer's activities took some time to leak out. When they did so Congress immediately mounted their own investigation and the British government appointed the Hunter enquiry on which Indians were represented. The Majority Report, signed by all the European members, criticised Dyer for firing without warning and for continuing to fire unnecessarily. The Minority Report, signed by the Indian members, was much more critical. Dyer was relieved of his command and sent home on sick-leave.

Dyer continued to claim that he had acted out of duty, 'my horrible, dirty duty', and O'Dwyer, his political superior, maintained that it was only Dyer's ruthlessness that had averted much worse disorders. Though the government's treatment of Dyer was approved in a Commons debate by 230 votes to 129, a House of Lords motion deploring the injustice shown to Dyer was passed by 40 votes. The *Morning Post* opened a fund to pay Dyer's defence costs and it raised the huge sum of £26 000, including a £10 cheque from Rudyard Kipling. It was as much the unofficial reaction to the Amritsar massacre as the massacre itself that affronted Indian opinion. Nehru commented on the affects the House of Lords decision had on him: 'I realised then, more vividly than I had done before, how brutal and immoral imperialism was and how it had entered into the souls of the British upper classes.' [cited in Brecher, p. 66]

M. Brecher, *Nehru* (1959)

After Amritsar British authority in India was never the same. Another inevitable consequence was the radicalising of the Indian nationalist movement. Gandhi launched the first of his civil disobedience campaigns. The Montford reforms were implemented in a mood of increasing disaffection, and were rejected by Congress. There were outbreaks of violence on the Malabar coast and a police station was set on fire at Chauri-Chaura. Gandhi was arrested in 1922 and sentenced to six years' imprisonment. Order was slowly re-established but the political climate remained stormy.

Hopes Unfulfilled: 1926–32

In 1926 a new Viceroy was appointed, Lord Irwin. He proved to be an inspired choice on Baldwin's part. Irwin was a devout Christian who developed a considerable admiration for Gandhi. He was determined to bring peaceful change to India. The new Secretary of State for India, Lord Birkenhead, on the other hand, had no faith in the Indian capacity for self-government. Birkenhead decided to advance the ten-year review of the working of the Montford reforms to 1927 so that he could determine the composition of the Commission appointed for the purpose, and if possible influence its findings. He appointed as its chairman Sir John Simon, whose Liberalism had never been more than skin-deep. The other members were all MPs though two Labour members were included, Vernon Hartshorn and Clement Attlee.

Birkenhead and Irwin made the fatal mistake of not including any Indians on the Commission. Its presence, one historian has remarked, was 'a political disaster'. [Spear, p. 350] The Commission raised unrealistic hopes and affronted Indian susceptibilities. Wherever it went it was greeted with hostility. Its progress was accompanied by demonstrations organised by the Congress party. At one of these, staged at Lucknow, Nehru himself experienced a charge of mounted police and it strengthened his determination to continue the struggle for independence. When the Simon Report eventually emerged in 1930 it confined its recommendations to self-government in the provinces. But at its annual meetings in 1928 and 1929 the Congress party had already passed resolutions calling first for dominion status within

Spear, *The Oxford History of Modern India*

one year, and in 1929 for complete independence, also to be achieved within a year. The gap between the two sides had widened.

Faced with this situation, Irwin decided that a conciliatory gesture was needed. On 31 October 1929 he announced with the cabinet's approval that 'the eventual issue of Indian constitutional progress would be the attainment of Dominion status.' For a time it looked as though Congress would be prepared to co-operate in the Round Table Conference which Irwin also suggested. But an angry debate in the House of Commons, in which Birkenhead and Churchill both attacked the pledge of dominion status, aroused doubts. Irwin was asked whether he could guarantee the immediate granting of dominion status, which he clearly had no power to do. The hopes raised were dashed. At the Lahore Conference which met in December 1929 Congress resolved to boycott the Round Table talks, to demand complete independence and to embark on a campaign of civil disobedience.

As a first step 172 members of the Congress party resigned their seats in provincial legislatures and in the legislative assembly. On 26 January 1930 Independence Day was proclaimed. An Indian Declaration of Independence was drawn up which echoed its American forerunner: 'We believe that it is the inalienable right of the Indian people, as of any other people, to have freedom and to enjoy the fruits of their toil ... we believe also that if any government deprives a people of these rights, and oppresses them, the people have a further right to alter it and to abolish it ....' [Brecher, p. 147]

Brecher, *Nehru*

In March 1930 Gandhi launched his own personal campaign of civil disobedience. He chose as his target the hated salt tax. By now aged 61, he marched from Ahmedabad to Nandi on the west coast of India, a distance of 241 miles, and on his arrival solemnly set about making illegal, and probably uneatable, salt. His gesture caught the Indian imagination and was copied throughout India. By the end of the year 60 000 political prisoners, including Gandhi and Nehru, were under arrest. There were outbreaks of violence at Chittagong in Bengal, Shotapur in Bombay Province and in Peshawar in the North West. Here the local Congress party took over the city for five days and two platoons of the Royal Garhwali Rifles refused to fire on a rioting crowd.

On 11 November the first session of the Round Table Conference opened in London, but without any representatives from Congress it could make little headway. In January 1931 Gandhi was released. Between 17 February and 5 March he had a series of talks with Lord Irwin. Churchill commented on 'the nauseating and humiliating spectacle of the one-time fakir, striding half naked up to the steps of the Viceroy's palace, there to negotiate and to parley on equal terms with the representative of the King-Emperor'. [Brecher, p. 171] But the talks were hard-headed and bore fruit. The civil disobedience campaign was called off and Gandhi agreed to take part in the next session of the Round Table Conference, a decision that was endorsed by Congress at its next conference at Karachi.

Brecher, *Nehru*

In September 1931 the second session of the Round Table Conference got under way, this time with Gandhi in attendance. It proved a fiasco. It soon got bogged down over the question of representation of minority groups in the projected federal assembly. Gandhi insisted that there should be no separate representation for minorities other than Muslims and Sikhs. He also urged that all such questions should be settled after rather than before the granting of dominion status. Though there was goodwill on both sides the session ended in deadlock. Gandhi returned to find a new and less sympathetic Viceroy, Lord Willingdon. Congress in the meantime had lent its support to a tax strike in the United Provinces where peasants had suffered from a very bad harvest. Gandhi condemned the Viceroy's emergency legislation, revived his civil disobedience campaign and in January 1932 was arrested yet again. The Congress party was banned and thousands of its supporters jailed. The path of conciliation, for the time being, was closed.

The Government of India Act, 1935

The Round Table Conferences and the Simon Commission were not entirely fruitless. Sir Samuel Hoare, who became Secretary of State for India in 1931, was determined that some progress should be made towards dominion status, and in this he was strongly supported by Baldwin. Over the next four years a long and complicated measure, the Government of India Act, went through all its various stages, finally becoming law in 1935. A White Paper containing the main proposals was presented to the House of Commons in 1933. This then went through a Joint Committee made up of members of the two Houses of parliament. It held 159 meetings and its work was only completed in November 1934. The Act itself was strongly opposed by one faction in the Conservative party which formed itself into the Imperial Defence League. It attracted the support of 70 Conservative MPs, including Carson, Brendan Bracken, Lennox Boyd and most notably, Churchill. The Conservative Party Conference, meeting at Bristol in October 1934, approved the government's proposals by only 540 votes to 523. Without Baldwin's advocacy it is likely that the Government of India Act would not have been passed.

The Act was based on two principles: an All India Federation at the centre to include all the princely states that could be induced to join; and full responsible government, that is to say, Indian ministers answerable to elected legislatures, at the provincial level. The electorate was widened to include 30 million people. This was a significant advance giving real power to Indian ministries, though provincial governors would retain special powers in emergencies. At the centre the proposals were a good deal less radical – 40% of the seats on the council of state and 33% of the seats on the legislative assembly were to be reserved for nominees of the princely states, lending a conservative bias to both bodies. The Viceroy would continue to be head of state and effective Prime Minister, responsible to a British Secretary of State and a British Parliament. He would retain powers over defence and external affairs. He would also have the right to act on his own initiative whenever he judged that there was a threat to the peace and tranquility of India. The central legislature would only come into operation when over half the princes had acceded to the federation, a goal that was never achieved.

K. Middlemas and J. Barnes, *Baldwin* (Weidenfeld & Nicolson, 1969)

The Act was attacked both in Britain for going too far and in India for not going far enough. Churchill dismissed it as 'a gigantic quilt, a jumbled crochet work, a monstrous sham built by the pigmies'. [Middlemas and Barnes, p. 714] Nehru, on the other hand, dismissed the Act as 'this new charter of slavery to strengthen the bonds of imperialist domination and to intensify the exploitation of our masses.' [Brecher, p. 222] Gandhi was more polite but equally cutting: 'India is still a prison, but the superintendant allows the prisoners to elect the officers who run the jail.' [Woodcock, p. 289]

Brecher, *Nehru*

Woodcock, *Who Killed the British Empire?*

Despite these criticisms Congress decided to allow party members to contest elections to the provincial legislatures. They won majorities in five out of the eleven provinces. Initially, Congressional politicians refused to take office until they received assurances that provincial governors would not use their emergency powers. Such a pledge the cabinet refused to give, but a conciliatory message from the Viceroy persuaded the Congress party to abandon that condition. In the end Congress party ministries were formed in seven provinces where they worked with reasonable success for the next two years. But no progress was made towards the creation of a federal government and legislature at the centre. The princes discussed terms of accession but came to no firm decision by the time war broke out in 1939. The Act revealed another limitation. In its emphasis upon majority rule it perhaps too readily assumed that Muslims would be content to be ruled by Hindu-dominated legislatures. In 1937 Jinnah, leader of the Muslim League, had indicated his willingness to co-operate with the Congress party in the forthcoming elections. But after they were over Muslim politicians found themselves cold-shouldered. In the United Provinces, for instance, an offer of coalition made to the League by Congress party candidates was withdrawn when Congress was seen to have a clear majority. In a Report commissioned by the Muslim League in 1938 it was concluded that Muslims were better off under British rule than under the Congress-dominated ministries.

The outbreak of the Second World War in 1939 exposed both the limitations of British policy and the constraints upon it. Lord Linlithgow, Viceroy since 1936, was fully within his rights in declaring that a state of war existed between Germany and the British Empire, including India. There was, as yet, no federal government for him to consult but he did not take the premiers of the provinces into his confidence, as he might have done. Congress, while sympathetic to the cause of anti-fascism, refused support for the war-effort unless India could participate as an independent nation. All Linlithgow could promise was dominion status at the end of the war. Congress duly ordered its ministries in the provincial governments to resign and the brief experiment in responsible government at the provincial level came to a premature end. Ironically, the resignation of the Congress ministries was hailed as 'A day of deliverance' by Jinnah, who pledged Muslim support for the British cause.

Anglo-Indian relations during the Second World War are reserved for separate treatment. Suffice it to say at this stage that British policy in the 1920s and 1930s had fallen far short of Indian aspirations; this meant that when war came, victory for the British Empire would take second place to the achievement of independence in the order of priorities so far as most Indian politicians were concerned. On the other hand, the Government of India Act of 1935 did provide a structure that might have proved workable had it not been for the religious divisions that separated Hindu and Muslim. Nor should the Amritsar Massacre, shameful as it was, blind us to the real efforts made by men such as Montagu, Irwin and Hoare to set India upon the road to self-government.

BRITAIN AND THE MIDDLE EAST ▬▬▬▬ D

Problems and Policies

Britain's influence in the Middle East was more extensive than ever before in her imperial history during the inter-war years. Egypt, despite achieving a nominal independence, remained effectively under British control. Aden, a Crown Colony since 1837, provided a base from which protectorates were eventually established over 25 sheikhdoms along the South Arabian coast. Britain appointed a political agent to the Sultan of Muscat and Oman, and through him controlled the Sultan's external relations. Britain also signed a series of treaties with the chain of territories on the West of the Persian Gulf: the Trucial States, Qatar, Bahrain and Kuwait. In most cases these treaties gave Britain exclusive rights to oil concessions within these tiny kingdoms in return for accepting the obligation to defend them from without.

With the destruction of the Ottoman Empire, Britain also became the mandatory power, with responsibility for all Ottoman territory between present-day Syria and the head of the Persian Gulf. British support for the Arab Revolt gave her a preponderant voice in the Arabian peninsula, where the rival houses of Ibn Saud and Hussein contended for power.

What were Britain's interests in this increasingly unstable area? First, the security of the Suez Canal; variously described as the 'lifeline' or the 'windpipe' of empire, the Canal linked Britain to India, Australia and New Zealand, and her possessions in the Far East. The protection of the Suez Canal remained a fundamental objective of British policy certainly up to 1956. Secondly, and growing in importance, came the safeguarding of Britain's oil supplies. In 1912 Winston Churchill, First Lord of the Admiralty at the time, took out a 51% shareholding in British Petroleum on behalf of the British government. The oil terminals at Basra and Haifa were obviously vulnerable targets which would be safer if included within Britain's sphere of influence. In addition there was the prospect of further discoveries. When Churchill, in a moment of frustration, suggested that Britain might pull out of Mesopotamia, Lloyd George rejoined: 'If we leave, we may find a year or two after we have departed that we have handed over to the French and the Americans some of the richest oil fields in the world.' [Gilbert, vol. IV, p. 818] It was a prescient warning.

M. Gilbert, *Winston S. Churchill*, vol. IV (1975)

A third interest, or perhaps it would be better to say obligation, was the fulfilment of Britain's promise to the Jews, in the Balfour Declaration, to support a national homeland for the Jewish People in Palestine. This directly contradicted a fourth interest, the promotion of good relations with the Arab states that were to develop out of the old Ottoman Empire. Finally, there was the overriding constraint of resources. In the economic climate of the 1920s and 1930s any reduction in defence expenditure was to be welcomed. If law and order could be preserved more cheaply through the selective use of airpower rather than by keeping large garrisons on the ground, so be it. The contradictions between these different interests do much to explain the uncertainties and shifts in Britain's Middle-Eastern policies. There could be no consistent course where so many competing claims had to be met.

Egypt

At least in Egypt British policy was relatively straightforward. Its aims were to maintain the security of the Suez Canal while, if possible, remaining on good terms with the host country through which the Canal ran. Faced with an outbreak of anti-British feeling in 1919, Allenby, the British High Commissioner, announced that it was Britain's aim

> to preserve the autonomy of that country [Egypt] under British protection, and to develop the system of self-government under an Egyptian ruler. The object of Great Britain is to defend Egypt against all external danger and interference by any foreign power, and at the same time to establish a constitutional system wherein, under British guidance so far as may be necessary – the Sultan and his Ministers and the elected members of the people may, in their several spheres, and in an increasing degree, co-operate in the management of Egyptian affairs.
> [Cross, p. 106]

C. Cross, *The Fall of the British Empire, 1918–1968* (1968)

But such a policy required a substantial British garrison to guard the Canal. Its presence was a constant source of resentment. A treaty was signed in 1922 under which Egypt's independence was recognised and the Sultan became King Fuad I. But the British High Commissioner still controlled Egypt's foreign policy. After the assassination of Sir Lee Stack, Governor-General of the Sudan, in 1924, Britain imposed a collective fine of £500 000 and withdrew all Egyptian troops from the Sudan which then came more directly under British control, a further source of grievance. In 1936 a second treaty was signed under which British troops would be confined to the Canal Zone and responsibility for the Sudan would be shared between Britain and Egypt. But when war broke out in 1939, though Egypt broke off relations with Germany she declined to declare war, even when her territory was invaded, and British rule was unofficially re-imposed on the Egyptian population. Britain's interference with Egyptian internal affairs had been a source of grievance ever since the suppression of Arabi Pasha's Revolt by Gladstone in 1881. Despite the nominal independence achieved by Egypt in 1936, Britain's strategic interests compelled her to remain a dominating influence and an unwelcome one.

At the end of the war, Britain had a large garrison in Mesopotamia, including 25 000 British and 80 000 Indian troops. Baghdad was occupied by British forces and the whole area was effectively under the rule of the British Commander-in-chief, General MacMunn. In March 1920 the arrest of an Arab sheikh for failure to pay his debts sparked off a revolt which lasted for about six months and whose suppression cost the British government some £32 million. When Churchill was made Colonial Secretary in January 1921, with particular responsibility for the whole of the Middle East, he made it his first concern to reduce the costs of administering this, to him, unwelcome acquisition. Two solutions suggested themselves. First, an Arab ruler had to be found who would be both friendly to Britain and acceptable to the people of Mesopotamia (henceforth to be known as Iraq). Secondly, the RAF must take over from the army the role of maintaining internal security.

Iraq

Churchill's choice lighted on Feisal, third son of Sherif Hussein of Mecca whom Britain had supported during the Arab Revolt. Feisal had recently been ousted from Syria where he had claimed the throne and was ready to accept an alternative reward, though he had no obvious links with Iraq. Churchill also approached Trenchard, the founder of the RAF, and won his approval in principle to the security role he envisaged for it.

Both these solutions were agreed to at the Cairo Conference which met in March 1921. Churchill telegraphed Lloyd George: 'I think we shall reach unanimous conclusion among all authorities that Feisal offers hope of best and cheapest solution.' Trenchard agreed to provide eight squadrons of aeroplanes and six armoured car companies in due course. On 15 August 1921 Feisal was duly 'elected' king of Iraq after a referendum. However, no sooner was he elected than he determined to assert his independence from the British government. He refused to accept the restrictions on sovereignty implied by Iraq's status as a mandate and demanded a direct treaty with Britain instead. Negotiations dragged on for over a year between Feisal and an increasingly irritated British government. In August 1922 Churchill complained to Lloyd George: 'we are paying eight millions a year for the privilege of living on an ungrateful volcano, out of which we are in no circumstances to get anything worth having'. [Gilbert, vol. IV, p. 817] However, a treaty was signed in October, under which Iraq became an independent state bound to Great Britain during the period of the mandate.

Gilbert, *Winston S. Churchill*, vol. IV

In 1930 the mandate formally came to an end but Iraq accepted a continuing British presence, particularly at the airbases at Basra and Habbaniya which provided useful staging posts en route to India. Iraq remained a political client of Great Britain so long as the Hashemite dynasty stayed on the throne. It survived until 1958 when Feisal II was overthrown and killed in a military coup.

In 1926 Iraq acquired the oil-rich territory of Mosul and the 'ungrateful volcano' became an important source of British oil imports. It could be argued that for nearly 40 years Britain's association with Iraq was beneficial to both parties, but in the long run it could not survive the pressures of radical Arab nationalism.

The problems faced by Britain in Egypt and Iran did not compare with the difficulties she faced in Palestine. The labyrinth of war-time diplomacy produced a situation to which there could be no easy solution. During the course of the war, it will be remembered, Britain had made three inconsistent if not explicitly contradictory undertakings. First, in the course of the MacMahon-Hussein correspondence, which went on from October 1915 to January 1916, Britain gave a pledge to 'recognise and support the independence of the Arabs in all regions within the limits demanded by the Sherif of Mecca'. However, in the same letter dated 24 October 1915 an exception was made: 'The two districts of Mesina and Alexandretta and portions of Syria lying to the West of the districts of Damascus, Homs, Hama and Aleppo cannot be said to be purely Arab, and should be excluded from the limits demanded.' [Fraser, p. 12] In the Sykes-Picot Agreement, signed in May 1916, two new Arab states were to be created in the areas between Damascus and Aqaba, but territory west of the river Jordan was to be placed under international control. Finally, in November 1917 the Balfour Declaration promised Britain's support for 'the establishment in Palestine of a national home for the Jewish people, ... it being clearly understood that nothing shall be done which may prejudice the civil and religious rights of existing non-Jewish communities ....' [Fraser, p. 18]

T. G. Fraser, *The Middle East, 1914–1979* (1980)

As well as the implied contradiction between the promises made in the MacMahon-Hussein correspondence (which said nothing about territory *south* of Damascus) and the Balfour Declaration, three matters were left dangerously vague: first, what was to be the exact status of a national home? Secondly, what were to be its frontiers? Thirdly, how large a Jewish population might it be allowed to attract?

There were similar uncertainties about Britain's motives and interests in Palestine. At the outset, the Balfour Declaration was issued with the interests of the Jewish people in mind and with the object of winning support from Jewish opinion in the United States for the allied war-effort. Balfour himself saw no reason for a British presence in Palestine. He would have preferred the United States to have assumed the responsibility of the mandatory power. In a conversation held between Lloyd George, Curzon and Churchill in June 1921 Churchill evidently expressed himself as 'very taken' with the suggestion that the United States might take over both Palestine and Mesopotamia, though he soon retracted when Lloyd George vented his disapproval. [Gilbert, vol. IV, p. 597]

Gilbert, *Winston S. Churchill*, vol. IV (1975)

On the other hand, the Chief of the Imperial General Staff suggested in a memorandum issued in December 1918 that a Jewish buffer state would be 'strategically desirable' for the protection of Egypt. French presence in Syria was thought in some British military circles to pose a threat to Britain's communications with India (shades of Napoleon's Egyptian campaign, perhaps). While the General Staff had concluded by 1923 that Palestine was a military encumbrance and nothing more, the other services and the Colonial Office advised a cabinet committee that year that a British military presence in Palestine was essential for the safeguarding of the Canal. Thus, what began as a disinterested gesture of support for the Jewish people became inextricably tied up with Britain's imperial strategy.

Between 1920 and 1921 a number of critical decisions were reached. At the San Remo Conference in 1920 the boundaries of British mandates in Palestine and Iraq were finally settled. Sir Herbert Samuel, previously a Liberal cabinet minister and himself a Zionist Jew, assumed the office of High Commissioner for Palestine. In April 1921 at the Cairo Conference presided over by Churchill it was decided to transfer the territory east of the river Jordan to another of Hussein's sons, Abdullah, who had already established himself in Amman and was threatening war on the French in Syria. At the time it seemed a tidy solution, and indeed it worked better than might ever have been expected. But it was a great source of disappointment to the Jews who would be denied access to this area, and it also prevented the possibility of transferring to Transjordan those Arabs who, rightly or wrongly, found themselves dispossessed by Jewish settlers. However, in 1923 the Council of the League recognised the division of Palestine and exempted Transjordan from the terms of the mandate.

THE BRITISH MANDATE IN PALESTINE

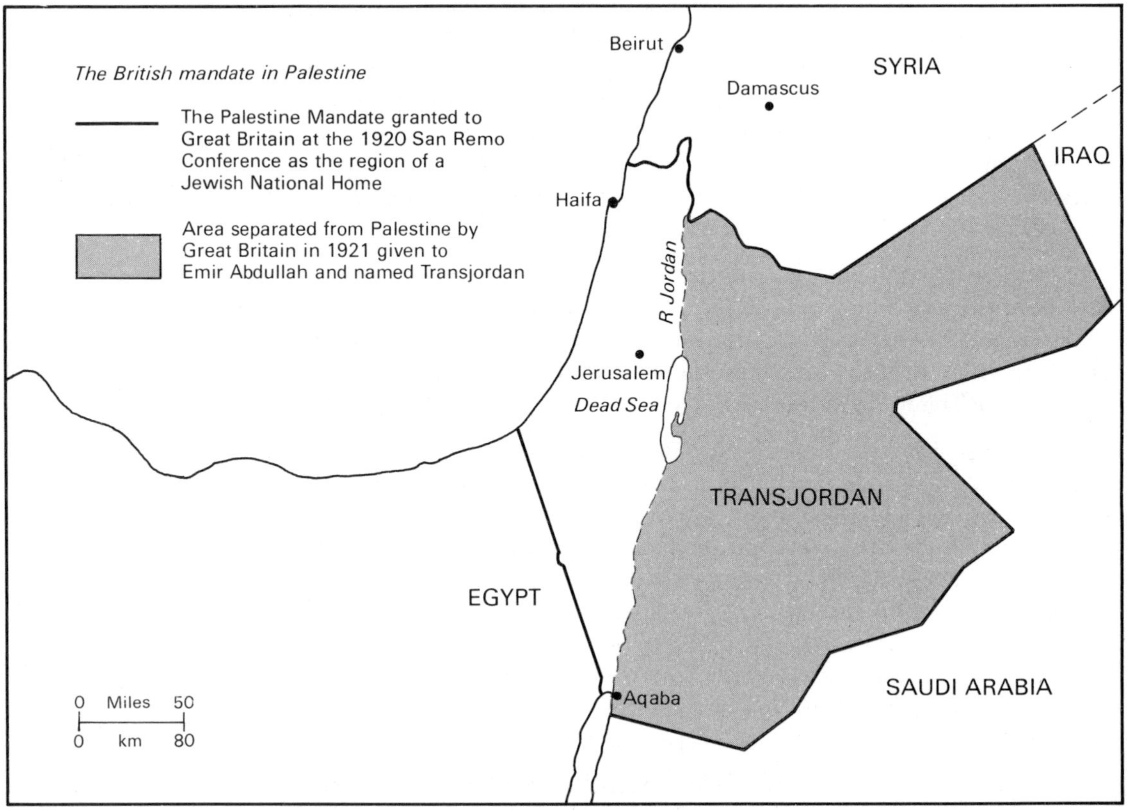

The British mandate in Palestine
The Palestine Mandate granted to Great Britain at the 1920 San Remo Conference as the region of a Jewish National Home
Area separated from Palestine by Great Britain in 1921 given to Emir Abdullah and named Transjordan
Beirut
SYRIA
Damascus
IRAQ
Haifa
R Jordan
Jerusalem
Dead Sea
TRANSJORDAN
EGYPT
Aqaba
SAUDI ARABIA
0 Miles 50
0 km 80

Once the frontiers had been settled it might have been hoped that stability would return to the area but two basic problems remained. Under the terms of the mandate Britain was required 'to facilitate Jewish immigration under suitable conditions'. She was also expected to prepare the inhabitants of Palestine for self-government. But the granting of representative government to the Arab population on the basis of majority rule would be certain to be followed by a total Arab ban on immigration. Britain was thus forced into the unhappy position of trying to restrain Jewish immigration within acceptable limits, while denying legitimate Arab demands for a say in their own future.

British policy between 1921 and 1930 was supposedly based on the concept of 'equality of obligation'. Churchill tried to reassure an Arab delegation who came to see him at Jerusalem in 1921 that 'a national home does not mean a Jewish government to dominate the Arabs'. [Sykes, p. 67] But in a newspaper article written in February 1920 Churchill had also envisaged the possibility of a Jewish state under the protection of the British Crown, which might contain 'three or four million Jews'. [Gilbert, p. 10] Sir Herbert Samuel, following an outbreak of Arab violence in 1921, placed restrictions upon Jewish immigration; but a British White Paper in 1922, while conceding that a Jewish national home did not mean 'the imposition of a Jewish nationality upon the people of Israel as a whole', emphasised that it was essential for the Jewish community to know 'that it is in Palestine as of right, and not on sufferance'.

C. Sykes, *Crossroads to Israel* (1965)

M. Gilbert, *The Arab-Israeli Conflict — Its History in Maps* (1974)

In fact, Britain had no consistent or coherent policy with regard to Jewish immigration but rather lurched from one position to another depending on where the pressures were most acute. Throughout most of the 1920s immigration averaged 8000–8500 a year, sufficient to cause growing resentment in Arab circles but not enough to upset the balance of population. In 1929 there were serious anti-Jewish riots in which 133 Jews were killed and 339 wounded. These disturbances provoked the setting up of two royal commissions and the publication of a government White Paper. The Shaw Commission sat in 1929, the Hope-Simpson Commission in 1930. Hope-Simpson recommended a limit of 50 000 on future Jewish immigration, a figure that was accepted in the government White Paper issued by Lord Passfield (better known as Sydney Webb) in 1930. But so much opposition was aroused in Zionist circles in England and America that no further action was taken on its recommendations.

It is just possible, though highly unlikely, that if Jewish immigration had remained at the annual level reached in 1931, 4075, Arab opposition might have been contained. But with the advent of Hitler to power in 1933 and the consequent persecution of the Jews in Germany, the pressures to increase immigration became irresistible. The figures speak for themselves:

Year	Number of Immigrants
1933	30 327
1934	42 359
1935	61 854

[Sykes, pp. 166–7]

Sykes, *Crossroads to Israel*

Britain was now faced with a dreadful dilemma. To allow Jewish immigration to proceed at such a rate could not but provoke furious Arab opposition; to restrain it meant condemning European Jews to discrimination, persecution, imprisonment and death. There was an alternative. If other countries could be persuaded to take the 600 000 or so German Jews whose lives might be at risk, the pressures on Palestine might be diverted. Such a solution was in fact suggested by President Roosevelt. In 1938 a conference met at Evian at which 31 countries were represented. But the offers made fell lamentably short of the numbers of entry permits needed. Nor, it must be said, were Zionists particularly anxious to see such a scheme succeeding because it would weaken the Jewish case for entry into Palestine.

In 1936 a serious Arab revolt broke out, directed as much against the British and moderate Arab leaders as against the Jews. It lasted for the next three years. In 1938 alone it led to the deaths of 69 British, 292 Jews and 1600 Arabs. Once again a royal commission was appointed. This one was headed by Lord Peel, grandson of the British Prime Minister, Sir Robert Peel. By common consent the Peel Commission was the most thorough and best equipped of all those which sought to find a solution to the Palestine problem. Its recommendations were both radical and realistic. It accepted that there was an irrepressible conflict between Arabs and Jews and that 'to maintain that Palestinian citizenship has any moral meaning is a mischievous pretence'. In such a case partition was the only answer. The commission also recommended an annual limit on immigration of 12 000 for five years, after which the position would be reviewed. Jews welcomed the recommendations, the Arabs did not. The Arab Revolt continued and in the hope of persuading other Arab states to use their good offices in bringing it to a halt, the Foreign Office then contacted the rulers of Iraq and Saudi Arabia. George Rendell, head of the Eastern Department in the Foreign Office, convinced himself as a result of these soundings that partition would have a disastrous effect on Arab opinion outside as well as inside Palestine. He converted Eden, the Foreign Secretary, to his view. Thus, when the Woodhead Commission was sent out to make detailed recommendations for partition, its terms of reference were so drafted that it might recommend 'that a workable plan could not be devised'. [Kedourie, p. 168]

E. Kedourie, *Islam in the Modern World* (1980)

When the Commission reported its findings in October 1938 it reserved such a tiny enclave for the Jews, 400 square miles, that there was no hope of this being accepted. Instead, the new Colonial Secretary, Malcolm MacDonald, convened a conference in London which was attended by delegates from Palestine, Egypt, Saudi Arabia, Yemen and Transjordan as well as Jewish delegates. Predictably, the two sides refused to meet each other and on 17 March the conference broke up without agreement. Britain was left with the responsibility of producing a policy on her own. On 17 May MacDonald announced the government's final initiative before the outbreak of the Second World War, the notorious White Paper of 1939. Partition was abandoned; immigration was limited to 10 000 a year for five years, with an additional 25 000 in the first year, amounting to 75 000 in all. No further immigration would be allowed without Arab acquiescence. The Jews felt bitterly betrayed. A year earlier, MacDonald had mentioned a figure of 400 000 immigrants but this figure had been steadily whittled down by the Foreign Office. The Chiefs of Staff had reported in January 1939 that 'the goodwill of Egypt and the Arab countries in the Near East' was 'of great importance to our Imperial strategy'. [Bethell, p. 61] Britain knew that in the event of war with Germany, Jewish opinion was bound to side with Britain, but Arab support would need to be bought. This was the reason for the White Paper. Forty years after the event, MacDonald defended his actions in these words: 'I'm not saying the White Paper was right. All I'm saying is that this was the reason for it and I'm damned if I can see what else could have been done.' [Bethell, p. 72] It was an appropriate epitaph on 20 years of good but misguided intentions.

N. Bethell, *The Palestine Triangle* (1979)

EMPIRE TO COMMONWEALTH ▬▬▬▬▬▬ E

If Ireland, India and Palestine showed the British Empire at its most vulnerable, at least there were positive gains to record in Britain's relations with the Dominions. The First World War made a re-definition of the imperial relationship inevitable. The sacrifices made by Dominion troops, while in one sense strengthening the emotional links with the mother country, also ensured that the Dominions would demand a greater say in the conduct of their external relations. British governments might still hanker after the 'diplomatic unity' of the Empire but such a concept became less and less acceptable to the Dominion governments.

The pressure to define dominion status more precisely came, as we have seen, from South Africa, Ireland and Canada (see p. 182). The formula arrived at in the Balfour Memorandum of 1926 had three elements: equality of status, free association and a common allegiance to the Crown. The implications of this formula still had to be worked out in practice. To some extent this was done in the Statute of Westminster, 1931. This stated, among other things that 'no Law made by the Parliament of the United Kingdom shall extend to any of the Dominions as part of the law of the Dominion otherwise than at the request and with the consent of that Dominion ....' Conversely, the repeal of the Colonial Laws Validity Act allowed Dominions to pass legislation in contradiction to British law. The Dominions did not take immediate advantage of the new powers extended to them but in effect they were now free to act as they wished. This was made clear in the case of *Moore* v. *the Attorney General for the Irish Free State* in 1932. The Judicial Committee of the Privy Council ruled that the Irish legislature 'can now pass acts repugnant to an imperial act'.

Further steps towards *de facto* independence were taken in 1930 when it was agreed that the Governor-General in each of the Dominions, as the monarch's representative, should be appointed on the advice of the Dominion government concerned. George V had objected to the appointment of Sir Isaac Isaacs as the first Australian Governor-General, but the King had to give way. Dominion governments also began the practice of appointing their own diplomatic representatives. Canada was the first to do so, appointing ambassadors to Washington, Paris and Tokyo. By 1936 she had been joined by Ireland and South Africa. At first the Foreign Office had tried to insist that all matters of imperial concern should be handled by the British ambassador on the spot, but this claim was officially abandoned in 1929.

Further weakening of imperial ties was demonstrated in the Chanak crisis in 1922 and in the attitude shown by the Dominions to the Treaties of Locarno in 1925. When Lloyd George appealed to the Dominions to send troop contingents to Asia Minor in September 1922 'in defence of interests for which they have already made enormous sacrifices', he met with a varied response. New Zealand and Newfoundland offered ready support. The Australian Prime Minister announced that 'In a good cause, we are prepared to venture our all; in a bad one, not a single man.' Mackenzie King, Prime Minister of Canada, flatly refused the appeal on the grounds that neither the Canadian cabinet nor its parliament had been consulted.

On the other hand, when Austen Chamberlain signed the Treaty of Locarno in 1925 the Dominions were explicitly excluded from its provisions unless they chose to be associated with it. Defending this procedure in a subsequent debate in the House of Commons, Chamberlain said:

> I could not go as the representative of His Majesty's Government, to meeting after meeting of the League of Nations, to conference after conference with the representatives of foreign countries and say 'Great Britain is without a policy. We have not been able to meet all the governments of the Empire and we can do nothing'.
> [Mansergh, p. 44]

N. Mansergh, *Survey of British Commonwealth Affairs, Problems of External Policy, 1931–1939* (1952)

Perhaps not surprisingly, though invited to do so, none of the Dominions signed the Treaties of Locarno at the subsequent Imperial Conference. The 'diplomatic unity' of the Empire was something of a chimera.

What then survived? In a formal sense the Empire had been transformed into a Commonwealth, but this metamorphosis merely changed one indefinable entity into another. In practical terms the machinery of empire was rationalised. The Colonial Office was divided into two in 1924 with a separate Office for Dominion Affairs. In 1930 this Office gained its own minister. But Imperial Conferences met at increasingly irregular intervals: 1921, 1923, 1926, 1930 and 1937. The Committee of Imperial Defence rarely had any Dominion representatives at its meetings, though Mackenzie King called in on occasions. Imperial contributions to defence were confined to the provision of base facilities and a handful of cruisers and destroyers until the inauguration of the Empire Air Training Plan in Canada in 1939. The economic links between Britain and the Dominions inevitably weakened as they developed their own industries and sought out different markets.

But when all this is said, the emotional ties remained and were if anything strengthened by the personification of the sole remaining bond joining the Dominions, the monarchy. George V and George VI took the Commonwealth very seriously, as did Edward VIII prior to his accession. George V abhorred royal tours; he only visited India once and never visited Canada, Australia, New Zealand and South Africa. But his sons were regularly dispatched round the globe, and made the monarchy visible as it had never been before to the Dominions.

Some indication of the importance attached to the monarchy by the Dominions can be seen in their reaction to the abdication crisis. When Edward VIII announced his determination to marry the twice-divorced Mrs Simpson in 1936, Baldwin canvassed the views of the Dominion premiers. Without exception they advised abdication rather than a morganatic marriage. General Herzog of South Africa argued that the first would be 'a great shock', the second 'a permanent wound'. If the link with the Crown had not mattered so much they would not presumably have been so concerned about the character of its wearer.

Final proof of the continuing importance of the Commonwealth connection came in 1939. Britain declared war on Germany on 3 September. Canada waited only until 7 September, the four-day delay being used to secure parliamentary approval. Mr Menzies of Australia announced that when Britain was at war, so was Australia. In New Zealand there was an equally immediate response, the Prime Minister declaring his support for Britain in these words: 'Where she goes, we go, where she stands, we stand.' In South Africa the position was a good deal more complex. The Nationalist Party under Dr Malan and part of the United Party under the Prime Minister, General Herzog, wanted a policy of neutrality. But General Smuts forced a debate in the House of Assembly and won enough Afrikaner votes to secure a majority for war by 80 votes to 67. Of the five Dominions, only Eire, still thwarted by the Ulster question, stood for neutrality. It was a remarkable demonstration of the residual strength of imperial sentiment which would surely not have survived had Britain not voluntarily surrendered so much of her imperial authority.

POINTS AT ISSUE

Ulster and the Irish Treaty

One of the continuing sources of controversy in Anglo-Irish history concerns the conduct of the negotiations which led up to the signing of the Irish Treaty in December 1921. It has been claimed by some historians that the Irish delegation were deliberately duped into signing the Treaty by assurances, first, that the British government would bring pressure to bear on Ulster to join up with the South and when that failed, by the offer of a Boundary Commission whose findings would render the continuance of Ulster as a separate entity politically and economically impossible. Much of the evidence rests upon the record of private conversations and the subsequent gloss placed upon them. In one case a critical document has disappeared. The point at issue is whether Lloyd George sought to deceive the Sinn Fein delegates or whether, in his search for a settlement, he followed up any opening without intentionally raising false hopes.

The record of the negotiations is a complex one, including as it does meetings in Dublin as well as London and what was said informally in private as well as in formal session. The following summary is not by any means comprehensive, but accurate, one hopes, so far as it goes.

30 October, 1921	A meeting between Arthur Griffith and Lloyd George at Churchill's house. In his account of this meeting to De Valera, Griffith recorded Lloyd George as saying: 'If I could give him personal assurances on these matters [the Crown, free partnership with the Empire and naval facilities] he would go down to smite the Die-Hards and would fight on the Ulster matter to secure "essential unity".' [Longford and O'Neill, *Eamon De Valera*, p. 157]
5 – 7 November	Meetings between Sir James Craig (premier of N. Ireland) and Lloyd George at which Craig made plain Ulster's refusal to accept the rule of an All Ireland Parliament.
8 November*	Tom Jones, Lloyd George's Secretary, suggested to Collins and Griffith the option of allowing Ulster to secede from a united Ireland, the frontier to be decided by a Boundary Commission.
12 November*	Meeting between Griffith and Lloyd George at which Griffith agreed not to oppose the suggestion of a Boundary Commission in view of impending Tory Party Conference. (It met on 17 November.)
13 November	Tom Jones showed Griffith a memorandum of this conversation which Griffith approved. (This document has since disappeared.)
25 November	Meeting between Griffith and De Valera in Dublin at which it was agreed to offer that 'Ireland shall agree to be associated with the British Commonwealth for purposes of common concern such as defence, peace and war ....' Ulster evidently was not discussed.

26 November– 2 December	Abortive negotiations in England over Oath of Allegiance.
3 December	Further meeting of Irish cabinet. Griffith agreed not to sign any document accepting allegiance to the British Crown but would bring any such document back to Dublin and refer it to the Dail.
4 December	Meetings between Burke and Duffy (intransigent members of Irish delegation) and Lloyd George. No agreement in sight. Meeting between Jones and Griffith. Collins was persuaded to see Lloyd George on the following morning.
5 December*	9.00 am Meeting between Lloyd George and Collins. Conference arranged for 3.00 pm
5 December	3.00 pm Meeting between Irish and British delegations. Griffith accepted inclusion in the Empire 'If Ulster comes in'. Lloyd George produced document of 13 November in which Griffith had agreed to the Boundary Commission. Griffith gave way: 'I said I would not let you down and I won't.' Lloyd George threatened war unless all signed.
6 December	2.10 am Griffith, Collins and Barton signed Articles of Agreement.

The critical differences in interpretation concern what Tom Jones said about the Boundary Commission to Griffith and Collins on 8 November*, what Lloyd George said to Griffith on 12 November* and what Lloyd George said to Michael Collins on 5 December*. G. Dangerfield argues that Lloyd George trapped the Irish delegates by holding out more than he could deliver:

> With Craig's intransigence now blocking the way to Unity, Lloyd George turned back to a plan which he had concocted as early as November 7. Tom Jones was to make the following suggestion to Arthur Griffith and Michael Collins: If an acceptable Treaty could be made, let Ulster be included in it, but let her Parliament have the right to contract out of this Treaty within a year of its final ratification. If the Ulster Parliament exercised this right, however, it would have to accept a Boundary Commission, appointed to determine the proper line between Ulster and the rest of Ireland in accordance with the wishes of the inhabitants and the national demands of geography and economics.
>
> On such a basis, *it was to be rather more than hinted*, [author's italics] a Boundary Commission would have to give large parts of Tyrone and Fermanagh, and smaller, but important sections of Down, Derry and Armagh to Southern Ireland. What was left of Ulster would then become entirely too small for political or economic survival and would fall like a ripe fruit into the lap of the Dublin Parliament.

At the meeting between Griffith and Lloyd George on 12 November Griffith agreed that he would not repudiate the Boundary Commission when it was presented to the Tory Party Conference.

> Griffith agreed; the idea was not his, he said; it was Lloyd George's: but he did not want to be obstructive. This was at once reported to Lord Birkenhead and Austen Chamberlain; 'I do not think that I have seen D. [Lloyd George] so excited about anything before,' Miss Stevenson recorded; [she was Lloyd George's personal secretary, and by this time also his mistress] and the next day the wily Jones brought the Boundary Commission idea in the form of a memorandum in the handwriting of Austen Chamberlain. Lloyd George and Jones had marked their quarry and run him down ...

In his account of the meeting between Lloyd George and Collins on 5 December Dangerfield says this: 'Griffith then talked Collins into meeting alone with Lloyd George at 9 the next morning; and here the Prime Minister, *who played with consummate artistry on the theme of a Boundary Commission and its fatal consequences for Ulster*, [author's italics] persuaded Collins to return for another conference at 3 pm'. [Dangerfield, *The Damnable Question*, pp. 334–5, 337] A more dispassionate account of these negotiations is given in Thomas Jones, *A Whitehall Diary*, edited by K. Middlemas. Middlemas writes of the 8 November meeting:

> T.J. gave the news of the impending break to the Irish delegates on 8 November and pointed out that if Lloyd George resigned, the alternative would be Bonar Law and a return to coercion. As if it were his own, he put forward Lloyd George's suggestion of a Boundary Commission, and this was at once attractive because it appeared to forecast the acquisition of a large part of Ulster by the South.

Of the meeting between Collins and Lloyd George on December 5, Middlemas writes: 'T.J. agreed to arrange another meeting between Lloyd George and Collins, and this time, on 5 December, Lloyd George said that the break would come on the question of "within or without" the Empire. Convinced that the North would be forced to come in because of her economic weakness, Collins agreed to the terms.' [Jones, *A Whitehall Diary*, vol. I, *1916–1925*, pp. 176–7]

The most reliable account of the final negotiations is probably that contained in F. S. L. Lyons's *Ireland since the Famine*:

> On 5 December he [Lloyd George] saw a reluctant Collins and found him anxious about the form of the Oath and still more about the question of Ulster. There was little common ground between them on the former question, but on the latter it seems that *Collins was only too ready to let himself believe that after the Boundary Commission had done its work* economic pressures would bring about the 'essential unity' of Ireland. [author's italics] [Lyons, p. 435]

Without a full record of what was said by each of the participants it is impossible to know who is right. But the onus of proof surely rests upon those who see a conspiracy where none may have been intended.

Books Cited

Earl of Longford and T. P. O'Neill, *Eamon De Valera* (Hutchinson, 1970)
G. Dangerfield, *The Damnable Question* (Constable, 1977)
T. Jones, *A Whitehall Diary*, K. Middlemas (ed.), vol. I, *1916–1925* (OUP, 1969)
F. S. L. Lyons, *Ireland since the Famine* (Weidenfeld & Nicolson, 1971)

BIBLIOGRAPHY BIBLIOGRAPHY BIBLIOGRAPHY BIBLIOGRAPHY BIBLIOGRAPHY BIBLIOGRAPHY
BIBLIOGRAPHY BIBLIOGRAPHY BIBLIOGRAPHY BIBLIOGRAPHY BIBLIOGRAPHY
BIBLIOGRAPHY BIBLIOGRAPHY BIBLIOGRAPHY BIBLIOGRAPHY BIBLIOGRAPHY
BIBLIOGRAPHY BIBLIOGRAPHY BIBLIOGRAPHY BIBLIOGRAPHY BIBLIOGRAPHY
BIBLIOGRAPHY BIBLIOGRAPHY BIBLIOGRAPHY BIBLIOGRAPHY BIBLIOGRAPHY
BIBLIOGRAPHY BIBLIOGRAPHY BIBLIOGRAPHY BIBLIOGRAPHY BIBLIOGRAPHY BIBLIOGRAPHY

CHAPTER 6
FURTHER READING

General

Essential
M. Beloff *Imperial Sunset* (Methuen, 1969)
C. Cross, *The Fall of the British Empire, 1918–1968* (Hodder & Stoughton, 1968)
G. Woodcock, *Who Killed the British Empire?* (Cape, 1974)

Recommended
M. Gilbert, *Winston S. Churchill, vols. IV and V* (Heinemann, 1975, 1977)
D. Judd, *Balfour and the British Empire*, (Macmillan, 1968)
N. Mansergh, *Survey of British Commonwealth Affairs, Problems of External Policy 1931–1939* (OUP, 1952)

Ireland

Essential
G. Dangerfield, *The Damnable Question* (Constable, 1977)
F. S. L. Lyons, *Ireland Since the Famine* (Weidenfeld & Nicolson, 1971)
A. T. Q. Stewart, *The Narrow Ground, Aspects of Ulster, 1609–1969* (Faber, 1977)

Recommended
T. P. Coogan, *Ireland Since the Rising* (Pall Mall Press, 1966)
Earl of Longford and T. P. O'Neill, *Eamon De Valera* (Hutchinson, 1970)
N. Mansergh, *The Irish Question, 1840–1921* (Allen & Unwin, 1975)
C. C. O'Brien, *States of Ireland* (Hutchinson, 1972)

India

Essential
P. Spear, *The Oxford History of Modern India* (OUP, 1978)
M. Edwardes, *The Last Years of British India* (Cassell, 1963)

Recommended
M. Brecher, *Nehru* (OUP, 1959)
A. Draper, *Amritsar, The Massacre that ended the Raj* (Cassell, 1963)

The Middle East

Essential
T. G. Fraser, *The Middle East, 1914 - 1979* (Arnold, 1980)
M. Gilbert, *The Arab-Israeli Conflict – Its History in Maps* (Weidenfeld & Nicolson, 1974)
E. Kedourie, *Islam in the Modern World* (Mansell, 1980)
C. Sykes, *Crossroads to Israel* (Collins, 1965)

Recommended
N. Bethell, *The Palestine Triangle* (Andre Deutsch, 1979)
D. Holden and R. Johns, *The House of Saud* (Sidgwick & Jackson, 1981)

Date	Social and Economic	Political	Foreign Affairs	The Empire and Ireland
1919	*Feb.* Sankey Commission appointed; report issued in June. *Feb.* National Industrial Conference. *Dec.* Cunliffe Committee Report. Addison's Housing Act.	*Oct.* Curzon replaced Balfour as Foreign Secretary. *Dec.* Lady Astor first woman to take seat as MP.	*Jan.* Paris Peace Conference opened. *Mar.* Comintern founded. *Jun.* Treaty of Versailles signed. *Jun.* German fleet scuttled. *Sep.* Treaty of St. Germain (Austria). *Nov.* Treaty of Neuilly (Bulgaria).	*Mar.* Rowlatt Acts in India. *Mar.* Anti-British riots in Egypt. *Apr.* Amritsar Massacre. 1919–21 'Troubles' in Ireland.
1920	*Feb.* National Debt peaked at £7830 million. Unemployment Act. Agriculture Act. Coal Mines Act (7 hour-day).		*Feb.* United States Senate rejected Treaty of Versailles. *Jun.* Treaty of Trianon (Hungary). *Jul.* Spa Conference (Reparations). *Aug.* Treaty of Sèvres (Turkey). Russo-Polish War; Greek-Turkish War.	*Dec.* Government of Ireland Act. Revolt in Iraq.
1921	*Apr.* Mines returned to private owners. *21 Apr.* 'Black Friday'; failure of Triple Alliance. *Aug.* Geddes Committee appointed. Safeguarding of Industries Act. Unemployment reached 2 million (15% of work force).	*Mar.* Bonar Law resigned Conservative leadership.	*Apr.* Reparations Bill fixed at £6600 million. *Nov.* Washington Naval Conference: treaty signed Feb. 1922; Anglo-Japanese alliance ended.	*Mar.* Cairo Conference; Feisal made king of Iraq. *Jul.* Truce in Ireland. *5 Dec.* Irish Treaty signed. Montford reforms in India.
1922	*Feb.* Geddes Axe; cuts in public spending. *Nov.* British Broadcasting Company given monopoly. Hyper-inflation in Germany.	*Jan.* Younger rejected Lloyd George's advice to have election. *19 Oct.* Carlton Club meeting; Lloyd George resigned. *23 Oct.* Bonar Law made premier. *15 Nov.* General Election; Conservative victory.	*Jan.* Cannes Conference. *Apr.* Genoa Conference. *Apr.* Treaty of Rapallo. *Aug.* Turkish offensive in Asia Minor. *Sep.* Chanak crisis. *Nov.* First conference at Lausanne.	*Jun.* Shelling of 'Four Courts' in Dublin; beginning of Irish Civil War. *Dec.* Irish Free State declared.

Date	Social and Economic	Political	Foreign Affairs	The Empire and Ireland
1923	Unemployment down to 1.2 million.	*May* Bonar Law resigned; Baldwin made premier *Oct.* Baldwin announced protection policy. *6 Dec.* General Election; inconclusive result.	*Jan. to Jul. 1924* French occupation of the Ruhr. *Jul.* Treaty of Lausanne (Turkey).	*Jul.* Ending of the Irish Civil War.
1924	Manufacturing output recovered to 1913 levels. Wheatley Housing Act.	*22 Jan.* MacDonald made premier of first Labour Government. *Jul. Workers' Weekly* Article (Campbell case). *Oct.* MacDonald defeated in Commons; resigned. *25 Oct.* Zinoviev Letter. *29 Oct.* General Election; Conservative Victory.	*Jan.* Dawes Committee appointed; report issued in July. New German currency. *Feb.* Diplomatic relations restored with Russia. *Aug.* Trade Treaty with Russia. *Oct.* Geneva Protocol adopted by many countries.	*Nov.* Assassination of Sir Lee Stack, Governor of Sudan; exclusion of Egyptians from Sudan.
1925	*Apr.* Return to Gold Standard. *Jun.* Threat to cut miners' wages. *31 July* 'Red Friday'; TUC support for miners. Widows', Orphans' and Old Age Pensions Act.	*Sep.* Samuel Commission appointed. Preparations for General Strike.	*Feb.* Britain refused to sign Geneva Protocol. *Oct.* Locarno Conference; Locarno Pact signed.	*Mar.* De Valera founded *Fianna Fail.* *Dec.* Boundary Agreement in Ireland.
1926	*Mar.* Samuel Commission Report. *30 Apr.* Lockout of Miners. *3–12 May* General Strike. Electricity Supply Act. British Broadcasting Corporation set up. Miners drift back to work.	*May* Simon attacked General Strike as unconstitutional. Churchill edited *British Gazette.*	*Sep.* Germany entered League of Nations.	*Oct.–Nov.* Imperial Conference; Balfour Draft on Commonwealth. *Apr.* Lord Irwin made Viceroy of India.
1927	Trades Disputes Act.		*May* Raid on Arcos offices; diplomatic relations with Russia suspended. *Aug.* Geneva Naval Conference; no agreement reached.	*Nov.* Simon Commission for India appointed.

Date	Social and Economic	Political	Foreign Affairs	The Empire and Ireland
1928	Churchill's Budget abolished rates for agricultural land and buildings; reduced rates on industrial building by 75%.	*May.* Votes for women over 21.	*Apr.* Churchill made ten-year-rule permanent (no war expected for ten years). *Aug.* Britain signed Kellogg–Briand Pact.	
1929	*Oct.* Wall Street Crash. Local Government Act; Poor Law Unions abolished.	*30 May.* General Election; Labour won most seats.	*Oct.* MacDonald visited United States. Preparations for Disarmament Conference.	*Oct.* Irwin promised Dominion Status for India. *Dec.* India Congress party voted for Independence. Anti-Jewish riots in Palestine.

The Years of Crisis, 1929–31

THE ECONOMIC BACKGROUND ━━━━━━━━━━ A

Introduction

1929 was a watershed both in world and British history. It was the year when the Wall Street Crash precipitated the great depression in the United States which in turn set off the economic blizzard that swept over Western Europe. 1929 was also the year which saw a Labour government with the largest number of seats, though not yet an outright majority, in the House of Commons. Such were the strains to which it was subjected that within two years the cabinet split and the pattern of domestic politics underwent a kaleidescopic shift which left the Conservative party in virtual command for the next 14 years.

Between 1924 and 1929 the economic and political indicators were generally favourable. World trade increased, unemployment declined, international relations generally became more harmonious. After 1929 all these trends were reversed. World trade declined, unemployment mounted and the international climate grew steadily worse. Britain could not insulate herself from these developments. On the contrary, her dependence on overseas markets and the central role played by the City of London in international finance made her particularly vulnerable to changes in the world economy. It is arguable that no British government could have sustained the shocks delivered by the Wall Street Crash to the international trading and financial system; but it is also possible that a more adventurous and resolute approach might have enabled the Labour government to ride the storm. What cannot be denied is that there were no obvious or easy solutions and that dependent as it was on Liberal support and on the backing of its own left-wingers, MacDonald's government had little freedom of manoeuvre.

The World Economy

The prosperity enjoyed by the United States and Western Europe in 1929 was unevenly shared and precariously balanced. Primary producing countries did not experience a comparable improvement in their national incomes as demand for their products failed to keep pace with the growth in industrial production. The mechanism of international trade rested to a great extent upon the extensive loans made by the United States, which had replaced Britain as the main source of overseas investment. Between 1919 and 1930 the United States invested $11 billion in Europe, much of it in the form of loans which could be recalled if the need arose. German reparations payments depended on this flow of funds. Most countries were now on the Gold Standard, but whereas France and the United States had plentiful gold reserves, Britain, which attracted a lot of short-term finance, was dangerously low in gold reserves and therefore vulnerable to speculative movements. Thus the health of Europe's economies was closely bound up with the health of the American one.

In October 1929 the Wall Street Crash was brought about by a sudden loss of confidence in the febrile condition of the American stock market. Share prices had been pushed to wholly unrealistic levels as a result of a speculative boom. On 24 October the bubble burst. In one day 13 million shares changed hands. Despite efforts to arrest the slide in share prices, once the process had begun it could not be halted. The consequences were devastating. By 1931 industrial production had fallen to 51% of its 1929 level and unemployment in the United States had reached 11 million. This caused a fall in the demand for European exports, aggravated by the Smoot Hawley tariff of 1930. The value of merchandise goods imported into the United States fell from $4339 million in 1929 to $1323 million in 1932. By 1930 the United States had also become a net importer of capital.

For Europe there were two obvious consequences. The loss of American markets and the decline in world trade brought about a fall in industrial production, reflected in the following figures:

Index of Industrial Output (Volume)

(1929 = 100)	*1932*
Britain	84
France	72
Germany	53

World trade had not recovered to its 1929 levels before Europe was overtaken by the Second World War.

The second consequence was the strain which the flight of American capital back to the United States imposed on the international monetary system. First Austria, then Germany and finally Britain suffered exchange crises. These in turn led to the abandonment of the Gold Standard, fixed exchange rates and free trade. By 1932 unemployment was as bad in Europe as it was in the United States. In the 1920s Britain had not succeeded in absorbing 'the intractable million' unemployed in the declining industries. But 1929 was the best year for industrial production since 1920 and without the Wall Street Crash, it is at least possible that the unemployment situation would not have got any worse. As it was the figures rose inexorably. It is not easy to be precise about the exact numbers as official statistics only take note of those who claimed unemployment benefit. But even on this basis, they reached nearly 3 million in 1932, and one estimate puts the total as high as 3 750 000, that is 23% of the working population. The visible trade balance was equally affected. Exports fell from £729 million in 1929 to £391 million in 1931.

The problem facing the Labour government was, as one committee report put it in 1930, that 'a severe world wide trade depression has been superimposed on our special national difficulties.' [Skidelsky, p. 164]

R. Skidelsky, *Politicians and the Slump, 1929–31* (1970)

Policy
Alternatives

R. Skidelsky, *Politicians
and the Slump,
1929–31* (1970)

It has become customary to divide policy-makers in the 1929–31 crisis into economic radicals and economic conservatives. [see Skidelsky, p. 11] The economic conservatives included civil servants at the Treasury, the authorities at the Bank of England, most industrialists and politicians of all parties – notably Philip Snowden in the Labour party, Neville Chamberlain in the Conservative party and Harold Samuel in the Liberal party. Some academic economists would also have supported the 'conservative' position, Professors Cannan and Gregory of London University for instance. Economic 'radicals' included economists such as Keynes, politicians like Lloyd George and Oswald Mosley, and trade unionists such as Ernest Bevin. This leaves out of account full-blooded socialists like James Maxton or John Wheatley who could see no way of making a capitalist economy work successfully.

Within these broad divisions there were numerous permutations in the range of policy alternatives that presented themselves. It was possible to be 'conservative on some issues' 'radical' on others. Many of these alternatives were canvassed in the 1929 election campaign. In 1928 a Liberal Study Group produced a policy document headed *Britain's Industrial Future*, advocating a massive injection of public spending on roads, housing, and other public works as a cure for unemployment. Lloyd George adopted most of these suggestions in the Liberal election manifesto '*We Can Conquer Unemployment*'. The Conservatives produced a rejoinder to this in a White Paper which demonstrated both the administrative and the financial objections to the Liberal proposals. The Labour party manifesto, '*Labour and the Nation*', written by R. H. Tawney, was less specific than the Liberal one but made 'an unqualified pledge to deal immediately and practically with unemployment'.

After their arrival in office the Labour government was deluged with advice, much of it from committees of its own devising. In November 1929 Snowden, the Labour Chancellor, set up the Macmillan Committee on Finance and Industry. It was presided over by a judge, Lord Macmillan, and contained two professional economists, four bankers, two industrialists and two Labour representatives. Its report did not finally emerge, however, until July 1931. In February 1930 MacDonald created the Economic Advisory Council made up of economists, industrialists and civil servants. He chaired it himself. Lastly, in March 1931, at the insistence of the Liberals, Snowden agreed to the appointment of the May Committee presided over by Sir George May, retiring secretary of the Prudential Assurance Company, whose task was to enquire into ways of reducing public expenditure. In addition to this, MacDonald also had the benefit of individual solutions to the problem of unemployment. In January 1930 Oswald Mosley, who had been given a roving brief to assist J. H. Thomas, the minister in charge of unemployment, produced his own memorandum. It contained the most radical of all the proposals made to the government, though none of them were adopted.

This readiness to seek advice exposes the weakness of the Labour government. Barred by the lack of an overall majority from pursuing socialist objectives, even had it wished to do so, the government had no policies of its own for dealing with the problems of capitalism. But in its defence the government might legitimately have pleaded that much of the advice it received was conflicting. It was of the Economic Advisory Council that Tom Jones made what has become a classic comment: 'Where five economists are gathered together there will be six conflicting opinions, and two of them will be held by Keynes.' [Jones, p. 19] Where economists disagreed there

T. Jones, *A Diary with
Letters* (OUP, 1954)

was little hope of reaching a consensus among businessmen, bankers, politicians and trade unionists.

At the risk of over-simplification the rival alternatives can be summarised as follows:

'Conservative' policies

1. *The Treasury view* (also supported by the Bank of England and Philip Snowden).
   Remain on the Gold Standard.
   Do not raise tariffs.
   Balance the budget (all expenditure to be financed out of taxation; unemployment insurance to be self-financing).
   Keep public expenditure as low as possible to prevent the diversion of capital from non-productive uses, and to relieve the pressure on interest rates.

2. *Protectionists* (Neville Chamberlain and the Empire Free Traders, such as Lords Beaverbrook and Rothermere).
   As above, except that Chamberlain advocated tariffs to protect British industry; Beaverbrook and Rothermere wanted to see tariffs used discriminately to favour imperial producers.

'Radical' policies

1. *Lloyd George*
   Remain on Gold Standard.
   Do not raise tariffs.
   Massive public investment over a two year period on roads etc., to be financed by borrowing.

2. *Oswald Mosley*
   Remain on Gold Standard.
   Stronger central government controls over the economy.
   Planned public investment over a wide range of economic activities.
   Protective tariff.

3. *Keynes*
   Public investment financed by borrowing, not necessarily on projects that would yield an economic return. The increase in purchasing power would help to stimulate demand in the economy as a whole. (Keynes had not yet worked out the full theoretical justification for this argument.)
   Protective tariff.
   Abandonment of Gold Standard (only after August 1931).

4. *Bevin*
   Unemployment benefits to be financed out of taxation.
   Public expenditure increases to be financed out of taxation.
   Protective tariff.
   Abandon Gold Standard.

There is no way of proving which, if any, of these policies would have proved successful. But the main indictment against the Labour government of 1929–31 is that none of them were consistently attempted. Economic policy decisions were made not as part of a coherent design, but in response to internal pressures and external events. To see why this should have been so we need to examine the political background.

Party policies in 1929: the Conservative attack on high taxation

THE POLITICAL BACKGROUND ═══════════ B

The Election of 1929

The 1929 General Election showed the British electorate to be remarkably evenly divided in its allegiance to the three major parties. The main results were as follows:

Party	Votes	%	Seats
Conservative	8 656 473	38.2	260
Labour	8 389 512	37.1	288
Liberal	5 308 510	23.4	59

The arbitrary working of the electoral system favoured the Labour party whose support was geographically concentrated in industrial areas, while it told against the Liberals who now became keen advocates of proportional representation.

On hearing the results the Conservative cabinet met to discuss whether to resign immediately or wait to be defeated in the House of Commons. Opinions were divided but Baldwin had no doubts and offered his resignation at once. On 7 June MacDonald became Prime Minister for the second time in his career. He was still dependent on Liberal support but his position was a good deal stronger than it had been in 1924. As leader of the largest single party he had an obvious claim to office; nor were the Liberals anxious to face another General Election. They were unlikely to bring about the government's defeat.

The second Labour cabinet relied less upon outsiders than the first one had done, but in other respects it was very much the same mixture of trade unionists and middle-class reformers. The key appointments were:

Prime Minister	Ramsay MacDonald
Chancellor of the Exchequer	Philip Snowden
Foreign Secretary	Arthur Henderson
Home Secretary	J. R. Clynes
Lord Privy Seal	J. H. Thomas
(with responsibility for unemployment)	
Chancellor of the Duchy of Lancaster	Oswald Mosley
(and also responsible for unemployment)	
Minister for Works	George Lansbury

MacDonald hated making appointments. In his diary for 7 June he confided: 'I have broken hearts – one man all but fainted when I told him he could not get what he expected. Most painful day in one's life. Not good experience for maintenance of respect for mankind.' [Marquand, p. 491] In fact, Henderson virtually demanded the Foreign Office and got it; this was the Department MacDonald would have liked himself (he had combined it with the premiership in 1924), and relations between the two men were never very good thereafter. Though he respected Snowden, MacDonald found him a heavy cross to bear at times, and the rigidity of Snowden's views meant that any change in economic policy could only be secured at the cost of his resignation, a political risk that MacDonald was never prepared to take. Of his other colleagues, MacDonald only felt at ease with J. H. Thomas whose incapacity soon led to his demotion to the Dominions' Office. George Lansbury was the only left-winger included in the cabinet, in a relatively minor post. Oswald Mosley's was the most adventurous appointment but by coupling him with J. H. Thomas, MacDonald left him straining at the leash.

D. Marquand, *Ramsay MacDonald* (1977)

What of MacDonald himself? He has been the victim of numerous unflattering epithets. Beatrice Webb once called him 'a magnificent substitute for a leader'; in a savage attack during a debate on the Trades Disputes Bill in January 1931, Churchill described MacDonald as 'a boneless wonder'. He certainly lacked Churchill's dynamic assurance. After the death of his wife in 1911 he was a lonely man, and probably rather a vain one. He never found it easy to get on with his colleagues and preferred the company of George V and Lady Londonderry to that of his fellow politicians. His main weakness was an inability to make up his mind. But when he saw his way clearly he could show plenty of courage and determination. He had resolutely opposed British participation in the First World War and was to show in 1931 an equal readiness to risk unpopularity by doing what he thought was right. One of the main difficulties confronting him in 1929 was to decide what were the right policies.

Even supposing he could secure cabinet agreement on what course to pursue, there was also the difficulty of getting Labour policies through the House of Commons and the House of Lords. MacDonald's position would have been a great deal easier had he been able to come to a working agreement with the Liberals. But three obstacles stood in the way: first, MacDonald's personal dislike of Lloyd George

Party Politics

whom he regarded as 'an unprincipled adventurer, who would do anything to get back into power'; [Marquand, p. 528]; then there was the price the Liberals demanded for their co-operation – proportional representation – which MacDonald was not willing to pay, at any rate initially; finally, there was no assurance that Lloyd George could command the loyalty of his fellow Liberals who quite frequently were to be found in different division lobbies. Force of circumstance in the end compelled MacDonald to come to some kind of working arrangement with Lloyd George but it was never an effective partnership. The House of Lords, with its built-in Conservative majority, was also prepared to use its delaying powers in the knowledge that it was unlikely to have its veto overridden.

Marquand, *Ramsay MacDonald*

Finally, MacDonald had to face the opposition of his own left wing. He had deliberately excluded the Clydesiders, James Maxton and John Wheatley, from the cabinet. He had earlier dismissed their prescriptions for dealing with unemployment as a collection of 'flashy futilities'. It was only to be expected that they would reply in similar coin. In April 1930 a left-wing group in the Independent Labour party broke away and formed their own enclave under Maxton's leadership. There were only 17 of them to begin with but they provided a vocal opposition to the government's policies from its own backbenches.

Thus, sniped at from the left and unsure of Liberal support on the right, MacDonald and his cabinet took office. It was hardly surprising that they ran into difficulties and that MacDonald's performance in the demanding role he had to play should have come in for such harsh criticism.

DOMESTIC POLITICS AND POLICIES, JUNE 1929–JULY 1931   C

Unemployment Just as unemployment had dominated the 1929 election campaign, so it became the pressing concern of the government during its short term in office. There were two aspects to the problem: the proper maintenance of those who through no fault of their own were without jobs; and the provision of employment to reduce the ranks of the jobless. Though action was taken on both aspects simultaneously, it will be convenient to treat them separately.

Maintenance of the unemployed rested on a series of Acts, the most important of which was the Unemployment Act of 1920. This covered 11 million workers. It was amended several times, perhaps most importantly by the Act of 1924 which required claimants to prove that they were 'genuinely seeking work' before being eligible for benefit. This was a major source of grievance with trade unions, whose members argued that if no work was available it was hardly fair to require proof of seeking it. The other problem that had arisen by 1929 was that the Unemployment Insurance Fund had run seriously into debt. The original intention had been that unemployment insurance should always pay for itself out of the contributions provided by employees, employers and the state. But with the increase in the numbers of unemployed, benefits could only continue to be paid through grants from the Treasury or public borrowing.

Margaret Bondfield, President of the Board of Trade, and responsible for the working of the scheme, took steps to deal with both problems. She appointed the Morris Committee to investigate the 'Not genuinely seeking work' clause, and a Royal Commission under Judge Holman Gregory to examine the financing of unemployment insurance.

The Morris Committee recommended certain changes, but at the insistence of the trade unions these were simplified to the adoption of the so-called Hayday formula. This replaced the 'NGSW' clause by the requirement that claimants must be prepared to take a suitable job if one were offered. They no longer had to prove that they had looked for one. These changes were incorporated into the Employment Act of 1930 which also made marginal increases in the benefits payable to dependants.

The Royal Commission produced an interim Report in July 1931. The majority recommended that statutory benefit should be payable only for 26 weeks, after which the unemployed would become a charge on the Treasury rather than the Unemployment Fund; that weekly contributions should be raised by one or two pence; and that benefits should be reduced in line with falling prices by 2/- a week for men and women. The TUC had recommended increases of 3/- per week. The Report met with a very hostile reception and the government made no attempt to implement its recommendations. The only further step taken was to introduce an Anomalies Bill designed to make it harder for married women, seasonal and intermittent workers and part-time workers to claim unemployment benefit. No solution was found to the financing of unemployment benefit. By 1930 the Treasury was contributing nearly £40 million, while the Fund was having to borrow between £40 million and £50 million. MacDonald was always sensitive to the charge that unemployment benefit might encourage 'spongers'. He made no attempt to implement the official Labour policy of financing all benefit payments out of taxation. But, equally, he did nothing to put the financing of unemployment benefit on a more rational footing and it would become an obvious target when there were calls for reductions in public spending.

Any efforts to provide employment had to be made against a background of considerable scepticism in many quarters. In Churchill's graphic phrase, Snowden and the Treasury mind embraced each other 'with the fervour of two long-separated lizards'. They shared the view that any increase in government spending was likely to have inflationary consequences and to divert resources from productive to non-productive uses. Snowden was always more worried about inflation than he was about unemployment: 'The microbe of inflation is always in the air.' [Skidelsky, p. 59] J. H. Thomas, the Minister nominally responsible for the government's unemployment policies, remarked in a speech given in January 1930: 'All that Government can do, when all is said and done, is infinitesimal compared with what business can do for itself.' [Skidelsky, p. 174]

Skidelsky, *Politicians and the Slump*

The one serious initiative that was suggested fell on stony ground. In January 1930 Oswald Mosley put forward a closely argued memorandum. It proposed both short- and long-term remedies for unemployment. In the short term there was to be an increase in spending of £100 million on roads and of £100 million by the Unemployment Grants Committee. Together with the raising of the school-leaving age to 15 and earlier retirement, Mosley calculated that this would provide 700 000 extra jobs. In the long term Britain's declining industries would have to be restructured behind the shelter of a tariff wall. This would require a considerable measure of government interference to be supervised by a much strengthened government machine. Mosley's memorandum was examined by a cabinet committee in May 1930 but was rejected on financial grounds as being far too extravagant. Shortly afterwards Mosley resigned and directed his energies into first the New party and then the British Union of Fascists. In June 1930 MacDonald removed Thomas to the Dominions' Office and put himself at the head of a cabinet committee to tackle unemployment. It was to be serviced by a new secretariat headed by Sir John Anderson. Together with the Economic Advisory Council, which had been initiated in January, there were now three bodies specifically charged with the task of finding solutions to the unemployment problem. But their combined labours proved remarkably barren. Anderson encouraged MacDonald in the belief that there was little to be done. He likened the government's position to that of 'the captain and officers of a great ship which has run aground on a falling tide; no human endeavour will get the ship afloat until in the course of nature the tide again begins to flow.' [Skidelsky, p. 244] Sir Henry Maybury, Chief Engineer Consultant to the Ministry of Transport, was little more encouraging. He regularly poured cold water on schemes to accelerate the road-building programme. At best, all he could suggest in the summer of 1930 was a scheme to eliminate level crossings and other minor hazards which might provide 16 000 jobs.

In the face of the theoretical objections advanced by the Treasury and the administrative difficulties anticipated by civil servants it is not difficult to understand why so little progress was made in providing extra employment. On one calculation, the government was responsible for only 60 000 extra jobs in 1930 at a time when the unemployment figures had risen to 2.5 million. [Pollard, p. 254] No one could fairly accuse the government of not trying, but their efforts were patently unsuccessful.

S. F. Pollard. *The Development of the British Economy, 1914–1980* (1983)

Coal Mines, Agriculture and Housing

The government's record in other fields showed a similar blend of good intentions and limited results. After the trauma of the General Strike the miners had been forced back to work at lower wages and the Conservative government had repealed the Seven Hours' Act. The Coal Mines Act of 1930 has been described as 'a patchwork of compromises to placate the divergent interests involved' [Skidelsky, p. 152] but it did at least reduce the working day to 7.5 hours. It set up the Coal Mines Reorganisation Commission with the aim of rationalising production through amalgamations and closures, and the Coal Mines National Industrial Board to regulate wages on a national basis. Unfortunately neither body had sufficient powers and the mine owners virtually ignored them. Nothing was done about the nationalisation of royalties, let alone the mines themselves. Effective change in the coal industry had to wait until the advent of the Attlee government in 1945.

Skidelsky, *Politicians and the Slump*

Where agriculture is concerned it was much the same story. In 1931 a Land Utilisation bill was passed in the House of Commons, but after a mauling in the Lords it merely provided the government with limited powers of compulsory purchase for the provision of small-holdings. As the Treasury refused to provide any money the Act was a dead letter from the start. More significant was the Agricultural Marketing Act of 1931. This enabled two-thirds of the producers of an agricultural commodity to prepare a scheme for organised marketing and with, Parliament's approval, this would then become compulsory for all producers of the commodity concerned. So long as there were no controls on the import of foreign foodstuffs such schemes could be of little benefit and the Act had no immediate result. However, it paved the way for the Agricultural Marketing Act of 1933 which did have significant effects and gave marketing boards considerable powers.

Arthur Greenwood, Minister of Health, was responsible for the Housing Act of 1930. This placed the emphasis on slum clearance. Local authorities were given £2 5s. a year for 40 years for every person re-housed and all local authorities with populations of over 20000 were required to prepare five-year schemes of slum clearance. The Act was suspended in 1931 but put into operation in 1934 and then, according to A. J. P. Taylor, 'more slums were cleared in the five years before the Second World War than in the preceding fifty years.' [Taylor, p. 352] The Housing Act has some claim to being the most successful of all the measures passed between 1929 and 1931.

A. J. P. Taylor, *English History, 1914–45* (Pelican, 1970)

Abortive Reforms

A number of other reforms were suggested, but came to grief either because of lack of support from the Liberal party or through the wrecking tactics of the House of Lords. In the King's speech of 1930 there were proposals to raise the school-leaving age to 15, to repeal the Trades Disputes Act of 1927, and to introduce a measure of electoral reform. On each of them the government's intentions were frustrated. The bill to raise the school-leaving age was hampered in its passage through the House of Commons by an amendment to delay its implementation until subsidies were provided for Catholic schools. More seriously the bill was rejected in the House of Lords by 168 votes to 22. MacDonald promised to invoke the Parliament Act but the government fell before he had the chance to do so.

The Liberals had promised to support a bill to repeal the Trades Disputes Act of 1927 in return for the introduction of the alternative vote in parliamentary elections. But the deal came unstuck. A Liberal Amendment to the Trade Union bill made it even less palatable to the unions than the Trades Disputes Act and repeal was therefore dropped. The Labour Party planned to include abolition of plural votes (enjoyed by those who owned business premises) and the university seats at the same time as introducing the alternative vote. Again, some Liberals rebelled and voted against the abolition of university seats. The House of Lords insisted on the retention of plural votes. In the face of these reverses, electoral reform expired. If the alternative vote had been introduced it might have changed the map of British politics. As it was, the Liberals lost their last chance of changing the electoral system to their advantage.

These defeats underlined the case for a better working relationship between Lloyd George and MacDonald and in the summer of 1931 there were some indications that a change was on its way. Lloyd George recorded a meeting at which MacDonald had indicated his wish for an alliance with the Liberal party and had held out hopes of a key post in the government for Lloyd George. But if such a change was contemplated it would have come too late. In July the 1931 crisis blew up and in August Lloyd George was laid low with a prostate gland operation. The realignment of British politics had to take place in his absence.

THE 1931 CRISIS AND THE FALL ▰▰▰▰▰▰▰ D
OF THE LABOUR GOVERNMENT ▰▰▰▰▰▰

The Economic Background

The 1931 crisis arose out of two different but related problems. The first was how to meet the pressure on Britain's gold reserves brought about by the sudden withdrawal of a huge volume of foreign deposits from London. The second problem was how to balance the budget (i.e. how to ensure that all prospective expenditure would be met by future revenue) at a time when the increase in unemployment was causing mounting deficits in the Unemployment Insurance Fund. Each problem on its own might have been tackled successfully. Their coincidence was fatal. Pressure on the pound could only be relieved by borrowing from overseas central banks, but they in turn would only lend on the assurance that the British government was pursuing appropriate economic policies which included balancing its budget. Conversely, attempts to balance the budget were to have such damaging political consequences that the confidence of foreign investors could not be sustained. The crisis was essentially one of confidence, both in the health of the British economy and in the capacity of the British government. Ironically, Ramsay MacDonald's government was to fall because of his determination to pursue responsible policies, and Britain was to leave the Gold Standard partly as a consequence of taking the steps needed to remain on it.

Pressure on Britain's gold reserves was brought to bear, initially at least, through a chain of circumstances unrelated to Britain's particular predicament. The international monetary scene began to darken on 23 March 1931 when Germany announced a plan for a Customs Union between Germany and Austria in defiance of the terms of the Treaty of Versailles. This greatly antagonised the French who were now determined to exact a high political price for their economic co-operation.

On 11 May the great Viennese bank, the Credit Anstalt, declared that it could no longer meet the claims of depositors. It owed \$100 million to foreigners who could no longer get their money out of Austria. This provoked a run on German banks who had even larger overseas creditors and could not possibly meet their obligations without foreign assistance. On 14 June the German Reichsbank raised their bank rate in an effort to restore confidence and attract foreign loans. On 16 June the Bank of England arranged to lend £4.5 million to the Reichsbank. On 20 June President Hoover of the United States suggested a one-year moratorium on all inter-governmental debt payments, including reparations. But the French were unwilling to forego their share and it was another two weeks before the moratorium came into effect. In the meantime the pressure on Germany's reserves continued. On 15 July the Reichsbank was compelled to declare exchange control, thus freezing all foreign deposits in Germany. On the same day MacDonald received a message from Washington offering American support for an international conference to be held in London to deal with Germany's financial plight. After prolonged manoeuvering between the British, French and German authorities the conference duly assembled on 20 July. But the French were only prepared to offer a long-term loan to Germany on condition that Germany would undertake to make no alteration to the Treaty of Versailles for the next 10 years. All that was achieved was an agreement to maintain existing short-term loans to Germany at their current levels. MacDonald commented bitterly in his diary: 'Agreement Germany needs help but French never heartily in and act as freezing mixture. They are solely responsible for the failure of the Hoover plan and the present position ....' [Marquand, p. 608]

Marquand, *Ramsay MacDonald*

By now the pound, too, was under pressure. Foreign investors, unable to withdraw their deposits from Germany, turned to London. Britain's short-term liabilities were twice the size of her gold and foreign currency reserves. Between 15 July and 7 August £33 million in gold and £33 million in foreign exchange was withdrawn from London, a quarter of the reserves. On 26 July the bank rate was raised from 3.5 to 4.5% and a loan of $50 million was negotiated with France and the United States. But these moves were still not sufficient to restore confidence in the pound.

It was at this stage that the second problem came to a head. It had become clear as early as February 1931 that with the increase in unemployment and the consequent drain on the Unemployment Fund, the budget could not possibly be balanced without reductions in expenditure, or increases in taxation, or a combination of the two. Following an acrimonious debate on 11 and 12 February Snowden accepted a Liberal proposal to set up a Committee on the lines of the Geddes Committee of 1921. On 17 March it was duly appointed, chaired by Sir George May and consisting largely of businessmen and accountants. It had one trade unionist, Alan Pugh of the Iron and Steel Trades Confederation. Its terms of reference were 'to make recommendations to the Chancellor of the Exchequer for effecting forthwith all possible reductions in National Expenditure, having regard especially to the present and prospective position of the Revenue'. On 30 July, at the worst possible moment, its Report was presented to the cabinet. The Report anticipated a budget deficit of £120 million, though this included borrowing by the Unemployment and Road Funds and the £50 million regularly earmarked for the Sinking Fund to reduce the National Debt. The committee recommended savings of £97 million to be achieved as follows:

Savings on Unemployment Insurance	£67 million
Reduction in teachers' salaries by 20%	14
Cut in service pay by 10%	2
Cut in police pay by 12.5%	1
Postponement of road schemes	8
Miscellaneous	5
Total	£97 million

[Skidelsky, p. 381]

Skidelsky, *Politicians and the Slump*

The remaining gap of £23 million would be met by increases in taxation.

On 31 July the Report was published without any kind of comment from the government. Parliament went into recess and the cabinet dispersed, MacDonald to his beloved Lossiemouth. The cabinet economic committee agreed to consider the Report on 25 August. They little realised how soon the storm was to break.

Coming on the heels of the first foreign exchange crisis, the May Committee Report provoked a further wave of speculation against the pound. Between 4 August and 11 August the Bank of England used up £11 million of its reserves and £11 million of the credits extended by the French-American loan in trying to support the pound. On 6 August Sir Edward Harvey, Deputy Governor of the Bank of England

Government Policies 1 August – 24 August

(Norman, the Governor, was ill) warned Snowden of the drain on the reserves and added that foreign lenders expected 'an immediate adjustment of the budget position'. Leaders of the London clearing banks conveyed the same message. On 8 August Snowden wrote to MacDonald urging an immediate meeting of the cabinet economic committee. On 10 August MacDonald returned to London and began the long process of negotiation which led to the fall of his government.

The government was faced with two unappealing alternatives. If Britain was to remain on the Gold Standard then the May Committee recommendations, or something like them, would have to be implemented. That was the minimum condition on which foreign lenders insisted. If the government was not prepared to impose the cuts required, no loans would be forthcoming and Britain would not be able to meet the claims of foreign creditors, which would in effect mean abandoning the Gold Standard. The overwhelming body of expert financial opinion was committed to keeping Britain on the Gold Standard, the two notable exceptions being Keynes and Ernest Bevin. In a scrawled letter to MacDonald on 5 August Keynes advised him that 'it is now nearly *certain* that we shall go off the existing parity at no distant date'. Instead of clinging to the Gold Standard he recommended MacDonald to form a new Currency Union 'which could be based on a gold unit obtained by devaluing existing units by not less than 25%'. [Marquand, p. 610] Bevin had made his views known in his evidence to the MacMillan Committee on Finance and Industry where he had argued that there could be no improvement in Britain's employment situation at the existing parity.

Marquand, *Ramsay MacDonald*

But Snowden, the banking community, the Treasury and most professional economists were convinced that it was vital to the financial stability of both Britain and Europe that Britain should stay on the Gold Standard. The spectre of inflation lurked behind any departure from it. MacDonald would have needed to have supreme confidence in his own and Keynes's judgment if he was to ignore this body of advice. Not surprisingly he preferred to accept it. Marquand comments: 'Keynes's advice was rejected; within a few days the Government's future had been staked on a defence of the parity; it was the most tragic, as well as the most disastrous mistake of MacDonald's life.' [Marquand, p. 614] But it was wholly understandable. Once committed to defence of the pound, MacDonald's remaining task was to win the cabinet's approval for the economic package that would be needed to win the support of the overseas central banks. The shape of the package had to satisfy not only them but also the Liberals, and preferably the Conservative party as well. This imposed a further constraint on the government. The budget would have to be balanced in such a way that the main burden fell on expenditure cuts rather than on increases in taxation. It was this condition that finally brought about the split in the cabinet, most of whom accepted the obligation to make revenue match expenditure.

The negotiations that took place between 12 August and 24 August were largely concerned with the relative shares of expenditure cuts and tax increases in achieving a balanced budget. The cabinet economic committee had its first meeting on Wednesday 12 August when it received the unwelcome news that Snowden now anticipated a budget deficit of £170 million, not the £120 million forecast by the May Committee. The committee produced its recommendations for the full cabinet on the following Wednesday 19 August. Taxation was to rise by £89 million, expenditure was to be cut by £78.5 million, out of which £43.5 million would be found by reducing the cost of unemployment insurance, though no direct cut in benefit was suggested. These proposals were argued over from 10.00 am to 10.30 pm, without agreement being reached on the changes in unemployment insurance.

On the following day the problems magnified. In the morning of Thursday 20 August MacDonald and Snowden met Chamberlain and Hoare (Conservatives) and Samuel and MacLean (Liberals); all the opposition leaders expressed their hostility to the projected tax increases and insisted that there must be further economies. At 3.00 pm that afternoon members of the economy committee had an equally fruitless meeting with the General Council of the TUC where they received a precisely opposite message. The General Council made clear its opposition to any cuts in teachers' or policemen's pay and to any reduction in unemployment benefit. When the cabinet met at 8.30 pm there was still no agreement on the size of the cuts in unemployment insurance. A TUC deputation which called on the cabinet economy committee at 9.30 pm urged a radically different policy to balance the budget: suspending the £50 million sinking fund payments and imposing extra taxes on dividends on government securities. There seemed to be no way out of the impasse.

MacDonald had not yet given up hope. When the cabinet met on Friday 21 August he urged them to accept an increase of £20 million in the cuts in unemployment benefit to bring the figure up to the £43.5 million suggested by the cabinet economy committee. But the cabinet divided on the question and the best MacDonald could get was an agreement to produce cuts amounting to £56 million in all. In the afternoon MacDonald was told by Harvey of the Bank of England and the opposition leaders that this was inadequate. Later in the evening Chamberlain declared that the opposition would unite to defeat the government if these were its final proposals. When the cabinet met yet again on Saturday 22 August it still refused to agree to the extra £20 million cuts needed, but it did authorise MacDonald to sound out the opposition to see whether they would be sufficient. This he did, and on securing their approval he put the same question to the Federal Reserve Bank in the United States.

No answer could be expected until the following day and the cabinet agreed to meet at 7.00 pm on Sunday 23 August. When it met the message from New York had not yet come. The cabinet adjourned to 9.00 pm. Then the news came through. The Federal Reserve Board would offer a loan of $100–$150 million on the understanding that France would provide a similar amount and that the government's spending cuts received the approval of the City and the Bank of England. All now hinged on whether the cabinet would accept the 10% cut in unemployment benefit needed to make up the £68.5 million total reduction in government spending. Nine members refused to do so. They were: Henderson, Clynes, Graham, Greenwood, Alexander, Johnston, Adamson, Addison and Lansbury. MacDonald had the support of Snowden, Thomas, Sankey, Passfield, Miss Bondfield, Morrison, Parmoor, Wedgwood Benn, Shaw, Amulree and Lees-Smith. If MacDonald's vote is counted he had a majority of 12–9. It was not enough. Hard as they had tried, MacDonald and Snowden had failed to convince the General Council of the TUC or enough of their colleagues to adopt the policies on which the country's economic survival was thought to depend.

The Formation of the National Government

The Political Consequences

After the split in his cabinet MacDonald was faced with three choices: he could resign the leadership and retire to the backbenches, unable to exert any further influence on the course of events; he could offer the collective resignation of the cabinet and go into opposition at the head of his party; or he could place himself at the head of a National Government made up of his own supporters in the Labour party, Liberals and Conservatives. MacDonald eventually decided on the third course, but it is far from certain when and why he made that decision.

It seems probable that the main influence was George V's. He saw MacDonald on three occasions over the weekend of 22–24 August and urged him each time to put himself at the head of a National Coalition. The first of these meetings occurred on the morning of Sunday 23 August, shortly after the King's return from Balmoral. MacDonald recorded in his diary: 'I explained my hopeless parliamentary position if there were any number of resignations. He said he believed that I was the only person who could carry the country through .... He again expressed thanks and sorrow ....' [Marquand, p. 630] On the Sunday afternoon George V saw Samuel and Baldwin who concurred in advising the King that if MacDonald could not carry the economy measures with Labour support it would be best for him to stay on as premier of a national government and do so with the support of the opposition. MacDonald, having failed to secure cabinet approval to the cuts in unemployment benefit that were needed, left Downing Street a second time that day, evidently remarking to Harvey as he did so: 'I'm off to the Palace to throw in my hand.' [Nicolson, p. 464] He arrived, according to the King's private secretary, Wigram, 'looking scared and unbalanced'. Again, George V urged him to stay and 'impressed upon the Prime Minister that he was the only man to lead the country through the crisis and hoped he would reconsider the situation.' [Marquand, p. 635] The King, at MacDonald's request, then agreed to hold a meeting with the two opposition leaders at 10.00 the following morning.

Marquand, *Ramsay MacDonald*

Nicolson, *George V* (Constable, 1952)

MacDonald returned to Downing Street to inform the cabinet of these arrangements. Finally, at the end of a hectic day, he saw Baldwin, Chamberlain and Samuel. Chamberlain recorded in his diary that MacDonald felt 'It would be of no use for him to join a Government. He would be a ridiculous figure unable to command support and would bring odium on us as well as himself.' [Marquand, p. 635] Chamberlain did his best to persuade MacDonald otherwise and may have succeeded. At any rate, when George V met the three leaders at Buckingham Palace on Monday morning, he told MacDonald that his resignation was out of the question,

K. Rose, *George V* (1983)

that by remaining at his post with such colleagues as were still faithful to him, his position and reputation would be much more enhanced than if he succumbed; the Prime Minister must come to some arrangement with Baldwin and Samuel to form a National Emergency Government which would restore British credit and the confidence of foreigners. [Rose, p. 376]

MacDonald this time did not demur. By 11.45 am agreement had been reached. Samuel drew up a seven-point memorandum, as follows:

1.   National Government to be formed to deal with the present financial emergency.

2.   It will not be a Coalition in the ordinary sense of the term, but co-operation of individuals.

3.   When the emergency is dealt with, the Government's work will have finished and the Parties will return to their ordinary position.

4. The economies and imports shall be equitable and shall generally follow the lines of the suggestions attached, designed to enable a loan to be raised in New York and Paris.

5. The elections which may follow the end of the Government will not be fought by the Government but by the Parties.

6. If there is any legislation which is necessary to pass for special departmental or other reasons and it is generally accepted by the different Parties it may be undertaken.

7. The Cabinet shall be reduced to a minimum.

[Middlemas and Barnes, p. 630]

K. Middlemas and J. Barnes, *Baldwin* (1969)

MacDonald then returned to Downing Street to inform his incredulous colleagues who had last seen him setting off to resign; he told them that 'in view of the gravity of the situation he had felt that there was no other course open to him than to assist in the formation of a National Government on a comprehensive basis for the purpose of meeting the present emergency.' The cabinet could do nothing but agree to hand in their resignations. Sankey proposed a vote of thanks to record 'their warm appreciation of the great kindness, consideration and courtesy invariably shown by the Prime Minister when presiding over their meetings.' But for many of the cabinet MacDonald's action was inexplicable and unjustifiable.

The composition of the new cabinet was settled shortly afterwards. It was made up as follows:

Prime Minister	MacDonald	
Chancellor of the Exchequer	Snowden	Labour
Dominions Secretary	Thomas	
Lord Chancellor	Lord Sankey	
Lord President	Baldwin	
Minister of Health	N. Chamberlain	Conservative
Secretary for India	Hoare	
President of the Board of Trade	Cunliffe-Lister	
Home Secretary	Samuel	Liberal
Foreign Secretary	Lord Reading	

There is little doubt that MacDonald hoped to recruit more Labour members into the government. He had warned junior ministers that he was committing political suicide and would not ask any of them to do the same, but added 'But ... perhaps some of us *would* be willing to travel the same road with him.' [Marquand, p. 643] He invited Cripps and Shinwell to stay on as Solicitor General and at the Mines Department respectively. Both declined. In all, there were five Labour ministers outside the cabinet, including Ramsay MacDonald's son, Malcolm. At the swearing in of new ministers MacDonald noted: 'Strange eerie feeling glancing around ... My worst fears re desertion of Party realised. We are like marooned sailors on a dreary island.' [Marquand, p. 645]

Marquand, *Ramsay MacDonald*

THE MASTER CHEMIST

PROFESSOR MACDONALD: "NOW IF ONLY THESE RATHER ANTAGONISTIC ELEMENTS WILL BLEND AS I HOPE,
WE'LL HAVE A REAL NATIONAL ELIXIR."

Punch 1931

224

N. Chamberlain,
Hoare.

Samuel, Sankey.

Cauliffe-Lister,
J.H. Thomas,
Reading.

Snowden, MacDonald,
Baldwin.

'At the swearing in of new ministers, MacDonald noted "Strange eerie feeling glancing round ... My worst fears over desertion of party realised. We are like marooned sailors on a desert island."' [Marquand, p. 465]

New Measures and the Gold Standard

The National Government took office for the specific purpose of implementing the changes in taxation and expenditure to which a majority of the Labour cabinet had, however reluctantly, agreed. On 10 and 11 September Snowden's Budget and the National Economy Bill were put before the House of Commons. Between them they provided for tax increases of £51.5 million and cuts in government expenditure of £70 million. The latter included a 15% cut in teachers' salaries, a 10% cut on average in the salaries of ministers, M.Ps, judges, members of the armed services and in unemployment benefit. Though the Labour cabinet had endorsed cuts of up to £56 million in the negotiations prior to the split, the party now swung round to oppose the whole package, much to MacDonald's disgust, and the debate held on the government's programme became increasingly acrimonious. In the meantime, the financial crisis appeared to have been averted. The Bank of England negotiated a credit of £80 million with New York and Paris; it looked as though the pound had been saved.

But on September 15 the government's hopes were dashed. Sailors in the Royal Navy at Invergordon only heard about the impending cuts through the press and the radio. They discovered that whereas an Admiral's pay was to be docked by 7%, that of an unmarried Able Seaman would go down by 13.5%. Discussions took place in the large canteen at Invergordon and it was agreed that the men would not take ships to sea on the forthcoming naval exercises. There were 12 000 men involved, serving on three battleships and two battle cruisers. It was not a 'mutiny' in the true sense of the word but it was construed as such by foreign investors. If the Royal Navy could not be trusted, how much less the continuing stability of the pound. On 16 September £5 million was withdrawn, on the 17th £20 million and on the 18th £18 million from the Bank of England's gold reserves. Within three days over half the credits negotiated earlier had been used up. Enquiries to the French and American financial authorities about the possibility of further support for the pound this time met with a frosty response. On 19 September the Bank of England requested to be relieved of its obligations under the Gold Standard Act of 1925; On 20 September the cabinet met to give its approval; and on 21 September Parliament repealed the Gold Standard Act.

There were two immediate consequences. The Bank of England was now no longer under an obligation to exchange gold for sterling; and the rate at which the pound was exchanged for foreign currencies was left to find its own level. It fell in relation to the dollar from $4.86 to the pound to $3.80 almost at once, and to $3.40 by the end of the year. The other dire consequences of leaving the Gold Standard failed to materialise. Montagu Norman, Governor of the Bank of England, remarked to an acquaintance: 'We have fallen over the precipice, missus, but we are alive at the bottom.' [Middlemas and Barnes, p. 664] In fact British domestic prices rose hardly at all, while British exports became more competitive as a result of the fall in the value of the pound. In terms of the dollar, for instance, British goods were now 30%

Middlemas and Barnes,
Baldwin

cheaper by December 1931 than they had been in August. By accident rather than design the government had stumbled into an exchange-rate policy that was evidently both appropriate and beneficial.

On the other hand, once Britain had left the Gold Standard most other countries felt compelled to follow suit. By the end of 1932 all except France had done so. The world economy entered upon an era of tariffs, import quotas and competitive depreciation of currencies which in the end were self-defeating. World trade stagnated. While it is arguable that in Britain's case leaving the Gold Standard had beneficial consequences, for the rest of the world the collapse of fixed exchange rates probably did more harm than good.

The Isolation of MacDonald

The political effect of leaving the Gold Standard was to make MacDonald more and more dependent on the Conservative party. His presence was no longer needed to defend the pound and the sacrifices he had called for now seemed to have been unnecessary. His relations with the Labour party grew steadily worse. Mistakenly he declined to attend a meeting of the Parliamentary Labour party to which he was belatedly invited on 28 August. When Parliament first assembled on 8 September 249 Labour members voted against the new government on a motion of confidence. Only twelve Labour members were prepared to support it and there were five Labour abstentions. On 12 September a delegate conference at MacDonald's own constituency of Seaham in Northumberland voted by 40–39 to ask for his resignation. On 28 September the National Executive Committee of the Labour party ruled that all members and supporters of the National Government should automatically and immediately cease to be members of the Labour party.

Coinciding with these developments was a growing pressure in Conservative ranks for a general election. On 21 September the 1922 Committee urged the need for an election on the issue of protection and their view was endorsed by the Conservative Business Committee on 24 September. MacDonald was not anxious to have an election, but after his expulsion from the Labour party on 28 September he ceased to oppose the idea. Before this could happen two difficulties would have to be resolved. The agreement reached between the party leaders at Buckingham Palace on 24 August had envisaged a temporary alliance to deal with the immediate crisis, after which the parties would revert to their ordinary position (see point 3). Any subsequent election would 'not be fought by the Government but by the Parties'. If MacDonald threw in his lot with the Conservatives and the Liberals he would be reneging on this agreement. And if the government was to go to the country it would have to be on an agreed programme.

Between 28 September and 5 October partial solutions were found to both problems. The Coalition parties retained their separate identities: Conservative, Liberal and National Labour (MacDonald and his supporters). But there were a whole series of local deals, reminiscent of the Coupon Election of 1918, to prevent Coalition party candidates standing against each other. In the end, 517 Conservatives, 160 Liberals and 21 National Labour candidates took the field under the Coalition umbrella.

So far as the agreed programme was concerned this could only be fudged. After the financial crisis of 1931 Conservatives had generally become convinced of the need for a protective tariff. Even Churchill, that inveterate free trader, had spoken in favour of tariffs in a debate on 8 September. But the Liberal leader, Samuel, and Philip Snowden were still equally committed to free trade. MacDonald, though by now himself an agnostic on the tariff question, was determined to support Samuel. There was no way of reconciling the two positions. Instead a formula was devised to accommodate them. On 5 October it was agreed that the National Government should go to the country 'on the general policy on which the Cabinet was unanimous, leaving discretion to the various Parties to deal with control of imports and tariffs on their own lines.' [Marquand, pp. 665–6] Parliament was dissolved on 7 October and the election was fixed to take place on 27 October.

Marquand, *Ramsay MacDonald*

The 1931 election took place in a mood of understandable bitterness. The Labour party felt betrayed by MacDonald and his supporters, while they, sensitive to the imputation, defended themselves by charging their former colleagues with at best irresponsibility, at worst dishonesty. The election was not fought on issues. MacDonald called for a 'doctor's mandate' to do whatever was necessary, but the Coalition parties could not even agree about tariffs, let alone any other policies. Inevitably Labour were portrayed as the party which sought to divide rather than to unite the nation. Snowden talked of 'Bolshevism run mad'. MacDonald waved worthless German mark notes dating from the 1922 German inflation before the electors as an awful warning of what a Labour victory might entail. Baldwin conducted a less strident campaign, but also succeeded in conveying the impression

The 1931 Election

Rose, *George V*

Middlemas and Barnes, *Baldwin*

that a vote for the Coalition would be a vote for 'sound, clean and honourable finance'. George V urged Hankey to break the habit of political neutrality and to cast his vote: 'I wish the National Government to get every vote possible.' [Rose, p. 382] Tom Jones, another Civil Servant, confessed that having been a Labour supporter he had 'voted Conservative for the first time in my life ... we had to do it.' [Middlemas and Barnes, p. 653]

It was almost certainly the reaction of people like Jones that led to the astonishing victory of the Coalition parties. Their combined vote came to 14.5 million, while the Labour vote fell by 1.5 million to 6 600 000. In terms of seats the results were even more devastating for the Labour party. Coalition candidates gained a total of 556 seats, 471 of whom were Conservative. The Labour party saw its representation at Westminster reduced from 269 in 1929 to 56. All the ex-cabinet ministers who had stayed in the party lost their seats, with the sole exception of George Lansbury. MacDonald at Seaham won against the official Labour candidate, his former agent, by nearly 6 000 votes. J. H. Thomas was equally successful. Sankey and Snowden, now elevated to the House of Lords, were not put to the test. For the Conservative party the 1931 election was an unqualified success, secured admittedly by good luck rather than good management. They gained over 200 seats. The Liberal vote went down by 3 million but, such are the vagaries of the British electoral system, their representation went up to 68, or 72 if the Lloyd George faction are included. For MacDonald himself the results left a bitter taste. He had announced at Seaham 'Labour I am and Labour I shall remain.' [Marquand, p. 670] Perhaps it was small wonder that he should reflect in his diary when the results were in 'It has all turned out too well. How tragically the Labour party has been let down ....' It was the tactics of the Conservative party he blamed, but he shared in their guilt.

Marquand, *Ramsay MacDonald*

POINTS AT ISSUE
POINTS AT ISSUE **POINTS AT ISSUE** POINTS AT ISSUE
POINTS AT ISSUE

Ramsay MacDonald and the Formation of the National Government

Ramsay MacDonald's action in putting himself at the head of a National Government in August 1931 was the most controversial episode in a controversial career. It has also been described as 'the greatest disaster that has befallen the country, and indeed the world since the war ....' [MacNeill Weir, *The Tragedy of Ramsay MacDonald*, p. 565] To his defenders, MacDonald in 1931 took the path of duty, preferring what he took to be the interests of the country to the claims of party or his own political future. To his opponents, rather than give up the premiership and its perquisites MacDonald was ready to betray his party and to throw in his lot with the opponents of the working class.

Human motivation will always remain a mystery and even with the benefit of MacDonald's diary we are in no position to judge whether finally it was vanity, ambition or a sense of duty that led him to act as he did. But the area of disagreement about his conduct can be narrowed down by examining the evidence of his contemporaries and by the official records that have now become available. There are two main indictments against MacDonald: first, that he was never a true socialist

POINTS AT ISSUE
POINTS AT ISSUE
POINTS AT ISSUE
POINTS AT ISSUE

and that he was scheming to join forces with the opposition parties, with whom his sympathies really lay, long before the crisis of August 1931; secondly, that when the crisis came he failed to take his cabinet colleagues into his confidence and deliberately manoeuvred them into a position where a cabinet split became unavoidable.

The two main sources on which these indictments rest are *The Tragedy of Ramsay MacDonald*, written by L. MacNeill Weir, a Labour MP and until August 1931 one of Ramsay MacDonald's personal private secretaries, and Philip Snowden's *Autobiography*. Weir's book, as the title suggests, is written from a partisan viewpoint, and while he saw a good deal of MacDonald between 1929 and 1931 he was on holiday in the Outer Hebrides during the fortnight which led up to the fall of the Labour government. Snowden's relations with MacDonald were never easy and his *Autobiography* was written after his resignation on the tariff issue in 1932.

On the first indictment, MacDonald's socialism, Weir writes:

> MacDonald was always the most accommodating of Socialists. His Socialism was of the kind that Sir William Harcourt meant when he said on a famous occasion: 'We are all Socialists now.' His Socialism is that far-off Never-Never-Land, born of vague aspiration and described by him in picturesque generalities. It is a Turner landscape of beautiful colours and glorious indefiniteness. He saw it not with a telescope, but with a kaleidoscope. It is as real and as remote as the garden of the Hesperides. Anyone can believe in it without sacrifice or even inconvenience.
>
> It is evident now that MacDonald never really accepted the Socialist faith of a classless world, based on unselfish service. It can be seen now that he never could have at heart believed in the principles of Brotherhood and self-denial, which are the bases of Socialism .... To renounce a position of honour and security for the sake of a principle is an act of patriotic devotion, which is rare in the modern world. MacDonald feared that he might have to make this sacrifice, and to avoid it, committed a great act of political treachery. [Weir, pp. xi–xii]

Weir also argues that the formation of the National Government had long been premeditated. He traces its origins back to the debate on the King's speech of July 1929:

> In view of the crisis of 1931, these words should be particularly noted: (MacDonald is speaking) 'I want to say something else. It is not because I happen to be at the head of a minority that I say this. The thought must be occurring to the minds of everyone who is aware of the very serious problems that this country has to face ... I wonder how far it is possible, without in any way abandoning any of our party positions, without in any way surrendering any item of our party principles, to consider ourselves more as a Council of State and less as arrayed regiments facing each other in battle.' [Weir, p. 212]

By early 1931 MacDonald was becoming estranged from the main body of the Labour party because of his failure to tackle unemployment.

> To MacDonald, therefore, at this time, the scheme of a 'National' Government, with himself at its head, was particularly attractive. As it practically abolished the Party system, it removed the danger of defeat. In the circumstances, too, supersession was impossible. It would give him tremendous power and authority. In the last analysis it came almost to dictatorship. [Weir, p. 311]

Weir cannot fix an exact date at which the first move was made but he argues that 'As early as the end of March, it became pretty well known that a "National" Government was in contemplation.' Despite lack of evidence beyond press speculation, Weir assumes that a project to set up a 'national' government had been planned long ahead and that when MacDonald returned to London from Lossiemouth on 10–11 August 1931 'He had come to London to carry out the plan that had been long devised, and the people whom he saw were those who were directly concerned in the coup d'etat.' [Weir, p. 359]

Finally, Weir's account of the fatal cabinet meeting on Sunday 23 August implies that MacDonald was expecting the eventual outcome:

> It appeared that, having delivered the alleged ultimatum of the Liberal and Conservative leaders on the question of unemployment benefit, he seemed to be merely waiting for a complete deadlock to arise. He had no advice to give, no recommendations to make, nothing helpful to add. He seemed to drop out of the discussion and to be waiting wearily for the anticipated deadlock. While the rest of the cabinet were at their wits' end suggesting, proposing, discussing, MacDonald sat absent-mindedly 'doodling' on a blotter. When the final discussion on that fateful Sunday night ended in a complete failure to reach agreement, MacDonald acted in a way that revealed that this development had been expected and duly provided for.

Having secured the resignations of his colleagues, MacDonald announced his intention to see the King to arrange a conference with the opposition leaders the following day.

> The members of the Labour cabinet naturally assumed on that night, 23 August, that Mr. Baldwin would be asked to form a government. But it is significant that MacDonald had something quite different in view. Without even informing them of his intention to set up a National Government with himself as Prime Minister, he proceeded to carry out his long-thought out plan.

Philip Snowden's *Autobiography* adds some corroborative support to this view:

> When the Labour cabinet as a whole declined to agree to a reduction of Unemployment Pay, Mr MacDonald assumed too hurriedly that this involved the resignation of his Government. He neither shewed nor expressed any grief at this regrettable development. On the contrary, he set about the formation of the National Government with an enthusiasm which shewed that the adventure was highly agreeable to him. [Snowden, vol. II, p. 953]

More damningly, Snowden gives this account of MacDonald's reaction to the break-up of the Labour government: 'The day after the National Government was formed he came into my room at Downing Street in very high spirits. I remarked to him that he would now find himself very popular in strange quarters. He replied, gleefully rubbing his hands: "Yes, tomorrow every Duchess in London will be wanting to kiss me".' [Snowden, vol. II, p. 957]

The most convincing defence of MacDonald is to be found in the biography by D. Marquand, published in 1977. Marquand concedes that MacDonald's socialism lacked a specific programme or indeed even an overall strategy. MacDonald wrote in 1905: 'Socialism marks the growth of society, not the uprising of a class.' While

he insisted that public ownership was the distinguishing mark of socialism, he had no plans for introducing it:

> For him, as for Marx, Socialism was a goal in the future towards which history was inexorably moving, rather than a set of values to be applied to the changing problems of the present: thus his theory offered no more guidance to a socialist faced with the practical tasks of government than Marx's had done. In place of the revolutionary utopianism of Marx, he offered, in effect, evolutionary utopianism – a kinder, but not in practice a more useful creed. [Marquand, p. 92]

In the absence of a clear-cut socialist programme and lacking the majority to carry it through, even had there been one, the Labour party must still demonstrate its fitness to govern. It must not run away from harsh decisions. Should it do so, then the national interest must come first:

> The case against forming a national government was, in essence, the same as the case against cutting unemployment benefit. It was based on the premiss that a Labour politician's chief function is to represent the organized working class, and that a party leader's chief duty is to keep his followers together. That view – a modern version of the view which Disraeli once expounded in his phillipics against Peel – has a great deal to be said for it; and it was both intolerant and unimaginative of MacDonald to assume that his colleagues who held it differed from him for base reasons. But they were at least as intolerant towards him. For he did not hold their view, and never had. In spite of later charges to the contrary, he was deeply attached to the Labour party; and, as we shall see, he never recovered from the emotional wounds inflicted by his separation from it. But he had always believed that party loyalty could conflict with higher national or international loyalties, and that it should come second if it did. That was why he had gone against his party in 1914: as he saw it, 1931 was 1914 all over again. He has often been accused of betraying his party, but if he had acted differently he would have betrayed his whole approach to politics. He and his party both paid a heavy price for his decision, and there can be little doubt in retrospect that the price was not worth paying. But it was his economics that were at fault, not his motives – his tragedy, not that he deserted to the enemy, but that he fought with characteristic courage in a battle that turned out to be unnecessary: and that in doing so he came near to wrecking the achievements of a lifetime. [Marquand, pp. 640–41]

As one might expect, the warmest defence of MacDonald comes from his son, Malcolm. He records in his diary a telephone conversation he had with his father on 23 August 1931:

> The decision will be taken tonight or tomorrow; and is in doubt. The PM thinks he may be in a minority, or else have a slight majority. He will carry on if he can. But it is more likely that the situation will be such that he has no alternative but to resign.
>
> If he wins in the cabinet the immediate crisis is over. But there is then of course the Party to face. There would be a tremendous fight there. But the PM's view is that the situation is so serious that, if necessary, he must commit his own political suicide in order to pull the country through the immediate financial crisis.
>
> If he is beaten in the cabinet, the Government will resign and the Tories come in. Shortly afterwards there would be an Election. The Labour party would in the meantime doubtless have carried a motion of censure on him and those who agreed with him, and would fight drastically on the 'claptrap programme' of Henderson and his friends. [Marquand, p. 632]

There is no suggestion here that MacDonald had *planned* to form a national government, though the possibility is perhaps envisaged in the reference to committing 'political suicide'. On the other hand, it is clear how far apart MacDonald already was from Henderson and the bulk of the Labour party. On this evidence it was not so much lack of integrity as insensitivity towards his colleagues for which MacDonald stands to blame. Certainly, whatever his motives, it would be difficult in view of the way the 1931 crisis was handled, to describe Ramsay MacDonald as 'perhaps the finest statesman that the British Labour Movement has yet produced', his son's loyal but flattering verdict. [MacDonald, *People and Places*, p. 15]

Books cited

L. MacNeill Weir, *The Tragedy of Ramsay MacDonald* (Secker & Warburg, 1938)
P. Snowden, *An Autobiography* (Ivor Nicholson and Watson, 1934)
D. Marquand, *Ramsay MacDonald* (Cape, 1977)
M. MacDonald, *People and Places* (Collins, 1969)

BIBLIOGRAPHY BIBLIOGRAPHY BIBLIOGRAPHY BIBLIOGRAPHY BIBLIOGRAPHY BIBLIOGRAPHY
BIBLIOGRAPHY BIBLIOGRAPHY BIBLIOGRAPHY BIBLIOGRAPHY BIBLIOGRAPHY BIBLIOGRAPHY
BIBLIOGRAPHY BIBLIOGRAPHY BIBLIOGRAPHY BIBLIOGRAPHY BIBLIOGRAPHY BIBLIOGRAPHY
BIBLIOGRAPHY BIBLIOGRAPHY BIBLIOGRAPHY BIBLIOGRAPHY BIBLIOGRAPHY BIBLIOGRAPHY
BIBLIOGRAPHY BIBLIOGRAPHY BIBLIOGRAPHY BIBLIOGRAPHY BIBLIOGRAPHY BIBLIOGRAPHY
BIBLIOGRAPHY BIBLIOGRAPHY BIBLIOGRAPHY BIBLIOGRAPHY BIBLIOGRAPHY BIBLIOGRAPHY

CHAPTER 7
FURTHER READING

Economic Background

Essential
P. Fearon, *The Origins and Nature of the Great Slump, 1929–32* (Macmillan, 1979)
R. Skidelsky, *Politicians and the Slump, 1929–31* (Pelican, 1970)
D. Winch, *Economics and Policy* (Fontana, 1972)

Recommended
D. E. Moggridge, *The Return to Gold* (CUP, 1969)
S. F. Pollard, *The Development of the British Economy, 1914–1980* (Arnold, 1983)

Political Background

Essential
D. Marquand, *Ramsay MacDonald* (Cape, 1977)
C. L. Mowat, *Britain between the Wars* (Methuen, 1955)

M. Pugh, *The Making of Modern British Politics* (Blackwell, 1982)

Recommended
K. Middlemas and J. Barnes, *Baldwin* (Weidenfeld & Nicolson, 1969)
K. Rose, *George V* (Weidenfeld & Nicolson, 1983)
P. Snowden, *An Autobiography 2 vols* (Ivor Nicholson & Watson, 1934)
L. MacNeill Weir, *The Tragedy of Ramsay MacDonald* (Secker & Warburg, 1938)

CHAPTER 8

The British Economy and the National Government

INTRODUCTION

The 1930s have gained a bad reputation; they have been described as 'the devil's decade' and 'the age of the pygmies'; books such as George Orwell's *The Road to Wigan Pier*, published in 1937 and Walter Greenwood's *Love on the Dole*, published in 1933, have conveyed the image of a Britain wracked by poverty and unemployment. The Prime Ministers of the decade, MacDonald (1929–35), Baldwin (1935–37) and Neville Chamberlain (1937–40) have been seen to be as inept in the handling of Britain's unemployment problems as they were to show themselves in dealing with the dictators. There are thus two problems to be explored: first, were the 1930s as grim as they have been painted? Secondly, if not, how much credit for this should go to the policies pursued by the National Government?

THE CONDITION OF THE BRITISH ECONOMY, 1931–39   A

It is now customary among economists to judge the health of an economy by applying to it four criteria: the rate of inflation, the rate of economic growth, the state of the trade balance and the rate of unemployment. In all four respects, the 1930s showed an improvement after the crisis years of 1931–32. The retail price index fell between 1929 and 1934 and prices rose only slowly thereafter. Inflation was no problem during the slump. The index of real national income (1900 = 100) rose from 130.1 in 1929 to 155.1 in 1936. Britain experienced an average annual rate of growth of between 2.2% and 3.3% over the decade as a whole, and according to one authority 'the mid 1930s, indeed, saw what has been called "the largest and most sustained period of growth in the whole of the inter-war period".' [Stevenson and Cook, p. 9] The index of industrial production fell from 100 in 1929 to 84 in 1931, but had recovered to 124 by 1937.

J. Stevenson and
C. Cook, *The Slump:
Society and Politics
during the Depression*
(1977)

The current trade balance showed a similar improvement. Despite the fall in the value of the pound after 1931, the terms of trade moved in Britain's favour (i.e. import prices fell faster than export prices). Britain in the mid-thirties was able to import 40% more goods for the same quantity of exports. C. L. Mowat calculates that the annual saving on import costs was equivalent to £400 million per annum. [Mowat, p. 435] Though visible trade remained in deficit, after invisible payments have been taken into account the current balance moved into equilibrium in 1933 and into surplus in 1934. There were small deficits thereafter, but none large enough to cause concern. Britain's share of world trade remained surprisingly constant, varying between 10.76% in 1929, 9.36% in 1931 and 9.87% in 1937, though it needs to be remembered that the volume of world trade fell rapidly between 1929 and 1934, and that the value of British exports fell from £729 million in 1929 to £365 million in 1932 before recovering to £521 million in 1937.

C. L. Mowat, *Britain between the Wars* (Methuen, 1955)

It is the final criterion of unemployment that upsets the picture of growing prosperity and stability, though here too, there was an improvement:

Registered unemployed in thousands

1929	1216	1935	2036
1930	1917	1936	1755
1931	2630	1937	1484
1932	2745	1938	1791
1933	2521	1939	1514
1934	2159		

[Stevenson and Cook, p. 286]

Stevenson and Cook, *The Slump: Society and Politics during the Depression*

While there was a more or less continuous fall in the numbers of unemployed (with a slight hiccough in 1938) from the 1932 total, even with the stimulus of rearmament, there were still over 1.5 million out of work in 1939. What these figures cannot reveal is the increase in total employment that took place during these years, where the fall in primary industries was more than counterbalanced by the rise in employment in the secondary and tertiary industries. Various estimates have been made of these changes and the following table represents an attempt to reconcile them:

Changes in Numbers Employed in thousands

	1921–31	1931–39	Total Change 1921 - 39
Primary Industries	− 466	− 419	− 885
Secondary Industries	− 491	+ 1050	+ 559
Tertiary Industries	+ 873	+ 1210	+ 2083
All Employment	− 74	+ 1841	+ 1767

[Pollard, p. 288]

S. F. Pollard, *The Development of the British Economy, 1914–1980* (1983)

Though unemployment remained obstinately high, it would appear from these statistics that it was caused not by a contraction in the labour market but by the failure to provide enough new jobs to cater for an increase in the size of the working population as well as the loss of jobs in the primary sector.

On closer analysis, what was happening to the British economy in the 1930s was an intensification of the trends which had become noticeable in the 1920s. The new growth industries in the Midlands and the South East expanded faster than they had done before; contraction in the old staple industries, with some exceptions, also proceeded more rapidly. Engineering output went up by 50% between 1927 and 1937. Car output reached a peak of 500 000 in 1937. The chemical industry opened new plants on Teesside and in North Wales. The electricity industry employed 325 000 directly by 1938 and through the new sources of power it made available, millions more indirectly. But four-fifths of the new factories built between 1932 and 1937 were located in the Greater London area where they provided two-thirds of the new jobs. [Stevenson and Cook, p. 14]

Stevenson and Cook,
*The Slump: Society and
Politics during the
Depression*

Ford's new factory at Dagenham under construction in 1931

In the old staple industries there was an opposing pattern of falling employment, for even when production was sustained it was usually accompanied by improvements in productivity (output per worker) which reduced the demand for labour. In the coal industry, for instance, total production had recovered to within 7% of its 1929 level by 1939, but output per worker had gone up by 33% since 1924 thanks to increased mechanisation, and 22% of miners were without jobs. The cotton industry suffered a very severe contraction. Spinning capacity fell from 56 million spindles in 1929 to 39 million spindles in 1939, with a corresponding fall in employment. Shipbuilding suffered worst of all from the depression, at any rate in the short term. In 1930 launchings from British yards amounted to 1.4 million tons. By 1933 this figure had fallen to 133 000 tons. 60% of all shipyard workers were without jobs. When Palmer's Shipyard in Jarrow closed in 1934, local unemployment rose to nearly 73%. A company called National Shipbuilders Security was formed in 1930

to buy up and put into cold storage excess shipyards. By 1934 it had acquired 139
berths with a shipbuilding capacity of 1 million tons. As world trade recovered and
rearmament got under way shipbuilding benefited from increased demand, and in
1937 920 000 tons of shipping were launched in British yards. Even so, in 1938
the unemployment rate among shipyard workers was still 21.4%. The only one of
the staple industries to see an actual increase in production was the iron and steel
industry. Production fell from 9.6 million tons in 1929 to 5.2 million tons in 1931,
but aided by tariffs and quotas and massive investment in the new steel plants at
Ebbw Vale and Corby, the industry staged a remarkable revival and achieved an
output of 9.85 million tons in 1935, increasing to 13.2 million tons in 1939. Here,
too, increases in productivity more than matched increases in production, and as late
as 1938 24.8% of workers in the industry were unemployed.

As a general proposition it would be true to say that in each of these four basic
industries, coal, cotton, shipbuilding and iron and steel, the unemployment rate in
1938 was twice what it was in other forms of employment. The concentration of

these industries in Scotland, Wales, Northern England and Northern Ireland explains the geographical disparities in unemployment rates indicated in the following table:

Stevenson and Cook,
The Slump: Society and
Politics during the
Depression

Unemployed as a Percentage of Insured Workers in Regions of Great Britain

	1929	1932	1937
London and S.E. England	5.6	13.7	6.4
S.W. England	8.1	17.1	7.8
Midlands	9.3	20.1	7.2
Northern England	13.5	27.1	13.8
Wales	19.3	36.5	22.3
Scotland	12.1	27.7	15.9
Northern Ireland	15.1	27.2	23.6

[Stevenson and Cook, p. 286]

These figures conceal further disparities. Single industry towns, like Jarrow, as we have seen, might have unemployment rates of over 70%. Merthyr Tydfil, whose coal went largely into exports, had an unemployment rate of 61.9% in 1934, the cotton town of Blackburn one of 46.8% in 1931. It was in areas such as these that long-term unemployment was at its worst. In Crook, County Durham, 71% of the unemployed had been without a job for five years in 1936; in the Rhondda valley it was 45%. The effect of the slump was thus to accentuate the chronic depression which the declining industries had suffered since 1921, and to sharpen the differences between the prosperous Midlands and South East and the rest of the country.

LIVING STANDARDS ▬▬▬▬▬▬▬▬▬▬ B

It is this disparity which best explains the apparent contradictions in the evidence about living standards during the 1930s. Here, too, the broad trends were generally favourable: life expectancy, the level of real wages, standards of physical health, housing conditions, consumer spending, all appeared to indicate an improvement in living conditions.

Life expectancy showed a fairly steady increase. The standardised death rate for England and Wales, which was 13.5 per 1000 in 1911–14, fell to 9.7 in 1931–36, and to 9.3 in 1937. Infant mortality rates fell from a national average of 80 per 1000 live births in 1920 to 60 in 1930 and 56 in 1940. Whereas during the First World War nearly two-thirds of those called up for military service were deemed to be physically unfit, in 1940, applying the same classification, only one-third fell into that category.

Though wage rates tended to fall between 1929 and 1934, prices fell faster: 'By 1938 average real wages were one-third higher than they had been in 1913, and the thirties alone saw a rise of the order of 15%.' [Stevenson and Cook, p. 18] The trend to smaller families also helped. Whereas live births per married woman averaged 5.71 between 1841 and 1850, this figure had dropped to 2.19 between 1925 and 1929. To George Orwell, family size was the critical factor that determined whether

Stevenson and Cook,
The Slump: Society and
Politics during the
Depression

a working-class family lived in decency or squalor: 'The best-kept interiors I saw were always childless houses or houses where there were only one or two children; with, say, six children in a three-roomed house it is quite impossible to keep anything decent.' [Orwell, p. 53]

G. Orwell, *The Road to Wigan Pier* (1931)

England's housing shortage was supposedly cured by 1939. It was certainly true that over three million houses were built in the 1930s, more than during any other decade in British history. Whereas there were 610 000 more families than houses in 1918, by 1939 there was an apparent surplus of 500 000 houses. A semi-detatched three-bedroomed house could be bought for £300 to £350. Mortgage rates were around 4.5%. This put house purchase within the reach of skilled artisans as well as the lower middle classes.

A London County Council Housing Estate at Barnes, 1929

Patterns of consumer spending reflected increased purchasing power and the range of new products on the market. Whereas in 1914 60% of working-class incomes would go on food and a further 10% on rent, it has been calculated that in 1937 the comparable figures were 35% and 9%, allowing 56% of incomes to be spent on other commodities. The 1930s saw the development of chain stores such as Woolworth's, Marks and Spencer and Littlewood's. Consumer durables such as vacuum cleaners, wireless sets, refrigerators, and gas and electric cookers became available for the first time. The 3 million motor cars owned by Britons in 1939 would not have been parked outside working-class homes, but as Orwell comments, 'Of course the post-war development of cheap luxuries has been a very fortunate thing for our rulers. It is quite likely that fish-and-chips, art-silk stockings, tinned salmon, cut-price chocolate [five two ounce bars for 6d.–2.5p], the movies, the radio, strong tea and the football pools have between them averted revolution.' [Orwell, pp. 80–1]

In 1938 the *Economist* boasted complacently: 'The British (working-class) consumer, in fact, has for several years been getting the best of both worlds. From 1929 to 1932 the fall in prices outweighed to his advantage the fall in employment. And from 1933 to 1937 the rise in employment outweighed to his advantage the rise in prices.' This comment would have raised, at best, a hollow laugh in any working-class home. For while there were undeniable improvements in living standards in the 1930s, two things need to be remembered. First, those standards were very low to start with; secondly, the long-term unemployed, and all their dependants, were substantially worse off in most cases, after losing their jobs.

Seebohm Rowntree, who had done his great survey of York workers in 1899, repeated the experiment in 1935–36. Applying a slightly more generous definition of poverty, he concluded that a family of five (man, wife and three children) needed an income of 43s.6d. (£2.17) exclusive of rent to remain above the poverty line. On this basis, 31% of working-class households in York were below it. Investigations by H. Tout in Bristol, one of the more prosperous cities in Britain, reached the conclusion that any unemployed man with three children or more and any old-age pensioner with only his pension to live on would suffer from poverty. Despite the prevalence of unemployment the length of the working week still averaged 48 hours and as late as 1931 only 1.5 million workers out of 18 million were entitled to any paid holiday. Mowat calculated that in 1934 73.5% of all families (8.6 million) earned less than £4.00 per week. For all of these people the margin between subsistence and reasonable comfort must still have been very narrow.

Even so, they were substantially better off than the unemployed. A survey of 800 families in Stockton on Tees in the 1930s showed that the average income of families where the wage earner was unemployed was 29s. 2¹/₂d. (£1.45), well below the Rowntree poverty line. The Pilgrim Trust, which carried out numerous investigations into the plight of the unemployed, established that far from encouraging men to live in idleness, unemployment benefit was usually some 45–66% lower than a man's previous wage. These figures were confirmed in a Ministry of Labour study in 1937, which showed that the average weekly insurance benefit paid to an adult man was 24s. 6d. (£1.22¹/₂), whereas the median wage rate of these men when last employed was 55s. 6d. (£2.77¹/₂). [Constantine, p. 27] There were instances, particularly in the unskilled trades, where the gap was much narrower, but in these cases it is the lowness of the wage rather than the lavishness of the dole that is cause for comment.

S. Constantine,
*Unemployment in Britain
between the Wars*
(1980)

The physical and psychological strains of unemployment also need to be taken into account. There was an evident correlation between the incidence of unemployment and mortality rates. Death rates in the families of the unemployed were 29.29 per 1 000, as against 21.01 per 1 000 in the families of those in work. Disease such as rickets, pneumonia, tuberculosis and heart disease were all more prevalent in the depressed areas. Infant mortality rates were nearly twice as high, as was the number of mothers who died in childbirth. The psychological impact of unemployment cannot be quantified, but the Chief Medical Officer to the Ministry of Health admitted in 1932 that it was the cause of mental depression, and individual case studies provide plenty of evidence to support that view. A Ministry of Labour survey in 1934 established that whereas 75.5% of those recently unemployed were physically fit, only 59.9% of the long term unemployed were in good physical condition. Unemployment was debilitating.

The obvious conclusion to be drawn from all this evidence is that life chances in the 1930s depended very much on where one happened to be born and bred. The aggregate figures on health, wages, housing and consumer spending undoubtedly support the view that living standards were rising. But for those living in the depressed areas the traditional picture of the 1930s as years of waste and deprivation still holds good.

C ▬▬▬▬▬▬▬▬▬▬▬▬▬▬ POLITICS AND POLICIES

Political Changes

Though the first National Government, formed in August 1931, contained only four Conservatives the results of the 1931 General Election soon changed its complexion. The huge Conservative majority within the National Coalition made it inevitable that when the cabinet was reshuffled in November most of the rewards would go to the Conservatives. They held eleven seats in the new cabinet, compared with the four held by National Labour and five held by Liberals. In terms of personnel the most important change came with the substitution of Neville Chamberlain for Philip Snowden as Chancellor of the Exchequer. Snowden went to the House of Lords but retained his seat in the cabinet as Lord Privy Seal. Government policy was largely the product of an inner grouping of Ministers,

The face of Unemployment: a white collar worker seeks a job at the Labour Exchange, Snow Hill, London, 1930

referred to by Chamberlain as 'the Six'; they consisted of MacDonald, Thomas, Simon, Runciman, Baldwin and Chamberlain himself. In October 1932 Snowden and the Liberal free traders, Samuel and MacLean, resigned from the cabinet after the Ottawa Conference. In June 1935 Baldwin and MacDonald virtually changed places, MacDonald handing over the premiership to Baldwin and taking his sinecure post as Lord President of the Council. Sankey was replaced as Lord Chancellor at the same time by Lord Hailsham and the last of MacDonald's Labour supporters in 1931, J. H. Thomas, was forced to resign in 1936 after a Tribunal of Inquiry found him guilty of leaking Budget secrets to two of his business associates. Thus, what had been in August 1931 a temporary coalition of individuals formed to deal with a particular emergency in effect became a Conservative administration masquerading as a National Government. Its hold on office was nonetheless confirmed by the electorate in the General Election of 1935, when Coalition candidates won 435 seats to Labour's 154, with 11.8 million votes compared to a Labour vote of 8.3 million.

By 1931 MacDonald was 65, Baldwin was 64. Neither could equal Neville Chamberlain in intellectual grasp or administrative capacity. While MacDonald continued to take a close interest in foreign affairs he was content to relegate domestic policy to the Chancellor of the Exchequer, as was Baldwin when he became Prime Minister. Thus the economic policies pursued between 1931 and 1937 were largely Chamberlain's, aided and abetted by Runciman at the Board of Trade and Sir Edward Hilton Young, Minister of Health. Chamberlain believed as firmly in balanced budgets as any of his predecessors. But he was also a convinced advocate of his father's policies of Protection and Imperial Preference. As Lord Mayor of Birmingham from 1915 to 1917 and as Minister of Health from 1924 to 1929 he had shown his passion for administrative efficiency and his genuine concern for improvement in social conditions. The policies of the National Government reflected these priorities.

Financial Policy

Chamberlain's budgets were all intended to balance. His first one in 1932 resulted in an unforeseen deficit of £32 million, which required an increase in taxation in 1933. But by 1934, with unemployment falling, he was able to restore the 10% cut in unemployment benefit and by 1935–36 the cuts in government salaries had been restored in full. In 1935 income tax was reduced from 5s (25p) in the pound to 4s 6d (22$\frac{1}{2}$p). The increases in defence expenditure which began in 1936 were generally met out of increases in income tax and a tax on profits imposed in 1937. But, while his budgets were strictly conventional, Chamberlain used to advantage the freedom of manoeuvre gained by leaving the Gold Standard. In April 1932 he inaugurated the Exchange Equalisation Account. The Bank of England acquired a large quantity of foreign exchange through the sale of Treasury Bills and it was able to use these funds to intervene on the foreign exchange market to stabilise the value of the pound. In consequence the Bank of England was freed from the need to maintain a high bank rate in order to support the pound. Bank rate (officially the rate of interest at which the Bank of England would lend money to the discount houses) fell to 2%, where it stayed for the next seven years. Bank rate determined all other interest rates which moved in sympathy with it, thus a low bank rate made borrowing cheaper and therefore encouraged investment.

Chamberlain was also able to reduce the burden of interest payments on the National Debt. He implemented a plan, inherited from Philip Snowden, to convert £2087 million of War Loan carrying an interest rate of 5% into a new loan where the rate of interest was only 3.5%. The overall saving amounted to £23 million per annum. 'Cheap money' and the reduction in the burden of the National Debt could not of themselves bring about economic recovery. There was no immediate increase in investment, and when it came from 1934 onwards it probably owed more to improvements in world trade and rising home demand than it did to low interest rates. But Chamberlain's financial policies won the confidence of the business community and in that way made an important contribution to Britain's economic recovery.

Chamberlain never seems to have had any doubts about the wisdom of Protection and Imperial Preference. In the speech announcing the Import Duties Bill in 1932 he explicitly paid tribute to his father, Joseph Chamberlain, who had first urged these policies in 1903, and it was more than family piety that caused him to speak with pride of the fulfilment of his father's aims:

Protection and Imperial Preference

> I believe he would have found consolation for the bitterness of his disappointment if he could have foreseen that these proposals which are the direct and legitimate descendants of his own conception, would be laid before the House of Commons, which he loved, in the presence of one [Austen Chamberlain] and by the lips of the other [Neville himself] of the two immediate successors to his name and blood. [Feiling, p. 205]

K. Feiling, *The Life of Neville Chamberlain* (1946)

The first step towards Protection was taken in November 1931 with the passage of the Abnormal Importation Act, giving the Board of Trade six months in which to impose duties of up to 100% *ad valorem* on goods entering the United Kingdom in abnormal quantities. 50% duties were imposed in the next few months on a whole variety of manufactures, ranging from pottery to radio parts. At the same time a Balance of Trade Committee was set up to investigate the tariff. It recommended an all round *ad valorem* duty of 10% with additional duties to be imposed at the discretion of an Import Duties Advisory Committee. When these proposals were put before the cabinet on 21 January 1932, they ran into strong opposition from Snowden and Samuel. For the time-being the breach was temporarily papered over by the notorious 'agreement to differ'. In view of the gravity of the economic situation and the need for unity, the cabinet agreed to suspend the principle of collective responsibility: 'It has accordingly determined that some modification of usual Ministerial practice is required, and has decided that Ministers who find themselves unable to support conclusions arrived at by the majority of their colleagues on the subject of import duties and cognate matters are to be at liberty to express their views by speech and vote.' [Snowden, p. 1012]

P. Snowden, *An Autobiography*, vol. II (1934)

Notwithstanding these objections, the recommendations of the Balance of Trade Committee were incorporated into the Import Duties Act. Sir George May was again wheeled out of retirement to head the Import Duties Advisory Committee, and on its advice duties on luxury goods were raised to 25% and on most manufactured goods to 20%. The net effect over the next three years was to leave about a quarter of British imports untaxed, a half paying duties of between 10–20%, and the remaining quarter paying duties of over 20%.

Protection was always coupled with Imperial Preference in Chamberlain's eyes. Ideally, it was hoped, Britain would be able to secure tariff-free entry for her manufactures into the Dominions in return for similar concessions for their primary products. Unfortunately this simplistic picture of two complementary economic systems no longer fitted the facts. The Dominions were beginning to industrialise themselves while British farmers were in competition with Dominion producers of wheat, beef and dairy products. Given these economic rivalries, it was not surprising that the Ottawa Conference, which met from 21 July to 21 August in 1932, achieved so little. Twelve individual agreements were signed. Britain offered tariff-free entry to most foodstuffs and raw materials from the Dominions, but the most she could get in return were agreements to give preference to British exports, not by reducing tariffs but by raising them yet further on non-British exports. In many cases these tariffs were already impossibly high.

The immediate effect of the Ottawa Conference was to bring about the resignations of Snowden, Samuel and Sir Donald MacLean. Their objections were primarily to the food taxes which would be imposed on foodstuffs from outside the Dominions. Snowden pointed out, not unreasonably, that the Dominions would have a free market here with protection all round against the foreigner, while their own markets would continue to remain highly protected against British manufactures. Whether either the Import Duties Act or the Ottawa Agreements had beneficial effects on the British economy has been much disputed. Britain's new tariffs gave her a bargaining weapon which she could use to secure more favourable terms for British exports. Some industries, most obviously iron and steel, certainly benefited from Protection. But exports fell even more rapidly than imports after the passage of the Act, and the industries which prospered in the 1930s were those which did not need protecting.

The Ottawa Agreements probably did no more than reinforce existing trends:

	% of UK Imports from Empire	% of UK Exports to Empire
1913	25.0	32.9
1924–29 (average)	26.8	35.2
1931	24.5	32.6
1933	34.3	36.0
1937	37.3	39.7

Most of the Dominions also based their currencies on the pound after the collapse of the Gold Standard, and this was probably a more powerful influence than Imperial Preference in encouraging the growing proportion of British trade within the Empire.

Policies for Unemployment

Feiling, *The Life of Neville Chamberlain*

Chamberlain had little faith in public spending as a cure for unemployment. He pointed out to the World Economic Conference in 1935 that public works were a panacea which Britain had tried and failed. He assured his hearers that in the seven years up to 1931 the state had spent £700 000 000, 'yet at no time had employment been found thereby during that time for over 100 000 men.' [Feiling, p. 241]

Direct government assistance to create jobs was limited to two main measures. In 1934 the Special Areas Act was passed. This recognised the particular problems of districts in Southern Scotland, the North East, West Cumberland and South Wales. Two Commissioners were appointed with powers to spend up to £2 million mainly via local authorities. The Act had so little effect that one of the Commissioners, Sir Malcolm Stewart, urged the need for a second experiment. His suggestions bore fruit in the Special Areas (Amendment) Act of 1937 which offered remissions on rates, rent and income tax to firms locating in the distressed areas. New industrial estates were built at Treforest, Gateshead and in the area outside Glasgow. How much work they provided is hard to say, estimates varying between 12 000 (A. J. P. Taylor) and 50 000 (S. Constantine). With unemployment in the areas concerned standing at 350 500, even on the most optimistic estimate government policies can have done no more than put a dent in the total without work. The only other measure was the North Atlantic Shipping Act 1934. This made a loan of £9.5 million to the Cunard Shipping Line for the building of the liners *Queen Mary* and *Queen Elizabeth* in order to capture a share of the prestigious North Atlantic passenger trade.

Having little faith in the efficacy of government expenditure to create employment, Chamberlain was all the more concerned to see that unemployment benefit was put on a rational footing and that it went only to those in need. By 1931 the system was in an unholy mess. Three kinds of assistance were available: statutory benefit, claimed as of right by all those covered by the insurance acts, which lasted for 26 weeks; transitional benefit, payable to the same groups of workers who had been without work for more than 26 weeks; and outdoor relief which covered all those not in the first two categories. Since 1929 the transitional benefit and outdoor relief had been administered by Public Assistance Committees, under the County and Borough Councils, and financed by the Treasury. Chamberlain's aim was to simplify the system and to make the Unemployment Fund actuarially sound, i.e. self-financing. The Unemployment Act of 1934 achieved both objectives. Part I of the Act set up an Unemployment Insurance Statutory Committee which would be responsible for all the short-term unemployed. It fixed the scales of contributions and benefits.

Under Part II all those who had exhausted their 26 weeks' entitlement to benefit, and those not covered by insurance, would come under an Unemployment Assistance Board (UAB) with its own staff of full-time officers. The Public Assistance Committees were left with exceptional categories such as old-age pensioners. The implementation of the Act caused a storm because in many cases the rates of benefit paid by the Unemployment Assistance Board were lower than those which the Public Assistance Committees had been paying. A Standstill Act had to be introduced in 1935 to head off the protests that were provoked, and it was not until 1937 that the UAB assumed its full responsibilities. But once in operation the two schemes worked well. The Insurance Fund for the short-term unemployed not only remained solvent but was able to reduce the level of contributions and raise the level of benefits. The UAB eventually brought most of the other groups in need under its wing, and the administrative structure created was of vital importance in dealing with the civilian casualties caused by the Second World War.

The one really unpopular feature of the government's unemployment policies was the Means Test. This was first introduced in September 1931 and was applied to all the unemployed who had exhausted their statutory entitlement. It was a Household Test and took into account the earnings of all members of the family, savings and any other sources of income. It acted as a disincentive to seek work; it led to evasion on the one hand and 'snooping' by Public Assistance Committee and UAB officers on the other; most seriously it damaged family relationships. Orwell commented:

Orwell, *The Road to Wigan Pier*

> The most cruel and evil effect of the Means Test is the way in which it breaks up families. Old people, sometimes bedridden, are driven out of their homes by it. An old age pensioner, for instance, if a widower, would usually live with one or other of his children; his weekly ten shillings goes towards the household expenses, and probably he is not badly cared for. Under the Means Test, however, he counts as a 'lodger' and if he stays at home his children's dole will be docked. So, perhaps at seventy or seventy-five years of age he has to turn out into lodgings, handing his pension over to the lodging house keeper and existing on the verge of starvation. I have seen several cases of this myself. It is happening all over England at this moment thanks to the Means Test. [Orwell, p. 70]

Conditions were relaxed slightly in 1934 when disability allowances and maternity benefit, and a small proportion of savings, were disregarded in calculating household income. But the main grievance remained. The legacy of the Means Test was to imbue all those subjected to it with a lasting dislike of needs-related benefits and a strong preference for a system of universal benefits, even if this meant their going to the undeserving as well. It has been claimed that provision for the unemployed in the 1930s was better than at any previous period in Britain's history, and that it compared favourably with what was available either in Europe or the United States. Such a claim is probably justified. But the zeal for economy meant that the unemployed were still treated with what now seems unnecessary parsimony. A more serious indictment of the government was its continued refusal to embark on any extensive system of public works. Both in Germany and the United States such ventures were tried. The German Autobahn network was built by mobilising the unemployed. In the United States President Roosevelt embarked on a series of measures, collectively known as the New Deal, to promote employment. Among the most successful of these ventures was the Tennessee Valley authority, which brought the Tennessee river under control and harnessed its force to the generation of electricity. Britain had no such monuments to the imaginative use of public money in the 1930s.

Agriculture

Where agriculture was concerned the government had fewer inhibitions and its policies brought about the biggest changes in the British agricultural scene since the repeal of the Corn Laws in 1846. The first important new departure was the Wheat Act of 1932, under which producers were guaranteed a standard price of 10/- (50p) per cwt; where the free market price fell below this figure the government would make up the difference, up to a limit of 27 million cwt. The limit was extended to 37 cwt in 1937. Under the Agricultural Adjustment Act of 1933, which built on the Agricultural Adjustment Act of 1931, groups of producers who chose to combine were now permitted to control output as well as prices. The government undertook to add protection against cheap imports where it was felt to be necessary. By 1939 such schemes were in operation for hops, milk, bacon and potatoes. The sugar beet industry, started in 1924, was also receiving subsidies of £5 million a year in the 1930s.

Under the Import Duties Act of 1932 the government was able to impose tariffs on all foodstuffs from outside the Empire. Horticultural produce, oats and barley were all protected in this way. The livestock industry was protected through the imposition of quotas on meat imported from non-Empire countries, and subsidies were given to British producers under the Cattle Industry (Financial Provisions) Act of 1934.

The overall effect of all these measures was to cost the British taxpayer about £100 million a year by 1939. Agricultural output increased in volume by one-sixth between 1931 and 1937. Wheat production rose from 20 million cwt to 30 million cwt, the number of pigs and poultry doubled. Thanks to the low level of world food prices, even with protection British food prices went up hardly at all. Farm incomes did not rise appreciably, but without protection they would have suffered a considerable fall. Most significantly for the future, British agriculture became a highly protected, organised and assisted industry.

Steps towards Nationalisation

Despite Conservative objections to interference with private enterprise, the national government in practice showed a pragmatic approach to the extension of state controls where there seemed to be a good case for them. Herbert Morrison, Minister of Transport in the second Labour government, had planned to integrate public transport in the London area. This was to be done by setting up the London Passenger Transport Board (LPTB) which would take over the bus, tram and underground services from private undertakings. A bill had been prepared in 1931 but the government fell before it could be passed. The National Government, to its credit, proceeded with the bill, which became law in 1933. The LPTB was given a monopoly of all public transport within 30 miles of Charing Cross, except for the main-line railways. Members of the Board were appointed by a panel of Public Trustees and its first chairman was the manager of the private underground railway. The Board was required to make a minimum return on capital. The success of the undertaking made it seem a suitable prototype for the industries that were to be nationalised by the Labour government after 1945.

The coal mining industry was also subjected to a further dose of government intervention. In 1938 royalties (payments due to the owners of the land on which collieries were situated) were nationalised. The owners were awarded £66.5 million in compensation, as recommended by independent arbitrators, to which the government added a further £10 million. A new Coal Commission was set up, empowered to order compulsory reorganisation with the aim of closing uneconomic pits. This Act, too, prepared the way for nationalisation of the industry in 1946.

Air travel since its inception had relied heavily on government assistance. In 1924 Imperial Airways was created to open up air routes within the Empire. It received generous government subsidies and had two government-appointed directors on its board of eight. It was joined in 1935 by British Airways, a private commercial undertaking which was responsible for flights to Europe. Both companies shared the London–Paris traffic. Partly to end the wasteful competition between the two companies, they were merged into the British Overseas Airways Corporation in 1939. The new body had a board of directors wholly appointed by the government, and came under the control of the Minister for Air.

Seen in perspective, the National government's economic policies did mark a significant departure from the rigid orthodoxies advocated by the Treasury in the 1920s. Two main pillars, the Gold Standard and free trade, had gone, one replaced by the Exchange Equalisation Account, the other by the Import Duties Act. But the third pillar, the belief in balanced budgets, was still firmly in place. This, as we have seen, inhibited any attempt to solve the unemployment problem either by an extensive system of public works as advocated by Lloyd George, or by the deliberate stimulus of consumption as was to be recommended by Keynes. Such economic recovery as did take place in the 1930s, it is now generally admitted, owed more to secular economic trends over which the government had little control than to government policies. Pollard concludes: 'The impetus came from a rising demand, which was based in the final analysis on the greatly improved terms of trade and on lowered real costs of production, and the main positive action of the Government consisted in channelling the additional demand into home-produced goods and services rather than imports.' [Pollard, p. 153] If this verdict seems ungenerous, it might be claimed that in setting up the Unemployment Assistance Board the government was also erecting the scaffolding on which Beveridge's Welfare State was to be built.

Pollard, *The Development of the British Economy*

OPPONENTS AND CRITICS D

The Nature of Opposition

Opposition to the National government took a variety of forms. Inside Parliament the Labour party was joined by Lloyd George and his supporters, and after 1932 by the Liberals who were still committed to free trade. Between 1931 and 1935 their combined number amounted to about 80 MPs. After the 1935 general election numbers increased to 180, but the National government continued to enjoy a commanding majority. The parliamentary opposition was never able to mount an effective challenge to government policy so long as the National parties remained united, which until 1940 they very largely did.

It may well have been the frustration engendered by this knowledge that provoked protests outside Parliament. While the Communist party attracted very little electoral support it was for a time able to exert considerable leverage by taking over the National Unemployed Workers' Movement. On the right, the Fascist party was equally unsuccessful in elections, but it too was able to attract a certain amount of support when it took to the streets. Finally, within the consensus that was still committed to parliamentary democracy and a capitalist economy there was an increasingly influential group of economists and politicians who argued for radical changes in the government's handling of the economy.

The Labour Party

Disastrous though the 1931 election had been in terms of seats for the Labour party, in terms of votes it did better than in any previous election with the exception of 1929. After 1935 most of the leaders who had lost their seats in 1931 were back in Parliament. Once again it became a credible alternative government. In the 1930s, as throughout its history, it was faced with a dilemma. If the Labour party was to

THE BRITISH ECONOMY AND THE NATIONAL GOVERNMENT

offer a radical socialist alternative to the policies of the National government it stood to frighten off its potential moderate supporters. But if it abandoned its socialist programme, as MacDonald had found to his cost, there would be nothing to distinguish its policies from those of the National government. A way out of the dilemma was found by committing the party to a full range of socialist objectives, while at the same time reasserting the party's faith in the parliamentary road to socialism. All overtures from the Communist party were firmly rebuffed and the Labour leadership would have nothing to do, officially at any rate, with extra-parliamentary action such as the hunger marches and demonstrations staged by the National Unemployed Workers' Union. Those who advocated a more militant approach, or an alliance with more extreme groups on the left, were liable to find themselves expelled from the party. MacDonald may have been regarded as a renegade after 1931, but his concern that the Labour party should be a reforming rather than a revolutionary one was shared by his successors in the leadership.

Inevitably there were splits and divisions both over tactics and over policy. The first occurred in 1932 when the Independent Labour party decided to disaffiliate, ostensibly because its members were unwilling to accept the code of discipline which prevented Labour MPs from speaking or voting against party policy. In practice, members of the ILP were opposed to the gradualist approach now favoured by the TUC whose influence predominated at party conferences. An alternative organisation, the Socialist League, took the place of the ILP inside the Labour party. Its leading members were Sir Stafford Cripps, John Strachey and Harold Laski. They continued to advocate the use of radical methods as well as radical policies.

In 1934 the party agreed on a detailed socialist programme: *For Socialism and Peace*. It promised full and rapid socialist economic planning under central direction; a full-scale extension of nationalisation including the public ownership of land; a state medical service; abolition of the Means Test; and the raising of the school-leaving age to 15. The Socialist League argued that any Labour government must arm itself with emergency powers on getting into office, but this suggestion was rejected.

In 1935 the party went through another leadership crisis. George Lansbury, who had replaced Arthur Henderson as Leader in October 1931, was a Christian pacifist. In the summer of 1935 it became clear that Italy was about to invade Abyssinia. The League of Nations canvassed support for a policy of economic sanctions to be applied should the need arise. Lansbury had announced his support for the League in August 1935, but when a resolution supporting the use of sanctions was moved at the Labour Party Conference at Brighton in October, Lansbury could not bring himself to condone the use of force which a policy of sanctions might entail. He made an emotive speech opposing the resolution. At this point Ernest Bevin accused Lansbury of inconsistency, and of 'taking your conscience round from body to body to be told what to do with it'. [Bullock, p. 568] Bevin's speech was brutal but effective. The Conference resolution was passed by 2 168 000 to 102 000. Lansbury resigned shortly afterwards, to be replaced by Clement Attlee, the Deputy Leader. In some ways it was a surprising, but as it turned out, inspired choice. Attlee was to remain Leader for the next 20 years. There were further splits between Left and Right in 1937 and 1939. In January 1937, Cripps urged that there should be a United Campaign of the Left, to include the Independent Labour party, the Socialist League and the Communist party. The National Executive Committee damned any suggestion of co-operation with the Communist party and the Socialist League was

A. Bullock, *The Life and Times of Ernest Bevin, vol. I* (1960)

expelled from the Labour party, a decision that was endorsed by the Conference when it met in October. One tangible result of this move was the founding of the *Tribune* newspaper by ex-members of the Socialist League. It became an important source of left-wing ideas.

A further attempt to join forces with all anti-fascist groups, including the Communists, was made by Cripps in January 1939. He urged a policy of peace by collective action, to include the Soviet Union. His proposals were circulated to local Labour parties and when he refused to withdraw his memorandum, he was expelled from the party, to be followed shortly afterwards by Sir Charles Trevelyan, Aneurin Bevan and G. R. Strauss.

There were few indications in 1939 that the Labour party was destined for power. It had increased its representation in 1935 in Parliament, but polled almost the same number of votes as in 1931, and though it won 13 by-elections between 1935 and 1939 these were on relatively small swings. But it had re-established itself as the main Opposition party after the split in 1931; and it had preserved its identity as a party committed to parliamentary democracy no less than to socialism. This was perhaps more of an achievement than it seemed at the time.

The Communist Party

The Communist party was never more than a token presence in terms of the electoral support it managed to attract. It polled 75 000 votes in 1931, 22 out of 26 candidates forfeiting their deposits (i.e. failing to get 12.5% of the vote). Only in the Rhondda did any Communist candidate get as much as 30%. In 1935, Communist candidates did, if anything, even worse, gaining 27 000 votes in all; they did, however, succeed in having one candidate elected, William Gallagher for West Fife. The party had no more success in its efforts to found rival trade unions through the so-called Minority Movement. With the rise of Fascism in Europe its appeal went up, only the Communists apparently being prepared to challenge Hitler in Germany and Franco in Spain. By 1942, at the height of its popularity, the Communist party had a membership of 56 000. Even so, in terms of representation in Parliament its influence was derisory.

In two other fields, however, the Communist party had more effect. The great depression exposed the weakness of capitalism and lent a new credibility to Marx's predictions. The failure of MacDonald's government to do anything about unemployment weakened the appeal of the Labour party. Many British intellectuals in consequence became converts to Marxism, some carrying their beliefs to the point where they were willing to collaborate with the Soviet Union. In 1931 the first Communist cell at Cambridge was set up. It recruited men whose names were to become notorious: Donald Maclean, Guy Burgess, Anthony Blunt, Kim Philby – the effects on the British intelligence service, which all these men managed to infiltrate, were devastating. Marxist ideas had a significant influence in the academic world. Historians such as Christopher Hill and E. J. Hobsbawm, scientists such as J. D. Bernal, literary critics like Arnold Kettle illustrate the growing tendency to apply a Marxist framework to academic disciplines. The image of the Soviet Union conveyed by the apparent success of Stalin's Five Year Plans and the democratic facade displayed by the 1936 Constitution also helped to make Communism more attractive. Sydney and Beatrice Webb, by this time elevated to the rank of Baron and Baroness Passfield, set the seal of respectability on Stalin's Russia after a carefully

Baron and Baroness Passfield, *Soviet Communism, a New Civilisation* (Longman, 1937)

guided tour on which they embarked in 1935. Their account of it, *Soviet Communism, a New Civilisation?* had the question mark omitted in its second edition in 1937. It seems, however, that the Webbs knew about the cruel realities of Soviet life but regarded them as necessary evils.

Another area where the Communist party achieved some success was in the leadership they gave to the National Unemployed Workers' Movement (NUWM). This had been founded by a Communist tool-maker, Wal Hannington, in 1921. Its ultimate goal was the abolition of capitalism, but in the meantime the Movement was more concerned to champion the rights of the unemployed, both to jobs and to reasonable subsistence allowances. The leaders of the Movement took their orders from Moscow and Hannington was elected to the Central Committee of the British Communist party in 1929. The NUWM devoted most of its energies to marches and demonstrations, the *Daily Worker*, for instance, calling for 'Mass struggle in the Streets'. Whether these were intended to bring about the collapse of the government or merely to draw attention to the grievances of the unemployed was never entirely clear. The Means Test fuelled support for the Movement and in 1932 there were a whole series of protests, culminating in a national rally in Hyde Park with contingents from 18 different starting points assembling there. The government drafted in 2000 police, arrested Hannington and refused to allow the marchers to present their petition to Parliament.

There was another upsurge of activity at the beginning of 1935, after the announcement by the Unemployment Assistance Board of reduced scales of benefit. It was reported that 300 000 workers took to the streets in South Wales, and there was an angry demonstration in Sheffield; the government was sufficiently alarmed to rush through the Standstill Act, delaying implementation of the new scales.

Ellen Wilkinson arrives with Jarrow Hunger Marchers at Hyde Park, November 1936

The march which caught the public imagination was the Jarrow Crusade, though this had little to do with the NUWM. It was organised by the Labour MP for Jarrow, Ellen Wilkinson, and the Mayor and Council of Jarrow. It had the blessing of all the churches in Jarrow and won wide support from trade unionists and local politicians. The 200 men who took over a month to do the journey of 300 miles were warmly received en route, and while they were not allowed to present the petition that had been drawn up in person they were entertained to tea in the House of Commons. The Special Branch reported that the conduct of the marchers had been 'exemplary'. The marchers captured the public's sympathy and more tangible support followed. Sir John Jarvis, Sheriff of Surrey, which had 'adopted' Jarrow in 1934, founded Jarrow Metal Industries and by 1938 the town had acquired a foundry, a tube mill, a ship-breaking yard and an engineering works.

The NUWM's much larger demonstration also took place in November 1936. It included ten contingents of marchers and the police estimated the numbers who assembled at Hyde Park at 12 000. On this occasion the Labour party gave its approval, Hannington appearing on the same platform as Clement Attlee. This was the last of the big organised protests — from 1936 onwards the NUWM devoted most of its energies to helping individuals through the jungle of the unemployment regulations. Altogether 2 000 cases were fought, in a third of which the NUWM was successful. The revolutionary potential of the NUWM was exaggerated, both by Moscow and the British government. In 1934 an Incitement to Disaffection Act was passed, making it a criminal offence to seduce any member of His Majesty's forces (including the police) from his duty or allegiance, and giving the police greater powers of search. Informers were infiltrated into the organisation and its leaders were not infrequently arrested, usually on charges of incitement. At its greatest, the NUWM claimed a membership of 100 000 with 386 different branches. It probably did more for the unemployed than either the TUC or the Labour party in terms of modifying the regulations governing the payment of benefit, but its leaders were very reluctant revolutionaries and such violence as the movement provoked owed as much to over-reaction by the police as to deliberate encouragement of disorder.

Fascism

Just as Fascism in Europe depended on a charismatic personality, Hitler in Germany, Mussolini in Italy, Franco in Spain, so in Britain its appeal rested largely on Oswald Mosley. After the failure to win cabinet approval for his plans for unemployment in 1930, and their rejection by the Parliamentary Labour party, Mosley founded his own New party in March 1931. This contested 24 seats in the 1931 General Election, polling 36 777 votes in all — 22 out of the 24 candidates forfeited their deposits. In 1932 Mosley visited Italy and came back resolved to imitate what he had seen there. In October the British Union of Fascists was founded with all the paraphernalia of a military-style organisation: uniform, salutes and parades. All were designed to reinforce loyalty and discipline. For a time, Mosley attracted quite a lot of support — William Morris, the future Lord Nuffield, contributed £50 000 to the New party, Lord Rothermere, proprietor of the *Daily Mail* and three other newspapers, gave his approval to the Fascist movement.

But as Fascism acquired its unpleasant overtones of anti-semitism and the use of violence towards its opponents, it lost its appeal. In June 1934 a mass meeting at Olympia was marked by the gratuitous brutality meted out to Anti-Fascist demonstrators by Mosley's strong-arm men. In April 1935, Mosley's own anti-semitic sentiments were clearly revealed in a speech he made at Leicester: 'For the first time I openly and publicly challenge the Jewish interest in this country, commanding commerce, commanding the press, commanding the cinema, commanding the City of London, killing industry with sweatshops. These Jewish interests are not intimidating and will not intimidate the Fascist movement of this age.' [Stevenson and Cook, pp. 204–5] In directing his hostility at the Jews, Mosley forfeited any support he might have had from radical politicians such as John Strachey, who at one time had sympathised with Mosley's economic ideas. Right-wing circles were also offended – Rothermere withdrew his support after the Olympia meeting. Mosley's only achievement, in fact, was to provoke violent reaction to the activities of his supporters, the most celebrated example of which was 'the battle of Cable Street' in October 1936. On this occasion anti-fascist groups, attempting to block a march planned by the fascists, clashed with the police who were there to protect the marchers. There were 88 arrests and 70 injuries. The fascists were unscathed.

Stevenson and Cook, *The Slump: Society and Politics during the Depression*

Oswald Mosley (second from R , front rank) leads a march through London's East End, April 1936

This event at least had a positive result. In December 1936 the government introduced the Public Order Act, banning the wearing of uniforms and allowing Chief Constables to prohibit marches and demonstrations with the Home Secretary's approval. The Act was invoked to stop all further marches in the East End of London where violence was likely to erupt. Shorn of this weapon, Fascism soon ceased to have much impact. Its 66 candidates in the 1937 municipal elections gained only 2 000 votes between them.

What has been called 'the civility' of British politics proved strong enough to contain extremist movements both on the Left and on the Right. London witnessed little of the street violence that broke out in Germany in the early 1930s. There were only two deaths in consequence of all the marches and demonstrations that took place in Britain, both of them in Belfast where the Irish dimension aggravated the situation. Most observers commented that unemployment tended to breed apathy rather than resentment. The NUWM discovered that, except in South Wales, it drew more support from areas where unemployment was relatively low than it did from the most depressed areas. The fact that unemployment in Britain was concentrated in the remoter parts of the country, making concerted action difficult, may also have had something to do with the lack of organised opposition. The dole, for all the criticism directed at it, took the edge off the sense of grievance. Perhaps, too, despite the persistence of class divisions and gross inequalities of wealth, the British people were still a remarkably united people. When the Prince of Wales toured South Wales in 1932 he was given a hero's welcome. The Silver Jubilee in 1935 was celebrated with greater enthusiasm in working-class districts than in middle-class suburbs. Such moods cannot be measured but they register a fundamental sense of community on which Britain's political stability ultimately depended.

Critics

While the slump persuaded some British intellectuals to reject capitalism altogether, others approached the problem differently. Could it not be made to work more efficiently? By far the most influential of these thinkers was J. M. Keynes, and he was supported by a wide variety of politicians, civil servants and other academic economists. There were groups such as Political and Economic Planning, founded in 1931, which contained civil servants, businessmen and academics, and the Pilgrim Trust, the brain child of an American millionaire, founded in 1930, which devoted a lot of its attention to investigating the problems of unemployment. Their combined efforts were to change the climate of opinion about the role of government in economic affairs, a change which has been christened the Keynesian revolution.

At the inevitable risk of oversimplification it may be argued that Keynes changed the whole approach to the problem of unemployment. Conventional economic analysis took the view that full employment was a natural condition to which any economy tended. It might be upset by the trade cycle, but left to themselves, economic forces would work themselves out to restore full employment. During a slump wages would fall, costs would come down and employers would take on more labour until the process of recovery was under way. Conventional economics also asserted that investment (i.e. the application of wealth to the production of factories, railways, machines etc.) depended on the level of savings. The Treasury opposed expenditure on public works because diverting savings into public expenditure would 'be merely to substitute less productive public investment for more productive private investment.' [Meade, 'The Keynesian Revolution' Keynes (ed.), p. 83]

M. Keynes (ed.), *Essays on John Maynard Keynes* (CUP, 1975)

In *The General Theory of Interest, Employment and Money*, published in 1936, Keynes upset both these fundamental ideas. He argued that it was perfectly possible

THE BRITISH ECONOMY AND THE NATIONAL GOVERNMENT

for an economy to operate at a level below full employment for an indefinite period of time, as indeed the British economy had been doing. Nor was there any guarantee that savings would find their way into productive investment. In an economy suffering from a high level of unemployment, so far from government spending pre-empting resources that would have been used more productively by the private sector, Keynes argued that government spending would stimulate consumption which would in turn promote more investment. In one celebrated passage he even denied that such spending need have any economic justification:

If the Treasury were to fill old bottles with banknotes, bury them at suitable depths in disused coal-mines which are then filled up with town rubbish, and leave it to private enterprise on well tried principles of *laissez-faire* to dig the notes up again ... there need be no more unemployment, and with the help of the repercussions, the real income of the community, and its capital wealth also, would probably become a good deal greater than it actually is. [Keynes, p. 129]

J. M. Keynes, The General Theory of Interest, Employment and Money (Macmillan, 1936)

Keynes also introduced the idea of the multiplier which he owed to one of his pupils, R. F. Kahn. Kahn pointed out that every initial injection of government spending would be spent several times over. A road-building programme, for instance, would yield income to the contractors and workers which would be spent on capital equipment and on consumer goods; the money received would be spent again, and so on, though at each stage a certain amount would leak out into savings. The importance of the idea lay in the realisation that a comparatively small injection of capital expenditure by the government could have ripple effects which would multiply the number of jobs created.

The implications for government policy arising out of *The General Theory* were far-reaching. If full employment was not a natural condition, then market forces could not be relied on to achieve it. But remedies were available. The level of employment depended on aggregate demand which Keynes analysed into the following components: Consumption, Investment, Government Expenditure and Exports minus Imports. If aggregate demand was insufficient to keep the country's resources fully employed, then it should be the government's task to raise it. This could be done either by reducing taxation (and so increasing consumption) or by increasing government expenditure, or by some combination of the two. Whether the government balanced its budget was, in Keynes's view, largely irrelevant. The economies pursued by the inter-war governments were actually self-defeating and made the employment situation worse rather than better. Keynes thus prepared the way for the managed economy in which governments would maintain full employment by sustaining aggregate demand at the appropriate level, through using the levers of taxation and public spending.

The publication of *The General Theory* in February 1936 caused a considerable stir. It met with a mixed reaction from professional economists, winning both praise and criticism. But of its importance there could be no doubt. In the next 10 years there were at least 300 articles written in professional journals arising out of the book. Its optimistic message that unemployment could be cured without resorting to all the apparatus of socialist planning gave Economics as a subject a new appeal. It lost its reputation as 'the dismal science' and attracted new generations of students.

The effect of the book on government policy is harder to trace. It certainly had no immediate impact. But in 1937 Keynes wrote three articles in *The Times* on 'How to avoid a slump', in which he urged an increase in public spending in the distressed areas. One of the senior officials in the Treasury, Sir Frederick Phillips, who was conversant with Keynes's writings, argued for the same policy at a cabinet committee meeting in August. The seed had been sown. It was really the Second World War which brought about general acceptance of Keynesian ideas. This can best be demonstrated by the White Paper on Employment Policy produced by the Treasury in 1944. This put forward as an attainable objective the maintenance of a high and stable level of employment. In committing the government to such a goal the Treasury admitted that it lay within its powers to determine the level of employment. This, in essence, was the Keynesian revolution.

The Treasury had been converted, but politicians still needed to be convinced. The Labour party had little difficulty in assimilating Keynes's prescriptions. So long as there was a private sector, capitalism might as well be made to work efficiently. To those who believed in a planned economy a managed economy was a perfectly acceptable half-way house. Though Keynes has been hailed as 'the saviour of capitalism', a claim he never made himself incidentally, the post-war Labour governments, at least until 1976, generally accepted the Keynesian way of looking at the economy and adopted the solutions he would have advocated for dealing with unemployment.

The conversion of the Conservative party to Keynes involved a much bigger breach with party doctrine. It took longer to accomplish and was never entirely whole-hearted. But a substantial section of the party was won over, including a future Prime Minister. In this context, Harold Macmillan's book '*The Middle Way*' has considerable importance. In the 1930s Macmillan was MP for Stockton on Tees, in the heart of the depressed North East of England. In a speech made to the Conservative party in 1958 he recalled the unemployment of those years: 'As long as I live I can never forget the impoverishment and demoralisation which all this brought with it. I am determined, as far as it lies within human power, never to allow this shadow to fall again upon our country.' [Macmillan, pp. xxiv–xxv] *The Middle Way* was published in 1938 and from the footnote references alone it is clear that it owed a great deal to *The General Theory*. Macmillan fully accepted the Keynesian diagnosis of the ills of capitalism and he drew up his own set of remedies. They included industrial reconstruction, a national investment board, the careful control of overseas trade and investment and the setting up of an economic council to co-ordinate the government's economic policies. His conclusion indicated the strength of his convictions:

H. Macmillan, *The Middle Way* (1938)

> My case is that, through the Economic Council and the bodies responsible for financial, foreign trade and industrial policy, the Government will be expected to achieve full employment of the labour and capital resources of the nation. It will be left with no excuse for failing to do so. For, although it will not control the enterprises engaged upon production, it will control the conditions to which these enterprises respond. If full employment does not result; if we are still enduring the paradox of poverty amidst potential plenty; then clearly it will be a result of the Government's failure to take full advantage of the powers and opportunities that lie ready to its hand to bring about the conditions in which productive enterprise would expand to a full capacity of prosperity, limited only by the economic resources of the nation. [Macmillan, p. 300]

THE BRITISH ECONOMY AND THE NATIONAL GOVERNMENT

When the Conservatives returned to power in 1951 the Keynesian consensus was already well established. There was no fundamental change in unemployment policies. For this Macmillan, who himself became Prime Minister in 1957, deserves a good deal of the credit. By his championship of Keynesian ideas in 1938 he had made them respectable, at least to the more forward-looking members of his own party.

The effects of the slump were far-reaching, and the failure of the national government to solve the problem of unemployment provoked a wide range of opposition and criticism. It was not, however, the more extreme among the government's opponents who had most impact. Paradoxically, perhaps, it was from critics in the ranks of the academic and political establishment that real changes in government policies towards the economy were to come.

POINTS AT ISSUE
POINTS AT ISSUE **POINTS AT ISSUE** POINTS AT ISSUE
POINTS AT ISSUE

Public Spending and Unemployment

The most controversial aspects of the policies pursued by the inter-war governments were the insistence on balanced budgets and the unwillingness to use expenditure on public works as a way of curing unemployment. These issues are as relevant to the 1980s as they were in the 1930s, and it is impossible not to be aware of the present debate (and the current unemployment figures) when looking at the arguments that surround economic policy between the wars.

Views about the wisdom or otherwise of government policy during this period inevitably reflect both the standpoint of the observer and the point in time at which he is writing. Up to about 1973 most historians and economists shared in the Keynesian consensus, though there were always a few dissentients. After 1973, with the evident failure of governments in Western Europe and in the United States to solve simultaneously the problems of inflation and unemployment, scepticism began to creep in, and by the 1980s a new consensus, based upon the monetarist theories of Milton Friedman, had captured right-wing circles both in this country and the United States.

The following excerpts illustrate, first the general criticisms made of the inter-war government in the light of Keynes's ideas, and secondly the growing reservations as to whether his policies, if applied, would have been any more successful.

S. F. Pollard, *The Development of the British Economy, 1914–67* (first published in 1962)

> In the wider sense, the new doctrine held that it was the duty of the Government, by budgetary as well as other means, to control the economy so as to keep it at a steady and high level of activity. This doctrine, common property and widely adopted now, made little impression on the Government in the 1930s. Sweden, Australia, New Zealand and, above all, the USA carried out policies which, however unconsciously, were in line with the new economics; but in Britain the pragmatic efforts of the Labour Government of 1929–31 to foster public works by the Development (Loan Guarantee and Grants) Act and the Colonial Development Act of 1929, and to admit more progressive economic thought by the Economic Advisory Council ... were a failure. Although Keynes made many converts among academic economists, it was not until the early years of the war that the new economics received official sanction in budgetary policy and elsewhere. It

POINTS AT ISSUE
POINTS AT ISSUE
POINTS AT ISSUE
POINTS AT ISSUE

followed from the new, and now generally accepted doctrine that British budgetary policy in the inter-war years was of a nature to aggravate the trade cycle.... Technically the reduction of the floating debt, partly by repayment and largely by funding, was highly successful, but the fact that the immense deflationary pressure was applied from April 1920 onwards, when the boom began to sag, greatly aggravated the effects and extent of the slump. Budgetary policy was similarly ill-timed in the recurring crises and difficulties of the remainder of the inter-war years. [Pollard, first edition (1962), pp. 209–10]

J. Meade, 'The Keynesian Revolution'

The revolution in practical governmental policy is of much greater importance and significance for the welfare of mankind. But it can be expressed and discussed in many fewer words. It is now universally recognised by governments, at least throughout the industrialised free-enterprise world, that it is one of their primary duties to control the level of total effective demand for goods and services. If demand is insufficient to provide full employment, it is the government's duty to raise it .... This general task of controlling the level of total effective demand was not recognised to be a duty of government before the Second World War; it has been generally so recognised since the war. [*Essays on John Maynard Keynes*, Keynes (ed.), pp. 87–8]

R. Skidelsky, 'The Reception of the Keynesian Revolution'

Even though the British political culture was highly resistant to change, we may ask why it was proof against the overwhelming *fact* of mass unemployment. The answer is that the existence of a new and unpleasant fact is not the same as the perception of the fact as a problem, and even if it is perceived as a problem, it may not be perceived as a crisis which has to be overcome if the system is to survive. In fact, the British political system survived the era of mass unemployment with comparative ease, even though the economy was thereby enfeebled and *entirely avoidable suffering* [author's italics] inflicted on millions of people.

Skidelsky goes on to argue that it was the Second World War which made possible the adoption of Keynesian techniques for managing the economy:

It has been very far from my intention to suggest that Keynesian theory and the fiscal techniques to which it gave rise have not played a vital part in winning peacetime acceptance for Keynesian policies. Nor do I deny that the prolonged experience of mass unemployment and the shorter though sharper experience of depression played their part in discrediting the old ideas. My argument rather is that it required the Second World War to convince men in all sections of society that a 'new age' requiring a 'new wisdom' had indeed arrived to stay. [*Essay on John Maynard Keynes*, Keynes (ed.), pp. 101–2, 105–6]

Doubts about the efficacy of Keynesian-style policies, had they been applied in the inter-war period, rest upon both practical and theoretical grounds. The practical objections relate to the specific nature of Britain's unemployment problem.

A. J. P. Taylor, *English History, 1914–1945* (first published in 1965)

Moreover, Keynes and his school did the wrong sum so far as Britain was concerned. They saw the problem as a permanent pool of unemployed men and unemployed resources, and proposed to dry out this pool by planned expenditure from public funds. This analysis was correct for the United States and still is. The British problem was at once simpler and more intractable. The old England of the declining staple industries had a surplus of resources which could not be brought back into use even by a lavish credit policy. The new England had reached in a later phase, something like full employment except during the world Depression. Public spending stimulated industries which were already prospering, without doing much to reduce those industries which were in decline. Yet prevailing opinion, including that of Keynes, rejected the alternative course of a directed or planned economy. Under such circumstances, the endless economic debates in parliament fumbled in the dark, occupying much time, creating much passion, leading to little result. [Taylor, p. 440]

S. Constantine, *Unemployment in Britain between the Wars* (first published in 1980)

Nor is it entirely certain that the world was waiting for Keynes. The monetary and fiscal solutions he proposed in his 1920s writings and in *The General Theory* might have checked cyclical depression, but it can be argued that he offered no solution to the structural problem which lay at the heart of regional unemployment. Government action to stimulate aggregate demand in the economy might have soaked up the pools of unemployment in the growing areas of the South and East, but it might have still left a severe problem in South Wales or Tyneside unless the demand generated by monetary and fiscal policies either revived existing industries in these areas (which is doubtful) or encouraged the settlement there of new industries. For that to happen government planning and direction of investment would probably be necessary and on this Keynes himself had little to say. The most practical programmes for government action were those like Macmillan's *The Middle Way*, which combined state direction of industry with the supporting financial policies for which Keynes's mature work provided the theoretical justification. Such proposals were not fully developed in the 1930s. In the light of the 1970s it can also be less easily claimed that the new economic thinking of the 1930s produced all the answers. [Constantine, p. 78]

One school of economists never accepted the validity of the Keynesian attack on classical economics. They differed with Keynes on a variety of grounds. Among the most outspoken of his critics was Harry G. Johnson, Professor of Economics at the London School of Economics, and also a Fellow of King's College, Cambridge.

In his essay *Keynes and British Economics*, published in 1975, Johnson attacks Keynes on several fronts. He is accused of getting the causes of mass unemployment wrong:

I have argued that the sources of the problem of mass unemployment with which *The General Theory* was concerned lay in severe monetary disturbance created by perverse monetary policies thoroughly reconcilable with the orthodox neo-classical tradition of monetary theory, and not in any inherent deficiency of capitalism requiring a new causal theory and a new set of policy prescriptions and governmental responsibilities.

Keynes is attacked for opportunism and inconsistency:

Thus Keynes realised fully, and exposed brilliantly in *The Economic Consequences of Mr. Churchill*, the adverse consequences for Britain of the return of the gold standard. But once that decision had become a part of the order of things, he absorbed it and turned to advocating public works as a way of increasing employment; and in 1931 he came out in favour of protection. These gyrations frequently made him seem inconsistent to his contemporaries; actually the examples cited can be easily reconciled by reference to the modern theory of second-best, but Keynes never spelled out such a theory. *The General Theory* represents the apotheosis of opportunism in this sense, in two ways. Mass unemployment had lasted so long that it appeared to the average man to be the natural state of affairs which economics was powerless to explain and political processes powerless to alter; a new theory of its causes that promised an easy cure was thus certain to sell, provided its author had impeccable professional credentials...

Finally, the Keynesian Revolution is blamed for 'encouragement to the indulgence of the belief of the political process that economic policy can transcend the laws of economics with the aid of sufficient economic cleverness, in the sense of being able to satisfy all demands for security of economic tenure without inflation or balance of payments problems, or less obvious sacrifice of efficiency and economic growth potentialities.' Johnson concludes: 'A good case could even be made to the effect that Keynes was too expensive a luxury for a country inexorably declining in world economic and political importance and obliged to scramble for dignified survival, to be able to afford.' [H. G. Johnson, 'Keynes and British Economics' in *Essays*, Milo Keynes (ed.), pp. 112, 115–116, 122]

The layman is in no position to adjudicate between the rival theories of professional economists. But common sense might incline him to argue that classical economics patently failed to explain the severity of the inter-war depression, or to cure it, and to note that Western Europe and the United States enjoyed nearly 30 years of full employment at a time when Keynesian ideas dominated the making of economic policy.

Books cited

S. F. Pollard, *The Development of the British Economy, 1914–80* (Arnold, 1983)
Essays on John Maynard Keynes, Milo Keynes (ed.), (CUP, 1975)
A. J. P. Taylor, *English History, 1914–1945* (Penguin, 1970)
S. Constantine, *Unemployment in Britain between the Wars* (Longman, 1980)

BIBLIOGRAPHY BIBLIOGRAPHY BIBLIOGRAPHY BIBLIOGRAPHY BIBLIOGRAPHY BIBLIOGRAPHY
BIBLIOGRAPHY BIBLIOGRAPHY BIBLIOGRAPHY BIBLIOGRAPHY BIBLIOGRAPHY BIBLIOGRAPHY
BIBLIOGRAPHY BIBLIOGRAPHY BIBLIOGRAPHY BIBLIOGRAPHY BIBLIOGRAPHY BIBLIOGRAPHY
BIBLIOGRAPHY BIBLIOGRAPHY BIBLIOGRAPHY BIBLIOGRAPHY BIBLIOGRAPHY BIBLIOGRAPHY
BIBLIOGRAPHY BIBLIOGRAPHY BIBLIOGRAPHY BIBLIOGRAPHY BIBLIOGRAPHY BIBLIOGRAPHY
BIBLIOGRAPHY BIBLIOGRAPHY BIBLIOGRAPHY BIBLIOGRAPHY BIBLIOGRAPHY BIBLIOGRAPHY

CHAPTER 8
FURTHER READING

The Economy

Essential

S. Constantine, *Unemployment in Britain between the Wars* (Longman, 1980)
S. F. Pollard, *The Development of the British Economy, 1914–1980* (Arnold, 1983)

Social Conditions

Essential

G. Orwell, *The Road to Wigan Pier* (Penguin, 1962)
J. Stevenson and C. Cook, *The Slump: Society and Politics during the Depression* (Cape, 1977)

Government Policies

Essential

A. Bullock, *The Life and Times of Ernest Bevin, vol. I* (Heinemann, 1960)
K. Feiling, *The Life of Neville Chamberlain* (Macmillan, 1946)
K. Middlemas and J. Barnes, *Baldwin* (Weidenfeld & Nicolson, 1969)

Recommended

P. Snowden, *An Autobiography, vols. I and II* (Ivor Nicholson & Watson, 1934)

Critics of Government Policy

Essential

H. Macmillan, *The Middle Way* (Macmillan, 1966)
D. E. Moggridge, *Keynes* (Fontana, 1976)

Recommended

R. F. Harrod, *The Life of John Maynard Keynes* (Macmillan, 1966)
M. Keynes (ed.), *Essays on John Maynard Keynes* (CUP, 1975)
R. Lekachman, *The Age of Keynes* (Penguin, 1966)
D. Winch, *Economics and Policy* (Fontana, 1972)

Fascism

Essential

R. Skidelsky, *Oswald Mosley* (Macmillan, 1975)

Recommended

C. Cross, *The Fascists in Britain* (Barrie & Rockliffe, 1961)

The Labour Party

Essential

H. Pelling, *A Short History of the Labour Party* (Macmillan, 1969)

LOCAL RESEARCH PROJECT

The argument over living conditions during the Slump continues. Possible lines of enquiry could be: local unemployment rates; the incidence of new factory building in the area concerned; housing developments; the level of means-tested benefits in comparison with local wage rates; and local health statistics.

Conditions during the Slump

Introductory

The best recent books are:
J. Stevenson (ed.), *Social Conditions in Britain between the Wars* (Penguin, 1977)
J. Stevenson and C. Cook, *The Slump: Society and Politics during the Depression* (Cape, 1977)

Suggested sources of information

N. Branson and M. Heineman, *Britain in the Nineteen Thirties* (Panther, 1981)

Three vivid if impressionistic accounts of England in the 1930s are:
George Orwell, *The Road to Wigan Pier* (Penguin, 1962)
J. B. Priestley, *English Journey* (Book Club Associates, 1984) and
S. P. B. Mais (ed.) *Time to Spare* (an anthology of the views of several unemployed workers) (Allen & Unwin, 1935).

Further sources

Until 1930 Boards of Guardians were responsible for the administration of Poor Relief. Thereafter Poor Relief became the responsibility, in most cases, of the Social Services Committees of County Councils. County Record Offices should have both sets of records: it should be possible to trace both rates of benefit and numbers in receipt of it from these sources. The Town Hall should be able to provide information about local housing and industrial development. Old established firms might be able to supply information about wage rates, and the Medical Officer of Health should be able to provide health statistics on infant mortality rates, for instance.

CHAPTER 9

Britain and the World, 1929–39: The Outbreak of the Second World War

A ▰▰▰▰ THE INTERNATIONAL BACKGROUND

The international climate after the Wall Street Crash became increasingly threatening, until the storm finally broke in 1939. It is tempting, with the advantage of hindsight, to argue that it could never have been averted. But that would be to acquit the policy-makers of the 1930s of all responsibility for the final outcome. Even if the limits within which they had to work were narrower than their opponents were prepared to admit, there were real choices to be made. The continuing debate over appeasement proves that both politicians at the time and the historians who have reconstructed their actions believe that the Second World War might have been prevented.

The Aggressor States

The world in 1929 can be crudely, but not inaccurately, divided into those countries who were bent on extending their territories and those who were contented with the status quo. Of the aggressor states, the first to resort to military action was Japan. Japan had emerged from the First World War as a significant naval power, as was recognised in the Washington Naval Agreement of 1922. She had substantial economic interests in mainland China, the collapse of whose government provided a standing invitation to Japanese intervention. Her government, nominally a constitutional monarchy under the Emperor Hirohito, was plagued by political violence and came increasingly under the domination of a military clique, bent on a programme of territorial expansion. If and when she chose to embark on her military conquests no European power had the will or the means to prevent her, and the United States was equally unwilling to get involved.

Britain was necessarily concerned because of her possessions in the Far East: Hong Kong, Malaya and Singapore. There were also British communities in Shanghai and Wei-Hai-Wei. The threat of Japanese aggression was a constant source of worry to British defence planners. The creation of a huge naval base at Singapore was begun in 1923, but not completed until 1938, by which time Britain could no longer supply the ships to guard it.

Since 1922 Italy had been effectively ruled by Benito Mussolini, self-styled Duce, though nominally Italy was also still a constitutional monarchy. In his early years of power Mussolini was content to consolidate his authority and to do what he could to improve the Italian economy. He is popularly credited with making the trains run on time, but he also had a hand in expanding Italian grain production. As his hold on power tightened his ambitions increased, and by 1932 he had decided on a programme of territorial expansion. There were several reasons for this. Fascist ideology was imbued with militaristic claptrap, of which the following slogans provide typical examples:

D. Mack Smith,
Mussolini's Roman Empire (1977)

'Better one day as a lion than a hundred years as a sheep.'
'War is to man as maternity is to woman.'
[Smith, pp. 47–8]

Benito Mussolini,
Duce of Italy
1922–42
(taken in 1923)

Having created an army, Mussolini wanted to use it. He was anxious to expunge the humiliation inflicted on Italian troops by Abyssinia at the battle of Adowa in 1896. He claimed, too, that Italy needed living space for her rapidly rising population, and that she would bring civilisation to the territories she acquired as Rome had done centuries earlier. Mussolini's ambitions were directed primarily at Abyssinia which abutted onto the colonies of Eritrea and Italian Somaliland, but he also coveted parts of the Balkan peninsula. Corfu was bombarded in 1923; Albania and Greece were both to become victims of Italian aggression in 1939 and 1940 respectively.

Lastly, there was Germany. Most Germans wanted to see the Treaty of Versailles revised. Such revision included the ending of restrictions on German armaments; the right to remilitarise the Rhineland; the recovery of Danzig and the Polish corridor; and the inclusion within the Reich of all German-speaking peoples, notably the Austrians and the Sudeten Germans. Hitler owed much of his popularity to the emphasis he placed on the attainment of these objectives. But what distinguished him from his predecessors in the German Chancellery was that Hitler was prepared to use force, or the threat of force. Nor would Hitler have been content with the re-establishment of Germany's frontiers as they were in 1914. If *Mein Kampf* is to be believed Germany also needed *Lebensraum* (living space) in Eastern Europe. Hitler reaffirmed this objective in a later book, written, but never published, in 1928. Despite the doubts cast by A. J. P. Taylor on Hitler's commitment to the long term ambitions described in *Mein Kampf* [see Taylor, pp. 68–9] in practice the invasion of Poland in 1939 and of Russia in 1941 both suggest that while Hitler was an opportunist when it came to the timing of his initiatives, he did not waver in the pursuit of his objectives.

A. Hitler, *Mein Kampf* (Hutchinson, 1940)

A. J. P. Taylor, *The Origins of the Second World War* (1961)

Adolph Hitler, Chancellor of Germany 1933–45 (taken on his way to the Reichstag on becoming Chancellor in January 1933).

In 1936 these three countries, Japan, Italy and Germany, came together in the Anti-Comintern Pact. While this was not a formal alliance it was an expression of certain shared characteristics: a sense of grievance, whether deserved or not; a willingness to resort to force; a contempt for the forces of internationalism such as the League of Nations; and an authoritarian style of government which tolerated no opposition and made no provision for constitutional change. Finally, there was an element of irrationality in the foreign policies pursued by each of these countries. While there might be a cold calculation of the risks of a particular stroke of policy, for instance Hitler's decision to remilitarise the Rhineland in 1936, it was just as likely that a decision would be taken on the spur of the moment in a mood of anger or pique. The unpredictable was always likely to happen and one of the main hazards Western statesmen faced in dealing with Hitler and Mussolini was the difficulty of gauging their intentions.

The Satisfied States

The main satisfied states of Europe were France and Britain. After her experiences in the First World War and the recovery of Alsace-Lorraine after it France had no further territorial ambitions. Rather she sought to construct a system of alliances with the countries of Eastern Europe, and if possible with Britain, that would enable her to restrain a resurgent Germany. Her defence policy was based upon the Maginot line, a huge fortification on her Eastern frontier with Germany, behind which French armies would shelter rather than proceed to disastrous offensives as they had done in 1914. France was a political democracy, but a deeply divided one. The political spectrum embraced semi-fascist right-wing groups such as the *Action Francaise* or the *Croix de Feu* and a significant Communist party (it polled 1 million votes in 1928) which took its instructions from Moscow. The French party system in conjunction with a system of proportional representation made it inevitable that no one party would ever command a majority in the Chamber of Deputies. Thus French governments between the wars were drawn from a series of shifting coalitions. The Bloc National represented the forces of the Right, the Cartel des Gauches those of the Left. On three occasions, 1928, 1932 and 1936, the Cartel won a handsome majority, but the divisions between the Radicals, the Socialists and the Communists prevented it from forming a stable administration. French politics in the 1930s produced a series of weak and short-lived governments with whom co-operation was never going to be easy.

Britain, as we have already seen, had problems enough with the territories for which she was responsible. Her interests could only be served by the maintenance of peace, and the same applied to Belgium and the Netherlands, the Scandinavian countries, Spain and Portugal. Those states which had succeeded the Austro-Hungarian Empire, Yugoslavia, Czechoslovakia and Poland, were all potential victims rather than aggressors, though Poland did cast covetous eyes at part of Czechoslovakia. None of these countries, it needs to be stressed, would have gone to war to bring about a change in their frontiers. In that sense they were satisfied.

Outside Europe proper were the two countries destined to become the Super Powers, the Soviet Union and the United States. After Lenin's first stroke in 1922 there was a struggle for power within the Soviet Union, eventually won by Stalin. In personal terms this led to first the exile and then the assassination of Trotsky, Stalin's main opponent, in 1940. In political terms it meant victory for Stalin's strategy of 'Socialism in One Country' rather than the continuous effort to promote world revolution, favoured by Trotsky and his supporters.

Internally, Stalin's policies in the 1930s involved the massive programme of industrialisation embodied in the Five-Year Plans and the attempt to boost agricultural production through the collectivisation of agriculture. But these years also witnessed the liquidation of the Kulaks (the richer peasants) and the notorious spy trials and purges which extended to the higher reaches of the Bolshevik party and to the commanders of the Red Army. That blueprint of political democracy, the 1936 Constitution, could not conceal, except from the most naive observer, the reality of Stalin's power and those henchmen whom he still trusted.

Russia's external policies showed the same gap between appearance and inner purpose. The emphasis on economic growth implied by Stalin's Five-Year Plans had as its corollary the need for Western economic co-operation, and there was a corresponding reduction in the activities of the Comintern. Whereas in the 1920s Communist parties in Europe had been officially discouraged from any form of co-operation with 'bourgeois' parties such as the German Social Democrats or the British Labour party, in the 1930s Stalin encouraged the formation of Popular Front governments in France and Spain. But the downfall of capitalism was postponed, not abandoned, as an objective. Stalin would do whatever he felt to be necessary in pursuit of Russia's security, even going to the lengths of allying himself with his most inveterate opponent, Hitler, in 1939. Western statesmen, in seeking to deter aggression by widening the anti-fascist front, were faced with an unappealing ally in the Soviet Union.

Nor was there much reliance to be placed on the United States. American foreign policy between the wars continued to reflect the isolationist mood which took the United States out of the League of Nations in 1920. This mood, if anything, was strengthened after the Wall Street Crash when tariff barriers went up and every European country adopted 'sauve qui peut' exchange rate policies. Franklin D. Roosevelt, President of the United States from 1933 until his death in 1945, was a good democrat and naturally sympathetic to Britain and France. But there was little he could do in the face of an isolationist-minded Congress. In 1935 the Nye Committee, set up to investigate the role of munitions sales in causing American entry into the First World War, concluded that the high profits made by American bankers and manufacturers had been instrumental in getting the United States involved. Partly in consequence Congress proceeded to pass the first of three Neutrality Acts. This banned the sale of arms and munitions to any belligerent. It denied to the President any discretion in applying the ban and thus prevented the United States from aiding its friends, while harming its enemies. Roosevelt vainly tried to have the Act repealed or amended. It was not until war had broken out in 1939 that it was made possible for belligerents to purchase arms, and then only on condition that they paid in cash and transported the arms in their own ships.

In the face of such strong Congressional opposition to any step which might involve the United States in Europe's affairs, there was little Roosevelt could do, beyond making suggestions or indicating his disapproval. In a press conference he gave in July 1937, Roosevelt admitted his limitations. Urged by the leaders of several countries to take the initiative for peace, Roosevelt commented that people were looking 'for somebody outside of Europe to come forward with a hat and a rabbit in it'. 'Well' he said, 'I haven't got a hat and I haven't got a rabbit in it.' [Dallek, p. 144] Messages sent to Hitler and Mussolini in April 1939, appealing for a ten-year guarantee of non-aggression against 31 potential victims, were greeted with contempt. Henry Wallace, one of Roosevelt's cabinet ministers, likened this effort to 'delivering a sermon to a mad dog'. [Dallek, p. 186] British politicians were thus

F.D. Roosevelt, President of the USA (1933–45)

R. Dallek, *Franklin D. Roosevelt and American Foreign Policy, 1935–1945* (1978)

faced with a dangerous and uncertain world. Of their potential allies, France was internally divided and committed to a defence policy that would enable her to protect her own borders, but do no more; the Soviet Union could be relied on to fish in troubled waters, but little else; and the United States was incapable of offering more than moral support.

BRITAIN AND THE WORLD, 1929–39: THE OUTBREAK OF THE SECOND WORLD WAR

POLICY MAKERS AND POLICIES

Prime Ministers		Foreign Secretaries	**The Makers of**
			Policies
1929–31 Ramsay MacDonald	(1929 –– August 1931)	Arthur Henderson	
1931–35 Ramsay MacDonald	(August – November 1931)	Lord Reading	
	(November 1931 – June 1935)	Sir John Simon	
1935–37 Stanley Baldwin	(June – December 1935)	Sir Samuel Hoare	
	(December 1935 – February 1938)	Anthony Eden	
1937–40 Neville Chamberlain	(February 1938 – December 1940)	Lord Halifax	

Permanent under-secretaries at the Foreign Office
1930–38   Sir Robert (later Lord) Vansittart
1938–46   Sir Alexander Cadogan

Whereas during the years prior to the outbreak of the First World War foreign policy had been very much the preserve of the Foreign Secretary, Sir Edward Grey, during the 1930s, the situation was rather more complex. Of the three premiers concerned, MacDonald by 1931 was something of a spent force though he took an active interest in disarmament; Baldwin never trusted his own judgment in foreign affairs and in any case preferred to preside over rather than to direct or lead his cabinet. Neville Chamberlain, on the other hand, could never see a problem without wanting to solve it. He was very much the architect of the government's foreign policy from 1937 onwards. He employed his own adviser, Sir Horace Wilson, whose influence was preferred to that of the Foreign Office. Chamberlain believed in personal diplomacy, visiting Hitler on three separate occasions and Mussolini once. He by-passed Eden to such an extent that Eden eventually resigned from the Foreign Secretaryship. From 1937–39 Chamberlain's control over foreign policy was virtually unchallenged. Of the Foreign Secretaries, Arthur Henderson's primary concern was disarmament and he resigned before trouble developed. Lord Reading's tenure of office was so brief that it requires no comment. Simon, who managed to occupy five different cabinet posts, one of them twice, in the course of a long political career, had both the qualities and the shortcomings of the good lawyer. He was so good at seeing all the sides of a case that he became the victim of one of Lloyd George's more accurate thrusts:

'Simon has sat on the fence so long that the iron has entered his soul.' [Taylor, p. 87] Both as Foreign Secretary and later as Chancellor of the Exchequer, Simon's inclination was always to seek the path of compromise and conciliation. His successor, Sir Samuel Hoare, was equally committed to seeking peaceful solutions; such was his zeal in the case of Abyssinia that it brought his career as Foreign Secretary to a premature if undeserved conclusion. Eden was of a different temperament. Instinctively distrustful of the dictators, he was less willing to make accommodations with them and his resignation in 1938 came as no surprise. Lord Halifax (formerly Lord Irwin), the Viceroy of India, was naturally in sympathy with Chamberlain's policies though less optimistic about their outcome. The qualities which enabled him to get on with Gandhi were seen to less advantage in his dealings with Hitler.

Taylor, *The Origins of the Second World War*

The two Permanent under-secretaries at the Foreign Office, Vansittart and Cadogan, played contrasting roles. Vansittart was violently anti-German. He acknowledged in one of his publications that he did not dislike all Germans, only 'the bloody-minded bulk'. [Gilbert and Gott, p. 24] Vansittart used all his influence to promote an anti-German front, even if this meant condoning the aggressive policies of Mussolini. His hostility to Germany was such an obstacle to Chamberlain's policies that he was moved sideways to the prestigious but meaningless post of Chief Diplomatic Adviser in 1938. Cadogan did not share Vansittart's anti-German views and was in any case much more of a civil servant.

M. Gilbert and R. Gott, *The Appeasers* (1963)

Other significant influences on policy were the strategically placed ambassadors who might tell their masters what they wanted to hear or, more rarely, might modify the views held in London. Undoubtedly the most influential of these was Sir Neville Henderson, British ambassador to Germany from 1937 to 1939. So sympathetic was Henderson to Hitler that he became known as 'our Nazi ambassador in Berlin'. During the Czech crisis in 1938 Henderson's views were reinforced by those of Lord Perth in Rome, Lord Chilston in Moscow and the British Minister in Prague, Basil Newton. [Rock, pp. 61–2]

W. R. Rock, *British Appeasement in the 1930s* (1977)

Two major institutional sources of influence were the Chiefs of Staff Committee and the Treasury. Each stressed the limitations upon Britain's freedom of action. The Chiefs of Staff regularly produced reports for the cabinet. One such report in 1933 led to the setting up of the Defence Requirements Committee consisting of Sir Maurice Hankey (still very much at the centre of affairs), Vansittart and Sir Warren Fisher, Permanent under-secretary at the Treasury. Fisher's inclusion underlines the importance of economic considerations in the making of defence and foreign policy. The cost of rearmament was an ever-present consideration and the Treasury's advice had a particular impact on Chamberlain as an ex-Chancellor of the Exchequer himself. If Britain could not rearm at the same pace as Germany this, as Halifax put it in 1937, placed 'a heavy burden on diplomacy'.

Public Opinion

In a democracy foreign policy has also to take note of public opinion. In the 1930s this appeared to have an influence at two levels. There was first what might be called the level of the political establishment. This included that 'Top People's' paper, *The Times*. It was edited by Geoffrey Dawson from 1912–19, and again from 1923–41. Dawson was a firm believer in the appeasement of Germany, and *The Times* editorials generally supported the German case. There was also the country-house set who gathered at places like Cliveden as guests of Lord Astor, or Blickling Hall, Norfolk, the home of Lord Lothian. Lothian was a typical establishment figure and though never in the cabinet (he was under-secretary for India in 1931—32 and ambassador in Washington in 1939—40) his advice was regularly sought, frequently quoted. To this world there also belonged the Oxford Union. In 1933 it debated the motion that 'This House will in no circumstances fight for its King or Country.' The motion was passed by 257 votes to 153. It is impossible to gauge what influence the expression of such sentiments may have had but it all helped to create a climate of opinion, both at home and abroad, in which appeasement could flourish.

At a more popular level, public opinion manifested itself in episodes such as the Fulham by-election in October 1933. On this occasion a Conservative candidate, advocating increases in defence spending, was defeated by his Labour opponent and a Conservative majority of 14 621 was transformed into a Labour majority of 4840. It was to this by-election that Baldwin referred in a celebrated speech made in 1936, when he was attempting to justify the delay in the rearmament programme:

> I put before the whole House my own views with appalling frankness. From 1933, I and my friends were all very worried about what was happening in Europe. You will remember at that time the Disarmament Conference was sitting at Geneva. You will remember at that time there was probably a stronger pacifist feeling running through the country than at any time since the War. I am speaking of 1933 and 1934. You will remember the election in the autumn of 1933, when a seat which the National Government held was lost by about 7000 votes on no issue but the pacifist... I asked myself what chance was there – when that feeling that was given expression to in Fulham was common throughout the country – what chance was there within the next year or two of that feeling being changed so that the country would give a mandate for rearmament? [Middlemas and Barnes, p. 970]

K. Middlemas and J. Barnes, *Baldwin* (Weidenfeld & Nicolson, 1969)

Another example, frequently cited, was the Peace Ballot carried out in 1934, whose results were published in June 1935. Of the five questions, most invited the answer 'yes' – for instance 'Should Britain remain a member of the League?' or 'Are you in favour of an all round reduction in armaments by international agreement?' But the final question was more instructive. It asked: 'Do you consider that, if a nation insists on attacking another, the other nations should compel it to stop by (a) economic and non-military measures (b) if necessary, military measures?' About 10 million out of 11.5 million votes answered yes to (a). On (b) the votes were 6 784 368 yes 2 351 981 no. It was not an overwhelming expression of pacifist sentiment, though sometimes interpreted as such.

R. C. Sheriff, *Journey's End* (1933) (Penguin, 1983)

R. Graves, *Goodbye to All That* (1929) (Cassell, 1957)

E. Blunden, *Undertones of War* (1928) (Penguin, 1984)

Perhaps more influential in moulding opinion were the experiences of those who had actually fought and suffered in the First World War. Almost without exception the literary harvest of poems, plays and autobiographies yielded by the war condemned its wastefulness and futility. The poems of Siegfried Sassoon or Wilfred Owen; the play *Journey's End* by R. C. Sheriff; Robert Graves's autobiography *Goodbye to All That*, Edmund Blunden's *Undertones of War* and Vera Brittain's *Testament of Youth* were powerful testimonies. No British politician could lightly embark on a policy which appeared to increase rather than diminish the prospect of a second war.

V. Brittain, *Testament of Youth* (1933) (Virago, 1978)

Policy Options

Faced with aggression, there were three possible responses, short of war, which British governments could make. They might choose to rely wholly on the League of Nations which had after all been set up as a peace-keeping organisation and which imposed on its members the obligation to resist an aggressor. Alternatively they could pursue a policy of collective security through a system of regional alliances such as the Treaties of Locarno. Finally they might hope to forestall an aggressor by meeting his legitimate demands, by appeasing him.

Appeasement did not acquire its pejorative overtones until the Second World War. Its recent dictionary definitions include: 'make calm or quiet; try to conciliate or bribe (potential aggressor) by making concession, freq. with implication of sacrifice of principles; soothe, satisfy.' [*Concise Oxford Dictionary*] As a policy appeasement was first intended to conciliate; only later did it come to seem more like bribery. There is another distinction to be made. Appeasement could take both a passive and an active form. In its passive form appeasement involved reacting to aggression by simply tolerating it. In its active form it meant anticipating the demands of a potential aggressor and seeking to meet them in advance. In these senses Baldwin and his fellow ministers were passive appeasers, Chamberlain was an active one.

If these were the policy options, what were the limiting factors which conditioned Britain's choices? Three stand out. First, there were Britain's global commitments. Her possessions in the Far East, India, the Mediterranean and North Africa compelled Britain to give priority to maintaining the sea links joining the Empire, and if necessary to defend its threatened outposts. Secondly, there was Britain's vulnerability to air attack. London was very much closer to Germany's western boundaries, let alone western France, than Berlin was to the airfields of East Anglia. In 1934 Churchill described London as 'the greatest target in the world ... a valuable fat cow tied up to attract the beasts of prey'. [Middlemas and Barnes, p. 781] Baldwin once concluded: 'The bomber will always get through.' Should it do so, it was calculated, each ton of bombs dropped would cause up to 50 casualties; daily raids of up to 700 tons worth of bombs might be expected. To combat such a threat Britain would need to build up her own bomber force to act as a deterrent, and a chain of fighter stations to intercept that of the enemy.

Middlemas and Barnes,
Baldwin

Finally there was the sheer cost of rearmament. The Treasury argued that any major increase in defence spending would have catastrophic effects on the balance of payments. Imported raw materials accounted for 30% of new weapons. The shortage of skilled workers would mean that their transfer to the armaments industry would reduce production of exports. Should Britain run a serious trade deficit, sterling would come under pressure, the value of the pound would fall, and import prices would rise. This alarming scenario was presented every time demands were made to increase defence expenditure. It was only pushed aside in February 1939 when the cabinet finally agreed that Germany posed a more immediate threat than the balance of payments.

The last and most significant determinant of British policy was the awful threat that Britain might find herself at war with Germany, Italy and Japan all at once. After the invasion of Abyssinia by Italy in 1935, the Defence Requirements Committee faced this possibility. It concluded: 'It is a cardinal requirement of our National and Imperial security that our foreign policy should be so conducted as to avoid the possible development of a situation in which we might be confronted simultaneously with the hostility of Japan in the Far East, Germany in the West, and any power on the main lines of communication between the two.' [M. Howard, 'British Military Preparations for the Second World War', Dilks (ed.), p. 112]

D. Dilks (ed.), *Retreat
from Power*, vol. I
(1981)

If there was any single objective underlying British foreign policy in the 1930s it was to prevent such a situation arising.

C ▪ THE MACDONALD-BALDWIN ERA, 1929–37

The signing of the Kellogg-Briand Pact in 1928 was the high water mark of international co-operation. Among the consequences of the Wall Street Crash in 1929 was the withering of that tender plant. This became apparent in the two areas where international co-operation was sought: disarmament and international finance. Britain played a leading part in both initiatives and failure was certainly not due to lack of endeavour on the part of British statesmen.

The Collapse of International Co-operation

There were two major efforts to reduce the level of armaments. In 1929 the five leading naval powers, Britain, the United States, Japan, France and Italy, met in London to seek a formula restricting naval armaments. Agreement was reached between Britain, the United States and Japan but France was unwilling to accept parity with Italy because of her additional commitments on the Atlantic as well as the Mediterranean, and these two countries did not sign the main Agreement. At the time Japan's compliance was seen as a major diplomatic achievement, an illusion only too soon to be dispelled.

In 1932 a World Disarmament Conference convened at Geneva, at which both Germany and Russia were represented. Arthur Henderson was chosen to preside. The main problem was Germany's claim for parity of treatment. This might be achieved by other countries agreeing to reduce their armaments to the German level or, more realistically, allowing Germany to drop the restrictions imposed on her by the Treaty of Versailles. Sir John Simon accepted the justice of the German claim to equality of status but France was unwilling to see any change in Germany's relative position unless accompanied by further safeguards for France's security, for instance the creation of an international peacekeeping force. Several times the Conference looked to be on the point of collapse. Germany temporarily withdrew in September 1932 and was only persuaded to return in December after a five-power conference in Geneva agreed that Germany should be offered 'equality of rights in a system which would provide security for all nations'. In January 1933 Hitler became German Chancellor. He did not show his hand at once and the detailed proposals on force levels suggested by Eden – British Minister for the League – in March 1933 met with apparent approval. The Conference then adjourned. When it reassembled in October, Simon presented an Anglo-French plan whereby armaments would be kept at existing levels for five years, under international supervision, after which time all the powers would disarm to Germany's level. This was Hitler's cue. The same day the proposals were presented the German delegation withdrew and, shortly after, Germany left the League of Nations as well. The Disarmament Conference limped on until 1934 but in Germany's absence it accomplished nothing.

More progress was made in the neighbouring city of Lausanne where a conference between Britain, France and Germany met to deal with the reparations problem, yet again, in 1932. MacDonald put forward a compromise suggestion which was finally accepted by both France and Germany. Germany undertook to make a final payment of 2.6 million marks to a European Reconstruction Fund, which would end all her financial obligations. Unfortunately this settlement was unpopular in Germany to the extent that it may well have helped the Nazis in the subsequent election. By the time the reparations issue was disposed of, other grievances had taken its place.

With the collapse of the Gold Standard in 1931 and 1932 international trade suffered from increasing currency fluctuations. It was with the intention of doing something to restore international financial stability that the World Economic Conference convened in London in June 1933, with 64 separate countries being represented. It was the last great international gathering before the outbreak of the Second World War. There was an inevitable clash of interests between those countries such as France who were still on the Gold Standard and those, like Britain and the United States, who had left it. France wanted to see a return to fixed parities. The United States preferred a flexible exchange rate which would allow domestic prices to rise and still enable American exports to be competitive. A compromise might have been reached had not Roosevelt rejected any suggestion that the United States should agree to stabilise the international value of the dollar. He defended his decision on the grounds that 'the sound internal economic system of a nation is a greater factor in its economic well-being than the price of its currency in changing terms of the currencies of other nations'. [Dallek, p. 54] The Conference dispersed without any tangible result. Chamberlain doubted whether anything came of it 'except that they had all been forced to think'.

Dallek, *Franklin D. Roosevelt and American Foreign Policy, 1933–1945*

No further efforts were made to recreate a stable international monetary system. Just as the countries of Europe began to rearm in earnest, so they turned their backs on co-operation in the economic sphere.

The Failure of the League: Manchuria, German Rearmament and Abyssinia

In September 1931 Japan used the excuse of a frontier incident at Mukden to invade Manchuria. China appealed to the League of Nations, and in November the Lytton Commission was despatched to investigate the position on the League's behalf. The Commission produced its report in October 1932. It admitted the validity of some of the Japanese grievances but condemned the Japanese invasion and recommended that Manchuria should have autonomous status under Chinese supervision. The League accepted these recommendations by 42 votes to 1 in February 1933. Japan – which had in the meantime annexed Manchuria, renaming it Manchukuo – ignored the League's rulings and resigned from it. Japan also engaged in another aggressive move against China, sending troops into Shanghai in 1932. British policy in both crises was to protest but not too loudly. While supporting the League's initiative over Manchuria, Britain could do no more than condemn Japan's refusal to abide by the League's rulings. Where the Shanghai incident was concerned, Britain actually rejected an American suggestion of a forcible joint protest, preferring to sponsor its own anodyne resolution through the League. A. J. P. Taylor defends British handling of the Manchurian question: 'In reality, the League, under British leadership, had done what the British thought it was designed to do, it had limited a conflict and brought it, however, unsatisfactorily, to an end.' [Taylor, p. 64] This is surely a somewhat perverse judgment. The League's recommendations were ignored and Japan's withdrawal underlined its lack of authority.

Taylor, *The Origins of the Second World War*

The next two episodes which helped further to discredit the League of Nations were inextricably linked. Having left the Disarmament Conference in 1933, it was only a matter of time before Germany repudiated the disarmament clauses of the

Treaty of Versailles. Mussolini had also decided by 1932 on the invasion of Abyssinia; it was to take place in 1935. Western statesmen were confronted with the dilemma that if they wanted to restrain Germany they would need to condone Italian aggression in Abyssinia; if they wished to restrain Italy, they would have to come to some agreement with Germany. It also needs to be remembered that neither Hitler nor Mussolini made their intentions clear and indeed were more likely to engage in deliberate deception.

Germany made the first move, announcing in March 1935 her adoption of conscription in blatant defiance of the Treaty of Versailles. This provoked a joint protest from Britain, France and Italy. Their heads of government and foreign secretaries met at Stresa in April. They solemnly resolved to maintain the existing treaty settlement of Europe and to resist any attempt to change it by force, an engagement known as the Stresa Front. Its formation clearly had little effect on Hitler. In May he repudiated the remaining disarmament clauses of the Treaty of Versailles.

Britain's response was to make what seems one of the least explicable of all the agreements signed with the dictators, the Anglo-German Naval Agreement. Preparations were made for this when Simon and Eden visited Hitler in March, and the detailed negotiations were completed under Baldwin's supervision in June. Germany was to have the right to build up to 35% of British capital ships and was to be allowed parity in submarines in exceptional circumstances. The Admiralty and the Foreign Office favoured the Agreement as did all the members of the cabinet, with the possible exception of Eden who wondered, rightly, how the French might react. Baldwin defended the Agreement, in private, on the grounds that if broken it would expose Germany's aggressive intentions: 'It may well be that we are on a road leading to war. If that is so, then this agreement is tantamount to erecting a danger sign on the road ahead.' [Middlemas and Barnes, p. 828] Whatever its justification the Agreement, signed without prior discussion with France or Italy, gravely damaged Anglo-French relations and exposed the inconsistencies of British policy, coming as it did, just after Britain had sponsored a resolution condemning German rearmament at the League of Nations. Germany could claim that her breaches of the Treaty of Versailles were now officially condoned.

Middlemas and Barnes,
Baldwin

If the Stresa Front had been damaged by the Anglo-German Naval Agreement, it was wrecked beyond repair by the Italian invasion of Abyssinia. This took place on 3 October 1935. It had long been anticipated and Mussolini had done what he could to prepare the ground. In January he reached an agreement with France under which both countries would act in concert to defend Austria in the event of a German attack. In return, France agreed to give Italy a free hand in economic matters in Abyssinia. Grandi, the Italian ambassador in London, also tried to sound out the nature of Britain's interest in Abyssinia. As a result of these overtures Britain produced a succession of plans under which Abyssinia might surrender certain parts of her territory in exchange for land which would give her an outlet to the sea. Emperor Hailie Selassie was prepared to accept British suggestions. Mussolini rejected them contemptuously, claiming that he wanted the whole of Abyssinia. The cabinet met on 21 and 22 August to consider the implications of Mussolini's intransigence. The Chiefs of Staff emphasised the dangers to Britain's naval strength of a conflict with Italy but the cabinet nonetheless decided that Britain should stand by her treaty obligations, keep in line with France on sanctions and give her full support to the League, to which Abyssinia had appealed.

THE SWEETS OF AGGRESSION

HAILE SELASSIE: "HAVE I GOT THIS RIGHT?—HE'S TAKEN NEARLY HALF OF WHAT I HAD AND NOW YOU GENTLEMEN WANT TO DISCUSS WHETHER HE SHOULD TAKE ANY MORE!"   *Punch 1935*

However, when Hoare, the new Foreign Secretary, met his French counterpart, Laval, at Geneva on 11 September, both men agreed that no steps should be taken which would provoke Italy into a European war. [Middlemas and Barnes, p. 886] This hardly corresponded with the ringing promise of support for the League which Hoare delivered on 12 September. He promised that HM's government 'will be second to none in its intention to fulfil, within the means of its capacity, the obligations which the Covenant lays upon it ....'

Middlemas and Barnes, *Baldwin*

When, a month later, the invasion took place, the League responded vigorously. On 7 October the Council adopted a report declaring that the Italian government had resorted to war in defiance of the Covenant. On 9 October the Assembly set up a committee to co-ordinate the steps to be taken. On 19 October a policy of sanctions was recommended to all member countries. Sanctions were to be imposed on imports from Italy and on a certain number of exports to Italy. Oil was not on the list because it could be imported from non-League sources, notably the United States.

Britain throughout the crisis attempted to pursue two policies: bringing increasing pressure to bear on Italy through tightening the screw of sanctions, and exploring the possibilities of a compromise solution along the lines of the British plan suggested in the first instance. Where sanctions were concerned oil was the vital commodity. Mussolini made it clear to the French that if oil were added to the list war would probably follow. On 2 December the British Cabinet held a critical meeting to decide what line to take on the oil issue. The Chiefs of Staff forecast a loss of four capital ships in the event of a naval conflict with Italy. They recommended further negotiations before any embargo was placed on oil and the cabinet concurred. Hoare, in the meantime, had been consulting with Laval who was also in touch with Mussolini. On 7 December Hoare met Laval in Paris and on 8 December the Hoare-Laval Plan was agreed. It went a lot further than the British plan of June 1935. In all, Abyssinia would lose about one-third of her territory, gaining in exchange a thin strip of land giving her access to the Red Sea. The British cabinet, to its consternation, received details of the Plan on 9 December and it was leaked to the French press on the same day. In both countries there was an immediate outcry. The British public had been led to believe that Britain would defend Abyssinia's interests to the utmost and there was an angry debate in Parliament. On 18 December the Cabinet decided that the Hoare-Laval Plan must be repudiated, and that Hoare himself must be induced to resign. In his resignation speech Hoare voiced no regrets and claimed that his policy still offered the best solution that Abyssinia could hope for. He may well have been right. Oil was never added to the list. Mussolini continued with his campaign of conquest, using bombs and poison gas on unarmed tribesmen. On 2 May 1936 Hailie Selassie fled his kingdom and on 9 May Mussolini declared its annexation by Italy. In a speech on 10 June Chamberlain described the continuation of sanctions as 'the very midsummer of madness'. On 18 June they were finally withdrawn.

The Abyssinian crisis showed both the League of Nations and British foreign policy in a very poor light. By failing to make sanctions effective the League exposed its impotence. Britain by pursuing two contradictory policies at the same time failed with both. After Britain's dealings with Mussolini Hitler was not likely to be impressed.

1936–37: British Defence Policy, the Remilitarisation of the Rhineland; the Spanish Civil War

British Defence Policy

As the international scene darkened Britain gradually began to rearm, but there was no blinding conversion to the need for a new defence policy and no rapid escalation in defence expenditure. Defence spending dropped to its lowest figure between the wars – £102 million in 1932. From that point onwards it steadily increased. In 1933 the 10-year rule (see p.162) that Britain need not anticipate a war for at least 10 years was finally abandoned. In 1934 expenditure on the RAF was increased with the aim of adding a further 41 squadrons (820 planes) to existing levels. This would provide a front-line strength of 1304 planes within the next five years. The 1935 Defence White Paper, issued in March, recognised the increasing threats to peace and concluded that 'Additional expenditure on the armaments of the three Defence Services can therefore no longer be postponed.' In May the rate of expansion of the RAF was doubled to provide a first-line strength of 1500 planes by 1937. Germany already had 2400 aircraft.

The Defence White Paper of 1936, issued on 3 March, envisaged further increases: two new battleships, one new aircraft carrier, four infantry battalions and another 250 aircraft. But these were all marginal increases rather than the major expansion of the armed forces for which Churchill was now calling. It was also at this time that a Minister for Co-ordination of Defence was appointed. Both the new office and the man appointed to fill it indicate the government's lukewarm approach to rearmament. The new minister was intended to adjudicate inter-service rivalries rather than to take charge of Britain's defences. Churchill, who desperately would have liked the job, was passed over, probably on Chamberlain's advice, and it went to Sir Thomas Inskip, a lawyer with no previous experience of the armed forces. Lord Cherwell, one of Churchill's cronies, commented that it was 'the most cynical thing that has been done since Caligula appointed his horse a consul'. [Gilbert, p. 716] In his first speech Inskip confessed 'I may say, with all sincerity, that it never occurred to me – I can say this in all seriousness – that I would ever be able to discharge these duties even if they were offered to me ..... I do not claim to be a superman.' [Gilbert and Gott, p. 351] Inskip's appointment was approved, nonetheless, by the First Sea Lord, Lord Chatfield, and he is credited with at least one critical decision – to build up Fighter Command in December 1937. But he was not the man to invigorate Britain's defence programme. In the Inskip Report, 1937, he accepted the Treasury reasoning that economic stability was 'the fourth arm of defence, without which purely military efforts would be of no avail'. [G. C. Peden, 'A Matter of Timing: the Economic Background to British Foreign Policy 1937–39', History, p. 16] This constraint continued to dominate Britain's rearmament programme until the spring of 1939. Until that year no provision was made for any expeditionary force and when Britain was faced with the next challenge to European security, she was in no position to meet it.

The Remilitarisation of the Rhineland, March 1936

It was perhaps to be expected that Hitler would choose the Abyssinian crisis as a suitable moment to repudiate another of the clauses of the Treaty of Versailles, and to march his troops into the Rhineland; he gave as his excuse the signing of a treaty of mutual assistance between France and Russia, which took place on 27 February. Britain and France had both envisaged the possibility. Eden, who succeeded Hoare as Foreign Secretary in December 1935, even recommended in a memorandum for the cabinet on 17 February 1936 that the ending of the Rhineland's status as a

Gilbert, *Winston S. Churchill*, vol. V, 1922–1939

Gilbert and Gott, *The Appeasers*

History (Feb. 1984)

THE GOOSE STEP

"GOOSEY GOOSEY GANDER,
  WHITHER DOST THOU WANDER?"
"ONLY THROUGH THE RHINELAND—
  PRAY EXCUSE MY BLUNDER!"

Punch 1935

demilitarised zone might be used as a carrot to persuade Germany into making a new security arrangement. When Hitler stole a march on Britain by moving his troops into the Rhineland on Saturday 7 March, Eden commented: 'By reoccupying the Rhineland Hitler has deprived us of the possibility of making to him a concession which might otherwise have been a useful bargaining counter in our hands in the general negotiations with Germany which we had it in contemplation to initiate ...' [N. Medlicott, 'Britain and Germany, the Search for Agreement' Dilks (ed.), p. 94–5] Eden's comment makes it quite clear that the British government would never consider the remilitarisation of the Rhineland a *casus belli*. This view was widely shared. Eden's taxi driver, taking him to No. 10 Downing Street, summed up the popular reaction: 'I suppose Jerry can do what he likes in his own back garden can't he?' [Middlemas and Barnes, p. 916], a remark more often attributed to Lord Lothian. [see Churchill, p. 157]

Dilks (ed.), *Retreat from Power*

Middlemas and Barnes, *Baldwin* (Weidenfeld & Nicholson, 1969)

W. S. Churchill, *The Gathering Storm* (Cassell, 1948)

The French were naturally more concerned. Flandin, the new Foreign Minister (Laval, like Hoare, had been forced to resign), came to London to urge the British government at least to consider adopting sanctions. In an interview with him on 12 March Baldwin made it quite clear that Britain was in no state to go to war and would not support the police operation which the French were contemplating. Britain's line throughout the crisis was to accept the remilitarisation as a *fait accompli*, and to see whether something might be salvaged from it in the form of new guarantees and non-aggression pacts. Hitler rejected all such suggestions and got his way without having to make any concessions.

Of British politicians, only Churchill pressed for a more resolute stance. At a meeting of the House of Commons Foreign Affairs Committee on 12 March he urged that 'we must fulfil our obligations under the Covenant and follow the procedure it enjoins – it is unthinkable that we should repudiate our signature of Locarno'. In an article in the *Evening Standard* the same day he stressed that there was only one way to preserve peace: 'the assembly of overwhelming force, moral and physical, in support of international law'. [Gilbert, vol. V, pp. 713–14] But only the French had forces available and without British support they were not prepared to act.

Gilbert, *Winston S. Churchill*, vol. V, 1922–1939

It has been argued on the basis of German records that had the invasion of the Rhineland been opposed, German troops would have been withdrawn – the operation was carried out by 22 000 men, many fewer than the French generals anticipated – but this is to be wise after the event. It is equally hard to see how any British Prime Minister could have taken a different line, granted the sympathy for Germany's case and the state of British armaments.

The remilitarisation of the Rhineland was nonetheless a major blow to the European security system. The Treaties of Locarno had been proved worthless. Germany now had a defended western border which effectively prevented France from bringing pressure to bear on Germany in the event of her eastern allies being attacked. The Maginot Line mentality was reinforced. Belgium, seeing the writing on the wall, asked to be released from her treaty obligations and opted for neutrality. The Maginot Line was thus never extended northwards beyond the French frontier with Belgium so that it ceased even to serve its defensive purpose, as France found to its cost in 1940. Finally, Hitler won an important psychological victory. He had gambled and won. He drew the appropriate lesson: 'The world belongs to the man with guts! God helps him.' [Craig, p. 691]

G. Craig, *Germany, 1866–1945* (1978)

The Spanish Civil War

Since 1931, when it came into existence, the Spanish Republic had been trying vainly to establish its authority both over its right-wing opponents in the army and the Church and over its more militant and anti-clerical supporters on the left. There were also strong separatist movements in Catalonia and in the Basque country. In 1932 a right-wing *coup*, led by General Sanjurjo, was successfully contained. In 1934 there was a communist-led revolt in the coal-mining area of Asturias which was put down with considerable brutality. One of the armies involved was commanded by General Franco. In the elections held in February 1936 the parties of the left won a decisive victory and a Socialist government, headed by Manual Azana, took office. Remembering what had happened at Asturias, many right-wing groups feared that Azana would play the role of a Kerensky (the Russian premier who preceded Lenin). Another military conspiracy was hatched to seize power from the Republican government. In July the plans came to fruition. All over Spain right-wing forces made a bid for power. Franco, who had been 'banished' to the Canary Islands, returned to Spain with contingents from the Army of Africa. But the Republic maintained its hold over Madrid and Barcelona, as well as in the North. In that sense the conspiracy failed. It led, instead, to a Civil War which lasted for nearly three years, cost the lives of over 600 000 Spaniards and was marked by atrocities on both sides.

The war can be seen as a right-wing counter-revolution to a democratically elected government. But it was also a class and a religious conflict. The Nationalists had the support of the Monarchists, the Catholic Church and the majority of the officer class. The Republicans were backed by the industrial working class, middle-class Liberals, Socialists and Communists. There was also a strong vein of anti-clericalism on the Republican side. The war was fought, like most civil wars, with great bitterness. It was the most traumatic event in Spanish history.

The war was important in the European context for two main reasons. First, Spain became for a time the arena where the forces of the Left did battle with those of the Right. The ideological dimension brought sympathisers from all over Europe to each side. Irish Catholics were to be found on the Nationalist side, Welsh coal miners on the Republican. Practically every European country as well as the United States supplied volunteers for the International Brigades who fought for the Republicans. When George Orwell was asked why he was going to Spain he replied: 'This fascism, somebody's got to stop it.' [Crick, p. 206] At the other end of the spectrum Pope Pius XII, on hearing the news of the fall of Madrid to the Nationalists in March 1939, wrote to Franco: 'Lifting up our hearts to God we give sincere thanks with your Excellency for Spain's Catholic victory'. [Thomas, pp. 602–3] Secondly, the war was important because the governments of European countries took a close interest in, and indeed helped to influence, its outcome. Hitler, and more particularly Mussolini, wanted a Nationalist victory. They also used the war as a testing ground for their new weapons and military techniques. The Soviet Union supported the Republicans, hoping to install a communist-led government in Madrid.

The French Popular Front government, led by Leon Blum, was naturally sympathetic to the Republic but afraid to antagonise right-wing sentiment in France by too overt support. Opinion in Britain was similarly ambivalent. The Labour party, most Liberals and some Conservatives sympathised actively with the Republicans. But there was also plenty of support for the Nationalists. The First Sea Lord, Chatfield, thought Franco 'a good Spanish patriot'. [Thomas, p. 258] English Catholics such as Douglas Jerrold and Arnold Lunn also backed the Nationalists.

B. Crick, *George Orwell, A Life* (Penguin, 1982)

H. Thomas, *The Spanish Civil War* (1961) (Hamish Hamilton, 1977)

Organisations such as the Friends of Nationalist Spain matched those which sprang up in defence of the Republic, the Friends of Spain, the London Committee for Spanish Medical Aid and the National Joint Committee for Spanish Relief.

Officially all the countries named adhered to a policy of non-intervention. By the end of August 1936 they had signed an agreement to this effect, and in September a Non-Intervention Committee was established to enforce the ban on the export of war material to Spain. The Non-Intervention Committee graduated, as Thomas puts it, from 'equivocation to hypocrisy and humiliation'. [Thomas, p. 264] Its lack of effectiveness can be seen in the foreign aid calculated to have been received by each side. Italy provided the Nationalists with approximately £80 million worth of war material in addition to the services of the 50 000 troops who fought in Spain. Italian submarines are credited with sinking at least 72 000 tons of merchant shipping. Germany's contribution was £43 million and 16 000 soldiers and airmen. It was a German squadron that bombed the little town of Guernica in April 1937, causing the death of 1600 out of its 7000 inhabitants. On the other side, Russia provided the Republicans with £63 million in gold, used for the purchase of weapons and a further £23 million worth of war materials. This assistance, which was on an official level, needs to be distinguished from the support provided through charitable organisations and the services of the International Brigades which were recruited from genuine volunteers. These did not breach the legal principles of Non-Intervention.

There can be little doubt that the failure of Non-Intervention stacked the odds against the Republic. Italian and German Assistance had a critical effect at various stages in the war though the Republic could not have survived as long as it did without Russian financial support. If arms had also been available to the Republic from France, Britain and the United States, Thomas concludes, the war might well have taken a different course.

The British government stuck blindly but consistently to a policy of Non-Intervention, carrying out the Agreement to the letter and doing what little it could to secure the compliance of other countries. In January 1937 the government signed a 'Gentleman's Agreement' with Mussolini under which both countries agreed to accept the status quo in the Mediterranean. Under the Foreign Enlistment Act the recruitment of British subjects to fight in Spain was forbidden. In September 1937 Britain sponsored a conference at Nyon to tackle the attacks, mainly by Italian submarines, on neutral shipping off Spanish coasts. A naval patrol was instituted in which, ironically, Italy participated. Mussolini boasted to Hitler that it would make no difference to Italy's naval operations. Thus while the fiction of Non-Intervention was maintained, in reality the Axis powers made Franco's victory possible.

In the event, Franco refused to join Germany and Italy in 1939, but the Spanish Civil War was still a serious defeat for France and Britain. A legitimate government had been overthrown by force. It was another defeat for the policy of appeasement. Russia became increasingly distrustful of France and Britain because of their failure to stop German and Italian support for the Nationalists. Conversely, the activities of the Spanish Communist party, particularly the purges carried out against their political rivals, disillusioned some members of the British Left. Orwell described these purges in *Homage to Catalonia* and drew attention to the fact that there could be a totalitarianism of the Left as well as of the Right. The mutual suspicions thus aroused made the formation of an anti-fascist front between France, Britain and the Soviet Union even less likely.

D ▬▬▬ THE CHAMBERLAIN YEARS, 1937–39:
▬ AUSTRIA, CZECHOSLOVAKIA AND POLAND

When Chamberlain replaced Baldwin as Prime Minister in 1937 British foreign policy gained a clearer sense of direction. One of his biographers describes Chamberlain as: 'Masterful, confident, and ruled by an instinct for order, he would give a lead, and perhaps impart an edge, to every question. His approach was arduously careful but his mind, once made up, hard to change.' [Feiling, p. 303] Inevitably Chamberlain took over responsibility for foreign policy. Eden resigned in February 1938 as much because of Chamberlain's refusal to consult him before taking an initiative as over differences in policy. While the Foreign Affairs Committee of the cabinet continued to meet it did so sporadically. There were no meetings for instance between 1 July 1937 and January 1938, nor, more significantly, between June and November 1938 when the Czech crisis was at its height. Chamberlain persisted in using his own intermediaries such as Sir Horace Wilson. He communicated directly, rather than via the Foreign Office, with ambassadors such as Sir Neville Henderson in Berlin. When the cabinet was brought into discussions on policy this was usually after critical decisions had been taken. During the Czech crisis Chamberlain confided only in those Ministers whose views he knew to be sympathetic: Hoare, Simon and Halifax. The historian of the Chamberlain cabinet writes:

> The conclusion may be that the Cabinet was far from being, as Churchill described it, 'twenty-two men of blameless party character sitting round an overcrowded table, each having a voice.' In reality they were deprived of secret Intelligence, unsure of what had been said, done and written, and unconsulted until the essential and irrevocable lines of policy had been devised by Chamberlain and accepted in the Prime Minister's foursome meetings. It was Prime Minister's rule. [Colvin, p. 167]

This being so it is in Chamberlain's private reflections, committed to his *Diary* or in letters to his sisters, that the best clues to the direction of British foreign policy between 1937 and 1939 are to be found. On taking office as premier in 1937 he wrote: 'I believe the double policy of rearmament and better relations with Germany and Italy will carry us safely through the danger period, if only the Foreign Office will play up.' [Feiling, p. 319] But he also confessed to the cabinet on his return from Munich in 1938 that he was 'oppressed' with a belief that 'the burden of armaments might break our backs'. Diplomacy and defence policies were thus closely linked and one of the objectives of better relations with Germany and Italy was to reduce the burden of rearmament.

Except in his assessment of the dictators, Chamberlain showed a hard-headed realism. There were few concessions he was not prepared to make in the interests of peace. In 1937, following Halifax's report of a visit he had made to see Hitler and Goering, Chamberlain concluded with this reflection: 'But I don't see why we shouldn't say to Germany: "give us satisfactory assurances that you won't use force to deal with Austria and Czechoslovakia and we will give you similar assurances that we won't use force to prevent the changes you want, if you can get them by peaceful means".' [Feiling, p. 333] Chamberlain was also ready to consider the return of Germany's colonies in West Africa and some arrangement to compensate her for the

Chamberlain and the Making of Foreign Policy

K. Feiling, *The Life of Neville Chamberlain* (1946)

I. Colvin, *The Chamberlain Cabinet* (1971)

loss of Tanganyika and German South West Africa. Where Italy was concerned he had already advocated giving up sanctions and he was ready to recognise the *de facto* annexation of Abyssinia without securing any concession in return. It was on this question that Eden finally resigned.

Feiling, *The Life of Neville Chamberlain*

Chamberlain had little faith either in the League of Nations or in collective security. He dismissed the prospect of American involvement. After Roosevelt's celebrated 'quarantine' speech in October 1937, calling for a concerted effort to 'oppose those countries who were creating a state of international anarchy', Chamberlain privately recorded: 'It is always best and safest to count on nothing from the Americans but words.' [Feiling, p. 325] And when Roosevelt in January 1938 suggested convening an international conference at New York, Sir Horace Wilson dismissed the idea as 'woolly rubbish'; Chamberlain requested the President to 'hold his hand for a short while'. No more came of the suggestion. He was equally sceptical about the Soviet Union, writing in March 1939: 'I must confess to a most profound distrust of Russia. I have no belief whatever in her ability to maintain an effective offensive, even if she wished to do so. And I distrust her motives which seem to me to have little connection with our ideas of liberty, and to be only concerned with getting everybody else by the ears.' [Feiling, p. 403] Where France was concerned Chamberlain was consistently unwilling to underwrite France's commitments to her East European Allies. During the Czech and Polish crises it was Britain who made most of the running and Chamberlain's policy which prevailed.

Feiling, *The Life of Neville Chamberlain*

Thus from 1937 until September 1939 Chamberlain conducted British foreign policy largely on his own, overruling the advice of those members of the cabinet who disagreed with him and being unwilling to take into account the views and interests of Britain's potential allies.

The Anschluss with Austria

Six months after Chamberlain took office Hitler held a critical meeting in Berlin attended by Goering, his Foreign Minister, Von Neurath, and his service chiefs. His adjutant, Hossbach, made a record of what was said, known subsequently as the Hossbach Memorandum. The exact significance of this document has been much disputed. It was called in evidence at the Nuremburg Trials, but A. J. P. Taylor has argued that it is an unreliable guide to Hitler's intentions. [see A. J. P. Taylor, pp. 131–4] At its face value the document gives a clear picture of Hitler's goals. There must be a drive to the East, the first stage of which would be the absorption of Austria and the destruction of Czechoslovakia. Hitler did not spell out an exact timetable and he considered several possible contingencies, but the policies he pursued in the next two years bore an uncanny resemblance to the objectives he had announced.

Taylor, *The Origins of the Second World War* (1961)

Hitler had long wanted an *Anschluss* (literally 'connection') with Austria. He had attempted to bring this about in 1934 when Austrian Nazis staged a coup against the Austrian government in which the Chancellor, Dolfuss, was killed. On this occasion Mussolini, who was apprehensive for the security of the North Italian frontier, moved Italian troops up to the Brenner Pass and Hitler heeded the warning. For the time being Austria was saved. But in 1936 Germany and Italy came together in the Axis Pact. They contributed jointly to the Nationalist side in the Spanish Civil War. By 1938 Hitler knew that he could count on Mussolini's acquiescence in any further attempt to incorporate Austria into the Reich.

On 12 February 1938 Von Schuschnigg, successor to Dolfuss, was summoned to Berchtesgaden, Hitler's private headquarters in Bavaria. Hitler insisted that Schuschnigg should include Nazis in his cabinet, in particular Seyss-Inquart as Minister of the Interior. Schuschnigg complied, but announced shortly afterwards on 9 March that a plebiscite would be held to enable Austrians to decide for themselves whether they wished to be joined with Germany. This was not at all to Hitler's liking. On 11 March he gave instructions that German troops should march into Austria and on 12 March they did so. Britain had little warning of the crisis. On 11 March Schuschnigg telephoned Halifax to ask his advice. Halifax, after consulting with the Prime Minister, replied that 'HM Government could not take the responsibility of advising the Chancellor to take any course of action which might expose his country to dangers against which HM Government was unable to guarantee protection'. [Colvin, p. 105] There was indeed little the British government could do beyond addressing a formal protest to Berlin. The *Anschluss* was duly completed and subsequently approved by a massive majority in a plebiscite held under Nazi auspices.

Colvin, *The Chamberlain Cabinet*

It was clear to everyone that Czechoslovakia would be the next item on Hitler's agenda. The country was now surrounded on three sides by German territory. The 3 million Sudeten Germans were getting increasingly restive and the Nazi party under the leadership of Henlein was attracting more support there. Indeed, at the cabinet meeting held on 12 March to consider the Anschluss, Halifax raised the question of how to prevent similar action being taken in Czechoslovakia. This was the problem to which Chamberlain now addressed himself.

The fortunes of Czechoslovakia dominated diplomacy in the summer of 1938. In the welter of speeches, messages, threats and counter-threats it is all too easy to lose the wood for the trees and to attribute either too much or too little significance to particular episodes in the story. In an attempt to clarify what was a highly complex and rapidly shifting situation it is helpful to set out the fundamental positions of the main participants. There can be no doubt that Hitler wanted to improve conditions for the Sudeten Germans by incorporating them into a racially homogeneous Germany. Whether at this stage he also wanted to bring about the disintegration of Czechoslovakia is less certain. It is equally clear that Chamberlain had some sympathy for the position of the Sudeten Germans and in his concern for peace was willing in the last resort to see the Sudetenland handed over to Germany, provided this could be done by negotiation rather than by force. France, linked by treaty to Czechoslovakia, was much more concerned to see that country's economic and defensive viability preserved, but would not act without a guarantee of British support. Italy had no direct interest in the Czech question, but was clearly not ready to face a European war in 1938 and Mussolini was therefore prepared to play the role of honest broker. The Soviet Union's policy is more of an enigma. Bound by treaty to France, the Soviet Union several times urged either action through the League of Nations or through a four power conference to restrain Germany. But Czechoslovakia showed little inclination to seek Russian assistance and Britain was positively anxious to prevent Russia getting involved.

Chamberlain was clear in his own mind that military intervention to save Czechoslovakia was out of the question. On 20 March he wrote: 'You have only to look at the map to see that nothing France or we could do could possibly save Czechoslovakia from being overrun by the Germans if they want to do it ... I have therefore abandoned any idea of giving guarantees to Czechoslovakia or the French

The Czech Crisis

in connection with her obligations to that country.' [Feiling, pp. 347–8] That being so, the best that could be hoped for was to persuade the Czechs to meet Hitler's grievances. At the meeting held with French ministers on 28 April this was the policy agreed. Benes the Czech President was to be advised to meet the demands of the Sudeten Germans for greater autonomy. On 20 May, when German troop movements on the German-Czech border caused the Czechs to mobilise some of their reserves, Britain caused it to be known that Germany should not count on Britain standing aside in the event of war, a somewhat surprising threat which Halifax soon repented. It was evidently the press reaction to this episode that caused Hitler to announce to his generals on 28 May: 'It is my unalterable intention to smash Czechoslovakia by military action in the near future.' He named 1 October as the operative date. [Craig, p. 705]

Feiling, *The Life of Neville Chamberlain*

Craig, *Germany, 1866–1945*

The Czech Crisis	Events
19 March	Russia suggested four power conference. Britain rejected suggestion.
28 April	Anglo-French talks between Chamberlain, Halifax, Daladier and Bonnet to consider Sudeten question. Benes to be urged to make concessions.
20–21 May	Crisis in German-Czech relations. Czech reserves mobilised.
28 May	Hitler's decision 'to smash Czechoslovakia'
16 June	British decision to send a mediator to Czechoslovakia. Lord Runciman chosen.
3 August–16 September	Runciman mission in Czechoslovakia.
30 August	Cabinet meeting in Britain. Decision not to warn Germany.
2 September	Litvinov suggested joint French, Czech, Russian Staff talks.
4 September	Czech government offered autonomy to Sudetenland.
6–12 September	Nazi Party Rally at Nuremburg.
13 September	Henlein demanded separation of Sudetenland from Czechoslovakia.
14 September	Chamberlain announced decision to see Hitler.
15 September	Meeting between Hitler and Chamberlain at Berchtesgaden.
17 September	Cabinet informed of terms discussed.
18 September	Anglo-French talks. Cession of Sudetenland agreed. Guarantee to be offered to Czechoslovakia.
22–3 September	Talks between Hitler and Chamberlain at Bad Godesburg. Hitler demanded immediate evacuation of Sudetenland.
24–5 September	Cabinet meetings to discuss Bad Godesburg terms.
26 September	Wilson sent to Berlin with warning to Hitler.
27 September	Mussolini approached by British ambassador to suggest conference.
28 September	Hitler consented to Munich Conference.
29–30 September	Munich Conference; Munich Agreement signed.

Ignorant of Hitler's intentions, Chamberlain continued to pursue a solution of the Sudeten question. The cabinet approved the despatch of the Runciman mission which arrived in Czechoslovakia on 3 August. Runciman was to act as a disinterested intermediary, though at one stage in the negotiations he allowed himself to be used as a British representative. The terms Runciman suggested were very largely accepted by Benes on 4 September. They offered autonomy to the Slovaks and to the Sudeten Germans, reserving defence, foreign policy and finance to the Czech government. But at the Nuremburg rally which opened on 6 September, Hitler launched a savage attack on the Czech government and promised the Sudeten Germans that they would be neither defenceless nor abandoned. On 13 September Henlein duly demanded complete separation of the Sudetenland from Czechoslovakia.

In the meantime the British government had been receiving unofficial representations from Germans opposed to Hitler, warning of Hitler's intentions to invade and urging the British government to take a strong stance. This might, it was argued, bring about Hitler's downfall. Chamberlain and Halifax were inclined to discount these approaches but they took the warnings seriously enough to raise them at a cabinet meeting held on 30 August, at which Henderson was also present. Halifax admitted his ignorance of Hitler's real intentions and posed the question of whether Britain would be justified in fighting 'a certain war now in order to forestall a possible war later on'. [Colvin, p. 141] He concluded that in the absence of proof of Hitler's determination to use force, all the British government could do was to 'try to keep Hitler guessing'. Chamberlain strongly supported Halifax. Only Duff Cooper expressed serious dissent, arguing that Britain should make it clear that 'we were thinking of the possibility of using force'. He had little support. Chamberlain summed up the feeling of the meeting: 'The Cabinet were unanimously of the view that we should not utter a threat to Hitler that if he went into Czechoslovakia we should declare war upon him.' [Colvin, p. 144] It was also agreed 'to keep Germany guessing as to our ultimate attitude'.

Colvin, *The Chamberlain Cabinet*

Before the next cabinet meeting took place, Chamberlain had warning of Hitler's intentions from a more reliable source. Herr Theo Kordt, Counsellor at the German Embassy — putting conscience before loyalty — saw Sir Horace Wilson on 6 September and warned him that Hitler was planning to invade Czechoslovakia on 20 September. On 7 September Kordt urged Halifax that a strong warning to Hitler might have the desired effect. Such a message was duly drafted. It declared that once France was involved in war on behalf of Czechoslovakia 'it seems to HM Government inevitable that the sequence of events must result in a general conflict from which Britain could not stand aside'. Henderson was to deliver the message to Ribbentrop (now Foreign Secretary) and the text was to be shown to Hitler. Henderson, attending on Hitler at Nuremburg, refused to deliver the note and, in response to his pleas, on 10 September he was excused from doing so. Neither Ribbentrop nor Hitler ever saw it.

Instead, another plan was devised. Chamberlain suggested to Simon, Hoare and Halifax the possibility of a personal visit to Hitler. This became known as Plan Z. On 13 September Chamberlain, with the approval of the three men in whom he had confided, decided to go ahead with Plan Z. On 14 September the rest of the cabinet were informed of his decision. They had not been consulted. They, nonetheless, gave their approval to what Simon described as Chamberlain's 'brilliant proposal'. From this point on Chamberlain bore personal responsibility for all the negotiations with Hitler.

The three visits which Chamberlain undertook to Germany are in one sense a tribute to his determination in the case of peace. If anyone deserves the credit for arresting the invasion of Czechoslovakia in 1938 it was Chamberlain. But he always went as the suppliant, and each time Hitler raised his terms Chamberlain sought to persuade his colleagues and allies to accept them.

At his first meeting on 15 September at Berchtesgaden, Hitler announced that he was interested only in the Sudetenland. Chamberlain replied: 'in principle I had nothing to say against the separation of the Sudeten Germans from the rest of Czechoslovakia'. It was a large admission for which Chamberlain had to secure the agreement both of the British cabinet and the French, quite apart from the Czechs themselves. On 17 September the cabinet considered Chamberlain's account of his conversations with Hitler. No decisions were taken. On 18 September the French ministers, Daladier and Bonnet, were summoned to London and after some hard bargaining it was finally agreed that the Czechs should be asked to cede to Germany districts mainly inhabited by the Sudeten Germans. Chamberlain reluctantly agreed to a joint Anglo-French guarantee of Czechoslovakia's new frontiers. The cabinet approved these proposals on 19 September and they were transmitted to Benes on 20 September. In the knowledge that he would get no support from Britain or France should he reject them, Benes reluctantly accepted the proposals.

But Hitler had not yet got all he wanted. When Chamberlain returned to Germany and met Hitler at Bad Godesburg on 22 September, Hitler demanded that the Sudetenland should be evacuated by 1 October and that the grievances of the Polish and Hungarian minorities also needed to be considered. Chamberlain was shocked but would still not be deflected from his search for a peaceful solution. Cabinet meetings were held on 24 and 25 September. Halifax now admitted to serious doubts about the wisdom of giving in to Hitler's demands. When the French ministers arrived on 25 September they too announced that it was time to call a halt. Chamberlain, seeing his policies in danger of collapse, made a last effort to keep negotiations going. On 26 September Sir Horace Wilson was dispatched to Berlin with a message which indicated British readiness to support France in the event of active hostilities between France and Germany. Wilson, who found Hitler in a furious mood, delayed delivering the message to Hitler until 27 September. On that day the British ambassador in Rome, Lord Perth, was also instructed to approach Mussolini with a request for his intervention.

On the evening of 27 September, with the prospect of war looming, Chamberlain broadcast to the British people. Among other things he said: 'How horrible, fantastic, incredible, it is that we should be digging trenches and trying on gasmasks here because of a quarrel in a far-away country between people of whom we know nothing ... I would not hesitate to pay even a third visit to Germany, if I thought it would do any good.' On 28 September he had his opportunity. News came through as Chamberlain was speaking in the House of Commons that Hitler had accepted Mussolini's suggestion of a Four Power Conference to be held at Munich. It assembled on 29 September and was attended by Hitler, Mussolini, Chamberlain and Daladier. Chamberlain's suggestion that the Czechs might also be invited to attend was rebuffed.

Neville Chamberlain, on his return, from Munich, holding the 'pit of paper'

The differences between the terms offered at Bad Godesburg and those agreed at Munich were relatively slight. German occupation of the Sudetenland would now be carried out in five stages rather than at one bound on 1 October. The boundaries of the new Czechoslovakia would be determined by an international commission. Those Czechs who wished to leave the Sudetenland would have six months to do so. More important than the details of the settlement in Chamberlain's eyes was the piece of paper he induced Hitler to sign after the formalities had been completed. Drafted by Chamberlain himself it concluded: 'We are resolved that the method of consultation shall be the method adopted to deal with any other questions that may concern our two countries, and we are determined to continue our efforts to remove every possible source of difference, and thus to contribute to assure the peace of Europe.' It was this piece of paper which Chamberlain waved to the crowds who greeted him on his return to Heston airport, and on which he relied when, echoing Disraeli, he said from the balcony at No. 10 Downing Street: 'This is the second time in our history that there has come back from Germany to Downing Street peace with honour. I believe it is peace for our time.'

E ▬▬▬▬ THE ENDING OF APPEASEMENT

When the debate on the Munich Agreement took place in the House of Commons, Chamberlain defended it in these terms: 'The real triumph is that it has shown that representatives of four great powers can find it possible to agree on a way of carrying out a difficult and delicate operation by discussion instead of by force, and thereby

The Collapse of Czechoslovakia

A GREAT MEDIATOR

JOHN BULL: "I'VE KNOWN MANY PRIME MINISTERS IN MY TIME, SIR, BUT NEVER ONE WHO WORKED SO HARD
FOR SECURITY IN THE FACE OF SUCH TERRIBLE ODDS."

Punch 1938

BRITAIN AND THE WORLD, 1929–39: THE OUTBREAK OF THE SECOND WORLD WAR

they have averted a catastrophe which would have ended civilisation as we know it.' But Duff Cooper, who had resigned from the cabinet in protest, put a less flattering gloss on the Agreement: 'We have taken away the defences of Czechoslovakia in the same breath as we have guaranteed them, as though you were to deal a man a mortal blow and at the same time insure his life.' Attlee was equally critical: 'This has not been a victory for reason and humanity. It has been a victory for brute force.' Churchill was bluntest of all: 'We have suffered a total and unmitigated defeat.' Of Chamberlain's efforts, Churchill went on, 'the utmost he has been able to gain for Czechoslovakia and in the matters which were in dispute has been that the German dictator instead of snatching his victuals from the table has been content to have them served to him course by course....' Despite such trenchant criticism, the Munich Agreement was approved by 366 votes to 144. There were 22 abstentions on the Conservative side. [Gilbert, vol. V, pp. 992 et. seq.]

M. Gilbert, *Winston S. Churchill, vol. V, 1922–1939* (1976)

Duff Cooper's misgivings were soon to be realised. In October the Poles acquired Teschen from Czechoslovakia; in November the Hungarian-Czech frontier was redrawn to Hungary's advantage. In January 1939 Slovak leaders visited Germany and their separatist movement was encouraged. When President Hacha, successor to Benes, dismissed the leaders of the Ruthenian and Slovak governments on 6 and 9 March respectively, the Slovaks appealed to Hitler for assistance. The elderly and inexperienced Hacha also made the journey to Berlin. He was threatened with the destruction of Prague unless he agreed to sign away Czechoslovakia's independence – Hacha gave way. On 15 March German troops entered Bohemia and Hitler spent that night in Prague.

So far as British opinion is concerned, this was the turning point. Up to March 1939 Hitler's aggressive moves had all taken place in the context of dismantling the Treaty of Versailles and had affected only German-speaking peoples. Now he had extended German rule over people of different nationality. He had also plainly broken the Munich Agreement and his pledge to Chamberlain. Even Henderson was disillusioned: 'It was the final shipwreck of my mission to Berlin', he commented. [Hayes, p. 290]

P. Hayes, *Modern British Foreign Policy* (A. & C. Black, 1981)

But the cabinet had not finally abandoned appeasement. Chamberlain's first reaction was simply to recognise that as Czechoslovakia no longer existed, Britain could no longer be bound to guarantee her frontiers. Halifax commented in the same vein to the British ambassador in France: 'The one compensating advantage that I saw was that it brought an end to the somewhat embarrassing commitment of a guarantee in which we and the French had been involved.' [Taylor, p. 209] On 17 March Chamberlain slightly changed his tone. In a speech delivered at Birmingham he discarded his prepared text on domestic policy and addressed himself to the international situation. He was unrepentant about Munich but went on to say that while there was hardly anything he would not sacrifice for peace, 'there is one thing I must except, and that is the liberty we have enjoyed for years, and which we would never surrender'. Nor should anyone suppose that 'because it believes war to be a senseless and cruel thing, this nation has so lost its fibre that it will not take part to the utmost of its power in resisting such a challenge if it ever were made.' [Feiling, p. 400] After March 1939 Chamberlain pursued appeasement with much less conviction and an awareness that war had become a more likely alternative.

Taylor, *The Origins of the Second World War*

Feiling, *The Life of Neville Chamberlain*

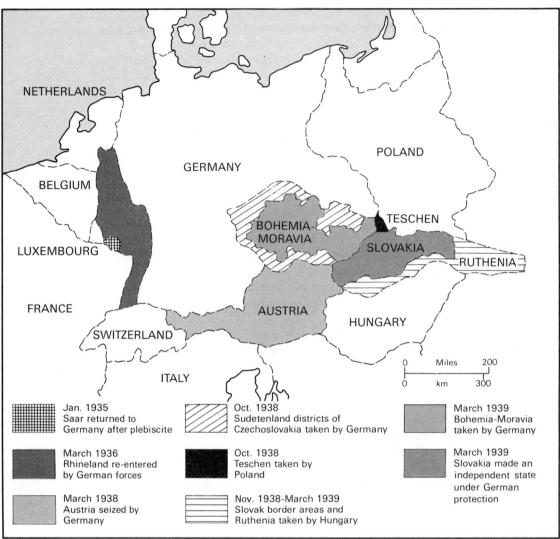

Jan. 1935
Saar returned to
Germany after plebiscite

Oct. 1938
Sudetenland districts of
Czechoslovakia taken by Germany

March 1939
Bohemia-Moravia
taken by Germany

March 1936
Rhineland re-entered
by German forces

Oct. 1938
Teschen taken by
Poland

March 1939
Slovakia made an
independent state
under German
protection

March 1938
Austria seized by
Germany

Nov. 1938-March 1939
Slovak border areas and
Ruthenia taken by Hungary

Rearmament

It has sometimes been claimed that Chamberlain deliberately bought time at Munich and that as a result Britain was much better placed for war in 1939 than she would have been in 1938. There is little evidence to support such a claim. No real change in British rearmament policy took place until the spring of 1939, and then it owed more to the Chiefs of Staff than to Chamberlain.

In the autumn of 1938 Chamberlain continued to support the Treasury view that Britain could not afford substantial increases in defence spending. Every request from the service ministers was carefully scrutinised. In October Kingsley Wood urged a substantial increase in the British bomber force, but this was turned down as was a request by Hore-Belisha in November for an improvement in the weapons provided for the Territorial Army. Chamberlain continually resisted suggestions from Churchill to establish a Ministry of Supply and he refused to consider the introduction of conscription.

But significant changes in government policy took place between February and April 1939. After the Munich Agreement it began to dawn on both French and British defence planners that a defenceless Czechoslovakia would be incapable of drawing off German forces in the event of a war between France and Germany. France would have to sustain the weight of a German attack unaided. The British ambassador in Paris wrote to Halifax in January 1939: 'It was no use pointing to the size of the British Navy or Airforce or talking of Britain's financial stability ... rightly or wrongly French public opinion wanted large numbers of British troops in Europe.' [Fraser, p. 20] In February the Chiefs of Staff delivered the same message: 'It is difficult to see how the security of the United Kingdom could be maintained if France were forced to capitulate and therefore defence of the former may have to include a share in the land defence of French territory.' [Howard, 'British Defence Policy', Dilks (ed.), p. 115] In consequence British defence policy underwent two major changes. It was decided on 22 February for the first time since 1918 to equip five regular divisions and two divisions of the territorial army for service on the Continent. In the longer term the army was to be expanded to 32 divisions. The corollary to this decision was the ending of the Treasury stranglehold over defence spending.

D. Fraser, *And We Shall Shock Them: The British Army in the Second World War* (Hodder & Stoughton, 1983)

Dilks (ed.), *Retreat from Power*

In April Chamberlain finally conceded the principle of compulsory military service. Under the Military Training Act selected year groups of 200 000 men were to be called up for military training. Only the first of such groups had been recruited when war broke out in September but a start had been made. Chamberlain also gave his approval to the setting up of a Ministry of Supply which came into operation under Leslie Burgin, a previous Minister of Transport, in July.

The rapid expansion in the size of the army created a situation in armaments manufacture of 'predictable chaos'. By the summer of 1939 even the regular divisions had only 'fifty per cent of their (totally inadequate) scales of anti-tank and anti-aircraft weapons, and about thirty per cent of their ammunition'. [Fraser, p. 22] The British army that went to the Continent in 1939 was both under-equipped and under-trained. But this was the inevitable consequence of years of neglect rather than the fault of those who tried, too late in the day, to make amends.

Fraser, *And We Shall Shock Them*

Fortunately it was a different story where the RAF was concerned. The chain of radar stations first proposed by Robert Watson-Watt in 1935 had been largely completed by 1939. Whereas in September 1938 the RAF had been equipped with one squadron of Spitfires and five of Hurricanes, by 1939, twenty-six squadrons were equipped with one or the other. The monthly output of aeroplanes had risen from 200 to 600, actually exceeding the German rate of production. Civil Defence had become the responsibility of Sir John Anderson and extensive preparations were made to deal with the threat of air raids.

It is a moot point whether Britain gained more than she lost by the year between Munich and the outbreak of war in 1939. Germany benefited by the elimination of Czechoslovakia and the acquisition of the huge Skoda armaments works in the Sudetenland. But by the end of 1939 Britain was devoting almost as large a share (21.4%) of GNP to defence as Germany (23.0%). Perhaps the greatest gain was the knowledge that no effort had been spared to keep the peace. After March 1939 the British public were much readier to face the threat of war from a man the aggressiveness of whose policies was now clear beyond dispute.

The Polish Crisis

New Guarantees

The cabinet met to consider the implications of the invasion of Czechoslovakia on 18 March 1939. It was generally agreed that the time had come to seek new allies and to extend Britain's protection to Hitler's next potential victims. Rumania had apparently already been threatened, Germany having demanded a monopoly of her exports – oil in particular – in return for German guarantee of her frontiers. Poland was another likely candidate and rumours soon reached the British government of an impending invasion, though this time they seem to have been unfounded. There were two possible strategies. One was to issue a four-power declaration involving Britain, Russia, France and Poland, promising joint opposition to any act of aggression committed against any one of them. The other was for Britain to enter into a series of individual agreements with threatened countries. Poland soon made it clear that she was unwilling to be associated with any arrangement that included the Soviet Union. In these circumstances the suggested joint declaration was dropped and it was decided instead to offer Treaties of Guarantee to Poland and Rumania.

The guarantee to Poland was made public in an answer to a prearranged parliamentary question on Friday 31 March. After referring to rumours of a German attack on Poland, Chamberlain stated that 'in the event of any action which clearly threatened Polish independence and which the Polish government accordingly considered it vital to resist with their national forces, HM Government would feel themselves bound at once to lend the Polish government all support in their power ...' [Colvin, p. 197] This guarantee, as Duff Cooper pointed out, gave to Poland the power to determine British policy, for it would be up to the Polish government to decide what constituted a threat to their independence. Further doubts about the treaty were raised after Colonel Beck, the Polish Foreign Minister, visited London from 4–6 April. Beck refused to join with Britain in a treaty of guarantee to Rumania. He also refused to be associated in any defensive arrangement made with the Soviet Union. Halifax commented later: 'An intelligent rabbit would hardly be expected to welcome the protection of an animal ten times its own size, whom it credited with the habits of a boa constrictor.' [Gilbert and Gott, p. 237] Beck's refusal may have been intelligible but it deprived the Anglo-Polish treaty of any real effectiveness. The treaty was not finally ratified until 25 August, but from now on it determined the drift of British policy.

Colvin, *The Chamberlain Cabinet*

Gilbert and Gott, *The Appeasers*

Undeterred by Beck's lack of co-operation, the British government proceeded to sign treaties of guarantee with Greece and Rumania, following Mussolini's invasion of Albania which took place on 7 April. In May an agreement was also reached with Turkey, providing for joint action against aggression in the Mediterranean. This willingness to extend the range of Britain's commitments stands in remarkable contrast to the reluctance shown by British politicians, right up to the Munich Agreement, to enter into any formal treaty, even with France. It can only be explained by the revulsion in sentiment that followed the collapse of the Munich Agreement. On any rational assessment of the balance of forces Poland was much less defensible than Czechoslovakia.

Anglo-Soviet Relations

The only way Poland could be protected was through a defensive agreement with the Soviet Union but this, as we have seen, was just what the Poles refused to consider. Thus every overture from the Soviet Union met with a cool reception. The

Joint Four Power Declaration suggested on 18 March was declined. On 18 April Litvinov's proposal of a Pact of Mutual Assistance between France, Britain and Russia caused considerable embarrassment. Cadogan, in his brief for the Foreign Affairs Committee, wrote: 'This proposal is extremely inconvenient. We have to balance the advantage of a paper commitment by Russia to join us in a war on one side against the disadvantage of associating ourselves openly with Russia. The advantage, to say the least, is problematical.' [Colvin, p. 200] The Chiefs of Staff were consulted on the military value of an alliance with Russia and on 24 April produced a somewhat sceptical report. But there was strong pressure in parliament and in the country for an agreement with Russia. A second *aide memoire* produced by the Chiefs of Staff in May took a more sanguine view: 'a full blown guarantee of military assistance between Great Britain, France and the Soviet Union offers certain advantages'. [Colvin, p. 211] There were also the dangers of throwing Russia into the hands of Germany, or of Russian neutrality to be considered. In view of such arguments the Chamberlain cabinet continued to pursue negotiations, though with what conviction it is hard to say.

Colvin, *The Chamberlain Cabinet*

One of those who participated, Lord Strang, has left his own account of those negotiations [Lord Strang, 'The Moscow Negotiations', Dilks (ed.), pp. 170–86] They went on both in London and Moscow from May to August. Strang stresses the amount of common ground reached before they were finally called off. The draft agreement envisaged a direct obligation to provide military assistance between France, Britain and Russia should any of them be attacked. Similar protection was to be offered to the following states: Estonia, Latvia, Finland, Poland, Rumania, Turkey, Greece and Belgium. But on two issues agreement could not be reached. The Russians wanted the guarantee of mutual assistance to cover 'indirect aggression'. By this they meant that should there be a change in the neutral or independent status of one of the minor countries mentioned, even if this occurred voluntarily it would still give Russia the right to intervene and to claim the support of her allies in any subsequent conflict. This undertaking, not surprisingly, the British government were unwilling to give. The second obstacle was Russian insistence that any diplomatic agreement must be accompanied by simultaneous agreements of military assistance. It was to make such agreements that an undistinguished team of British admirals and generals left London for Leningrad on 5 August. They arrived in Moscow on 10 August and the talks went on until 17 August. British dilatoriness has been blamed for their failure but the real explanation for this was the stance adopted by the Polish government. Beck made this clear to the French ambassador: 'I cannot admit that in any measure whatever there can be discussions about the use of part of our territory by foreign troops. This is for us a question of principle. We have no military agreement with the Russians. We do not wish to have one.' [Strang, p. 179] Faced with this objection the Russian military authorities saw no point in continuing the discussions, and on 17 August they came to an end.

Dilks (ed.), *Retreat from Power*

Unknown to Britain and France, on 14 August Ribbentrop sent a letter to the German ambassador in Moscow, offering to come in person 'to lay the foundations for a final settlement of German-Russian relations'. [Taylor, p. 259] Molotov, who had replaced Litvinov in May, expressed interest. On 20 August Hitler sent a personal message to Stalin urging that Ribbentrop should be received. Stalin consented. On 23 August Ribbentrop arrived. In contrast to the interminable Anglo-French-Russian negotiations, within a matter of hours the Nazi-Soviet Pact had been agreed. It provided for a 20-year Non-Aggression Treaty and it stated in

Taylor, *The Origins of the Second World War*

The signing of the Nazi-Soviet Pact, 23 August 1939 (L to R Ribbentrop, Molotov and Stalin)

a secret protocol that in any territorial rearrangement of Eastern Europe, Germany would recognise Russian claims to Eastern Poland and to the Baltic states.

Germany was now safe from a war on two fronts, should she choose to attack Poland. On 22 August, in anticipation of the Pact, Hitler boasted to his generals: 'Now Poland is in the position in which I wanted her ... I am only afraid that at the last moment some swine or other will submit to me a plan of mediation.' [Craig, p. 712] On 26 August he ordered the invasion of Poland to proceed, though rapidly countermanding the orders when it became clear that he could not count on Mussolini's support. The delay was only temporary. On 1 September German troops crossed the Polish border and Warsaw was bombed.

Craig, *Germany, 1866–1945*

The Final Crisis

With the signing of the Nazi-Soviet Pact, war looked inevitable in London, too, though last-minute attempts continued to be made to avert it. On 25 August the British government confirmed the Treaty of Mutual Assistance with Poland, hoping that this might have some deterrent effect on Hitler. The Treaty did not state specifically that Danzig was covered, though there was a secret protocol to that effect. It has been argued that Halifax was still hoping that a deal over Danzig might be privately negotiated and on 26 August he asked Mussolini to make it clear to Berlin that 'if a settlement were confined to Danzig and the Corridor, it did not seem to us that it should be impossible ... to find a solution without war'. [Hayes, p. 313] While Britain employed Mussolini as an intermediary, the Germans called into service a Swedish businessman, Dahlerus, who shuttled between London and Berlin from 25 August to 30 August, relaying terms from one government to the other.

P. Hayes, *Modern British Foreign Policy* (A. & C. Black, 1981)

Whether any of these initiatives had a chance of success seems doubtful. While Britain would have been prepared to accept changes in the status of Danzig and the Polish Corridor, the Polish government was not. In view of Hitler's actions on 1

September it also seems highly unlikely that he would have settled for a compromise. The final break came when the Polish government refused a demand to send a plenipotentiary to Berlin, with full powers to negotiate, at 24-hours' notice. Even Chamberlain conceded that this was more than the Poles could be asked to do.

When Halifax was informed that German troops had crossed the Polish border and that Polish towns had been bombed, he assured the Polish ambassador that 'if the facts were as stated, I had no doubt that we should have no difficulty in deciding that our guarantee must at once come into force'. [Colvin, p. 244] That decision was not, however, reached as easily as Halifax implied it would be. The cabinet meeting on 1 September did not decide on what form the ultimatum to Germany should take. It was left to Halifax to draft the Note which Henderson was instructed to deliver to the German government. The Note read: 'Unless the German Government has suspended all aggressive actions against Poland and is prepared to withdraw their forces from Polish territory HM Government will without hesitation fulfil their obligations to Poland.' No time limit was attached for German compliance and Henderson was instructed to say that he was not delivering an ultimatum. Halifax was still hoping for Italian mediation and did not want to prevent this by imposing a time limit. However, when the cabinet met again on 2 September and no German reply having arrived, the mood changed. The Polish ambassador, Raczynski, was called in and made a heartfelt plea for the implementation of the Anglo-Polish guarantee. Hore-Belisha spoke strongly in favour of an ultimatum with a time limit and the cabinet agreed on a deadline of midnight. That was as far as it got.

Colvin, *The Chamberlain Cabinet*

After the cabinet meeting was over Halifax contacted the French government and discovered that they wanted a time limit of 48 hours. Thus when Chamberlain rose to speak in the House of Commons at 7.30 that evening it was in the awareness that no agreement had yet been reached with France. Chamberlain had an expectant audience, prepared to hear that positive steps had been taken to assist Poland. Instead, Chamberlain merely recalled the history of the recent negotiations, and made no reference to the ultimatum to which the cabinet had agreed earlier in the day. He was greeted with a stunned silence. Arthur Greenwood, acting leader of the Labour party in Attlee's temporary absence, was cheered by both sides when he got up to reply. Robert Boothby, an opponent of appeasement, cried out 'You speak for Britain.' [Nicolson, p. 419] Greenwood did so. Why, he asked, when Poland was being bombed and attacked, had the British government vacillated for 34 hours? He accused Chamberlain of 'imperilling the very foundations of our national honour'. After the debate, Greenwood saw Chamberlain in his room and warned him that unless the inevitable decision for war had been taken by the following day, 'it would be impossible to hold the House'. [Gilbert and Gott, p. 308] Chamberlain's colleagues were equally disturbed at his failure to mention the ultimatum. Simon led a deputation consisting of himself, Hore-Belisha, Anderson, de la Warr and Walter Elliot to see the Prime Minister, after Greenwood. They put the case very forcibly for a declaration of war.

H. Nicolson, *Diaries and Letters, 1930–1939* (1966)

Gilbert and Gott, *The Appeasers*

Chamberlain and Halifax had an uncomfortable dinner together. At 9.30 pm Halifax learned that Mussolini would not press Hitler to withdraw his troops, nor would he request a conference on Britain's conditions that all German troops must be withdrawn before a conference could be held. The cabinet met again at 11.30 pm and Chamberlain, for once, asked their advice. It was finally agreed that an ultimatum requiring German troops to be withdrawn from Poland should be delivered at 9.00 am on 3 September, to expire at 11.00 am. Henderson duly delivered the ultimatum. No German reply was received. At 11.15 the Prime Minister broadcast to the nation to tell the British people that they were at war. In the House of Commons later that day Chamberlain confessed his failure: 'Everything that I have worked for, everything that I had hoped for, everything that I have believed in during my public life, has crashed in ruins ....' But he concluded in a more hopeful note: 'I trust I may live to see the day when Hitlerism has been destroyed, and a liberated Europe has been re-established.' [Feiling, p. 416]

Feiling, *The Life of Neville Chamberlain* (1946)

POINTS AT ISSUE
POINTS AT ISSUE **POINTS AT ISSUE** POINTS AT ISSUE
POINTS AT ISSUE

Appeasement and the Munich Settlement

British foreign policy in the 1930s continues to be a subject of intense historical interest and the source of continuing historical controversy. Almost every episode from the Manchurian crisis of 1931 to the Anglo-Soviet negotiations in 1939 has been ear-marked as the critical turning-point in the slide towards the Second World War. Of these episodes, the one which has attracted most attention is probably the Czech crisis of 1938. There are good reasons for this. First, it showed appeasement in its most positive form. Secondly it was one of the rare occasions when Britain was in a position to act rather than react to events, and when an alternative policy was open to her. Had Chamberlain chosen to strengthen rather than to weaken French resolve and to associate the Soviet Union with British and French opposition to Hitler he could have done so. Thus, both at the time and in the writings of later historians the Czech crisis and the Munich agreement have been the subject of fierce debate.

The critics initially had the best of the argument because the Munich agreement signally failed to achieve its purpose. But in 1961 A. J. P. Taylor produced a resounding defence of British policy in his book *The Origins of the Second World War*. He did not establish a new orthodoxy, however, and with the opening of the cabinet records in 1967 the critics returned to the attack. More recently historians have tended to emphasise the constraints under which British politicians had to operate. The following excerpts can do no more than illustrate the rival viewpoints, but they should serve to indicate the continuing vitality of the argument.

The Defence of Munich

K. Feiling, *The Life of Neville Chamberlain* (Macmillan, 1946) *From Chamberlain's correspondence: 11 September, 1938*

Over and over again Canning lays it down that you should never menace unless you are in a position to carry out your threats, and although, if we have to fight I should hope we should be able to give a good account of ourselves, we are certainly not in a position in which our military advisers would feel happy in undertaking to begin hostilities if we were not forced to do so .... [Feiling, p. 360]

Feiling's conclusions on the Munich Agreement:

> No, he was not deceived, neither by Hitler's moods nor by the exultant relief of London; 'all this will be over in three months', he said to Halifax as their car struggled through the crowd, and he had prepared his statement for Hitler to sign in hope but also in calculation. For if it were honoured well and good; if repudiated, it would brand the guilty party before all mankind. This also he spoke of on the journey home.
>
> The middle path, which he stressed, would be arduous, easy to misrepresent and easy to miss. He must exploit a hope as though he believed it to the hilt, deny surrender without boasting of victory, entrench a firm position by rearming and yet give no cause for war, and submit to provocation for a greater end till time were on his side.' [Feiling, p. 382]

A. J. P. Taylor, *The Origins of the Second World War*

> Leon Blum expressed French feeling best when he welcomed the agreement of Munich with a mixture of shame and relief. With the British, on the other hand, morality counted for a great deal. The British statesmen used practical arguments: the danger from air attack; the backwardness of their rearmament; the impossibility, even if adequately armed, of helping Czechoslovakia. But these arguments were used to reinforce morality, not to silence it. British policy over Czechoslovakia originated in the belief that Germany had a moral right to the Sudeten German territory, on the grounds of national principle; and it drew the further corollary that this victory for self-determination would provide a stabler, more permanent peace in Europe. The British Government were not driven to acknowledge the dismemberment of Czechoslovakia solely from fear of war. They deliberately set out to impose this cession of territory on the Czechs before the threat of war raised its head. The settlement at Munich was a triumph for British policy which had worked precisely to this end; not a triumph for Hitler, who had started with no such clear intention. Nor was it merely a triumph for selfish or cynical British statesmen, indifferent to the fate of far off peoples or calculating that Hitler might be launched into war against Soviet Russia. It was a triumph for all that was best and most enlightened in British life; a triumph for all those who had preached equal justice between peoples; a triumph for those who had courageously denounced the harshness and short-sightedness of the Treaty of Versailles. [Taylor, p. 189]

The Critics of Munich

M. Gilbert and R. Gott, *The Appeasers*

This is a study both of the policy of appeasement and the policy-makers. The book's approach is indicated in the Foreword:

> This is a history of British policy towards Nazi Germany, and of the men who supported and opposed it. It shows in some detail how British policy was formed, how it was carried out, and why it was misconceived, in the light of warnings received at the time from trained diplomats like Vansittart, Rumbold and Kennard; and experienced politicians like Amery, Eden and Duff Cooper .... Those who supported appeasement after October 1938 did so for two reasons. Munich 'bought' a year of peace, in which to rearm. It brought 'a united nation' into war, by showing Hitler's wickedness beyond doubt. Both these reasons were put forward by the Government, and accepted by many who could not check them. Both were false.
>
> If a year had been gained in which Chamberlain could have strengthened Britain's defences and equipped the country for an offensive war, there should be evidence of growing strength, growing effort, and growing Cabinet unity. But while some members of the Cabinet sought to use the 'bought' year, others did not. Chamberlain and his closest advisers were unwilling to allow the Minister for War, Hore-Belisha, to introduce

conscription. The Air Minister, Kingsley Wood, failed to achieve the needed air parity with Germany. Machines were not lacking. Will power was. Germany, not Britain, gained militarily during the extra year. German forces were strengthened by Czech munitions, western forces weakened by the loss of the Czech Army and Air Force.

Munich showed the Soviet Union that western resolve could be broken. Democracies had sacrificed one of their number. In England the First Lord of the Admiralty resigned. He saw the moral, as well as the military implications of the betrayal. In 1938 France had been willing to fight, but Chamberlain overruled Daladier. In the 'bought' year, French courage failed. Britain, having abandoned Anglo-French interests once, could not abandon them again. France lapsed into defeatism. [Gilbert and Gott, p. 11–12]

On the Munich settlement itself, the authors quote without comment Benes's broadcast to the Czech people on 5 October:

We did our utmost to reach understanding with other nationalities, and we went to the extreme limit of possible concessions. Do not expect from me a single word of recrimination. But this I will say, that the sacrifices demanded from us were immeasurably great and immeasurably unjust. This the nation will never forget, even though they have borne these sacrifices quietly. [Gilbert and Gott, p. 181]

Among the effects of the Munich Agreement the authors also cite the plight of German Social Democrats in the Sudetenland:

Wenzel Jaksch flew to London. He begged for visas for the Sudeten Social Democrats. Few visas were forthcoming. He visited Lord Runciman, and reminded him of how he had come to Prague as 'the friend of all and the enemy of none'. He had befriended the Henleinists. How was he going to help the German democrats? Jaksch asked for visas. Runciman replied: 'I believe that the Lord Mayor is opening a fund for you all, and if so you will certainly find my name on the list of contributers.' The necessary visas were never granted. Many of Jaksch's associates perished in German concentration camps ....'

Ian Colvin, *The Chamberlain Cabinet*

Colvin criticises Chamberlain first for his failure to consult or be guided by the cabinet:

....Chamberlain was a shy autocrat and made his own policy in silence before he made it Cabinet policy. If appeasement began as a common Cabinet policy, it was he who gave it such an emphasis as to add a pejorative sense to the word. I can, moreover, find no example in two and a half years of Cabinet meetings in which the discussion in Cabinet altered his mind on a subject, though he was known to alter it between Cabinets. In forming our view of him, we must read his own evidence about the decision to go to Berchtesgaden when confronted with intelligence reports from Germany – 'on Tuesday night I saw that the moment had come and must be taken if I was not to be too late. So I sent the fateful telegram and told the Cabinet next morning what I had done.' There has been absolutely no evidence since that such haste was necessary or indeed that he was so advised at the time. Subsequent events illustrated the wisdom of not evading Cabinet responsibility.

Colvin identifies three main indictments against the Chamberlain cabinet:

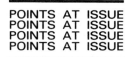

> The three broad issues upon which the Chamberlain Cabinet stands at the bar of history are that with a large Parliamentary majority it failed to rearm in time; that it surrendered over Czechoslovakia in 1938, when it need not so have done; and that it failed in 1939 to achieve an alliance with Russia, thus entering war with less effective allies than could have been found in 1938.

Where the Czech crisis is concerned Colvin criticises the failure to take seriously enough the internal threat to Hitler's authority: 'It is evident from Lord Halifax's descriptions and other personal recollections that there was more than the solid testimony of Herr von Kleist that showed some cracks in the edifice of the Third Reich. We know of none that described Hitler as bent on war and sure of absolute support.' [Colvin, p. 268] The British government cannot, Colvin argues, justifiably excuse their caution on the grounds of

> their inner knowledge that France was divided and unlikely actively to honour her obligations; .... If we recall the Chautemps-Delbos visit to London in November 1937, we find the two French ministers firm enough about the pledge to military action in aid of Czechoslovakia 'Whatever the nature of the aggression'. When Daladier and Bonnet visited in April 1938, they were equally affirmative that an Anglo-French *Entente* would be efficacious. Although the timidity of Bonnet later became a byword, had not the ebb of French confidence in the summer of 1938 something to do with the absolute refusal of the British to accept a new commitment, or even to say that in no circumstances would they take action?

Colvin concludes: 'Since British strategy then envisaged in any case a long war, in which a blockade rather than a land offensive against Germany would be decisive, the inference is strong that Austria should have been the storm signal and Czechoslovakia the *casus belli*.'

The debate continues. William R. Rock has summarised the argument in *British Appeasement in the 1930s*. On Munich he has this to say:

> The controversy over Munich will never be settled. It is too easy to take alternative views and accumulate arguments. Thus it comes down to a matter of feeling and instinct rather than reason and logic. That Munich was essentially inescapable, even wise, given the circumstances of 1938, is a weighty proposition. But that Britain should never have fallen into that predicament is also quite compelling. Whether Britain would have done better to have fought, if necessary, in 1938 instead of waiting until one year later may be debated endlessly, both with regard to her military preparations relative to Germany's and the extent to which Munich was essential to educating the British in the ways of depraved men and therefore basic to their later conviction that war, as never before in history, was right. But to put excessive emphasis on the 'validity' of Munich is to miss a broader point about it as an extension of appeasement. Whether Munich was right or wrong, it was a shameful, humiliating, alarming experience. And for Chamberlain and some of his colleagues to interpret it as a constructive achievement on the way to peace with justice and reconciliation with Germany was downright deceitful, especially as the prime minister himself was not convinced that Munich had made peace any more secure. After Munich, appeasement was a clearly misguided and misguiding policy. [Rock, p. 91]

Books cited

A. J. P. Taylor, *The Origins of the Second World War* (Hamish Hamilton, 1961)

K. Feiling, *The Life of Neville Chamberlain* (Macmillan, 1946)

M. Gilbert and R. Gott, *The Appeasers* (Weidenfeld & Nicolson, 1963)

I. Colvin, *The Chamberlain Cabinet* (Gollancz, 1971)

W. R. Rock, *British Appeasement in the 1930s* (Arnold, 1977)

BIBLIOGRAPHY BIBLIOGRAPHY BIBLIOGRAPHY BIBLIOGRAPHY BIBLIOGRAPHY BIBLIOGRAPHY
BIBLIOGRAPHY BIBLIOGRAPHY BIBLIOGRAPHY BIBLIOGRAPHY BIBLIOGRAPHY BIBLIOGRAPHY
BIBLIOGRAPHY BIBLIOGRAPHY BIBLIOGRAPHY BIBLIOGRAPHY BIBLIOGRAPHY BIBLIOGRAPHY
BIBLIOGRAPHY BIBLIOGRAPHY BIBLIOGRAPHY BIBLIOGRAPHY BIBLIOGRAPHY BIBLIOGRAPHY
BIBLIOGRAPHY BIBLIOGRAPHY BIBLIOGRAPHY BIBLIOGRAPHY BIBLIOGRAPHY BIBLIOGRAPHY
BIBLIOGRAPHY BIBLIOGRAPHY BIBLIOGRAPHY BIBLIOGRAPHY BIBLIOGRAPHY BIBLIOGRAPHY

CHAPTER 9
FURTHER READING

The literature on international history between 1919 and 1939 is enormous. The following list is highly selective. For further guidance consult the bibliographies in books indicated with an asterisk.

General

Essential

A. Adamthwaite, *The Making of the Second World War** (Allen & Unwin, 1977)
A. J. P. Taylor, *The Origins of the Second World War* (Hamish Hamilton, 1961)

Recommended

E. Wiskemann, *Europe of the Dictators* (Collins, 1966)

Individual Countries

Essential

Germany
A. Bullock, *Hitler, A Study in Tyranny* (Penguin, 1969)
W. Carr, *Arms, Autarky and Aggression: A Study in German Foreign Policy 1933–1939* (Arnold, 1972)
G. Craig, *Germany, 1866–1945* (OUP, 1978)

France
A. Adamthwaite, *France and the Coming of the Second World War, 1936–1939* (F. Cass, 1977)
J. Nere, *The Foreign Policy of France from 1914–1945* (Routledge and Kegan Paul, 1975)

Italy
D. Mack Smith, *Mussolini's Roman Empire* (Penguin, 1977)

The United States
R. Dallek, *Franklin D. Roosevelt and American Foreign Policy, 1933–45* (OUP, 1978)

Russia
J. Erikson, *The Soviet High Command, 1918–1941* (Macmillan, 1979)

British Policy and Policy Makers

Essential

I. Colvin, *The Chamberlain Cabinet* (Gollancz, 1971)
D. Dilks (ed.) *Retreat from Power, Studies in Britain's Foreign Policy of the Twentieth Century,* vol. I *(1906–1939)* (Macmillan, 1981)
W. R. Rock, *British Appeasement in the 1930s** (Arnold, 1977)

Recommended

M. Cowling, *The Impact of Hitler: British Politics and Policy, 1933–1940* (CUP, 1975)
M. Gilbert, *The Roots of Appeasement* (Plume Books, 1978)
M. Gilbert and R. Gott, *The Appeasers* (Weidenfeld & Nicolson, 1963)
W. N. Meddlicot, *British Foreign Policy since Versailles, 1919–1963* (Methuen, 1968)
W. N. Meddlicot, *The Coming of War in 1939* (Historical Association, 1963)
K. Middlemas, *The Diplomacy of Illusion: The British Government and Germany, 1937–1939* (Weidenfeld & Nicolson, 1972)
H. Nicolson, *Diaries and Letters, 1930–1939* (Collins, 1966)
J. W. Wheeler-Bennett, *Munich, Prologue to Tragedy* (Macmillan, 1966)

Individual Biographies and Memoirs

Essential

A. Eden, *The Memoirs of Anthony Eden, Facing the Dictators* (Cassell, 1962)
K. Feiling, *The Life of Neville Chamberlain* (Macmillan, 1946)
M. Gilbert, *Winston S. Churchill,* vol. V, *1922–1939* (Heinemann, 1976)

Recommended

D. Carlton, *Eden* (Allen Lane, 1981)
Sir N. Henderson, *Failure of a Mission, Berlin, 1937–39* (Putnam, New York, 1940)
Viscount Templewood (Sir S. Hoare), *Nine Troubled Years* (Collins, 1954)
D. C. Watt, *Personalities and Policies: Studies in the Formulation of British Foreign Policy in the Twentieth Century* (Greenwood Press, 1976)

Britain and the Second World War

MAIN FEATURES OF THE WAR ▬▬▬▬▬▬ A

The Combatants

Allied Forces

1939   Poland (September – October)

     Britain and the British Empire (September 1939 – August 1945)

     France (September 1939 – June 1940)

1940   Norway (April – May 1940)

     Denmark (April 1940)

     Holland (May 1940)

     Belgium (May 1940)

     Greece (October 1940 – May 1941)

1941   Yugoslavia (April 1941)

     Russia (June 1941 – August 1945)

     United States (December 1941 – August 1945)

Axis Forces

1939   Germany (September 1939 – May 1945)

1940   Italy (June 1940 – September 1943)

1941   Japan (December 1941 – August 1945)

The Second World War falls into two distinct phases. At the outset it was largely a European war, fought between Britain, France and those countries invaded by Germany on the one hand, and by Germany and Italy on the other. Poland was conquered in the first six weeks of the war, though a Polish government in exile was set up in London, and thousands of Poles continued to fight on the Allied side. In April 1940 the war was extended to Scandinavia, with the German invasion of Denmark and Norway. The Norwegian government, too, took refuge in Britain. In May, Belgium and Holland were invaded. The Dutch royal family fled to Britain; the Belgian king on the other hand, decided that he could serve his people best by seeing through the German occupation with them. In June 1940 Mussolini declared war on Britain and France, anticipating France's surrender by a matter of days. In October he attacked Greece. In March 1941 Hitler also turned his attention to the Balkan peninsula. He signed a Tripartite Pact with Yugoslav ministers on 25 March but this was repudiated by the Serbian people and its rejection resulted in the German invasion of Yugoslavia which took place in April. Having conquered Yugoslavia, German troops advanced into Greece, whose government surrendered on 21 April. By the spring of 1941 the whole of Western Europe was under Nazi domination except for Britain and the neutral countries of Sweden, Switzerland, Spain and Portugal. In November 1942 German troops moved into the unoccupied zone of France to complete Hitler's *Festung Europa*.

The second phase of the war opened with the German invasion of Russia on 22 June 1941. This, as Churchill said, altered the values and relationships of the war. It also made Germany's defeat possible. From now on Russia was to absorb the greater weight of the German war machine. While the achievements of Anglo-American forces in North Africa, Italy and North-West Europe must never be discounted, it needs also to be remembered that the Soviet Union was to lose 20 million casualties in the ensuing conflict, compared with a total of 400 000 suffered by the British and 300 000 by the Americans.

In December 1941 the Japanese attack on Pearl Harbour finally brought the United States into the war. It made an Allied victory, if not inevitable, at least highly probable. In the euphoria of the moment Churchill, in his own words, 'went to bed and slept the sleep of the saved and thankful'. Thus, for the first two years of the war, Britain was fighting for her survival. After the fall of France in June 1940 and before the invasion of Russia in June 1941, she stood alone against the Axis powers. This was, indeed, 'Her finest hour'. But from June 1941, Britain's role became a supporting one as the two superpowers of Russia and the United States geared their very different economic systems to the demands of war and assembled their forces. With the entry of Japan into the war the Pacific now became an important theatre of operations and the European war became a world war.

War Aims

As the scale of the war changed, so did the aims of the combatants. There is some reason to believe that Chamberlain was still hoping for a negotiated peace until the *Blitzkrieg* launched by Hitler in May 1940. Chamberlain believed that the German economy would collapse under the pressure of economic blockade – a forlorn hope, but while it persisted he refused to escalate the war. Air raids on Germany were strictly confined to attacks on naval units and to the dropping of leaflets on centres of civilian population. The invasion of Norway and Denmark, the bombing of Rotterdam and the assault on France ruled out any such hopes. After the fall of France, in a broadcast to the German people on 19 July, Hitler held out vague prospects of peace. He announced his willingness to recognise the British Empire, providing Germany could have Egypt and Iraq, and professed himself willing to negotiate with a friendly British government containing Lloyd George and presided over by the Duke of Windsor. Both men at certain times had expressed their admiration for Hitler. Churchill and the cabinet would have none of it. On 3 August Churchill defined Britain's peace terms in response to a Swedish offer of intervention. He required 'effective guarantees by deeds, not words ... from Germany, which would ensure the restoration of the free and independent life of Czechoslovakia,

A. J. P. Taylor, *English History, 1914–1945* (Pelican, 1970)

Poland, Norway, Denmark, Holland, Belgium and above all, France, as well as the effectual security of Great Britain and the British Empire in a general peace ....' [Taylor, p. 596] There would be no compromise peace with Germany.

Partly to win American support, partly out of a genuine wish to make clear the moral basis of the Allied cause, in August 1941 the Atlantic Charter was drawn up at a meeting between Roosevelt and Churchill at Placentia Bay, Newfoundland. The document was framed at Churchill's request by Sir Alexander Cadogan, Permanent under-secretary at the Foreign Office. As a statement of war aims it might be compared with Wilson's Fourteen Points though it was even less specific. The Charter made clear that on the Allied side the war was not being fought for any territorial goal; that the rights of all peoples to self-government should be upheld; that there should be freedom of trade, freedom of the seas, and equal access to the world's raw materials. Hopes were expressed for economic collaboration and for a peace 'that will afford to all nations the means of dwelling in safety within their own boundaries, and which will afford assurance that all the men in all the lands may live out their lives in freedom from fear and want.' [Dilks (ed.), p. 400] Though the United States was not yet a combatant, Roosevelt signed the Charter, as did representatives of all the Allied governments in exile.

D. Dilks (ed.), The Cadogan Diaries (Cassell, 1971)

But the war had first to be won. As its ferocity increased and as it became clear that there were no bounds to Hitler's ambitions, a starker and simpler formula took the place of the Atlantic Charter. At the Casablanca Conference, held in January 1943, Churchill and Roosevelt conferred with the Joint Chiefs of Staff to concert Allied strategy. They also discussed war aims, and though in the communiqué issued after the Conference there was no specific reference to these, in a press conference held on 24 January Roosevelt observed: 'Some of you Britishers know the old story - we had a General called U. S. Grant. His name was Ulysses Simpson Grant, but in my and the Prime Minister's early days he was called "Unconditional Surrender" Grant. The elimination of German, Japanese and Italian war power means the unconditional surrender by Germany, Japan and Italy.' [Lewin, p. 181] Churchill and the War Cabinet gave their endorsement to this statement. For better or worse, the Allies were now committed to a peace without conditions. Those Germans who plotted Hitler's downfall were now handicapped by the knowledge that any government which replaced Hitler's would still have to accept any peace terms the Allied powers chose to impose. According to one historian of the German Resistance, Gerhard Ritter, 'As the sole peace terms were to be "unconditional surrender" not only did most of his generals, but even men of the opposition ... refused to relieve the tyrant by revolution from such a disaster ....' [cited in Fuller, p. 279] In their defence the Allies could argue that only such an unequivocal goal could have kept them together. There were serious enough divisions on all sides and at least the formula of 'unconditional surrender' eliminated the possibility that one partner might make peace behind the backs of the others. But now that victory was the sole war aim, any moral constraints on how it was to be achieved virtually disappeared. This can be seen in the Casablanca directive issued to the commanders of the British and American Bomber forces shortly after the Casablanca Conference. It stated: 'Your primary aim will be the progressive destruction and dislocation of the German military, industrial and economic system, and the undermining of the morale of the German people to a point where their capacity for armed resistance is fatally weakened ....' [Hastings, p. 185] The Dresden Air Raid in February 1945 and the dropping of atomic bombs on Hiroshima and Nagasaki in August 1945 were the

R. Lewin, Churchill as War Lord (1973)

J. F. C. Fuller, The Conduct of War (Methuen, 1961)

M. Hastings, Bomber Command

logical consequences of a war strategy that had as its ultimate goal the unconditional surrender of the opposition.

'The Second World War was to see a curious blend of mass participation and deadly esoteric duels between technological experts.' [Howard, p. 120] The Second World War involved the people of the warring powers more directly and more completely than the First World War. It was rightly christened 'The People's War'. This was partly the consequence of airpower, partly because of the demands imposed on the economy by the quantity and variety of weapons required. Bombing brought civilians into the front line — up to December 1941 more British civilians had been killed by enemy action than British servicemen. It was safer to be a mess waiter in Aldershot than a docker in Liverpool. The merchant navy suffered more casualties (33 000 − 17%) in proportion to its size than did any of the armed services. The distinction between the front-line soldier on the Western Front and the civilian separated from him by the English Channel, which had been such a marked feature of the First World War, disappeared.

Total War and Technology

M. Howard, *War in European History* (1976)

There was no hesitation about introducing conscription as there had been in 1915. The principle of compulsory military training had already been accepted in 1939, so no further legislation was needed. In 1941 the British government introduced the direction of labour, extending it to women without domestic responsibilities. By 1941, 49% of the British people were being employed by the government in one capacity or another. As the threat of invasion approached in 1940 all those capable of holding a rifle (even if there weren't any rifles to be held) were recruited into the Home Guard (later on to be brilliantly and affectionately satirised in the TV programme, 'Dad's Army'). Rationing of food, clothing and petrol affected everybody, as did the application of 'utility' standard specifications to the manufacture of a wide range of consumer goods. The war was an all-pervading presence which disrupted the lives of everyone, to a greater or lesser extent.

The war also imposed huge demands upon the economy. Superimposed on the demand for guns and shells which had caused such a strain in 1914 was the demand for aeroplanes, tanks, wireless sets, and all the sophisticated weaponry that came to be required on the battlefields of the Second World War. The ratio of combatant soldiers to those required to keep them fed and supplied changed significantly as armies became more mobile. Hard choices had to be made. The decision to support the Strategic Air Offensive in 1942 meant fewer aeroplanes to protect Allied convoys. Because cereals fed directly to people had a higher food value than when fed to animals, meat production went down and the proportion of land devoted to arable farming increased. Every resource, including manpower, had to be carefully husbanded.

While the war required the mobilisation of the working population, its fortunes were also determined by the achievements of a small number of scientists and technologists whose influence was out of all proportion to their numbers. A few examples must suffice. The German magnetic mine, caused to explode by the electrical field surrounding a ship's hull, was countered by the device of 'degaussing'; RADAR and its associated developments enabled hostile aeroplanes to be identified in time for fighters to be sent to intercept them. Later on it was used to guide aircraft to their targets. An electronic 'war' was as much part of the struggle for aerial superiority as the design of aircraft or the conduct of operations. Two developments require particular emphasis. Radio was the essential form of communication in the Second World War. It was used to link national headquarters with operational commands; to co-ordinate the deployment of ships at sea; and to make possible the co-operation of tanks, aircraft and infantry on the battlefield. But radio communication was vulnerable to interception. Since 1974 it has become known that the Allies were intercepting and deciphering most of the high-level radio traffic that passed between German, Italian and Japanese commands and embassies. This was made possible, first by the smuggling into Britain of a replica of the German cypher machine known as ENIGMA, and secondly by the devoted and sometimes inspired work of the code breakers at Bletchley Park, officially known as the Government Code and Cipher School. So important was this work that it has been claimed by one historian that all those histories of the Second World War written in ignorance of ENIGMA 'are fundamentally, misleading, inadequate and out of date ...' [R. Lewin, 'A Signal Intelligence War in The Second World War', Laquer (ed.), p. 185] The information garnered at Bletchley Park became known as 'Ultra'. It gave the British knowledge of the organisation of Goering's Air Fleets in 1940, forewarning of the impending invasion of Russia in 1941, and the state of Rommel's supplies during the North African campaigns and the dates and composition of the convoys sent to relieve him. The precise date of the German landings on Crete in 1941 was forecast to the point where the British commander, General Freyberg, was heard to remark as the German gliders and parachutists arrived: 'They're dead on time.' [Lewin, p. 157] For much, but not all, of the war Britain was able to intercept Admiral Doenitz's instructions to his U-boat commanders. U-boat sinkings of merchant shipping were very much higher during the period from February to December 1942 when the U-boat cipher defied the code breakers. Ultra's final contribution to the war was to provide proof that the German High Command had swallowed the Allied deception plan made for the invasion in 1944. Several Panzer divisions were kept from the Normandy beachhead by the fear of another invasion in the Pas de Calais which never came.

W. Laquer (ed.), *The Second World War, Essays in Military and Political History* (1982)

R. Lewin, *Ultra Goes to War* (1978)

The most expert of the technologists' accomplishments was, of course, the development of nuclear weapons – a more obvious and direct instance of their influence on the outcome of the war could not be found. The use of nuclear weapons in 1945 brought the war with Japan to a speedy end; it also ushered in a new era in man's potential for self-destruction and in that sense the Second World War, through the 'deadly esoteric duels' it provoked, continues to exert its baleful effects.

Methods of Warfare and the Role of the Armed Forces

The Second World War was dominated by two innovations which had only made a limited contribution in the First: the tank and the aeroplane. Used in combination, as they were by Hitler in 1939 and 1940, they made possible the *Blitzkrieg* (lightning war). The tank dominated the battlefield in North Africa where it was in its element. Tanks were also important in every other theatre and there was no return to the static trench warfare of 1914. But to every weapon there is an antidote; in the case of the tank it was primarily the German 88mm dual purpose aircraft/anti-tank gun, which was capable of destroying any British tank throughout the war. The notion that tanks could operate independently of infantry or artillery support was soon dispelled, particularly in the narrow ground between the ridge of the Appenines and the sea up which the Allies painfully advanced in 1943–44, or in the Normandy 'bocage' country. Armoured warfare certainly changed the roles of infantry soldiers and gunners but all three arms were needed on the battlefield. There were no repetitions of the Somme and on the whole British generals showed themselves to be much more careful of their men's lives than they had been in the First World War. Altogether, 145 000 British soldiers were killed.

Airpower was the decisive factor on the battlefield. It would not guarantee success, but no army could hope to win without aerial superiority. Until 1942 Hitler generally held the advantage in this respect and he scarcely lost a battle, let alone a campaign. But from the battle of El Alamein onwards the tables were turned. By 1944 the Allies enjoyed complete air superiority both on the Western and the Eastern fronts and it ensured their eventual success.

The further claim that airpower alone could win wars was to be disproved. It was made first by an Italian Colonel, Giulio Douhet, whose book *Command of the Air* was first published in 1921. Douet claimed that once command of the air had been achieved the destruction of the enemies' cities and industrial centres would bring about collapse within a matter of weeks. His views were shared by Air Chief Marshal Sir Hugh Trenchard, founder of the RAF, and by Air Marshal Harris, head of Bomber Command from 1942 to 1945. In 1938 Bomber Command 'still claimed that by attacking the Ruhr it could bring the German War Machine to a standstill in two weeks' [Strachan, p. 155] and though Harris altered the time-scale he persisted in his belief that, granted the necessary resources, Bomber Command could win the war on its own. As we shall see, this proved to be an illusory hope.

G. Douhet, *Command of the Air* (Faber & Faber, 1943)

H. Strachan, *European Armies and the Conduct of War* (1983)

The war at sea showed many of the characteristics of the First World War. Britain's survival still depended on keeping the sea lanes open. This time there was no German High Seas Fleet to guard against, but there were several fast and powerfully armed battleships that could be used as commerce raiders: the *Graf Spee*, *Bismarck*, *Prince Eugen*, *Scharnhorst*, *Gneisenau* and *Tirpitz*. Though Germany had only 57 submarines when the war began, the U-boat once again emerged as the most serious threat to the British war effort. The battle of the Atlantic, as Churchill christened the duel between the U-boat and the Allied convoys, was the battle Churchill most feared he might lose. Indeed, without mastery of the sea the resources of the United States in men and materials would have been of no avail.

Britain's armed forces all had vital roles to perform: the army to win back the territories lost to Germany in the first years of the war, in addition to defending Britain's imperial possessions in Africa, the Mediterranean and the Far East; the RAF to defend Britain's airspace, to win air superiority over the battlefields where British troops were deployed and, most controversially, to destroy the German economy and break down German morale; and the Royal Navy to counter the threats to the movement of men and supplies from German capital ships and submarines, and to support the deployment of troops and, if necessary, their evacuation, wherever coastal operations were involved.

The sense of euphoria which captured the British public in 1914 was lacking in 1939. There was no rush to join up in the fear that the war might be over by Christmas; rather a dogged realisation of the pain and suffering that war would bring, allied, this time, to a more justifiable conviction about the rightness of the cause. Of all the combatants, Britain and the Empire fought longest. Protected by the Channel, Britain escaped the rigours of enemy occupation. But the war was nonetheless a long ordeal which strained all the resources of her people.

The Phoney War

From September 1939 to April 1940 Britain might hardly have been at war. Though an expeditionary force was sent to the Continent under Lord Gort, its role was strictly defensive. The RAF confined their activities to sporadic raids on German shipping and dropping leaflets on German cities. Only at sea was there a reminder that this was a real war. The aircraft carrier *Courageous* was sunk in September and the battleship *Royal Oak* in October, both by German U-boats. The *Graf Spee* sank eight British merchant ships in the South Atlantic before being brought to bay by three British cruisers in December. The *Graf Spee* took temporary refuge in Montevideo harbour before emerging 24 hours later to scuttle herself rather than face destruction from the waiting British ships. But this was the only victory to be recorded, and it hardly justified Chamberlain's unwise boast in the House of Commons on 4 April that 'Hitler had missed the bus'. In truth, Britain had no effective war strategy at this stage, as can be seen by some of the desperate expedients that were contemplated. Churchill, ever a fertile source of ideas – some crack-brained, others not – suggested floating mines down the Rhine or bombing the oil wells in Baku. But before either of these ventures could be tried another complication set in. On 30 November 1939 Russia invaded Finland. There was a wave of sympathy for the Finns and in a gesture which did more credit to their hearts than their heads the British and French governments promised to send an Anglo-French force of 100 000 men to Finland's assistance. Behind this promise Churchill had a concealed purpose. In the belief that the German war effort might be halted by cutting off supplies of vital raw materials, Churchill clutched at the straw offered by the possibility of cutting off the supply of high-grade Swedish iron ore. In winter the Baltic was frozen and the only route by which the ore could reach Germany was through the Norwegian ice-free port of Narvik. German ships were safe from attack provided they stayed within the three-mile territorial limit of the Norwegian coast. Churchill proposed to use the Anglo-French expedition to Finland to seize Narvik and to destroy the Swedish iron ore mines at the same time. Needless to say, the Norwegian and Swedish governments refused to allow the passage of the Anglo-French force across their territory and when Finland made peace with Russia on 12 March the excuse to intervene had disappeared. But if the excuse had gone, the motive had not. The plan to aid Finland was replaced by a plan to 'invade' Norway.

The Norwegian Campaign

The Norwegian campaign was badly planned and badly executed. Hitler, no doubt anticipating Allied moves, gave orders for a combined air and sea attack on Norway on 9 April 1940, the same day chosen by Britain and France for their initiative. Within hours German paratroops had seized Oslo and German forces had occupied the other main ports: Trondjheim, Bergen and Narvik. Instead of landing on 'friendly' soil the British and French were now faced with the task of dislodging a well-trained and well-armed opponent. Two attacks were to be mounted, one on Trondjheim, one at Narvik. The attack on Trondjheim never took place. Instead troops were landed at Namsos to the North and Aandalsnes to the South. Both groups were evacuated without having achieved anything on 2 May. The attack on Narvik met with more success, falling to Allied forces on 28 May but it was impossible to sustain such an isolated success, and on 8 June Narvik too was evacuated. In the naval operations which took place during the Norwegian campaign the honours were more evenly shared. Britain lost the aircraft carrier *Glorious* and two destroyers, the Germans two cruisers and ten destroyers, with some damage to their other capital ships as well.

The Norwegian campaign, for which Churchill was largely responsible, paradoxically led to the fall of the Chamberlain government and Churchill's elevation to the premiership. A recent historian comments:

> The influence of Churchill was generally deplorable: his boldness and imagination on this occasion were not — as was generally and mercifully the case — checked by a strong Chiefs of Staff Committee. The mixture of ignorance and interference from London was seldom creditable. If the first campaigns of the British in long wars tend to be ineptly launched and incompetently executed, Norway was no exception. [Fraser, p. 52]

D. Fraser, *And We Shall Shock Them, The British Army in the Second World War* (1983)

The BEF and the Fall of France

The performance of the BEF a few days later was little better. On 10 May Hitler ordered Operation Sichelschnitt (Sickle Cut) to begin. As expected, Army Group B under General Bock invaded Belgium and Holland. Allied plans had been drawn up on the assumption that the Germans would repeat the strategy of the Schlieffen Plan. What they had not anticipated was the advance of seven Panzer Divisions in Army Group A, under General Von Runstedt, through the Ardennes forest. This force smashed its way through what little opposition it encountered and by 19 May it had reached Abbeville on the Channel coast. The French armies were now fatally split with the BEF surrounded on three flanks. In accordance with pre-arranged plans, as soon as the German offensive began the BEF had advanced to the river Dyle. Under the pressure of Army Group B the Belgians retreated, finally surrendering on 27 May. Gort found himself in an impossible position. He was ordered to mount an offensive on 22 May to his south-west on the flank of Army Group A, while to the north he faced the danger of being cut off entirely from the Channel. Gort wisely ignored the order and concentrated on getting his force safely evacuated. Meanwhile, the German offensive rolled on. Boulogne was evacuated on 26 May and Calais, after a brave defence, also surrendered. The only port now left in Allied hands was Dunkirk.

Dunkirk: waiting for evacuation

On 26 May the decision was taken to evacuate the BEF and Vice Admiral Ramsay was put in charge of the operation. Nothing was yet said to the French whose assistance was vital for the defence of the perimeter surrounding the beaches and the port of Dunkirk. The French Admiral at Dunkirk, Admiral Abrial, demanded an explanation. It was given on 28 May when the decision was also taken that British and French troops should play an equal role in defence of the perimeter and should be evacuated in equal numbers. Over the next week, 338226 soldiers were taken off the beaches and the mole at Dunkirk harbour – 124999 of them were French. The BEF left all their transport, heavy weapons and tanks behind. As Churchill said in the House of Commons: 'We must be very careful not to assign to this deliverance the attributes of a victory. Wars are not won by evacuations.' [Churchill, vol. II, p. 102] But Dunkirk was a triumph of a kind and the one redeeming feature of a disastrous campaign.

W.S. Churchill, *The Second World War*, vol. II (Cassell, 1949)

It was not yet the end of the war in France. On 30 May two divisions were shipped to France to take part in the defence of Brittany. On 16 June in desperation Churchill, with the cabinet's approval, offered Paul Reynaud, the French premier, the opportunity of a permanent union with Great Britain. Reynaud declined the offer and resigned the following day, to be succeeded by Marshal Petain who was convinced that France must pull out of the fight. On 22 June an armistice was signed between France and Germany. Fortunately by that time most of the 160000 British troops still in France had been evacuated, apart from the luckless 51st Highland Division which was surrounded and compelled to surrender at St Valéry. So ended Britain's first continental engagements in the Second World War. It would be nearly four years before British troops returned to the scene.

There were two unhappy sequels to the fall of France. Churchill was desperately anxious to prevent French naval units falling into the hands of the Germans. Those at Alexandria were effectively immobilised but those at Oran posed a more serious problem. The local commander was offered four choices: to sail his ships to a British port and join forces with the Royal Navy; to sail his ships to a British port and have his crews repatriated to France; to sail to a West Indian port, and have his ships de-militarised, or handed over to the United States; or to sink his own ships. The French admiral, on the instructions of the Vichy government, refused all these offers. Reluctantly and with the full approval of the War Cabinet Churchill ordered the destruction of the French fleet. At 5.55 pm on 3 July the British opened fire. Within nine minutes one French battleship had blown up, two had run aground and 1250 French sailors had been killed. This action, coming less than a month after Churchill's offer of union between France and Britain, left a nasty taste; but it convinced any doubters of Britain's determination to carry on the fight.

The second episode was the attempt of British marines and members of the Free French under General de Gaulle to capture Dakar – Operation Menace. It was a classic example of incompetence. Security was appalling; a squadron of French warships was able to sail from Toulon through the straits of Gibralter unhindered to Dakar's defence; De Gaulle's forces met with an unexpectedly hostile reaction when they attempted to land on 23 September; two British warships were damaged. Within two days the operation was called off. It has been immortalised in Evelyn Waugh's trilogy, *Sword of Honour*.

E. Waugh, *Sword of Honour* (Penguin, 1970)

There was no doubt in Churchill's mind, nor in the minds of the British people, that the struggle must go on. In his broadcast to the country on 18 June 1940 he said: 'Let us therefore brace ourselves to our duties, and so bear ourselves that, if the British Empire and its Commonwealth last for a thousand years, men will still say "This was their finest hour".' Of Hitler's determination to invade Britain there is less certainty. To guarantee success he would need to have control over the Channel and mastery of the air. On 16 July he issued a directive declaring his intention to prepare a landing operation against England 'and if necessary carry it out'. On 31 July he gave orders for a massed air offensive against England in August, to be followed by a cross-Channel assault in September, 'if we have the impression that the English are smashed'. [Craig, p. 722] Hitler may have been hedging his bets, but invasion barges were assembled, and though there was no attempt to co-ordinate the three fighting services, if Goering's boast that the Luftwaffe could destroy Britain's power to resist had come true, an invasion could certainly have been improvised; this was evidently Hitler's intention. The Battle of Britain was therefore to prove vital to Britain's survival.

Operation Sea Lion and the Battle of Britain

G. Craig, *Germany 1866–1945* (OUP, 1978)

Making Spitfires

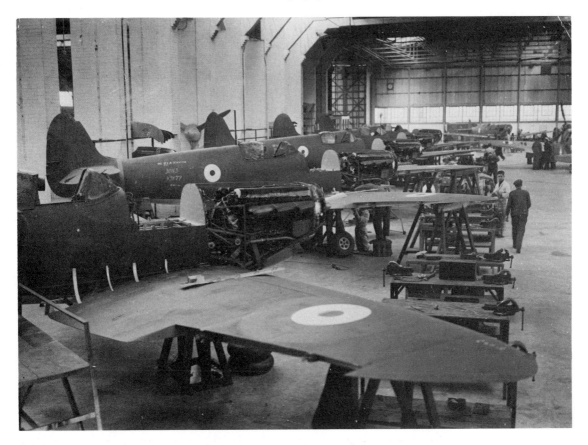

It began on 10 July with attacks on British convoys and lasted until 17 September when Hitler gave orders to postpone the invasion indefinitely. At the outset the Luftwaffe had 4549 aeroplanes, made up of medium bombers (Heinkels, Dorniers and Junkers) and fighters (the Messerschmitts 109 and 110). The RAF had 2913 aeroplanes of which about 800 were fighters (Spitfires and Hurricanes). The Spitfire was the fastest plane on either side but the Hurricane was outpaced by the Messerschmitt. The Germans had the advantage of experience and a large supply of trained pilots; the British had the benefit of radar but were desperately short of pilots. About 3000 took part in the Battle of Britain, many of them straight from flying school. The critical issue was whether Britain's supply of pilots would run out before German willingness to press on with their attacks.

Between 10 July and 30 August the Luftwaffe concentrated its attention on British shipping and raids on coastal towns – German losses comfortably exceeded those of the RAF – but from 30 August to 6 September it switched its attacks to southern airfields and in one week 185 British fighters were destroyed. At one point only two airfields in the South of England were operational. The RAF lost 20% of its fighter strength, a loss rate that could not have been sustained much longer. Fortunately, fate intervened. On 24 August a German airman inadvertently dropped his bomb load on London. Churchill immediately ordered retaliatory raids on Berlin. This so angered Hitler that on 7 September he ordered Goering to make London the Luftwaffe's next target. It was bombed continuously until 2 November.

L. Deighton, *Fighter*
(1977)

The decision to abandon the attacks on airfields probably saved the RAF, though at the expense of the citizens of London, 30 000 of whom were killed in the Blitz. On 15 September (which became Battle of Britain Day) 50 German aircraft were shot down – the RAF claimed 185 – and it became clear to Goering that the destruction of the RAF was still far from being accomplished. By remaining intact, as Len Deighton has put it, Fighter Command won the Battle of Britain. [Deighton, p. 200] Aircraft losses are harder to compute because of the tendency on each side to exaggerate the score of likely 'kills'. The following figures seem to be generally accepted:

German aircraft lost	1773
British aircraft lost	915

though the British figure still leaves about 1000 Spitfires and Hurricanes lost for which no official explanation has been given.

Many reasons have been advanced for Britain's success: the superiority of her fighters, the use of radar, Air Chief Marshal Dowding's careful control of the battle, the fact that it was fought mainly over English soil thus enabling British pilots who parachuted to safety to fight again, and the mistaken tactics employed by the Luftwaffe. While these matters remain a matter of controversy, few will dissent from Churchill's eloquent tribute to the British pilots who bore the brunt of the battle: 'Never in the field of human conflict has so much been owed, by so many, to so few.' The immediate effects of the Battle of Britain were to frustrate any plans Hitler might have had for the invasion of Britain. In the longer term Hitler's failure in the west accelerated his decision to turn east. He was already contemplating a war with Russia in 1940. With the shelving of Operation Sea Lion, it was only natural that Operation Barbarossa should take its place.

The entry of Italy into the war in June 1940 created another theatre of operations for British forces, extending from the Mediterranean to Abyssinia in the south and Syria in the north. This whole area became known as the Middle East and came under the command of the British Commander-in-Chief based at Cairo, General Archibald Wavell. Britain's interests in the Middle East derived first from her imperial possessions: Gibraltar, Malta and Cyprus in the Mediterranean; Egypt, British Somaliland and the Sudan in North Africa; Palestine, Transjordan and Iraq in the Middle East proper. Though Egypt and Iraq were nominally independent they were still treated as British territories. Britain was also concerned to safeguard her oil supplies in the Persian Gulf and to prevent any possible German threat to this area. Finally, the Suez Canal, though it ceased to be used for merchant ships between 1940 and 1943, was still regarded as an imperial waterway whose protection was of paramount importance.

North Africa and the Mediterranean

THE MEDITERRANEAN AND THE NORTH AFRICAN THEATRE, 1941–43

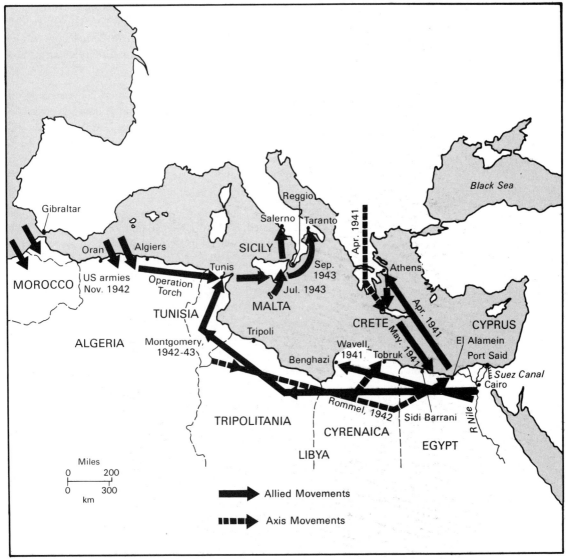

How vital these interests really were is a matter of dispute. A. J. P. Taylor argues that the British rationalised their Mediterranean strategy by arguing that the defeat of Italy would weaken Hitler and provide a back door into Europe, but that 'the British were in the Mediterranean because they were there. This simple statement of fact determined the main weight of Great Britain's military effort until the late days of the Second World War.' [Taylor, p. 634] He sees no evidence of German ambitions in the Middle East or any realistic prospect of a Turkish alliance. Whatever the reasons, the Middle East theatre was given a high priority by Churchill and in the long run it became the scene of some notable victories.

Taylor, *English History 1914–1945* (Pelican, 1970)

Quite how important Churchill considered the Middle East can be seen by his decision to send an armoured brigade to Egypt via the Cape of Good Hope on 16 August 1940 before the threat of invasion had lifted. In the short term the results of this decision were spectacularly successful. Marshal Graziani's invasion of Egypt from Libya was halted at Sidi Barrani and in February 1941 Wavell's counter-attack took British troops as far west as Benghazi and led to the capture of 130 000 prisoners and 500 tanks. A four-pronged attack on Abyssinia followed, with British troops advancing from the Sudan, Kenya, Eritrea and Italian Somaliland. Addis Ababa fell on 6 April and by the end of June 1941 the Italian Empire in Africa was at an end.

The British navy had two successes to its credit as well. On 14 November 1940 torpedo-carrying aircraft disabled three Italian battleships at Taranto and on 27 March 1941 three heavy cruisers and two destroyers were sunk by Admiral Cunningham's fleet off Cape Matapan. ENIGMA played an important role in both these victories. Cunningham knew of the Italian fleet's plans to intercept a British convoy and he was able to convince the Japanese consul at Alexandria that the British fleet had no intention of sailing to meet it by having a timely round of golf. The British fleet achieved complete surprise.

But these triumphs were short-lived. In April 1941 Germany invaded Greece. The War Cabinet, with Wavell's approval, agreed to send 60 000 British troops to the aid of the Greeks, a quixotic and as it proved unavailing effort. The Greeks were unable to stem the German advance and their Prime Minister advised that British troops be evacuated before they were caught. Most of them had done no fighting before they were taken off from the Peloponnesus, leaving 11 500 behind to be captured. Many of those who escaped were added, without arms or ammunition, to the garrison of Crete directed by General Freyberg. The Germans launched a sustained aerial bombardment of Crete on 14 May which went on for nearly a week, and on 20 May German paratroopers landed at the island's three airfields. Only at one airfield, Maleme, did the German troops manage to secure control, but it sufficed. Once again, the British army had to be evacuated; this time they left 13 000 casualties behind them.

The third blow to Britain's military pride took place in North Africa where Rommel, a recent arrival, caught the British army by surprise in Cyrenaica and recovered most of the ground lost by the Italians in February. The safe arrival of a convoy of tanks at Alexandria prompted Churchill to demand a counter-attack from Wavell. Largely untrained in the new tanks with which they were now equipped, the British army met with another defeat in Operation Battle Axe on 15–16 June. Out of 200 British tanks at the start of the battle only 40 remained serviceable at the end. It was the German 88 which did most of the damage. 'Fighting against it', writes General Fraser, 'resembled engaging with a carving knife a man armed with a long spear'. [Fraser, p. 158]

Fraser, *And We Shall Shock Them, the British Army in the Second World War*

Despite their victories over the Italians, British armies had been worsted in every encounter they had so far had with the Germans. The tide had still to turn.

C ▰▰▰▰ BRITAIN AND THE GRAND ALLIANCE

It was clear from the outset of the war that Britain would need American assistance if she were to survive. By the summer of 1940 her plight was desperate. After the losses of equipment in France and with the growing U-boat threat, Britain was in acute need of weapons and escort vessels for convoy duties. In these circumstances it was fortunate that the British Prime Minister was the son of an American mother, Lady Jenny Churchill, and married to an American wife, the former Clementine Hozier. Churchill had a natural sympathy for the United States and he developed a close *rapport* with the American President, Franklin Roosevelt, which is reflected in their correspondence.

Britain and the United States

Until December 1941 Churchill was in the position of a suppliant. Roosevelt was a sympathetic listener but he had to contend with isolationist pressures in Congress, and until November 1940 would do nothing that might jeopardise his chances of re-election. American co-operation was thus limited to what Roosevelt could persuade Congress and American public opinion to accept. In November 1939 he had secured the amendment of the Neutrality Acts to allow Britain and France to purchase arms under the 'cash and carry' provisions. But it was still not possible for Britain to borrow money in the United States because of the Johnson Act, 1934, which forbade loans to any country defaulting on its loans. Britain had still not repaid all the money borrowed during the First World War.

In May 1940, in response to Churchill's plea for help, Roosevelt gained permission from Congress to release from United States ordnance stores 500000 First World War rifles and 900 75mm field guns. In September he signed the Destroyer Deal under which the United States provided Britain with 50 old destroyers in return for 99-year leases for United States bases on British islands in the Caribbean and in Newfoundland. In December Churchill put forward two further requests: for financial assistance to purchase American arms and for American help in the protection of Atlantic convoys. Both requests were met. Roosevelt's advisers calculated that Britain had less than $2 billion in foreign reserves to meet arms purchases of $5 billion. To meet this financial dilemma Roosevelt coined the idea of Lend-Lease. Using the analogy of the good neighbour who lends his garden hose to put out his neighbour's fire, Roosevelt argued that the United States should provide Britain with the arms she needed to avert the Nazi threat.

On 29 December Roosevelt delivered one of his celebrated Fireside Chats to the American people urging that America must become 'the great arsenal of democracy'. It met with an enthusiastic response. For his part, Churchill declared: 'Give us the tools and we will finish the job.' Congress complied with Roosevelt's wishes and on 11 March 1941 the Lend-Lease Bill became law. It gave the President authority to 'sell, transfer title to, exchange, lease, lend or otherwise dispose of' any article of defence to any foreign government. Under its provisions the Allies were supplied with £50 billion worth of military equipment.

Roosevelt met Churchill's second request by occupying Iceland on 7 July 1941 and by undertaking responsibility, with the Canadian government, for the escort of all convoys from the American coastline to a mid-ocean meeting place, on the 26 degree west meridian. This inevitably brought German U-boats into conflict with American escort vessels. On 4 September the United States destroyer *Greer* dropped depth charges on a German U-boat and following this incident, Roosevelt made it clear that any German or Italian submarine entering American 'defensive waters' would be attacked on sight. But Americans were still reluctant to take the final steps to war. This was shown by the narrow majorities in favour of a bill to amend the Neutrality Acts, to allow American merchant ships to be armed, and to enter war zones to deliver supplies to friendly ports. The Act squeezed through by 50 votes to 37 in the Senate, and 212 votes to 194 in the House in November 1941.

Fortunately for Great Britain, the Japanese left no room for further hesitation when they bombed Pearl Harbour on 7 December. Roosevelt delivered a War Message to Congress whose approval was necessary for a declaration of war on 8 December. With one dissentient Congress gave its approval. Three days later, on 11 December, Germany and Italy declared war on the United States, thus averting the possibility which Churchill feared above all that the two conflicts would remain separate: Britain v. Germany, and the United States v. Japan. Hitler consulted none of his advisers before taking this step and Mussolini fell into line. By their actions they ensured that Britain and the United States were now united in a common cause.

Britain and Russia

Churchill became well aware through ENIGMA intercepts and other sources that Hitler was planning an attack on the Soviet Union in June 1941. On 10 June the Russian ambassador in London, Ivan Maisky, was treated to a detailed account of German troop movements on the Russo-German border throughout the previous month. But Stalin refused to believe the evidence presented to him and when the offensive opened on 22 June it caused greater surprise in Russia than it did in Britain.

Churchill had no doubts about how Britain should respond. On the night before the Russian invasion he said to John Colville, one of his secretaries, in this connection: 'If Hitler invaded Hell, I would at least make a favourable reference to the Devil in the House of Commons.' [Lewin, p. 77] On the evening of 22 June in a broadcast to the British people, he went further: 'The Russian danger is therefore our danger, and the danger of the United States, just as the cause of any Russian fighting for his hearth and home is the cause of free men and free people in every quarter of the globe.' [Gilbert, p. 1121]

Lewin, *Churchill as Warlord*

M. Gilbert, *Churchill, Finest Hour* (Heinemann, 1983)

In November 1941 Eden, the Foreign Secretary, visited Stalin and arrangements were made to supply Russia with arms round the North Cape of Norway, an extremely hazardous journey that proved very costly in terms of ships and men. A Russian delegation, headed by Molotov, the Russian Foreign Secretary, arrived in Britain in May 1942, and after a good deal of wrangling a treaty of mutual assistance was signed on 26 May. All reference to the post-war settlement of frontiers was deliberately omitted, it being clear already that this would be highly controversial.

Thus by the summer of 1942 the Grand Alliance was effectively in being. It was in many respects an artificial creation, brought to birth by Hitler, and it did not survive the war. But while it lasted there was at least a measure of co-operation, and the Allies were agreed upon their main objective, the defeat of Germany.

From 1942 onwards Britain could no longer decide where or how the war was to be fought, and as the United States came to provide a larger share of the men and materials involved there was a gradual shift in responsibilities. But Churchill and the British Chiefs of Staff continued to play a notable part in determining Allied strategy and their views sometimes prevailed. Through the Joint Chiefs of Staff Committee, set up in January 1942, there was a genuine partnership and whatever frictions had to be overcome, it worked. Though the Soviet Union had little direct influence on Anglo-American strategy the Russians were kept informed, and the constant pressure from Moscow to open a Second Front had an important bearing on the conduct of the war.

Britain and Allied Strategy

Strategic policy decisions were taken at a series of Conferences and high-level meetings between the heads of government or their representatives. For the sake of convenience they are listed below:

January 1942	ARCADIA Conference in Washington between Churchill and Roosevelt.
June 1942	Further meetings between Churchill and Roosevelt in Washington.
August 1942	Churchill's first meeting with Stalin in Moscow.
January 1943	SYMBOL Conference at Casablanca between Churchill and Roosevelt.
May 1943	TRIDENT Conference in Washington between Churchill and Roosevelt.
August 1943	QUADRANT Conference at Quebec between Churchill and Roosevelt.
November 1943	SEXTANT Conference at Cairo between Churchill and Roosevelt.
November 1943	TEHERAN Conference between Churchill, Roosevelt and Stalin.
December 1943	Further meetings between Churchill and Roosevelt at Cairo.
September 1944	OCTAGON Conference at Quebec between Churchill and Roosevelt.
February 1945	YALTA Conference between Churchill, Roosevelt and Stalin.

At the ARCADIA Conference in January 1942 the vital decision was taken to give priority to the defeat of Germany rather than Japan, a decision that owed much to Churchill's advocacy. Various means to that end were discussed under their curiously chosen code names: BOLERO, ROUND UP, SLEDGEHAMMER, GYMNAST and TORCH. The essential difference of opinion arose over when to launch the invasion of Europe. Churchill, well aware of the dangers of a combined operation, and the fighting qualities of the German army, favoured attacking Germany in the

Mediterranean and delaying the invasion of Europe until the Allies had time to build up an overwhelming superiority of forces. The Americans were anxious to see a Second Front established as soon as possible. On his second visit to Washington in June 1942 Churchill secured American agreement to his proposals and operation TORCH, the landing of American troops in North Africa, was put in train. At the same time it was decided to go ahead with BOLERO, the build-up of forces in Britain in preparation for the invasion of France, now scheduled to take place in 1943.

Churchill then made his first visit to Stalin to whom he had to break the news that there would be no Second Front in 1942. Stalin was predictably furious. Partly to mollify him Churchill held out hopes of a Second Front in 1943, and he also threw out a suggestion for a joint attack on the North of Norway – Operation JUPITER – to the consternation of the British Chiefs of Staff. No more came of this suggestion. The Casablanca Conference in January 1943 produced a detailed set of strategic objectives: the defeat of the U-boat threat, aid to Russia, the occupation of Sicily, the heaviest possible bomber offensive on Germany, amphibious attacks on Germany on a limited scale and the preparation of the strongest possible force 'in constant readiness to re-enter the continent as soon as German resistance is weakened to the required extent'. These objectives were spelt out more precisely at the Washington Conference held in May 1943. It was decided to press ahead with the invasion of Sicily (Operation HUSKY) and a date was fixed for Operation OVERLORD (the invasion of Europe): it was now to be 1 May 1944. At the first Quebec Conference, held in August 1943 Churchill conceded that the command of OVERLORD would have to go to an American, and the Americans also put forward a plan for a simultaneous invasion in the south of France, to be code-named ANVIL.

Two months later, Roosevelt and Churchill again conferred, this time at Cairo, in preparation for their meeting with Stalin. Chiang Kai-Shek was also present on this occasion and most of the time was spent, to Churchill's chagrin, in discussing Far Eastern strategy. At the Teheran Conference which took place immediately afterwards a mood of surprising amity prevailed. The Communiqué issued after the Conference stated: 'The Military Staffs of the Three Powers concerted their plans for the final destruction of the German forces. They reached complete agreement as to the scope and timing of the operations which will be undertaken from East, West and South, and arrangements were made to ensure intimate and continuous co-operation.' Stalin announced, almost casually, that the Soviet Union would declare war on Japan immediately after Germany's surrender, so throwing into the melting pot all the plans that had been discussed at Cairo. Churchill reflected his view of the Conference in his inimitable words: 'There I sat with the great Russian bear on one side of me, with paws outstretched, and on the other side the great American buffalo, and between the two sat the poor little English donkey who was the only one ... who knew the right way home.' [Pelling, p. 546] It was the high water mark of Allied unity but the Teheran Conference also symbolised the arrival of the two super powers and the comparative eclipse of Britain's independent influence.

H. Pelling, *Winston Churchill* (Macmillan, 1974)

While wrangles continued, for instance over the allocation of landing craft to OVERLORD, or the Italian campaign, and over the conduct of the campaign in North-West Europe in 1944–45, the main Allied strategy was confirmed at the Teheran Conference. At Cairo, on his way home, Roosevelt announced his decision to appoint General Eisenhower to the command of Operation OVERLORD. Shortly after, Montgomery was appointed to take charge of the invasion forces. The subsequent Conferences at Quebec and Yalta were more concerned with the making of peace than the conduct of war and will be looked at in that context.

D ▰▰▰▰▰▰▰ THE BRITISH CONTRIBUTION TO
▰▰▰▰▰▰▰▰▰▰▰▰ ALLIED VICTORY, 1941–45

The entry of the United States and the Soviet Union into the war did not diminish the intensity of the British war effort. The British economy was more highly mobilised for war than the German one and British forces played an equal, sometimes the major role in most of the Anglo-American campaigns that followed, at any rate until 1944.

After the defeat of the British army in Operation BATTLE AXE Churchill removed Wavell from his Middle East Command and replaced him by General Auchinleck. Auchinleck, at Churchill's urging, planned another offensive – Operation CRUSADER – which began on 18 November 1941. This was a long and confused battle extending over 3000 square miles and involving 30 000 vehicles. It was a partial success, causing Rommel's retreat from Egypt and relieving Tobruk. By 25 December the British were back where they had been in February 1941. But Rommel's army was still intact. On 21 January 1942 he launched a limited offensive which took the 8th Army by surprise and by February he had won back much of the ground that had been lost. It was a humiliating coda to Operation CRUSADER.

The North African Campaign

In May 1942 Rommel struck again. In the ensuing five weeks, though considerably outnumbered – Rommel had 560 tanks to Britain's 849 – he gained a major victory. British forces were out-manoeuvred and outfought. The major disaster was the surrounding of Tobruk and its surrender on 21 June. Its garrison of 30 000 were all taken prisoner. The 8th Army retreated to the ridge of El Alamein, only 60 miles from Alexandria, and here Auchinleck constructed a defensive line which held out against all Rommel's offensives for the next three months. But Churchill was unimpressed. On his visit to Cairo in August 1942 he ordered another change of command. General Harold Alexander was appointed to succeed Auchinleck as Commander of Middle East Forces, and Lieutenant-General Gott replaced Ritchie in command of the 8th Army. Gott was unfortunately killed when his aircraft crashed as he was coming to Cairo to take up his command. On the advice of Alan Brooke, Chief of Staff, Churchill then appointed Lieutenant-General Montgomery in his stead. Montgomery had commanded a division with some success in France in 1940. Since then he had proved his abilities as a trainer of soldiers, though he was unfamiliar with desert warfare. He proved to be beyond question the most successful British general in the Second World War. He planned his battles with meticulous care; he showed an iron resolve in the pursuit of his objectives; and he had the priceless ability to communicate his sense of purpose to all those under his command. Against these merits his vanity, his prickliness and his unwillingness to give credit where it was due, while they damaged his reputation, did not detract from his success as a commander. After his arrival the 8th Army suffered no more defeats.

It might be argued that Montgomery arrived at an opportune moment. From August 1942 the British enjoyed aerial superiority; the 8th Army easily outnumbered the Afrika Corps, both in men and tanks; Rommel's supply lines were stretched and the convoys supplying him constantly liable to interception. Ultra provided Montgomery with intelligence that was far better than anything available to his opponent. When the Americans landed in Algeria in November, Rommel faced an enemy on two fronts. Whatever the reasons, the combination of improved generalship and superior numbers proved at last successful. On 23 October the battle of El Alamein began. Montgomery had 230 000 men and 1030 tanks to pit against Rommel's 100 000 men and 500 tanks. It was not an easily won victory and it cost the British 13 500 casualties, but it broke Rommel's army. Altogether 30 000 were taken prisoner and the route to Tunisia lay open. Much hard fighting lay ahead. The American forces which landed in November under Operation TORCH were defeated at the battle of Kasserine Pass in February 1943. The battles of Medenine and Mareth in March 1943 showed the German capacity to resist. But the eventual outcome was not in doubt. Hitler, as unwilling to admit defeat in North Africa as he had been at Stalingrad, refused to permit the evacuation of any German troops. On 7 May the Axis armies were finally cornered as the Allies entered Tunis and 238 000 surrendered. North Africa was now in Allied hands.

The Italian Campaign

It had already been decided at the Casablanca Conference in January 1943 that the defeat of the Axis forces in North Africa should be followed by the invasion of Sicily. This took place on 10 July. It was the largest combined operation to have been mounted and met with comparative success. The conquest of the island was not so easily accomplished and the German withdrawal was skilfully carried out, 27 000 men escaping across the Straits of Messina to fight again.

But the fall of Sicily had one beneficial effect. On 24 July, by order of the Grand Fascist Council, Mussolini was removed from office and arrested. He was succeeded by Marshal Badoglio who requested secret negotiations with the Allied commanders on 15 August. These were agreed to but the insistence on 'unconditional surrender' complicated the issue, and it was not until 8 September that armistice terms were finally agreed. By that time the Germans realised what was happening. They rushed troops into Italy and took over the administration of the country. The Allied advance up the Italian peninsula was thus to be hotly contested. On 3 September Montgomery's forces landed at Reggio, followed shortly after by the landing of American troops at Salerno on 9 September. The Salerno landings were carried out in the face of considerable opposition and it became apparent that the conquest of Italy would be as hard a task as any the Allies had had to undertake. The mountainous terrain favoured the defender and because of the narrow fronts to which the Allied armies were restricted on either side of the Appenines their superior numbers were of little advantage. Thus the Italian campaign developed into a long slogging match reminiscent of the battlefields of the First World War. Its strategic justification was that it tied down over 20 German divisions that might have been used against the Allied invasion of France, but the price paid was a heavy one. German strategy was based on the preparation of a series of defensive lines across the Italian peninsula, the most important of which was the Gustav line stretching from Gaeta in the west, through Cassino, and east across the mountains to the Sangro valley and the Adriatic. It took the Allies three months to reach the Gustav Line. There they halted. A major obstacle to their advance was the hill on which the founder of monasticism in the West, St Benedict, had placed his monastery, Monte Cassino, and it was here that the fiercest fighting of the whole campaign took place.

The deadlock was broken in January 1944 with two operations. An Allied force of two divisions was landed behind the German lines at Anzio and a terrific assault, supported by aerial bombardment, was launched on the German positions round Cassino. Alexander gave his approval to the bombing of the monastery itself fearing that it was being used for artillery spotting. Neither operation was immediately successful. The Anzio landing was immediately countered by Kesselring, the German commander, and rather than becoming a springboard for an attack, Anzio became a beleaguered bridgehead that was only maintained with difficulty. The attack on Cassino ended in stalemate. In May, a second offensive, known as Operation DIADEM was undertaken. The Germans finally retreated from the Gustav line, Cassino falling on 18 May. At the same time an American Corps advanced east from Anzio, and though the German armies were not surrounded as had been hoped, they were forced into a rapid retreat, north of Rome. On 4 June, Allied troops entered Rome, two days before D-Day. German forces then retreated to the Gothic Line, an even stronger defensive position than the Gustav Line. In the autumn of 1944 a series of costly offensives failed to breach it and by the end of December winter called a halt to military operations.

In April 1945, now supported with overwhelming superiority in air power, armour and artillery, the Allies put in their final offensive. On 20 April Polish troops entered Bologna, cutting the links between the German 10th and 14th Armies. On 28 April German delegates arrived at Alexander's headquarters and on 2 May German forces surrendered unconditionally. The Italian campaign yielded no easy victories but it absorbed a considerable part of the German army and was finally crowned with triumph.

The Battle of the Atlantic

There were two essential preliminaries to the final land campaigns which brought about Germany's defeat: the battle of the Atlantic and the Strategic Air Offensive. Both lasted throughout the war but the essential victories were won in 1943 and 1944 respectively.

There were two main threats to be faced in the battle of the Atlantic. The first was presented by the handful of fast and powerfully armed German battleships which could wreak fearful havoc on all but the most strongly defended convoys were they ever to get loose; the second threat was the constant war of attrition waged by U-boats which reached its peak in the spring of 1943. The threat from German capital ships was countered relatively easily. Their location was usually known and every sortie was closely monitored. After the sinking of the *Graf Spee* in 1940 there were no further alarums until the *Bismarck* and *Prince Eugen* were spotted moving from their Norwegian anchorage through the Denmark strait into the North Atlantic, in May 1941. On 24 May the *Bismarck* encountered *HMS Hood* and *HMS Prince of Wales*. Her good shooting caused the destruction of the *Hood* within minutes. But all available British ships were put onto the *Bismarck*'s scent, and three days later, having been immobilised by a torpedo from a British aircraft, the *Bismarck* herself went to the bottom.

In February 1942 two powerful battle cruisers, *Scharnhorst* and *Gneisenau* made their way, without being intercepted, up the English Channel. *Scharnhorst* was sunk in December 1943. *Gneisenau* was so badly bombed in Kiel harbour that she never took to sea again. The *Tirpitz*, moored in a Norwegian fjord for much of the war, proved more useful as a potential threat than in actuality. Her greatest success was gained in July 1942, though she took no part in the operations. Rumours that the *Tirpitz* had left her anchorage caused the Admiralty to order the escort group guarding the Arctic convoy PQ 17 to withdraw, and the convoy to scatter. The results were devastating. Attacks by German U-boats and bombers resulted in the loss of 25 out of the 36 merchant ships in the convoy. A closer watch was kept on the *Tirpitz* thereafter. She was put out of action after an attack by midget submarines and eventually sunk in 1945 by Bomber Command. German capital ships required the Royal Navy to provide heavier convoy escorts than would otherwise have been necessary but otherwise their impact was relatively slight.

It was the opposite with the U-boat. Though Germany began the war with only 57 U-boats, by the end of 1942 Admiral Doenitz had 393 available. Sinkings by U-boats rose alarmingly. In 1941, 432 Allied ships were sunk, in 1942 this rose to 1160, and in the first three weeks of March, 97 ships were sunk. In one convoy, intercepted by 40 U-boats, 21 ships were sunk for the loss of a single U-boat. Such rates of sinking could not be tolerated for very long and at the Casablanca Conference in January 1943 it was agreed that precedence must be given to defeating the U-boat threat. In fact Allied counter-measures were already beginning to take effect. In December 1942, Bletchley Park cracked the Triton cipher now being used by U-boat Command. The addition of an extra rotor to the Enigma coding machine in March caused a temporary setback but by the end of the month this problem had also been overcome. In April and May 1943, 56 U-boats were sunk, causing Doenitz to order the withdrawal of his submarines from the Atlantic. They never returned in such numbers.

A conference was held in Germany in 1978 to establish the reasons for the failure of the German U-boat offensive. In the concluding report a number of factors were cited: the extension of air cover across the whole of the Atlantic, finally achieved in 1943 with the use of very long-range aircraft such as the Liberator; improved radar; better anti-submarine weapons; and the employment of escort groups carefully trained in anti-submarine warfare. But pride of place must surely go to the cryptographers at Bletchley Park. The Germans never knew that their codes had been broken; in 1943 the Admiralty became aware that theirs had. The incidence of sinkings by U-boats corresponds very closely with the ability of the Admiralty to read U-boat signals and this was finally and fully achieved in March 1943. Whatever the reasons, from that date on the Atlantic became a relatively safe seaway and the huge build-up of men and supplies needed for the invasion could proceed unhindered.

The Strategic Air Offensive

No aspect of the Allies' conduct during the Second World War has been the subject of as much controversy as the Strategic Air Offensive, both in relation to its effectiveness and to its morality. What is not in doubt is the faith placed by Bomber Command in area bombing and the costs in human and economic terms of sustaining it.

There were several phases to the Bombing Offensive. From May 1940 until November 1941 Bomber Command carried out a series of fruitless raids with no very clear pattern or purpose. Casualties were higher for bomber crews than they were for German civilians – 37 planes were lost out of 400 in one raid on Berlin, a loss-rate that if sustained would allow an average squadron only 10 missions before it would have to be fully replaced. A statistical survey based on the interpretation of aerial photographs indicated that on a moonlit night two out of five planes dropped their bombs within five miles of the target. With less visibility the ratio was nearer to one in fifteen. For every ten tons of bombs dropped, one bomber was lost.

The British Bombing Offensive: Air Chief Marshall Harris planning targets, July 1943

Two inferences were drawn from these figures: first that to have any effect the scale of air raids must be greatly increased; secondly that until and unless bombing techniques could be greatly improved the only targets Bomber Command could be relied on to hit were large built-up areas. In February 1942, Air Chief Marshal Harris was made head of Bomber Command and he proceeded to apply these lessons. They were given further justification in a minute produced for the Chiefs of Staff by Lord Cherwell, Churchill's scientific adviser, on 30 March. Cherwell argued, on the basis of British experience, that if only half of the 10 000 bombers which he expected to be available in 1943 were to drop their bomb loads on the built-up areas of 58 German cities, each with over 100 000 inhabitants, and assuming a notional life of

14 trips for each plane, then over one-third of the German population 'would be turned out of house and home'. 'There seems little doubt', Cherwell argued, 'that this would break the spirit of the people.' [Hastings, pp. 127–8] Cherwell's views were disputed by some of his fellow scientists, notably Sir Henry Tizard, but the Air Minister, Sir Archibald Sinclair, and the Chief of Air Staff, Sir Charles Portal, called Cherwell's paper 'simple, clear and convincing'. Churchill agreed. In a paper composed for the War Cabinet on 21 July 1942, he made his views clear:

Hastings, *Bomber Command*

> We must regard the Bomber offensive against Germany as at least a feature in breaking her war-will second only to the largest military operations which can be conducted on the Continent until that war-will is broken. Renewed intense efforts should be made by the Allies to develop during the winter and onwards ever-growing, ever more accurate and ever more far-ranging Bomber attacks on Germany. [Lewin, p. 103]

Lewin, *Churchill as Warlord*

Cherwell's Minute coincided with the arrival in fairly large numbers of the first four-engined bombers, Stirlings, Halifaxes and in July, the first Lancasters. They were also equipped with *Gee*, a radio-pulse system by which the navigator could determine his exact position. The policy of area bombing could now get under way.

It began with raids on Lubeck and Rostock on 28 March 1942, coastal targets which were easy to find, poorly defended and highly combustible. The first 1000 bomber raid took place on Cologne on 30 March. For the next ten months Bomber Command averaged over 2000 sorties per month. Over 1200 aircraft were lost during the same period. In January 1943 the Casablanca Conference gave its seal of approval to a bombing policy aimed at undermining the morale of the German people. The arrival of the 8th United States Airforce required some co-ordination of British and American bombing strategy. The Americans adopted a policy of daylight raids, carried out by highly armed Flying Fortresses and aimed, where possible, at particular targets, for instance oil refineries and the ball bearing factories at Schweinfurt. In April 1943 an Operational Committee laid down that such efforts 'should be completed and complemented by RAF bombing attacks against the surrounding industrial areas at night....' [Hastings, p. 185] These recommendations formed the basis of *Pointblank*, the directive issued to both airforces on 10 June 1943. Harris interpreted his orders to suit his own belief that the indiscriminate bombing of German cities was the quickest way to end the war. Between March and July 1943 there were 43 major raids, mainly on the Ruhr, and a further 33 raids between July and November.

Hastings, *Bomber Command*

Preparations for the invasion brought a change in policy. Between April and June 1944 most of Bomber Command's efforts were devoted to attacks on transport centres in France, while the American airforce had considerable success in its attacks on oil refineries. During the course of the invasion itself the energies of both forces were directed to the support of the Allied armies.

The final phase of the bombing campaign began in July 1944 with a return to area bombing. Portal tried to persuade Harris to concentrate on oil targets but Harris refused to abandon his policy of attacking cities on an ever-increasing scale. The most notorious example of this saturation bombing were the four raids launched on Dresden between 13 February and 2 March 1945. These raids originated with Churchill, who enquired of the Air Ministry what it intended to do about 'blasting the Germans in their retreat from Breslau'. [Hastings, p. 341] Churchill was anxious to impress the Russians with Bomber Command's capabilities. The Air Staff suggested raids on Dresden, Leipzig, Chemnitz and Berlin. An official request for such raids was submitted by the Russians at Yalta on 4 February and the Chiefs of Staff gave their approval on 6 February. Dresden was the victim of this decision. Between 30 000 and 100 000 people are calculated to have been killed and the city was virtually destroyed in the fire-storm created by the combination of high explosive and incendiary bombs dropped. The raids aroused the public conscience and led Churchill to produce a revised memorandum on bombing policy for the Chiefs of Staff:

> It seems to me that the moment has come when the question of bombing German cities for the sake of increasing the terror, though under other pretexts, should be reviewed. Otherwise we shall come into the control of an utterly ruined land .... The destruction of Dresden remains a serious query against the conduct of Allied bombing. I am of the opinion that military objectives must henceforward be more strictly studied in our own interests rather than those of the enemy. [Hastings, pp. 343–4]

Hastings, *Bomber Command*

Portal regarded this as a serious slur on Bomber Command and persuaded Churchill to revise the wording of the Memorandum, omitting all reference to Dresden. But Harris saw the original draft and wrote angrily, and revealingly, to Bottomley, Deputy Chief of the Air Staff, 'I would not regard the whole of the remaining cities of Germany as worth the bones of a British grenadier. The feeling over Dresden could easily be explained by any psychiatrist. It is connected with German bands and Dresden shepherdesses ....' [Hastings, p. 344] But this time Harris's protests were to no avail. The Chiefs of Staff formally decreed an end to area bombing on 16 April 1945.

Operation Overlord and the Conquest of North-West Europe

Planning for the invasion of Europe began in earnest with the appointment of Lieutenant-General Frederick Morgan as Chief of Staff to the Supreme Allied Commander (COSSAC) in April 1943. Morgan recruited an Anglo-American staff and for the next twelve months they devoted themselves to the enormous task of landing over one million men on the continent of Europe. The operation, Morgan wrote in his initial report, 'is fraught with hazards, both in nature and in magnitude, which do not obtain in any other theatre of the present world war.' Final decisions about the invasion had to wait until the appointment of the Supreme Commander, Eisenhower, and the ground forces commander, Montgomery, in December 1943. But a lot had been accomplished before Montgomery assumed responsibility for Operation Overlord. Detailed reconnaissance of the French coastline led, almost inevitably, to the choice of the Normandy beaches as the point of entry. They were within easy reach of Allied air cover, not too heavily defended and gave good access to the surrounding countryside.

Montgomery accepted most of COSSAC's recommendations but he was alarmed at the limited frontage on which the invasion was planned, with only three divisions going ashore in the first wave. He argued strongly for increasing the frontage to allow five divisions to be put ashore and won his point, though it meant delaying the invasion for a further month in order to get hold of the 1000 extra landing-craft required. It was finally decided to land units from the American 12th Army Group

on the two western beaches, Utah and Omaha, while British and Canadian units from the 21st Army Group would land on the eastern beaches of Gold, Juno and Sword. The date planned for the operation was 5 June.

Apart from getting the men and vehicles ashore in the face of enemy opposition there was also a huge logistical problem to be overcome. It was calculated that every American infantryman needed the equivalent of 30 lb a day to keep him fit for battle. The British figure was 20 lb. The total volume of supplies the Allied armies needed amounted to 26 000 tons per day. Two solutions were adopted. Mulberry harbours, huge caissons of concrete, were floated across the Channel to form breakwaters against which ships could unload; and PLUTO (pipe line under the ocean) was laid to supply petrol to the vast numbers of vehicles required. Neither expedient worked as well as it had been hoped. The American Mulberry harbour was destroyed in a storm that took place from 19 to 23 June and PLUTO only began to work really effectively from January 1945. Even so, while the supply problem on occasion delayed the tempo of the advance, particularly after the Allied breakthrough in August, 1944 Allied troops were always better supplied than their German opponents.

The balance of forces before the invasion showed that the Germans had 59 divisions in France, 41 North of the Loire, to face 23 divisions in the 12th United

States Army Group under General Omar Bradley, and 17 divisions in the 21st Army Group under Montgomery. The Allies enjoyed a 3–1 advantage in quantity of tanks but had no tank to rival the German Tiger and Panther. In artillery, the Allies had three guns to every two German ones. Each side had roughly equivalent numbers of infantry. But the Allies had two great advantages. The German armies had 3000 miles of coastline to defend and their inadequate intelligence prevented them from knowing when or where the invasion would take place. This prevented them from concentrating their forces, and, in the reputed words of Frederick the Great, 'He who defends everything defends nothing'. The Allied deception plan convinced the German high command that the Normandy landings were only a preliminary diversion to distract attention from a much larger enterprise in Pas de Calais which never materialised. The other major advantage held by the Allies was aerial superiority. On D-Day the *Luftwaffe* flew just over 300 sorties, the Allied airforces flew 12 000.

THE SITE OF THE INVASION, 1944

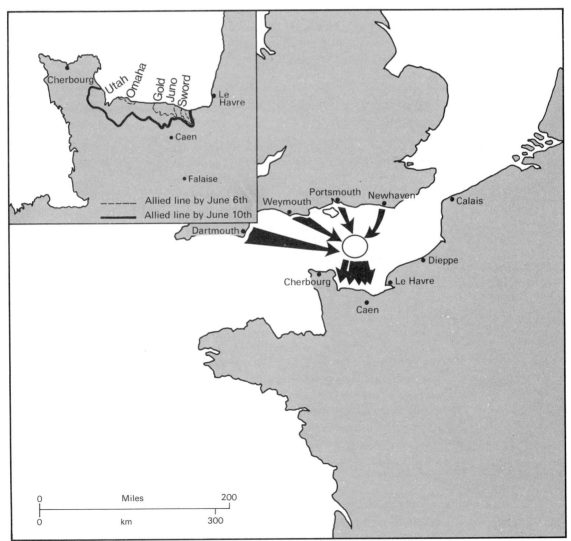

The success of the invasion was not a foregone conclusion. Both Hitler and Rommel were convinced that it could be halted on the beaches. Alan Brooke remained sceptical almost to the last moment. The only precedent, the raid launched on Dieppe as a trial run in 1942, had been catastrophic. But, thanks to complete mastery of the sea and the air, the element of surprise, and the sheer courage of the men involved at critical times and places, D-Day itself was a major triumph.

After delaying the start of the operation for 24 hours because of bad weather, Eisenhower gave orders for the go-ahead on 6 June. In rapid sequence three airborne divisions were landed at either flank of the beach head, a huge aerial bombardment of the beach defences and a naval bombardment followed. From 6.30 am onwards landing-craft began debouching their cargoes of infantry, engineers and tanks onto the beaches. Except at Omaha, where the Americans sustained 2 000 casualties, the landings went surprisingly well. By the end of the first day a beach head 25 miles long and to an average depth of 5 miles had been established.

The next phase of the operation was not so successful. The Normandy *bocage*, small fields bordered by thick hedgerows and interleaved with steep valleys and hillsides, was ideal terrain for the defender. The well-placed tank or anti-tank gun could do awful damage to Allied armour, and infantry were equally vulnerable to concealed machine guns. Montgomery had hoped to reach Caen on the first day; it took him six weeks. Two offensives had to be called off because of the high casualties sustained. In one attack the *Green Howards* lost 26 officers and 250 of their other ranks. Caen was eventually captured only after high-level bombing had virtually destroyed it.

On 17 July Montgomery ordered Operation Goodwood, an attempt to break through the German defences with three armoured divisions. It went disastrously wrong, the British losing 400 of their tanks, 36% of their armoured strength. But while Goodwood was a serious reverse, both to British arms and to Montgomery's reputation, it had one beneficial consequence. It helped to draw German Panzer divisions away from the American thrust further south. When the American armies turned east they were able to trap German forces in the Falaise pocket. On 15 August the gap was sealed and Allied air power pounded the entrapped German divisions unmercifully. The battle for Normandy was settled. It had cost Germany 450 000 men, of whom 240 000 were killed or wounded, while Allied casualties were 209 672.

For a brief moment it looked as though victory was at hand. Paris was liberated on 25 August, Brussels on 3 September. At this point the first serious rift in Allied strategy became apparent. On 1 September Eisenhower took over Montgomery's responsibilities as commander of all ground forces. Eisenhower believed in a slow and cautious advance on Germany on a broad front, probing and advancing where the enemy was weakest. Montgomery favoured an all-out thrust in the north, aimed at securing the Ruhr before the winter. The shortage of fuel required a choice to be made, but Montgomery saw a chance of putting his strategy into effect by using airborne troops. Eisenhower gave his approval and Operation MARKET GARDEN was conceived.

The purpose of the operation was to seize all the river crossings in Holland in preparation for a rapid advance which would enable the Ruhr to be attacked from the north. The plan was to drop airborne divisions at Eindhoven, Nijmegen and

Arnhem (this was Market); as soon as the river crossings had been captured British armour would advance, linking up with the airborne forces and establishing a corridor that would lead into Germany – Operation Garden. The First British Airborne Division was given the task of capturing the bridge over the Rhine at Arnhem, some 64 miles inside the Dutch border. It was as General Browning, Commander of the British Airborne Corps, feared it might be, 'a bridge too far'. The first phases of the operation went reasonably well with the bridges at Eindhoven and Nijmegen being captured successfully. But the British Airborne Division only succeeded in securing the northern end of the Arnhem bridge and were unfortunate to find the 11th Panzer Corps re-fitting in their area. The ten miles of road between Nijmegen and Arnhem was bordered by flooded fields slowing down the forces sent to link up with the Airborne division to snail's pace. After nine days of bitter fighting the few British survivors at Arnhem were instructed to withdraw south across the Rhine. MARKET GARDEN cost the Allies 17 000 casualties, more than they had lost on D-Day. The British First Airborne Division was destroyed. Of the 10 000 men who landed at Arnhem, 7872 became casualties. German casualties over the whole operation are calculated at between 7500 and 10 000.

But while the Germans had won a tactical victory they could not prevent the inexorable build-up of Allied forces and the continuing impact of Allied air power. Between 15 December and 23 January 1945 Hitler attempted a final desperate offensive in the Ardennes. Aided by bad weather, which prevented flying, 21 German divisions attacked the American front. The offensive met with initial success but as with the German offensive in March 1918, when it was held it threw the Germans off balance and they had used up their precious reserves of fuel. The fighting capacity of the German army had not been destroyed but all hope of a counter-attack had now disappeared. British forces took part in the final operations on the German frontier. On 8 February Operation Veritable was launched at German positions in the Reichswald Forest; it was, as one British historian has described it, 'a killing match, slow, deadly and predictable'. [Fraser, p. 390] British and Canadian casualties totalled 15 500, but it was the last battle of its kind. On 23 March the Rhine was finally crossed. By 20 April British troops had advanced 200 miles into Germany. On 30 April Hitler committed suicide. On 4 May a German delegation met Montgomery on Luneburg Heath and on 8 May the unconditional surrender of Germany was finally announced. Now only Japan was left in the field.

Fraser, *And We Shall Shock Them*

E ▬ BRITAIN AND THE WAR AGAINST JAPAN

In 1937 Japan captured Pekin and by 1939 most of China's eastern seaboard was in Japanese hands. Japan now turned covetous eyes towards South East Asia. What she wanted was guaranteed access to the raw materials with which this area was so well endowed, oil and rubber in particular. There were conflicts within Japanese policy-making circles on how far to go in securing this objective. On any rational assessment of force-levels Japan could hardly expect to defeat Nationalist China, where Chiang-Kai-Shek was still in the field, Britain and the United States. Those who argued for war gambled on the hope that a quick victory might enable Japan to establish her hold over South East Asia before her opponents were ready, and that its recovery would prove too expensive for Britain and the United States to undertake. They proved right in their first assumption, wrong in their second.

Japan joined the Anti-Comintern Pact in 1936 and welcomed the defeat of France in 1940. In September of that year Japan gained permission from the Vichy government to occupy the northern provinces of Indo-China. In April 1941 Japan signed a non-aggression treaty with the Soviet Union, thus safeguarding her rear from attack. In July, Japanese troops moved into the rest of Indo-China. Britain and the United States protested, but neither country was anxious to risk a war. They agreed to freeze Japanese assets held in Britain and the United States and to impose an embargo on the export of war materials to Japan. The Dutch government-in-exile also banned the export of oil from the Dutch East Indies. After their meeting at Placentia Bay, Newfoundland in August 1941 Churchill and Roosevelt sent a warning to the Japanese government that 'Any further encroachment by Japan in the South-West Pacific would produce a situation in which the United States government would be compelled to take counter-measures, even though these might lead to war between the United States and Japan.' [Gilbert, pp. 1254–5] Japan now had to face a situation in which nine-tenths of her oil supply had been cut off. Suggestions of a meeting between Roosevelt and the Japanese Premier, Prince Konoye, came to nothing and on 16 October Konoye was replaced by General Tojo who belonged to the militant faction. Tojo's government decided on a final attempt at a negotiated settlement with the United States, but while negotiations were proceeding, preparations were set in hand for war; these were to be completed by the beginning of December, in readiness for a declaration of war should negotiations fail.

Gilbert, *Churchill, Finest Hour* (Heinemann, 1983)

The Japanese strategy had two main objectives: to wipe out the American Fleet at Pearl Harbour, the only naval force able to challenge the Japanese navy; and to occupy a belt of territory stretching from Burma in the west through Java and Sumatra in the south to the Gilbert Islands in the east. The whole operation was to be completed in about three months. Phase One was to begin with attacks on Hong Kong, Malaya and the Philippines and was timed to coincide with the carrier-based attack on Pearl Harbour.

Neither Britain nor the United States had made any effective preparations for meeting the Japanese attack. When it was learned that Tojo had replaced Konoye the Defence Committee of the British government agreed to send out the new battleship *Prince of Wales* to join the *Repulse* at Singapore, in the hope that this gesture might act as a deterrent to Japanese aggression. A War Office memorandum on 30 November still held that a war with Japan 'might be so severe as to prejudice our chances of beating Germany. Our policy must therefore be – and is – avoidance of war with Japan.' [Gilbert, p. 1262] But that option was effectively closed when the Japanese received American terms requiring the Japanese to withdraw all their forces from China and Indo-China as a condition of any settlement. On 1 December the Japanese Emperor ratified his government's decision to go to war and to implement the plans already made. At 6 am on Sunday 7 December Japanese planes bombed Pearl Harbour. On 8 December Japanese forces began their attacks on Hong Kong and Malaya.

Gilbert, *Churchill, Finest Hour*

So far as Britain was concerned the war against Japan bore a depressing similarity in its early stages to the war against Germany. Inadequate preparations, lack of air support, confused orders and a general unreadiness to meet a well-trained and determined opponent led to a sequence of disasters.

The sequence began with a Japanese attack on Hong Kong. Garrisoned by only six battalions and five batteries of artillery the colony had no hope of holding out indefinitely, but the Governor had been instructed to resist as long as possible. The Japanese attack started on 8 December 1941 and it was completed on 25 December. The British forces suffered 4000 casualties to no very good purpose.

Hong Kong

Malaya and Singapore should have been eminently defendable, to outward appearances at least. The only land frontier was a narrow isthmus adjoining the neutral state of Thailand. Britain had a huge naval base at Singapore and by 1942 a garrison of 90 000 troops. But Britain's position was weaker than it looked. The defence of Malaya had been planned on the assumption that at least 400 fighters would be available. Airfields were prepared in the north of the peninsula from which they would be able to operate. These airfields would have to be defended, if only to deny their use to the enemy. The long coastline on both sides of the Malayan peninsula gave the Japanese a wide range of options when choosing where to invade. Finally, the only naval units available to defend this extensive coastline were the battleship *Prince of Wales*, the battle cruiser *Repulse* and four destroyers. No aircraft carrier accompanied them. Nor did General Percival, the British Commander-in-Chief, get any of the aircraft he had requested. He had at his disposal only 141 serviceable aircraft, none of which could match Japanese fighters. Whether these limitations made Percival's task impossible or not, it must also be conceded that the defence of Malaya was also badly handled and that the troops whose task it was were in many cases incompetent to carry it out.

Malaya and Singapore

The invasion began on 8 December in the north-east. On 10 December the *Prince of Wales* and the *Repulse* were sunk by Japanese torpedo bombers. By 15 December Japanese troops had advanced 100 miles. Every defensive line established by Percival was either outflanked or infiltrated; there were no major engagements. By 1 February all Allied troops had either been captured or withdrawn to Singapore Island itself. The defence of the Island was handled no more skilfully than the defence of Malaya, and the situation was worsened by Japanese air raids on the town of Singapore. When the Japanese captured the Island's water-supply Percival had no option open to him but to surrender. Altogether 130 000 Allied soldiers went into captivity, a larger number than the Japanese invading force. It was the worst defeat ever inflicted on a British army.

The attack on Singapore coincided with a Japanese advance into Burma, where the British suffered another humiliating defeat. With only two divisions at his disposal General Alexander, who was hastily put in command in March 1942, decided that Rangoon could not be held. The city was evacuated on 6 March, leaving British forces virtually stranded. There was no road to India and the troops could only straggle back using jungle paths and tracks, abandoning all their heavy equipment as they did so. Within three months the Japanese had captured all British possessions in the Far East. Their recovery would take much longer.

Burma

Before this process could begin British forces needed to be re-built. It was fortunate that they could call on the abilities of General Sir William Slim for this task. Slim was appointed to command the 14th Army in October, 1943 and he did for it what

Montgomery did for the 8th Army in even more difficult circumstances. He addressed himself to three problems: supply, health and morale. Questions of supply were solved in a variety of ways: the use of air transport, road building, even, at one stage, construction of prefabricated rafts. But after Slim's arrival his troops never found themselves without the necessary supplies. On the health problem he sought the best medical advice. It was badly needed. For every man evacuated because of wounds, 120 went sick – 84% of combatant troops contracted malaria. Slim insisted that the proper drugs should be made available and taken and as a result health standards improved enormously. Slim, like Montgomery, had the ability to communicate with men of all ranks and nationalities. To restore morale he spent much of his time visiting different units and he gave the 14th Army a new pride in itself.

By 1944 the recovery of Burma could begin. As it happened, the first British advance coincided with a Japanese offensive and both sides clashed for the possession of three bases linked by road: Dinapur, Kohima and Imphal. Though surrounded by Japanese troops their garrisons were kept supplied by air and eventually the Japanese called off their attacks. On 22 June the links between Kohima and Imphal were restored. It was the turning-point in the Burma campaign. By now British forces outnumbered Japanese ones and were much better supplied and equipped. A new offensive was undertaken in February 1945 which resulted in the capture of Mandalay on 20 March and of Rangoon on 4 May. Slim and the 14th Army had succeeded in turning the tables.

Hiroshima and Nagasaki

Britain played little part in the final stage of the war against Japan. Although British scientists made a vital contribution to the building of the atomic bomb, the decision of when and where to use it was reserved for the American President, as Commander-in-Chief of their armed forces. Under the Quebec agreement of 1943 Britain did have the right to be consulted, but this seems to have been a formality rather than a right to share in any decision-making. On 30 April 1945 Field-Marshal Wilson, head of the British Joint Staff Mission in Washington, reported to London that the Americans were thinking of dropping an atomic bomb and he requested guidance on the form in which British consent should be given. On 2 July he was instructed to convey the British government's approval at the next meeting of the Anglo-American Combined Policy Committee. It was anticipated that the American President would discuss the whole question at the Potsdam Conference which was just about to start. When Truman did raise it, Churchill gave full approval to the use of the atomic bomb. [Thorne, p.533]

C. Thorne, *Allies of a Kind* (Hamish Hamilton, 1978)

The first trial bomb was detonated successfully on 16 July. By this time a British General Election had been held and on 26 July Attlee became Prime Minister. It was therefore to him that Truman gave the news. In his autobiography, Attlee, in typically laconic style, describes what happened: 'I recall very well President Truman telling me that the atomic bomb had been tried out at Los Alamos and how he had informed Stalin of this. Stalin made no comment, though it must have given him a bad shock.' [Attlee, p. 149] It did not evidently shock Attlee and even had the British been consulted over the dropping of atomic bombs on Hiroshima on 6 August and on Nagasaki on 9 August it is unlikely that they would have voiced any objections. Britain's reaction to the news was one of overwhelming relief. The qualms of conscience came later.

C. R. Attlee, *As it Happened* (Heinemann, 1954)

The Second World War cost the lives of some 30 million people. Britain's share in this horrific total was about 400 000. Such aggregates cannot measure the hardships and sacrifices endured by individuals. Though the Second World War left no literary legacy comparable with that left by the First, this does not mean that the agonies endured by the combatants were any the less. In his book *The Sharp End of War* John Ellis has vividly recreated the experiences of the front-line soldier in the Second World War. He points out that casualty rates of those in the battle zone were as high as those suffered on the Western Front between 1914 and 1918. Death in a burning tank or aeroplane was no more endurable than death in a dug-out or shell-hole. The reason why the British army suffered relatively fewer casualties between 1939 and 1945 than between 1914 and 1918 was simply that a much higher proportion of soldiers were required to serve behind the front line. For those involved in battle the reality was always hellish. The Second World War may have been necessary to bring about the defeat of Nazi tyranny but the moments of triumph should never be allowed to obscure the human costs.

J. Ellis, *The Sharp End of War* (1980)

POINTS AT ISSUE
POINTS AT ISSUE **POINTS AT ISSUE** POINTS AT ISSUE
POINTS AT ISSUE

The Strategic Air Offensive

The Strategic Air Offensive has been attacked both on grounds of its relative ineffectiveness and its immorality. After the War the *United States Strategic Bombing Survey, Overall Report (European War)* established the extent of the damage inflicted to German cities and to the German economy by bombing, and the German government also produced its own calculations arrived at by the Federal Statistical Office in Wiesbaden. The United States *Survey* concluded:

> During the period from October 1939 to May 1945 the Allied Air Forces, primarily the RAF, dropped over one-half million tons of high explosives, incendiaries and fragmentation bombs ... on 61 cities .... These cities included 25 000 000 people ... attacks are estimated to have totally destroyed or heavily damaged 3 600 000 dwelling units, accounting for 20 per cent. of Germany's total residential units, and to have rendered homeless 7 500 000 people. They killed about 300 000 people and injured some 780 000. [cited in Fuller, p. 282]

The German figures indicate that 593 000 civilians were killed and 3.37 million dwellings were destroyed. During the same period, Bomber Command suffered the highest casualty rate of any of the armed services, with 55 573 killed and a further 9784 captured. The United States *Survey* also calculated that Britain devoted between 40 and 50% of her war production to her airforce.

Arguments over the effects of strategic bombing centre upon whether it seriously affected Germany's capacity to make war. Figures released after the war showed that German war production reached its peak in the first half of 1944. The raids on urban areas evidently had little effect on the working population:

> Under ruthless Nazi control they showed surprising resistance to the terror and hardships of repeated air attack, to the destruction of their homes and belongings, and to the conditions under which they were reduced to live. Their morale, their belief in ultimate

victory ... and their confidence in their leaders declined, but they continued to work efficiently as long as the physical means of production remained. The power of a police state over its people cannot be underestimated. [Fuller, p. 285]

Fuller concludes that the indiscriminate attacks on German cities were ineffective and that whatever numbers may have been engaged in making heavy bombers for the RAF 'they were largely wasted on an operation which Churchill once called an "experimental horror".' [Fuller, p. 287]

Economic historians agree that 'German industry proved astonishingly resilient in the face of bombing'. [Hastings, p. 350] But there is no doubt that raids on specific targets did have very damaging effects in some cases. A recent appraisal of the evidence is given by Hew Strachan:

The exclusive focus on the strategic bombing offensive had a number of consequences which in military terms were deleterious. The RAF was reluctant to switch aircraft to the battle of the Atlantic, it was loath to train bomber pilots for airborne operations and it scorned interdiction raids. And yet, on the air force's own terms, the strategic bombing offensive was a failure. Nonetheless, in many other ways its achievements were considerable. In 1942 it gave the British and Americans their only means of retaliating directly against Germany. It required 2 million Germans to man anti-aircraft batteries rather than swell the front line forces. It forced the *Luftwaffe* to switch its fighters from the Eastern front, and later from northern France, to the protection of Germany. Finally, without it, Germany's economic expansion in 1942–44 would have been even greater. Industry had to disperse and thus production was delayed. Raids on marshalling yards isolated goods and by 15 March 1945 German car loadings had been cut by 85 per cent. Transport was hampered by the attack on oil production. In April 1944 Germany produced 175 000 tons of aviation spirit, but then from June until the end of the war she manufactured only a further 197 000 tons. Therefore Germany, unlike the United States, could not develop her war economy in optimum conditions. Arguably these achievements vindicated the pre-war advocates of strategic bombing, albeit not on the terms they themselves set. [Strachan, pp. 179–80]

The moral equation is no easier to solve. The Blitz on British cities was undertaken from exactly the same motives as the policy of strategic bombing, to terrorise the civilian population. In the final months of the war Hitler began deploying the pilotless plane – the V1, otherwise known as the 'flying bomb' – and rockets – the V2s – against London. These were indiscriminate weapons of destruction. There were few in Britain who were prepared to challenge the view that Hitler, and the German people, deserved a taste of their own medicine. In March 1943 the *Sunday Dispatch* argued that: 'It is right that the German population should "smell death at close quarters". Now they are getting the stench of it.' [Hastings, p. 174] A handful of protests were raised. Richard Stokes, a Labour MP, constantly challenged the government to admit in public what it was doing in private, deliberately bombing civilian targets. Lord Salisbury expressed doubts to Sinclair, the Secretary of Air, at Harris's threat to continue bombing 'until the heart of Nazi Germany ceases to beat', particularly if this was to mean the deliberate killing of women and children. The most articulate attack on the policy of strategic bombing was delivered by Bishop Bell of Chichester. In a speech to the House of Lords on 9 February 1944 he said:

I fully realise that in attacks on centres of war industry and transport the killing of civilians when it is the result of bona fide military activity is inevitable. But there must be a fair balance between the means employed and the purpose achieved. To obliterate a whole town because certain portions contain military and industrial establishments is to reject the balance .... [Hastings, p. 177]

Bell's protest had little effect, and he was passed over for the archbishopric of Canterbury when a vacancy arose in 1944.

The moral doubts surfaced when the war was over. Harris, alone of British commanders, was not honoured with a peerage. Less justifiably, those aircrew who had endured the dangers and discomforts of a tour of bombing missions were not granted a separate campaign medal. Perhaps the scale of destruction brought about by the Second World War makes all rules of war irrelevant, but it is hard to quarrel with the final verdict of Max Hastings: 'The obliteration of Germany's cities in the Spring of 1945, when all possible strategic justification had vanished is a lasting blot on the Allied conduct of the war and on the judgment of senior Allied airmen.' [Hastings, p. 350]

Books Cited

Major-General J. F. C. Fuller, *The Conduct of War, 1789–1961* (Methuen, 1961)
M. Hastings, *Bomber Command* (M. Joseph, 1979)
H. Strachan, *European Armies and the Conduct of War* (Allen & Unwin, 1983)

BIBLIOGRAPHY BIBLIOGRAPHY BIBLIOGRAPHY BIBLIOGRAPHY BIBLIOGRAPHY BIBLIOGRAPHY
BIBLIOGRAPHY BIBLIOGRAPHY BIBLIOGRAPHY BIBLIOGRAPHY BIBLIOGRAPHY BIBLIOGRAPHY
BIBLIOGRAPHY BIBLIOGRAPHY BIBLIOGRAPHY BIBLIOGRAPHY BIBLIOGRAPHY BIBLIOGRAPHY
BIBLIOGRAPHY BIBLIOGRAPHY BIBLIOGRAPHY BIBLIOGRAPHY BIBLIOGRAPHY BIBLIOGRAPHY
BIBLIOGRAPHY BIBLIOGRAPHY BIBLIOGRAPHY BIBLIOGRAPHY BIBLIOGRAPHY BIBLIOGRAPHY
BIBLIOGRAPHY BIBLIOGRAPHY BIBLIOGRAPHY BIBLIOGRAPHY BIBLIOGRAPHY BIBLIOGRAPHY

CHAPTER 10
FURTHER READING

General

Essential

B. Collier *A Short History of the Second World War* (Collins, 1967)
H. Strachan, *European Armies and the Conduct of War* (Allen & Unwin, 1983)

Recommended

Major-General J. F. C. Fuller, *The Conduct of War, 1789–1961* (Methuen, 1961)
M. Howard, *War in European History* (OUP, 1976)
R. Lewin, *Churchill as Warlord* (Batsford, 1973)
W. Lacquer (ed.), *The Second World War, Essays in Military and Political History* (Sage Publications, 1982)

The Army

Essential

J. Ellis, *The Sharp End of War* (David & Charles, 1980)
D. Fraser, *And We Shall Shock Them, The British Army in the Second World War* (Hodder & Stoughton, 1983)

Recommended

N. Hamilton, *Monty: The Making of a General* (Hamish Hamilton, 1981)
    Monty: Master of the Battlefield (Hamish Hamilton, 1983)

The Navy

Essential

S. W. Roskill, *The War at Sea*, vols 1–3 (HMSO, 1954)

Recommended

M. Middlebrook, *Convoy* (Penguin, 1978)

The RAF

Essential

L. Deighton, *Fighter* (Cape, 1977)
M. Hastings, *Bomber Command* (M. Joseph, 1979)

Recommended

M. Middlebrook, *The Nuremburg Raid* (Allen Lane, 1973)

PARTICULAR CAMPAIGNS

Dunkirk

Essential

N. Harman, *Dunkerk, The Necessary Myth* (Hodder & Stoughton, 1980)

North Africa

Essential

C. Barnett, *The Desert Generals* (William Kimber, 1960)

Recommended

M. Carver, *El Alamein* (Batsford, 1962)
    Tobruk (Batsford, 1964)
D. Irving, *The Trail of the Fox: A Life of Field Marshal Erwin Rommel* (Book Club Associates, 1977)

Italy

Essential

W. G. F. Jackson, *The Battle for Italy* (Batsford, 1976)

Recommended

F. Majdalany, *Cassino, Portait of a Battle* (Longman, 1957)

The Far East

Essential

Sir J. Smyth, V.C., *Percival and the Tragedy of Singapore* (MacDonald, 1971)
Sir W. Slim, *Defeat into Victory* (Cassell, 1956)

The Invasion, 1944

Essential

M. Hastings, *Overlord, D-Day and the Battle for Normandy* (M. Joseph, 1984)
J. Keegan, *Six Armies and the Battle for Normandy* (Cape, 1982)

Intelligence

Essential

R. V. Jones, *Most Secret War: British Scientific Intelligence, 1939–1945* (Hamish Hamilton, 1978)
R. Lewin, *Ultra Goes to War* (Hutchinson, 1978)

BRITISH MILITARY, NAVAL AND AIR OPERATIONS, 1939–45

	LAND FORCES			THE WAR AT SEA	THE WAR IN THE AIR
Date	Europe	Africa	Far East		
1939	Period of Phoney War.			*Sep.* Sinking of *Courageous*. *Oct.* Sinking of *Royal Oak*. *Nov.* German use of magnetic mine. *Dec.* Sinking of *Graf Spee*.	Leaflet raids on Germany.
1940	*Apr.–Jun.* Norwegian campaign; landings at Namsos, Andalsnes and Narvik. All evacuated by June. *10 May* German Blitzkrieg. *29 May –3 Jun.* British forces evacuated from Dunkirk. *22 Jun.* France surrendered.	*Jul.* Italian invasion of British Somalia. *Sep.* Italian invasion of Egypt halted. *Dec.* British Offensive into Libya.		*Jul.* Sinking of French fleet at Oran. *Sep.* Unsuccessful attempt to land forces at Dakar. *Nov.* Battle of Taranto; Italian fleet damaged.	*May –Jun.* Air cover for BEF. *Jul.–Sep.* Battle of Britain. *Sep.–Nov.* London Blitz.
1941	*Apr.* British forces sent to Greece; withdrawn to Crete. *May* Fall of Crete; 30 000 British prisoners.	*Feb.* British occupied Benghazi. *Apr.–Jun.* British gained Abyssinia. *Jun.* Failure of Operation Battle Axe. *Nov.* Failure of Operation Crusader.	*8 Dec.* Japanese attack on Malaya and Hong Kong. *25 Dec.* Fall of Hong Kong.	*Mar.* Battle of Cape Matapan; Italian fleet damaged. *24 May* Sinking of *Hood*. *27 May* Sinking of *Bismarck*. *10 Dec.* Sinkings of *Repulse* and *Prince of Wales*. Sinkings by U-boats of 432 ships.	Ineffective air raids on Germany.
1942	*Aug.* Unsuccessful raid on Dieppe.	*Jun.* German offensive; fall of Tobruk to Rommel. *Jul.–Sep.* German attacks held at Al Alamein. *23 Oct.–5 Nov.* Battle of El Alamein. *Nov.* United States landings in Algeria. Operation TORCH.	*15 Feb.* Fall of Singapore. *Mar.* Fall of Rangoon. British armies retreated to India.	*Jul.* Convoy PQ 17 destroyed. Worst year for Battle of Atlantic; 1160 ships sunk. German attacks on Malta convoys.	*Feb.* Harris appointed to head Bomber Command. *Mar.* First 1000 bomber raids on Lubeck, Rostock, Cologne.

	LAND FORCES			THE WAR AT SEA	THE WAR IN THE AIR
Date	Europe	Africa	Far East		
1943	*Jul.* Invasion of Sicily. *Sep.* Landings in Calabria and at Salerno.	*Feb.* Battle of Kasserine Pass. *Mar.* British broke Mareth line. *May.* Allied capture of Tunis.	Recruitment of India National Army. Wingate's landings behind Japanese lines.	*Mar.* German naval codes cracked. *Apr.–May* 56 U-boats sunk. Continuous air cover over Atlantic achieved.	*Jan.* Casablanca Conference approved air raids to break German morale. *Jun.* Pointblank bombing directive to RAF and USAAF. Continuous raids on Ruhr.
1944	*Jan.* Anzio landings. *May* Fall of Cassino to Allies. *4 Jun.* Fall of Rome to Allies. *6 Jun.* Operation Overlord (D-Day). *9 Jul.* Caen captured. *17 Jul.* Operation Goodwood. *17–26 Sep.* Operation Market Garden (Arnhem).		*Feb.* Japanese attack in the Arakan. *Apr.–Jun.* Sieges of Imphal and Kohima. *Jul.* Japanese offensive called off.	*Nov.* *Tirpitz* finally destroyed. Allied command over Channel and Atlantic secured.	*Apr.–Jun.* Air support for invasion. *Jun.* Germans launched first V1 rocket. *Jul.* Allies returned to area bombing. *Sep.* Germans launched V2.
1945	*Jan.–Feb.* Ardennes offensive contained. *Feb.* Operation Veritable (Reichswald Forest). *27 Mar.* Crossing of Rhine. *8 May* German surrender.		*Jan.* British offensive in Burma. *Mar.* British capture of Mandalay. *May* British capture of Rangoon.		*Feb.* Dresden air raids. *Apr.* End to area bombing ordered.

CHAPTER **11**

The War at Home

A ▬▬▬▬▬▬▬▬▬▬▬▬▬▬▬ WARTIME POLITICS

Chamberlain detested war. Six weeks after it began he confessed: 'How I do hate and loathe this war. I was never meant to be a war minister, and the thought of all those homes wrecked with the *Royal Oak* [sunk by a German U-boat on 14 October] makes me want to hand over my responsibilities to someone else.' [Feiling, p. 420] But his iron sense of duty, mixed with a natural reluctance to step down from the premiership, kept Chamberlain in office. The outbreak of the war made little immediate difference to the political scene. Neither the Liberals under Archibald Sinclair, nor the Labour party under Attlee responded to Chamberlain's invitation to join a National Government, unlike Churchill who accepted the offer to return to the Admiralty with alacrity.

Chamberlain went some way towards the Lloyd George precedent of 1916, creating a War Cabinet of about ten. It included his old trusted colleagues, Halifax, Simon and Hoare; the service ministers, Churchill (Admiralty), Kingsley Wood (Air), Hore Belisha (Army); the Minister for Military Co-ordination, Lord Chatfield; and, finally, Lord Hankey, whose indispensibility had yet to be discounted. It was an old team, whose average age, Churchill calculated, was 64.

But there was a fatal lack of purpose in the conduct of the war, stemming from Chamberlain's continuing hopes of a negotiated peace. The BEF remained on the defensive in France, the RAF was allowed to do nothing that might prompt German retaliation. At home there was no real effort to co-ordinate the work of government departments concerned with production and supply. Conservative MPs who joined the armed forces, of whom there were 95, brought to the notice of their former colleagues the desperate shortages of equipment, especially in the army. Chamberlain's subsequent Cabinet changes did little to inspire confidence. Hore-Belisha was sacked for no very good reason in January 1940; Sir Samuel Hoare exchanged jobs with Kingsley Wood. In April, Chatfield resigned as Minister for Co-ordination of Defence because there was nothing for him to do. Churchill was made Chairman of the Military Co-ordination Committee in his stead, but his authority was never clearly defined. Coming on top of Chamberlain's fatal remark on 4 April that Hitler 'had missed the bus', the failure of the Norwegian campaign a month later destroyed the credibility of his government. It was put to the test in the motion put down for debate by the Labour party on 27 May. Technically a Motion on the Adjournment, it was a debate on the government's conduct of the war, and when the House divided

The Fall of Neville Chamberlain

K. Feiling, *The Life of Neville Chamberlain* (Macmillan, 1946)

it became a vote of censure. The debate has been vividly described in Harold Nicolson's Diaries. [Nicolson, pp. 76–80] The most effective speeches were evidently those made by Sir Roger Keyes, Leopold Amery and Lloyd George. Keyes, in the uniform of an Admiral of the Fleet, attacked the ineptitude with which operations at Trondjheim had been carried out; Amery, in a more wide-ranging attack, quoted the words of Oliver Cromwell to the Rump Parliament, pointing at Chamberlain: 'You have sat too long for any good you have been doing. Depart, I say, and let us have done with you. In the name of God, go!' Lloyd George, while attacking the government, did his best to shield Churchill from blame. When Churchill refused to disclaim responsibility, Lloyd George still came to his rescue: 'The right hon. Gentleman must not allow himself to be converted into an air raid shelter to keep the splinters from hitting his colleagues.' [Addison, p. 97]

Chamberlain made the tactical error of treating the criticism of his government as a personal attack on his leadership (which in a sense it was): ' "I have", he says with a leer of triumph, "Friends in this House".'. [Nicolson, p. 78] It may have been this, as much as anything else, which persuaded many Conservative MPs either to vote with the Opposition or to abstain. The government still had a majority (281 to 200) but 38 Conservative MPs and eight other normal supporters of the government went into the Opposition Lobby and 60 more Conservatives abstained. Normally the government had a majority of 213.

Chamberlain's resignation was not yet inevitable. Nor was it certain that Churchill would succeed him. On 9 May Chamberlain consulted the Labour leaders, Attlee and Greenwood, to see whether the Labour party would enter a coalition. Attlee indicated that he thought this unlikely were Chamberlain to remain Prime Minister, but that he would have to consult the National Executive of the party which was at that moment having its annual conference at Bournemouth. At 5.00 pm on 10 May Attlee phoned Chamberlain, confirming that while the party would not serve under Chamberlain, 'it would take its full and equal share as a full partner in a new government under a new Prime Minister which would command the confidence of the nation'. [Addison, p. 100] This settled the issue of Chamberlain's resignation but it did not resolve the question of his successor.

Having seen the Labour leaders on 9 May Chamberlain had a vital conversation with Halifax, Churchill and the Conservative Chief Whip, Margesson. Chamberlain raised the question of whom he should recommend to George VI to be invited to form the new government. In the account of this conversation, made the same day in his diary, Halifax wrote:

> PM said I was the man mentioned as the most acceptable. I said it would be hopeless position. If I was not in charge of the war (operations) and if I didn't lead in the House, I should be a cypher. I thought Winston was a better choice. Winston did not demur. Was very kind and polite but showed that he thought this right solution. [Gilbert, p. 302]

As German armies swept into Belgium and France on 10 May, Chamberlain had second thoughts about resigning at such a critical moment. But Kingsley Wood urged him not to delay and at the third meeting of the War Cabinet that day Chamberlain announced to his colleagues his intention to resign. He saw George VI as soon as the meeting ended and after George VI had indicated his preference for

H. Nicolson, *Diaries and Letters, 1939–45* (1967)

P. Addison, *The Road to 1945 – British Politics and the Second World War* (1975)

Nicolson, *Diaries and Letters*

Addison, *The Road to 1945*

M. Gilbert, *Winston S. Churchill, Finest Hour* (1983)

J. W. Wheeler-Bennett, *King George VI – His Life and Reign* (1958)

Halifax, Chamberlain advised the King that 'Winston was the man to send for'. [Wheeler-Bennett, p. 444]

It is pleasant to record that this change in leadership was effected with little of the bitterness that surrounded Lloyd George's replacement of Asquith in 1916, and it is to the credit of both Chamberlain and Churchill that they continued to work well together in the few remaining weeks that Chamberlain still had to live. Chamberlain stayed on in the War Cabinet as Lord President of the Council, until an operation for cancer forced his retirement. After his death, Churchill delivered a generous tribute in the House of Commons; in his letter to Chamberlain's widow he wrote: 'I felt when I served under him that he would never give in: and I knew when our positions were reversed that I could count upon the aid of a loyal and unflinching comrade.' [Gilbert, p. 901]

Gilbert, *Winston S. Churchill, Finest Hour*

The Direction of the War

In his Memoirs written in 1949, Churchill recalled his emotions on the night he became Prime Minister: 'I was conscious of a profound sense of relief. At last I had the authority to give direction over the whole scene. I felt as if I were walking with destiny, and that all my past life had been but a preparation for this hour and for this trial.' [Churchill, vol. II, p. 10] It was fortunate for Britain that at this moment her Prime Minister had such sublime confidence in himself. In his introspective moments Churchill, nonetheless, examined his performance more critically: 'Each night I try myself by Court Martial to see if I have done anything effective during the day. I don't just mean pawing the ground, anyone can go through the motions, but something really effective.' [Gilbert, pp. 758–9] In a speech delivered in 1954 he made a modest assessment of his contribution to victory: 'It was the nation and the race dwelling all round the globe that had the lion's heart. I had the luck to be called on to give the roar.' [Gilbert, p. 318] The 'roar' was important. It was Churchill's ability to articulate the mute determination of ordinary people to resist Hitler that gave them the courage to do so. His speeches to the House of Commons nearly always succeeded in hitting the right note, unlike Chamberlain's, even at moments of disaster. His broadcasts to the country, while they may have antagonised a few by their rhetorical flourishes, carried conviction to the majority that however hard the road might be, victory would ultimately be won.

W. S. Churchill, *The Second World War*, vol. II (Cassell, 1949)

Gilbert, *Winston S. Churchill, Finest Hour*

But Churchill was much more than a voice. He was Chairman of the War Cabinet and Minister of Defence. He conducted in person most of the important international negotiations with Britain's international partners, Roosevelt and Stalin. He barely took a day off, except when ill, throughout the war. He regularly worked a 70-hour week, even if at unconventional hours. The war was never out of his thoughts and while his readiness to interfere with almost any aspect of it was a constant trial to his subordinates, his constant probings, suggestions and demands at least imparted a sense of urgency to all who came under his scrutiny.

Churchill reduced the size of the War Cabinet initially to five members: himself, Chamberlain (Lord President of the Council), Halifax (Foreign Secretary), Attlee (Lord Privy Seal) and Greenwood (Minister without Portfolio). Of these men only Attlee and Churchill remained by 1945. Chamberlain retired in October 1940; Halifax went as Ambassador to Washington in December 1940; Greenwood retired to become Leader of the Opposition in 1942. The most important additions were Sir John Anderson who took Chamberlain's position; Sir Kingsley Wood (Chancellor of the Exchequer) and Ernest Bevin (Minister of Labour), both of whom joined in October 1940; Eden who replaced Halifax; and Beaverbrook who served in a variety of capacities: Minister for Aircraft Production, Minister of Supply, Minister of Production and Lord Privy Seal. He was an awkward colleague whose presence was more trouble than it was worth. Others who were recruited at different times were Oliver Lyttleton, Minister for Production, and Sir Stafford Cripps who was briefly Leader of the House of Commons. The *ad hoc* nature of Churchill's appointments to the War Cabinet indicated the particular preoccupations of the moment rather than any clearly defined set of priorities, and though it continued to meet regularly and to underwrite all major policy decisions, the real planning went on elsewhere.

Churchill Broadcasts to the nation

Defence policy was the responsibility of the Defence Committee (Operations) on which sat the Prime Minister, the Foreign Secretary, the three service ministers and the three Chiefs of Staff. In practice the key decisions were usually taken by the Chiefs of Staff Committee made up of the Chief of the Imperial General Staff, the First Sea Lord and the Chief of the Air Staff. This committee met every day. When Churchill was not present his own staff officer, General Ismay, deputised for him. Churchill thus kept in close touch with every aspect of the war. When important decisions had to be taken he would take the chair himself.

At the outset of the war the Chiefs of Staff consisted of Field-Marshal Ironside (Chief of the Imperial General Staff); Admiral of the Fleet Sir Dudley Pound; and Air Chief Marshal Sir Cyril Newall (Chief of the Air Staff). In May 1940, Sir John

Dill replaced Ironside and was himself succeeded in October by General Alan Brooke. In the same month, Air Chief Marshal Sir Charles Portal replaced Newall. The final change took place in 1943 when Sir Dudley Pound, who had had a stroke, was succeeded by Admiral of the Fleet, Sir Andrew Cunningham. Of these appointments, Alan Brooke's was the most important. Brooke was never afraid to challenge Churchill. When commanding British forces in France after Dunkirk, Brooke insisted in the course of a half-hour telephone conversation that British troops must be allowed to withdraw. Churchill gave way. As CIGS Brooks was able to contain Churchill's wilder flights of fancy, though it cost him many hours of lost sleep. The combination of Churchill's restless intelligence and the sober sense of reality which the Chiefs of Staff brought to defence planning proved, as an eye witness, Lieutenant-Colonel Sir Ian Jacob, reported 'a formidable combination'. [Gilbert, p. 326] Churchill never overruled the advice he was given and the disasters which did occur, Dakar, Crete, Singapore, for instance, were the outcome of decisions which the Chiefs of Staff had approved.

Gilbert, *Winston S. Churchill, Finest Hour*

Churchill's preoccupation with winning the war inevitably meant that he had less to do with the Home Front. It had been his intention that Chamberlain, as Lord President of the Council, should co-ordinate the work of the Home Departments involved, particularly the Home Office, the Ministry of Labour, the Ministry of Supply and the Treasury. On Chamberlain's retirement, Anderson took over this role and performed it very efficiently. When he became Chancellor of the Exchequer in 1943 he kept responsibility for Manpower Planning and if anyone can be said to have played the same role in Home Policy that Churchill did in Defence it was Anderson. He was aided by two powerful Labour ministers: Ernest Bevin as Minister of Labour and Herbert Morrison as Home Secretary. Attlee came into his own when he became Deputy Prime Minister in 1943, where he showed the gifts of chairmanship that made him such a successful Prime Minister in 1945. Other successful appointments were those of Lord Woolton who became Minister of Food in April 1940 and then Minister for Reconstruction in 1943; Lord Leathers, appointed as Minister of Transport in May 1941; and Oliver Lyttleton as Minister of Production in March 1942. At the time, the appointment of Beaverbrook as Minister for Aircraft Production in August 1940 was hailed as a stroke of genius. He certainly brought great energy to the task, though a less frenetic approach might have been equally successful.

Though Churchill never had a 'Garden Suburb' of private advisers like Lloyd George, he continued to place great reliance on one or two trusted cronies, notably Professor Lindemann, who became Lord Cherwell in 1941, and Sir Desmond Morton, who had supplied him with information about German air strength before the war. On scientific matters Cherwell was hard to refute, but in other areas of policy he could sometimes be outflanked.

Churchill was also rarely able to resist unconventional and original ideas, sometimes to the public benefit, at other times not. He backed investigation of the idea that German radio beams might be guiding bombers to their targets, in which he proved absolutely right. He supported the idea of Mulberry Harbours, another profitable scheme. But his championship of Wingate who urged the dropping of the equivalent of a division of troops to operate behind Japanese lines, to be supplied entirely by air, proved expensive both in lives and equipment. It never had Slim's approval.

Churchill enjoyed power and was never afraid to exercise it. He once said:

R. Lewin, *Churchill as Warlord* (Batsford, 1973)

> Power in a national crisis, when a man believes he knows what orders should be given, is a blessing ... The loyalties which centre upon number one are enormous. If he trips he must be sustained. If he makes mistakes he must be covered. If he sleeps he must not be wantonly disturbed. If he is no good he must be pole-axed.' [Lewin, p. 24]

Churchill never hesitated to dismiss those commanders or ministers who failed in his estimation: Wavell, Auchinleck, Admiral North, or Sir John Reith, for example. Reith never forgave him. But he was willing to put his own leadership to the test. He willingly accepted debates on his conduct of the war. In May 1941 after the fall of Crete, a motion of censure was defeated by 477 votes to 3. In July 1942 after the loss of Singapore and the fall of Tobruk, he still survived a vote of no confidence with remarkable ease by 476 votes to 25 (and 40 abstentions). After the battle of El Alamein his position was unassailable, and there were no further challenges to his leadership. But it made no difference to the way he treated his colleagues or the House of Commons. He may have been a warlord but he was never a dictator.

Party Politics during the War

On the outbreak of war in 1939 a party truce was officially agreed. Under the terms of the Parliament Act, 1911 a General Election should have been held in 1940, but an Act was passed in that and every succeeding year to suspend an election until the war should be over. Thus the House of Commons reflected the balance of parties produced in the 1935 General Election throughout the war. It was also agreed that when vacancies arose, by-elections would not be contested by the three major parties. Seats would go to candidates selected by the parties already in possession. Randolph Churchill became MP for Preston in 1940 under this arrangement.

When the National Coalition government was formed by Churchill in May 1940 there was no longer an effective Opposition and party politics in the House of Commons virtually came to a halt. Lees-Smith, an elderly Labour MP, acted as Leader of the Opposition as a matter of convenience until 1942 when Arthur Greenwood replaced him, but the role was purely a procedural one. Hopes were voiced at various times that the spirit of comradeship engendered by the war might persist when the war was over, bringing a permanent end to party strife. In May 1941 Churchill, having deplored the prospect of a General Election at the conclusion of hostilities, added:

> 'I may say, however, that some of the ties and friendships which are being formed between members of the administration of all parties will not be very easy to tear asunder, and that the comradeship of dangers passed and toils endured in common will for ever exercise an influence upon British national politics far deeper than the shibboleths and slogans of competing partisans.' In June 1941, Arthur Greenwood voiced the same hopes: 'Among my colleagues representing other political points of view I have found a strong and sincere wish, not merely to avoid the mistakes made after the last war, but to cooperate in the fullest measure in working together to restore the shattered fabric of our civilisation ....' [Addison, p. 165]

The facade of a united government supported by a united Parliament continued for most of the war. The Chief Whips of the major parties shared the same office and

Churchill's policies were defended by Labour as well as Conservative spokesmen. But under the surface the old divisions remained. Churchill, against his wife's wishes, was elected leader of the Conservative party in October 1940, on Chamberlain's retirement. His Conservative reflexes appeared whenever any step to be taken looked likely to threaten the existing social order. He opposed the work of the Army Bureau of Current Affairs; he gave a distinctly lukewarm reception to the Beveridge Report; he forced his supporters to reverse an amendment that would have given equal pay to teachers in the 1944 Education Act.

On the other side of the House, Aneurin Bevan accused Churchill of having an ear 'so sensitively attuned to the bugle note of history that he is deaf to the raucous clamour of contemporary life ....' [Addison, p. 126] Bevan, sometimes joined by Shinwell, kept up a constant sniping at Churchill and delivered a slashing attack on him in the 'No Confidence' debate of July 1942. Though the official Labour leadership remained loyal to the government, there were several occasions, notably after the debate on the Beveridge Report, where Labour backbenchers voted against government policies.

Addison, *The Road to 1945*

There was more opposition to the government outside Parliament. The *Daily Mirror* aroused Churchill's anger by its outspoken criticism of the government's failings to the point where he threatened to have the paper closed down. The *Daily Worker* was actually banned for eighteen months from January 1941. The best evidence of growing discontent with government policies is to be found in the by-elections that were contested. No seats previously held by Labour candidates were lost but in 1942 three seats that had been Conservative went to independent candidates, one of them being Tom Driberg, standing as a Socialist.

Also in 1942 Sir Richard Acland founded the Common Wealth party. Acland was elected as a Liberal MP for Barnstaple in 1935, but by 1940 he had become a convert to his own idealistic brand of socialism, based on the doctrines of Christianity. The party at its peak had only 15 000 members but it was generously endowed and its largely middle-class membership was active and committed. It put up candidates in several by-elections, winning three seats at Eddisbury (April 1943), Skipton (June 1944) and Chelmsford (April 1945). The most remarkable by-election result, however, was the triumph of Charles White standing as an Independent Socialist with Common Wealth party support in West Derbyshire. The seat was practically a pocket borough in the gift of the Duke of Devonshire. Members of the Cavendish family had held it without a break from 1885, apart from the years 1918–23. White was the son of the Liberal MP who had broken the pattern. In February 1944 Colonel Hunloke, son-in-law to the Duke of Devonshire, resigned. With indecent haste the Marquess of Hartington, the Duke's son, was nominated as the Conservative candidate. Despite Churchill's personal support Hartington was defeated and a Conservative majority of 5500 was transformed into a victory by 4500 votes for the Independent Socialist, Charles White.

In October 1944 the National Executive Committee of the Labour party resolved that it would contest the General Election, when it came, as an independent party. After the war in Europe had ended on 8 May 1945, Churchill invited the Labour members of the Coalition to continue in the government until the war with Japan was over. Attlee, Dalton and Bevin were in favour of this course, but they were overruled in the NEC and this decision was endorsed by the Annual Conference of the party, then meeting at Blackpool. Attlee, in his reply to Churchill, argued strongly for an election to be held in the autumn. But Churchill, anxious to gain what advantage he could from victory in Europe, fixed the date for 5 July. Parliament was dissolved on 15 June and the National Coalition government was replaced by a caretaker government drawn exclusively from the Conservative party. The hopes entertained in 1941 were dashed and the party battle was resumed.

THE WAR ECONOMY B

War-Time Planning

With the experience of the First World War to guide it, the British government never underestimated the task facing it in the Second World War. This time there was no pretence of 'business as usual'. On 1 September 1939 the government passed the first of several Emergency Powers Acts, giving it all the authority it needed to interfere in the nation's affairs. Within weeks a host of new ministries had been added to the Ministry of Supply which Chamberlain had created in July 1939: Information, Food, Economic Warfare, Home Security, Shipping, Labour. In 1940 Churchill set up the Ministry of Aircraft Production; in 1941 the Ministry of Labour added National Service to its responsibilities; and in 1942 the Ministry of Production came into existence. The Civil Service increased from 388 000 in April 1939 to 719 000 by July 1943. There was no shortage of 'planners'. But all this administrative activity needed to be co-ordinated and it depended on a flow of accurate and up-to-date statistics. It was not really until 1941 that the effective planning of the war effort really began. It was in that year that serious shortages of labour first became apparent; the Central Statistical Office was able to provide the necessary facts and figures and for the first time the Budget was designed to relate government expenditure to the real resources available rather than to what could be raised in taxes.

There was no exact equivalent to Churchill and the Chiefs of Staff Committee for running the domestic side of the war. There evolved instead a series of Cabinet Committees: the Lord President's Committee for Home Affairs, the Food Policy Committee, the Manpower Requirements Committee and the Production Executive. Eventually the Ministry of Production became the main co-ordinating body on the supply side, while the Treasury continued to be responsible for financial policy. Just as there was no economic supremo comparable with Churchill's role as Minister of Defence, there was no long-term economic strategy. Planning took the form of responding to particular needs and demands as they arose, whether a shortage of shipping space or a shortage of coal miners. But this approach at least had the virtue of flexibility and government ministers and civil servants became increasingly skilful at anticipating problems and working out solutions to them.

Manpower

The best example of the government's handling of the economy is to be found in its approach to manpower. It became obvious by January 1941, by which time virtually all the unemployed had been absorbed, that the country's manpower requirements could not be met without the shoe pinching somewhere. Bevin, as Minister of Labour, took three important initiatives. He set up a Register of Protected Establishments whose workers would not be so liable to call-up; he began to use his authority to direct people to essential work (32 000 directives were issued between July 1941 and June 1942); finally, he introduced the Essential Work Order under which employers could not dismiss workers without approval, nor could workers leave their jobs without permission, subject to arbitration.

In July 1941 the Ministry of Labour embarked on a further study of manpower resources and concluded that there would be a shortfall of 300 000 if all the demands of the services and the munitions industries were to be met. The age of call-up was extended in both directions, downwards to 18 and upwards to 51; all people of both sexes from the age of 18 to 60 were required to undertake some form of national service. In December 1941 Bevin introduced conscription for single women between the ages of 20 and 30, extended to 51 in 1943. Altogether 460 000 served in the women's equivalent of the armed forces: the Women's Royal Naval Service, the Women's Auxiliary Airforce and the Auxiliary Territorial Service. The majority, however, worked in industry in Royal Ordnance factories; another 100 000 or so worked in the Women's Land Army. In addition to their regular war work most men and women were also expected to assist in one of the voluntary services such as the Auxiliary Fire Service, or the Home Guard. Direction of labour went furthest, perhaps, in the method adopted for recruitment of miners. Under the Bevin scheme introduced in December 1943 one out of ten new conscripts would be chosen by ballot to work in the mines. The scheme was far from popular and it provided only 45 000 miners.

By July 1944, 4.5 million men and 460 000 women were in the armed forces. Another 3.5 million were employed on war work of one kind or another. Out of a working population of 22 million this meant that 8.5 million extra workers had to be found as a result of the war. They were recruited from the unemployed, non-essential industries and services, and from those who would otherwise have stayed at home. But there were at least a million men over 65 (including Churchill) at work, too. Working hours varied but were rarely less than 50 hours a week and in 1940 sometimes reached 70 hours. The one compensation for the strains imposed on the working population was the ending of unemployment. The official figure fell to 60 000 in 1943.

No other country, except perhaps for the Soviet Union, used its manpower as intensively as Britain during the Second World War. Conscientious Objectors, of whom there were 59 000 were directed to work on the land or to continue in their occupations; reliable prisoners-of-war were also employed on the land. Despite the loss of freedom which direction of labour and conscription brought with them there was little opposition. The public accepted the obligations brought by the war because they applied to everyone, and because the country was fighting for its survival.

Industry

The government controlled industry both directly and indirectly. The Royal Ordnance Factories were run by the Ministry of Supply and by 1942 they were employing 300 000 workers. In addition the government provided a large number of 'shadow' factories for firms engaged in war production. The government met the running costs while leaving the management in private hands. There were 265 such factories working for the Ministry of Supply, the Admiralty and the Ministry for Aircraft Production.

Other forms of control were achieved by the allocation of raw materials, quotas and licences and the establishment of manufacturing standards to which producers had to adhere. Such standards were intended to economise on the use of labour and raw materials, hence the name 'Utility' given to them. They were first applied to textiles, but furniture, pottery and a wide range of consumer goods eventually came to bear the 'utility' label. The prices of these goods were also strictly controlled. Whether the economies achieved justified all the bureaucratic interference which the Utility scheme entailed is doubtful. On the other hand it did ensure that the basic needs of consumers for household goods were met, if not very adequately.

The war had mixed effects on British industry as a whole. Non-essential industries and services such as textiles, pottery, clothing, construction and retailing all suffered from loss of manpower and lack of investment. Whereas in 1938, £214 million was invested in new capital equipment, equivalent to 5% of the National Income, it has been calculated that by 1945 the loss of capital equipment through depreciation, even allowing for new investment, amounted to £1000 million. Where no investment had taken place such industries would be ill fitted to meet the challenge of post-war competition.

Many industries, however, benefited from the stimulus of war. This was most obviously the case with the aircraft industry. Production rose from 7000 planes in 1938 to 26000 in 1943 and 14000 engineering works and 1.7 million workers were engaged in the manufacture of aircraft. This in turn stimulated demand for new alloys and aluminium, and for machine tools and as a result these industries also expanded. The war accelerated technical progress in the electronic and chemical industries – 12 million radio valves were produced in 1940 and the figure rose to 35 million in 1944. The chemical industry made rapid strides in the development of insecticides such as DDT, new drugs and artificial fibres such as rayon and nylon. The engineering industry as a whole emerged greatly strengthened by the war, most branches increasing the numbers of employees by between 30% and 50%.

Two more general effects may be noted. The enhanced role of the scientist in warfare gave him a corresponding importance in the war-based industries which were required to meet his specifications, for instance in the manufacture of radar sets. The research scientist became a more familiar figure in industry, at any rate in the more enterprising firms, and research departments built up during the war were maintained after it. The war also stimulated improvements in production methods: 'The necessities of war taught new methods of mass-production, of industrial control and management, of design and quality control, and spread this knowledge among a host of sub-contractors.' [Pollard, p. 204] Such changes cannot be quantified but they do something to compensate for all the energies devoted to essentially destructive purposes.

S. F. Pollard, *The Development of the British Economy* (1983)

Agriculture

Agriculture was the industry which benefited most from the war. It was known from the outset that one acre of wheat would produce the same food equivalent as seven acres of grassland, and with the pressing need to save shipping space the more self-sufficient Britain could become the better. In 1939 the balance between arable and grassland was as follows:

Arable	*Grassland*
12 million acres	17 million acres

By 1943 these proportions had effectively been reversed. Arable acreage was now 18 million, compared with 11 million acres now devoted to grassland. These changes were brought about through a combination of incentives and penalties. Farmers were offered £2 for every acre of grassland they put under the plough. County War Agricultural Executive Committees went round inspecting every farm to make sure that the land was being properly farmed and as a result 400 000 acres were taken over where the existing farmers were found to be unsatisfactory. The application of fertilisers improved yields for all the main crops. Wheat, for instance, rose from 17.7 cwt per acre to 19.7 cwt per acre. The extra demand for labour created by the conversion to arable farming was met by increasing mechanisation – the number of tractors used increased from 56 000 in 1938 to 203 000 in 1946. While there were inevitably some falls in livestock production, cereal production went up considerably and the potato crop doubled.

Land Girls bringing in the harvest on Britain's largest wheatfield on the Sussex Downs (uncultivated for the previous twenty years)

Farmers benefited from direct subsidies totalling £37 million a year by 1945. Their prices were guaranteed and so, in effect, were their markets. Farm incomes kept well ahead of price increases and the agricultural labourer gained a well-deserved and long overdue improvement in his wages. By 1945 agriculture was more prosperous than it had been for 70 years and the foundations of Britain's most successful post-war industry had been laid.

Paying for the
War and the
Control of
Inflation

The government faced the same problem in 1939 as it had done in 1914. How was the war to be paid for without causing an unacceptable level of inflation? Keynes addressed himself to this problem, and his advice, while not accepted in its entirety, was the main influence on government policy. Keynes publicised his views in two articles in *The Times* published in October 1939, and in a pamphlet entitled *How to Pay for the War*, which came out in February 1940. The essential problem, as Keynes saw it, was that the transfer of resources to war-time requirements would inevitably bring a fall in the supply of consumer goods. Unless consumer demand could be held down, prices would be bound to rise. Keynes's solution was to restrain demand by high taxation. Such a policy was bound to be unpopular with the trade unions but if part of the taxes raised were in the form of post-war credits, to be released when the war was over, this would sugar the pill. Keynes also argued for family allowances to be introduced to ease the burden on large families. Though the post-war credits scheme was not implemented on the scale Keynes recommended the main thrust of his argument was accepted. The proportion of government expenditure met by taxation rather than borrowing rose steadily throughout the war, as the following figures indicate:

J. M. Keynes, *How to Pay for the War* (Macmillan, 1940)

	Total Tax Revenue £ million	Total Deficit £ million	Of which raised by Public Borrowing £ million
1939	980	490	352
1940	1382	2115	1550
1941	2143	2828	2553
1942	2563	2909	2576
1943	3052	2826	2972
1944	3262	2672	2792
1945	3265	2131	2442

Receipts from direct taxes rose by 300%, the standard rate of income tax eventually reaching 50p in the pound. Receipts from indirect taxes, mainly on beer and tobacco, rose by 160%.

Official encouragement of savings through the National Savings Movement, lack of anything much to spend money on, and some carefully tailored inducements such as National Savings Certificates, meant that the government was generally able to raise all the loans it needed at an average interest rate of 3%. This was a big improvement on the First World War when the rate had averaged 5%. It meant that, while the National Debt in 1945 was three times as high as it had been in 1919, total interest charges were only 56% higher. The burden of servicing the debt was much less of a problem in 1945 than it had been after 1919.

Inflation was also kept in check by price controls, subsidies and rationing. Price controls applied to all rationed goods, to rents and to 'Utility' products. By 1944, 95% of all household expenditure went on goods that were subject to price controls. Subsidies used to keep down food prices were introduced as an emergency measure in 1939 and maintained throughout the war. By 1945 they amounted to £250 million a year. It was one way of keeping the retail price index down and thus reducing the pressure for wage increases.

Rationing came in by stages and was designed partly to prevent the prices of goods in short supply from rocketing, partly to ensure fair shares. It began in January 1940 and was applied first to bacon, butter and sugar. By the end of the year meat, tea, cheese, sweets and jam had all been added to the list. Amounts were small but were carefully calculated to meet nutritional needs. In 1942 clothes rationing was introduced and a system of points was applied to certain foodstuffs. The monthly allocation of 20 points might largely be blown on one luxury, such as a tin of salmon, or stretched to cover bulkier but less appealing foods. Lord Woolton, Minister of Food from 1940–43, broadcast regularly to the country, whilst the 8.15 am spot on the radio was filled every day by 'Kitchen Front' whose ingenious recipes were designed to make very ordinary ingredients such as carrots more palatable.

According to the government's own figures, the cost of living rose by roughly 30% during the course of the war. The government index was heavily weighted towards food prices and a differently weighted index would have produced a higher rate of inflation. Even so, by the standard of the late 1960s and 1970s the government's achievement was a remarkable one and it certainly helped to make the strains of war more bearable.

The Balance of Payments

While the internal problem of paying for the war was effectively solved, the external one was not. In 1939 Britain's gold and dollar reserves amounted to £450 million, nothing like enough to meet the cost of the additional armaments she needed to import, as we have seen. But the problem was made worse by the loss of export markets on the European continent after 1940, and the diversion of resources from production for exports to production for the war. Exports fell in volume terms to one-third of their pre-war level. The proportion of the labour force engaged in producing exports dropped from 9% to 2%. Britain experienced a large visible trade deficit every year between 1939 and 1945, and by 1945 had accumulated a total debt of £3355 million.

Lend-lease met the immediate problem but it did not quite live up to its reputation as 'the most unsordid act in history'. The Lend-Lease Act had to be renewed each year and increasingly stiff conditions were attached to it. British exports were not allowed to contain any raw materials provided under lend-lease and Britain was required to sell all her capital assets in the United States. When the war ended lend-lease was abruptly halted and this emphasised Britain's growing dependence on the American economy and her continuing need for American economic aid.

The British economy was successfully mobilised for war. Every resource, including labour, was effectively deployed. Prices were held down while rationing and subsidies ensured that the burdens were shared, if not equally, at least with a sufficient appearance of fairness to win public support and co-operation for the war effort. On the debit side capital equipment in many areas of industry and the transport network had to be gravely neglected, and the fall in exports led to a mounting trade deficit. While the physical destruction caused by bombing did not rival that inflicted on Germany, it was still serious – 222 000 houses were destroyed and another 5 million badly damaged, apart from the disruptive effects which air raids had on the infrastructure. These were the economic legacies of the war.

RECONSTRUCTION ===================================== C

Motives

'The demand for social reform at home sprang up as suddenly as a gust on a still day, and continued to blow with increasing force.' [Addison, p. 104] One of the effects of the ordeal endured by Britain in 1940 – Dunkirk, the Battle of Britain and the Blitz – was to strengthen the conviction in all levels of society that Britain must become a better place to live in when the war was over. The War Aims Committee, set up at the urging of Duncan Sandys when the Battle of Britain was at its height, had as one of its terms of reference: 'To consider means of perpetuating the national unity achieved in this country during the war through a social and economic structure designed to secure equality of opportunity and service among all classes of the community.' [Addison, p. 122] J. B. Priestley, the well-known author and broadcaster, spent much of his time travelling round the country talking to various groups. According to him while the first topic of conversation was always the state of the war, 'Topic Number Two, running Number One very close, was always the New World after the war. What could we do to bring our economic and social system nearer to justice and decency? That was the great question ....' [Addison, p. 162]

Addison, *The Road to 1945*

The war thus established a mood to which politicians in all parties felt bound to respond. The social reforms achieved or anticipated by the Coalition government were often designed by experts and technocrats such as Keynes or Beveridge. But their implementation depended on the support they were given in government circles and the enthusiasm with which they were received by the public. The war also had the effect of bringing the parties closer together. United for the purpose of winning the war, there was also something approaching a consensus in the War Cabinet's plans for peace.

The first of many Government Committees for Reconstruction was appointed under the chairmanship of Arthur Greenwood in January 1941. It held only four meetings before Greenwood left the War Cabinet. His post was taken first by Sir William Jowitt and then in 1943 by Lord Woolton. The new priority given to Reconstruction can be seen in the high-powered membership of the Committee at this time. It included the Chancellor of the Exchequer, Sir John Anderson, Attlee, Bevin and Morrison on the Labour side, R. A. Butler and Oliver Lyttleton on the Conservative side. Numerous other bodies were also concerned with planning for the future. On the economic side, Political and Economic Planning, the National Institute for Social and Economic Research, the Oxford Institute of Statistics and the London School of Economics were all engaged in finding solutions to post-war economic problems. The Town and Country Planning Association was only one of a variety of groups dedicated to improving the environment. A Medical Planning Committee was set up in August 1940 to review the country's medical services.

The strong Labour presence in the War Cabinet allied to pressure groups inside and outside Parliament and backed by a growing body of public opinion provided an impulse towards social reform which Churchill, even when he wished to do so, was unable to resist.

The first significant step was the publication of the Beveridge Report. This had its origins in a committee set up under Beveridge's Chairmanship in June 1941 to investigate and to sort out the anomalies in the existing system of National Health Insurance, which covered some workers but not others. Beveridge seized the opportunity to produce his own blueprint for the Welfare State. He circulated a Memorandum to fellow members of the Committee, stating that the aim of social insurance should be to provide a minimum standard of living for all. He based his plans on three assumptions: the provision of a National Health Service; the maintenance of full employment (defined as a maximum rate of unemployment of 8.5%); and a system of family allowances. The Committee took evidence from 127 individuals and groups and the Report was finally published on 1 December 1942. In essence it recommended the unification of all existing schemes of benefit; flat rate contributions from all employees; and benefits calculated to provide an adequate standard of living when earnings were interrupted, for whatever reason. The scheme was more revolutionary in its assumptions than in its detailed recommendations. It was to be self-financing and as both contributions and benefits were to be uniform, very little redistribution of income would occur. Beveridge also accepted that it would take years before pensions reached a satisfactory level if the scheme was to remain financially viable.

The Beveridge Report

But these qualifications mattered less than the promise of 'cradle to grave coverage' to the general public. Altogether 635 000 copies of the Report were sold and a Gallup poll indicated that 86% of the population were in favour of its recommendations. The popular radio programme *It's That Man Again* (ITMA) probably caught the current public perception of the Report as well as anything. One of ITMA's characters, His Fatuity, the Minister of Social Hilarity, remarked: 'I've been up the last three days and nights reading the first chapter of a book called "Gone with the Want", by that stout fellow Beveridge.' [Calder, p. 527]

A. Calder, *The People's War: Britain 1939–1945* (1969)

Some Conservatives, including Churchill, had considerable doubts about the Beveridge Report on the grounds of expense, the encouragement it would give to 'scrounging' and the unreasonable expectations it might arouse. Having given the Report maximum publicity on the Overseas Service of the BBC, the government then clamped down on discussion of it. A pamphlet written for the Army Bureau of Current Affairs by Beveridge himself was withdrawn on the instructions of the War Office. Churchill announced to the War Cabinet on 14 February that the government would plan but not legislate on the Report's recommendations.

In the debate held in the House of Commons on a motion welcoming the Report, no date was given for its implementation. Labour backbenchers insisted on tabling an amendment calling for prompt legislation with the result that 121 MPs voted for the amendment, including 97 Labour MPs; 45 Conservative MPs belonging to the recently formed Tory Reform Committee also put their names to an amendment calling for the immediate setting up of a Ministry of Social Security. In the end, the government's own proposals were published in September 1944. They embodied most of the principles of the Report and formed the basis of the National Insurance Act passed by the Labour government in 1946. Family Allowances for the second child and subsequent children were introduced in one of the final acts passed by the Coalition government in 1945.

Health

One of the assumptions on which the Beveridge Report was based was the provision of a National Health Service. In 1939 the provision of health care in Britain was arbitrary and often inadequate. There were about 1000 Voluntary Hospitals, kept going through charitable bequests, flag days and other such fund-raising activities. There were also about 1000 Local Authority Hospitals run by Local Authorities and financed out of the rates. The Voluntary Hospitals tended to take short stay patients who required operations, the Local Authority Hospitals looked after the chronically sick and elderly and were often almost indistinguishable from the Victorian workhouse. General Practitioners had three classes of patient: panel patients, covered by the National Insurance Acts; the families of panel patients whose medical expenses were often met through clubs formed for the purpose; and private patients who paid for all the treatment they received. The distribution of hospitals and GPs was unfair to the poorer parts of the country, for instance there were seven times the number of GPs per head of population in London as there were in South Shields.

The Blitz placed an immediate strain on the hospital service. It led to the creation of an Emergency Hospital Service under which voluntary and local authority hospitals were commandeered. Nurses and doctors were paid by the government and treatment was free. Originally intended to meet the needs of those injured by enemy action, it became increasingly hard to draw the line and in practice free hospital treatment was given to most of those who needed it. On 9 October 1941 the Minister of Health recognised the position and promised that a National Hospital Service would be established after the war. The Medical Planning Commission, set up in August 1940, produced an interim report in May 1942. It recommended the establishment of a National Health Service, available to all, with salaried GPs operating from Health Centres. In February 1943 the government accepted the idea of a National Health Service in principle and in a White Paper produced early in 1944 laid out the admirable objectives it should be designed to achieve:

(1) To ensure that everybody in the country – irrespective of means, age, sex or occupation – shall have equal opportunity to benefit from the best and most up-to-date medical and allied services available.
(2) To provide, therefore, for all who want it, a comprehensive service covering every branch of medical and allied activity ....
(3) To divorce the care of health from questions of personal means or other factors irrelevant to it .... [Calder, p. 540]

The War Cabinet did not give its unanimous approval to the White Paper. Beaverbrook urged its rejection. The British Medical Association, dominated by wealthier GPs from the more prosperous parts of the country, voiced its disapproval of many features of the White Paper, thus anticipating the struggle that was to be waged between Bevan and the BMA between 1946 and 1948. Even so, it was a Conservative minister, Henry Willink, who defended the White Paper, both in Cabinet and in the House of Commons. The National Health Service owed its conception, if not its birth, to the Coalition government.

Education

Education was, as it still is, the cinderella of government departments. Rather to Churchill's surprise, R. A. Butler, one of the breed of progressive and intelligent younger Tories, when offered a diplomatic post or the Presidency of the Board of

Education, chose Education. With his deputy, Chuter Ede, who was a former teacher, they produced a wide-ranging Education Act that determined the structure of secondary education in Britain for the next generation. Among the positive achievements of the Act were the raising of the school-leaving age to 15 (finally implemented in 1947); the establishment of a clear division between primary and secondary education at the age of 11; a solution to the divisive issue of Church schools which were now allowed to opt for voluntary-aided or voluntary-controlled status; and a recognition by all local authorities of their obligation to provide nursery and further education where possible, as well as the statutory requirement to provide schooling for all children between the ages of 5 and 15.

Unfortunately the Act was also based on a dubious premiss. In 1943 the Norwood Committee on examinations and the curriculum produced a Report which argued, without much justification, that children fitted naturally into three categories: those best suited to an academic, literary and scientific education; those who were suited to a technical education; and those who could deal with 'concrete things' more easily than 'ideas'. By a happy coincidence these categories also happened to match the existing structure of grammar, technical and elementary schools. It was a relatively easy operation to separate the primary from the secondary departments of the elementary schools and to rename the senior schools as Secondary Moderns. The eleven-plus examination was introduced to determine which school a child would go to at the age of eleven, on the basis of aptitude and ability. In theory, all three kinds of school were to enjoy 'parity of esteem' but in practice the eleven-plus examination soon came to be seen not as a sign-post but as a hurdle. The tripartite system of education became known to its critics as the tripartheid system.

An unsuccessful effort was also made to integrate the private sector, which educated the wealthiest 10% of the country's children, into the maintained sector. The Fleming Report which came out in 1944 recommended that fee-paying schools should take up to 25% of their intake from maintained schools, local authorities finding the fees. Few were prepared to do so and the independent sector survived unscathed, though also unsubsidised except in the cases of the children of officers and diplomats serving abroad. If the changes in the educational system were more cosmetic than substantial, Butler could at least take credit for ending the religious divisions which had so bedevilled English education in the nineteenth century. Church schools were protected without being favoured, and the clause in the Act requiring the school day in maintained schools to begin with an act of worship and the inclusion of religious instruction in the curriculum provided a safeguard against those who accused the maintained sector of having a purely secular approach to education.

Town and Country Planning

Until the Second World War the State played almost no part in determining how land was to be used and developed. In 1942 only 3% of land in Britain was subject to any form of development scheme. The government's attention was drawn to the question of land use and distribution of the population by the threat of strategic bombing. In 1937 the Barlow Commission was appointed specifically to consider the existing distribution of the population in the light of this threat. Its Report came out in 1940 and recommended that the government should assume responsibility for the pattern of land use throughout the country, for instance by restricting development in the South-East, encouraging the movement of industry to areas of high unemployment, and relieving urban congestion by the creation of new towns. The majority who signed the Report were not prepared to recommend any increase in executive powers to achieve these ends, but the implications of the Report were still far-reaching.

While the Report made little impact in 1940, when the government had other considerations on its mind, the Blitz raised in immediate form the problem of what was to be done with bombed cities. In October 1940 Churchill appointed Sir John Reith, formerly Director General of the BBC, to be Minister of Works. Reith took a broad view of his responsibilities. He encouraged the London County Council to produce its own County Plan. He appointed two committees, the Scott Committee to investigate the use of the countryside, and the Uthwatt Committee to examine the problems of Development of Land. In February 1942 Reith had the status of his Ministry elevated to 'Works and Planning' but he did not unfortunately survive to enjoy it. He was dismissed by Churchill the same month, largely it would seem to appease Conservative critics. Nor, it must be said, had Churchill ever liked Reith very much, referring to him in private as 'that wuthering height'. But Reith's work bore fruit in the Report of the Uthwatt Committee in 1942. It recommended that the rights of development in all land outside built-up areas should be vested in the state and that urban authorities should be able to purchase any land they needed for development purposes at 1939 prices. These proposals were much too radical for the Conservatives in the Coalition government, but steps in this direction were taken which by the setting up of a Ministry for Town and Country Planning in 1943, and the passage of the Town and Country Planning Act in 1944 gave local authorities greater powers of compulsory purchase. The party consensus broke down on the land question. Conservatives had always been sensitive where property rights in land were concerned, while nationalisation of the land was still supposedly one of the Labour party's objectives. In practice the Labour manifesto in 1945 made no such commitment, but the 1947 Town and Country Planning Act did adopt the recommendations of the Uthwatt Committee over the development of land.

Full Employment

In some ways the most important, if least conspicuous change in government policy produced by the Second World War was the attitude to employment. The Beveridge Report had as one of its necessary assumptions the maintenance of full employment and the knowledge that Beveridge intended to extend his own researches into this area evidently encouraged the government to forestall him. Lord Cherwell wrote on 20 October 1943: 'It seems most desirable that the government should make proposals about this [employment policy] at an early date, in any event before Sir William Beveridge brings out his plan which will no doubt be boosted in the press like his social insurance scheme.' [Addison, p. 243] In the event, the government's White Paper on Employment was published in May 1944, beating Beveridge's own publication, *Full Employment in a Free Society* by a short head.

Addison, *The Road to 1945*

The government White Paper was an amalgam of Keynesian ideas modified by Treasury scepticism. Keynes himself had little to do with it, though one of his disciples, James Meade, who had been seconded to the Economic Section of the War Cabinet, had a considerable influence on its proposals. It began with a resounding promise: 'The Government accepts as one of its primary aims the maintenance of a high and stable level of employment.' The White Paper envisaged a shortage of manpower for the first few years after the war. Physical controls would be needed to manage the transition from a war to a peacetime economy. Thereafter, aggregate demand would have to be sustained by the encouragement of exports, the support of private investment, the careful timing of public investment, and the regulation of consumption by varying the level of insurance contributions. The White Paper deliberately ruled out the use of budget deficits to stimulate demand during a recession, provoking Keynes to comment that the document was 'a praiseworthy groping towards the light', but he deplored 'the undue timidity attributable to muddled thinking and the tenacity of error'. [Addison, p. 246]

Addison, *The Road to 1945*

J.M. Keynes, economic adviser to the Government, whose ideas were reflected in the White Paper on Full Employment

Though the government gave their official approval to the White Paper when it was debated in Parliament, it was attacked from the Left and from the Right. Aneurin Bevan argued that it was a sham, designed to discredit Socialism by removing any justification for nationalisation. Ralph Assheton, the recently appointed Chairman of the Conservative party, also claimed that the White Paper promised more than could possibly be performed. Whatever its critics might say, the White Paper was a vital landmark, all the same. Thereafter economic policy was to be cast in a Keynesian mould and governments of both parties proceeded for the next 30 years on the assumption that full employment was an attainable objective.

It can readily be argued that the Second World War created a new consensus in British politics between the front benches of the Labour and Conservative parties. The commitments to a Welfare State, to a National Health Service and to a managed economy were shared by the leaders of both parties. The rhetoric of the 1945 General

Election, particularly on the Conservative side, tended to conceal this fact. But when the dust had settled it became clear that the Second World War had brought about a significant shift to the left in the Conservative party, while the teachings of Keynes enabled the Labour party to live with a reformed capitalism. Politicians of both parties had more in common than they were willing to admit.

William Beverage, explaining the Beverage Report

THE WAR AND SOCIAL CHANGE ▬▬▬ D

The Experience of War

It is impossible to generalise about the impact of war on the British people. For those living on the Channel Islands it meant four years of German occupation; for Londoners it meant living with the constant fear of air raids, and 97 consecutive nights of bombing in 1940–41. For those living in remote rural areas, insulated from the effects of rationing by local produce, the war might have had very little effect on daily life, apart from the arrival of evacuees or girls in the Women's Land Army.

Some experiences were universal. Apart from those in essential occupations, everyone was liable to call-up, either in the armed forces or in industry. There were units of the Home Guard in the Hebrides and in the Scilly Islands. The BBC provided a national service of news and comment and a variety of programmes such as ITMA, the Brains Trust and the broadcast talks following the 9 00 pm news which united the country as never before. Few families were unaffected by the demand for labour; the population perforce became more mobile and 60 million changes of address were recorded during the war, equivalent to every household moving twice.

For many people the war brought a widening of social horizons. The million and a half children evacuated mainly from the slums of Britain's industrial cities in 1939 brought home to those in more comfortable parts of the country just what social deprivation could mean. Class barriers came down as perils and hardships were shared in the air raid shelter or in the queue. People from widely different social backgrounds were brought together in the Auxiliary Services such as the Fire Service or the Home Guard. Members of the middle class who found themselves working down a coal mine or on a factory floor gained a new insight into industrial Britain. A railway worker commented: 'We got the closest we've ever been to the classless society, not in the distribution of wealth but in the attitude of the people.' [Harrington and Young, p. 27]

W. Harrington and P. Young, *The 1945 Revolution* (1978)

Air Raids

The most dramatic and visible effect of the war on the civilian population was bombing or the threat of bombing. From 1 September 1939 to 17 September 1944 every household went through the nightly ritual of putting up the 'blackout', designed to eliminate every chink of light. Even in the quietest year of the war, 1943, there was barely a night without a raid taking place somewhere. The last German rocket fell on British soil as late as March 1945.

Air raid damage in Coventry

London was much the worst affected city, suffering 30 000 deaths from air raids and damage to 60% of houses. It was the capital, too, which had to bear the brunt of the 8000 V1s (flying bombs) and 1054 V2s (rockets) that were aimed at this country. The worst disasters all happened in London: 600 were killed or injured when a direct hit struck Balham Tube Station. A V1 which landed on the Guards' Chapel in June 1944 killed 119 people and injured a further 102. But other cities also suffered severely. In November 1941 Coventry was subjected to 11 hours of bombing resulting in 554 deaths. Ports such as Bristol, Liverpool, Southampton and Portsmouth all came in for heavy raids. In 1942 the so-called Baedeker raids were directed at towns renowned for their architectural distinction: Exeter, Norwich, York, Bath and Canterbury.

Air raids caused the deaths of 60 595 civilians and injuries to a further 86 182, while 2 350 000 people had the devastating experience of being 'bombed out' and losing all their visible possessions.

Living Standards

According to one estimate: 'In general it would be broadly true to state that personal consumption was stabilised at the previous skilled artisan level and that of other classes cut down to approach it.' [Pollard, p. 345] The demand for labour brought an end to unemployment. Price controls kept the cost of living broadly in line with wage increases, and the extra hours worked meant that weekly earnings kept ahead of inflation. Weekly earnings went up by 75% on average, prices by between 30 and 40%. Most people were better off, and the addition of a second income as women went to work might bring a substantial improvement to a family's finances. But there were still some painful disparities. Curiously it was those in the armed services who were worst off. The pay of a private soldier was roughly half that of a munition worker and it required constant increases in the marriage and children's allowances to keep his family out of poverty. The British serviceman was paid roughly a quarter of what his American counterpart could expect, leading to the well known, if anonymous, comment that there was nothing wrong with Americans apart from their being 'over-paid, over-sexed, and over here'.

Pollard, *The Development of the British Economy*

Increases in taxation affected all groups in the community. Seven million workers entered the income-tax bracket for the first time, though the blow was softened by the introduction of *Pay as You Earn*, under which tax was deducted by the employer at source. But tax rates were highly progressive and there was an excess profits tax of 100%. Wage earners paid between 13 and 17% of their incomes in tax; those on salaries and with private means paid between 30 and 44%. There was thus some redistribution of income, though it did not go very far as can be seen from the following figures:

Percentage share of all income after tax received by:	*1938*	*1947*
The Top 1%	14	11
The Top 10%	38	30
The Top 50%	73	70

Rationing had a much more visible effect in equalising living standards. Lord Woolton's plea for fair shares was generally accepted. Rationing was popular because it guaranteed that everyone would get the essential quantities of foods that were in short supply. It has been claimed that the nation's health improved as a result of rationing. The poorest classes in the community benefited from the extension of free school milk and meals and from controlled prices, while the introduction of wholemeal bread and the shortages of sugar and foods rich in cholesterol such as eggs, butter and bacon provided the wealthy with a healthier diet. Statistics support the claim. Death rates, infant mortality rates and suicide rates all declined during the war. The incidence of tuberculosis, which rose briefly, was checked. If life for the majority was drab, it was not unhealthy.

Unlike the First World War, the Second did not bring any specific improvement in the status of women; but it may have had a greater effect on their long-term aspirations. If women were to be conscripted it was not unreasonable for them to claim equality of treatment and equal pay became the burning issue in industry. The engineering industry unwillingly conceded that after eight months doing a man's work, a woman should be entitled to a man's pay. Various expedients were adopted by employers to evade this obligation and there was a serious strike at the Rolls Royce works in Hillingdon in 1943 before the management would agree to eliminate pay differentials between men and women. It is significant that when an amendment was successfully tacked on to the Butler Education Act in 1944, providing equal pay for men and women teachers, Churchill insisted that the vote be reversed on the following day. The battle for equal pay had still to be won, despite some successful skirmishes. In January 1944 women in the engineering industry were still being paid roughly half what men were earning.

The war had less tangible effects. Many women had the chance to do important jobs, both in the services and in industry. The number of domestic servants declined from 6% of the working population before the war to 3% after it. The Parliament elected in 1945 contained 25 women MPs, the majority in the Labour party.

Greater sexual licence was an inevitable consequence of war-time separations. The divorce rate rose from 10000 in 1939 to 25000 in 1945, while the one-parent family was viewed less critically. But these changes might have taken place anyway, and it would certainly not be true to say that the war weakened family ties. As after the First World War, many women returned readily enough to the domestic roles of wife and mother. The post-war boom in the birth rate suggests that the rearing of children was still seen as an attractive alternative to a career when there was little opportunity to combine the two.

Changes in the Role of Women

The bargaining power of labour was strengthened in the Second World War as it was in the First. This time, however, there was a National government almost from the start and a powerful trade unionist, Ernest Bevin, in the War Cabinet. Trade union membership rose from 6298000 in 1939 to 8803000 in 1946. The Amalgamated Engineering Union more than doubled its membership, partly by including women for the first time, to reach a total of 909000. Bevin's union, the Transport and General Workers' topped the million mark.

Bevin insisted that collective bargaining must be allowed to continue, but only under constraints. He tried to insist on compulsory arbitration and strikes were officially banned under Order 1305. In practice, as other governments have discovered, strikes cannot be prevented by government *fiat*. In 1943 there were 1785 strikes

Changes in the Position of Organised Labour

causing the loss of 1.8 million working days. The figures for 1944 were worse: 2194 strikes and a loss of 3.7 million working days. The government's impotence was demonstrated by the strike at Betteshanger in the Kent coalfield in 1942. The local leadership were imprisoned and 1000 miners were fined up to £3.00 per head. Only nine fines were paid. Most strikes were confined to the coal industry, still plagued by bad industrial relations, engineering and the docks. They rarely lasted longer than a week and only had a serious effect on output in the coal industry.

Bevin's position in the War Cabinet ensured that the TUC's voice was heard on a number of issues. Its advice was sought on rationing, pricing policy and the dilution of labour. George Woodcock, then Head of the Research and Economic Department at the TUC, described the relationship in these terms:

Harrington and Young,
The 1945 Revolution

> The Government had two motives – morale and help. They wanted to keep us sweet, not on the outside criticizing and we put to them things they would have missed ... We had regular committees with the Minister of Labour. We also had regular meetings with the Ministry of Food and with the Board of Trade on clothes rationing. These committees were totally different from the *ad hoc* deputations between the wars. They were regular – monthly, fortnightly or even more often. [Harrington and Young, p. 127]

Another development was the introduction of Joint Production Committees on which Unions and Management would both be represented. They were started on the initiative of the Ministry of Supply in Royal Ordnance Factories. The government gave their official blessing to the idea but refused to make such committees compulsory. Even so, by 1943 there were 4500 JPCs or their equivalents, covering some 3.5 million workers. Unfortunately, by 1948 only 550 survived and industrial relations reverted to the adversary relationship which has had such damaging consequences.

Bevin also did something to protect the living standards of those workers who were not unionised. The Catering Wages Act of 1943 set up a Catering Wages Commission with power to determine wages, hours and holidays for all who worked in the industry. In 1945 he renamed the Trade Boards first established by Churchill in 1908 as Wages Councils, and extended their scope. By 1950, 4.5 million workers came under their umbrella.

After the humiliating defeat inflicted on the trade union movement by the failure of the General Strike in 1926, the Second World War brought a recovery in its power and status. The position of the manual worker improved during the war partly as a result of this recovery. But more important than the gains made by trade unions was the shift in public opinion that took place during the war, leading to the first outright victory for the Labour party.

Changing Attitudes

Changes in public opinion are notoriously difficult to measure and have to be inferred from a variety of evidence, ranging from public opinion polls to by-election results, the comments of informed observers and circulation figures of books and newspapers. Haphazard as it may be, the evidence can at least indicate a trend, and that trend between 1939 and 1945 was steadily towards the Left. The popularity of J. B. Priestley's broadcasts after the 9 00 pm news; the support for anti-Conservative candidates at by-elections; the growing circulation of the *Daily Mirror*, which went up from 1 750 000 to 3 000 000 during the course of the war; and the growing demand for the *Penguin Specials* on social and economic issues: all indicate an increasing sympathy for a more socially just society.

The main church leaders shared this concern. In January 1941 a Conference was held under the auspices of the Industrial Christian Fellowship at Malvern where doubts were raised about the ethics of capitalism. William Temple, who became Archbishop of Canterbury in 1942, had at one time been a full member of the Labour party. His book, *Christianity and the Social Order*, one of the *Penguin Specials*, called for an end to inherited wealth, priority for wages over dividends and a long list of social reforms.

W. Temple, *Christianity and the Social order* (Penguin, 1942)

A good indicator of the shift in public opinion can be seen in attitudes towards the Soviet Union. After June 1941 the disillusion created by the Nazi-Soviet Pact was dispelled. Russia was now a gallant ally and as its economic system proved capable of resisting the strains of war, so Communism came to seem less pernicious. After the siege of Stalingrad, a silver sword was forged in honour of the city and exhibited round the country before being sent as a personal tribute from George V to the people of Stalingrad. Moore-Brabazon, Minister for Aircraft Production after Beaverbrook, tactlessly remarked in July 1941 that it would suit Britain best if Germany and Russia fought each other to a standstill. His views were angrily repudiated and he was dropped at the next cabinet re-shuffle in February 1942. Most revealing of the change in official attitudes is the reception given to George Orwell's *Animal Farm*. This was a none too carefully disguised satire on the Soviet Union's totalitarian system of government. When Orwell sought a publisher in 1944, the manuscript was first rejected by Gollancz for being too hostile to Communism and then when Jonathan Cape considered it, a Ministry of Information official advised against publication because of the damage it might do to Anglo-Soviet relations. [Crick, p. 315] Faber and Faber also turned it down, and the book was finally published by Warburg in August 1945. When the political and literary establishment were so concerned about the danger of offending the Soviet Union it was hardly to be expected that the man in the street should be critical. The prison camps of the Gulag Archipelago were invisible before 1945 and the spectre of Communism no longer a threat to left-wing causes.

B. Crick, *George Orwell, A Life* (Penguin, 1982)

This impression was confirmed by the results of a survey carried out by the Home Intelligence Unit of the Ministry of Information in 1942. The survey investigated the evidence for signs of 'home-made socialism'. All but two of the thirteen regions reported that 'something of the kind was in the making'. In its summary of the various regional reports, 'Home Intelligence concluded that the chief characteristics of the movement were

  (a) Its non-political character.
  (b) The impetus it has received from the Russian success.
  (c) A general agreement that 'things are going to be different after the war'.
  (d) A revulsion against 'vested interests', 'privilege', and what is referred to as 'the old gang'.
  [Addison, p. 163]

Addison, *The Road to 1945*

The more enlightened members of the Conservative party shared in the new concern for social justice. The Tory Reform Committee, formed in 1943, recalled Disraeli's goal of one nation and urged the need in one of its pamphlets 'to rebuild our country after the war not with the thought of money gain but with the thought of social purpose'. [Harrington and Young, p. 124] Churchill was prevailed on to go some way towards recognising this objective. In an important speech given in March 1943 he announced his support for compulsory national insurance and the maintenance of full employment; he also emphasised the need for improvements in education, housing and in the health services. A year later he repeated these pledges and introduced the idea of pre-fabricated houses as a short-term measure to ease the housing problem. Whichever party had won the General Election in 1945 would have been committed to an extensive programme of social reform.

Harrington and Young,
The 1945 Revolution

The 1945 General Election

The 1945 General Election can be interpreted in two ways. It can be seen, in one sense, merely to have ratified the changes which had already taken place in British political attitudes, the Labour government inheriting much of its programme from the Coalition. The goals had already been determined. On this view, all the Election did was to give to Attlee rather than Churchill the opportunity to put the Coalition's policies into effect. Alternatively, one can see the 1945 Election as a major turning-point in British politics, comparable with the 1832 Reform Act or the Liberal landslide in 1906. It was, after all, the first time that the electorate had returned a Labour government with an absolute majority, able to put its policies into effect without hindrance. At the time, the second view prevailed. In the remoter fastnesses of the Conservative party the announcement of the result was like the sound of the tocsin in the French Revolution. With the advantage of hindsight, it is the continuity between the policies of the Coalition and the Labour governments that catches the eye.

The Election began to all intents and purposes on 21 May 1945 when the Annual Conference of the Labour party voted overwhelmingly against Churchill's suggestion that the Election might be postponed until after the ending of the war with Japan. Churchill then resigned, formed a caretaker government from his own supporters and dissolved Parliament on 15 June. The 1945 Election has been neatly summarised as a conflict 'between a flamboyant personality whose policies seemed non committal and a committee policy advocated by a man who seemed to lack personality'. [Harrington and Young, p. 147] Churchill was used as the Conservatives' trump card. The Election manifesto was even titled: 'Mr. Churchill's Declaration of Policy to the Electors.' It reiterated the pledges on Full Employment, National Insurance and a National Health Service made in 1943; but it was studiously vague about controls and about how the new social benefits were to be financed. It made no reference to nationalisation. Nonetheless, taken as a whole, Addison concludes 'it was a sober restatement of the new wartime consensus'. [Addison, p. 265] Unfortunately for the Conservatives, the positive aspects of the Churchillian programme disappeared during the course of the campaign.

Harrington and Young,
The 1945 Revolution

Addison, *The Road to
1945*

The Labour manifesto, '*Let Us Face the Future*' was an equally sober document. It was essentially a team effort – neither Attlee's name nor his photograph appeared. Labour's programme made the same commitments to a Comprehensive Insurance Scheme, a National Health Service and improvements to Housing and Education but it differed from the Conservative manifesto in two important respects. It acknowledged the need to continue with physical controls in the interests of fairness:

'Homes for the people must come before mansions for the few.' The Labour party also made a specific promise to nationalise the Bank of England, fuel and power, internal transport and iron and steel. The Labour Manifesto cost twice as much as Mr Churchill's *Address*. It was also much better produced.

How much difference the campaign made to the eventual outcome is impossible to say. Each side made notorious gaffes. In his first election broadcast Churchill made a gross error of taste and judgment: 'I declare to you from the bottom of my heart that no Socialist system can be established without a political police. They [Labour] would have to fall back on some sort of *Gestapo*, no doubt very humanely directed in the first instance ....' Attlee, called on to comment, charitably attributed the inspiration of the remark to Beaverbrook, but on this occasion Beaverbrook was not to blame. It was Churchill's own blunder. Nor was it only Churchill who made the unfortunate link between the Labour party and Britain's erstwhile enemies. Lieutenant-Colonel A. P. Wise, standing for Epping where he was defeated, described Socialism as 'only Fascism with a dirty shirt'. Captain H. Balfour, Conservative candidate for Portsmouth, made a similar gibe: 'The Socialist state of Cripps is the same as the Fascist state of the Blackshirts'. [Harrington and Young, p. 164]

Harrington and Young,
The 1945 Revolution

Labour blunders were less serious. Harold Laski, Chairman of the Labour party, suggested that Attlee, who had been invited by Churchill to attend the Potsdam Conference, could not commit the Labour party to any policy which had not previously been endorsed by the National Executive Committee. This led to the charge that any Labour Prime Minister would be 'a mere tool in the hands of a non-Parliamentary body ...' [Attlee, p. 145] The Conservatives exploited the Laski bogey for more than it was worth, and it failed to frighten the electorate.

C. R. Attlee, *As it Happened* (1954)

The Election aroused intense interest. Every Election broadcast, ten for each of the two major parties, and four for the Liberals, attracted huge audiences. Public meetings were crowded out. Churchill's progresses were heartily cheered, even by those who had no intention of voting for him. After a ten-year gap the British electorate took their responsibilities very seriously and the eventual results tallied closely with a Gallup poll published by the *News Chronicle* on 11 July. Polling started on 5 July and continued until 19 July to allow those serving overseas or away on holiday to have the chance to vote. The results were declared on 26 July. They were as follows:

Party	Total Vote	%	Seats
Conservative	9 888 306	39.8	213
Labour	11 955 152	47.8	393
Liberal	2 248 226	9.0	12
Communist	102 780	.4	2
Commonwealth	110 634	.4	1
Other	640 880	2.0	19
Total			640

There was a swing of about 12% to the Labour party whose vote went up by about 3.6 million. The Conservative vote fell by 1.7 million. In terms of seats, Labour gained 227, the Conservatives lost 172. Thirteen Conservative ministers of cabinet rank lost their seats, including Harold Macmillan, Brendan Bracken and Duncan Sandys. Margaret Roberts, the future Margaret Thatcher, was 'amazed' at the result. Churchill was less surprised; he had had premonitions of defeat. But he kept his sense of humour: 'He confessed that it was distressing after all these years to abandon the reins of power. Someone said: "But at least, sir, while you held the reins, you managed to win the race." "Yes" said Winston, "I won the race – and now they have warned me off the turf."' [Nicolson, p. 479] When Clementine Churchill consoled her husband with the suggestion that his defeat might be a blessing in disguise, he remarked: 'At the moment it seems quite effectively disguised.' To his doctor, Lord Moran, he was more philosophic. Moran charged the British people with ingratitude. Churchill answered at once: 'Oh, no, I wouldn't call it that. They have had a very hard time.' [Calder, p. 585]

Nicolson, *Diaries and Letters, 1939–45*

Calder, *The People's War*

BIBLIOGRAPHY BIBLIOGRAPHY BIBLIOGRAPHY BIBLIOGRAPHY BIBLIOGRAPHY BIBLIOGRAPHY BIBLIOGRAPHY
BIBLIOGRAPHY BIBLIOGRAPHY BIBLIOGRAPHY BIBLIOGRAPHY BIBLIOGRAPHY BIBLIOGRAPHY BIBLIOGRAPHY
BIBLIOGRAPHY BIBLIOGRAPHY BIBLIOGRAPHY BIBLIOGRAPHY BIBLIOGRAPHY BIBLIOGRAPHY BIBLIOGRAPHY
BIBLIOGRAPHY BIBLIOGRAPHY BIBLIOGRAPHY BIBLIOGRAPHY BIBLIOGRAPHY BIBLIOGRAPHY BIBLIOGRAPHY
BIBLIOGRAPHY BIBLIOGRAPHY BIBLIOGRAPHY BIBLIOGRAPHY BIBLIOGRAPHY BIBLIOGRAPHY BIBLIOGRAPHY
BIBLIOGRAPHY BIBLIOGRAPHY BIBLIOGRAPHY BIBLIOGRAPHY BIBLIOGRAPHY BIBLIOGRAPHY BIBLIOGRAPHY

CHAPTER 11
FURTHER READING

War Time Politics

Essential
P. Addison, *The Road to 1945 – British Politics and the Second World War* (Cape, 1975)
M. Gilbert, *Winston S. Churchill, Finest Hour* (Heinemann, 1983)
W. Harrington and P. Young, *The 1945 Revolution* (Davis-Poynter, 1978)

Recommended
C. R. Attlee, *As it Happened* (Heinemann, 1954)
A. Bullock, *The Life and Time of Ernest Bevin, vol. II* (Heinemann, 1967)
B. Donoughue and G. W. Jones, *Herbert Morrison* (Davis-Poynter, 1973)
K. Harris, *Attlee* (Weidenfeld & Nicolson, 1982)
J. W. Wheeler-Bennett, *King George VI – His Life and Reign* (Macmillan, 1958)

The Effects of the War on Society and the Economy

Essential
A. Calder, *The People's War: Britain 1939–1945* (Cape, 1969)
A. Marwick, *Britain in the Century of Total War* (Bodley Head, 1968)
A. S. Milward, *The Economic Effects of Two World Wars on Britain* (Macmillan, 1972)
S. F. Pollard, *The Development of the British Economy* (Arnold, 1983)

Recommended
M. Bruce, *The Coming of the Welfare State* (Batsford, 1961)
E. R. Chamberlin, *Life in Wartime Britain* (Batsford, 1972)
D. Fraser, *The Evolution of the British Welfare State* (Macmillan, 1983)
H. Nicolson, *Diaries and Letters, 1939–45*, Nigel Nicolson (ed.) (Collins, 1967)
J. A. Winter (ed.), *War and Economic Development* (CUP, 1975)

LOCAL RESEARCH PROJECT

The Effects of the Second World War

As with the First World War it is possible to trace the effects of the war through the experiences of individuals and particular units. Air power added a new dimension to warfare. Squadrons both in Fighter Command and in Bomber Command were usually tied to particular airfields, and their histories can be followed through, as with county regiments. Another obvious line of enquiry is to investigate the effects of air raids on particular cities.

The Second World War required the mobilisation of the whole working population and the control of all the nation's resources. The reach of central government extended further than it had ever done before. The effects of such control could be studied in relation to the evacuation of children during the Blitz; the extension of rationing; the direction of labour; and the organisation of emergency services such as the Air Raid Precaution Service, the Home Guard and the National Fire Service.

Changes in public attitudes to the war, and in attitudes to the form society should take when the war was over, might be assessed through the editorials and correspondence columns of local newspapers. Most political activity was suspended during the war, but there were some by-elections, and these would repay investigation.

Suggested sources of information

Introductory

Autobiographies

Out of a wide selection, these are among the best:

P. Cochrane, *Charlie Company* (North Africa and the Italian Campaign) (Chatto & Windus, 1977)

R. Hillary, *The Last Enemy* (the RAF and the Battle of Britain) (Pan Books, 1969)

J. F. W. Mallallieu, *Very Ordinary Seaman* (the Arctic Convoys) (Mayflower Books, 1978)

R. Rhodes-Jame, *Chindit* (the Burma Campaign) (John Murray, 1980)

R. Trevelyan, *The Fortress* (the Italian Campaign) (Penguin, 1956)

The best account of the experiences of the front-line soldier is to be found in John Ellis, *The Sharp End of War* (David & Charles, 1980). M. Middlebrook's *The Nuremberg Raid* (Allen Lane, 1973) gives an authentic account of one of Bomber Command's least successful air raids.

The domestic impact of the war is best described in Angus Calder's *The People's War, 1939–1945* (Cape, 1969), and this may be supplemented by A. Marwick's *Britain in the Century of Total War* (Bodley Head, 1968). *Living through the Blitz* (Collins, 1976) by Tom Harrisson gives a selection of observers' reports on the impact of bombing on civilian morale and attitudes. M. Wainwright's *The Bath Blitz* (Kingston Press, 1982) is an admirable study of the effects of an air raid on a British city. P. Addison, *The Road to 1945* (Cape, 1975) is the best guide to changes in public attitudes.

Further sources

The best source on the impact of the war is undoubtedly the Mass Observation Archive presently kept in Sussex University Library. The Archive was compiled from contributions sent in by observers all over the country who were commissioned for the purpose. It covers the years 1937 to 1950, and is open to researchers, providing an appointment has been made with the archivist beforehand. An anthology from the Archive has already been published, *Speak for Yourself*, Angus Calder and Dorothy Sheridan (eds.) (Cape, 1984). A paperback edition is to be published by the OUP in 1985.

Local newspapers should again be a useful mine of information, and the local County Record Office will probably have records of the emergency services and correspondence with central government departments.

For more recent decades such as this one, another source becomes available. There are plenty of eye witnesses of, and participants in, the events of the Second World War waiting to be interrogated if they can only be identified. Friends and relatives can provide an initial contact in many cases. Regimental histories and museums could be another starting point. Finally, the local newspaper and a telephone directory together should be able to provide some clues.

TIME CHART 1930–45

Date	Social and Economic	Political	Foreign Affairs	The Empire and Ireland
1930	*Feb.* Economic Advisory Council set up. *Mar.–May* Mosley Memorandum considered and rejected. *Dec.* Unemployment reached 2.5 million. Employment Act, Coal Mines Act. Greenwood Housing Act.	*May* Mosley resigned from cabinet. House of Lords rejected educational and electoral reforms.	*May* Young Plan on Reparations.	*Mar.* First Civil Disobedience campaign in India. *Jun.* Simon Commission Report. *Jun.* Iraq Mandate ended. *Oct.* Passfield White Paper restricted Jewish immigration. *Nov.* First Round Table Conference on India.
1931	*Mar.* May Committee appointed. *Jul.* May Report published. *Jul.–Aug.* Foreign Exchange crisis. *11 Sep.* Snowden's Budget, Means Test. *15 Sep.* Invergordon Mutiny. *21 Sep.* Britain left Gold Standard.	*Feb.* Mosley founded New Party. *23 Aug.* Cabinet split. *24 Aug.* National Government formed. *28 Sep.* MacDonald expelled from Labour party. *27 Oct.* General Election; victory for National government. *Nov.* Second National Cabinet formed.	*Sep.* Japanese invasion of Manchuria.	*Jan.* Gandhi released. *Sep.* Second Round Table Conference. *Dec.* Statute of Westminster.
1932	*Mar.* Import Duties Act. *Apr.* Exchange Equalisation Account set up. *Aug.* Ottawa Trade agreements. Bank rate down to 2%.	*Jul.* ILP disaffiliated from Labour party. *Sep.* Resignations of Sankey, Sinclair and Snowden. *Oct.* British Union of Fascists founded.	*Feb.–Jul.* World Disarmament Conference. *Jun.* Lausanne Conference on Reparations. *Oct.* Lytton Report on Manchuria.	*Jan.* Gandhi rearrested. *Mar.* De Valera became Irish premier. *May* Oath of Allegiance ended. *Jul.* Start of tariff war between Britain and Ireland.
1933	*Jun.–Jul.* World Economic Conference in London. Agricultural Marketing Act. Agricultural Adjustment Act. London Passenger Transport Board set up.		*Jan.* Hitler Chancellor of Germany. *Feb.* Japan resigned from League. *Mar.* F. D. Roosevelt inaugurated. *Oct.* German withdrawal from League. *Jun.–Jul.* World Economic Conference.	

Date	Social and Economic	Political	Foreign Affairs	The Empire and Ireland
1934	Unemployment Act; Unemployment Assistance Board set up. 10% cut in unemployment benefit restored. Special Areas Act. North Atlantic Shipping Act.	*Jun.* Fascist Rally in Olympia.	*Jun.* Nazi Purge. *Jul.* Dolfuss (Austrian Chancellor) murdered. *Sep.* Russia admitted to League.	
1935	*Feb.* NUWM demonstrations in South Wales and Sheffield.	*Jun.* MacDonald replaced by Baldwin. *Oct.* Lansbury replaced by Attlee as leader of Labour party. *14 Nov.* General Election; Conservative victory.	*Mar.* Germany adopted conscription. *Apr.* Stresa Conference. *Jun.* Peace Ballot results published. *Jun.* Anglo-German Naval Agreement. *Oct.* Invasion of Abyssinia; sanctions. *Dec.* Hoare-Laval Plan; Hoare resigned.	Irish Nationality Act. Government of India Act.
1936	*Oct.* Battle of Cable Street. *Nov.* NUWM demonstration in London. *Oct.–Nov.* Jarrow Crusade. Publication of Keynes's *General Theory of Interest, Employment and Money.*	*Jan.* Death of George V. *Dec.* Abdication of Edward VIII. Public Order Act.	*Mar.* Remilitarisation of Rhineland. *May* Hailie Selassie left Abyssinia. *Jun.* Sanctions ended. *Jul.* Start of Spanish Civil War. *Sep.* Non-Intervention Committee set up. *1 Nov.* Axis Pact announced.	*Apr.–Oct.* Arab revolt in Palestine. *May* Lord Linlithgow made Viceroy of India. *Aug.* Treaty with Egypt. *Dec.* Irish External Relations Act.
1937	Special Areas (Amendment) Act.	*May* Chamberlain replaced Baldwin. *Oct. Tribune* founded.	*Apr.* Bombing of Guernica. *Oct.* Roosevelt's Quarantine speech. *Nov.* Halifax's visit to Germany.	*Dec.* New Irish Constitution; claim to 32 Counties.
1938	Coal Royalties nationalised. Publication of Macmillan's *The Middle Way.*	*Feb.* Eden resigned as Foreign Secretary. *Dec.* Duff Cooper resigned as First Lord of Admiralty.	*Feb.* German Anschluss with Austria. *Mar.–Sep.* Czech crisis (see p. 286). *29 Sep.* Four Power Conference at Munich, Munich Agreement.	*Apr.* Tariff war ended. *Apr.* Britain gave up Irish Treaty ports. *Oct.* Peel Commission recommended Partition of Palestine.

Date	Social and Economic	Political	Foreign Affairs	The Empire and Ireland
1939	*Apr.* Military Training Act passed. *Jul.* Ministry of Supply set up. Unemployment down to 1.5 million.	*Jan.* Cripps expelled from Labour party. *Sep.* War Cabinet formed; Churchill to Admiralty.	*Mar.* Hitler occupied Czechoslovakia. *Mar.* Treaty of Guarantee to Poland. *Apr.* Treaties of Guarantee to Rumania and Greece. *May* Treaty of Guarantee to Turkey. *Aug.* Military talks with Russia. *23 Aug.* Nazi-Soviet Pact announced. *25 Aug.* Anglo-Polish treaty confirmed. *1 Sep.* Invasion of Poland. *3 Sep.* Britain declared war on Germany.	*May* White Paper limiting immigration into Palestine. *Sep.* All Dominions except Ireland declared war on Germany. *Sep.* Provincial governments resigned in India. Empire Air Training Plan in Canada.
1940	*Jan.* Food rationing introduced. *Jan.* Barlow Report published. *May* Ministry of Aircraft Production set up. *Aug.* Medical Planning Committee set up. *Sep.–Nov.* London 'Blitz'.	*Jan.* Dismissal of Hore-Belisha. *7–8 May* Debate on conduct of war. *10 May* Chamberlain resigned; Churchill made premier; War Cabinet reduced to five. *Oct.* Churchill elected leader of Conservative party.	*Apr.* Germany attacked Norway and Denmark. *Jun.* Italy declared war on Britain and France. *Jul.–Sep.* Battle of Britain. *Sep.* Destroyer deal with United States. *Oct.* Italy declared war on Greece.	*Aug.* British Somaliland invaded.
1941	*Feb.* Committee on Reconstruction set up. *Mar.* Lend Lease started. *Apr.* First budget based on resources. *Dec.* Conscription of women. Central Statistical Office set up.	*May* Vote of Confidence won by 477–3.	*Mar.* Germany defeated Yugoslavia. *Apr.* Germany defeated Greece. *Jun.* Germany invaded Russia. *Aug.* Atlantic Charter signed. *7 Dec.* Pearl Harbour. *8 Dec.* Japan attacked Hong Kong, Malaya. *Dec.* Germany, Italy declared war on United States.	*Jan.* British Somaliland recovered. *May* Revolt in Iraq.

Date	Social and Economic	Political	Foreign Affairs	The Empire and Ireland
1942	*Feb.* Ministry of Production set up. *May* Ministry of Fuel and Power set up. *Aug.* Scott Committee Report published. *Sep.* Uthwatt Committee Report published. *Dec.* Beveridge Report published. Clothes rationing introduced.	*Jul.* Vote of Confidence won by 476 to 25. *Jun.* Commonwealth party founded.	*Jan.* Arcadia Conference in Washington. *May* Treaty of alliance with Russia.	*15 Feb.* Surrender of Singapore. *Mar.* Japanese invasion of Burma. *Mar.* Cripps Mission to India. *Aug.* Congress passed 'Quit India' resolution; leaders arrested. *Aug.–Nov.* Civil disobedience campaign.
1943	*Feb.* Ministry of Town and Country Planning set up. *Jun.* Catering Wages Act passed. Unemployment down to 60 000.		*Jan.* Casablanca Conference. *Aug.* Quebec Conference. *Sep.* Armistice signed with Italy. *Nov.* Teheran Conference.	*Apr.* Malta awarded George Cross. *Oct.* Wavell made Viceroy of India.
1944	*Feb.* White Paper on National Health Service. *May* White Paper on Full Employment. *Jul.* Fleming Report on independent schools. *Aug.* Butler Education Act. *Nov.* Town and Country Planning Act.	*Feb.* West Derbyshire by-election won by Independent Socialist.	*Sep.* Second Quebec Conference.	
1945	*Mar.* Wages Councils replaced Trades Boards. *May* Family Allowances Act passed. By 1945, 220 000 houses destroyed; 60 595 killed in air raids.	*21 May* Labour party voted to end Coalition. *15 June.* Caretaker government. *Jul. 5–19* General Election; first overall Labour majority. *27 Jul.* Attlee made premier.	*Feb.* Yalta Conference. *8 May* German surrender. *Jul.* Potsdam Conference. *6 Aug.* Atomic bomb on Hiroshima. *9 Aug.* Atomic bomb on Nagasaki. *15 Aug.* Japanese surrender.	Burma recaptured.

CHAPTER 12

Conflict and Consensus, 1945–79

A ▬▬▬▬▬▬▬▬▬▬▬▬▬ PROBLEMS AND POLICIES

It has been calculated that the Second World War cost the British economy the equivalent of £7000 million, or a quarter of the national wealth. These losses were made up as follows:

Britain's Economic Problems in 1945

	£ million
Sale of overseas investments	1000
Increase in loans and sterling balances held by foreign countries	3000
Damage to property	1500
Depletion of gold and dollar reserves	152
Shipping losses	700
Depreciation and obsolescence of plant	900
Total	7252

More seriously, Britain had lost two-thirds of her export trade. In 1945 exports totalled £350 million, imports £2000 million. The central problem facing all post-war governments was how to make good this gap and to keep the balance of payments in equilibrium.

In 1945 approximately 5 million men and women were employed in the armed services. Their redeployment in civilian occupations would require a massive increase in the provision of jobs if full employment was to be maintained. Inflation had been successfully contained during the war by the imposition of taxation, rationing, wage and price controls. But it was doubtful for how long a war-weary population would submit to the continuation of these restraints. It could be anticipated that rising expectations would put an increasing strain on resources just at a time when more would have to be diverted into exports. Inflation was as serious a threat in peacetime as it had been during the war.

Every post-war government also had to face the problem of how to sustain a high level of economic growth, partly because it was only through economic growth that higher living standards could be achieved, partly because in an increasingly competitive economic environment a high rate of growth would be needed to win and to hold on to valuable export markets.

Economists have recommended a variety of solutions to these problems. A trade deficit may be corrected in several ways. Imports can be restrained through the use of quotas or tariffs; exports can be encouraged through the allocation of resources, the provision of export credits or by holding down domestic consumption. Devaluing the exchange rate should have the effect of reducing the price of exports to foreigners, while raising the cost of imports to domestic consumers. Assuming that both groups are responsive to changes in price, this should lead to an increase in the volume of exports and a fall in the volume of imports. All these devices were tried at one time or another.

Full employment depends on the maintenance of a high level of aggregate demand. A Keynesian-minded Treasury after 1945 and commitments by both parties to full employment ensured that until the 1970s Keynesian-style techniques to regulate the level of demand were used by successive Chancellors of the Exchequer. Tax rates and levels of public spending were altered not to balance the Budget but either to inject into or to withdraw from the economy the spending power needed to sustain full employment without risking inflation. A further refinement was the adoption of a wide range of regional policies designed to secure an even spread of employment throughout the country.

There was less unanimity about how to tackle inflation, for here treatment depended on diagnosis. If inflation was caused, as Keynes and his followers tended to argue, by the pressure of demand on limited resources, or by the effect of excessive wage demands on costs and prices, then the appropriate policies would be to reduce demand by increasing taxation and to reduce wage costs by some form of wage restraint. If, as Milton Friedman (the increasingly influential American economist) maintained, inflation is a monetary phenomenon which can wholly be explained by excessive increases in the supply of money, then its cure is simply a matter of restraining monetary growth. Until 1976 or so Keynesian remedies were the ones adopted. But as inflation and unemployment began to rise simultaneously in the 1970s the emphasis changed and control of the money supply assumed a new importance in economic policy.

The need to promote economic growth provoked a wide range of suggestions. At one end of the political spectrum the best governments could do was to create a competitive climate in which initiative and enterprise would be encouraged by, for instance, controlling monopolies and abolishing restrictive practices; at the other end state control of 'the commanding heights of the economy' (the phrase was Aneurin Bevan's) was urged as a necessary stage to a fully planned economy. In between these two positions a wide range of initiatives were to be suggested. Economies of scale were to be promoted through the encouragement of mergers (the Industrial Reorganisation Commission); small businesses were to be encouraged through tax concessions; labour was to be persuaded to move from the service into the manufacturing industries (the Selective Employment Tax); industry was to be made more efficient through the work of Development Councils (the National Economic Development Council and its satellites).

Governments of both political persuasions were agreed on the desirability of all these objectives. The problem each faced was how to reconcile the different policies needed to achieve them. Restraint of domestic consumption to free resources for exports might have the effect of increasing unemployment. Encouragement of economic growth, on the other hand, might precipitate a balance-of-payments crisis by causing a rapid increase in the import of raw materials.

The economy was also particularly vulnerable to outside influences. A rise in commodity prices, as in 1950–51 or in 1973–74, could have devastating effects on the terms of trade. A fall in world demand, as in 1974, was bound to affect employment. Economic policy was thus less a consistently pursued strategy than a series of attempts to square the circle, punctuated by desperate responses to sudden emergencies.

A fifth objective of economic policy was not shared by both parties. With its commitment to equality the Labour party sought, with varying persistence, to bring about a redistribution of wealth. This might be secured by progressive taxation, by increasing public expenditure on the social wage (social security benefits, expenditure on health and education for instance) and ultimately by confiscation, through death duties or the capital transfer tax, as it came to be called. Conservatives, on the whole, resisted such policies, arguing that high taxation had a disincentive effect on the creation of wealth from which all stood to benefit. But with this exception, Labour and Conservative Chancellors of the Exchequer pursued policies which were in many respects interchangeable, at any rate until the arrival of Margaret Thatcher at No. 10 Downing Street.

The Political Framework

Election results, 1945–83

Year	CONSERVATIVE			LABOUR			LIBERAL		
	Vote (million)	%	Seats	Vote (million)	%	Seats	Vote (million)	%	Seats
1945	9.9	39.8	213	11.9	47.8	393	2.2	9.0	12
1950	12.5	43.5	298	13.2	46.1	315	2.6	9.1	9
1951	13.7	48.0	321	13.9	48.8	295	0.7	2.5	6
1955	13.2	49.7	344	12.4	46.4	277	0.7	2.7	6
1959	13.7	49.4	365	12.2	43.8	259	1.6	5.9	6
1964	12.0	43.4	304	12.2	44.1	317	3.0	11.2	9
1966	11.4	41.9	253	13.0	48.0	363	2.3	8.5	12
1970	13.1	46.4	330	12.1	43.0	287	2.1	7.5	6
1974 (Feb.)	11.8	37.9	297	11.6	37.1	301	6.0	19.3	14
1974 (Oct.)	10.4	35.9	277	11.4	39.2	319	5.3	18.3	13
1979	13.6	43.9	339	11.5	36.9	268	4.3	13.8	11
1983	13.01	42.4	397	8.4	27.6	209	*7.9	25.4	23

* This figure includes votes for the Social Democrats, a party formed by a breakaway group of Labour MPs in 1981. They entered into an electoral agreement with the Liberals, known as the Alliance, prior to the 1983 General Election. Of the 23 seats gained, Liberals won 17, Social Democrats 6.

Year	S.N.P.			PLAID CYMRU		
	Vote (million)	%	Seats	Vote (million)	%	Seats
1966	0.128	0.5	—	0.06	0.2	—
1970	0.3	1.1	1	0.1	0.6	—
1974 (Feb.)	0.6	2.0	7	0.1	0.6	2
1974 (Oct.)	0.8	2.9	11	0.1	0.6	3
1979	0.5	1.6	2	0.1	0.4	2
1983	0.3	1.1	2	0.1	0.4	2

D. E. Butler and
A. Sloman, *British
Political Facts*
(Macmillan, 1975)

[Butler and Sloman, pp. 184–6 (amended)]

The 40 years since 1945 have not yet seen any major change to the two-party system which was re-established at the end of the Second World War. As can be seen from the figures in the Chart the Conservative share of the total vote has never fallen below 35.9%, and until 1983, the Labour share never dropped below 37%. In the 1950s the two major parties gained over 96% of the vote, and until 1974 they continued to attract the support of at least 80% of the electorate. It is true that there were signs that the pattern was being broken, first in 1964 when the Liberals gained 11.2% of the vote, and again in 1974 when their share rose to 19.3%. This year also witnessed a sudden rise in support for Welsh and Scottish Nationalism, the Scottish National party gaining eleven seats, and Plaid Cymru two in the October 1974 election. Support for all three parties dropped off in 1979 but by 1983 the emergence of the Social Democratic party and internal divisions within the Labour party caused a dramatic fall in the Labour vote to its lowest figure (8.4 million) since 1931. The share of the vote gained by the two largest parties fell correspondingly to 67.8%.

But the 'first past the post' system, under which there are no prizes for coming second, has ensured that the increased support for the Liberal party (and their Social Democrat allies) has never been reflected in seats won in the House of Commons. In February 1974, when the Liberal vote reached its peak, whereas the average vote per Conservative MP elected was 39 000 with a corresponding figure of 38 000 for every Labour MP, the average vote per Liberal MP was 352 000. Reasonably enough, the Liberal party has continued to protest at the unfairness of the electoral system but neither of the major parties has been prepared to sacrifice its own electoral advantage for the doubtful benefit of an increased Liberal presence in the House of Commons.

Two consequences have followed. The British electoral system has failed to register, in terms of seats, the loss of support for the two major parties; conversely it has magnified the effect of relatively small swings between them. Until 1983 there was no widespread or deep-seated shift in allegiance to one of the major parties comparable with the gains made by the Labour party in 1945. But even changes at the margin were sufficient to bring about changes in governments and subsequent reversals of policy.

Politically, the period divides up into five distinct phases: the Labour governments, 1945–51; the 13 years of Conservative rule, 1951–64; the second Labour administration under Harold Wilson, 1964–70; the Conservative government of Edward

Heath, 1970–74; and a third Labour government, first under Wilson and then under James Callaghan, 1974–79. The economic boundaries are rather different. Until 1970 the British economy was growing more or less continuously, and the problems of inflation and unemployment were contained without too much difficulty. There was a corresponding degree of consensus between the two main parties. From 1970 onwards the economic problems magnified and each party moved further away from the middle ground in their efforts to find solutions.

Two general characteristics may be observed; first, the 'swing of the pendulum', which has produced alternate Labour and Conservative governments, if not at regular intervals then at least in regular sequence. Between 1945 and 1984 Labour has been in power for 17 years, the Conservative party for 22. The second characteristic is what has come to be known as 'adversary politics'. Each party confronted the same problems and in many ways was forced to adopt identical policies for dealing with them. But each party has felt impelled to attack, and in some cases to reverse, the policies of its opponents. The differences have been magnified by political rhetoric. The intense arguments in the House of Commons and on television screens have often concealed a common agreement about objectives and a common failure to achieve them.

B   THE WORK OF THE LABOUR GOVERNMENTS, 1945–51

The Labour governments of 1945–51 were historic for a number of reasons. For the first time in its history the Labour party had a large overall majority over all other parties in the House of Commons (393–247). It enjoyed continuing support, losing only one by-election between 1945 and 1950. The Labour vote actually went up in the elections of 1950 and 1951. The Labour government succeeded in translating all its manifesto pledges into law; and perhaps most remarkable, in view of later developments, it avoided, until 1951, any serious splits and divisions. Few governments can boast such a successful record.

Personnel, the Party and the Programme

The government was headed by Clement Attlee, leader since 1935. Attlee's reputation has fluctuated. He was never 'a sheep in sheep's clothing' – an epigram doubtfully attributed to Churchill. His unassuming manner concealed a strong will and he succeeded in holding together a cabinet of powerful and disparate personalities. By all accounts he was an admirable chairman but he had his blind spots. Harold Wilson described him as 'tone deaf' on any economic question. [Morgan, p. 383] He greatly offended Aneurin Bevan by criticising him for failure to appear in evening dress on a formal occasion – Attlee was a stickler for such formalities. He could be abrupt to the point of callousness when dismissing a colleague; and he was very sparing of praise. More seriously, he has been accused of losing his grip at moments of crisis, notably during the 'convertibility' crisis of August 1947 (see p. 381), and again at the time of the split with Bevan in March 1951. [Morgan, pp. 345, 449] But whatever his weaknesses, his tenure of power was marked by more solid achievements than those of any of his successors.

K. O. Morgan, *Labour in Power, 1945–1951* (1984)

Attlee's most important supporter was Ernest Bevin, former General Secretary of the Transport and General Workers Union and Minister of Labour in the Churchill Coalition. To his own, and many others' surprise, Bevin was made Foreign Secretary. Here his robust anti-Communism enabled the Labour government to pursue what was in effect a bi-partisan foreign policy which appealed more to the Conservative party than it did to left-wingers in the Labour party. Attlee shared Bevin's views completely and Bevin, in return, gave his total loyalty to Attlee, firmly resisting any challenges to Attlee's leadership.

Attlee and Bevin en route to the Potsdam Conference just after Labour's election victory in July 1945

Herbert Morrison, previously a highly successful chairman of the Labour Group on the London County Council and Home Secretary under Churchill, was made Lord President of the Council and Leader of the House of Commons. He supervised domestic policy and was responsible for seeing the legislative programme through Parliament.

The new Chancellor of the Exchequer was Hugh Dalton. Dalton was a product of Eton and King's College, Cambridge, where he had studied Economics. He joined the Fabian Society while still an undergraduate and despite his social background, was firmly committed to the full Labour programme. As Chancellor, he put a higher priority on maintaining full employment than on containing inflation and he was to prove a useful ally to Aneurin Bevan when it came to financing the Health Service.

Sir Stafford Cripps, President of the Board of Trade, also came from an upper middle-class background. He was a man of strong Christian convictions but his political allegiance had been given to a variety of causes. By 1945 he had returned to the main stream of the Labour party and was to prove, when he became Dalton's successor at the Treasury, a surprisingly successful Chancellor of the Exchequer.

These five men were the core of the new government. One other deserves notice – Aneurin Bevan, who became Minister of Health. Bevan had learned his politics in the South Wales Coalfield and he was the most actively committed Socialist in the government. He accepted much of the Marxist indictment of capitalism but remained firmly wedded to Parliament. He was to prove an effective and constructive minister with a remarkable ability to win over his opponents in the medical profession.

While the members of the Attlee government differed in the strength of their commitments to Socialism they were all agreed on the main planks of the Labour manifesto: the extensive programme of nationalisation, the implementation of the Beveridge Report and the creation of the National Health Service. This agreement was shared by the other organisations in the party, the National Executive Committee, the Trade Union Congress and the Annual Conference. For a rare period in its chequered history the Labour movement was united, enabling its government to put through the most extensive legislative programme of any post-war administration. But the government's first priority was to ensure the country's economic survival, for this was the necessary foundation on which all its other achievements rested.

The Handling of the Economy: Balance of Payments

The balance of payments problem was the first to demand attention. In August 1945 President Truman abruptly announced the ending of Lend-Lease. Britain's continuing dependence on the United States for a whole range of imports made it imperative to negotiate a loan until such time as Britain's exporting industries had recovered. Keynes was despatched to Washington. He requested a loan of $6000 billion. In the end, he had to settle for $3700 billion, repayable over 50 years, at a rate of interest of 2%, payment of which would begin in 1951. Two further conditions were attached to the loan. Britain would have to dismantle her system of imperial preference and sterling would have to be made freely convertible in 1947. The Canadian government provided a further loan of $1500 billion. The cabinet agreed to the terms of the loan and it was approved in the House of Commons by 345 votes to 71.

The loan provided only a temporary respite. The deficit on the current balance of payments was £295 million in 1946, rising to £442 million in 1947. Whereas 42.5% of all imports into Britain came from the New World, only 14% of British exports went there in return. By July 1947 Britain's monthly trade deficit with the United States was running at $500 million. It was at this critical moment that the Labour government was obliged under the terms of the American Loan to announce that sterling was now freely convertible. This meant that any holder of pounds could use them to purchase dollars from the Bank of England's dwindling reserves. Within a month these had fallen by $542 million. On 21 August the government announced the suspension of convertibility. It had proved disastrous. But the shock injected a new note of realism into the economic policy. Dalton introduced an emergency budget designed to cut dollar imports. Unfortunately for Dalton he announced his intentions to a journalist of the *Star*, prior to his Budget speech, and for this indiscretion he was compelled to resign. But this had the beneficial consequence of bringing to the Treasury the one man in the Labour government who both understood the seriousness of Britain's economic position and had the resolution to do something about it — Sir Stafford Cripps.

Cripps concentrated his efforts on improving Britain's export performance, partly by reducing home demand, partly by providing incentives to exporters. He was remarkably successful. By 1949 exports had risen to 150% of their 1938 level. Britain's economic recovery was also assisted by the more generous response shown by the United States to Europe's economic plight. The ending of Lend-Lease in 1945 and the harsh terms of the United States Loan in 1946 were replaced in 1948 by the Marshall Plan. Under the Plan, Britain received economic aid to the value of $1263 million in 1948–49. The net result of Cripps's policies and American generosity was that Britain's balance of payments were in surplus for 1948 (+£7 million), 1949 (+£38 million) and 1950 (+£297 million).

The level of Britain's gold and foreign currency reserves, however, remained dangerously low. Under the Bretton Woods Agreement of 1944 the British government was committed to maintain the exchange rate of the pound to the dollar at $4.03. Despite Britain's improving trade performance in 1949, a bad set of monthly trade figures led to a wave of speculation against the pound in fear of a possible devaluation. Cripps, ill in a Swiss sanatorium, had always opposed devaluation. But on 21 July a group of young Economic Ministers, which included Strachey, Strauss, Jay and Wilson, reached the view that devaluation was now inevitable. On 29 July Attlee was given approval by the cabinet to take whatever steps he thought necessary and Wilson was deputed to carry this message to Cripps. Cripps reluctantly concurred with the decision to devalue the pound and on 29 August it was decided to reduce its value to $2.40, a fall of 30.5%. This decision was conveyed to the American government early in September and was finally announced by Cripps on 19 September. Devaluation has been hailed as a success and condemned as a failure. K. O. Morgan writes: 'The immediate consequences of devaluation were wholly satisfactory. The drain on the reserves was checked; exports soon began to flow again, especially to North America. The gold and dollar deficit shrank from $539 million in the third quarter of 1949 to a mere $31 million in the final quarter.' [Morgan, p. 386] Pollard is less complimentary:

Morgan, *Labour in Power*

In many ways, the devaluation was a turning point. It marked the failure of the Government's economic policy before its defeat at the polls in 1951. It was a flagrant violation of the Bretton Woods Agreement, in spirit if not in letter (the Fund being forced to sanction it as a virtual *fait accompli*), and contributed no little to its weakness and to the general disillusionment with the post-war international institutions. [Pollard, pp. 239–40]

S. F. Pollard, *Development of the British Economy 1914–1980* (1983)

Whatever view is taken of devaluation, the reserves did rise and the balance of payments surplus of £297 million in 1950 was the highest recorded during the Attlee administration. Unfortunately for Britain, 1950 also brought the outbreak of the Korean War. This led, among other things, to the stockpiling of raw materials by the United States and a consequent rise in Britain's import prices. This provoked another balance of payments crisis in 1951, with a current account deficit of £419 million. For this outcome the Labour government could not be held responsible and while mistakes may have been made both in the handling of convertibility in 1947 and in devaluation in 1949, there can be no doubt that the improvement in Britain's export performance left the British economy much better placed in 1951 than it had been in 1945.

The Labour government's record on unemployment was remarkably successful. Although the Beveridge Report had postulated a figure of 8.5% as likely, in practice unemployment rarely rose above 2%. It reached its highest level in the early months of 1947 when the combination of a fierce winter coupled with a coal shortage led to short-time working in industry and pushed the unemployment rate up to over a million. But the average figure for the year was only 480 000 and unemployment then dropped to 308 000 in 1949 and 314 000 in 1950. The government owed its success both to the good sense of its own policies and to favourable trends in the world economy. Dalton managed to keep interest rates down by pursuing a deliberate 'cheap money' policy. This encouraged both private investment and capital spending by local authorities. Public expenditure, much of it on post-war reconstruction, was kept at a high level. Growing world demand aided British exports. In these circumstances Keynesian-style policies for stimulating demand were hardly needed and in fact the government had a budget surplus every year after 1946. From the vantage point of 1984 it might appear either that the Labour government's employment policies were peculiarly inspired or that the government was exceptionally fortunate in its circumstances. In fact, both explanations have some validity. The real triumph of the Labour government was to achieve full employment without serious inflation. This was achieved, in the first instance, by maintaining controls on prices and by continuing to ration goods that were in short supply. Sir Stafford Cripps, Chancellor of the Exchequer from 1947 to 1950, was also successful in persuading the TUC to adopt a policy of wage restraint, both in 1948 and in 1949.

Full Employment

Though this policy was finally rejected in September 1950 for three precious years wages rose more slowly than prices, and the rate of inflation remained below 5% until 1951; the rise in import prices following the Korean War and the ending of voluntary wage restraint then pushed up the rate of inflation to 11.8%. It could be argued that the formula was only successful for a time and that industry was held back by the persistence of controls, but in the long run, as Keynes once remarked, 'we are all dead'. In the short term, Labour's policies for inflation and employment patently worked. The years 1945–51 were also years of rapid economic growth.

Control of Inflation

Domestic capital formation proceeded at an annual rate of 10.6% of net national product, on average, between 1948 and 1952. The annual increase in manufacturing output was 8% and the *per capita* increase (i.e. the growth of productivity) in all industry was 3%. This led to an annual rate of growth in real terms in the national income of 2%. This compared favourably with the rate achieved at any other period in Britain's economic history, and with the rate of her competitors in Western Europe and North America.

Economic Growth

Thus, in terms of the economic objectives outlined at the beginning of the chapter, the Labour governments of 1945 to 1951 were remarkably successful. This was not so apparent at the time, when the country appeared to lurch from one balance of payments crisis to another and living standards barely rose. But if life was austere the achievements were considerable.

Nationalisation

Clause Four, Section Four of the Labour Party Constitution, adopted in 1918, stated as Labour's aim 'To secure for the workers by hand or by brain the full fruits of their industry, and the most equitable distribution thereof that may be possible upon the basis of the common ownership of the means of production, distribution and exchange, and the best obtainable system of popular administration and control of each industry and service.' This commitment has remained, despite Hugh Gaitskell's attempt to have Clause Four removed at the Labour Party Conference in 1959. The party's attachment to nationalisation rests on a variety of motives. In the first place, perhaps, it represents a step towards a fairer society which has always been at the heart of the party's purposes. The private ownership of capital inevitably tends to promote inequality, whereas public ownership implies, even if it does not always result in, a sharing of the national wealth. The Marxist wing of the party has supported nationalisation as an essential element in a planned economy and because, according to Marxist reasoning, the contradictions within capitalism would in any case bring about its collapse. Finally, nationalisation has been defended on pragmatic grounds because it may lead to greater efficiency; the nationalisation of electricity, for instance, makes possible a national grid; nationalisation of transport, it was hoped, would lead to an integrated transport system.

Nationalisation was supported for all these reasons in 1945. If motives were mixed, so were views about which industries should be included, and about the form nationalisation should take. There were no doubts within the Labour party about the primary objectives: the fuel industries (coal, gas and electricity); docks, railways and inland waterways; the Bank of England; and cable and wireless. There were doubts about road transport, and serious divisions over the iron and steel industry.

There was also considerable uncertainty about how the nationalised industries should be organised, financed and controlled. Herbert Morrison advocated running the industries through semi-autonomous boards which would have an 'arm's length' relationship with the government and this was the pattern that was adopted. Existing shareholders were to be compensated for the full market value of their shares; more surprising, perhaps, was the decision that trade union representatives should not be allowed to sit on the controlling boards. This condition had led to a fierce argument between Bevin and Morrison in 1932 over the composition of the London Passenger Transport Board, with Morrison opposing trade union representation. By 1944, for rather different reasons, the General Council of the TUC had come round to Morrison's view:

It will be essential, not only for the maintenance and improvement of the standards and conditions of workpeople, but because of the power of independent criticism that they can exert, that the trade unions shall maintain their complete independence. They can hardly do so if they are compromised in regard to Board decisions which are not considered to be in their members' interests by the fact of their representatives' participation in them. [Pelling, p. 77]

H. Pelling, *Labour Governments, 1945–51* (1984)

Ironically, nationalisation thus perpetuated the adversary relationship between management and unions which characterised much of private industry in Britain, and at a time when West Germany was pioneering a system of worker representation both in public and privately owned concerns, the Labour party deliberately rejected this opportunity. It has proved an expensive mistake.

The financial obligations of the industries to be nationalised were not thought out very clearly, either. In most cases the industry concerned was under an obligation 'to break even', taking one year with another. But nothing was said about pricing policies or about the provision of capital for investment. Thus, despite the grandiose ambitions of Clause Four, the nationalisation programme of the Labour government was in practice confined in nearly every case to those industries for which a good case could be made on pragmatic grounds – about 20% of British industry as a whole. Manufacturing industry was left untouched, as were agriculture and the service industries. Public ownership made little difference to the work force. Perhaps the most significant change was the removal from the industries concerned of the commercial constraints to which they had been subject under private ownership. However, nationalisation was to bring in its train a whole series of problems.

The process of nationalisation went through remarkably smoothly, and is summarised below:

Industry	2nd Reading of Bill	Royal Assent	Vesting Day	Numbers Employed in 1951
Bank of England	29 Oct. 1945	14 Feb. 1946	1 Mar. 1946	6 700
Coal	29 Jan. 1946	12 Jul. 1946	1 Jan. 1947	765 000
Civil Aviation	6 May 1946	1 Aug. 1946	1 Aug. 1946	23 300
Cable and Wireless	21 May 1946	6 Nov. 1946	1 Jan. 1947	9 500
Transport	16 Dec. 1946	6 Aug. 1947	1 Jan. 1948	888 000
Electricity	3 Feb. 1947	13 Aug. 1947	1 Apr. 1948	176 000
Gas	10 Feb. 1948	30 July 1948	1 Apr. 1949	143 000
Iron and Steel	15 Nov. 1948	24 Nov. 1949	15 Feb. 1951	292 000
TOTAL				2 304 200

[Pelling, p. 90]

Pelling, *The Labour Governments, 1945–51*

Nationalisation of the Bank of England has been described by one prominent City figure, Nicholas Davenport, as 'a great non-event'. [Morgan, p. 101] On vesting day Bank shares became Treasury Stock and the Governor and Directors were in future to be appointed by the Chancellor of the Exchequer, but the Bank retained its semi-independent status. The existing Governor, Lord Catto, and his deputy, Cameron Cobbold, were both re-appointed to their positions, one trade unionist was made a Director. Nationalisation of cable and wireless equally made little difference. The operating company was now to be wholly rather than partly owned by the government, but no changes in management were involved. Civil Aviation had already been partially nationalised by the Conservative government before the war. Labour policy merely involved a division of the existing British Overseas Airways Corporation (BOAC) into three concerns: BOAC itself, now responsible for long-distance routes; British European Airways; and South American Airways. The changes aroused little opposition and the massive costs of developing airlines could not have been met without government intervention.

Morgan, *Labour in Power*

Much of the electricity supply industry had already been taken over by Baldwin's government in 1926. All that happened under Labour was the transfer to the British Electricity Authority of the generating stations still under private or municipal control and the setting up of 14 regional boards which would have responsibility for distribution. This measure was also generally welcomed.

Nationalisation of the coal industry had been recommended by the majority of the Sankey Commission's members in 1919 and the industry's record since then had only strengthened the case for nationalisation. A first step was taken with the nationalisation of Coal Royalties in 1938 and during the war the Reid Committee had recommended the reorganisation of the industry, with the aim of concentrating production in the larger and more economic pits. The mine owners, strongly supported by Churchill, continued to resist any form of public ownership, however, and without Labour's strong commitment to it, nationalisation of coal would never have gone through. Unfortunately, while there was no hesitation about the objective little had been done by way of detailed preparation. Shinwell, who had been Minister for Mines in 1924 and again from 1929–31, complained somewhat unreasonably when given responsibility for the coal industry in 1945 that 'nothing practical and tangible existed'. [Pelling, p. 79] The Morrison pattern was eventually adopted. A National Coal Board was set up under the chairmanship of Lord Hyndley, previously a mining company director. Two trade unionists were also appointed: Walter Citrine, previously General Secretary of the TUC, and Ebby Edwards, a former general secretary of the National Union of Miners. Each had to sever their links with the trade union movement and sat on the Board in their private capacities. Compensation to shareholders totalled £164 000 000, given in the form of fixed interest bearing government securities. This saddled the NCB with a considerable burden for in good and lean years alike these fixed interest payments would have to be met out of the industry's earnings. Nationalisation of the coal industry was met with acclaim in the coal fields and it was certainly the most popular of all the government's nationalising measures. But Attlee's prediction that the Coal Board was going in to bat on 'a sticky wicket' proved more accurate than his belief that 'it would score a great many sixes'. [Pelling, p. 80]

Pelling, *The Labour Governments*

Nationalisation of the coal industry at the pithead

CONFLICT AND CONSENSUS, 1945–79

Nationalisation of the transport industries should ideally have led to an integrated transport system, and this was certainly the objective of the Transport Act. A National Transport Commission was set up with five separate executives under it for railways, docks, inland waterways, road transport, London transport and hotels. The only serious controversy arose over the attempt to bring small firms into public ownership. Small road operators whose journeys were limited to a radius of forty miles were issued with 'C' licences; in the end the Government relented and such firms were not taken over. The number of 'C' licences rose sharply after nationalisation.

Nationalisation of the gas industry could be justified on the same grounds as were used for electricity. Most gas production was already in the hands of municipal authorities and a nationally controlled distribution network made obvious sense. The Gas Bill was introduced in 1948. It set up a Gas Council with overall responsibility for the industry and 14 area boards which corresponded where possible with the Electricity Boards. The Act should have gone through without difficulty had the Conservative party not used it as a weapon to delay the nationalisation of steel which was waiting its turn – 800 amendments were tabled, most of them trivial, for instance whether nationalisation should be spelt with an 's' or a 'z'. (The Oxford Dictionary allows both.) The Standing Committee on the Bill had to sit continuously for 50 hours at one point, but the Bill got through on schedule.

Nationalisation of the iron and steel industry was much the most contentious of Labour's measures. There were serious doubts among civil servants; Sir Edward Plowden, for instance, described it as 'an act of economic irresponsibility'. Two Labour MPs, Alfred Edwards and Ivor Thomas, opposed it. Edwards was expelled from the party and Thomas resigned from it in consequence. The steel unions were also divided. The Iron and Steel Trades Confederation supported 'full and immediate nationalisation', but Lincoln Evans, general secretary of the Iron and Steel Workers Union consistently opposed nationalisation. A further obstacle was provided by the House of Lords. Knowing that the House of Lords would certainly reject any bill to nationalise iron and steel, the Government had either to reduce the delaying powers of the Lords from two years to one year or face the prospect of postponing nationalisation until after the forthcoming General Election. It was these pressures which determined the uncertain course of the Iron and Steel Bill. The House of Lords' delaying power was indeed reduced to one year by the Parliament Act of 1949, the Iron and Steel Bill having been introduced in October 1948. In all, 107 companies, employing 200 000 workers, were to be taken over, but the general structure of the industry was to be left largely unimpaired.

In the end a compromise was reached between Labour and Conservative leaders in the House of Lords under which the passage of the Iron and Steel Bill was agreed to on condition that vesting day would be delayed until after the next general election. It was not in fact until 15 February 1951 that the iron and steel industry finally and briefly passed into public ownership.

By the end of 1949 Labour's programme of nationalisation had effectively been accomplished. But two main questions still remained to be resolved. Were the industries taken into public ownership to be treated as commercial undertakings, subject to the same laws of supply and demand as firms in the private sector? Or were they to take into account wider social costs and benefits? Secondly, if nationalisation was appropriate for some industries, where was it sensible to draw the line? Answers to these questions have still to be found.

The Welfare State

National Insurance

The Labour party was committed to the implementation of the Beveridge Report as was the Conservative party by 1945. Two Acts were passed whose purpose was to extend and consolidate existing legislation. The National Insurance Act of 1946 brought under the same umbrella all the benefits which had previously been the responsibility of different departments: unemployment insurance (Ministry of Labour); Workmen's Compensation (Home Office); and Sickness Benefit (Ministry of Health). Rates of benefit were fixed at 26/- per week for a single person and 42/- per week for a married couple, which represented a slight increase, in real terms, on pre-war scales. In a non-inflationary age it was hopefully anticipated that revision of these scales would only need to take place at five-yearly intervals. Contributions were fixed at a level intended to make the scheme self-financing. The self-employed were to pay 5/9d. per week, the employed 4/7d. per week. Maternity grants and allowances and a death grant to cover funeral expenses were also introduced. The Act built on foundations previously laid by Lloyd George in 1911, 1912 and 1920 and involved no new principle. But Insurance was now made compulsory and the benefits provided were intended to cover all the hazards of human existence.

For those who for one reason or another still slipped through the net, the National Assistance Act, passed in 1948, provided a further safeguard. This Act swept away the last vestiges of the Victorian Poor Law. Those not covered by National Insurance, the chronic sick for instance, and those whose benefits were inadequate were now able to claim further financial help from the National Assistance Board. A further measure of protection was provided by the Industrial Injuries Act of 1948. This raised the benefit payable to those disabled at work, for instance miners suffering from pneumoconiosis, to 40/- a week and made the State rather than the employer responsible for payment.

Britain could at last claim to have a comprehensive system of insurance which would remove the burden of financial hardship from those in need. The scales of benefit have never been as lavish as critics of the Welfare State have sometimes maintained and the number of those who exploited the system was never as great as those who have failed to claim the benefits that were their due. Nonetheless, once the State entered upon a commitment to underwrite a fully comprehensive and universal system of insurance it became increasingly difficult to set finite limits to expenditure. So long as the national income was increasing, benefits could be allowed to increase broadly in line with wages and prices and problems did not arise. But with mounting unemployment and an actual fall in output, as was experienced in the late 1970s, the implicit conflict between beneficiaries and taxpayers became more explicit. Thus, while there was virtual unanimity in 1945 about the desirability of the National Insurance and National Assistance legislation put through by the Labour government, the scale of benefits and contributions has come to be an increasing source of friction.

The National Health Service

A National Health Service had been envisaged in the White Paper produced by the Coalition Government in February 1944, but the form it would take had still to be agreed with the medical profession. The new Minister of Health, Aneurin Bevan, was determined to have a Health Service that would be both free (in the sense that treatment would not be related to the ability to pay for it) and comprehensive. On the recommendation of his chief civil service adviser, Sir John Hawton, Bevan decided that all hospitals must be taken over, apart from the main teaching hospitals for whom separate arrangements would be made. To ensure an even spread of doctors throughout the country, the sale and purchase of practices would have to be forbidden and doctors would not be allowed to set up in practice in areas where there were already enough of them. On these matters, Bevan was not prepared to bargain. But he was prepared to be flexible on other issues. Consultants were to be allowed to take private patients and to treat them in pay beds in National Health Service hospitals. General practitioners were to receive remuneration in the form of a basic salary, a capitation fee based on the number of NHS patients on their lists, and on any fees gained from private patients. Doctors would also be free to decline to have any patient on their list, just as patients would be free to change doctors when they wished. In this way, Bevan hoped to preserve the sanctity of the doctor–patient relationship. Bevan also offered to provide £66 million to compensate those doctors who had bought their practices but would now be prevented from selling them.

The National Health Service Act embodying most of these proposals was passed in November 1946. It was to come into force on 5 July 1948. But despite Bevan's concessions, the British Medical Association waged a determined campaign to make

Anevrin Bevan with some nurses on 5 July 1948, the day the national health service came into operation

the scheme unworkable. A referendum held under its auspices in December 1946 voted by 54% to 40% to suspend all negotiations with the Minister. The deadlock continued for over a year. In February 1948 the Government had a debate on the question of its determination to inaugurate the National Health Service on the date appointed. Bevan dealt in detail with each of the BMA's objections: the abolition of the sale and purchase of practices; the provision of a basic salary; the difficulties which the scheme would bring to partnership agreements; and the possible loss of legal rights which doctors might now have to face. Despite his reassurances, a plebiscite held shortly after the debate revealed that 45 569 doctors were still against joining the scheme as against 4735 in favour. The deadlock was finally broken in April 1948. At Lord Moran's suggestion, Bevan made a pledge in the House of Commons that no whole time salaried medical service would be established. He hoped that this would free doctors from the fear that they were to be turned into 'salaried civil servants'. This was enough to tilt the scales.

A second plebiscite still revealed a majority – 25 942 to 14 620 – against joining the NHS. But only a bare majority of GPs were now against the scheme. The Council of the BMA debated the results for seven hours and then, reluctantly, recommended their members to join.

On 5 July 20 000 (over 90%) decided to do so. Within two months, 93% of the population had registered as NHS patients. The somewhat hysterical campaign waged by the BMA proved to have been unnecessary as well as unsuccessful. In 1956 the Guillebaud Committee, appointed in 1953 by a Conservative Minister of Health, Ian Macleod, to investigate the NHS, produced its report. It concluded that while there were some weaknesses in the organisation, the NHS had been framed on sound lines, and that 'it would be altogether premature at the present time to propose any fundamental changes in the structure of the National Health Service'. Thus the Conservative party which had voted against the second and third readings of the National Health Service Bill in 1946 and again against the Government's motion to proceed with its inauguration in 1948, finally came round to accept the structure which Bevan had created.

Housing

Bevan was also responsible for Housing. Bombing had destroyed or damaged thousands of dwellings and there were still large areas in the England of the first industrial revolution where slums needed to be cleared. Skilled manpower and building materials were in short supply so that house-building inevitably got away to a slow start. Bevan concentrated his efforts on encouraging local authorities to add to their stocks of council housing and he laid down improved standards to which they were to adhere. Rival claims on resources from different government departments led to the creation of a powerful standing cabinet committee on housing chaired by Attlee. A Housing Production Executive was also set up in April 1946. The pace of construction increased from 139 000 houses completed in 1947 to 227 000 in 1948. The total number of houses built between August 1945 and December 1951 reached 1 016 349. The annual average figure was well below the target of 300 000 houses a year which Churchill set for Macmillan in 1951, but it was still no mean achievement.

Education

The continuity between the war-time Coalition and the Labour government is seen at its clearest in the sphere of education. Ellen Wilkinson, Minister of Education from 1945 to 1947, and her successor, George Tomlinson, both accepted without question the basic features of the 1944 Education Act and their educational policies were shaped by it. Ellen Wilkinson attached most importance to the raising of the school-leaving age to 15. It was agreed that 1 April 1947 should be the date at which this change would come into effect and Miss Wilkinson successfully resisted an attempt in the cabinet to postpone it. Both Ministers and many Labour MPs had been educated at maintained grammar schools and were anxious to retain this ladder of advancement. There was a general acceptance of the tripartite system of secondary schools provided for by the 1944 Act in the Ministry of Education, and in the cabinet. But doubts about the fairness of the eleven-plus examination surfaced as early as 1946 and in that year the Annual Conference passed a resolution condemning the system of selective schools. In 1950 a working party was set up by the National Executive Committee. In its Report the working party recommended the adoption of a system of comprehensive schools and in the election manifesto of July 1951 the party made a somewhat vague pledge 'to extend our policy of giving all young people equal opportunities in education'. But it was not until 1964, with the return of the next Labour government, that any steps could be taken to redeem that pledge.

The Achievement

When Attlee announced the inauguration of the National Insurance Act and the National Health Service on 4 July 1948 he said: 'They give security to all members of the family.' This was the essence of the Welfare State. Critics on the left could complain that the system of compulsory and comprehensive insurance and the provision of free medical treatment did little to affect the distribution of wealth. Private medicine and private education continued to flourish. The English class system reappeared in much of its old vigour once the mood of war-time unity had evaporated. Critics on the right attacked the whole concept of a Welfare State. Beveridge disliked the term because it implied rights rather than duties, even though he himself contributed much to its architecture. In the 1980s right-wing circles coined the phrase 'Nanny State' to voice their disapproval of a society where the State was given so much responsibility for the welfare of its citizens. Seen in perspective, the achievements of the Attlee government were still very considerable. Building on the foundations laid by Lloyd George in 1911–12, and supported by the war-time consensus arrived at by the Coalition government, Attlee and his team filled in the gaps in social security and removed from every family in the land the fear that ill health would bring either financial strain or would have to go untreated. Those who criticised the Welfare State for the generosity of its provisions were very rarely those who suffered from the hazards against which the Welfare State was designed to give protection. More difficult to meet is the criticism that the legislation passed between 1945 and 1951 failed to end poverty. Groups at risk such as old age pensioners, or one-parent families were still vulnerable because the statutory benefits were too low to provide an adequate standard of living. Unless they were prepared to claim extra support through National Assistance they were likely to go cold and hungry. Deaths from hypothermia could still occur. But such cases do not invalidate the achievement. No government after 1945 has attempted to dismantle the structure created by Attlee. It has needed refining and extending, in some cases trimming. The obligation of the State to ensure the well-being of all its citizens continues to be acknowledged even when it has not been met.

Further Measures

Besides the programme of nationalisation and its contribution to the Welfare State the Attlee government was also responsible for a number of other measures of considerable importance. Some were passed with party advantage in mind, others had a more general purpose. The first of the partisan measures was the repeal of the Trades Disputes Act of 1927. When the Act was passed the Labour party had promised to repeal it at the first available opportunity and in 1946 this promise was duly met. Repeal restored trade unions to the legal position they had enjoyed in 1906, in effect giving them complete immunity from the damages caused by industrial action undertaken for whatever reason. In the generally conciliatory relationship that existed between the TUC and the Labour party from 1945 to 1951 no doubts were felt about the freedom restored to trade unions. Things were to change in subsequent Labour governments.

The Labour party was also anxious to implement the principle of 'One man, one vote' by ensuring that no-one should enjoy two or more. This required the abolition of the 'business' vote which allowed owners of business premises an additional vote, and of the university seats for Oxford, Cambridge and the Scottish Universities which gave an extra vote to graduates of those universities. The Representation of the People Act, passed in 1948, ended these anomalies.

Despite the anachronistic composition of the House of Lords, the government showed itself less ready to attempt wholesale reform, much less abolition, of the Upper House. In the democratic mood of 1945 there was little danger of an hereditary chamber using its delaying powers to frustrate the will of the elected government. It was only when such a danger did materialise in the case of steel nationalisation that the Parliament Bill was framed to deal specifically with this threat. In the end, the Parliament Bill, reducing the delaying powers of the House of Lords to one year, was passed over the House of Lords veto by going through three successive sessions in the House of Commons and it became law in 1949. None of these measures would have been passed by a Conservative government but they met with general acquiescence.

There was a less partisan purpose in the Labour party's concern for the environment. Four important Acts were passed: the Distribution of Industry Act, 1946; the New Towns Act, 1946; the Town and Country Planning Act, 1947; and the National Parks and Access to the Countryside Act, 1949. Their total effect was to give both to national and to local governments a much greater degree of control over land usage and the location of industry. The Distribution of Industry Act offered a carrot in the shape of various grants and allowances to firms that would settle in the old depressed areas. The Town and Country Planning Act, among many other provisions, required all firms to obtain an Industrial Development Certificate before embarking on any industrial building, thus giving the government power to steer new industry to areas of high unemployment. The New Towns Act set up a number of government-financed corporations to develop new towns. By 1950, 15 such corporations had been set up, eight of them in the home counties. They bore fruit in places such as Basildon, Stevenage, Harlow, Milton Keynes near London, and further afield, in places such as Cumbernauld in central Scotland. The National Parks Act created a National Parks Commission with power to designate 'extensive areas of beautiful and relatively wild country' where special controls over development would apply. The Lake District, Snowdonia and the Peak District were the first to be selected. The Act ensured that the British countryside would be protected from the vandalism of commercial developers and it helped to make areas of outstanding natural beauty more accessible to the general public.

A final measure deserving to be mentioned was the Monopolies Act of 1948. The Labour Government's attitude towards the structure of private industry was ambivalent. Unwilling to endorse a policy of cut-throat competition, it was at the same time averse to the exploitation of the consumer by monopolists, or through the operation of restrictive practices such as price-fixing agreements. The Government's approach was typified by the Monopolies Act which set up a Monopolies and Restrictive Practices Commission, with powers to investigate any industry where one third of the output or more was in the hands of a single producer. The Commission had powers to make recommendations but no more than that. By 1951 only two minor industries had been investigated and no further action had been taken. The Act was a timid foray into the jungle world of take overs and mergers that was to characterise much of British industry in the 1950s and 1960s.

The End of Labour Rule

By 1949 the majority of the Labour party manifesto's plans had been realised and it was clear that the government would have to go to the country some time in 1950. Attlee canvassed the views of some of his colleagues but was evidently most impressed by the views of Cripps, who urged that the election should be held before rather than after the Budget, traditionally due in March or April. On 10 January 1950 Attlee announced that the election would be held on 23 February. The Labour Manifesto was largely produced by Herbert Morrison and Michael Young, secretary of the Research Department. It contained an undertaking to nationalise a ragbag assortment of industries, including industrial assurance, shipbuilding, ICI Ltd, water supply, the sugar industry and the cement industry. Tate & Lyle mounted an effective advertising campaign to show the serious effects that nationalisation of the sugar industry would have, and there was little logic about the choice of the other industries marked for State control. During the campaign itself the emphasis was rather on the government's record in maintaining full employment. When polling day came, Labour's total vote went up to 13.2 million, but its share of the vote fell to 46.1% and its majority was reduced to five over all other parties. This outcome was described by Dalton as 'the worst possible result. We have office without authority or power, and it is difficult to see how we can improve our position.' [Pelling, p. 230] Attlee felt much the same: 'It was, of course, obvious that with so slender a majority our position in the House of Commons was going to be very difficult, and that we could not embark on any major controversial measures, but the King's Government had got to be carried on, whatever the difficulties.' [Attlee, p. 196] The difficulties soon magnified. In July 1950 the Korean War broke out, imposing further strains on the balance of payments and requiring a big increase in defence spending. In October, Cripps was forced to resign because of ill health. In March 1951 Bevin had to be persuaded to give up the Foreign Office, also on the grounds of health. Attlee himself had to go into hospital the same month, just at a time when internal divisions in the party came to a head.

Pelling, *The Labour Governments*

C. R. Attlee, *As it Happened*

These divisions arose out of the Korean War. To meet the new threat posed by the Communists it was decided almost to double defence expenditure, to the point where it would absorb 14% of the Gross National Product. This decision was taken by the full cabinet but it created dissension. Hugh Gaitskell, who had replaced Cripps as Chancellor, had the task of raising £4700 million over the coming three years to meet the new defence budget. In the circumstances he was not prepared to see spending on the National Health Service rise by £30 million, as the new Minister of Health, Hilary Marquand, requested. A compromise was eventually struck under which Gaitskell agreed to an increase in expenditure from £393 million to £400 million on condition that charges were introduced to meet half the cost of dentures and spectacles. Bevan, who had been moved rather against his will to the Ministry of Employment, was not prepared to concede any departure from the principle of a free health service. He had also come to have considerable doubts about the scale of Britain's rearmament, having initially supported the increases. Disappointment over not getting the Foreign Office, which went to Morrison on Bevin's resignation, and jealousy of Gaitskell may also have contributed to his refusal to accept the compromise. Gaitskell introduced his budget on 10 April. On 22 April, *Tribune*, the left-wing periodical founded by Cripps in 1937, produced a savage attack on Gaitskell, comparing him with Philip Snowden in 1931. *Tribune* was edited by Jennie Lee, Bevan's wife, and Michael Foot, his devoted supporter. On 23 April Bevan delivered his resignation speech in which he attacked not only the imposition of charges for teeth and spectacles but the whole of the government's defence policy, arguing that the burden would prove insupportable. He was joined the following day by Harold Wilson, then a rising young minister at the Board of Trade, and by John Freeman, a junior minister at the Ministry of Supply. Though at the time these three were relatively isolated, they soon became the nucleus of a much larger group of disaffected MPs known as the Bevanites, and the argument over health service charges was only the first of a series of debilitating clashes between Bevan and Gaitskell.

The Government, harried by a merciless opposition, found that its paper-thin majority required the constant presence of members and ministers in the House of Commons if parliamentary defeats were to be avoided. The stress was considerable and got to the point where it was putting the health of some members at risk. King George VI, whose health was also a matter of concern, was planning to visit Australia in the spring of 1952. Attlee, anxious to spare the King the anxiety that he might have to be recalled in the middle of a royal tour, decided that another election must be held in the autumn of 1951, somewhat to the dismay of some of his colleagues. The date was fixed for 25 October. The 1951 Labour Manifesto did not mention the word Socialism, and contained no specific proposals beyond the promise to maintain full employment and to build 200 000 houses a year. The only reference to nationalisation was the statement: 'We shall take over concerns which fail the nation.' Despite, or perhaps because of, the vagueness of the Labour programme, the party's total vote again went up to a figure of 13.9 million, the highest ever recorded by any British political party, and the largest share (48.8%) of the vote that Labour had ever secured. But whereas in 1950 475 Liberal candidates had stood, in 1951 their numbers were reduced to 109. The Liberal vote tended to go to the Conservative rather than the Labour party and as a result, the Conservative vote also went up, this time to 13.7 million. Many Labour votes were 'wasted' in piling up huge majorities in working-class constituencies, while Conservatives made gains in marginal seats. As a result, the Conservative party finally gained a narrow but sufficient majority of 17 seats over all other parties (321–304). In view of the Labour party's troubled fortunes in the previous year, it was perhaps not surprising that the results were greeted with relief rather than disappointment. Dalton even described them as 'wonderful'. No one expected that 13 years in the wilderness were to come.

C ▬▬▬▬ THE YEARS OF CONSENSUS, 1951–70

In retrospect the years 1951–70 look like a golden age so far as the British economy was concerned. Unemployment never rose beyond one million and was more often well below that figure. The average annual rate of inflation between 1946 and 1960 was 4.5% a year and until 1969 it stayed within single figures. Britain's rate of economic growth may have been sluggish by continental standards but it averaged at least 2% a year. Living standards steadily improved, with real wages improving by about 20% between 1955 and 1970. Harold Macmillan was quite entitled to say, as he did in June 1957: 'Most of our people have never had it so good.' Anthony Crosland in his book *The Future of Socialism*, published in 1956, was even able to write: 'We stand in Britain on the threshold of mass abundance.'

The Economic Context

A. Crosland, *The Future of Socialism* (1956) (Cape, 1981)

Britain benefited from the general expansion in world trade that took place during these years. For much of the time the terms of trade moved in Britain's favour, with raw material prices falling in relation to the price of manufactured exports. The creation of the European Economic Community in 1957 brought economic stability to Western Europe from which Britain was also to benefit, just as she did from the rapid growth in the American economy during this period.

There were darker sides to the picture, however. The balance of payments remained a continuing source of concern, with deficits on the current balance (visibles + invisibles) in 1951, 1954, 1960, and in every year between 1964 and 1968. Unemployment remained disturbingly high in some parts of the country and the regional imbalance between the prosperous South East and Midlands and the old depressed areas in Scotland, Wales, Northern England and Northern Ireland was not corrected. While inflation never reached the levels of 1975, it remained a constant threat. Industrial relations, closely related to the movement of wages and prices, became increasingly acrimonious, and provoked a series of attempts to reform the process of collective bargaining.

Most seriously of all, Britain's rate of investment tended to lag behind that of her competitors; productivity in industry rose more slowly than it did elsewhere; and from about 1966 onwards an absolute fall in industrial employment began to set in. Both political parties had to face these problems and to a considerable extent they tried to apply the same solutions. The *Economist* coined the term '*Butskellism*' in 1951 to describe the consensus which it discerned between the policies of Butler and Gaitskell. Both parties were committed to the maintenance of full employment through the management of the economy, and to the improvement of the welfare state through increases in public expenditure. Thus, while elections continued to be hotly fought, they made less difference to policy than might have been expected, and the general improvement in the nation's economic position helped to soften the edges of party conflict.

Political Changes, 1951–70

From 1951 to 1964 the Conservative party enjoyed an unbroken hold on political power that was almost unprecedented in peace-time. Furthermore, at every election their position grew stronger. The Conservative majority of 17 in 1951 rose to 58 in 1955 and to 100 in 1959. For the first four of these years Churchill returned to the premiership; aged 77 he resisted his wife's advice to retire and, despite two strokes, only did so in 1955 at the behest of his senior cabinet colleagues. He took little interest in domestic policy, leaving the handling of the economy in the hands of R. A. Butler, Chancellor of the Exchequer; industrial relations in the hands of Sir Walter Monckton, Minister of Labour; and the fulfilment of the Conservative election pledge to build 300 000 houses a year to Harold Macmillan, the new Minister of Housing.

Anthony Eden at the outset of the Suez crisis, July 1956

In 1955 Anthony Eden at last succeeded to the premiership. Eden had already served 15 years as the heir apparent, Churchill having indicated as early as 1940 that he wished Eden to succeed him. Perhaps, as Eden himself put it, this long wait 'helped to dampen my exhilaration when the time came to succeed.' [Eden, p. 266] For Eden, too, foreign affairs took precedence over domestic considerations. The Suez crisis, coupled with Eden's own ill health, brought his premiership to a premature conclusion in January 1957 and the Conservative party was faced with the first of two succession crises. This time there was no crown prince available and there was no clear-cut procedure for choosing a leader. On this occasion the Queen took advice from the elder statesmen of the Conservative party, Churchill and Lord Salisbury, before sending for Harold Macmillan to form a government. Macmillan's premiership was marked by a more dynamic approach to domestic policy, reflecting Macmillan's own experience as Member for Stockton-on-Tees and his strong opposition to unemployment. Until 1962 his reputation grew steadily. But, concerned by what he took to be a lack-lustre performance as Chancellor of the Exchequer by Selwyn Lloyd, he dismissed Lloyd in 1962, together with six other members of the cabinet, an event that soon became known in political mythology as 'the night of the long knives'. Macmillan was also badly let down by his Secretary for War, John Profumo, who falsely denied both to Macmillan and to the House of Commons that he had shared the favours of a certain Miss Christine Keeler with

Two Conservative Premiers: Harold Macmillan and Lord Home shortly before Macmillan's resignation in October 1963

Captain Ivanov, a naval attaché at the Russian embassy. Trivial in itself, this incident reflected badly on Macmillan's judgment and was exploited to the full by the Opposition. Finally, Macmillan was also struck by illness on the eve of the Conservative Party Conference in October 1963. On doctor's orders he announced his resignation. This led to another succession crisis. It was won this time by Lord Home, the Foreign Secretary, who was pressed into service largely because senior Conservatives could not agree about the merits of the two more obvious claimants, Lord Hailsham and Butler. Home's appointment was not universally welcomed either. A peer, who confessed unwisely to doing his economics with the aid of matchsticks, did not convey the image of a dynamic and classless party. Two members of Macmillan's cabinet, Enoch Powell and Ian Macleod, refused to serve under Home and it was little surprise when, after sustaining a narrow defeat in the 1964 election, the Conservative party readily accepted Home's resignation in 1965. Before he resigned, Home made sure that the party should adopt a new procedure for choosing his successor. Instead of 'the usual processes of consultation', all Conservative MPs were now to be given a vote, and a succession of ballots would be held until a leader emerged with over 50% of the votes cast. On this occasion, Edward Heath was chosen with 150 votes to 133 for Reginald Maudling and 15 for Enoch Powell.

A. Eden, *Full Circle* (Cassell, 1960)

The Labour party, meanwhile, had been going through a succession of internal crises. From 1951 to 1957 the Bevanites were a continual source of trouble to the Party leadership. Bevan himself resigned from the Shadow Cabinet in 1954 because he refused to support the creation of the South East Asia Treaty Organisation (SEATO). In April 1955 he was so openly critical of Attlee in a debate on defence policy that a majority of Labour party MPs (141 to 112) voted that the Party Whip should be withdrawn from him. When Attlee resigned the party leadership in December 1955, Bevan's conduct virtually put him out of the running. In the ensuing election he gained only 70 votes compared to Gaitskell's 157.

More serious divisions erupted in 1959 and 1960. In 1959 Gaitskell unwisely, if honestly, raised the issue of Clause Four at the annual Conference which followed Labour's third election defeat. He wanted the party to acknowledge the limits to nationalisation. In his speech to the Conference he said that Clause Four confused ends and means.

P. M. Williams, *Hugh Gaitskell* (OUP, 1982)

> It lays us open to continual misrepresentation ... It implies that we intend to nationalise everything, but do we? The whole of light industry, the whole of agriculture, all the shops, every little pub and garage? Of course not. We have long ago come to accept a mixed economy ... the view of 90 per cent of the Labour Party - had we not better say so instead of going out of our way to court misrepresentation? [Williams, pp. 324–5]

But Clause Four was an article of faith with many trade union leaders and party activists. Gaitskell failed to carry the Conference with him and created unnecessary divisions within the party by raising a sleeping dog that would have been better left to lie.

In 1960 there was another row, this time over nuclear disarmament. Two powerful trade unions, the Transport and General Workers and the Amalgamated Engineering Union, were persuaded to cast their block votes in favour of unilateral nuclear disarmament. The party leadership was still committed to Britain's retention of nuclear weapons in line with her commitment to the NATO alliance. The unilateralist motion was carried at the Annual Conference held at Scarborough in 1960 by 400 000 votes. Gaitskell refused to accept the decision vowing that 'We will fight and fight and fight again to bring back sanity and honesty and dignity, so that our Party with its great past may retain its glory and its greatness.' [Williams, p. 358–9] Gaitskell did less than justice to the motives of those who supported the unilateralist case, but he was convinced in his own mind that unilateral renunciation of nuclear weapons by the British government was incompatible with membership of NATO, to which the majority of the Labour party was still firmly wedded.

M. Williams, *Hugh Gaitskell* (OUP, 1982)

Hugh Gaitskell at the time of his election to the Labour leadership in 1955

In November 1960 he successfully held off an unprecedented challenge to his leadership from Harold Wilson, defeating his rival by 166 votes to 81. He then worked hard to secure a change in the party's policy on nuclear weapons. By the time the next Annual Conference took place he had succeeded. This time the Conference backed the official policy by 4 526 000 votes to 1 756 000, a victory that was achieved by persuading three of the six largest trade unions to change their stance. But Gaitskell did not live long to enjoy his success. Tragically, in January 1963 he died of a virus disease at the age of 56. His death had been preceded by that of his old rival, Aneurin Bevan, who also died sadly early in 1960. Of the Attlee government of 1945–51 only Harold Wilson survived. Though Wilson enjoyed a not entirely undeserved reputation for facing both ways – perhaps a necessary attribute in any leader of the Labour party – he won a comfortable victory in the leadership election, coming top on the first ballot and defeating George Brown by 144 votes to 103 on the second.

In the 1964 General Election Labour's appeal was directed at the white-collar rather than the manual worker. Wilson made much of the technological revolution. Selective intervention, rather than nationalisation, was to be the recipe for economic growth. Two new ministries were promised: one for Economic Affairs, one for Technology. Though the Labour vote actually fell by 10 000 votes on the 1959 figure, the Conservative vote dropped by over a million, much of it going to the Liberals. The Labour party emerged with an overall majority of four, but unlike Attlee in 1951, Wilson headed a fresh team, determined to hold on to office. After 18 months in power Wilson picked a propitious moment to hold another election and this time the Labour vote went up by 800 000.

Wilson now had a comfortable overall majority of 96 and for the second time in its history a Labour administration was in a position to carry out its own policies.

The Management of the Economy

Conservative Policies

'Britain was trying to reconcile full employment, stable prices, economic growth, the defence of sterling and a world role. It was a hopelessly over-ambitious task.' [Bartlett, p. 163] This comment, made in relation to the British economy in 1959, could be applied to the whole period between 1951 and 1970. With the best will in the world no government could have hoped to meet all these objectives simultaneously. In practice, successive Chancellors of the Exchequer changed their policies in accordance with the needs of the moment, steering a path between the twin evils of unemployment and inflation where possible, but every now and then having to subordinate every other priority to the need to deal with the balance of payments. As banker to the sterling area Britain was in a peculiarly vulnerable position, particularly after sterling became convertible in 1958. The level of gold and foreign currency reserves was never adequate to meet the sudden demands that were placed on them when there was a run on the pound. Such speculative movements tended to be sparked off by an unfavourable set of trade figures. This gave to the balance of payments an importance it did not warrant and economic policy revolved accordingly round Britain's foreign trade account.

C. J. Bartlett, *A History of Post-War Britain, 1945–1974* (1977)

The other factor that came to play an increasingly important role in economic policy was the growing bargaining power, and the willingness to use it, of the trade union movement. The understanding established between Cripps and the TUC between 1947 and 1949 was never re-established and governments of both political persuasions had to contend with wage demands that were less and less easy to contain.

Churchill's government had enjoyed an unusually favourable economic climate. The fall in raw material prices brought the balance of payments back into surplus in 1952 and Butler was able to bring rationing to an end. He also removed all the war-time controls that were still in force. His term of office was marked by an investment boom and a shortage of labour. Share prices doubled, production rose by 4–5% a year, roughly in line with inflation. Macmillan, who succeeded Butler in 1955 as Chancellor, faced a balance of payments deficit of £115 million and resorted to a series of deflationary measures designed to reduce domestic consumption. They were evidently successful and the balance of payments remained in surplus for the rest of the decade.

As Prime Minister, Macmillan's chief worry was inflation. In 1957 he set up the Committee on Prices and Productivity, headed by Lord Cohen, hoping to secure a national consensus on the level of wage increases which the country could afford. The TUC refused to participate. At the end of 1957 another foreign exchange crisis convinced the new Chancellor, Peter Thorneycroft, that inflation must be held down, if necessary by restraining public expenditure. In his Budget plans for 1958 he refused to make allowances for anticipated price increases in departmental estimates, compelling ministers to make real cuts in their expenditure plans. A gap of £50 million still had to be bridged. Macmillan refused to accept the need for this further cut and this led to the resignations of the whole Treasury team: Thorneycroft, Nigel Birch and Enoch Powell. At the time Macmillan dismissed the resignations as 'these little local difficulties'. To a later generation of Conservatives they came to look more like heroic gestures in defence of much needed monetarist policies. Heathcote Amery replaced Thorneycroft and continued in office until 1961 when he was replaced by Selwyn Lloyd. Lloyd tried to deal with the problem of inflation by introducing a 'pay pause', to last for six months. It could only apply to government employees and those in the nationalised industries – where private industry was concerned the government could merely exhort. Needless to say, the pay pause was seen by the trade unions as unfairly discriminatory and they refused an invitation to take part in the National Incomes Commission which was set up in 1962.

Selwyn Lloyd was succeeded by Reginald Maudling in 1962. Both Macmillan and Maudling were committed to a policy of expansion and as unemployment rose to 800 000 in 1963 Maudling determined to inject a stimulus to consumption in his 1964 Budget. There were tax cuts of £270 million and increases in grants and allowances to the depressed areas. But, as his critics feared, the immediate consequence was a surge in imports which resulted in a balance of payments deficit of nearly £700 million. No Conservative Chancellor had succeeded in reconciling economic growth with balance of payments equilibrium; nor had the problem of wage inflation been solved.

Labour Policies, 1964–70

The balance of payments deficit inherited from the Conservatives was to be the burden which dominated the economic policies of the Labour government. It was not just the need to reverse the trade deficit that demanded attention. Wilson was committed to the defence of sterling at its existing parity of $2.80 to the pound. When the subject of devaluation was raised in November 1964 he said to Crossman: 'You're talking nonsense. Devaluation would sweep us away. We would have to go to the country defeated. We can't have it.' [Howard (ed.), p. 47] Refusal to accept devaluation as a solution meant that every time there was a balance of payments deficit the pound came under pressure, which could only be met by cobbling together huge loans from the International Monetary Fund and overseas central banks. The parallels with 1931 were all too clear, particularly when Lord Cromer, the Governor of the Bank of England, urged cuts in public expenditure in order to restore foreign confidence.

A. Howard (ed.), *The Crossman Diaries – Selections from the Diaries of a Cabinet Minister, 1964–1970* (Hamish Hamilton, 1979)

The government's immediate response to the balance of payments deficit in 1964 was to impose a 15% surcharge on all tariffs, which was technically a breach both of the General Agreement on Tariffs and Trade, signed by Britain in 1947, and of the European Free Trade Agreement which Britain had joined in 1957. But

Callaghan's first Budget showed no such sense of urgency. It abolished prescription charges and increased old age pensions. This frightened overseas investors into the belief that an irresponsible government would soon be forced to devalue and there was an immediate run on the pound. A loan of £3 billion was negotiated which provided a temporary solution but balance of payments deficits continued to occur in 1965, 1966 and 1967. Wilson and Callaghan maintained their opposition to devaluation; in 1966 Callaghan declared that those who advocated devaluation 'are calling for a reduction in the real wage standard of every member of the working class of this country. Devaluation is not the way out of Britain's difficulties.' But by the autumn of 1967 this position was no longer tenable. A bad set of monthly trade figures sparked off another wave of speculation against the pound and this time no further loans could be raised. Devaluation was inevitable. Unfortunately, rumours that it was about to happen went unchecked and there was heavy selling of sterling in the few days before the announcement was made. Finally, on 18 November 1967 the pound was devalued a second time from $2.80 to the pound to $2.40, a fall of 14.3%. Roy Jenkins, who replaced Callaghan as Chancellor in December 1967, had a clearer grasp of priorities than his predecessor and the seriousness of Britain's international financial position made the harsh remedies he prescribed acceptable. In both his 1968 and 1969 Budgets he imposed cuts in expenditure and increases in taxation, with the aim of reducing domestic consumption so as to cut imports. The raising of the school-leaving age was postponed; prescription charges were imposed; and Britain's forces east of the Suez Canal were withdrawn.

In the short term these deflationary policies achieved their objective. Britain had a balance of payments surplus in 1969 which was sustained until 1972. But the 8% growth in exports was achieved by a diversion of output rather than an increase and unemployment started to creep up.

Labour's long-term hopes were fixed on the new Department of Economic Affairs, headed by George Brown, which was intended to act as a counter-weight to the restrictive policies of the Treasury. The Department produced its first National Plan in September 1965. This took the form of 'indicative planning'. It set out a number of targets for each sector of the British economy, based largely on aspiration rather than firm evidence. An average annual growth rate of 3.8% was thought to be feasible which, had it been achieved, would have increased real Gross National Product by 25% in the space of five years. But the deflationary measures that had to be adopted to correct the balance of payments deficit and to satisfy foreign lenders soon made the National Plan redundant. The targets were tacitly ignored and then officially abandoned in the second edition of the Plan, *The Task Ahead*, produced in 1969. Wilson's hope that the tension between the Treasury and the Department of Economic Affairs would prove 'creative' was also dashed. Crossman commented as early as January 1965 that 'the division of power between the Treasury and the DEA is a development for which we are having to pay a heavy price in divided authority and dissension in central planning.' [Howard (ed.), p. 58] Brown soon became disenchanted with his position, and was glad to move to the Foreign Office in 1966. Though Wilson himself took over the DEA in 1967, this made little difference and he gave it up to Peter Shore in 1968. The Department came to an inglorious end in 1969, when the Treasury was restored to its undisputed dominance.

Howard (ed.), *The Crossman Diaries*

The second major initiative taken by the Government was the attempt to provide an institutional framework for the adjustment of wages and prices. In 1964 Brown secured trade union approval to a policy statement, the Declaration of Intent, under which wage and price increases were to be related to improvements in productivity. In 1965 the National Board for Prices and Incomes came into existence; its purpose was to monitor all wage and price increases. Initially it had no powers, but under the Prices and Incomes Act of 1966 it was given authority to limit wage and price increases. A six months' freeze was imposed, to be followed by a period of 'severe restraint'. The rate of price increases was held down to 2.5% in 1967 but it proved impossible to win trade union acquiescence for the policy of wage restraint for more than two years, and by 1969 wage rates were again rising ahead of productivity. The Board subsequently calculated that its effect had been to reduce incomes by not more than 1% a year during the period of its operation. That may have been an unduly pessimistic assessment. But the Board was unpopular both with trade unions and employers and its abolition by the Heath government in 1970 came as no surprise.

The Public Sector

Superficially, nationalisation continued to be a serious bone of contention between the two major parties. Clause Four, as we have seen, remained firmly entrenched in the Labour Party Constitution, while Conservative bodies such as Aims of Industry continued to voice their outright hostility to the principle of public ownership. But much of this was shadow boxing. In practice, changes in the size of the public sector were marginal. In 1953 the Conservatives, in line with their manifesto promises, returned the iron and steel industry to private ownership. But Richard Thomas and Baldwin's, the huge steel firm in South Wales, remained under public ownership and an Iron and Steel Board was set up to supervise investment in the industry with the aim of bringing some measure of co-ordination to it. Road transport was also de-nationalised, but here too the Transport Commission was allowed to keep much of its long-distance lorry fleet. No changes were made to the other nationalised industries.

The Labour Manifesto in 1964 contained a firm undertaking to re-nationalise the iron and steel industry and to reorganise the country's water supplies. Despite their narrow majority, the government went ahead with the Iron and Steel Bill, but were held up until 1966 by two of their backbenchers, Woodrow Wyatt and Desmond Donnelly. Donnelly subsequently resigned from the party in 1968. With a large majority behind it, nationalisation went through comfortably enough in 1966 and virtually restored the position to what it had been in 1951. No action was taken over the water proposals and suggestions that 14 large public companies might be taken over also came to nothing.

No solution was found by either party to the problem of how to reconcile the commercial and the social obligations of nationalised industries. A Conservative White Paper in 1961 tried to bring some uniformity into how industries should interpret their statutory financial obligations, as defined in the various nationalising acts; but otherwise gave little guidance. In 1963 Dr Beeching, the new head of British Rail, did his best to close down those railway lines which could be defined as 'uneconomic'. In 1967 a more far-reaching White Paper, produced under Labour auspices, urged nationalised industries to adopt the same techniques for investment appraisal and price setting as were adopted by the best private firms, indicating how close the two parties now were in their attitudes to the public sector. Nor could

Government
and Industry

Labour or Conservative ministers resist the temptation to interfere with the investment, pricing and wage policies of the nationalised industries when it suited them to do so. Thus the public sector remained uneasily poised between the need to make ends meet and to provide employment. It was a dilemma which has still to be resolved.

The Private Sector

Between 1951 and 1964 there was little direct intervention in private industry by Conservative governments but one important new institution was created. In 1961 Macmillan set up the National Economic Development Council with the aim of bringing together government, industry and the trade unions in the common pursuit of economic growth. Its powers were minimal, but it at least provided a forum in which the two sides of industry could meet each other in a reasonably harmonious atmosphere. It also spawned a number of little 'Neddies' (National Economic Development Councils) for particular industries, which probably did more for industrial co-operation than the parent body.

The Labour Government of 1964 came into office with high hopes of harnessing the government's motive power to the technological revolution. A Ministry of Technology was set up with this end in view. Its first head was Frank Cousins, an ex-General Secretary of the Transport and General Workers' Union. Beyond endorsing the decision to proceed with the highly expensive Anglo-French airliner, the *Concorde*, the ministry had little to show for its activities before Cousins resigned over the compulsory incomes policy that was introduced in 1966. His successor, Tony Benn, played a more active role. Under his supervision the Industrial Reorganisation Corporation came to birth. Its purpose was chiefly to bring together firms engaged in similar fields of production on the popular but unproven assumption that the larger the enterprise the more productive it was likely to be. In some cases the IRC acted as midwife to mergers, in others it took a direct stake in private firms. The most celebrated and least successful of its ventures was the merger it sponsored between Leyland Motors and the British Motor Corporation; this called into existence an unwieldy giant that never looked like surviving. By 1971 the IRC had also taken shares in eleven companies, most of them very small.

The government also passed an Industrial Expansion Act in 1968. This enabled the government to buy shares in private industry and was attacked as a device for backdoor nationalisation. In practice, its purpose was to provide risk capital for research and development, though later on it was to be used to rescue firms in difficulties. All these measures, coupled with the 1967 White Paper, helped to blur the lines between public and private enterprise. It became increasingly hard to distinguish between the 'lame ducks' and the 'wounded heroes' of private industry, just as it was difficult to decide which loss-making activities in the public sector could be allowed to continue.

Another area of government intervention was the location of industry. In 1963 the Conservative Government designated the Board of Trade as the Ministry for Industry, Trade and Regional Development. Lord Hailsham had already been appointed Minister with special responsibility for the North East. The Labour Government imposed strict controls on office development in London in 1965, and between 1966 and 1967 brought in a wide range of grants and allowances with the aim of persuading firms to locate in the old depressed areas. Regional Development

Grants of up to 45% of new investment in buildings and plant were payable in the Special Development Areas such as Liverpool, while a Regional Employment Premium was paid to all industrial employers on behalf of their employees in all the assisted areas. The net effect of these measures, it has been calculated, was to add about 330 000 jobs to the areas concerned, though whether they added to total employment is much more problematical.

Common to both the Macmillan and the Wilson governments was a reluctance to upset the existing balance between the public and the private sectors, except in the case of steel; and a willingness to experiment with various forms of intervention into private industry with the purpose of improving its efficiency, while also making it serve the public good. If success did not attend these efforts this only reflected the intractability of the problems, and the limited capacity of any government to bring about solutions to them.

The Conservative governments between 1951 and 1964 produced little in the way of institutional reform, with one notable exception. The Life Peerages Act of 1958 enabled the Prime Minister to recommend for life peerages a wide range of distinguished men and women whose presence soon rejuvenated the House of Lords. They came to include ex-trade union leaders such as Hugh Scanlon, ex-Vice Chancellors of universities such as Lord Bullock, and previous Directors of the BBC such as Lord Swann. In 1963 Wedgwood Benn, who, much against his wishes, had inherited his father's title in 1960, secured the passage of a private member's bill which enabled peers to renounce their titles if they so wished. Ironically the next beneficiary of this Act was Lord Home who had to sit in the House of Commons if he was to become Prime Minister in 1964.

The Labour party also took up the cause of reform to the House of Lords. Discussions began with the leaders of the other parties in November 1967, and a substantial measure of agreement was reached. In its final form the government's Parliament No. 2 Bill proposed a two-tier chamber made up of life peers, hereditary peers of first creation, law lords and bishops who would be able to sit and vote; and a second tier of hereditary peers by succession, who would become 'non-voting' peers. There would be a retiring age of 72 and each incoming government would be allowed to create enough new life peers to give it a majority over the Opposition. The delaying powers of the House were to be reduced to six months. But the committee stage of such an important constitutional measure had to be taken on the floor of the House of Commons where the bill was strongly opposed, for quite different reasons, by Enoch Powell and Michael Foot. So successful were their delaying tactics that in April 1969 the cabinet decided not to proceed further. According to Crossman there had never been much enthusiasm for it.

Another nettle which the Labour party grasped, only to drop, was trade union reform. In 1965 Wilson appointed a Royal Commission under Lord Donovan to investigate every aspect of the trade unions. The Report, published in 1968, identified a number of weaknesses in Britain's system of industrial relations. It called attention to the fragmentation of collective bargaining through the number of unions involved and to the widespread prevalence of informal agreements which were difficult to enforce. The Report recommended that where possible formal agreements

Institutional Reforms

should replace informal ones and it also called for a Commission of Industrial Relations to assist the process. It did not recommend any changes in the law.

Barbara Castle, Minister for Employment and Productivity, accepted the recommendations, but because of the high level of unofficial strikes (they accounted for 95% of the days lost by industrial action in 1967) she and the Prime Minister agreed that tougher action would be needed as well. In her White Paper, christened ironically *In Place of Strife*, she advocated the introduction of penal sanctions (fines) to be imposed in a limited number of cases, for instance, where an unofficial strike was called in defiance of the official leadership. Neither the TUC nor the National Executive Committee of the Labour party were willing to accept these provisions, and after a bruising series of cabinet meetings, Wilson and Mrs Castle discovered that a majority of their colleagues were not willing to either. In June 1969 the White Paper was dropped and Wilson had instead to be satisfied with a 'Solemn and Binding Agreement' on the part of the TUC to use their best endeavours to prevent inter-union disputes and unofficial strikes. At the time it seemed like a serious rebuff. In practice it may be doubted whether the proposed legislation would have made very much difference. Perhaps the worst consequence of the failure of the Castle bill was that it encouraged the Conservative party to persevere with their much more radical, and as it transpired, unworkable proposals.

B. Castle, *In Place of Strife* (HMSO, 1969)

The third initiative taken by the Labour government was the attempted reform of the Civil Service. Another Royal Commission, this time under Lord Fulton, a former civil servant himself, was set up in 1965. Its report also came out in 1968. The Commission identified six main weaknesses: 'the cult of the generalist and the amateur'; the complexity and rigidity of the class structure; the failure to give responsibility to specialists such as engineers and scientists; the lack of enough skilled managers; the absence of contact between members of the Civil Service and the rest of the community; and the inadequacy of personnel management and career planning. Recommendations included the setting up of a Civil Service Department under the direct supervision of the Prime Minister; better training facilities; and the abolition of the existing system of grades and classes and its replacement by a much less rigid and simpler structure. Wilson immediately implemented the more specific recommendations. A Civil Service Department was set up and a Civil Service College was established with three centres in London, Sunningdale and Edinburgh. But Lord Crowther Hunt, a member of the Commission, was highly sceptical about the seriousness with which the other reforms were tackled. In his book *The Civil Servants*, published in 1980, he claimed that the cult of the generalist and amateur still flourished, and he was probably right in doing so. The Civil Service Department came to an inglorious end when it was abolished by Mrs Thatcher in 1981.

P. Kellner and Lord C. Crowther–Hunt, *The Civil Servants – an inquiry into Britain's Ruling Class* (MacDonald, 1982)

Social Reforms

Though there were discernible differences in the attitudes of the two major parties on social issues, these were not necessarily reflected in party divisions on particular issues. Some Conservatives voted for abolition of the death penalty, for instance, while many Labour MPs were more sympathetic to Conservative policies on immigration than the official leadership. In most cases legislation was inspired less by party doctrine than by private initiatives, or it emerged in response to particular needs. Both parties played a part in the expansion of higher education. The Macmillan government appointed the Robbins Commission in 1961 to investigate existing provision and the Report firmly recommended a doubling of university places to 218 000 within 10 years and an increase in places in higher education as a whole to 319 000. The government accepted the recommendation and eight new universities were founded. The Labour government maintained this expansion, granting university status to the Colleges of Advanced Technology. University education was made more widely available to those without formal qualifications through the Open University of the Air, which came into existence in 1969.

While there was general agreement over the need to expand higher education, there were important differences between the parties on secondary education. The Labour party was committed to the principle of comprehensive schooling and to the abolition of the eleven-plus examination. As Minister of Education, Anthony Crosland sent round a circular (10/65) to all local educational authorities requiring them to submit plans for the reorganisation of secondary education on comprehensive lines. By 1969, 129 out of 163 authorities had done so. By 1970 over one million children (a third of the secondary school population) were being educated in comprehensive schools.

Freedom of choice was extended in many different areas. In 1954 the powerful commercial television lobby persuaded the Conservative Government to end the BBC's monopoly over broadcasting. In the 1960s, with a sympathetic Home Secretary, Roy Jenkins, to give them a fair wind two private members' bills brought a more liberal approach in the field of sexual morality. In 1967 the Sexual Offences Act removed the criminal stigma from homosexual acts committed by consenting adults in private; the bill was sponsored by Leo Abse, in line with the recommendations of the Wolfenden Report. In the same year David Steel's Abortion Act made abortion legal in carefully defined circumstances. It is probable that these three measures had a greater effect on the lives of ordinary people than all the nationalising statutes put together.

Until the 1960s there was no need for an immigration policy. But, partly as a result of direct encouragement by the British government, anxious to recruit labour to staff the railways and the hospitals, partly because of economic pressures in the West Indies and the Indian sub continent, immigration figures began to rise rapidly. In the 1950s the annual average was between 30 000–40 000. In 1961 it reached 100 000. Both parties ultimately came to accept the need to limit immigration, while at the same time trying to ensure that those immigrants already here were treated as equal citizens and were protected against discrimination. In 1962 the Commonwealth Immigration Act introduced a voucher system under which only those with jobs to go to would be allowed in to the country. There was no limit on the entry of dependants of those already here. At the time Gaitskell objected strongly to what he called 'this miserable, shameful, shabby bill'. [Williams, p. 385] When the Labour government came to power in 1964 it made no attempt to reverse the Act, but by way of compensation it passed a Race Relations Act in 1965, making incitement to racial hatred a criminal offence and banning all racial discrimination in public places.

Williams, *Hugh Gaitskell*

When the Kenya government announced in 1968 that it proposed to deny citizenship to all Kenyan Asians the government bowed unwillingly to public pressure and as Home Secretary, Callaghan introduced a bill depriving the Kenyan Asians of the automatic right of entry into Britain which, as British passport-holders, they still enjoyed. It was in the context of increasing immigration that Enoch Powell made the notorious speech in which, like the Romans, he claimed to see 'the **River Tiber** foaming with much blood'. It was, to say the least, an unhelpful remark and cost Powell his job in the Shadow Cabinet, Heath commenting that the speech was 'racialist in tone and liable to exacerbate racial tensions'.

The party consensus on immigration was thus preserved, at any rate for the time being. But as the decade ended it became clear that Britain's social fabric would be subjected to an additional strain.

THE YEARS OF DIVISION, 1970–79 ▨▨▨▨▨▨▨ D

The Economy

Between 1970 and 1979 the conventional indicators of Britain's economic health all took a turn for the worse and the same was true for the United States and Western Europe. Oil prices quadrupled between 1973 and 1974 and there was a similar boom in commodity prices at the same time. Partly as a result of these events there was a world recession, beginning in 1974, and the long post-war period of uninterrupted economic growth came to a halt. So far as Britain was concerned the figures below tell the story.

	Price Inflation (annual rate of increase)	Unemployment (thousands)	% of Labour force
1970	6.4	519	2.5
1971	9.4	724	3.3
1972	7.1	899	3.6
1973	9.2	575	2.6
1974	16.1	542	2.5
1975	24.2	866	3.9
1976	16.3	1332	5.3
1977	15.9	1450	5.7
1978	8.2	1381	5.7
1979	13.2	1500	5.8

[Madgwick, Steeds and Williams, p. 122 (amended)]

P. J. Madgwick,
D. Steeds and
L. J. Williams, *Britain Since 1945*
(Hutchinson, 1982)

Britain's rate of economic growth, sluggish by continental standards at the best of times, was negative (i.e. there was a real decline in Gross National Product) in 1974 and 1975, and again in 1980 and 1981. Some undesirable records were broken. The visible trade deficit reached the alarming total of £5351 million in 1974 and the rate of inflation soared to nearly 25% in 1975, leading Dennis Healey, Chancellor of the Exchequer, to comment that Britain was looking over the edge of an abyss. The only sign of comfort was the development of North Sea Oil which began to come on stream in 1976. By 1979 production reached 75 million tonnes and contributed £8 billion to the balance of payments. This was still not sufficient to put Britain into surplus, indicating that the deficit on other visible trade was still increasing, particularly in manufactured goods. The Keynesian remedies were apparently working no longer. Under Keynesian theory inflation should have come down as unemployment went up, with wage demands falling and employers ceasing to bid for labour. But in the 1970s that relationship no longer obtained. Over the decade as a whole both inflation and unemployment went up together. In 1979 Sir Geoffrey Howe maintained in his first Budget speech as Chancellor that demand management had 'been tested to destruction'. The commitment to maintain full employment shared by both parties since 1945, could no longer be acknowledged by either of them.

Harold Wilson chose what he hoped would be a propitious moment to go to the country: June 1970. For once the public opinion polls proved unreliable. Much to everyone's surprise except Wilson's – 'I was one of the few who had doubts, though I would have found it hard to rationalise them.' [Wilson, p. 790] – the government was defeated, losing 60 seats overall, while the Conservative party made a net gain of 68. Heath duly became Prime Minister with a comfortable majority of 40 over all other parties.

Prior to the election Heath had held an important conference with other senior Conservatives at Selsdon Park, near Croydon. It had been decided that a sharp break with Labour policies was necessary. The days of consensus were over. Labour's

The Political Background

H. Wilson, *The Labour Governments, 1964–1970, A Personal Record* (Penguin, 1974)

Two Conservative Leaders still on speaking terms: Edward Heath and Margaret Thatcher in July 1979 with Lord Haisham

Incomes Policy was to be scrapped; state intervention into private industry ended; and a greater reliance was to be placed on market forces. Prices would be held down through greater competition. Finally, trade unions were to be subjected to legal constraints. Within two years, Heath had been forced by rising inflation and unemployment to execute a U turn. Incomes policy was restored; private firms such as Rolls Royce and British Leyland were receiving government subsidies; and the Industrial Relations Act, passed in 1971, was being largely ignored. In June 1972, faced with another balance of payments crisis, the pound was 'floated'. The statutory incomes policy introduced by Heath in 1972 was challenged in the spring of 1974, by the National Union of Mineworkers which refused to accept the tight pay limits imposed on every other industry. Heath decided to hold a General Election in the hope that the public would rally to his support in the face of this defiance of the authority of parliament. Like Wilson in 1970, Heath miscalculated. Though his party won a larger share of the vote (37.9% to Labour's 37.1%) the Labour party gained 301 seats to the Conservatives' 297. The Liberal party, with 14 seats, held the balance. Jeremy Thorpe, leader of the Liberal party, declined Heath's invitation to come to some kind of working agreement. Wilson, in these unpropitious circumstances, took office for a second time with some reluctance.

As Heath and the Conservative party had moved to the right in 1970, so the Labour party had moved to the left. The Labour manifesto in 1974 contained proposals to nationalise the aircraft and shipbuilding industries; to set up a National Enterprise Board with an unspecified list of companies that might be taken over; to make comprehensive education mandatory; and to bring about 'a fundamental

A change of leadership in the Labour party: James Callaghan after Wilson's resignation in March 1976

and irreversible shift in the balance of power and wealth in favour of working people and their families'. (*Labour's Programme*, 1973) In the absence of a clear majority the government could do little to realise this programme and Wilson contented himself with restoring some stability to the country and getting the miners back to work after a moderate increase in their wages had been conceded. By October he felt ready to risk another election. Though there had been a slight swing to the Labour party it was not enough to give them a decisive majority. The final result showed Labour with a majority of only three over all other parties. The position was not quite as precarious as it looked. The Opposition parties included 277 Conservatives, 13 Liberals, 11 members of the Scottish National party and 3 members of Plaid Cymru (the Welsh Nationalists). There were few, if any, issues on which these different groups were prepared to unite to bring down the government. Conversely, the government could use the promise of devolution as a bargaining counter to keep the Liberals and the Nationalist parties on its side. Relying on its tiny majority, in 1975 and 1976 the Labour party pressed ahead with its controversial policies. The aircraft and shipbuilding industries were nationalised. An act was passed to make comprehensive reorganisation of schools compulsory. The Conservative Industrial Relations Act was repealed. The National Enterprise Board was set up. These objectives accomplished, in March 1976 Harold Wilson announced his resignation. He had been in politics since 1945 and since 1900 only Baldwin had served longer as a peace-time Prime Minister. Ambition had been fully satisfied. In the leadership contest which followed James Callaghan was strongly challenged by Michael Foot, the candidate of the left wing and Aneurin Bevan's natural heir. Callaghan won by 176 votes to 137 on the third ballot.

The Conservative party had also changed its leader by this time. Heath's position had become increasingly vulnerable after his two election defeats in 1974. Backbench MPs found him disconcertingly difficult to talk to, but more significant was the growing feeling that Heath had not stuck as firmly as he should have done to the right-wing policies agreed at Selsdon Park. A Party Committee headed by Home, now back in the Lords, recommended that when in opposition the leader should submit himself annually for re-election. Heath agreed to do so in 1975. On the first ballot Margaret Thatcher, who had been selected as standard bearer for the right wing, despite her comparative lack of cabinet experience (she had only been Minister for Education), defeated Heath by 130 votes to 119. On the second ballot she gained an overall majority, with 146 out of 271 votes cast. Her victory marked, as it was intended to, a decisive shift to the right in the orientation of the Conservative party.

By 1977 the Labour party had lost its overall majority after a series of by-election defeats, some in normally safe seats such as Workington. Callaghan was determined to stay in office and in March he came to an agreement with David Steel, the new leader of the Liberal Party. The Pact ruled out any socialist-inspired legislation but it committed the Labour party to a policy of devolution for Scotland and Wales, while the Liberals promised their support to the government's economic measures. The devolution proposals, published in 1977 and enacted in 1978, provided separate parliaments for Scotland and Wales with varying powers, but they were still subject to the overriding authority of Westminster and dependent for finance on block grants. Unfortunately for the government a backbench amendment was incorporated into the bills under which the approval of 40% of the total electorate was needed before the acts would come into force. When voting took place in March 1979 it produced the following results:

P. J. Madgwick, D. Steeds and L. J. Williams, *Britain Since 1945* (Hutchinson, 1982)

	Turnout	Yes % electorate	No % electorate	Yes % vote	No % vote
Wales	58.3	11.8	46.5	20.3	79.7
Scotland	62.9	32.5	30.4	51.6	48.3

[Madgwick, Steeds and Williams, p. 183]

As can be seen in Wales support for devolution was minimal, while in Scotland, despite the gains made by the SNP, less than a third of the electorate were prepared to support it. In these circumstances the Nationalist parties had little to gain from continuing to support the Callaghan government. The pact with the Liberals had already ended in November 1978. The Labour party was also coming under increasing pressure from those who should have been its natural supporters. In the autumn and winter of 1978 a series of damaging strikes took place against the government's increasingly restrictive pay policy in the public sector. They affected water supplies, the National Health Service and refuse collection. Callaghan refused to hold a long anticipated election. But in April 1979 the Opposition parties finally agreed to join forces and the government was defeated on a motion of no confidence by one vote. The only precedent within living memory was the defeat of Ramsay MacDonald in 1924 and Callaghan met the same fate. Forced to resign at an inopportune moment, with a disaffected party, it was hardly surprising that he was defeated in the ensuing election. The Conservative party under their forceful new leader gained a majority of 43 seats over all other parties with 43.9% of the vote. Labour's share dropped to 36.6%. It was an unhappy sequel to the triumphs of 1945.

POINTS AT ISSUE POINTS AT ISSUE **POINTS AT ISSUE** POINTS AT ISSUE POINTS AT ISSUE POINTS AT ISSUE POINTS AT ISSUE

Socialism and the Labour Governments, 1945–51

A source of continuing debate among both historians and politicians is the extent to which the Labour governments of 1945 – 51 pursued Socialist objectives. Did the Attlee governments merely produce 'welfare capitalism', as R. H. S. Crossman argued in 1952 [*New Fabian Essays*, pp. 26–7] or did the 1945 election mark a much more distinctive move to the left? Views about the nature of the Labour achievement are inevitably coloured by the political standpoint of the observer and by the perspective in which the years 1945–51 are seen. Thus, to those on the hard left of the Labour party, the story of the Attlee governments is one of unfulfilled hopes and missed opportunities. Those on its social democratic wing are much more likely to praise its constructive achievements in the face of difficulties.

POINTS AT ISSUE
POINTS AT ISSUE
POINTS AT ISSUE
POINTS AT ISSUE

The governments' reputation has also fluctuated with the passage of time. In the 'revisionist' sixties the Attlee Government, with its commitment to nationalisation, looked positively radical. To the Marxist Left, whose hold on the Labour party strengthened after 1979, Labour's social reforms could be dismissed as an example of late-Victorian philanthropy. No attempt at a final verdict can yet be made. Instead, two groups of excerpts have been chosen, first to indicate what some members of the Labour government saw themselves as doing; secondly to demonstrate the different verdicts on the Attlee governments reached by later historians.

Contemporary views

(a) *Attlee*

> The Labour Party came to power with a well-defined policy worked out over many years. It had been set out very clearly in our Election Manifesto and we were determined to carry it out. Its ultimate objective was the creation of a society based on social justice, and, in our view, this could only be obtained by bringing under public ownership and control the main factors in the economic system.
>
> Nationalisation was not an end in itself but an essential element in achieving the ends which we sought. Controls were desirable not for their own sake but because they were necessary in order to gain freedom from the economic powers of the owners of capital. A juster distribution of wealth was not a policy designed to soak the rich or to take revenge, but because a society with gross inequalities of wealth and opportunity is fundamentally unhealthy. [Attlee, pp. 162–3]

(b) *Aneurin Bevan*

From a speech delivered on 4 July 1948 at a political rally in Manchester on the occasion of the inauguration of the National Health Service:

> The eyes of the world are turning to Great Britain. We now have the moral leadership of the world and before many years we shall have people coming here as to a modern Mecca, learning from us in the twentieth century as they learned from us in the seventeenth.

Earlier in the speech, Bevan, in a reference to the Means Test made the remarks for which he was better remembered:

> 'That is why no amount of cajolery can eradicate from my heart a deep burning hatred for the Tory Party that inflicted those experiences on me. So far as I am concerned they are lower than vermin. They condemned millions of first-class people to semi-starvation.' [Foot, pp. 237–8]

A later speech in 1949 to the Labour Party Conference at Blackpool summed up Bevan's philosophy more generously:

> I would point out that in some way or another the conception of religious dedication must find concrete expression, and I say that never in the history of mankind have the best ideas found more concrete expression than they have in the programme we are carrying out. 'Suffer the little children to come unto me' is not now something which is only said from the pulpit. We have woven it into the warp and woof of our national life, and we have made the claims of the children come first .... What is national planning but an insistence that human beings shall make ethical choices on a national scale? .... The language of priorities is the religion of Socialism.' [Foot, p. 263]

(c) Hugh Gaitskell

Gaitskell did not advocate nationalisation on purely practical grounds, but he knew that practical arguments were indispensable to convince others. Early in 1949, with the experience of office, he set out his views on nationalisation to a student audience 'Not an *end* in itself', say his notes. 'Our socialism is ... [aimed at eliminating] the three evils of individualism – *Inequality, Insecurity, Inefficiency.*'

He referred also to:

(a) *Concentration of economic power exercised without responsibility*
Now much modified by (i) Govt. controls (ii) Trade Union strength. It *still* counts.
(b) *Spiritual* aims – undesirability of concentrating on *material* ends ... doubtful how far this changes at top except under nationalisation. All the same desire to serve the community important ... make *democracy* an end in itself and need to acknowledge this in our policy. [Williams, p. 129]

(d) Ernest Bevin

We believe as good Social Democrats, that it is possible to have public ownership, great advance and social development, and with it maintain what I think is the most vital thing of all, liberty. I don't believe the two things are inconsistent, and never have. If I believed the development of socialism meant the absolute crushing of liberty, then I should plump for liberty, because the advance of human development depends entirely on the right to think, to speak and to use reason, and allow what I call the upsurge to come from the bottom to reach the top.' (from a speech delivered to American correspondents on 22 December 1947. [cited in Bullock, p. 92]

Histories of the Labour Governments

(a) The first full history of the Labour governments was written by D. N. Pritt in 1963. He says in his Preface: 'Although I lived close to the events I have to relate, as a member of the Parliament of 1945–50, I did not grasp the full tragedy of the story until I came, a decade later, to marshal the facts, look at them as a whole, and put them down on paper.' Pritt was a left-winger who was expelled from the official Labour party for supporting the Soviet invasion of Finland in 1940. He was elected as an Independent Labour MP for Hammersmith in 1945, but lost his seat to the official Labour candidate in 1950.

He concludes:

What went wrong? Why were our great hopes and opportunities frustrated and lost? Why was so little achieved, so little changed, so much left intact? Why was there no real advance towards socialism? And why, in the face of all that, did the right wing leaders keep pretty firm control of the Labour Party and of policy all through the years of betrayal, and for two more General Elections after the defeat of 1951? ...
The failure lay with the leadership; it was certainly not due to the strength of the forces of monopoly capitalism, who at the moment had neither morale nor confidence, and knew little of how the post-war world might shape or how long they might hope to last. A few shrewd blows at the start would have meant an end to their power, and the Labour Party could not merely have carried the building of a socialist Britain a very long way, but they could have given moral leadership to the whole of Europe ....

STARTING WRONG

What went wrong from the start? The Government, overwhelmingly right-wing in composition and outlook, far more conscious of the supposed 'enemy in the left' than of the real enemy that the electorate had sent them to power to conquer, accepted the capitalist *status quo*, political and economical, as if it were a law of nature, and never really sought to alter the class-structure of the nation, to attack the seats and sources of power, or even to weaken the ruling class. [Pritt, pp. 454–5]

(b) The next account, much more balanced in approach, was written by Roger Eatwell in 1979. Eatwell argues that there was something of a gap between the Labour claim to be working to create the 'Socialist Commonwealth of Great Britain', as stated in the Labour Manifesto, and the actual policies carried out:

Labour's welfare legislation considerably extended the pre-war services, but much of it had been anticipated by war time coalition planning .... Probably the main field where Labour was more radical was health, but the NHS system introduced in 1948 contained many problems, notably the existence side by side of a state and private sector. By 1951 the Government was trying to cut back expenditure in this field, and preparing the way for a vision of private affluence and public squalor ....

The Nationalisation programme took up considerable Parliamentary time; the iron and steel bill was an especially controversial one. By 1951 ten per cent of the work force were in the nationalised industries. However, the industries concerned were either derelict, or public service industries; even iron and steel was a dubious asset commercially .... Overall, Labour's nationalisation programme involved no clear gradualist strategy. It reflected piecemeal optimism, an approach reinforced by demands from Trade Unions for specific pieces of nationalisation ....

The most obvious economic change between pre-war and post-war Britain was full employment, a change which had a major effect in reducing poverty and raising living standards .... But it is doubtful whether the Governments' policies had much to do with this. A massive post-war cyclical boom was almost certainly more important than the Governments' efforts at planning and Keynesian demand management. Indeed, by the late 1940's physical planning was taking a less and less important role in economic policy ...

Eatwell sees Labour policy as getting steadily less socialist during the life of the government:

In 1945 Labour had proclaimed in its manifesto that it was socialist and 'proud' of it; in 1951 it was more evasive. By the late 1940's its ethical side had virtually disappeared, it began to stress more efficiency and prosperity – problematic issues in view of its record in other spheres, and the fact that they were issues on which other parties were well equipped to fight. [Eatwell, pp. 153–8]

(c) The most vigorous defence of the Labour government is produced by one of its most recent historians, K. O. Morgan, in his account *Labour in Power, 1945–1951* (1984). While Morgan concedes that nothing approaching a socialist revolution took place and that 'British society in general showed little outward change' [Morgan, p. 492], he sees very significant differences between the policies of the Labour party

and those of the Conservative opposition in 1945. He argues that the Attlee government

> had a clear record of achievement and of competence, which acted as a platform for successive governments, Conservative and Labour, throughout the next quarter of a century. The advent of a monetarist Conservative Government under Mrs Thatcher in 1979 signalled the first real attempt to wrench Britain out of the Age of Attlee. It received a huge endorsement at the polls in 1983. Yet until late 1983 at least, the economic record of well over three million unemployed, a severe contraction of manufacturing industry, eroding public and social services, and some threat of social and racial disorder, did not suggest that this alternative ideological approach had so far provided more coherent or acceptable answers to Britain's acknowledged problems. [Morgan, p. 494]

Not only was the Attlee government successful in its economic policies. Its commitment to its socialist convictions was maintained:

> Neither can these policies be reasonably characterized by mild centrism, a precursor of the SDP of the 1980s, nor by a betrayal of the inheritance of socialist convictions through the constraints of office and the blandishments of an allegedly right-wing civil service and the social establishment. On the contrary, the consensual nature of the Labour Government's programmes can be exaggerated. The National Health Service, several nationalization measures, the independence of India were all fiercely resisted at times by the Conservatives or outside pressure groups. In many cases, the most radical option was taken up. Cripps as Chancellor retained a commitment to high social spending, for all the rigours of austerity. Attlee himself, from the nationalization of hospitals to the recognition of Communist China, often confirmed Kenneth Younger's, perhaps surprising, view of him as 'the outside-left' member of the Cabinet. It was a gifted administration, a Government of prima donnas in many ways, but one in which the broad vision of Bevin, the managerial skills of Morrison, the spartan intensity of Cripps, the ebullient authority of Dalton, the charismatic appeal of Bevan, the intellectualism of Gaitskell, the experience of Addison, the administrative flair of Wilson, and the gut class loyalty of Griffiths, Isaacs, Shinwell and others all welded into some kind of coherent whole. The socialist ideal still retained its validity for all these men and women, with Attlee himself anxious to reinforce it. But this ideal was combined with executive competence in most areas and a zest for power rare in the somewhat innocent annals of the British left. [Morgan, pp. 495–6]

Books Cited

R. H. S. Crossman, *New Fabian Essays* (Turnstile Press, 1952)

C. R. Attlee, *As it Happened* (Heinemann, 1954)

M. Foot, *Aneurin Bevan* (Davis-Poynter, 1973)

P. M. Williams, *Hugh Gaitskell* (OUP, 1982)

A. Bullock, *Ernest Bevin, Foreign Secretary* (Heinemann, 1983)

D. N. Pritt, *The Labour Government 1945–51* (Lawrence and Wishart, 1963)

R. Eatwell, *The 1945–1951 Labour Governments* (Batsford, 1979)

K. O. Morgan, *Labour in Power, 1945–1951* (Clarendon Press, 1984)

BIBLIOGRAPHY BIBLIOGRAPHY BIBLIOGRAPHY BIBLIOGRAPHY BIBLIOGRAPHY BIBLIOGRAPHY
BIBLIOGRAPHY BIBLIOGRAPHY B**CHAPTER 12**GRAPHY BIBLIOGRAPHY BIBLIOGRAPHY
BIBLIOGRAPHY BIBLIOGRAPHY BIBLIOGRAPHY BIBLIOGRAPHY BIBLIOGRAPHY BIBLIOGRAPHY
BIBLIOGRAPHY BIBLIOGRAPHY BIBLIO**FURTHER READING**OGRAPHY BIBLIOGRAPHY BIBLIOGRAPHY
BIBLIOGRAPHY BIBLIOGRAPHY BIBLIOGRAPHY BIBLIOGRAPHY BIBLIOGRAPHY BIBLIOGRAPHY
BIBLIOGRAPHY BIBLIOGRAPHY BIBLIOGRAPHY BIBLIOGRAPHY BIBLIOGRAPHY BIBLIOGRAPHY

General

Essential

C. J. Bartlett, *A History of Post-War Britain, 1945–1974* (Longman, 1977)

V. Bogdanor and R. Skidelsky, *The Age of Affluence* (Macmillan, 1970)

Chris Cook and J. Stevenson, *The Longman Handbook of Modern British History* (Longman, 1983)

A. Sked and C. Cook, *Post-War Britain, A Political History* (Penguin, 1979)

Recommended

P. Calvocoressi, *The British Experience, 1945–1975* (Bodley Head, 1978)

D. Childs, *Britain since 1945, a Political History* (Benn, 1979)

P. J. Madgwick, D. Steed and L. J. Williams, *Britain since 1945* (Hutchinson, 1982)

D. McKie and C. Cook, *The Decade of Disillusion British Politics in the 1960s* (Macmillan, 1962)

K. Robbins, *The Eclipse of a Great Power, Modern Britain 1870–1975* (Longman, 1983)

A. Sampson, *The Changing Anatomy of Britain* (Coronet Books, 1982)

The British Economy, 1945–79

Essential

The Annual Abstract of Statistics (HMSO)

R. Bacon and W. Eltis, *Britain's Economic Problem, Too Few Producers* (Macmillan, 1970)

R. E. Caves (ed.), *Britain's Economic Prospects* (Allen & Unwin, 1968)

R. E. Caves and L. Krause (eds.), *Britain's Economic Performance* (Brookings, 1980)

J. C. R. Dow, *The Management of the British Economy* (CUP, 1960)

S. F. Pollard, *The Development of the British Economy* (Arnold, 1983)

A. R. Prest and D. J. Coppock (eds.), *The UK Economy, 9th edn* (Weidenfeld & Nicolson, 1982)

Recommended

Sir N. Chester, *The Nationalisation of British Industry* (HMSO, 1977)

British Economy Survey, various issues (OUP)

Studies in the British Economy, various titles (Heinemann Educational Books)

S. Brittan, *Steering the Economy* (Pelican, 1971)

M. Stewart, *Keynes and After* (Penguin, 1970)

Political Developments, 1945–79

Essential

D. Butler and A. Sloman (eds), *British Political Facts,* 4th edn (Macmillan, 1975)

S. H. Beer, *Modern British Politics* 2nd edn (Faber and Faber, 1982)

C. Cook and J. Ramsden (eds) *Trends in British Politics since 1945* (Macmillan, 1978)

F. Stacey, *The British Government, 1966–1975, Years of Reform* (OUP, 1975)

K. O. Morgan, *Labour in Power, 1945–1951* (Clarendon Press, 1984)

Recommended

C. Cook, *A Short History of the Liberal Party, 1900–1976* (Macmillan, 1976)

P. Jenkins, *The Battle for No. 10 Downing Street* (Knight, 1970)

A. Michie and S. Hoggart, *The Pact: The Inside Story of the Lib-Lab Government, 1977–78* (Quartet Books, 1984)

H. Pelling, *The Labour Governments, 1945–51* (Macmillan, 1984)

R. Rhodes James, *Ambitions and Realities in British Politics 1964–70* (Weidenfeld & Nicolson, 1972)

Biographies and Memoirs

Essential

A. Bullock, *Ernest Bevin, Foreign Secretary* (Heinemann, 1983)

R. H. S. Crossman, *The Crossman Diaries,* ed. A. Howard (Hamish Hamilton, 1979)

M. Foot, *Aneurin Bevan, vol II, 1945–1966* (Davis-Poynter, 1973)

K. Harris, *Attlee* (Weidenfeld & Nicolson, 1982)

H. Wilson, *The Labour Government, 1964–70, A Personal Record* (Weidenfeld & Nicolson, 1971)

Final Term: The Labour Government, 1974–1976 (Weidenfeld & Nicolson, 1979)

Recommended

C. R. Attlee, *As It Happened* (Heinemann, 1954)

R. A. Butler, *The Art of the Possible* (Hamish Hamilton, 1971)

Barbara Castle, *The Castle Diaries, 1964–1970* (Weidenfeld & Nicolson, 1984)

  The Castle Diaries, 1974–1976 (Weidenfeld & Nicolson, 1980)

B. Donoughue and G. Jones, *Herbert Morrison* (Davis–Poynter, 1973)

Lord Home, *The Way the Wind Blows* (Collins, 1976)

H. Macmillan, *Memoirs, vols 1–6* (Macmillan, 1966–73)

H. Pelling, *Winston Churchill* (Macmillan, 1974)

P. M. Williams, *Hugh Gaitskell* (OUP, 1982)

LOCAL RESEARCH PROJECT

1945–80 Parliamentary Elections, the Welfare State

In the period after 1945 History shades into its related disciplines of Sociology, Politics and Economics, and it becomes increasingly difficult to draw a clear dividing line between the past and the present. Almost any aspect of contemporary Britain would be worth investigating at the local level, whether it be the changes in the organisation of local government or regional differences in unemployment. The following suggestions are intended only as examples of the kind of study that might be feasible.

The fortunes of the main political parties could be traced at the local level through the history of individual constituencies. It would be well worth investigating how closely local results mirrored national ones, and the part played by local issues and local personalities in determining them.

Another possible area would be the development of the Welfare State. This could involve the inauguration of the National Health Service in a particular locality, and any subsequent changes in the level of health care. The working of the National Insurance and National Assistance Acts could be studied through the local office of the Department of Health and Social Security, and the operation of Welfare Services through the local authority.

Suggested sources of information

Introductory

British Political Facts, D. Butler (ed.) and A. Sloman, 4th edn (Macmillan, 1975)

Keesings Archives

D. Fraser, *The Evolution of the British Welfare State* (Macmillan, 1982)

Further sources

Local newspapers should give adequate coverage of elections. Local party headquarters and the County Record Office may have copies of past campaign literature.

Most hospitals were in existence before the National Health Service came into operation in 1948. Their individual histories could indicate the quality of health care both before and after the introduction of the NHS. Hospital records are also likely to be found in the County Record Office.

The local office of the Department of Health and Social Security can usually supply copies of the full range of leaflets on benefits and contributions currently in force. There is no better way of appreciating the range and complexity of Britain's Welfare State.

CHAPTER **13**

Britain and the World, 1945–79

A ▬▬▬ BRITAIN AND THE CHANGING ▬▬▬ BALANCE OF POWER

'Britain had entered the Second World War as an independent great power, but she no longer possessed that status when she emerged from it.' [Kennedy, p. 362] Such a verdict is easy to pronounce with the wisdom of hindsight. In 1945 the situation looked rather different. With 5 million men in the armed forces and a further 4 million engaged in their support, Britain's contribution to the Allied war effort fell not far short of that of the United States. Alone of the Allied powers who met at Yalta and Potsdam in 1945 Britain had fought from the first to the last day of the Second World War. British forces were stationed in Germany, Italy, North Africa, Greece, India and Burma in 1945. They would soon return to Hong Kong, Malaya and Singapore. Churchill had played a leading part in all the Allied conferences that took place between 1941 and 1945. He expected to be treated as an equal by Stalin and Roosevelt. Though he likened himself to 'a poor little English donkey' seated between 'the great Russian Bear' and 'the great American Buffalo' at the Teheran Conference in 1943, it was the donkey 'who knew the right way home'. [Pelling, p. 546] In terms of her commitments, responsibilities and experience Britain was still a great power. It was a Labour Prime Minister, Harold Wilson, who as late as 1964 stated in a speech at the Guildhall: 'We are a world power and a world influence or we are nothing.' [*The Times*, 17 November 1964]

The Situation in 1945

P. M. Kennedy, *The Realities behind Diplomacy 1865–1980* (1981)

H. Pelling, *Winston Churchill* (1974)

But there was an alarming disparity between this claim and the resources needed to sustain it. By 1945 the emergence of the two superpowers, Russia and the United States, was clearly visible. Though Russia had sustained 20 million casualties in the Second World War she had inflicted 75% of the losses suffered by the German army, and by the end of the war had a huge advantage over the Western powers in conventional armaments and manpower. Her tanks and aircraft were the equal of any other country. Her expertise in rocketry was to astonish the world with the launching of the first Sputnik (space satellite) in 1957.

The United States in 1945 alone possessed the capacity to manufacture nuclear weapons. Subjected neither to bombing nor invasion, the American economy had thrived under the stimulus of war production. American industry and agriculture had expanded their capacity and the United States by 1945 was not only the richest country in the world; by virtue of her possession of nuclear weapons, she was also the most powerful.

Britain's economic position by comparison was dire. Within months of the ending of hostilities she was forced to negotiate a loan from the United States, and when that ran out, to seek further relief. Her economic survival depended on making manpower available for her export industries. Every attempt to increase defence spending imposed strains on the economy. Thus while Britain enjoyed the illusion of great power status, or perhaps it would be better to say had to bear that burden, she never commanded the resources to match her responsibilities. This did not mean that she had a negligible influence on international affairs. Britain, both for reasons of her history and her geographical position, stands at a point where three sets of international relationships meet. She is at the centre of the Commonwealth; she is linked to Western Europe; and for much of the past 40 years she has claimed, sometimes deservedly, sometimes not, a special relationship with the United States.

The Commonwealth connection, to put it at its lowest value, has given Britain a point of contact with many of the developing countries of the Third World, both in Africa and Asia. Despite her reservations about European integration, Britain's defence policy has been wedded to that of Western Europe since 1949. And while the relationship with the United States may at times have lost its special flavour, it is still true to say that Britain has been the most reliable ally of the United States and the main beneficiary of American aid and support. Dean Acheson, American Secretary of State from 1949 to 1953, made an observation in 1962 which has now achieved the status of a cliché: 'Britain has lost an empire and has not yet found a role.' It would perhaps be truer to say that between 1945 and 1979 Britain had too many roles to play. The difficulty facing British statesmen was which one to choose.

Makers of Policy

	Prime Minister		Foreign Secretary
1945–51	Attlee		Bevin
		1951	Morrison
1951–55	Churchill		Eden
1955–57	Eden		Selwyn Lloyd
1957–63	Macmillan	1957	Selwyn Lloyd
		1960	Lord Home
1963–64	Lord Home	1963	Butler
1964–70	Wilson	1964	Gordon-Walker
		1965	Stewart
		1966	Brown
		1968	Stewart
1970–74	Heath	1970	Lord Home
1974–76	Wilson	1974	Callaghan
1976–79	Callaghan	1976	Crosland
		1977	Owen

No radical changes in the allocation of responsibilities for the conduct of diplomacy have occurred since 1945. The relative power and influence of the Foreign Secretary in relation to the Prime Minister has varied according to the personalities involved. It has been suggested that Attlee gave a much freer hand to Bevin than Chamberlain did, for instance, to Halifax or Eden: 'You don't keep a dog and bark yourself and Ernie was a very good dog.' [Harris, p. 268] But Attlee and Bevin saw eye to eye on most issues in any case, and when Bevin was ill it was Attlee who deputised for him. A similar relationship existed between Churchill and Eden, though there were occasional disagreements between the two, for instance over British participation in the European army that was mooted in 1950. When Eden became Prime Minister in 1955, with his long experience as Foreign Secretary, he found it impossible to delegate responsibility to Selwyn Lloyd and handled the Suez crisis virtually by himself. Eden's successors were generally unwilling to leave foreign affairs to their Foreign Secretaries. Macmillan took a leading part in the negotiation of the Nuclear Test Ban Treaty. Wilson changed his Foreign Secretaries three times in the course of his first premiership, and insisted on handling all critical negotiations himself. George Brown resigned in disgust in 1968 after failure to consult him about measures to be taken in an international currency crisis. Heath, with an experienced Lord Home at his elbow, still preferred to handle the vital talks that led to Britain's successful application to join the EEC himself. Both Wilson in his second premiership, and Callaghan, kept a close eye on foreign affairs. It is safe to say that of the Foreign Secretaries who have held office since 1945 only Ernest Bevin and Eden took significant personal initiatives. Responsibility in the main rested with the Prime Minister.

K. Harris, *Attlee*, (Weidenfeld & Nicolson, 1982)

The Foreign Office continued to play its traditional role. Bevin, despite his working-class background, made no changes to the permanent officials he inherited; Sir Alexander Cadogan, ex-Etonian, remained as Permanent under-secretary until his retirement in 1946. Bevin refused to make political appointments to the top posts in the Foreign Service because of the damage this might do to the career structure. He was determined to maintain the high calibre of the men who advised him. Members of the Foreign Service for their part showed an equal liking and admiration for their boss. On his 70th birthday all the staff contributed to present Bevin with an enormous birthday cake. It was an unprecedented gesture which indicated the community of outlook between the Foreign Secretary and his Department.

During Attlee's premiership the cabinet was rarely consulted on foreign policy issues. No cabinet committee was appointed to handle overseas policy and, more damningly, the decision that Britain should proceed with an independent nuclear deterrent was confined to the few members of the cabinet who were directly involved: Attlee, Bevin, Cripps, Morrison, Greenwood, Dalton and Wilmot. Eden was similarly unwilling to submit his policies during the Suez crisis to the scrutiny of the full cabinet. Macmillan launched his initiative to take Britain into the Common Market in December 1960 before taking the cabinet into his confidence. Where serious divisions over policy did occur, however, the cabinet could not be ignored. One such occasion was the suggestion that a British force might be sent to the Straits of Tiran during the Arab–Israeli War of June 1967. Wilson and Brown were evidently in favour of such an initiative but were overruled in the cabinet. [Crossman, p. 315] A more serious division developed in 1975 over whether Britain should accept the renegotiated terms of entry into the EEC. Seven members of the Labour cabinet were opposed to acceptance and it was only by using the device of a referendum that the Prime Minister was able to get his way. Foreign Affairs were a regular item on the agenda at cabinet meetings, but in most cases the Prime

A. Howard (ed.), Richard Crossman, *The Crossman Diaries, selections from the Diaries of a Cabinet Minister 1964–1970* (1979)

Minister and the Foreign Secretary had agreed on the line to be taken in advance, and most cabinet ministers were too busy with their own departments to query what had been decided.

If the cabinet played little part in the formulation of foreign policy this was even more true of Parliament. For most of the post-war period there was in any case a consensus between the two front benches on foreign policy issues. Bevin's severest critics were to be found on his own backbenches. Eden found himself much in accord with Bevin's policies: 'In Parliament I usually followed him in debate and I would publicly have agreed with him more, if I had not been anxious to embarrass him less.' [Eden, p. 5] The fault-line on most foreign policy issues ran not between the major parties but between the right and left wings of the Labour party. Thus a Labour government could almost always count on Conservative support when threatened by its own backbenchers; conversely, right-wing rebels on the Conservative side could expect no help from the Labour party, except in relation to the EEC. On only two foreign-policy issues were there serious confrontations between the two major parties. In 1956 the Labour Opposition was strongly critical of the Anglo-French invasion of Egypt, and in 1972 there was furious, if somewhat artificial, objection by the Labour party to the European Communities Act under which Britain entered the EEC. It may reasonably be concluded that Britain's foreign policy was made primarily by the Prime Ministers and Foreign Secretaries concerned, subject to the advice they received from the Foreign Office and the Chiefs of Staff, and subject to the approval of the cabinet, when it was consulted. When there was opposition in Parliament, it was never powerful enough to bring about changes in policy.

Sir A. Eden, *Full Circle* (1960)

The Aims of Policy

It is a truism to say that the aim of foreign policy is to maintain the national interest. The problem lies in defining the national interest. According to Bevin's biographer, he saw it in these terms: 'the security of the United Kingdom and its overseas possessions against external attack; the continued financial and economic as well as political independence of Britain; the right of its people to trade freely with the rest of the world, their right to maintain a policy of full employment and a decent standard of living.' [Bullock, p. 109] With these goals all his successors would have concurred. With the exception of the last two, so would most of Bevin's predecessors. What had changed in 1945 was the international context in which these aims were to be pursued. There were three essential differences from the pre-war world: first, the dominant position held by Russia and the United States, to which reference has already been made; second, the growing tension between the Communist states of Russia and Eastern Europe on the one hand and Western Europe and the United States on the other; thirdly the growing strength of nationalist sentiment in the old colonial empires of Holland, France and Britain. Britain's relations with the superpowers, her role in the Cold War and her changing attitude to Western Europe form the subject for the rest of this chapter. Her response to the challenge of nationalism in the Empire is reserved for the final one. This division, it must be admitted, is in some ways an unnatural one. The interests of the British Empire entered into the calculations of every Foreign Secretary, just as there was frequently an international dimension to be considered in Britain's dealings with her colonies or former colonies. But the process of de-colonisation developed its own momentum. The Colonial Office retained its separate identity until 1966 when it was merged with the Commonwealth Relations Office, and this in turn was absorbed into the

A. Bullock, *Ernest Bevin, Foreign Secretary* (1984)

Foreign Office in 1968. While these changes reflected the diminution of the empire, for the first 20 years after 1945 foreign and imperial policy were the responsibility of different cabinet departments, and they merit separate treatment.

B ▬▬▬▬▬▬▬ BRITAIN AND THE COLD WAR

The apparent amity displayed by the three Allied leaders at the Teheran Conference in 1943 proved to be misleading. By 1945 sharp disagreements had materialised over the terms of the peace settlements. By 1947 mutual distrust had reached a point where no further agreement seemed to be possible. By 1949 the world was divided into two armed camps. Whether this development was inevitable is one of those questions to which historians can give no certain answer. What will be attempted here is to suggest reasons for the development of the Cold War and then to trace the stages through which it progressed.

The Origin of the Cold War

In explaining the Cold War there is one immediate problem. The motives and actions of Western politicians are now reasonably well documented. Under the 30-year rule most British government records for the period 1945 to 1954 are now open to investigation. But no such licence operates in the Soviet Union. Russian motives can only be inferred from public statements and actions. Russian policy is thus open to the constant danger of misinterpretation and misrepresentation. Actions may speak louder than words but we can still only guess at the motives which informed them.

Three such motives have commonly been attributed to explain Russian foreign policy after 1945. In the first place the Soviet Union has a vested interest in the triumph of Communism, and a positive duty to bring it about. The *Communist Manifesto* concludes with an appeal to the workers of the world to 'unite and throw off your chains'. Karl Marx's grave in Highgate Cemetery is still an official shrine on the itinerary of any visiting Soviet dignitary. There is no sign in Russian circles that his words have lost their relevance, whatever view may be taken in Pekin. It has also been argued that the Soviet Union has displayed the same expansionist tendencies that characterised the Russia of Peter the Great and Catherine the Great. The urge to dominate Eastern Europe, Turkey, Iran and Afghanistan has a long historical pedigree. On the other hand, defenders of Soviet policy can point to the continuing fear of attack by capitalist countries. Allied intervention in the Russian Civil War of 1918–19; fears of a possible alliance with Nazi Germany in 1938, when Russia was excluded from the Munich Conference; finally, the unprovoked invasion of Russia by Germany in 1941; all these events lent a certain credibility to Russian apprehension. It might be claimed that Russian expansion was primarily defensive in character, its purpose being to surround the Russian heartland with a ring of friendly buffer states. The real, and in the present state of the evidence, unanswerable question, is whether the Soviet Union after 1945 was motivated by fear or ambition. Western statesmen have, for the most part assumed that it was ambition, and their responses to Russian policy have been based on that assumption. It would be surprising, perhaps, if the Russians did not reach similar conclusions about Western policies. Thus, what to Britain and the United States may have seemed perfectly reasonable defensive preparations, in Soviet eyes took on the appearance of menacing threats.

K. Marx, *Communist Manifesto* (1848) (Penguin, 1969)

Before equating the policies of the two sides, however, two further points need to be made. Stalin's Russia, as was publicly admitted at the Twentieth Communist Party Congress in 1956, was a dictatorship where the cult of personality flourished. The liquidation of the Kulaks (the class of wealthy Russian peasants which emerged in the 1920s) and the notorious purges and show trials of the 1930s were echoed after 1945 in the treatment of dissidents such as Boris Pasternak and Alexander Solzhenitsyn and in the denial of basic political rights, to form political parties, for instance. Once the gloss of the wartime alliance had worn off the Soviet Union re-emerged in its true colours as a totalitarian dictatorship. Russian counter accusations of the heartlessness of capitalist economic systems and the gross inequalities to which they give rise may have had some validity. But they were less applicable to a Britain whose government was committed to maintaining full employment and extending the Welfare State. It needs finally to be remembered that in the initial stages of the Cold War at least, the pressures for change came from the Soviet Union. It was the apparently remorseless spread of Communist regimes across Eastern Europe that provoked the first hostile responses from the West.

The Breakdown of Trust, 1944–46

Wartime Negotiations

It was clear in the final stages of the war that the chief problems the Allies would have to resolve would be the treatment of Germany and the settlement of Eastern Europe. Both these issues were in fact the ones on which agreement could not be reached. The first sketch of a possible settlement was drawn up in a meeting between Churchill and Stalin held in Moscow in October 1944. Churchill's inimitable account deserves to be quoted in full:

> The moment was apt for business, so I said, 'Let us settle about our affairs in the Balkans. Your armies are in Rumania and Bulgaria. We have interests, missions and agents there. Don't let us get at cross-purposes in small ways. So far as Britain and Russia are concerned, how would it do for us to have ninety per cent. of the say in Greece, and go fifty-fifty about Yugoslavia?' While this was being translated I wrote out on a half-sheet of paper:
> Rumania
>   Russia 90%
>   The others 10%
> Greece
>   Great Britain
>   (in accord with the United States) 90%
>   Russia 10%
> Yugoslavia 50%–50%
> Hungary 50%–50%
> Bulgaria
>   Russia 75%
>   The others 25%
> I pushed this across to Stalin, who had by then heard the translation. There was a slight pause. Then he took his blue pencil and made a large tick upon it and passed it back to us. It was all settled in no more time than it takes to set down. [Churchill, p. 198]

W. S. Churchill, *The Second World War*, vol. VI, *Triumph and Tragedy* (1954)

Yalta

But by the time the Allied leaders next conferred at Yalta in February 1945 disagreements were already coming to the surface. Arrangements were made for the Allied occupation of Germany and its division into three zones, Russian, American and British. A fourth French zone was subsequently added. But the Russians put in a claim for $20 000 million in reparations, a sum Churchill considered far too large. He pointed out to Stalin that 'if you wanted a horse to pull your waggon you had to give him some hay'. This homely analogy had little effect on the Russian leader. Stalin also claimed that each of the 16 republics that made up the USSR should be entitled to seats at the United Nations, the organisation that was to replace the League. This was whittled down to three seats by the end of the Conference. Much the most serious disagreements arose over the future of Poland. There were three points at issue: the composition of the new Polish government; Poland's frontiers, both on the East and the West; and how and when free elections were to be held.

Stalin wanted recognition to be given to the Soviet-sponsored and Communist-dominated government that had been set up at Lublin, south of Warsaw. Churchill and Roosevelt, to a lesser extent, were anxious to see the inclusion in any future Polish government of members of the Polish Government-in-Exile that had been set up in London, and to ensure that proper recognition was given to the interests of the 150 000 Poles who were serving in the Allied armies. Stalin wanted to extend Russia's frontiers to the Curzon line, recovering the territory that had been lost in the Russo-Polish war of 1920, while Poland would be compensated by extending her Western frontier to the line of the Oder and Western Neisse rivers. Churchill and Roosevelt accepted that there would have to be some revision of Germany's Eastern frontier, but feared that extending Poland's gains to the Western Neisse would mean the inclusion of up to 8 million Germans within Poland's new boundaries. Churchill was anxious for Western observers to be able to supervise elections which should be held as soon as possible. Stalin argued that this was a matter for the Polish government to decide. For the time being these disagreements were shelved, but none of them were resolved and it was clear that another conference would have to be held as soon as Germany had been defeated.

Potsdam

Between Yalta and the Potsdam Conferences several developments occurred to worsen relations. On 6 March a Soviet-dominated administration was installed at Bucharest. On 21 April a treaty of alliance was signed between Russia and the Lublin government; and 16 Polish resistance leaders, invited to Moscow under promise of safe conduct to discuss the broadening of the Lublin regime, had been arrested. Churchill took two initiatives in response. On 29 April he addressed a long personal letter to Stalin, voicing his complaints and concluding:

> There is not much comfort in looking into a future where you and the countries you dominate, plus the Communist Parties in many other States, are all drawn up on one side, and those who rally to the English speaking nations and their associates or Dominions are on the other. It is quite obvious that their quarrel would tear the world to pieces and that all of us leading men on either side who had anything to do with that would be shamed before history. [Churchill, p. 433]

Churchill, *Triumph and Tragedy*

Churchill also urged Truman, who had succeeded Roosevelt as President of the United States, not to withdraw American troops from those parts of Germany that were to be in the Russian zone before the Potsdam Conference convened. In this he was unsuccessful.

Meanwhile, in Britain the decision had been taken to hold a General Election. Quite by accident it took place during the Potsdam Conference, which convened on

15 July 1945 and adjourned on 2 August. The election campaign opened on 15 June, polling took place between 5 July and 19 July, and the results were announced on 26 July. Thus at a critical stage in the negotiations Churchill and Eden were replaced by Attlee and Bevin. Nothing could illustrate better the continuity of British policy than the ease with which this transition was accomplished. Churchill, as we have seen, invited Attlee to accompany him to the opening stages of the Conference, and Attlee flatly rejected Harold Laski's view that he could attend only as an observer. In correspondence with Churchill, Attlee agreed that 'there seemed to be a great public advantage in preserving and presenting to the world at this time the unity on foreign policy which we maintained through the last five years'. [Bullock, p. 67] Bevin, who much to his surprise, was made Foreign Secretary in the Attlee cabinet on July 28, fully concurred. He, too, had been a member of the Coalition government. While the personnel of the British delegation at Potsdam changed half way through the Conference, its policies did not.

Bullock, *Ernest Bevin*

Allied Leaders at Potsdam, July 1945: Stalin, Truman and Churchill

The Conference succeeded in settling the final boundaries of the zones of occupation, including special arrangements for Berlin which would be jointly occupied by the four powers, Russia, the United States, Britain and France. But Bevin objected as strongly as Churchill had done to the extension of Poland's Western boundary to the Oder-Western Neisse line. There were also disagreements about reparations. In the end, a compromise formula tying up the two issues was agreed by James Byrnes, the American Secretary of State, and Molotov, the Russian Foreign Minister. Bevin had no choice but to comply. Poland gained the boundary it wanted and the Russians undertook to return to the Western Zones an equivalent proportion of the value of the industrial goods they were to receive in reparations in the form of food, coal and raw materials. The Potsdam Conference papered over the cracks that were beginning to separate East and West. While in theory Germany was to be treated as a single unit, both economically and politically, as each country now began to extract reparations from its own zone this meant that the economic division of Germany began from the first days of the Allied occupation. Because most of Germany's agriculture was located in the Russian zone, Britain and the United States were soon faced with the task of feeding much of the German population in their zones and they thus had every incentive to get the German economy going again. Russia, who had suffered much more severely, was anxious to extract whatever she could from her zone. After Potsdam the prospects of a united Germany steadily receded.

EAST EUROPE IN 1945: THE POLISH FRONTIER

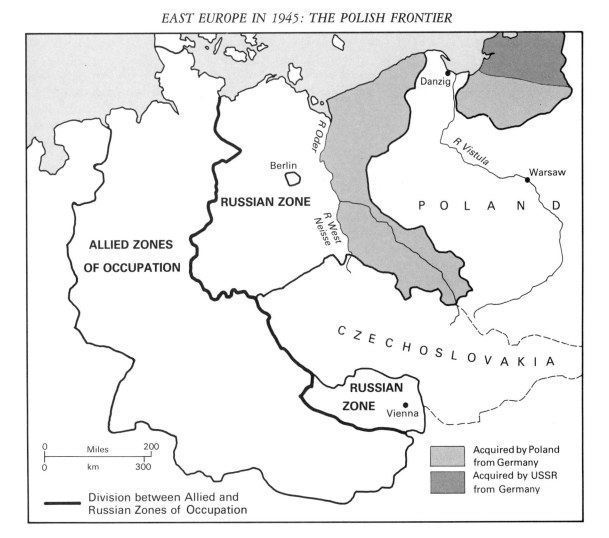

Labour's Foreign Policy 1945–46

After the Potsdam Conference, Attlee and Bevin took stock. Neither man had any illusions about the nature of the Soviet threat. Attlee's impressions of Stalin had been formed in the first stages of the Conference: 'Reminded me of the Renaissance despots – no principles, any methods, but no flowery language – always Yes or No, though you could count on him if it was No.' [Harris, p. 267] In September, in a letter to a left-wing MP, Fenner Brockway, he widened his condemnation: 'It's no good thinking that moral sentiments have any sway with the Russians, there's a good deal of old-fashioned imperialism in their make-up, you know. Their foreign policy has been carried on in much the same way from the days of Catherine the Great ....' [Harris, p. 245] As a powerful trade union leader, Bevin might perhaps have been expected to take a more flattering view of the Soviet Union. Much was made of a remark he made to the Labour Party Conference at Blackpool in May 1945: 'Left understands Left but the Right does not.' But, as Alan Bullock has pointed out, this remark was made in reference to the failure of the Conservative government to come to terms with the Popular Front established by Leon Blum in France, in 1936. Bevin never showed the slightest sympathy with Communism, either in Britain or abroad. He had an old-fashioned faith in the British Empire and was even more sensitive to the threat of Soviet expansion than Attlee.

K. Harris, *Attlee*
(Weidenfeld & Nicolson, 1982)

The next two years saw a steady deterioration in Anglo-Soviet relations. This became evident in the series of conferences that were held between the Foreign Ministers of the four Allies in an attempt to agree on peace terms with their former enemies. The first such conference was held in September 1945 at Lancaster House in London, to discuss peace treaties with Italy, Rumania, Bulgaria, Hungary and Finland. There were disagreements over the Italian-Yugoslav border, with Russia supporting the Yugoslav claim to Trieste, and over the fate of Italy's North African colonies, to which Russia laid a claim. Britain and the United States opposed Russia on both these issues, needless to say, and the conference adjourned without reaching any agreement. Before it reconvened in December, Russia aroused further British suspicions by her actions in the Middle East. Demands were made by Soviet Armenia for the return by Turkey of Kars and Ardahan which had been Turkish since 1921. Russia also gave her support to an independence movement in Azerbaijan in the North of Iran. In December an autonomous republic was proclaimed there, and it looked as though the Soviet Union was preparing to intervene in force in Iran. When the Foreign Ministers met again in Moscow on 17 December Bevin raised these matters. He had little support from Byrnes and was pilloried in the Soviet press as the exponent of British imperialism. But the Conference had one important outcome. President Truman concluded that Byrnes had done less than justice to the British case. In his *Memoirs* he commented: 'There isn't a doubt in my mind that Russia intends an invasion of Turkey and the seizure of the Black Sea Straits .... Unless Russia is faced with an iron fist and strong language another war is in the making .... I do not think we shall play compromise any longer .... I'm tired of babying the Soviets.' [Truman, pp. 492–3] From the beginning of 1946 the British and Americans were more closely in step, an impression that was confirmed by the speech which Churchill delivered, at Truman's invitation, at Fulton, Missouri on 5 March 1946. In it he said: 'From Stettin in the Baltic to Trieste in the Adriatic, an iron curtain has descended across the Continent. Behind that line lie all the capitals of the ancient states of Central and Eastern Europe .... Police governments are prevailing in nearly every case, and so far, except in Czechoslovakia, there is no true democracy.' [Pelling,

p. 566] Neither Bevin nor Attlee knew what Churchill was going to say beforehand, but neither dissented subsequently. Churchill sent an explanatory telegram to Attlee on 7 March, to which Attlee replied thanking him for 'your long and very interesting telegram' and also for the support Churchill had given on the American loan. There was no hint of criticism. On Bevin's reaction, Bullock comments: 'It was impossible for him as Foreign Secretary, or for anyone else, to be as forthright as Churchill in addressing the Americans; he certainly was not going to repudiate him or do anything to weaken the impact of his words.' [Bullock, p. 225] Churchill's speech received a much more hostile reception in the Labour press, while *Pravda* was violently critical. In this worsening atmosphere two further conferences were held, the first in Paris in April and May, the second in New York in November and December. They were not wholly barren. By December agreement had finally been reached on the status of Trieste – it was to become an international city – and on Italy's former colonies in North Africa which were to become independent. Peace treaties were signed with Italy, Rumania, Hungary, Bulgaria and Finland. But the German problem was no nearer solution. In the autumn of 1946 Britain and the United States made preparations to unite their two zones for economic purposes, a move which was strongly resisted by both France and Russia. By the end of 1946 the main features of Labour's foreign policy were clear. Every move to extend Russian influence, whether in Eastern Europe, the Mediterranean or the Middle East, would be opposed, preferably in concert with the Americans. If this led to confrontation, this was the price that had to be paid. An alternative view was reflected in an amendment tabled by 58 Labour MPs in November 1946. It called on His Majesty's Government to recast its conduct of international affairs so as 'to provide a democratic and constructive alternative to an otherwise inevitable conflict between American capitalism and Soviet communism in which all hope of World Government would be destroyed.' [Bullock, p. 328] In the subsequent division, no votes were cast for the amendment, but there were 130 abstentions. That such fears could be expressed, and should receive so much support, is an indication of the distance the world had travelled since 1945.

H. S. Truman, *Memoirs*, vol. I (1958)

H. Pelling, *Winston Churchill* (1974)

Bullock, *Ernest Bevin*

British Defence Policy

The Search for Security

Faced with the apparent threat of Soviet expansion the Labour Government adopted two approaches. Britain's own defences had to be kept in a good state of repair and a system of collective security was gradually established. Both approaches depended on Europe's economic recovery and the continuing support of the United States. So far as conventional forces were concerned British demobilisation proceeded relatively slowly. Substantial British forces were kept in Germany, and conscription was maintained. Defence spending fell from £1736 million in 1946, 20% of GNP, to £700 million in 1948. But as the international climate worsened it rose again to reach a total of £1112 million by 1951–52. The period of conscription was reduced to 12 months in 1947, but was increased to 18 months in 1948 and again to two years in 1950 when defence expenditure absorbed 10% of GNP, a higher proportion than that of any other Western country including the United States.

The Labour Government also decided to proceed with the development of nuclear weapons. At the Quebec Conference in 1943 the United States had promised to share all its discoveries in relation to atomic energy with Britain. But a suspiciously minded Congress passed the Macmahon Act in 1946, forbidding the exchange of atomic information with any other country, including Britain. In these circumstances, Britain had no alternative but to develop her own atomic research programme. In September 1945 a cabinet committee, known as GEN 75, was set up with responsibility for all questions relating to atomic energy. An advisory committee of civil servants and military personnel, headed by Sir John Anderson, now a Conservative MP, was also created. These two committees were responsible for Britain's atomic energy programme. A critical meeting of GEN 75 took place on 25 October 1946 at which it was decided to proceed with the development of a British nuclear weapon. Dalton and Cripps opposed the idea on financial grounds, but the Chiefs of Staff were in favour, as was Bevin who argued that it was 'important for the Union Jack to fly over a British bomb'. [Morgan, p. 282] In January 1947, GEN 75 was replaced by a smaller cabinet committee, GEN 163, on which Dalton and Cripps were no longer represented, and work on the British atomic bomb was started in earnest. Attlee had no doubts about the rightness of this decision: 'If we had decided not to have it, we would have put ourselves entirely in the hands of the Americans. That would have been a risk a British Government should not take .... There was no NATO then. For a power of our size and with our responsibilities to turn its back on the Bomb did not make sense.' [Harris, p. 288] In fact Britain's first atomic bomb was not exploded until 1952, and it must be questioned whether its possession then added greatly to Britain's security at a time when the two superpowers already commanded such a lead in atomic weapons and delivery systems.

K. O. Morgan, *Labour in Power 1945–1951* (Clarendon Press, 1984)

K. Harris, *Attlee* (Weidenfeld & Nicolson, 1982)

The Treaty of Dunkirk

More important than the British decision to proceed with the development of an independent nuclear deterrent was the creation of a system of collective security in Europe, and winning American support for it. The first move in this direction was the Treaty of Dunkirk, signed with France in March 1947. This was a defensive alliance, which was to last for 50 years and pledged the signatories to come to each other's assistance in the event of an attack by Germany. It had a curiously anachronistic ring to it, and Germany in 1947 could hardly be said to pose a threat to anybody. Bevin never fully overcame his suspicion of the Germans, and the Treaty provided some reassurance to France when Germany became integrated into the Western security system. The Treaty's real significance lay in Britain's evident willingness to enter into a formal commitment with another country.

The Truman Doctrine

At the same time as she was assuming a new responsibility in Western Europe, Britain decided that she could no longer afford to sustain an old one in the Mediterranean. Since 1944 British troops had been stationed in Greece to support the royalist Greek government against the Communist-led guerilla movement ELAS. The scale of assistance was considerable. At one time there were 80 000 British troops in Greece, and the costs of British support in 1945–46 came to £132 million. In January 1947, with a serious coal shortage and British industry on half-time because of it, Dalton decided that the price was too high. On 30 January Bevin reluctantly concurred and it was decided that aid both to Greece and Turkey would have to cease by 31 March. Bevin secured one concession. The Greeks would not be told until an approach had been made to the United States to see whether they would step in instead.

The Americans had already been alerted to the possibility of British withdrawal, but it was still a shock when the British ambassador in Washington informed them on 21 February that within six weeks British troops would be withdrawn from

Greece. This makes all the more remarkable the rapidity and scale of the American response. On 12 March Truman made his historic address to Congress which formed the basis of the Truman Doctrine. In the course of it he said:

> I am fully aware of the broad implications involved if the United States extends assistance to Greece and Turkey .... At the present moment in world history nearly every nation must choose between alternative ways of life. The choice is too often not a free one. One way of life is based upon the will of the majority and is distinguished by free institutions, representative government, free elections, guaranties of individual liberty, freedom of speech and religion, and freedom from oppression. The second way of life is based upon the will of a minority forcibly imposed upon the majority. It relies upon terror and oppression, a controlled press and radio, fixed elections, and suppression of personal freedoms. I believe that it must be the policy of the United States to support free peoples who are resisting attempted subjugation by armed minorities or by outside pressures ....

On 22 May Congress duly voted £400 million for aid to Greece and Turkey. To some observers the Truman doctrine was unnecessarily abrasive and divided the world too sharply into black and white. Gladwyn Jebb, a British Foreign Office official at the time, thought the speech 'hasty and ambiguous'. George Kennan, a respected member of the State Department, considered it 'doctrinaire and inflammatory'. But both Bevin and Attlee responded to Truman's message 'with warm enthusiasm'. [Morgan, p. 253] One thing the Truman Doctrine did make absolutely clear was that from now on the United States would be the main Allied protagonist in the Cold War.

K. O. Morgan, *Labour in Power 1945–1951* (Clarendon Press, 1984)

The Marshall Plan

This impression was soon reinforced. In March 1947 the State Department, at the prompting of Dean Acheson, the Under-Secretary of State, launched a series of investigations into all those countries that might need American economic and military assistance. On 28 April George Marshall, now Secretary of State, returned from a visit to Europe convinced that economic aid to Europe was vital. A report presented to the State Department by its under-secretary for Economic Affairs, Will Clayton, concluded: 'without further prompt and substantial aid from the United States, economic, social and political disintegration will overthrow Europe.' [Bullock, p. 402] These were the circumstances that led to Marshall's celebrated speech at Harvard on 5 June, usually taken as the starting point of the Marshall Plan. In his speech, offering American economic aid, Marshall made two vital points. Firstly he stressed the non-partisan purpose behind the American offer: 'Our policy is directed not against any country or doctrine but against hunger, poverty, desperation and chaos. Its purpose should be the revival of a working economy in the world so as to permit the emergence of political and social conditions in which free institutions can exist.' Secondly, Marshall emphasised that Europe must assume responsibility for its own economic recovery: 'It would be neither fitting nor efficacious for this government to undertake to draw up unilaterally a programme designed to place Europe on its feet economically. This is the business of Europeans. The initiative, I think, must come from Europe.' [Vaughan, pp. 22–4] Bevin heard a report of the speech by the BBC correspondent in Washington, Leonard Miall, on his bedside radio. He at once grasped its importance and in the next few weeks devoted all his energies to co-ordinating the European response for which Marshall had called.

Bullock, *Ernest Bevin*

R. Vaughan, *Post-War Integration in Europe, Documents of Modern History* (1976)

He proposed joint action to the French Foreign Minister, George Bidault, on 9 June. He contacted the Dutch and Belgian governments. The Russians were also informed. Talks were held with American officials on 24 June, and on 27 June a vital series of meetings between Bevin, Molotov and Bidault were held in Paris. Whether these negotiations were entered into seriously by either side is reserved for further discussion. (see Points at Issue) Suffice it to say that after five days Molotov made it clear that Russia would refuse to participate in any collective arrangement with the United States, and Britain and France announced their determination to proceed. Subsequently 22 countries were invited to take part in a Committee for European Co-operation. Eight refused, reluctantly in some cases. All were from the Eastern bloc. In April 1948 the Organisation for European Economic Co-operation was formally set up in Paris. It included the following countries: Austria, Belgium, Denmark, France, Greece, Ireland, Iceland, Italy, Luxemburg, the Netherlands, Norway, Portugal, the United Kingdom, Sweden, Switzerland and Turkey. In the same month Congress finally passed the Foreign Assistance Bill under which Marshall Aid was provided for the OEEC to administer. Between 1948 and 1951 the total given to Europe was \$12 billion, of which Britain's share was \$2.6 billion. In the debate held on the treaty under which Britain was to receive Marshall Aid, Cripps described it as 'an act of great immediate generosity'. Left wing doubts about the Truman Doctrine were generally silenced by Marshall Aid, and the House approved the treaty by 409 votes to 12.

The Treaty of Brussels and NATO

The refusal of Marshall Aid by Russia and her satellites marked a final parting of the ways. The Foreign Ministers' Conference, which met in New York in December 1947, ended in mutual recrimination, with no further meetings planned. Soviet pressures on Eastern Europe increased, and the few remaining opposition leaders were either removed or went into exile. [see Bullock, pp. 483–4] In September 1947 the Communist Information Bureau (the Cominform) was established in Moscow, where it began a furious ideological barrage against Western leaders. Attlee and Bevin were singled out: 'A special place in the imperialists' arsenal of tactical weapons is occupied by the utilisation of the treacherous policy of the right-wing socialists like Blum in France, Attlee and Bevin in Britain ....' [Bullock, p. 484] In February 1948 Czechoslovakia, the last bastion of democracy in Eastern Europe fell to a Communist coup. The lesson to be drawn from these developments was that Europe must unite militarily as well as politically.

Bullock, *Ernest Bevin*

Bevin again took a lead in prompting action and in March 1948 the Treaty of Brussels was signed by Britain, France, Belgium, the Netherlands and Luxemburg. It was to last for 50 years and pledged its signatories to come to the aid of any of their number who was attacked. The Treaty also created a Consultative Council, made up of the Foreign Ministers of the five signatories, a committee of the five Defence Ministers and a Permanent Military Committee based in London. The initial steps towards an integrated defence policy for Western Europe had now been taken. But without American military assistance the Treaty was worth little more than the paper it was written on. It was vital to involve the United States. A series of meetings were held at Bevin's suggestion between 22 March and 1 April under the chairmanship of the American ambassador in London, Lew Douglas, with this in mind. Out of their deliberations the North Atlantic Treaty Organisation was eventually to emerge.

The reality of American support for the Brussels Treaty was demonstrated before the acceptance of any formal commitment. Russia had long been suspicious of the economic integration of the Western zones of occupation in Germany, fearing rightly, as it turned out, that this would lead to their political integration. In May 1948 the Allied powers announced a plan to bring in a new currency as a way of tackling the inflation which was damaging the German economy. The Russians retaliated by threatening to introduce a new Soviet-backed currency in the whole of Berlin, West as well as East, and by withdrawing their representative on the four-power *Kommondatura* for the city. The Western powers refused to be dissuaded from proceeding with their currency reform, whereupon Russia imposed a blockade on all road and rail routes to Berlin from the Western zone.

West Berlin had 2.5 million German inhabitants, enough food for 36 days and enough coal for 45. The Allies were faced with three choices: to acquiesce in the blockade and allow West Berlin to become part of the Soviet zone; to break the blockade by force; or to supply the Western zone by air. It was evidently a British RAF officer, Air Commodore Waite, who convinced the British and American commanders, General Robertson and General Clay, that the third solution was feasible. The Berlin airlift duly went ahead. It lasted for 11 months, Britain providing one-third of the flights, a quarter of the supplies and the greater part of the ground organisation. Less well known is the fact that the British government also agreed to the stationing on British aerodromes of B29 bombers supported by F80 fighters. They were armed with atomic weapons. Russia did not yet have the atomic bomb. It is at least conceivable that had the Berlin blockade developed into a shooting war the Americans would have been prepared to use their nuclear weapons.

While the blockade was in progress secret talks were proceeding in Washington with the aim of extending the Treaty of Brussels to Washington. In November 1948 Truman scored a surprising victory in the American presidential elections, and with his return to the White House this removed the last serious obstacle in the way of the negotiations. The final draft of the North Atlantic Treaty was finally agreed on 15 March 1949. The vital clause was Article 5:

> The Parties agree that an armed attack against one or more of them occurring within the area defined below shall be considered an attack against them all; and consequently that, if such an armed attack occurs, each of them in exercise of the right of individual or collective self-defence recognised by Article 51 of the UN Charter, will assist the party or parties so attacked by taking forthwith such military or other action, individually and in concert with the other parties, as may be necessary to restore and assure the security of the North Atlantic area.

The Treaty was signed by the following countries: Britain, France, Belgium, the Netherlands and Luxemburg (the Brussels Treaty powers); Italy, Norway, Denmark, Iceland, Portugal, the United States and Canada. Bullock concludes that securing American commitment to NATO was 'the peak of Bevin's achievement as Foreign Secretary .... and one which for over 30 years, has provided the security and confidence which Bevin sought for Western Europe'. [Bullock, p. 645]

Bullock, *Ernest Bevin*

Britain and the Cold War, 1949–79

Britain, NATO and the United States

Since 1949 British membership of NATO has been the fundamental influence on British foreign policy. Britain's armed forces are at NATO's disposal, her diplomacy has been conducted with a careful regard to the views of her partners in the alliance. As the United States is by far the most powerful member of the organisation, her influence has been the greatest. Whereas up to 1949 it was arguable that Britain played a genuinely independent role in international affairs, since that date, with rare exceptions, her policies have generally been aligned with those of the United States. There is a further contrast. In 1945 the United States took a more optimistic view of Soviet intentions than Britain did and it was the British who tried to stir the Americans into action to combat the threat of Russian expansion, whether in Eastern Europe or the Middle East. After 1949 these roles were reversed. British influence, when it was exercised at all, was generally aimed at achieving some kind of accommodation with the Communist bloc, both with regard to Russia and China. Having encouraged the United States to come to the defence of Western Europe, Britain discovered that she had helped to launch a crusade whose text was the Truman doctrine and whose goals extended around the globe. British opposition to the Soviet Union was generally based on pragmatic grounds. The United States saw the contest in ideological terms.

The Korean War

The first overt challenge to the post-war settlement occurred on 25 June 1950 when North Korean troops crossed the 38th parallel into South Korea. Truman's response was immediate. The Security Council of the United Nations was called into special session. As Russia was boycotting the UN at the time, Truman was able to secure unanimous support for a resolution calling on all members to assist in compelling North Korea to withdraw its forces. The British government, both as a loyal ally of the United States and as a dutiful member of the UN had no hesitation in endorsing Truman's actions. Attlee, in a broadcast to the country, compared the North Korean invasion to the aggression which had led to the Second World War. He warned his audience: 'The fire which has started in distant Korea may burn down your home.' [Harris, p. 456] Britain did what she could to assist. Rearmament was accelerated, conscription extended to two years and a Commonwealth Brigade sent out to Korea where it gave distinguished service.

K. Harris, *Attlee*
(Weidenfeld & Nicolson, 1982)

By the end of September 1950 UN troops had reached the 38th parallel. But neither Britain nor the United States were at this stage prepared merely to see the restoration of the status quo. On 7 October Bevin sponsored a resolution at the UN calling for all appropriate steps to be taken to ensure stability *throughout all Korea*, and for elections to be held under UN auspices for the establishment of a unified, independent and democratic government in the sovereign state of Korea. General MacArthur, the UN Commander, interpreted this as a mandate to invade North Korea and on 9 October he did so. Warnings from the Indian Prime Minister, Nehru, that this might provoke Chinese intervention were ignored. On 26 November the Chinese retaliated in strength. Taken by surprise, the Americans were soon in headlong retreat. On 30 November at a press conference Truman unwittingly conveyed the impression that the United States was considering the use of nuclear weapons, and that the final decision on their use would be taken by the theatre commander, the mercurial MacArthur. This caused such alarm in Britain that an emergency cabinet meeting was held at which Attlee was commissioned to fly to see

Truman, his first crossing of the Atlantic for five years. Attlee arrived in Washington on 4 December and had several talks with Truman. He returned reassured, and reported to the cabinet:

> The President had entirely satisfied him about the use of the bomb. He had assured the Prime Minister that he regarded the atomic bomb as the joint possession of the United States, the United Kingdom and Canada, and that he would not authorise its use without prior consultation with the other two governments save in an extreme emergency – such as an atomic attack on the United States which called for immediate retaliation. [Harris, pp. 465–6]

K. Harris, *Attlee* (Weidenfeld & Nicolson, 1982)

The Korean War lingered on until 1953, Britain maintaining her military support until the armistice was finally signed. The frontier was re-established along the 38th parallel. Eden, Foreign Secretary at the time, commented: 'Thanks to the decision of President Truman and those who upheld him, the worst Korean tragedy was averted. The warning was clear, the invasion was stayed, the balance restored.' [Eden, p. 28]

Eden, *Full Circle*

Britain, the United States and the Far East, 1949–54

The Korean War brought to public attention the change in regime that had taken place in Pekin the previous year, when the Chinese Communist Party had won its final victory over the Nationalist leader, Chiang Kai Shek. Britain and the United States were sharply divided in their attitudes to the new China. For Britain, the triumph of Communism was an unwelcome fact that had to be recognised. The United States, which had invested much more heavily in aid to Chiang Kai Shek, refused to recognise the new Chinese government on the grounds that to do so would be to condone an illegal regime. Britain was thus forced into the ambiguous position of according diplomatic recognition to the Pekin government while denying it the right to representation at the United Nations where Chiang Kai Shek retained his seat. There were also differences of view over Indo-China.

Britain had first been involved in this area in 1946 when British troops occupied part of the peninsula, prior to the return of the French. There followed an eight-year war between the Communist-led Vietminh in North Vietnam and the Pathet Lao in Laos on the one side and a series of French-backed puppet governments in South Vietnam, Cambodia and Laos on the other. Eden doubted as early as 1951 whether the French had much chance of military success. When Molotov suggested in January 1954 that a conference might be held, including China, to reduce tension in international relations, Eden seized the opportunity. An international conference at which Communist China, France, Russia, the United States and Britain would be represented was arranged to meet at Geneva in May. Before the Conference met the Vietminh launched a fierce assault at a key French defensive position, Dien Bien Phu. Its loss was critical. The French government put in an urgent plea for American air support. Eden did his best to dissuade the United States from getting involved and he refused to associate Britain with a declaration, suggested by the Americans, that the United States and France would be prepared to use military means to check the expansion of Communism in South East Asia.

At the Geneva Conference which met from May to July, Eden and Molotov acted as joint chairmen and enjoyed a surprisingly good working relationship. Agreement was finally reached on 21 July. Laos and Cambodia were to be neutralised; a temporary frontier between North and South Vietnam was to be drawn, just south of the 17th parallel, pending free elections; and a supervisory commission made up of representatives from Poland, India and Canada was set up to police the agreements. The Americans refused to sign the final communiqué. The Geneva Agreements proved to be only a temporary break in the long agony of the Vietnam War, but Britain could at least claim to have played an honourable part in the attempt to end it.

The Problem of Germany

While Britain and Russia reached agreement over Indo-China, no such accord proved possible where Germany was concerned. There were two related and insoluble aspects to the German problem. Granted the huge superiority in conventional forces enjoyed by the Russians (they were calculated to have 175 divisions to the West's 14 in 1950) some German contribution to NATO came to be seen as essential. The United States began pressing for this as early as 1950. Inevitably such a move would bring West Germany firmly into the Western camp and make the problem of German reunification a great deal more difficult. The second continuing difficulty was the status of West Berlin. As the division of Germany came to assume a more permanent character the Russians argued, not without some justification, that the arrangements made at Potsdam no longer had any relevance. The special status accorded to West Berlin was thus a continuing source of grievance to the Russians. Its prosperity, boosted by American investment, was a constant reproach to the poorer Eastern sector of the city; it also provided a loophole through which it has been calculated as many as 4 million East Germans made their way to the freer and lusher pastures of West Germany between 1951 and 1961. Conversely, West Berlin was seen as a touchstone by which to judge the sincerity of Western support for West Germany and for democratic institutions. Though there was a tacit recognition that while the West might deplore Russion actions in Eastern Europe they would not interfere with them, this licence could not be allowed to extend to West Berlin.

The Berlin blockade ended in May 1949 without changing anything, except in so far as it had made clear the West's determination to maintain their presence in West Berlin. In the summer of 1949 the Federal Republic of Germany, made up of the British, French and American zones, came into existence. Its form was defined in a Basic Law, rather than in a formal constitution, to indicate the provisional character of the new state. The first elections were held in August 1949 and resulted in a victory for the Christian Democrats led by Konrad Adenauer. In September 1950 the state of war between the Western powers and West Germany was officially declared at an end and the armies of occupation became part of Germany's defences. In April 1951 a German Foreign Ministry was set up, with its own diplomatic representation.

Steps were also taken to integrate German forces into the Western security system. The French, who were distinctly apprehensive about such a move, suggested the Pleven Plan, christened after its author. This was designed to produce a European army in which German units up to battalion level might be included. Britain welcomed the Pleven Plan, but declined to have anything to do with it. After two years of fruitless negotiation, the French National Assembly turned it down in August 1954. The problem was eventually solved as a result of an idea of Eden's. He suggested widening the Treaty of Brussels to include Italy and Germany. This would subject German forces to some overall limits, eventually agreed at 12 divisions. Agreement was reached at a nine-power conference held in London and Paris in October 1954. To secure French compliance Eden undertook to keep four British divisions and the

British Tactical Airforce on the mainland of Europe. France was reassured. West German sovereignty was recognised by the European partners in 1954, and the German Federal Republic joined NATO in 1955.

The strengthening of NATO was matched by a corresponding increase in Soviet capability. In 1949 Russia exploded her first atomic bomb. In 1953, only one year

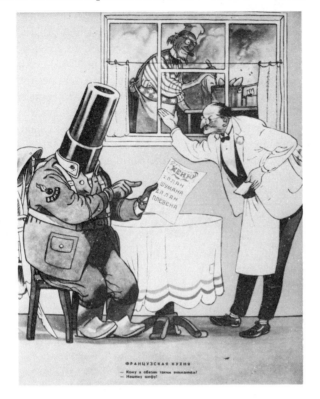

A Russian view of the Cold War (The menu reads: Schuman Plan Pleven plan)

after the United States, she detonated her first hydrogen bomb. In response to the inclusion of West Germany within NATO the Warsaw Pact was formed in 1955. The rearmament of East Germany was already under way. In these unpropitious circumstances the Geneva Conference, which convened to discuss the future of Germany in 1955, had little chance of success. All suggestions for German reunification came to grief on the same obstacle – the Russians insisted that a reunited Germany must not be allowed to remain in NATO while the Western powers insisted that she should be. The one positive consequence of the Conference was an invitation from Eden to Khruschev and Bulganin, the Russian leaders who had succeeded Stalin, to visit Britain. This they did in April 1956. The visit passed off reasonably amicably but did not yield any concessions from either side.

Between 1955 and 1959 Britain gave careful consideration to the Rapacki plan suggested by a Polish minister, Adam Rapacki. The Plan called for a demilitarised zone in central Europe from which all nuclear weapons and missile sites would be banned, and a general reduction in armaments. Macmillan, on a visit to Moscow in 1959 reverted to these suggestions, but by that time the German Federal Republic was in no mood to accept any reduction in its defences, while Khruschev also made it clear that there could be 'no roll back of Socialism from the People's Democracies'. [Northedge, p. 246]

The Berlin problem came to a head for a second time in 1958. In November Khruschev sent a letter to Western leaders announcing that Russia intended to hand over her rights of occupation in East Berlin to the East German government unless in the meantime the West would agree to make West Berlin a demilitarised 'free city'. The threat was a double-edged one. It would require the West to recognise the East German regime, which so far it had resolutely refused to do, and to withdraw Western troops from West Berlin. For the next three years this threat was held over the West and it undoubtedly contributed to the worsening climate in East–West relations. A conference held at Geneva in 1959 failed to arrive at any solution. Careful preparations were made for a Paris 'summit' in 1960, but it ended almost before it had begun. Khruschev confined his visit to a denunciation of American policies after a spy plane, a U2, had been shot down over Soviet territory. Whether Khruschev used the incident as an excuse for disrupting the Conference, or whether he was genuinely affronted by the evidence of American espionage has yet to be determined. The failure of the Paris Conference was not a happy augury for the presidency of John Kennedy, which saw the world approach closer to a nuclear war than at any other time in the Cold War.

F. S. Northedge,
Descent from Power:
British Foreign Policy
1945–1973 (1974)

EAST EUROPE IN 1955: THE WARSAW PACT

Britain and the Crisis in East–West Relations: 1961–63

In 1962 for the first time in her history Britain faced the threat of 'annihilation without representation'. By 1960 the two superpowers had acquired missile-carried nuclear weapons against which there was no credible defence, and the fate of the world depended on decisions made in Moscow and Washington. In practice, Britain was able to exercise some influence on the final outcome, but this was largely due to the warm relationship that grew up between President Kennedy and Harold Macmillan. The two men met for the first time in December 1961 shortly after Kennedy's inauguration, and the mutual trust established there was an important factor when the Cuba crisis blew up in 1962.

There were two main sources of tension in 1961, in separate hemispheres but closely related. Khruschev, as we have seen, was pressing for a change in the status of West Berlin. The United States was anxious to bring about the removal of Fidel Castro, the Marxist leader who had seized power in Cuba in 1958. The two crises evolved simultaneously. On 17 April 1961 an ill-fated expeditionary force of 1400 Cuban exiles was landed at the Bay of Pigs on the Cuban coastline. Their arrival had been anticipated and the expedition was a humiliating failure for which Kennedy had to acknowledge full responsibility, although he had not planned the operation. In June, Kennedy met Khruschev for a series of talks in Vienna. The talks ended acrimoniously and inconclusively, with Khruschev threatening to sign an East German Peace Treaty in December.

The Berlin Wall

In August, Khruschev gave orders for the construction of the Berlin Wall, sealing off all access from the East to the Western sectors of the city. An armed and carefully policed frontier now separated all of East Germany from the West, and the loophole by which refugees could escape through West Berlin was finally closed. Though he did not make good his threat over the treaty with East Germany, Khruschev then embarked on a more dangerous tactic. In October 1962 American photographic reconnaissance revealed incontrovertible evidence of the installation of medium range ground-to-ground missiles in Cuba, presumably capable of being fitted with nuclear warheads. From the outset, Kennedy was clear about his objectives. They were to compel Russian withdrawal of the missiles without the United States having to make any concessions on Berlin, or elsewhere. Three options were considered to secure these objectives: to 'take out' the missile bases by an air strike; to invade Cuba by air and sea; or to impose a blockade round the island preventing the arrival of any more missiles or other weapons. Kennedy appointed a special committee of advisers, the most important of whom was his brother, Bobby, but he also telephoned Macmillan every night throughout the crisis, both to keep the Prime Minister informed and to seek his advice. Macmillan, while offering support, urged caution. He strongly deprecated an invasion and he emphatically resisted a suggestion from Washington that NATO should be put on "full alert": 'I said that "mobilisation" had sometimes caused war. Here it was absurd, since the additional forces made available by "*Alert*" had *no* military significance.' [Macmillan, p. 190] Kennedy accepted the advice to move cautiously, which was also offered by his brother. A blockade was instituted and Soviet ships carrying missiles turned away rather than face American inspection. On 26 October Khruschev wrote the first of two letters implying that the Soviet presence in Cuba might be withdrawn if the United States would guarantee the island against foreign invasion. A second letter, less conciliatory, was ignored, and within two days the crisis was over. The missiles were removed and the United States gave an undertaking that Cuba would be safe from invasion.

H. Macmillan, *Memoirs,* Vol. VI, *At the End of the Day* (1973)

In his reflections on the crisis, Macmillan wrote: 'We were "in on" and took full part in (and almost responsibility for) every American move. Our complete calm helped keep the Europeans calm.' [Macmillan, p. 216] This perhaps unduly complacent conclusion cannot conceal the fact that there was nothing Britain could have done to prevent the United States from unleashing a nuclear war over the Cuban issue, had they chosen to do so.

The Cuban missile crisis, nonetheless had some beneficial effects. It led to the 'hot-line' agreement enabling the heads of state in Washington and Moscow to talk to each other at any time, thus reducing the risk of war by accident. It also helped to pave the way for a nuclear test-ban treaty. This was something particularly close to Macmillan's heart and he devoted the final months of his premiership to promoting it. After his encounter with Khruschev at Vienna, Kennedy was unwilling to get involved in high-level negotiations with the Soviet Union unless he could see a real chance of progress. Macmillan did much of the necessary spade work. The final break-through owed something to the Russian willingness to concede at last the principle of inspection, though this did not extend to underground tests. On 8 August 1963 the Partial Nuclear Test Ban Treaty was signed by Britain, Russia and the United States, banning all atmospheric nuclear tests. Neither China nor France, the other nuclear powers, were ready to sign it at this stage but it was the most significant measure of disarmament achieved since the ending of the Second World War.

British Foreign and Defence Policy, 1963–79

'Defence must be the servant of foreign policy, not its master.' (*Defence Review*, 1966) While British governments paid lip-service to this principle, in practice defence considerations have very much determined Britain's international role in the last two decades. Rising defence costs in the 1950s and 1960s forced Britain to place greater reliance on the nuclear 'shield'. In 1957 Britain exploded her first H-Bomb and the RAF was expanded to strengthen Britain's nuclear capability. The V bomber force (Vulcans, Valiants and Victories) was developed to carry the new weapons. In 1960 conscription was ended and by 1962 the total numbers in the armed forces had been reduced to 375 000. But no sooner was the V bomber force available than it became obsolete because of the improvement in missile technology. Britain's ventures in this field proved unsuccessful. *Blue Streak*, an air-to-ground missile, had clearly failed by 1960. The American substitute, *Skybolt*, was cancelled in 1962. It was in these circumstances that Macmillan made the *Polaris* agreement with the United States, at Nassau, in December 1962. Under the agreement the United States offered to provide Polaris missiles (launched from submarines and with a range of 3000 miles), less the nuclear war heads to go with them, for use in British submarines. The submarines were normally to be assigned as part of a NATO nuclear force 'except where Her Majesty's Government may decide that supreme national interests are at stake'. [Macmillan, p. 555] It was on this saving clause that the independence of Britain's nuclear deterrent now rested.

Macmillan, *At the End of the Day*

The Polaris agreement made Britain dependent on American nuclear technology. The incoming Labour government in 1964 promised to renegotiate the agreement but failed to do so. *Polaris* escaped the defence cuts in 1968 on the grounds that by then it was relatively cheap, the capital costs having already been met. Britain's reliance on American-supplied nuclear weapons has inevitably made her more dependent on the United States, and this dependence was reinforced in 1984 with the arrival of Cruise missiles under American control.

The other influence on British foreign policy has been the burden of defence spending at times of economic crisis. Until 1967 Britain was determined to maintain an armed presence in the Middle East (Aden and the Persian Gulf) and in the Far East (Hong Kong and Singapore). In the 1966 Defence White Paper, Denis Healey, Minister for Defence, put forward suggested cuts amounting to £400 million. How these were to be achieved without a reduction in Britain's defence commitments was not made clear. The Minister for the Navy, Christopher Mayhew, resigned because of the cancellation of plans to build an aircraft carrier. Crossman, attending his first meeting of the Overseas and Defence Policy Committee, in October 1966 urged that 'We should make a proper basic foreign policy change and not merely whittle down the defences while maintaining our commitments ....' [Crossman, p. 237] He described the proposed cuts as 'a futile attempt to remain Great Britain, one of the three world powers, while slicing away our defences'. The devaluation crisis of 1967 brought a necessary touch of realism to the debate. In the Defence White Paper of 1969 there were cuts of £110 million in 1969–70 and of £210 million for 1972–73. All British forces were to be withdrawn from the Far East by 1971, except those in Hong Kong and the Persian Gulf. The Americans protested strongly. George Brown, Foreign Secretary at the time, reported 'the appalling onslaught to which he had been submitted, first by Dean Rusk (Secretary of State) and then by a State Department official whose theme had been, – "Be British, George, be British – How can you betray us?"' [Crossman, p. 394] But there was no turning back. When Heath

Howard (ed.), *The Crossman Diaries*

became Prime Minister in 1970 he made a brief attempt to reverse the policy of withdrawal, but without much success. Arab rulers showed little desire for a British presence in the Gulf and plans for a five-power naval force based on Singapore came to nothing.

The reduction in Britain's overseas commitments made between 1968 and 1971 marked the point at which Britain's transition from a world to a European power was officially acknowledged by British governments. It is an appropriate moment at which to consider Britain's relations with the European movement and the European Economic Community.

BRITAIN AND EUROPE C

The European Movement

The movement for European unification drew its support from many different sources. There was, in the first place, a common sense of revulsion in many quarters against the nationalism which had twice within living memory helped to fuel two world wars. This was particularly the case in those countries which had experienced invasion and occupation. It is perhaps no accident that the founder members of the EEC – France, Germany, Italy, Belgium, the Netherlands and Luxemburg – had all suffered those experiences. Secondly, there was the growing fear of Soviet power and the spread of Communism. Both France and Italy had strong Communist parties and it was the right-wing Catholic-based parties in Europe as a whole that were most enthusiastic for European unity. The United States was constant in its advocacy of European integration, both because this would strengthen Europe in the face of possible Soviet aggression and because Americans could see no reason why a federal system of government which suited them should not be equally applicable to an area considerably smaller than the United States. The Second World War had also brought about the collapse of European empires. The Italians lost all their colonies in North Africa; the Dutch failed to re-establish their hold over the Dutch East Indies; France pulled out of Indo-China in 1954, most of her West African colonies in 1960 and Algeria in 1962. The age of imperialism was over and it was natural for the countries of Europe to turn inwards rather than outwards.

The adoption of economic growth as a policy goal was a further incentive towards economic integration. The removal of tariff barriers and the establishment of a large free market for goods and services would, it was thought, help to promote more competition, greater opportunities for specialisation and a corresponding improvement in efficiency. At the same time the creation of a regional trading bloc would give Europe greater bargaining power with the rest of the world.

Finally, there was the influence of individual politicians committed in various ways to the European ideal. Of these men, perhaps the most important was Jean Monnet, a French civil servant, who devoted all his energy to the cause of European unity. Vital support also came from Robert Schuman, a citizen of Alsace, who fought in the German army in the First World War and in the French Resistance in the Second. Schuman was successively Minister of Finance, Justice and Foreign Affairs in governments of the Fourth Republic between 1946 and 1958, and he played a vital part in the creation of the European Coal and Steel Community in 1950–51.

Konrad Adenauer, Chancellor of West Germany from 1949 to 1963, and Alcide de Gasperi, Italian Foreign Minister from 1944 to 1954, were also sympathetic to the idea of a united Europe. Winston Churchill gave the movement his blessing. In a speech given at Zürich in 1946 he called for 'a United States of Europe', and he was made honorary chairman of a conference which met at the Hague in May 1948 to represent the various interests that were pressing for some form of European association.

Within the broad spectrum of support for a united Europe there were many shades of opinion on how far the process should be encouraged to go. Three main viewpoints can be identified. First were those like de Gaulle who believed in a *Europe des Patries*, in which European nation states would retain their separate identities but would agree to co-operate on matters of trade and defence through treaties and mutual agreements. Secondly, there were the so-called 'functionalists' who supported the idea of common policies, for instance in relation to coal and steel, atomic energy, agriculture, trade and industry; they were also prepared to accept the need for supra-national authorities to implement such policies. Finally, there were the 'federalists', whose goal was a European government responsible to a sovereign European parliament. It was the second variant which proved to be the most practicable and which is now embodied in the Treaty of Rome and in the institutions of the European Economic Community.

The Process of Integration

The first landmark to be reached was the establishment in April 1948 of the Organisation for European Economic Co-operation (the OEEC). Its purpose was the co-ordination of Marshall Aid. With the ending of Marshall Aid in 1960, the OEEC was joined by Canada and the United States and was retitled the Organisation for European Co-operation and Development, the OECD. Both organisations had transatlantic links and were thus unsuitable vehicles in which to carry the purely European movement. Such a vehicle came into existence as the result of a meeting of the European Congress at the Hague in May 1948. The Congress was organised by the International Committee of the Movements for European Unity. As a result of its deliberations the European Movement gained a formal structure, the Council of Europe. The form it should take was finally agreed in May 1949. There were to be two parts: a Committee of Ministers, which was simply an arrangement for regular inter-governmental meetings, and a Consultative Assembly which was to be made up of delegates from the Parliaments of the member states. The Assembly could discuss only those matters referred to it by the Committee of Ministers and neither body could do more than make recommendations. As Professor Northedge has rightly commented: 'The Churchill call "fiat Europe!" of 1946 had ended in a mere talking shop.' [Northedge, p. 151] A more fruitful development took place in May 1950 when Robert Schuman presented the Plan which now bears his name. It had actually been conceived by Jean Monnet as a way of ending Franco-German hostility by bringing together their coal and steel industries. Its purpose was as much political as economic. The Plan was warmly welcomed by Adenauer and was also strongly supported by Acheson, the American Secretary of State. The Benelux countries were invited to join and in 1951 the European Coal and Steel Community came into

Northedge, *Descent from Power*

operation. It provided for the free movement of coal and steel throughout the member countries, and it also set up four institutions to conduct the working of the community:

a High Authority assisted by a Consultative Committee
a Common Assembly
a Special Council of Ministers
a High Court of Justice.

The ECSC represented the first example of the functionalist approach to European integration, and proved to be so successful that it became the blueprint on which the EEC based itself.

When Germany and Italy signed the Treaty of Brussels in 1954 the Western European Union (WEU) was formed to supervise the execution of the Treaty, through a Council representing the member states. A link was also established with the Council of Europe whose wider membership included the neutral states of Ireland and Sweden. A complicated formula was devised to preserve the neutrality of these two states under Article 9 of the revised treaty. The Article provided that 'The Council of Western European Union shall make an Annual Report on its activities and in particular concerning the control of armaments to an Assembly composed of representatives of the Brussels Treaty powers to the Consultative Assembly of the Council of Europe.' [Vaughan, pp. 29–30] By 1954 Western Europe thus had five separate organisations: the OEEC; the Council of Europe; the ECSC; the Western European Union; and the Assembly referred to in Article 9 of the Brussels Treaty. Many of the member states were also in NATO. While in one sense this proliferation of organisations reflected the strength of the impulse towards integration, their variety also reflected the confused aims and motives which characterised the European movement. The accompanying chart will, it is hoped, clarify the picture.

Vaughan, *Post-War Integration in Europe*

European organisations in 1954

MEMBERSHIP

OEEC (1948)	*The Council of Europe* (1949)
Austria	Belgium
Belgium	Denmark
Denmark	France
France	Ireland
Greece	Italy
Iceland	Luxemburg
Ireland	Netherlands
Italy	Norway
Sweden	Sweden
Switzerland	United Kingdom
Turkey	
United Kingdom	Germany (1950)
Germany (1949)	

ECSC (1949)	Western European Union (1954)	NATO (1949)
Belgium	Belgium	Belgium
France	France	Canada
Germany	Luxemburg	Denmark
Italy	Netherlands	France
Luxemburg	United Kingdom	Iceland
Netherlands		Italy
	Germany	Netherlands
	Italy	Norway
		Portugal
	(It was an Assembly made up of representatives	United Kingdom
	of the above countries in the Council of Europe	United States
	to which the WEU made its Annual Report.)	
		Germany (1955)

Such was the success of the ECSC, however, that a special conference of Foreign Ministers of the Six (Germany, France, Italy and Benelux) was held at Messina in 1955 to see what further steps might be taken. The Messina Conference resolved to submit to an inter-governmental committee proposals for a common market in all commodities traded between themselves. It also proposed the creation of an atomic energy pool. This committee, chaired by Paul Henry Spaak, the Belgian Foreign Minister, produced a report which was discussed at a series of meetings in 1956; these culminated in the Treaty of Rome and the Treaty setting up Euratom. Both were signed in Rome on 25 March 1957 and came into effect on 1 January 1958.

The Treaty of Rome has 248 Articles and is not easily summarised. Its essential principles are nonetheless clear. Its purpose is to create a common market among the member states and to harmonise their economic and social policies so as 'to promote throughout the Community a harmonious development of economic activities, a continuous and balanced expansion, an increase in stability, an accelerated raising of the standard of living and closer relations between the States belonging to it.' [Treaty of Rome, Article 2] The Treaty provided for the removal of all barriers to the free movement of goods, labour and capital within the Community and for the adoption of a common external tariff to be imposed on goods entering the Community. Special provision would be made for the ex-colonies of member states. Common policies for agriculture and transport were envisaged. A period of 15 years was to be allowed in which these changes could be accomplished. The Treaty also defined the institutions which would be responsible for the Community. They were largely borrowed from the ECSC, and were as follows: the Council of Ministers the European Commission, the European Assembly and the Court of Justice. Final power would rest with the Council of Ministers, where a system of weighted majorities would operate. The European Parliament was initially to consist of members drawn from each of the individual Parliaments of the Six and would have only two powers: to dismiss the Commission and to approve the Community Budget.

By 1968 the transition period had been completed, five years earlier than intended. Two other significant developments had also taken place. In 1962 the main features of the Common Agricultural Policy were agreed. Target prices were to be fixed for most agricultural commodities and these would determine the prices paid by consumers. All commodities unsold would be purchased by the Commission through a fund created for the purpose. They would then either be stored, destroyed or exported. European farmers were guaranteed a high price for their products and an assurance that they would be paid for all they could produce. Mountains of beef and butter and lakes of wine were to be an inevitable consequence of the CAP.

The other significant development arose out of France's decision to boycott the Community in 1965 in protest at the means adopted to finance the CAP. After seven months, France was persuaded to return on the understanding that where very important national interests were at stake a unanimous decision would be required in the Council of Ministers. This proviso became known as the Luxemburg Agreement. It gave in effect the power of veto to any member country. But it failed to make clear who was to determine what was a 'very important interest' or on what criteria. The Luxemburg Agreement provided a safeguard against the erosion of national sovereignty, but it introduced an element of ambiguity into the Treaty of Rome which has still to be resolved.

Britain and Europe, 1945–61

British attitudes

Britain, it has often been remarked, is an island off but not of Europe. The Commonwealth connection, the special relationship with the United States, Labour's determination to retain full control over the British economy, and a long history of insularity, all these factors disposed the British government in 1945 to view European integration with suspicion. As Jean Monnet has pointed out, Britain having suffered neither conquest nor invasion, unlike France or Germany, 'felt no need to exorcise history'. [Monnet, p. 306] There was also a strong feeling that Britain was different from the other countries of Europe. The point was put unequivocally in a paper presented to the cabinet in October 1949 by Bevin. It concerned Britain's attitude to the Council of Europe, and after stressing that Britain should 'do nothing now to undermine the general hopes of solidarity and co-operation which the Council has aroused in Europe' it went on to say: 'We must remain, as we have always been in the past, different in character from other European nations and fundamentally incapable of wholehearted integration with them.' [Bullock, p. 734] The United States of Europe for which Churchill called in 1946 was not intended to include Britain.

J. Monnet, *Memoirs*, R. Mayne (translator) (Collins, 1978)

Bullock, *Ernest Bevin*

Indeed, subsequent British actions have led some commentators to give Churchill's words a Machievellian interpretation:

A. Spinelli, *The Growth of the European Movement Since the Second World War*, M. Hodges (ed.), *European Integration* (1972)

> Churchill's initiative had been conditioned by English policy. Great Britain had abandoned every prospect of taking part in some kind of European union, and in fact was in the midst of the Great Socialist experience inaugurated by the Labour Party. The British, by tradition, opposed any kind of political consolidation of Europe, since it could mean the creation of a great Continental power. But the presence of Russian imperialistic policy prevented Great Britain from taking a position openly against European integration, which would have meant against the United States and indirectly in favour of Russia. To get out of this diplomatic entanglement, Churchill came up with an idea both clever and cynical. The British would take over the role of guardian of the European movement, which they would guide so as to make sure that a real union would never be achieved ...' [A. Spinelli, p. 58]

Such a view exaggerates the sense of purpose that informed British attitudes to Europe, but it is fair to say that where Britain was involved with European organisations her influence was generally used to minimise any infraction of national sovereignty. When the Council of Europe was being discussed Britain succeeded in diminishing the role and powers of the Constituent Assembly. Similarly, while giving her approval to the Pleven Plan and the projected European Defence Community, Britain refused to consider integrating her forces into a European army.

446

Britain and the ECSC

The clearest example of Britain's lukewarmness towards European integration is to be found in her reaction to the Schuman Plan. Fearing a hostile British reaction, Schuman first outlined his proposals to Acheson and Adenauer in May 1950. Bevin was not told until the four Foreign Ministers met on 11 May in London. He protested strongly at Britain's exclusion from the preliminary soundings. Britain's position was not made any easier by the publication shortly after of a joint communiqué in Bonn where it was announced that Germany agreed in principle to the French Plan. The British government refused to make such a commitment in advance of negotiations and for that reason refused to take part in them when they opened in Paris on 3 June. Britain played no part, therefore, in the formation of the European Coal and Steel Community. Acheson commented that this refusal was 'the greatest mistake of the post-war period' [Acheson, p. 385] but in the prevailing climate of opinion it was probably inevitable.

D. Acheson, *Present at the Creation* (1970)

THE EEC AND EFTA, 1957–61

Britain did send an observer to the Messina talks in 1955 and was represented in the negotiations conducted by Spaak in 1955–56 which led up to the Treaty of Rome. But she withdrew from them when the future structure of the EEC became clear. After the Treaty of Rome was signed Britain was faced with the prospect of a tariff-free area from which she would be excluded. Proposals were made through the OEEC for some kind of association to be formed between the Six and the other members of the OEEC. A Committee under the chairmanship of Reginald Maudling, a member of the British cabinet, was set up to investigate this possibility. It met intermittently throughout most of 1958. But Britain was only prepared to see a Free Trade Area extended to industrial goods and not to agricultural commodities. The Six were not willing to accept this compromise and the negotiations came to a halt in November 1958.

Britain and EFTA

After this failure Britain and the other countries of the OEEC met to consider whether they could reach agreement among themselves. A series of meetings took place in Oslo and Stockholm. In December 1959 the Stockholm Convention was agreed and came into force in January 1960. It established the European Free Trade Area covering the following countries: Austria, Britain, Denmark, Norway, Portugal, Sweden and Switzerland, otherwise known as 'the Seven'. The one explicit purpose of EFTA was the removal of tariff barriers and quotas between the member countries. There was no intention to harmonise economic policies in other respects, and no supra-national institutions were set up to enforce the terms of the Convention. EFTA was thus no substitute for the EEC. Its membership added up to a total of about 90 million, compared with over 200 million in the EEC. The member countries were widely separated geographically and very much dominated by Britain. There is little doubt that many British politicians saw EFTA as a temporary arrangement, designed to keep the Seven together during further negotiations with the EEC and within two years of EFTA's formation Britain's first application for membership of the EEC was on the table.

Britain's attempts to enter the EEC, 1961–67

U. Kitzinger, *Diplomacy and Persuasion: How Britain Joined the Common Market* (1973)

The Change of Heart

In 1961 British policy towards Europe underwent a change of heart. Whereas in 1949 the Foreign Office had declared Britain to be incapable of wholehearted integration with European nations, between 1961 and 1967 British politicians of both parties did their best to convince European leaders that this was just what the British people wanted.

How is this change to be explained? Uwe Kitzinger in his book *Diplomacy and Persuasion*, published in 1972, lists 'five milestones on the road to Damascus'. They were: the Suez crisis in 1956; the abandonment of Blue Streak in 1960; the sterling crisis of that year; the fate of the 1960 Summit Conference when a British Prime Minister tried to play a major role at the top table for the last time; and finally, the growing evidence that on all the accepted criteria of economic growth (investment, manufacturing output, share of world trade) the countries of the EEC were doing markedly better than Britain.

Harold Macmillan, who was chiefly responsible for the decision to apply for membership, gave somewhat different arguments in his Address to the Commonwealth Prime Ministers in September 1962. On economic grounds, Macmillan pointed out that Britain's trade with the Commonwealth was declining, while it was increasing with the EEC. In 1939 the Commonwealth took 41% of British exports, in 1961 that figure had fallen to 35%. Britain could not possibly provide a market for all Commonwealth products; nor could she hope to finance the investment needed by the less developed Commonwealth countries. Commonwealth countries would stand to benefit from British entry to the EEC in both these respects. Macmillan also pointed out that as industry became more sophisticated so it demanded more investment, longer production runs and larger markets. He compared the textile industry of the nineteenth century with the car industry of the twentieth. Britain desperately needed the large tariff-free market offered by the EEC if she was to keep abreast of technological change.

More important, if anything, were the political arguments. Macmillan recognised the European idea that lay behind the Common Market:

> with the development of the European idea there has come a resurgence, a new vigour in all aspects of European life, in music, arts, science, industry. There is something here of that release of the spirit which lifted Europe out of the mediaeval period into the Renaissance and the modern world. Europe, which Spengler saw as decadent and declining, is once more seeing a great Renaissance. [Macmillan, p. 530]

Macmillan, *At the End of the Day*

Britain could not afford to stand aside from this development: 'The fact that our people from this small island had spread themselves to other continents and throughout the seven seas made it a tempting delusion that we had ceased to be Europeans. But for this mistake both we, and you, gentlemen, have paid a heavy price. Twice in my lifetime we have been brought to the brink of destruction by this fallacy.' Macmillan's sense of history, far from blinkering his outlook, gave him the flexibility of mind necessary to see when a change of attitude was needed.

The First Application

In December 1960 Macmillan circulated to members of the cabinet a document that he called the Great Design, calling for a renewed effort to unite Western Europe. On 27 February 1961 Edward Heath was dispatched with the cabinet's approval to see the European Council of Ministers. On 22 July the cabinet took the unanimous decision to seek British membership of the EEC. In the subsequent debate held on 2 and 3 August the government gained a comfortable majority of over 100 for its initiative. The rest of 1961 and the whole of 1962 were taken up with detailed negotiations between Britain and the Six, and between Britain and her Commonwealth partners. There seems to be little doubt that acceptable terms could have been agreed had it not been for the intransigence of General de Gaulle. This first became apparent at the private talks held between Macmillan and de Gaulle at Rambouillet on 15–16 December 1962. De Gaulle refused to believe that Britain was really a European power. He saw British entry into the Community as likely to alter its character and to import unwanted American influence in to Europe. This impression was reinforced by the Polaris Agreement which Macmillan negotiated with Kennedy at Nassau a few days after the Rambouillet meeting. On 14 January 1963 de Gaulle held a press conference at which he announced his opposition to British entry, and on 29 January the French representative at the Council of Ministers imposed a veto on further negotiations. In his *Memoirs* Macmillan recounts a story told to him by Christopher Soames, the British Minister of Agriculture. According to Soames, his opposite number gave this explanation for de Gaulle's opposition:

Macmillan, *At the End of the Day*

> Mon cher. C' est tres simple. Maintenant, avec les six, il y a cinq poules et un coq. Si vous joignez (avec des autres pays), il y aura peut-etre sept ou huites poules. Mais il y aura *deux* coqs. Alors – ce n' est pas aussi agréable. (My dear fellow. It's very simple. Now, with the six, there are five hens and one cock. If you join, with the others, there will be perhaps seven or eight hens. But there will be *two* cocks. This would not be such a happy state of affairs.) [Macmillan, p. 365]

The Second Application

The Labour Party leadership initially took an agnostic line on the question of British entry into the EEC. Gaitskell, perhaps surprisingly, professed to find the whole question 'always a bore and a nuisance'. [Williams, p. 390] But he was very concerned that the interests of the poorer Commonwealth countries should be protected and came to feel, as the negotiations progressed, that they were being sacrificed to Macmillan's enthusiasm for entry on any terms. It is at least possible that had de Gaulle not imposed his veto the Labour party would have opposed entry on Macmillan's terms.

P. M. Williams, *Hugh Gaitskell* (OUP, 1982)

The Labour Government of 1964–70 gradually came round, however, to support for British entry. There were several reasons for this change. The Commonwealth objections lost a good deal of their force as Commonwealth countries began to take precautionary steps to find other markets, for instance in Japan. Wilson's commitment to 'the white hot technological revolution', announced in 1964, made him at least as anxious as Macmillan to secure the large tariff-free market needed to sell Britain's new products. The special relationship with the United States became tarnished as a result of the Vietnam War and Britain's patent inability to have any influence upon its outcome. Finally there were several committed marketeers in the Labour cabinet, notably George Brown, Michael Stewart and Roy Jenkins.

The whole question of entry was considered at an important cabinet meeting held at Chequers on 22 October 1966. Serious differences of opinion were voiced which anticipated the later divisions in the party on this issue. [see Crossman, pp. 233–37] On this occasion a split was avoided and the meeting ended with an announcement by Wilson that he and George Brown would make a tour of European capitals to clarify the doubtful issues. The results of these soundings were announced to the cabinet on 21 March 1967. After a second meeting to discuss the Common Market on 6 April Crossman concluded: 'And Harold got so warmed and carried away that he made it absolutely clear that he's now a completely converted Common Marketeer.' [Crossman, p. 305] On 2 May the cabinet met to approve a Statement announcing the government's intention to apply for entry to the EEC. Though Crossman identified seven unqualified opponents of entry in his own mind in the cabinet, there was no sign of resignation or protest. When the Statement was debated in the House of Commons on 10 May the government motion had a majority of 488 to 62, 51 Labour backbenchers abstaining, 34 voting against the motion.

Howard (ed.), *The Crossman Diaries*

Despite Wilson's optimistic account of his interview with de Gaulle, the General delivered his second veto on 27 November. On this occasion he gave as his reason the parlous state of the British economy. The pound had just been devalued. In a press release de Gaulle said: 'The Common Market is incompatible with the British economy as it stands, in which the chronic balance of payments deficit is proof of its permanent imbalance ....' [Kitzinger, p. 38] Wilson attributed de Gaulle's continued opposition to 'the mortal sin of Atlanticism', while in his *Memoirs* George Brown repeated the farmyard analogy of hens and cocks, this time crediting the remark to de Gaulle himself. [Brown, p. 220] Whatever the reasons, it was clear now that no further progress would be possible until de Gaulle was out of the way.

Kitzinger, *Diplomacy and Persuasion*

G. Brown, *In my Way* (Gollancz, 1971)

Ending the Deadlock

Relations between Britain and France inevitably cooled after de Gaulle's second veto. They were not improved by *"L'affaire Soames"*. Christopher Soames, now British ambassador in Paris, had an informal interview with de Gaulle in February 1969, an account of which was given to the German Chancellor and subsequently released to the press. De Gaulle claimed that his views had been deliberately distorted to imply that he favoured a loosening up of the Community. What had been intended as a friendly initiative backfired completely.

However, in May 1969 de Gaulle resigned. In the ensuing presidential election Georges Pompidou, de Gaulle's preferred successor, won with a comfortable majority of 58% on the second ballot. Though he belonged to de Gaulle's party, Pompidou did not share his suspicion of Britain. At a Common Market summit in December 1969 he declared himself in favour of enlarging the Community. The main obstacle to Britain's entry, if not yet out of the way, was at least no longer immovable.

Negotiations for Entry

In the General Election of 1970 both parties announced their intention to renew Britain's application. The new Prime Minister, Edward Heath, was probably the most committed Marketeer on either side of the House of Commons. He had handled the Macmillan negotiations in 1961–62, and was eager to take up the challenge a second time. The negotiating procedure was long and complicated. Three other countries, Ireland, Denmark and Norway, were also seeking admission and each had its delegation at Brussels and Luxemburg. So far as the Six were concerned negotiations were nominally controlled by the President of the Council of Ministers, an office which rotated every six months. In practice most of the detailed work was done by the Permanent Representatives on the Council, but really contentious issues had to be resolved at prime-ministerial level.

So far as Britain was concerned there were six major problems to be settled: Britain's Budget contribution; the timescale for the adoption of Community preferences; the protection to be given to New Zealand dairy producers; the protection to be given to Commonwealth sugar producers; the question of Britain's sterling balances and the use of sterling as a reserve currency; and the question of Community access to British fishing grounds. Negotiations began on 30 June 1970, and were not finally completed until Britain signed the Treaty of Accession on 22 January 1972. The real breakthrough occurred at a meeting between Heath and Pompidou on 20–21 May 1971 when French objections to British entry were at last removed, and the main terms were agreed by the end of July. The bargaining was hard and the compromises finally achieved indicate the gaps that had to be bridged.

The problem of the Budget was the most difficult. Under existing Community arrangements all member states were to contribute the import duties collected

Britain's Successful Application, 1970–73

through the Common External Tariff, the variable import levies on foodstuffs imported from outside the Community, and a percentage of the proceeds of a Value Added Tax. These contributions were used to meet the costs of administration and to finance the Common Agricultural Policy through the Guidance and Guarantee Fund which bought up food surpluses. Britain's problem, still be be resolved, arose from the fact that she imported much of her food from outside the Community, while her small and efficient agricultural sector had little need of support. She was bound to contribute more than she received. But the main point at issue in 1971 was the size of her contribution. Britain's initial offer was 2–3%, which met with a derisive response. It was finally agreed that Britain should meet 8.64% of the Budget in 1973, rising to 18.9% in 1978, in monetary terms, £150 million and £350 million respectively.

Entente Cordiale? Edward Heath greets President Pompidou on his visit to London in March 1972

On the question of Community preferences Britain had hoped initially for a period of seven years in which to adjust her tariffs to those of the Community. This was reduced to five years. New Zealand dairy producers were given protection through a quota system. Britain guaranteed to take a gradually diminishing quota of butter and cheese from New Zealand, falling to 71% of current levels by 1977. Commonwealth sugar producers, notably in the West Indies and Mauritius, were protected by the Commonwealth Sugar Agreement due to expire in 1974. They were given 'bankable assurances' that the Community 'will have as its firm purpose' the safeguarding of their interests once the Agreement had run out. So far as the sterling balances were concerned, Britain conceded the need to reduce them and to bring to an end sterling's role as a reserve currency. British fishing interests were to be protected by a 12-mile limit in a few specified areas, pending a long-term review of the whole question.

Whether these terms could have been improved is very doubtful. The Conservative negotiating team, headed by Geoffrey Rippon, picked up the negotiating brief that had been prepared for the Labour government by the Foreign Office and used it without alteration. Several Labour ministers, including Michael Stewart, George Brown, George Thomson, Roy Jenkins and Harold Lever, subsequently conceded that a Labour government could have done no better. Even so, Heath discovered that while by July 1971 he had won over the members of the EEC to Britain's entry, he still had to convince a majority in the House of Commons that the terms were acceptable.

The Struggle in Parliament

'It would not be in the interests of the Community that its enlargement should take place except with the full hearted consent of the Parliaments and Peoples of the member states.' (Edward Heath)

'We have applied for membership of the EEC, and negotiations are due to start in a few weeks' time. They will be pressed with determination with the purpose of joining an enlarged Community provided that Britain's and essential Commonwealth interests can be safeguarded.' [*Labour Party Manifesto*, 1970]

Despite the Labour party's apparent enthusiasm for joining the Common Market, indicated in the 1967 application and in the 1970 Manifesto, serious rifts began to appear in the party's ranks as negotiations proceeded. This, combined with the emergence of a small but committed group of anti-marketeers in the Conservative party, meant that the Heath government nearly came to grief in the process of securing parliamentary approval to the terms of accession.

Until July 1971 Labour criticism of the terms of entry was muted. But two developments caused a change in outlook. There was growing evidence of working-class and trade-union opposition to entry, mainly based on the fear of rising food prices and the threat to employment that would follow if Britain adopted the CAP and abolished her protective tariffs. The growing unpopularity of the Conservative government's policies, particularly the Industrial Relations Act of 1971, meant that there was an increasing readiness to use the European issue to bring about the government's defeat. A Special Labour Party Conference, held in July 1971, to consider the party's attitude to entry evoked a wide variety of views hostile to the EEC, ranging from dislike of 'Golden Delicious' apples and continental beer to suspicion of the Krupp family. In response to such sentiments a number of the Shadow Cabinet began to shift their ground. By July Callaghan, Healey and Crosland had all indicated their opposition to the terms so far negotiated. At the Special Conference, Wilson declared his view that the terms for New Zealand and Commonwealth sugar producers were unacceptable. On 28 July the National Executive Committee voted by 16 votes to 6 to recommend the rejection of the government's policy. In September the TUC passed by acclamation a resolution sponsored by the TGWU to oppose entry 'on the terms now known'. In October the Labour Party Conference, meeting at Brighton, approved the NEC Resolution of 28 July by 5 073 000 votes to 1 032 000. On the Conservative side, government Whips calculated that there were about 20 MPs who were strongly opposed to Britain's entry into the Common Market on any terms and another 20 whose votes were in doubt.

The political arithmetic in the autumn of 1971 presented Heath with a difficult problem. If the Labour party remained united in their opposition to the terms of entry and were joined by all the potential Conservative rebels, his government would be defeated. Thus British entry into Europe and the survival of the Heath administration were indissolubly linked. The connection between the two issues explains the elaborate political manoeuvres of the next few months.

The first stage in the contest was the debate held on a government motion approving the decision to join the Communities, 'on the basis of the arrangements which have been negotiated'. The debate was held from 21 October to 28 October. Heath announced a few days beforehand that the Conservatives would be allowed a free vote, in the hope that this would encourage Labour pro-marketeers, who were subject to the Party Whip, to vote for the motion. His hopes were realised. The voting on 28 October was as follows:

	Votes For	Votes Against
Conservative	282	39
Labour	69	198
Liberal	5	1
Other		6
Total	356	244

Keesings Archives
(Longman, 1971)

The Government had a majority of 112.
[Keesings Archives, 1971, p. 24.930]

But the Government was still not home and dry. While in ordinary circumstances Treaties do not require parliamentary sanction, in the case of Britain's accession to the Treaty of Rome special legislation was needed to translate much of its procedures into British domestic law. The European Communities Bill was drafted for this purpose. It had twelve clauses, the most important of which was clause two under which Community Treaties and Community Laws would become 'enforceable Community Rights'. The abruptness with which this transition was to be accomplished offended many of the Labour pro-marketeers who were now also under considerable pressure from the Party Whips and their constituency associations to assist the Opposition in bringing down the government. Heath's majority on the second reading of the European Communities bill fell to eight. On 17 February Heath saw each of the Conservative rebels, and warned them that defeat on the Bill would mean the resignation of his Government. In the end Heath scraped home. After 102 divisions, on one of which his majority fell to 4, the Bill passed its third reading by a majority of 17 on 13 July 1972.

On 1 January 1973 Britain finally joined the European Economic Community. The events of the preceding year made it all too clear that she did so with many reservations, and in the face of considerable opposition.

Britain and the EEC, 1973–79

Renegotiations and the Referendum

In the course of the internal arguments surrounding the passage of the European Communities Bill the NEC held an important meeting on 22 March 1972 when it was decided by 13 votes to 11 to submit the decision on joining the EEC to a referendum. On 29 March the shadow cabinet also gave approval to a referendum by eight votes to six, reversing a decision made only two weeks earlier. This change of course was too much for Roy Jenkins who resigned from his post as Deputy Leader. George Thomson and Harold Lever also resigned from the shadow cabinet. Their resignations had little effect.

When the 1974 General Election took place the Labour Manifesto contained a pledge to renegotiate the terms of entry, and to submit them to a referendum. On Wilson's return to Downing Street after his slender victory, Callaghan was made Foreign Secretary with responsibility for conducting the new round of negotiations.

The terms finally agreed made no difference to the principles on which Britain had entered. But there were some minor improvements in the working of the CAP, and concessions were made on Britain's Budget contribution. Better terms were also secured for Britain's ex-colonies in the Third World who were promised tariff-free entry for many of their products under the Lomé Convention. Finally the Labour government secured assurances that the EEC would not seek to prevent further measures of nationalisation, regional aid or financial assistance to particular industries.

On 26 February 1975 the government presented a White Paper proposing that a referendum should be held on the simple question: 'Do you think that the United Kingdom should stay in the European Community?' The White Paper was approved by 312 votes to 262. On 18 March Wilson announced that the cabinet would recommend a 'Yes' vote, but he had to admit that it had split 16 to 7 on this issue. The opponents of entry were Michael Foot (Employment), Tony Benn (Industry), Peter Shore (Trade), Barbara Castle (Social Services), Eric Varley (Energy), William Ross (Scotland) and John Silkin (Planning and Local Government). By any criteria they made up a formidable group and between them held several of the key economic ministries concerned with Europe. No comparable situation had occurred since 1931, but Wilson was determined not to be caught like MacDonald. He was able to keep the party together by the device of the referendum. The seven dissentients agreed not to speak against the government's policy in the House of Commons, thus preserving the fiction of collective responsibility. Eric Heffer, who broke this understanding, was duly dismissed from his post as Minister of State for Industry. While Ministers were free to argue against a 'Yes' vote in the campaign leading up to the referendum, they promised to accept the people's verdict. In the House of Commons the Parliamentary Labour party voted by 145 votes to 138 to reject membership of the EEC in the debate on the renegotiated terms of entry. But with most Conservatives voting in its favour the government had a majority of 223 (390 to 170).

After a heated campaign, in which the pro-marketeers were both better organised and more generously financed, the British people came down heavily in favour of staying in Europe. The voting was as follows:

| For | 17 378 000 | 67.2% |
| Against | 8 470 000 | 32.8% |

This, it might have been thought, would settle the issue once and for all. But trade union opposition persisted and through the use of the block vote, motions calling for withdrawal from the EEC were successfully passed at Labour Party Conferences in 1978 and 1979. The Labour party election manifesto in 1979 contained a pledge to take Britain out of the EEC unless there were substantial changes to it. The anti-European stance adopted by the left wing of the Labour party, despite the approval given to the EEC by European Socialist parties, has been one of the most depressing and sterile features of Britain's relations with Europe.

The Consequences of Entry

Economists were evenly divided on whether Britain stood to benefit from entry into Europe. The damaging impact effects (higher food prices, costs to the balance of payments, the loss of Commonwealth preferences) had to be estimated against the dynamic effects (the stimulus of a large tariff-free market to greater specialisation, economies of scale and more efficiency). There have been similar divisions of opinion on the actual effects, now that Britain has been a member for over 10 years. The plain truth of the matter is that there is no way by which the gains and losses consequent on British entry can be computed. The British economy was subjected to all sorts of other influences after 1973 as well as the changes imposed by the conditions of entry. Bad harvests in 1973 kept EEC prices lower than world prices. The quadrupling of oil prices, on the other hand, caused a downturn in world trade which had a depressing effect on the EEC as well as on Britain. Another rise in oil prices in 1979 had similar effects. The depressed state of the British economy between 1973 and 1979 may have owed something to the tougher competition faced by British home producers after the loss of protection. It is equally arguable that Britain would have fared even worse outside the EEC.

Seen in perspective, it is the political changes wrought by the European Economic Community that have been the most significant. Between 1870 and 1945 France endured three German invasions. In 1947 the Treaty of Dunkirk was signed to guard her against a fourth. But in 1963 a 50-year treaty of friendship was signed between France and Germany. This was both a consequence of and a contribution to the improved relationship between the two countries that began with the Schuman Plan. Britain was drawn into both world wars because of her commitment to a stable Europe, safe from the domination of one country. She may be an offshore island, but her destinies still lie in Europe. Her rightful place is within the European Economic Community, as all governments since 1961 have belatedly come to accept.

POINTS AT ISSUE POINTS AT ISSUE **POINTS AT ISSUE** POINTS AT ISSUE POINTS AT ISSUE POINTS AT ISSUE

Marshall Aid and the Cold War

Soviet refusal to participate in the Marshall Plan has often been seen as a decisive moment in the Cold War. Bullock makes this comment on the meeting between Bevin, Bidault (the French Foreign Minister) and Molotov at which this decision was taken: 'In retrospect, it has seemed to most historians that this meeting was a turning point in relations between the Soviet Union and the West and to some extent this was felt by those who took part at the time.' [Bullock, p. 417]

Two issues are at stake. Was the Marshall Plan envisaged primarily as a weapon in the Cold War, or was it aimed at the economic regeneration of Europe as a whole? Secondly, was it seriously hoped to include the Soviet Union in the Marshall Aid programme, or was the invitation simply a cosmetic exercise, designed to throw the onus of dividing Europe onto the Soviet Union when the invitation was declined?

The most detailed account of the birth of the Marshall Plan is to be found in Joseph M. Jones, *The Fifteen Weeks*, published in 1956. The negotiations leading to Russian rejection of Marshall Aid are best covered in Bullock's biography of Bevin. The evidence presented here has been drawn from these two sources.

The Purpose of Marshall Aid

Jones suggests that Marshall Aid had a dual purpose. He cites a study made by members of the Foreign Aid Committee:

> These men reasoned that the primary objective of United States policy towards Europe should be to bring about conditions in Europe and in our relations with the USSR which would convince Soviet leaders to decide that their interests were better served by negotiating a political and economic settlement and collaborating with the United States on European matters rather than continuing a policy of unilateral expansion – in other words, we should press Soviet leaders to trade a policy of collaboration with regard to Europe as a whole for immediate material benefits to the Soviet Union and its satellites. A second objective should be to strengthen Western Europe and increase its Western orientation under our leadership so that we would be better able to resist in the event the Soviet Union should decline to collaborate. It was uncertain whether we could attain our primary objective, this being a matter of Soviet choice, or whether we should have to concentrate on our secondary objective. [Jones, p. 243]

American policy makers differed over the primacy given to these two objectives. Those who saw Marshall Aid as an extension of the Truman Doctrine favoured the first. In an important speech delivered by Dean Acheson on 8 May at Cleveland, Mississippi the link was made quite explicitly:

> Since world demand exceeds our ability to supply, we are going to have to concentrate our emergency assistance in areas where it will be most effective in building world political and economic stability ....
>
> This is merely common sense and sound practice. It is in keeping with the policy announced by President Truman in his special message to Congress on March 12 on aid to Greece and Turkey. Free peoples who are seeking to preserve their independence and democratic institutions and human freedoms against totalitarian pressures, either internal or external, will receive top priority for American reconstruction aid. [Jones, p. 279]

But George Kennan and the Policy Planning Staff took a wider view of Europe's problems and in a paper presented on 23 May 1947 stressed the need to give American aid a more philanthropic purpose:

> Steps should be taken to clarify what the press has unfortunately come to identify as the 'Truman Doctrine', and to remove in particular two damaging impressions which are current in large sections of American opinion. These are
> (a) That the United States approach to world problems is a defensive reaction to Communist pressure and that the effort to restore sound economic conditions is only the by-product of this reaction and not something we would be interested in doing if there were no Communist menace;
> (b) That the Truman Doctrine is a blank check to give economic aid to any area in the world where the Communists show signs of being successful. It must be made quite clear that the extension of American aid is essentially a question of political economy in the literal sense of that term and that such aid will be considered only in cases where the prospective results bear a satisfactory relationship to the expenditure of American resources and effort. [Jones, p. 252]

This paper was considered at a meeting in Secretary of State Marshall's office on 27 or 28 May. Marshall raised the question 'Is it wise to direct a proposal such as thus to all Europe? What will happen if the Soviet Union should decide to come in on a co-operative recovery program?' Acheson argued that 'it would be a colossal error for the United States to put itself in a position where it could be blamed for the division of Europe.' He doubted whether the Russians could accept a plan which would require them to disclose information about their economic and financial condition, but 'It would be best to make the offer an open one and then see if and how and when the Russians would fit in.' Kennan concurred, but stressed the possible advantages of Russian participation: 'The Soviet Union and satellites were great producers of food and raw materials that Western Europe needed, and east–west trade was highly important.' [Jones, p. 253]

In the speech which launched the Marshall Plan, delivered at Harvard on 5 June, Marshall went some way towards the Kennan view: 'Our policy is directed not against any country or doctrine but against hunger, poverty, desperation and chaos.' But he went on to say:

> Any government that is willing to assist in the task of recovery will find full co-operation, I am sure, on the part of the United States Government. Any government which maneuvers to block the recovery of other countries cannot expect help from us. Furthermore, governments, political parties, or groups which seek to perpetuate human misery in order to profit from them politically or otherwise will encounter the opposition of the United States. [Jones, p. 282]

The veiled warning indicated the suspicious tone in which the offer was made.

The Paris Negotiations, 27 June – 2 July 1947

The Russians were invited to make any observations on Marshall's offer on 13 June, and they accepted Bevin's invitation to a Conference in Paris on 27 June. Prior to the Conference, Bevin had meetings both with French and American officials. There can be little doubt that his main concern was to prevent the Russians from delaying or blocking the American offer. The American ambassador in Paris, Caffery, reported to Marshall on 18 June 'The British feel that Russian participation would tend greatly to complicate things and that it might be best if Russian refused invitation.' [Cited in Bullock, p. 407] On the other hand, at a meeting with American officials on 24 June Bevin had remarked that he thought the Marshall Plan was 'the quickest way to break down the iron curtain' [Bullock, p. 414], and he certainly hoped that the East European states could be brought in. Bullock summarises Bevin's approach to the Conference in these terms: 'Bevin's anxiety was not so much that Molotov would break up the conference with a flat refusal of the American offer and the Anglo-French invitation, as that he would try to impose conditions which might lead the Americans to withdraw their offer or at least so delay action on the European side as to make American aid arrive too late to prevent an economic collapse, in France and Italy at least.' [Bullock, p. 418]

When the Conference assembled, three sources of disagreement between the Russian and the Anglo-French positions became apparent. The Western powers proposed that the European states must first get together and formulate a joint plan for economic recovery; Molotov argued that it should be up to each state to prepare its own shopping list. The Conference could then present a combined list of needs

to the United States. The United States intended that aid should be available to Germany and Italy. Molotov insisted that no ex-enemy states should be included. Finally, Molotov objected to the setting up of an organisation under the control of the larger states for the purpose of administering Marshall Aid. This, he claimed would be an infringement of national sovereignty. Two days before the Conference ended Bevin had a conversation with the American ambassador in which Bevin said: 'I am glad that the cards have been laid on the table and that the responsibility will be laid at Moscow's door. They have tried to sabotage it in the conference room as I knew they would.' [Bullock, p. 421]

From this evidence it would seem that for Bevin the division of Europe was an accomplished fact before the Conference ever convened and that he saw it as his first priority to prevent Russia from blocking the American initiative. How anxious the Soviet Union was to accept the American offer and to improve relations with the West is much more difficult to judge. Molotov came to Paris with a large delegation and at least gave the appearance of being willing to negotiate, and the objections he made to the Western proposals were not without validity. But he delivered a warning that if Britain and France persisted with their proposals, this would have damaging consequences, and Russia refused to allow any of the East European states to accept Marshall Aid. Just as the offer of American economic assistance could not be separated from the political context in which it was made, neither could its rejection. By 1947 it would seem that mutual suspicions were already too deep to be removed by generous gestures, whatever their motives.

Books cited

A. Bullock, *Ernest Bevin, Foreign Secretary* (Heinemann, 1984)
J. M. Jones, *The Fifteen Weeks, February 21 – June 5, 1947* (Viking Press, 1956)

BIBLIOGRAPHY BIBLIOGRAPHY BIBLIOGRAPHY BIBLIOGRAPHY BIBLIOGRAPHY BIBLIOGRAPHY
BIBLIOGRAPHY BIBLIOGRAPHY BIBLIOGRAPHY BIBLIOGRAPHY BIBLIOGRAPHY BIBLIOGRAPHY
BIBLIOGRAPHY BIBLIOGRAPHY BIBLIOGRAPHY BIBLIOGRAPHY BIBLIOGRAPHY BIBLIOGRAPHY
BIBLIOGRAPHY BIBLIOGRAPHY BIBLIOGRAPHY BIBLIOGRAPHY BIBLIOGRAPHY BIBLIOGRAPHY
BIBLIOGRAPHY BIBLIOGRAPHY BIBLIOGRAPHY BIBLIOGRAPHY BIBLIOGRAPHY BIBLIOGRAPHY
BIBLIOGRAPHY BIBLIOGRAPHY BIBLIOGRAPHY BIBLIOGRAPHY BIBLIOGRAPHY BIBLIOGRAPHY

CHAPTER 13
FURTHER READING

General

Essential

P. M. Kennedy, *The Realities behind Diplomacy, 1865–1980* (Allen & Unwin, 1981)

F. S. Northedge, *Descent from Power: British Foreign Policy 1945–1973* (Allen & Unwin, 1974) (See bibliography for a useful guide to particular aspects)

Recommended

P. Darby, *British Defence Policy East of Suez, 1947–1968* (OUP, 1973)

W. N. Medlicott, *British Foreign Policy since Versailles* (Methuen, 1968)

D. C. Watt, *Personalities and Policies* (Longman, 1965)

Biographies and Memoirs

Essential

A. Bullock, *Ernest Bevin, Foreign Secretary* (Heinemann, 1984)

W. S. Churchill, *The Second World War*, vol. VI, *Triumph and Tragedy* (Cassell, 1954)

A. Howard (ed.), *Richard Crossman, The Crossman Diaries, Selections from the Diaries of a Cabinet Minister 1964–1970*, (Hamish Hamilton, 1979)

Sir A. Eden, *Full Circle* (Cassell, 1960)

H. Macmillan, *Memoirs*, vols. IV, V and VI (Macmillan, 1960–73)

H. Pelling, *Winston Churchill* (Macmillan, 1974)

Recommended

See books suggested for Chapter Twelve.

Britain and the Cold War

Essential

See Bibliography in Bullock, *Ernest Bevin, Foreign Secretary* for a guide to Revisionist Literature on the Cold War.

D. Acheson, *Present at the Creation* (Hamish Hamilton, 1970)

E. Luard (ed.), *The Cold War* (Thames and Hudson, 1964)

H. S. Truman, *Memoirs*, 2 vols. (Doubleday, 1958)

Recommended

J. M. Jones, *The Fifteen Weeks, February 21 – June 5, 1947* (Viking Press, 1956)

G. F. Kennan, *Russia, the Atom and the West* (OUP, 1958)

P. Seabury, *The Rise and Decline of the Cold War* (Basic Books, New York, 1967)

Britain and Europe

Essential

M. Camps, *Britain and the European Community, 1955–1963* (OUP 1964)

European Unification in the Sixties (OUP, 1967)

U. Kitzinger, *Diplomacy and Persuasion: How Britain Joined the Common Market* (Thames and Hudson, 1973)

R. Vaughan, *Post-War Integration in Europe, Documents of Modern History* (Arnold, 1976)

Recommended

E. Barker, *Britain and a Divided Europe, 1945–70* (Weidenfeld & Nicolson, 1971)

M. Hodges, (ed.), *European Integration* (Penguin, 1972)

For up to date information on the EEC consult the Commission of the European Communities, 20 Kensington Palace Gardens, London W8 4QQ.

CHAPTER 14

The Retreat from Empire

A ▬▬▬▬▬▬▬▬▬ THE BRITISH EMPIRE IN 1945

Once the British Empire recovered the territories lost to Japan it emerged undiminished from the Second World War. Bevin even hoped at one point to add to its size by acquiring the right to occupy Cyrenaica and Tripolitania in North Africa. Thus in 1945, despite the imminence of its fall, the British Empire covered as large an area of the globe as it had ever done. As in the First World War, the white Dominions all came to Britain's aid. So did India where no fewer than three million Indian soldiers volunteered to serve in the British army. While there was also serious opposition to the continuance of British rule in India, elsewhere there was little apparent threat to Britain's imperial position.

The Effects of War

The Statute of Westminster of 1931, it will be recalled, had given *de facto* independence to the Dominions of Australia, Canada, New Zealand, South Africa and Ireland. The constitutional status of the 80 or so other territories in the Empire varied enormously. Some, such as Jamaica or the Gold Coast, were Crown Colonies with elected legislatures, usually still dominated by an 'official' nominated majority. Others, such as Cyprus or the Sudan had unique relationships with the British government, reflecting the circumstances under which they had been acquired. India, too, was a law unto itself. Despite this variety, within 20 years most of these territories underwent a similar metamorphosis, so that by 1965 they became sovereign states inside, or in a few cases, outside the Commonwealth. The rapidity of this transformation has to be explained.

Forces making for change developed both within and without the Empire. Within there was first the widening gap between Britain's resources and the cost of sustaining an effective imperial presence. In 1930 total defence spending, including India's contribution, came to £154 million. In 1972 the figure reached £2 582 million. Even after allowing for inflation of about 700% this still meant that Britain was spending roughly twice as much on defence in real terms in 1972, without an Empire to defend, as she had been doing in 1930. The costs of the Second World War also imposed a heavy burden on the British economy which left little to spare for imperial policing.

Imperial sentiment was very much weaker by the end of the Second World War, though these things are impossible to measure. A poll conducted in 1947 established that three-quarters of those asked could not tell the difference between a dominion and a colony, while half could not name a single British possession. The social goals promised by the first Labour government took precedence over imperial considerations and there was a sense of psychological detachment from Britain's imperial heritage and a general disinclination to fight for its preservation. Britain had also signed the Atlantic Charter in 1941, undertaking 'to uphold the rights of all people to choose the form of government under which they will live'. Despite his mental reservations, Churchill could not prevent others from applying this principle to the British Empire.

The force of nationalism was a powerful solvent. The extraordinary popularity enjoyed by leaders such as Gandhi and Nehru in India, Nkrumah and Kenyatta in Africa, Makarios in Cyprus and Nasser in Egypt hardly needs stressing. The extension of mass communications and the emergence of an educated middle class in Britain's dependent territories resulted in a series of challenges to British rule wherever it was being exercised.

Britain had also to contend with the hostility of both the Soviet Union and the United States. In the Marxist creed imperialism was the final stage of capitalism and ripe for overthrow. The Soviet Union naturally supported anti-colonial movements which were regarded as necessary preliminaries to the establishment of socialism. Leaders such as Kenyatta were wooed by invitations to visit Moscow. It would be a mistake to detect the hand of the Soviet Union in every anti-colonial rising but the threat of Marxism was a powerful encouragement to British governments to settle with moderate nationalist leaders, for fear of something worse.

J. Morris, Farewell The Trumpets (1978)

American policy, while never so hostile to the British Empire as that of the Soviet Union, was initially very suspicious. Roosevelt maintained that 'the British would take land anywhere, even if it were only a rock or a sandbank'. [Morris, p. 464] He suggested that Hong Kong be handed over to Chiang Kai Shek at the end of the war. Truman clashed seriously with Britain over Palestine in 1946, and Dulles was unwilling to support British initiatives in the Middle East in 1955 and 1956. It was only in the 1960s that Britain's few remaining imperial possessions came to be seen as a source of stability by the United States.

G. Woodcock, Who Killed the British Empire? (1974)

Finally, just as the security of India had been used to justify the acquisition of large parts of the Empire — Aden, Egypt, parts of the Persian Gulf, for instance, so the loss of India in 1947 had the opposite effect. For as Lord Curzon had argued in 1908, once India was lost 'Your ports and your coaling-stations, your fortresses and your dockyards, your Crown colonies and protectorates will go too ....' [Woodcock, p. 301]

The Official View

K. O. Morgan, Labour in Power, 1945–1951 (Clarendon Press, 1984)

In 1942, shortly after the battle of El Alamein, Churchill announced that he had not become the King's First Minister 'in order to preside over the liquidation of the British Empire'. This was a view with which Ernest Bevin would almost certainly have concurred. He wanted to see Britain playing a more extensive role in the Middle East: 'This is essential to our survival as a great power.' [Morgan, p. 193] He tried to persuade Attlee against what he regarded as too precipitate a withdrawal from India. He sought to maintain Britain's informal empire by maintaining alliances with states such as Jordan and Iraq. The official leadership in both major parties accepted the view that Britain's role as a great power depended on the retention of her Empire.

But there was an equally strong and to some extent opposite approach, best illustrated by the policy pursued by Arthur Creech-Jones, Colonial Secretary in the Labour government from 1945 to 1951. A Command Paper No. 7533 during his tenure of office declared that it must be British policy 'to guide the colonial territories to responsible self-government within the Commonwealth in conditions that assure to the peoples concerned both a fair standard of living and freedom from aggression from any quarter'. [Morris, pp. 505–6] To that end, the Labour Government established the Colonial Development Corporation, responsible, it must be admitted, for the disastrous attempt to grow ground nuts on a commercial scale in East Africa, and more importantly, the Colombo Plan in 1950. This provided £1 868 million to be spent on the underdeveloped parts of the Commonwealth and it was raised by the wealthier members, including Britain. Official policy was thus a blend of two attitudes: a desire to protect the strategic interests on which Britain's status as a great power depended; and a concern to promote the welfare of the peoples still within the Empire while preparing them for self-government. In some cases the two objectives collided, notably in the Middle East. It was in these instances that the process of withdrawal proved most painful. But there were also arguments over the pace of retreat. British politicians had to balance the need to leave behind them a viable system of government against the threat of worse disorders if they stayed. India was a case in point.

Morris, *Farewell The Trumpets*

B ▬▬▬▬▬▬▬▬▬▬▬▬▬▬▬▬ BRITAIN AND INDIA

In 1939 Lord Linlithgow, the British Viceroy, pledged the support of British India to the Allied cause. Unfortunately he did so without consulting a single Indian. It was a serious blunder, the first of several, which damaged Anglo-Indian relations during the war. The British government never abandoned its initial position that any constitutional advance would have to wait until the end of hostilities, and it failed to secure the help of those moderate Indian nationalist leaders who were sympathetic to the British cause in the fight against Nazism.

India during the War

Indian leaders were divided on how to respond to the war. Gandhi, while totally opposed to Nazism, was not prepared to modify his belief in non-violence and consistently opposed any support for the British war effort. Nehru's position was much more complex. His sympathies were initially with Britain. He opposed using England's distress for political advantage, writing to a friend in May 1940: 'I think it would be wrong for us at this particular moment, when Britain is in peril to take advantage of her distress and rush at her throat.' [Brecher, p. 267] But he insisted that support could only be given in return for real constitutional advance. More ruthless nationalists like Subhas Chandra Bose believed that Britain's plight was India's opportunity. Bose went first to Germany, then to Japan and finally to Singapore, where he took command of the Indian National Army which was recruited from those Indian prisoners of war captured during the Japanese invasion of Malaya. About 20 000 out of a possible 60 000 joined the INA and took part in the Burma Campaign on the Japanese side.

M. Brecher, *Nehru* (1977)

Mohammed Ali Jinnah, leader of the Muslim League, on the other hand, strongly supported the British cause and urged his co-religionists to join the Indian Army. He took this course in the hope that it would win Britain's support for an independent Pakistan. The majority of Indian opinion supported the policy adopted by Congress of non-co-operation, erupting at times into more violent forms of opposition.

The war had little direct effect on India until the Japanese assault on Malaya in December 1941. But the fall of Singapore on 15 February 1942 and of Rangoon on 8 March altered the situation completely. India itself was now under threat of invasion. Churchill's immediate response was to send out Sir Stafford Cripps to see whether a compromise could be achieved with the Indian nationalist leaders. Cripps arrived in India on 25 March. He was authorised to promise dominion status at the end of the war, its form to be determined after a constitutional conference in which the Princes, as well as representatives from British India, would be included. In the short term Cripps also offered the hope that leaders of the political parties might be invited to join the Viceroy's Executive Council. Nehru evidently felt that an agreement on these lines might have been achieved. But Cripps had no more to offer, and Gandhi would settle for nothing short of full independence at once. He described the offer as 'a post-dated cheque on a failing bank'. On 7 August the All India Congress Committee passed a fateful resolution calling for Britain to quit India, on the grounds that 'it is no longer justified in holding the nation back from endeavouring to assert its will against an imperialist and authoritarian government .... The Committee resolves, therefore, to sanction ... the starting of a mass struggle on non-violent lines on the widest possible scale ....' [Brecher, p. 287]

The British reaction was tactless and counter-productive. All the Congress leaders, including Nehru and Gandhi, were arrested. They were not to be released until June 1945. This action sparked off the most serious outbreak of violence since the Indian Mutiny. According to official figures, 1028 were killed and 3215 were injured between 9 August and 30 November. Over 100 000 were arrested. The violence died down by the end of the year but it distracted the attention of the British army during a critical period in the campaign against Japan. More seriously, with all the leaders of the Congress party in jail all political progress came to a grinding halt. The bottling up of the opposition meant that when it was released the pressure on Britain for a rapid withdrawal was all the greater.

Negotiations and the Road to Partition, 1945–47

As the war approached its end in Europe, the new British Viceroy, Archibald Wavell, decided that another effort must be made to break the constitutional impasse. After lengthy discussions with the Coalition cabinet in the spring of 1945 he returned to India with proposals for constitutional change 'within the framework of the 1935 Government of India Act'. A Conference of political leaders was arranged to take place at Simla on 25 June, and the chief members of the Congress party were released from prison so that they could participate. Unfortunately the Conference reached deadlock on the issue of how the Muslim members of the reconstituted Executive Council were to be chosen. Jinnah insisted that they must all be nominated by the Muslim League, which was committed to a separate Pakistan. Congress could not accept such a restriction. The rivalry between Congress and the Muslim League thus surfaced at the very outset of the negotiations; it persisted throughout and led ultimately to Partition as the only viable solution. On 14 July Wavell adjourned the

Conference. On 26 July the new Labour government took office. Attlee, who had been a member of the Simon Commission in 1930 and had also chaired the India Cabinet Committee in the Coalition government, naturally assumed the main responsibility for the Labour government's India policy. He appointed Lord Pethwick-Lawrence, a man known for his sympathy towards Indian nationalism, to be the new Secretary of State. Attlee had no doubts in his own mind that the time had come for Britain to leave India. But he was very anxious to prevent Partition, and the next two years were largely taken up with negotiations to see whether an independent India could not also be united, despite the rivalries between Hindu and Muslim.

India's Last Viceroy Lord Louis Mountbatten and his Wife, with Gandhi

On 26 March 1946 a Cabinet Mission consisting of Pethwick-Lawrence, Cripps and A. V. Alexander (First Lord of the Admiralty) arrived in Delhi to canvass opinions. It soon became clear to the Commission that all previous schemes for an All-India Government would be unacceptable to the Muslim League. On 16 May

they produced a plan of their own. It envisaged a three-tier structure. The central government would control foreign policy, defence and communications; all other matters would be dealt with by the provincial governments. But a third intermediate tier would be created for 'selected purposes in common'. Provinces would be associated in groups of their own choice at this level of government. This arrangement would permit the Muslim-dominated provinces in the North West and in Bengal to be linked together while remaining inside a united India. It was an ingenious, if complicated, scheme and for a time it looked as though it was going to be accepted. But there were doubts about the interpretation of the group provisions. On 10 July Nehru made an inflammatory speech in which he said that the grouping scheme would probably never come to fruition. On 27 July the Muslim League withdrew its support for the plan and called for Direct Action in favour of a united Pakistan. This led in turn to serious rioting in Calcutta in which at least 4000 were killed. Further efforts to bring Nehru and Jinnah together failed and India drifted closer to civil war.

India's first Prime Minister, Pandit Jawaharlal Nehru

At this point Attlee and Wavell began to part company. In September 1946 Wavell produced a contingency plan called Operation Breakdown under which British personnel would evacuate the Hindu parts of India by 31 March 1947, while British troops would continue to garrison the Muslim areas in the North, prior to their withdrawal by 31 March 1948. This solution appalled Attlee and he decided that Wavell must be replaced. His choice lighted on Lord Louis Mountbatten, formerly Supreme Allied Commander in South East Asia. It proved an inspired one as Wavell generously recognised: 'Dickie's personality may perhaps accomplish what I have failed to achieve.'

Attlee also took another vital initiative. On 20 February 1947 he announced to the House of Commons that Britain would leave India by 1 June 1948 at the latest. He justified this decision to the cabinet by arguing that 'the time had now come to make a final effort, by the issue of this statement, to compel the two political parties in India to face the realities of the situation and collaborate in framing a new Constitution.' [Harris, p. 379] Mountbatten, prior to accepting the post of Viceroy, had asked for, and received, the power to make his own decisions on India. When he arrived on 20 March 1947 he used his authority to the full. In the next two months he had 133 recorded interviews with Indian leaders. He established a close rapport with Nehru. By mid-April he concluded that Partition was the only possible solution for India. Nehru gave his reluctant assent, and this was perhaps Mountbatten's most important achievement. On 2–3 June a final conference took place at which Nehru and Jinnah both gave their approval to what was now the Mountbatten Plan. It provided for two Dominions to be created, India and Pakistan. Each province would be free to join the Dominion of its choice, the decision being made in some cases by the Provincial Legislatures, in others by referenda. Nothing was said about the Princes who would apparently therefore be free to join either India or Pakistan, or to assert their independence – and this proved to be a serious omission. The Plan also made possible the acceleration of British withdrawal. The date finally agreed was 15 August 1947, nine months earlier than the deadline Attlee had suggested. The Muslim League gave its approval to the Plan by 400 votes to 8, and the All India Congress Committee (AICC) also assented by 153 votes to 29. Gandhi continued to voice his opposition to Partition but accepted its inevitability. On 4 July the India Independence Bill received its second reading in the House of Commons without a division; it was given the royal assent on 15 August, the day on which the Independence of India and Pakistan was joyfully proclaimed. A mere 73 days had elapsed between the acceptance of Partition and the attempts to implement it.

K. Harris, *Attlee* (Weidenfeld & Nicolson, 1982)

The Effects of Partition

The precipitate haste with which the Partition of India was carried out must bear at least some of the responsibility for the unhappy aftermath of Independence. Three problems remained to be resolved after the agreement reached between Hindu and Muslim leaders on 2–3 June 1947. How were the frontiers between the border areas of India and Pakistan to be determined? How were the 600-odd princely states to be integrated into the two new Dominions? How were the religious minorities (Muslims in India, Hindus and Sikhs in Pakistan) to be guaranteed protection? All these problems had still to be faced on 15 August.

With regard to the first problem, a British barrister, Sir Cyril Radcliffe, was appointed to chair Boundary Commissions for Bengal and the Punjab. He was assisted by two High Court judges nominated by the Congress party, and two nominated by the Muslim League. As might have been expected, on most contentious issues the Commission split along party lines, with Radcliffe's being the deciding voice. Inevitably some of his judgments were disputed and the award of one small but important area, Gardapur, which had a small Muslim majority, to India for largely economic reasons, sparked off the first outbreak of violence and caused Pakistan to doubt Radcliffe's impartiality. The final frontiers between India and Pakistan continued to be disputed long after the Boundary Commissions had completed their work.

The India Independence Act made no reference to the 600 princely states, beyond stating that Britain's paramount rights over their defence, foreign affairs and communications would cease with Independence. The Indian Congress party was naturally afraid that if the Princes opted for independence, as they were presumably entitled to do, this would lead to the 'Balkanisation' of India. On 15 June 1947 the AICC stated that no state would be allowed 'to declare independence and to live in isolation from the rest of India'. Foreign recognition of the independence of any princely state would be regarded as 'an unfriendly act'. On 25 July Mountbatten urged the Princes to accede either to India or to Pakistan. Under these pressures, by 15 August all but three had done so. The three exceptions were the tiny state of Junagadh, adjoining Kashmir, Hyderabad in central India, and Kashmir itself, an area of great strategic importance in the North of India. Junagadh and Hyderabad were ruled by Muslim Princes, but in each case the majority of the inhabitants were Hindu. In Kashmir the position was reversed, the Maharajah being Hindu while a majority of his subjects were Muslim.

Junagadh and Hyderabad were successfully absorbed into India after military occupation by the Indian army in 1947 and 1948 respectively. In 1948 Kashmir was invaded both by India and Pakistan and temporarily partitioned by the United Nations. In 1957 India annexed the eastern half of the state. In 1965 war broke out for a second time on the Kashmir question and it has still to be finally settled.

The third problem, that of religious minorities, has proved equally intractable. In 1947 it was worst in the Punjab. There was a large concentration of Hindus and Sikhs in West Pakistan and an equally large number of Muslims in the eastern part of the Punjab on the Indian side of the border. Such were the religious tensions that neither group felt that they could safely remain where they were. It has been estimated that 7.5 million Muslims moved into West Pakistan, while 5.5 million Hindus and Sikhs went in the opposite direction. There were similar movements of population, though not on the same scale, in East Pakistan. The flight of refugees was accompanied by frenzied outbursts of popular violence, especially in the Punjab. Trains taking Sikhs and Hindus from Lahore to Amritsar, for instance, were stopped and their passengers massacred. In one such incident 2000 died. Casualty figures for all post-Independence violence have been variously estimated at 200 000 to 500 000.

The Indian leaders did their utmost to stop the killings. Mountbatten was urged to return and head an Emergency Committee, which he did. Gandhi toured Bengal ceaselessly and promised a fast to death unless the violence ended. Nehru intervened personally to prevent Hindus from looting Muslim shops in Delhi and rescued two Muslim children from a Hindu mob. These gestures had an effect. Gandhi's appeal for moderation provoked his assassination by a Hindu extremist in January 1948, but his death did not lead to a further wave of reprisals. It was his last service to the India which he had done so much to create.

Britain's departure from India was indelibly stained by the communal violence which accompanied and followed it. Three wars have subsequently taken place between India and Pakistan, in 1948, 1965 and 1971. As a consequence of the third of these wars, East Pakistan broke from West Pakistan to form the new State of Bangladesh. In 1984 the holy city of Amritsar was the scene of another massacre as militant Sikhs were expelled from the Golden Temple which they had turned into a fortress. Could it have been different? It seems unlikely. In 1945 Britain was faced with an impossible dilemma, partly of her own making. Such was the pent-up demand for independence that to have delayed granting it any longer would have placed an intolerable burden on the civil and military authorities in India, as they themselves were forced to admit. But the antagonism between the two main religious communities prevented all Britain's attempts to create a united India. Partition was decided on as a last but inevitable resort. The haste with which it was executed may be seen either as a miracle of improvisation or as an abdication of responsibility. In the circumstances of 1947 it was perhaps the only option available. But it was hardly a matter for self-congratulation.

Something was salvaged, all the same. Mountbatten was asked to stay on as Governor-General of the New India. In Pakistan, Jinnah assumed that office himself. Though both States declared themselves republics in 1949 they were admitted to the Commonwealth, of which they have remained valued members. India, for so long the Jewel in the Crown, finally gained her independence in a spirit of goodwill on both sides and the long, often painful story of the *Raj* was transformed into a more equal and fruitful relationship.

INDIA AT INDEPENDENCE, 15 AUGUST 1947

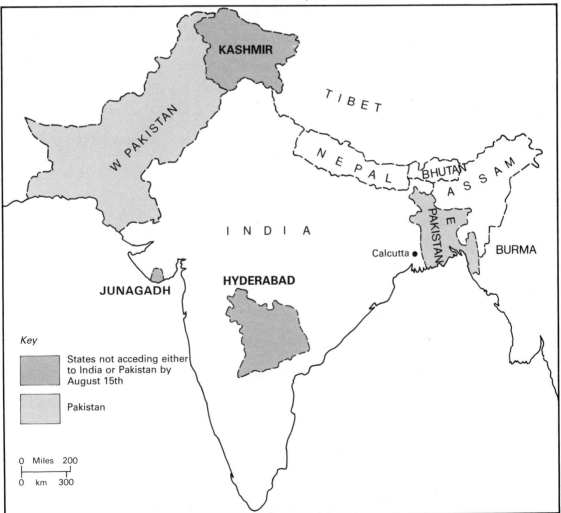

With the loss of India, Britain had no further strategic interest in the two adjoining parts of the Indian sub-continent, Burma and Ceylon. Much of Burma had been occupied by the Japanese in the Second World War and some Burmese politicians had collaborated with the Japanese administration. For a brief period an attempt was made to restore British rule under the restored British Governor, Dorman-Smith. But Attlee soon came to the conclusion that it would be better to come to terms with the strong nationalist movement led by Aung Sang. In December 1946 Aung Sang was invited to London and on 27 January 1947 an agreement was signed granting dominion status to his provisional government. Unfortunately, Aung Sang and all his ministers were assassinated in July 1947 by gunmen from a rival faction. But a new government under another member of Aung Sang's party, Thakin Nu, took over. A treaty granting Burma its full independence was signed on 17 October 1947 and in January 1948 Burma left the Commonwealth and became a sovereign republic.

Ceylon had already made considerable progress towards self-government and by 1931 was the only British colony where full adult suffrage was allowed. Ceylon also escaped Japanese invasion. Perhaps for these reasons her transition to dominion status was smoothly accomplished and took effect from February 1948. Britain retained the right to use the harbour at Trincomalee and Ceylon, unlike Burma, elected to remain in the Commonwealth.

BRITAIN AND THE MIDDLE EAST ═══════ C

The Principles of British Policy

With the loss of India, Burma and Ceylon it might have been expected that Britain's interest in the Middle East would wane, as Curzon had prophesied. But this was not the case. As late as August 1949 Bevin presented a paper to the cabinet in which he stressed Britain's concerns in the area:

A. Bullock, *Ernest Bevin, Foreign Secretary* (1984)

> In peace and war, the Middle East is an area of cardinal importance to the UK, second only to the UK itself. Strategically the Middle East is a focal point of communications, a source of oil, a shield to Africa and the Indian Ocean, and an irreplaceable offensive base. Economically it is, owing to oil and cotton, essential to United Kingdom recovery. [Bullock, p. 113]

Britain's imperial policy in the Middle East was largely governed by these considerations.

In 1945 Britain still had direct control over Gibraltar and Malta. Cyprus had been formally annexed in 1914. Under the 1936 Treaty with Egypt Britain retained the right to keep troops in the Canal Zone and shared with Egypt responsibility for the Sudan. In the Red Sea, Aden was a British colony and British suzerainty was recognised in many of the Sheikdoms along the south coast of the Arabian peninsula and in the Persian Gulf. Britain had the right to station troops and to maintain aerodromes in Iraq. She had close ties with Jordan whose army was commanded by a British officer, Sir John Glubb. Finally, as the mandatory power she was responsible for Palestine. In the light of Bevin's cabinet paper, British withdrawal from any of these areas was likely to be undertaken with reluctance and it is significant that Britain's only attempt at gunboat diplomacy after 1945 occurred in the Middle East during the Suez Crisis. Whether a British military presence was really needed in the Middle East is another matter. Attlee doubted whether it was. But the Chiefs of Staff continued to urge the need for a *place d'armes*, and Bevin supported them. Various places were suggested: Egypt, Palestine, Kenya, Cyprus. All had to be abandoned in the end. But whereas the retreat from India was an act of deliberate policy, Britain's withdrawal from the Middle East took place in a disconnected sequence of untoward events.

Palestine

The Effects of War

The Second World War made the Palestine problem more insoluble than ever. The holocaust of the Jews, which reduced the number of European Jews from 10 million to about 4.25 million, gave to Zionism a moral force which it had not previously enjoyed. British politicians, Bevin among them, were generally unwilling to recognise that Jewishness was a matter of nationality as well as of religion. After 1945 such a position was much harder to maintain. Zionists could maintain, as most of them did, that only a Jewish state in Palestine could provide the protection needed for the practice of the Jewish religion.

The strengthening of Zionism was matched by a corresponding increase in Arab national consciousness. The Arab League was founded in 1945. The cause of the Palestinian Arab was certain to be defended by the Arab states on Palestine's borders: Syria, Lebanon, Iraq, Jordan and Egypt. Thus Britain was faced with a vociferous demand to increase the number of permitted immigrants into Palestine by Jews who regarded Europe as little better than a Jewish cemetery; but any such increase was certain to be resisted by the Palestinian Arabs and their neighbours who rightly feared that the ultimate goal behind the increase was the establishment of a Jewish state. After 1945 Britain also had to face a well-organised and armed Jewish militia, the Haganah, spearheaded by two terrorist organisations, the Irgun Zwei Lumi and the Stern Gang, who were prepared to use the same resistance tactics that the British had encouraged in German-occupied Europe.

British Policy

The most recent statement of British policy was the White Paper of 1939 which had proposed a total limit of 75 000 Jewish immigrants over a five-year period. The Labour party had opposed the White Paper in 1939 and there was general sympathy in the party for the Zionist movement. In the 1944 policy statement, *International Post-War Settlement*, it had been suggested that the Jews should be allowed to become the majority in Palestine: 'Let the Arabs be encouraged to move out as the Jews move in.' [Pelling, p. 127] At the Party Conference in 1945 there were strong calls for an end to restrictions on immigration. But Bevin had never been a convinced Zionist and within weeks of gaining office he had come round to the Foreign Office view, remarking to Attlee: 'Clem, about Palestine, according to my lads in the office we've got it all wrong. We've got to think again.' [Harris, p. 390] This change of heart is confirmed by Harold Beeley, the Foreign Office official responsible for

H. Pelling, *The Labour Governments, 1945–51* (Macmillan, 1984)

K. Harris, *Attlee* (Weidenfeld & Nicolson, 1982)

briefing Bevin on the Palestine question. A Cabinet Committee on Palestine, which met on 8 September 1945 confirmed the importance to Britain of Arab opinion:

> Unfortunately the future of Palestine bulks large in all Arab eyes ... to enforce any such policy (to which they object) and especially one which lays us open to a charge of breach of faith, is bound seriously to undermine our position and may well lead not only to widespread disturbances ... but to the withdrawal of co-operation on which our Imperial interests so largely depend. [Report of the Palestine Committee, 8 September 1945, cited in Bullock, p. 171]

British policy after 1945 was the same, in essentials, as in 1939. Nothing should be done which would antagonise Arab opinion. There was some relaxation of immigration policy, a total of 1500 a month now being allowed into Palestine. But with over 200 000 Jewish displaced persons clamouring for entry this was hardly likely to satisfy Zionist organisations nor their sympathisers in Europe and the United States. If Bevin's policy was to have any chance of success he needed to secure American support. But Truman had a certain sympathy for Zionism and the Jewish vote in places like New York was sufficiently large to have a distinct influence on American Middle East policy. The inability of Britain and the United States to agree on a common approach to the Palestine problem helps to explain the ignominious failure of British policy.

The British Search for a Solution, 1945–47

For about 18 months, from July 1945 to February 1947, the British Government struggled without avail to secure an agreement that would be acceptable to both Jews and Arabs. On 13 November 1945 Bevin managed to secure the appointment of an Anglo-American Committee to make recommendations on the future of Palestine. Its report came out on 1 May 1946. It recommended the immediate admission of 100 000 immigrants; the ending of restrictions on the purchase of land by Jews; and it urged the ending of terrorism and illegal immigration. The report was rejected both by Jewish and Arab authorities. The Chiefs of Staff and the Foreign Office advised against accepting the immigration recommendations because of the harm this would do to relations with the Arab states, but President Truman immediately announced his support for the admission of 100 000 immigrants. This led to the first rift in Anglo-American relations. The British cabinet concluded that it would only agree to this figure if illegal Jewish military organisations were disbanded, and if the United States would accept responsibility with Britain for implementing the recommendation. Neither condition was satisfied.

On 22 July 1946, the King David Hotel in Jerusalem was blown up by the Irgun Zwei Lumi, with the loss of 91 lives, many of them British. This event strengthened British determination to oppose concessions on Jewish immigration. The United States also announced its opposition to a compromise plan for dividing Palestine into autonomous regions under a bi-national central government. The low point in Anglo-American relations was reached on 4 October when Truman reaffirmed publicly his support for the immediate admission of 100 000 Jews, despite Attlee's plea that he should postpone the announcement. Attlee wrote to Truman: 'I have received with great regret your letter refusing even a few hours grace to the Prime Minister of the country which has the actual responsibility for the government of Palestine ....' [Harris, p. 396] Granted this division between British and American

K. Harris, *Attlee* (Weidenfeld & Nicolson, 1982)

472

policy, little progress was made in the Conference which convened in London in September 1946, particularly as it was boycotted by Arab and Jewish leaders in Palestine.

In January 1947 a new round of talks began. By this time Truman had come round to the idea of Partition. Bevin at one time looked like accepting it too, but the Chiefs of Staff and the Foreign Office continued to be strongly opposed and Bevin evidently accepted their reasoning. In a memorandum addressed to the cabinet on 14 January 1947 he expressed the fear that Partition 'would contribute to the elimination of British influence from the whole of the vast Moslem area lying between Greece and India. This would have not only strategic consequences, it would also jeopardise the security of our interest in the increasingly important oil production of the Middle East.' [Bullock, p. 365] Instead of Partition, Bevin produced his own plan. Palestine would be placed under the Trusteeship of the United Nations for five years, before becoming a bi-national state; Jews and Arabs would be given powers of local self-government; and immigration would be stepped up to 96 000. As might have been expected 'this plan was also rejected by both sides' causing Bevin to admit to Attlee: 'I am at the end of my tether.' [Harris, p. 297] On 14 February the cabinet decided to hand Palestine over to the United Nations, a decision that was announced to the House of Commons on 18 February. Notice was also given that British troops would be withdrawn when the Mandate expired on 14 May 1948. It was an admission of defeat.

Bullock, *Ernest Bevin*

The End of the Mandate, 1947–48

Britain's responsibility for Palestine still had a year to run, however, and her position became increasingly isolated and exposed. The United Nations Special Committee on Palestine was set up in May 1947 and produced its report in September. By seven votes to four the Committee advocated Partition, with Jerusalem under the control of the United Nations. 150 000 immigrants were to be admitted over a two-year period, during which Britain's responsibility as the mandatory power would continue to be exercised. On 20 September the British cabinet considered these proposals. Bevin declared them to be 'manifestly unjust to the Arabs' and the cabinet approved without dissent his view that Britain should decline any responsibility for a settlement with which she so strongly disagreed. When the report was debated in the United Nations on 26–29 November the British delegate abstained. However, with both the United States and the Soviet Union voting in its favour, the report was carried by 33 votes to 13. There were 10 abstentions, Britain's among them.

In the next six months a state of undeclared war gradually incubated in Palestine. Syrian irregulars crossed the border as soon as the General Assembly's vote was announced. The families of all British civilians and non-essential officials were evacuated from Palestine as early as February 1947. By May 1948 most British troops had also been removed. On 14 May the state of Israel was proclaimed and was immediately recognised by the United States. It was also invaded by the neighbouring Arab states: Egypt, Transjordan, Lebanon, Syria and Iraq. Britain, having anticipated just such an event, could do nothing to prevent it. United Nations efforts to end the conflict began in May 1948, with the appointment of Count Bernadotte of Sweden to act as a mediator. A succession of cease-fires were agreed, only to be broken as each side sought the advantage. Bernadotte himself was assassinated, almost certainly by Jewish extremists. By January 1949 Israel had pushed back the invaders, gaining a further 8000 square miles of territory in the process. The Arab states accepted defeat, if only temporarily, and by the summer of 1949 Israel had negotiated truces with each of them. Britain gave a somewhat belated recognition to the new state of Israel in January 1949.

The Labour government inherited an impossible situation in Palestine. Between 1945 and 1948, 338 British lives were lost and £100 million were spent in a vain attempt to quell the forces of Jewish and Arab nationalism, and to separate the contending factions. It may be that Britain would have done better to recognise earlier than she did the inevitability of making concessions to pro-Zionist opinion, certainly in relation to immigration. But in view of the Arab reaction to Partition it can hardly be claimed that Britain was unduly sensitive to Arab susceptibilities. Israel's success in the 1948–49 war meant that her new boundaries were considerably larger than those envisaged in the United Nations award. Unlike the United States, Britain could claim no credit for Israel's emergence. Nor could she gain any gratitude from the Arab states following their defeat. Such was the unhappy sequel to the Balfour Declaration. Though Britain had surrendered responsibility for Palestine to the United Nations, she could not ignore the new situation created by the first Arab-Israeli war. She continued to provide arms to Iraq, Egypt and Jordan, while France and the United States provided assistance to Israel. In order to prevent an arms race in which the Soviet Union might get involved, a Tripartite Declaration was signed on 25 May 1950 between Britain, France and the United States. It laid down that applications for arms should only be considered 'in the light of legitimate self-defence'. It also pledged the Three Powers to take action both within and outside the United Nations should they discover that preparations were being made to violate the agreed armistice lines, a promise that was to be flagrantly broken in 1956.

Britain and Iran, 1951–54

No sooner was the Palestine problem disposed of than Britain had to face another difficulty in the Middle East. By 1950 Iran had become the largest oil-producing state in the Middle East and was the chief source of Britain's oil imports from that area. A British company, Anglo-Iranian, owned many of the oil fields and the huge refinery at Abadan, the largest in the world. The company was not generous in its payment of royalties to its host country and by 1951 negotiations on this question had broken down. In April an extreme nationalist government, headed by Dr Mussadiq, took office in Iran. On 2 May he announced the nationalisation of the Anglo-Iranian Oil Company.

The cabinet considered military intervention. It was strongly advocated by Morrison, the Foreign Secretary, and by Shinwell, Minister of Defence. The Chiefs of Staff were also in favour of action. A plan for the forcible occupation of Abadan Island was drawn up. But Gaitskell and Attlee were against the use of force and after a series of cabinet meetings the balance of opinion went in their favour. On 26 July it was decided to resume negotiations with the Iranian government. A mission headed by Richard Stokes, the Lord Privy Seal, who had business contacts in Iran, went to Teheran in August. It failed to secure an agreement but Stokes advised Attlee to continue negotiations. Morrison was still pressing for military action, but he was overruled and on 27 September the cabinet decided to refer the dispute to the United Nations. On 4 October all British personnel were withdrawn from Abadan and the refinery was closed down.

Mossadiq remained in power until 1953, but after his removal relations were re-opened with the British government. Lengthy negotiations then took place on the re-opening of the Iranian oil industry and an agreement was finally reached in July 1954. An international consortium was formed in which Anglo-Iranian held a large share to produce and market Iranian oil. The Iranian government agreed to pay compensation of £25 million, spread over 10 years. The oil soon started flowing again, and by 1955 had yielded £31 600 000 to the Iranian government. Eden was largely responsible for the success of these negotiations. His patience when dealing with Iran contrasts surprisingly with his handling of the Suez crisis.

The End of British Occupation, 1945–54

At the end of the war Britain had over 150 000 troops in Egypt and, under the Treaty of 1936, the right to keep them there for another 10 years. The Canal Zone, an area the size of Wales, was under British control and Britain also shared with Egypt responsibility for the Sudan. All these privileges were greatly resented by the Egyptian government, and were raised at the United Nations as early as 1946. For its part, the British government, concerned for the security of the Suez Canal, would only contemplate evacuating British troops if Egypt would enter some kind of regional security pact and would guarantee to maintain the Base facilities so that they could be used again if necessary. Britain also insisted that the Sudanese people should have the right of self-determination when they were ready for independence. Abortive negotiations on both these issues took place in 1946, 1949 and 1951. In October 1951 the Egyptian government announced the ending of the 1936 Treaty and of the condominium of 1899 giving Britain joint responsibility for the Sudan. The British Foreign Minister at the time, Herbert Morrison, reacted angrily and threatened military action. But he was overruled by Attlee and before any further steps could be taken a General Election intervened, Attlee resigning on 26 October. The incoming Conservative government also decided against armed intervention.

In July 1952 King Farouk was overthrown in a military coup. He was replaced first by General Neguib and in 1954 by Colonel Nasser. Neguib was ready to separate the issue of the Sudan from the question of Britain's military presence in Egypt. In 1953 an Agreement was signed under which the Sudanese people would be allowed to determine their own future at the end of a three-year transition period. In January 1956 the Sudan gained its independence and chose not to be incorporated into Egypt. Nasser forced his way into power in March 1954, but at this stage Eden did not view him with the hostility he later came to feel and in July 1954 the Canal Base Agreement was signed between the British and Egyptian governments. British troops were to evacuate the Base within 20 months, but the installations would be maintained by a joint group of British and Egyptian technicians, and Britain would have the right to re-activate the Base in the event of an armed attack on Egypt or any member of the Arab League. The last British troops left the Canal Zone in June 1956. The two major issues that had divided Britain and Egypt had been resolved. Eden had shown himself to be conciliatory and flexible, too much so for some right-wing members of the Conservative party.

The Background to the Suez Crisis

The sudden deterioration in Anglo-Egyptian relations that took place between 1954 and 1956 was caused partly by Nasser's increasingly aggressive policy, partly by British perceptions of that policy. In his book *A Philosophy of the Revolution*, which has been likened to *Mein Kampf*, Nasser located Egypt in the centre of three circles

Britain and Egypt, 1945–56

embracing the Arab, Islamic and African worlds. He saw it as his task to encourage nationalist movements throughout Africa, and in 1954 these included the *Mau Mau* rebellion in Kenya and the war against French settlers in Algeria. He announced his intention to exterminate Israel. He refused to take the Western side in the Cold War and was ready to do business with the highest bidder. There can be little doubt that by 1956 he came to be seen by Eden as a latter-day Hitler who must be stopped, and if possible removed, before his aggressive policies could be shown to have succeeded. British policy during the Suez crisis was based on that premiss.

The first serious disagreement occurred over the Baghdad Pact, a defensive alliance signed between Turkey and Iraq in February 1955. Britain encouraged the Pact and joined it herself in April, partly because she was anxious to strengthen the Middle East against Soviet incursions, partly because it enabled her to renew her right to keep airbases at Habbaniya and Shaiba in Iraq. Pakistan and Iran also joined, in September and November respectively. But Nasser was strongly opposed to the Pact which he saw as an attempt to divide the Arab world and as a challenge to his leadership. The United States was also unwilling to join. A British attempt to persuade King Hussein of Jordan to become a member in December 1955 was successfully frustrated by Nasser, who also persuaded Hussein to dismiss the British commander of the Jordanian army, Sir John Glubb, though the decision to do so was Hussein's alone.

The second point of conflict occurred over the financing of the Aswan High Dam. In December 1955 the United States and Britain decided to supplement a World Bank Loan for the purpose of building this dam on the Nile with a further $400 million. This decision was reached after Nasser's announcement that he intended to purchase arms from Czechoslovakia, and the purpose of the loan was to keep Nasser in the Western orbit. But by March 1956, following Nasser's activities in Jordan, Lloyd had decided that British policy must be realigned. At a cabinet meeting on 21 March he argued 'Instead of seeking to conciliate or support Nasser, we should do our utmost to counter him and uphold our true friends'. [Lloyd, p. 60] A message was sent to the British ambassador in Washington at the same time urging that 'we should not give Nasser the money for the dam unless he genuinely changed his attitude towards Western interests in the Middle East'. In May Lloyd met Dulles, the American Secretary of State, at a NATO Council meeting in Paris. According to Lloyd, both men agreed to let the Aswan Project 'wither on the vine'. Though the American government gave the British government no notice before taking the final step, it can have come as no surprise when Dulles announced on 19 July 1956 that the offer of a loan to the Egyptian government had been withdrawn. On 20 July Britain followed suit.

S. Lloyd, *Suez 1956, A Personal Account* (Cape, 1978)

Nasser may have been contemplating nationalisation of the Suez Canal for some time, but the American announcement certainly prompted Nasser's next step. On 26 July he made a public speech in Alexandria in which he declared that the days of alien exploitation were over; the Canal and all its revenues would belong entirely to Egypt: 'We shall build the High Dam and we shall gain our usurped rights ....' [Nutting, p. 145] Nasser assumed control of the Suez Canal Company's offices in Egypt, imposed martial law in the Canal Zone, and forbade all employees of the company to leave their jobs. Shareholders, however, were to be offered compensation at 26 July prices.

A. Nutting, *Nasser* (Constable, 1972)

British Reactions to the Nationalisation of the Canal

British policy following Nasser's action had both long-and short-term objectives. In the short term, compensation must be secured for the illegal seizure – theft was Eden's term – of the Canal, and the Canal must as a minimum condition be placed under international control. In the long term it was hoped that Nasser could be so humiliated that he would be rejected by the Egyptian people. To achieve these objectives two courses of action were considered. The Chiefs of Staff were instructed as early as 27 July to prepare an invasion plan, to be known as Operation Musketeer for the seizure and occupation of the Canal. The Foreign Office, meanwhile, would seek to achieve a peaceful solution by bringing diplomatic and economic pressures on Nasser. Both courses were pursued simultaneously. Unknown to the British, the French were also conducting secret negotiations with Israel. As the diplomatic options were gradually eliminated Eden turned to a military solution, in collusion with France and Israel. The story of the intermediate negotiations, conferences and conversations, which went on from 27 July to 29 October is a long and complex one and has already gone through many different versions. At the risk of over-simplification we shall concentrate on Britain's role in the crisis, exploring first the attempts to find a diplomatic solution and then the Suez operation itself.

The Search for a Diplomatic Solution

It is impossible to grasp Britain's role in the Suez crisis without knowing something of the motives of the other participants. Israel had a long-standing quarrel with Egypt. Israeli shipping had been barred from the Suez Canal and from the Straits of Tiran. Egyptian raids had been launched across the Israeli border in the Gaza strip. Nasser had promised to eliminate Israel. But Britain had a treaty with Jordan and Iraq. She was unlikely, in the first instance at any rate, to do anything that would antagonise those two countries. Hence, throughout the crisis Britain sought to distance herself from Israel and never admitted complicity. France regarded Nasser as primarily responsible for the Algerian War which had broken out in November 1954. Guy Mollet, the French Prime Minister, took the same view of Nasser as did Eden and would have been equally glad to see him removed. The United States, on the other hand, was much more ambivalent in its attitude to Nasser. Dulles and Eisenhower certainly disliked his flirtation with the Soviet Union, but they were not willing to risk antagonising Arab opinion as a whole. With an impending presidential election Eisenhower was anxious, to say the least, not to involve the United States in hostilities, certainly not on behalf of British and French claims to control a Canal which was of little direct importance to American economic interests. Dulles was to say at one stage that Nasser must be made 'to disgorge' the Canal, but he was never prepared to support the use of force to achieve that end. Britain's main diplomatic efforts were directed at creating a body of opinion, including the United States, that would support Britain's initial objectives, the safeguarding of the Canal.

There were three main initiatives. The first of these was the London Conference, which lasted from 16 to 23 August, attended by 18 nations. Six principles were agreed, recognising Egyptian sovereignty over the Canal, but also providing protection for the users of it. An international board was to be set up to run the Canal, the British government assuming, quite wrongly, that the Egyptians would be incapable of doing so. Sir Robert Menzies, Prime Minister of Australia, put these conditions to Nasser in talks which lasted from 3 September to 9 September, without success.

The second initiative came from Dulles who suggested on 11 September that a Canal Users' Association should be set up, to which dues would be paid and which would deal with all problems of Canal passage. But at a press conference on 12 September Dulles said that if an American ship sailing under the auspices of the Suez Canal Users' Association was stopped: 'we do not intend to shoot our way through. It should go round the Cape'. [Lloyd, p. 77] This, according to Selwyn Lloyd, was enough to damn the scheme as it clearly had no teeth behind it.

S. Lloyd, *Suez 1956, A Personal Account* (Cape, 1978)

The final attempt at a negotiated settlement was made through the Security Council of the United Nations from 2 October to 13 October. That this was a seriously intended effort is not in doubt, certainly as far as the British Foreign Secretary is concerned. Britain put forward a two-part resolution. The first recapitulated the principles agreed at the London Conference. They were as follows:

1. that there should be free and open transit through the Canal without discrimination, overt or covert;
2. that there should be respect for Egyptian sovereignty;
3. that the operation of the Canal should be insulated from the politics of any country;
4. that the level of dues should be fixed by agreement between users and owners;
5. that a fair proportion of the dues should be allotted to development;
6. that affairs between the Suez Canal Company and the Egyptian government should be settled by arbitration, with suitable terms of reference and suitable provision for the payment of the sums due.

[Lloyd, p. 159]

S. Lloyd, *Suez 1958, A Personal Account* (Cape, 1978)

The second part required Egypt to propose a system that would conform with the six principles. The Security Council vote on this resolution on 12 October accepted the first part unanimously. The Soviet Union and Yugoslavia voted against the second part, thus in effect vetoing the resolution. The gap between the two sides was a relatively narrow one, at least on the surface. Had Nasser been willing at this stage to come forward with some specific proposals, the crisis might have been over. Unfortunately Eden's patience was now at an end and British attention shifted to the military alternative.

The Military Solution

France and Israel, it is now clear, were the originators of the plan for a concerted attack on Egypt. Vital talks were held in Paris on 20 and 21 September at which the possibility was first mooted. Mollet gave his guarded approval on condition that Britain could be brought in, for only Britain had the bombers available to put the Egyptian air force out of action. At the very moment when Lloyd was negotiating in New York a vital meeting was taking place at Chequers between Eden, the Under Secretary at the Foreign Office, Anthony Nutting (Lloyd's deputy), Gazier, acting French Foreign Minister, and Challe, Chief of the French Air Staff. Challe put forward a possible plan of action:

> The plan, as he put it to us, was that Israel should be invited to attack Egypt across the Sinai peninsula and that France and Britain, having given the Israeli forces enough time to seize all or most of the Sinai, should then order 'both sides' to withdraw their forces from the Suez Canal in order to permit an Anglo-French force to intervene and occupy the Canal on the pretext of saving it from damage by fighting. Thus the two powers would be able to claim to be 'separating the combatants' and 'extinguishing a dangerous fire' while actually seizing control of the entire waterway and of its terminal ports, Port Said and Suez. [Nutting, p. 93]

A. Nutting, *No End of a Lesson, the Story of Suez* (1967)

THE RETREAT FROM EMPIRE

Eden was plainly drawn to the idea, but Nutting was appalled at what he considered 'a sordid manoeuvre'. Nutting subsequently resigned because he could not support the government's policy.

On 16 October a meeting of senior ministers took place to consider the French proposals. Those present included Eden, Kilmuir (Lord Chancellor), Macmillan (Chancellor of the Exchequer), Lord Home (Dominions Secretary) and Lloyd who arrived half way through the meeting. No decisions were reached except that Lloyd and Eden were to see Mollet and Pineau (French Foreign Minister) that afternoon. There is no official record of their discussions. On 18 October a full cabinet agreed that should Israel attack Egypt, Britain and France would be justified in intervening to protect the Canal. On 22 October Lloyd made a further visit to Paris, this time *incognito*. Here he met Ben Gurion, the Israeli Prime Minister, as well as the French politicians. According to his own account, Lloyd 'tried to make it clear that an Israeli-French-British agreement to attack Egypt was impossible', because of the hostility this would arouse against British nationals in Arab countries. [Lloyd, p. 184] All he would undertake to do was to report back to his colleagues on the conversations that had taken place. This he did on 23 October. In the evening Pineau arrived for further talks: 'The main point was greater precision about the actions we would take if Israel attacked Egypt.' [Lloyd, p. 186] Further consultation was felt to be necessary and on 24 October Patrick Dean, an Under-Secretary at the Foreign Office, was dispatched to Paris, it being Selwyn Lloyd's turn for Question Time in the House of Commons. It was at this meeting that Dean, on behalf of the British Government, signed a document which set out precisely the military operations contemplated by the Israeli government, and the Anglo-French action that would follow it.

S. Lloyd, *Suez 1956, A Personal Account* (Cape, 1978)

The memoirs of two of the Frenchmen who were present, Pineau and Thomas (private secretary to the French Minister of Defence), give a full account of this document. Article 1 announced the Israeli intention to drop parachutists near the Mitla Pass in order that they could reach the Canal the following day, so justifying British intervention. Article 2 'registered the intention of the British and French governments to issue simultaneous ultimatums to Egypt and Israel, calling upon them to cease fire, to withdraw their forces to a distance of 10 miles from the Canal and in the case of Egypt to submit to a temporary Anglo-French occupation of the Canal Zone in order to safeguard navigation through the waterway'. [Warner, '*Collusion' and the Suez Crisis of 1956* in Wilson (ed.), p. 141]

K. M. Wilson (ed.), *Imperialism and Nationalism in the Middle East – The Anglo-Egyptian Experience* (1983)

On 25 October the Cabinet gave its approval to this document though how much of it its members saw must remain in doubt. Lloyd concludes his account of the meeting as follows: 'Eventually it was agreed, without dissent, that if Israel attacked we would act as Eden proposed.' [Lloyd, p. 190]

S. Lloyd, *Suez 1956, A Personal Account* (Cape, 1978)

On 29 October Israel duly launched its attack on the Mitla Pass and elsewhere across the Gaza strip. On 30 October, in accordance with the arrangements previously made, Britain and France delivered their ultimatums to Egypt and Israel to withdraw 10 miles from the Canal. Israel readily accepted. She still had some distance to go. Egypt, equally naturally, refused. In New York, Britain and France vetoed a Security Council Resolution calling for all countries to refrain from using force in the Middle East. On 31 October the British and French airforces launched a series of strikes at Egyptian airfields. There was then a delay while the invasion force which had assembled at Malta made its way slowly across the Mediterranean.

Before it could arrive an American-sponsored resolution was debated in the General Assembly of the United Nations on 2 November. It called for an immediate cease-fire and for all member states to refrain 'from introducing military goods in the area of hostilities'. The resolution was passed by 64 votes to 5, those in the minority being Britain, France, Israel, Australia and New Zealand. Despite this majority, well over the two-thirds required for a binding resolution, the Anglo-French invasion went ahead. On 5 November paratroopers were dropped at Port Said, to be followed by a naval bombardment and the landing of sea-borne troops on 6 November.

The Suez Crisis: Colonel Nasser defends the Nationalisation of the Suez Canal at a Conference in Cairo on 25 August 1956

From a military point of view the operations were a great success – 20 miles of the Canal were occupied within 24 hours, and casualties were light. The whole of the Canal could probably have been occupied within a week. But the diplomatic consequences were disastrous. Britain had alienated most of the Commonwealth and the United States, which had been left entirely in the dark. Almost before it had begun, the British government decided to end the Suez operation. On 3 November Britain abstained in the vote on a Canadian resolution in the General Assembly calling for a United Nations Emergency Force to garrison the Canal. By 6 November, the government was ready to support the idea. A severe run on the pound, and the vital knowledge that he could expect no support from the United States, convinced Macmillan that the operation must be halted. At a cabinet meeting held on 6 November at 9.30 am it was decided to order a cease-fire. The French were informed at lunch-time. At midnight on 6 November the cease-fire came into effect. By December, all British and French troops had been evacuated from Egypt.

The Aftermath

Two countries benefited from the Suez operation: Israel and Egypt. For Britain it was an unmitigated disaster. Far from protecting the Canal, Nasser used the excuse of invasion to block it, sinking 47 ships filled with concrete at strategic places. Britain's oil supplies were reduced by the destruction of four pumping stations on the Iraq pipeline. Saudi Arabia imposed an embargo on oil exports to Britain. Nasser's authority, so far from being diminished, was greatly strengthened in the eyes of the Arab world. Britain had alienated her allies in the Commonwealth. Her actions were repudiated by the Baghdad Pact. Anglo-American relations were severely strained. Worst of all, perhaps, Britain lost her reputation for integrity in the conduct of international relations. The fiction that Britain and France were intervening to separate Israeli and Egyptian forces was barely credible at the time and has now been thoroughly exposed. This was Eden's tragedy. In the longer term, the Suez crisis marks the point at which Britain's dependence on the United States was made brutally clear, and it brought to an end the preponderant role which Britain had sought to play in the Middle East. In every succeeding crisis it is the United States which has made the running. The Canal was blocked for six months. However, when it was re-opened in March 1957 Britain had found alternative sources of oil and the introduction of super-tankers made the journey from the Persian Gulf round the Cape of Good Hope as economical as the journey through the Red Sea and the Canal. Ironically, the Suez crisis proved that the Suez Canal was no longer indispensable.

Blockships sunk at the Port Said entrance to the Suez Canal: the Consequences of Anglo-French Action to keep the Canal open

The Last Outposts: Cyprus, Aden and Malta

C. Cross, *The Fall of the British Empire, 1918–1968* (1968)

Cyprus

The Suez crisis did not bring about any immediate change in Britain's Middle East policy. If anything, it appeared to underline the need for Britain to retain a strong military presence in the Middle East. With the evacuation of the Canal Zone between 1954 and 1956 an alternative base was required. The choice fell on Cyprus. In July 1954 Henry Hopkinson, Minister of State at the Colonial Office, spelled it out: 'Nothing less than continued sovereignty over this island can enable Britain to carry out her strategic obligations to Europe, the Mediterranean and the Middle East.' [cited in Cross, p. 310] In many respects it was an unfortunate choice. The island had no good harbours. More seriously the population of 600 000, four-fifths Greek, one-fifth Turkish, was passionately divided, the Greek element looking for union with Greece (ENOSIS), while the Turkish element looked to Constantinople for protection. Inevitably there was growing resentment at British rule, complicated in this case, as in Ireland and India, by the fears of the minority population for their security once British authority was removed.

Serious opposition to British rule began in 1956, led by Archbishop Makarios and Colonel Grivas, one leading the political wing and the other the military wing of the national movement known as EOKA. Its aims were union with Greece, its methods those of every terrorist movement. Soon the British forces on the island were busy quelling a rebellion. Makarios was exiled to the Seychelles islands in 1956 and a policy of repression was pursued with a great deal of violence on both sides. In 1957 Macmillan, who succeeded Eden as Prime Minister in January, decided that a change of policy was needed. Macmillan visited the Greek and Turkish premiers. Makarios was allowed to return to Greece, though not yet to Cyprus. Sir Hugh Foot, known for his abilities as a conciliator, was made Governor of the island. After prolonged negotiations, which included the Greek and Turkish governments as well as Cypriot leaders, an agreement was finally hammered out. In August 1960 Cyprus gained its independence, Britain retaining sovereignty over two base areas at Akrotiri and Dhekelia.

But the careful constitutional safeguards to protect Turkish interests could not overcome the animosity of centuries between the Greek and Turkish communities. Civil war broke out in 1963 and was only quelled by the intervention of the United Nations. In 1974 the Turks invaded Cyprus, leading to the partition of the island. Britain's role in these events was confined to her participation in the UN peace-keeping force, but at least she could claim to have conducted an honourable withdrawal.

Aden and the Aden Protectorate

The last major outpost in the Middle East to be abandoned was Aden. Still concerned to protect Britain's oil supplies in the Persian Gulf, in 1959 the British government brought into existence the South Arabian Federation. This was an unwieldy amalgam of semi-feudal Sheikdoms on the south coast of the Arabian peninsula. It was hoped that their conservative influence would counterbalance the more sophisticated urban population in Aden itself. Aden was developed as a military base with as many as 18 000 troops being stationed there. But nationalism, encouraged from Cairo, was at work here too. In 1963 the National Liberation Front began a campaign for independence, to be joined shortly afterwards by the Front for the Liberation of South Yemen, a rival organisation. Faced with this opposition, the Labour government decided in 1967 that there was no case for staying in Aden. On 29 November 1967 Aden too gained its independence. Crossman commented, revealingly: 'It now looks

A. Howard (ed.), *Richard Crossman, Crossman Diaries*

as though we'll get out of Aden without losing a single British soldier, chaos will reign soon after we've gone, and there'll be one major commitment cut – thank God.' [Crossman, p. 348] In fact, Aden became the People's Republic of South Yemen under a Marxist government. It did not join the Commonwealth.

Malta and Gibraltar

Malta's connection with Britain dated back to the Napoleonic Wars. Its people earned the George Cross for their valour under German bombardment in the Second World War. But with the ending of a large British naval precence in the Mediterranean, its harbours and dockyards were needed no longer. In 1955 a parliamentary delegation approved a scheme for making Malta an actual part of the United Kingdom, but Britain was not willing to assume the financial obligation of bringing up the Maltese standard of welfare to the British one and the idea fell through. Malta was finally granted its independence in 1964.

Gibraltar, the oldest British possession in the Mediterranean, remains in British hands chiefly because that is where the inhabitants want it to be. In a referendum held in 1967 on whether to stay British or join Spain, 44 voted for Spain, 12 138 voted to remain under British rule.

Britain's withdrawal from the Middle East was a long and painful process. It took so long because the interests to which Bevin referred were held to require a physical British presence for their protection. In a world of growing national sensibilities, such a policy proved an anachronism. The lesson was finally learned, but only after some costly mistakes.

D ▬▬▬▬▬▬▬▬▬▬▬▬ DECOLONISATION

The Granting of Dominion Status/Independence

The Process of Decolonisation

	West Africa	East Africa	Central Africa
1956		Sudan	
1957	Gold Coast (Ghana)		
1960	Nigeria	British Somaliland	
1961	Sierra Leone	Tanganyika (Tanzania. 1964)	
1962		Uganda	
1963		Kenya Zanzibar (joined Tanzania 1964)	
1964			Nyasaland (Malawi) N. Rhodesia (Zambia)
1965	Gambia		
1966			Bechuanaland (Botswana) Basutoland (Lesotho)
1968			Swaziland

	West Indies	South East Asia	Elsewhere
1957		Malaya (Malaysia, 1963)	
1960			Cyprus
1962	Jamaica Trinidad and Tobago		
1963		North Borneo (joined Malaysia)	

	West Indies	South East Asia	Elsewhere
1964			Malta
1965			Maldive Is.
1966	Barbados		
	British Guiana (Guyana)		
1967			Aden
1968			Mauritius
			Maldive Islands
1973	Bahamas		

Cross, *The Fall of the British Empire*

Herbert Morrison remarked during the Second World War that to give independence to any of Britain's African colonies would be like 'giving to a child of ten a latch key, a bank account and a shot gun'. [Cross, p. 262]

The Colonial Office in 1945 would have tended to agree with him. In the period following the Second World War its paternalist role was expanded. Staffing increased by 45%. Total expenditure on the colonies which had been a mere £3 million in 1930 rose to £40 million in 1950. The Colonial Development Corporation was established with a capital of £100 million to promote economic development. Though advance to majority rule and independence within the Commonwealth was certainly envisaged, the progress towards these goals was expected to be leisurely, taking at least a couple of generations. In practice, as can be seen from the accompanying table, within the space of about 10 years (from 1957 to 1967) the greater number of Britain's colonies gained their independence. In 1959 there were ten members of the Commonwealth (Britain, Canada, Australia, New Zealand, South Africa, India, Pakistan, Ceylon, Ghana and Malaya). In 1967 there were 27.

There are two main reasons for the rapidity of the process. First there was the emergence of articulate local leaders, committed to the cause of national independence and able to communicate their message through the press, radio and political parties. In 1945 a little-noticed but highly significant meeting took place in Chorlton Town Hall, Manchester. Among those attending were Nkrumah (Gold Coast) and Kenyatta (Kenya). This self-styled Pan-African Rally produced a statement of aims: 'We are determined to be free ... therefore we shall complain, appeal and arraign. We will make the world listen to the facts of our condition. We will fight in every way for freedom, democracy and social betterment.' [Hatch, p. 262] In virtually every British colony leaders imbued with such ambitions were to be found: Hastings Banda in Nyasaland, Kenneth Kaunda in Northern Rhodesia, Julius Nyerere in Tanganyika, Joshua Nkomo in Southern Rhodesia, apart from Nkrumah and Kenyatta whom we have already mentioned.

J. Hatch, *Britain in Africa from the Fifteenth Century to the Present* (1969)

These men were able to attract a growing body of support. For all of them there were no adequate staging-posts short of independence and majority rule. Thus the careful checks with which successive British governments hoped to slow down the pace of advance proved to be worthless as the nationalist current began to flow.

The second explanation is to be found in the British reaction to these growing pressures. It is noticeable that it was during the 13 years of Conservative rule from 1951 to 1964 that decolonisation proceeded most rapidly. For this most of the credit should go to Macmillan. In 1960 he made a six weeks' tour of Africa and he summed up his impressions in a celebrated speech made to the South African Parliament (where it fell on deaf ears). He concluded with these words:

> Fifteen years ago this movement (nationalism) spread through Asia. Many countries there of different races and civilisations pressed their claims to an independent national life. Today the same thing is happening in Africa. The most striking of all the impressions

I have formed since I left London a month ago is of the strength of this African national consciousness. In different places it may take different forms, but it is happening everywhere. The wind of change is blowing through the continent.

Macmillan thought it better to ride with the wind than against it. It was easier for a Conservative Prime Minister to dismantle the Empire than it would have been for a Labour Prime Minister. He could be certain of Labour support and the right-wing rebels who opposed him, such as Lord Salisbury, were easily isolated. There were other pressures, too. The United Nations, increasing every year as more ex-colonies joined its ranks, was a constant source of criticism. By 1960 the French had decided to leave Algeria and the Belgians to leave the Congo. The Suez crisis, the Mau Mau emergency, the struggle against EOKA in Cyprus all helped to weaken Britain's resolve to hang on to her colonies. Finally, Britain's first application to join the Common Market in 1961 shifted the focus of attention to Europe.

Thus, a growing demand for independence met a door that was already opening. To this there were two exceptions. Where there was a strongly entrenched settler community, as in Kenya and Southern Rhodesia, the prospect of African majority rule was not to be welcomed; while in the rest of Africa the process of decolonisation proceeded relatively smoothly, in these two colonies the going was very much rougher.

West Africa

Decolonisation in Africa

The first African colony to gain its independence was the Gold Coast. Serious opposition to British rule was vented for the first time in 1948, when riots broke out at Accra in which 29 people were killed and a government enquiry was sent to investigate. It recommended substantial constitutional improvements. Nkrumah outflanked the moderate African leadership by demanding immediate majority rule. He was arrested for his inflammatory speeches, but in the elections that were held in 1951 his Convention People's party won 48 out of the 84 seats and Nkrumah, campaigning from gaol, won a notable personal victory. The Governor decided to take a calculated risk and invited Nkrumah to join the Executive Council as Leader of the government. By his evident moderation in the next few years Nkrumah was able to convince the British government that he was capable of governing the colony on his own and in 1957 the Gold Coast gained dominion status. It was renamed Ghana. With Ghana leading the way, Britain's other West African colonies were sure to follow. Nigeria, the largest state in Africa in terms of population, became independent in 1960, Sierra Leone in 1961 and Gambia in 1965.

At the time it was believed that the Westminster model of democracy (a Prime Minister and cabinet responsible to an elected Parliament, with an organised Opposition) could readily be transplanted to the alien soil of Africa. In practice, the plant rarely survived. Nkrumah adopted the title of 'Redeemer' and became the victim of his own grandiose ambitions to become the leader of black Africa. He was removed by a coup in 1966. Nigeria, whose federal constitution was an attempt to hold together three very different peoples, the Hausa, the Yoruba and the Ibo, was torn by a savage civil war from 1966 to 1970. Whether a longer period under British tutelage would have made any difference it is impossible to say. But the political structures devised for the new African states took little account of tribal divisions and expected a degree of political sophistication for which their previous history had done little to prepare them.

Eastern and Central Africa

British Somaliland, Tanganyika and Uganda all gained their independence with little difficulty between 1960 and 1962. With Kenya it was a different matter. Kenya's white population rose from 12 000 in 1945 to 50 000 by 1955. It took over the best land in the White Highlands and the settlers who dominated the Kenya Legislative Council did their best to block African political advancement. These grievances sparked off the first significant opposition in 1951. Led by Jomo Kenyatta, the Kenya African Union campaigned for more representation for Africans on the Legislative Council and for land reform to give the Kikuyu a greater share of the cultivable land. The opposition initially took the form of protests and demonstrations. But in 1953 it took a more ugly form in the Mau Mau movement. This adopted terrorist methods and was also linked with a rejection of all forms of European culture. It was directed as much against Africans who refused to support the movement as against the white settlers, and in fact 10 times as many Africans were killed as were Europeans. Mau Mau provoked an equally ugly response. Kenyatta was tried and sentenced for complicity, though this was never finally proved. Over 1000 terrorists were hanged and 80 000 were kept in detention. In one widely publicised episode 11 African prisoners in one of the camps were clubbed to death for refusal to work. In 1957 African representation on the Legislative Council was increased and a serious effort was made to operate a multi-racial government. But this concession came too late. Ian Macleod, who became Colonial Secretary in 1960, determined to break the deadlock. The state of emergency which had lasted for seven years was brought to an end and a conference was summoned to consider constitutional reform. In 1961 Kenyatta was released. A new Constitution was finally put into operation in April 1963. Kenyatta's party won two-thirds of the votes in the ensuing election and Macmillan concluded that independence ought to follow internal self-government. 'Nothing could be gained by delay; everything might be won by a sign of confidence.' [Macmillan, pp. 293–4] On 12 December 1963 Kenya gained its independence and settled down to a much more stable future than had been anticipated. The goodwill established between Kenyatta and the British government was well illustrated by his request for British assistance in quelling mutinies in the Kenya army in 1964, assistance which was readily given.

H. Macmillan, *Memoirs, vol. VI, At the End of the Day* (Macmillan, 1973)

The most difficult problem facing the British government in Africa was what to do with Southern Rhodesia. Here a white community of 200 000 ruled an African population of 4 million. Under the 1923 Constitution Southern Rhodesia enjoyed virtual self-government. In consequence no steps had been taken to give the Africans any form of political representation. To the north lay the colony of Northern Rhodesia with a white population of 66 000 with about 2 million Africans, and the colony of Nyasaland with a white population of 6800 and an African population of 2.5 million. The Conservative solution to the Rhodesian problem was to set up the Central African Federation, made up of these three colonies. It was hoped that the integration of their economies would be of mutual benefit, for instance through the building of the Kariba Dam on the river Zambesi. But it was also hoped that by enabling Africans to participate in the federal Parliament the path might be opened to a multi-racial society. No Africans were consulted about the scheme, and they feared that it would merely prove a device to enable the white element in Southern Rhodesia to extend its authority over the other two colonies. African opinion was against the Federation from the start.

Nonetheless it came into existence in 1953 with high hopes, and for eight years successive British governments strove to make it work. But as African resistance mounted in Northern Rhodesia and Nyasaland the Southern Rhodesian government moved further towards the right. The liberal-minded Garfield Todd was ousted from the premiership in 1957 and it became clear that there was little prospect of political advancement for Africans in that part of the Federation. In 1958, Hastings Banda returned to Nyasaland to conduct a campaign for the right to secede from the Federation, and a similar agitation developed under Kenneth Kaunda's leadership in Northern Rhodesia.

In 1959 Macmillan sent out a commission under Walter Monckton to investigate the working of the Federation. Its report concluded that while the Federation had proved of real economic benefit 'African distrust has reached an intensity impossible, in our opinion, to dispel without drastic and fundamental changes within the structure of the association itself and in the racial policies of Southern Rhodesia.' [Macmillan, p. 299] Following the report a series of attempts were made to make the Federation more acceptable to African opinion. Southern Rhodesia adopted a new constitution which provided limited representation for the African population. Africans were granted 15 seats in an Assembly of 65. But all these efforts failed. In 1962 Nyasaland gained an African majority on its legislative council and immediately requested to leave the Federation. Permission was granted. Northern Rhodesia put in a similar request. By 1963 it was clear that the Federation must come to an end. R. A. Butler was sent out to preside over the final negotiations which took place at the Victoria Falls in June 1963. Some of the economic links were retained but the Federation was officially terminated on 31 December 1963.

The ending of the Federation brought with it a further problem. If Nyasaland and Northern Rhodesia were to be granted independence, as now seemed highly probable, what justification was there for denying the same privilege to Southern Rhodesia? Macmillan describes the divisions in the Conservative party on this issue: 'There were some who felt that it was unrealistic to refuse an independence which we could not in fact prevent. There were others who were deeply concerned about the future of the African population and felt that even if we were powerless we ought not in honour to grant independence without effective safeguards for African progress.' [Macmillan, p. 328]

H. Macmillan, *Memoirs*, vol. VI, *At the End of the Day* (Macmillan, 1973)

Macmillan retired from the scene before any decision was reached on this question, but in April 1964 the Home Government drew up Five Principles to which the Rhodesian government would have to assent before independence would be granted. The Five Principles were as follows:
1. The principle and intention of unimpeded progress to majority rule, already enshrined in the 1961 Constitution, would have to be maintained and guaranteed.
2. There would need to be guarantees against retrogressive amendment of the Constitution.
3. There would have to be immediate improvement in the political status of the African population.
4. There would have to be progress towards ending racial discrimination.
5. The British Government would need to be satisfied that any basis proposed for independence was acceptable to the people of Rhodesia as a whole.
[Lord Home, p. 250].

Lord Home, *The Way the Wind Blows* (Fontana, 1978)

When Wilson became Prime Minister in June 1964 he accepted the Five Principles as the basis for negotiations with Ian Smith, Rhodesia's new premier; six days of talks in Salisbury, Rhodesia in October 1965 between the two men failed to provide an agreement. It was clear that the Smith government had no intention of proceeding to African majority rule within the forseeable future. On 11 November Smith announced a Unilateral Declaration of Independence and Britain was faced with an awkward challenge to her authority. Wilson protested strongly enough, but he also made it clear that the British government had no intention of using force to prevent Rhodesia's illegal action, and whether he was right to make public this intention so early in the crisis has been seriously questioned. The only other weapon open to the British government was the use of economic sanctions. These were agreed on by the Commonwealth Prime Ministers, meeting at Lagos in January 1966, where Wilson made the unwise claim that their effects would be felt 'within weeks rather than months'. Nothing could have been further from the truth. With access through South Africa and Portuguese Angola, Rhodesia was able to evade sanctions without any great hardship and they never looked like achieving their objective. Further talks were held on HMS *Tiger*, based at Gibraltar, in December. Some progress was made between Smith and Wilson but the Rhodesian cabinet refused to endorse concessions Smith had been prepared to make. At this point Wilson went to the United Nations and secured the organisation's backing for mandatory sanctions to be applied to Rhodesia. Britain's negotiating position now hardened. It was based on the formula No Independence Before Majority African Rule (NIBMAR). The Rhodesian

Ian Smith and Harold Wilson after talks at No. 10 Downing Street, 7 October 1965. The talks failed to avert a Unilateral Declaration of Independence by Rhodesia in November

THE RETREAT FROM EMPIRE

question lingered on, unsolved. Another round of talks was held on HMS *Fearless*, also at Gibraltar, in October 1968. These merely confirmed that both sides were disagreed on fundamental issues, i.e. unimpeded progress to majority rule.

The advent of a Conservative government under Edward Heath in 1970 led to a fresh initiative. Lord Home, now Foreign Secretary, visited Smith and reached a tentative agreement on a complex series of proposals, mainly designed to provide for a very gradual increase in African representation in the Rhodesian Parliament. But these proposals would have to be acceptable to the Rhodesian people as a whole. A Commission, headed by Lord Pearce, a High Court Judge, was sent to gauge African opinion. It concluded that the great majority of Africans were against the proposals. No African leader could recommend a settlement short of the NIBMAR formula. This was the last hope of a negotiated settlement. It was followed by guerilla war marked by increasing savagery on both sides which ended only in 1979.

Rhodesia finally gained its independence as the new State of Zimbabwe in 1980. British troops were sent out to supervise the elections and to assist in disarming the guerillas, tasks they accomplished with great success. Macmillan confessed that the concluding years of his premiership 'were haunted, not to say poisoned, by the growing tensions in the countries constituting the Central African Federation' [Macmillan, p. 295], while Wilson doubted whether any British government had ever had to face a problem so complicated and so apparently insoluble as the Rhodesian question. As in Palestine, the politicians of one generation had to bear the consequences of mistakes made by their predecessors. Hard as they undoubtedly tried, they could not prevent a violent outcome.

H. Macmillan, *Memoirs*, vol. VI, *At the End of the Day* (Macmillan, 1973)

Decolonisation in the Far East

Britain's colonies in the Far East were all occupied by the Japanese during the Second World War, but Britain showed no inclination to abandon them when the war was over. Against American wishes Hong Kong was reoccupied under the terms of the 99-year lease which Britain had signed in 1898. British planters returned to the rubber estates in Malaya. The tin mines were reopened. Malaya was soon making an important contribution to the sterling area through her exports of these commodities. The territories of Sarawak and North Borneo changed their anomalous status and became Crown Colonies in 1946.

The transition to independence in Malaya and Singapore was delayed by the outbreak of a Communist-led rebellion in 1948. The Communists were mainly Chinese and drew little support from the Malay population. They thus lacked the favourable environment in which to operate which Mao Tse Tung laid down as one of the conditions of success for a guerrilla movement. The British commander, General Templer, succeeded in isolating the rebels by a shrewd combination of anti-guerrilla operations and re-settlement of villages which might otherwise have become refuges. Gradually the war was won. Unfortunately both Britain, in Cyprus, and the United States, in Vietnam, drew the wrong lessons from these operations. Templer was successful because he had the majority of the population on his side. Once the emergency was over, there were no further barriers to constitutional advance. In 1957 Malaya gained its independence under the guidance of Tunku Abdul Rahman who became its hereditary ruler.

In 1963 the Federation of Malaysia came into being, consisting of Malaya, Singapore, Brunei, North Borneo and Sarawak. Indonesia also laid claim to the three last territories, even though their peoples had voted in a referendum to accede to Malaysia. War broke out on this issue between the two countries. Britain had assumed responsibility for Malaya's defence in 1957 and British forces were sent out to meet the threat from Indonesia. This they did successfully and when the war ended in 1966, Malaysia's integrity was guaranteed. Singapore, however, chose to leave the Federation in 1965. It was an amicable enough separation and Singapore stayed in the Commonwealth where her Prime Minister, Lee Kwan Yew, became one of its leading lights.

Hong Kong still survives as a Crown Colony, Britain's last imperial possession in the Far East. But her future, under an agreement signed in 1984, rests with Communist China.

Decolonisation in the West Indies

Britain's Empire in the Caribbean, acquired over centuries in a series of colonial wars, was a heterogeneous collection of islands and enclaves in Central America. They varied in size from Anguilla, with a population of 5000, to Jamaica with a population of 1.6 million. Their populations are similarly mixed, Jamaica's for instance being largely negroid while Trinidad and British Guiana (now Guyana) have large Indian minorities.

The main problem in handing over power in this part of the world was to ensure that the new units of government would be viable economically and politically. Anticipating this difficulty, Britain tried to persuade the West Indian colonies to adopt some form of federation. This was eventually accepted in 1957 when the West Indian Federation came into existence. But there was little sense of Caribbean nationality. The loyalty of the islanders went first to their own island, then to Britain. Local jealousies and the problems of distance conspired to make federation unwork-able. In 1962 Jamaica and Trinidad both decided to leave the Federation on achieving independence and without these two major participants the Federation collapsed. Britain dealt with the problem of the smaller islands by enabling them to become Associated States within the Commonwealth, the British government retaining responsibility for diplomacy, defence and economic aid.

Unfinished Business

The British Empire is now confined to a few islands such as St Helena and Ascension Island, and those territories which prefer to remain linked to Britain rather than to unite with a less desired neighbour. They include Gibraltar, the Falkland Islands and, stretching a point, Northern Ireland. Gibraltar's future is still uncertain but so long as its inhabitants continue to express a strong preference for British rather than Spanish rule their wishes are likely to be respected.

The Falkland Islands

There can be little doubt that the British government would have been ready to negotiate sovereignty over the Falkland Islands with Argentina at any time in the last 20 years, had the islanders themselves been ready to accept Argentinian rule. In 1967 the Labour Government entered negotiations with Argentina and Michael Stewart admitted in the House of Commons that sovereignty could be conceded if the Government concluded that it was in the islanders' own interests. In 1970 David Scott, the foreign office official responsible for the Falkland Islands, proposed that the Argentinian Government should woo the islanders by providing regular air and mail services: 'the Argentinians should be told that while Britain would not countenance the rape of the Falklands, it would actively encourage their seduction'. [Sunday Times Insight Team, p. 48] In 1980 Nicholas Ridley, a Junior Minister at the Foreign Office, canvassed the possibility of a leasehold arrangement under which Argentina would get the freehold of the islands, while the islanders would be given the protection of a long lease. The length of the lease was not specified but a period of between 30 and 99 years was envisaged.

Sunday Times Insight Team, *The Falklands War* (1982)

This proposal was strongly criticised in the House of Commons by both left-wing Labour MPs who disliked the prospect of handing over the Falklands to a dictatorial junta in Argentina, and by right-wing Conservatives who believed the wishes of the islanders must be paramount. In the Falklands themselves the Legislative Council voted by 8 to 1 to freeze all negotiations over sovereignty. The sequel is well known. On 2 April 1982 the Falkland Islands were invaded by Argentinian forces and what one hopes will be Britain's last imperial war took place. A Task Force was rapidly organised and sent to the South Atlantic. In an operation which compared very favourably for speed of execution with the Suez venture, British troops landed and brought about an Argentinian surrender. By 13 June the fighting was over. It had cost over 1000 Argentinian lives and 255 British ones, but it did not solve the problem. So far as Britain is concerned, the Argentinians wrecked their claim to sovereignty by the manner in which they pursued it. 'Fortress Falklands' has been developed to resist any future threat. That is how matters stand at the time of writing.

Northern Ireland

As was explained in Chapter One (p. 21) there are good reasons for treating the problems of Ireland in the context of the British Empire. This is no less the case when it comes to Northern Ireland. It was the 'Plantation' of Ulster by English and Scottish Protestants in the seventeenth century that gave to the Province its particular characteristics, and its peculiar relationship to the United Kingdom. In those two senses, the problem of Ulster is also a legacy of Empire.

There was nothing new about the Ulster Problem in 1945. The South still laid claim to the Six Counties while the Protestant majority in Ulster remained fierce in its determination to remain in the United Kingdom. Britain's policy, too, was unchanged. If the people of Ulster could be persuaded to join with the South, as both Asquith and Lloyd George had urged them to, the British government would have gladly given its blessing. But so long as the majority wished to remain in the United Kingdom they must be allowed to do so. This was confirmed in the Ireland Act of 1949.

Until 1965 Ulster remained fairly quiet and there are scarcely any references to it in histories of the period. There was even a false dawn in 1965 when Sean Lemass, Prime Minister of Eire, met Terence O'Neill, Prime Minister of Ulster, the first occasion on which two Irish premiers had even spoken directly to one another. But there were still serious Catholic grievances in the North. Discrimination in the allocation of council housing and in employment was rife. The rigging of electoral boundaries, for instance in Londonderry, allowed Protestant-dominated councils to be elected in areas where Catholics were in the majority. Worst of all, the polarisation of politics round religious allegiances ensured that a Protestant majority continued to dominate the Stormont (the Northern Irish Parliament) and that all Northern

Ireland's political leaders were drawn from the Protestant community. Steps were taken to remedy some of these grievances. Council housing for instance was put in the hands of a non-sectarian Housing Executive and electoral boundaries were changed. But these improvements did not come in time to avert the formation of a Northern Ireland Civil Rights Movement in 1967. Before long it was infiltrated by members of the IRA and what began as peaceful demonstrations became occasions for violent confrontation between Catholics and Protestants.

In January 1969 the first really serious clash occurred. There were fears of further violence when the Orange Day parades were staged in August, and British troops were sent out to keep the peace. At this time, too, the IRA split into two factions, the Official and the Provisional Wings. The Provisionals were ready to escalate the level of violence. In February 1971 the first British soldier was killed and by the end of the year the death toll of soldiers and civilians had reached 175.

On 30 January 1972 an illegal civil rights march in Londonderry led to the killing of 13 participants by British soldiers, an event that passed into Irish mythology as 'Bloody Sunday'. After further bomb outrages in England, the Heath government decided to take over responsibility for law and order. The Northern Irish premier, now Brian Faulkner, was not prepared to agree to this, so the Northern Ireland Assembly was suspended and direct rule from Westminster imposed on the Province.

The newly appointed Secretary for Northern Ireland, William Whitelaw, nonetheless did his best to find a constitutional solution to the grievances of the Catholic minority. In October 1973 he presented proposals under which proportional representation would be introduced for assembly elections; a Northern Ireland Executive would be formed from the chairmen of assembly committees, the chairmanships being shared between the Protestant and Catholic members; a Bill of Rights would be introduced; and there would be further links with the South.

These proposals were accepted by the Irish Government and the Protestant leadership in Northern Ireland in the Sunningdale Agreement, signed on 9 December 1973. A Council of Ireland was to be set up and the Dublin government accepted that there could be no change in the status of Northern Ireland without the consent of the majority. In January 1974 Direct Rule came to an end and the experiment in power-sharing began. Faulkner became leader of the Executive and Gerry Fitt, the Catholic Leader of the Social Democratic Labour party, his deputy. It was the best chance of reconciliation between the two communities that had so far been offered. Unfortunately, the IRA continued its activities – it had no interest in a compromise solution. Some Protestant opinion was equally hostile to the idea of power-sharing and to the Council of Ireland. In the elections for the Westminster Parliament in February 1974, 11 out of the 12 Northern Irish seats went to opponents of the Sunningdale Agreement. Though the Ulster assembly actually did ratify the Agreement when it met in May 1974 the Ulster Workers Council organised a strike in protest. Wilson was neither prepared to negotiate with the strikers nor to intervene with force to defeat the strike. Faulkner had little option but to resign. The Sunningdale Agreement broke down almost before it began and direct rule had to be re-imposed. In May 1975 the Labour government summoned a constitutional convention to which representatives were elected. On this occasion the United Ulster Unionist Council, which now represented the intransigent wing of the Unionist party, won a comfortable majority. There was no prospect of the convention reaching a settlement that would be acceptable to the Catholic minority.

For the next four years the killing continued, punctuated by particular outrages on both sides, such as the murder of Earl Mountbatten or the indiscriminate revenge carried out on innocent Catholics by the Ulster Volunteer Force. In 1979 no end was in sight and the next five years did little to lighten the prospect. By 1984 over 2000 people had been killed in Northern Ireland since the troubles began in 1969. Yeats's words about Southern Ireland, written in 1921, are still unhappily relevant to the problems of Ulster:

> Things fall apart; the centre cannot hold.
> Mere anarchy is loosed upon the world,
> The blood-dimmed tide is loosed, and everywhere
> The ceremony of innocence is drowned;
> The best lack all conviction, while the worst
> Are full of passionate intensity.

The Ulster Problem again: Barricades in the Falls Road, Belfast, 16 August 1969

E ▬ THE SURVIVAL OF THE COMMONWEALTH

The transition from Empire to Commonwealth can be traced through the changes in Britain's imperial machinery. In 1945 there were three Departments of State with imperial responsibilities: the Dominions Office, the Colonial Office and the India Office. By 1968 they had all disappeared. The first to go was the India Office in

Changes in Organisation and Definition

1947; at the same time the Dominions Office was restyled the Commonwealth Relations Office. In 1966 the Colonial Office was merged with the Commonwealth Relations Office, and in 1968 the CRO was itself absorbed by the Foreign Office. In 1964 a Commonwealth Secretariat was established to take over responsibility for Commonwealth organisation.

The only definitions of the Commonwealth current in 1945 were the statements made in the Balfour Memorandum of 1926 and the Statute of Westminster of 1931. (see Chapter 6, p. 199) Among the qualifications for membership was 'common allegiance to the Crown'. Neither India nor Pakistan were willing to recognise the continuing authority of the King-Emperor when they gained their independence in 1947 but each wished to maintain the Commonwealth connection. A new formula had to be devised. At the 1949 Commonwealth Prime Ministers' Conference a declaration was drawn up making the British monarch simply Head of the Commonwealth, without defining either his rights or duties in that capacity. The purposes of the Commonwealth were similarly vague: 'The United Kingdom, Canada, Australia, New Zealand, South Africa, India, Pakistan and Ceylon hereby declare that they remain united as free and equal members of the Commonwealth of Nations, freely co-operating in the pursuit of peace, liberty and progress.' [Cross, pp. 252–3] This change was given statutory effect when Queen Elizabeth II succeeded George VI in 1952. Under the Royal Titles Act of 1953 she became 'Elizabeth II, by the Grace of God of the United Kingdom of Great Britain and Northern Ireland and of her other Realms and Territories, Queen, Head of the Commonwealth, Defender of the Faith ....' Each Commonwealth country was free to define the Queen's position as it wished, so long as the phrase 'Head of the Commonwealth' was included in the title given to her.

Cross, *The Fall of the British Empire*

Another formal change of greater significance was the British Nationality Act, passed in 1948. Hitherto all the inhabitants of the Empire and Commonwealth were subjects of the British Crown, enjoying in theory at least the same rights as inhabitants of the United Kingdom. Under the Act in question British citizenship was now confined to those living in the United Kingdom or in the colonies still under British rule. Though not intended at the time as a discriminatory measure, it was the first clear admission that Commonwealth citizenship was not the same thing as British citizenship.

Changes in the Character of the Commonwealth

Until 1945 Britain and the self-governing Dominions made up a relatively homogeneous group of countries. They were all, economically, fairly well-developed; their populations, except in the case of South Africa, were of largely European stock; their political systems, again with the exception of South Africa, were variants of parliamentary democracy based on universal suffrage. There were two unwritten rules governing the relations between them. Britain undertook to consult the Dominions on matters of defence and international affairs; and there was a general disposition not to interfere with the internal affairs of any member of the Commonwealth.

Changes in the composition of the Comonwealth inevitably brought changes in its character. By 1957, with the admission of India, Pakistan, Ceylon, Ghana and Malaya, the number of old Dominions, including Britain, was exactly matched by members of the Third World. By 1967 Third-World countries were comfortably in the majority. Whereas the preoccupations of the Commonwealth before 1939 had been trade and defence, from about 1960 onwards the Commonwealth turned the focus of its attention to issues such as racial discrimination and neo-colonialism. Inevitably this wider membership brought with it divergences in outlook and in some cases actual conflicts between member states.

It was on matters of race that divisions were most acute. In 1960 South Africa, following a referendum on the issue, became a Republic. This required her to apply for re-admission to the Commonwealth. What would normally have been a formality was made the occasion for her exclusion. At the 1961 Commonwealth Prime Ministers' Conference Malaya proposed that South Africa should not be admitted unless she changed her policies of *apartheid*. A test was imposed. Would she accept Black High Commissioners from Nigeria and Ghana at Pretoria? The Prime Minister, Verwoerd, refused to make any concessions and rather than have his application turned down, withdrew it. Macmillan regretted the Commonwealth's decision but he accepted the justification for it.

Britain's own policy came under fire during the Rhodesia crisis. Several Commonwealth countries felt that Britain was not doing enough to bring down the Smith regime or to prevent the blatant evasion of sanctions. Tanzania temporarily resigned from the Commonwealth on this issue in 1966.

But it was Britain's immigration policies that placed the greatest strain on the Commonwealth. With almost a quarter of the world's population apparently entitled to come and settle in Britain, some form of restraint was inevitable once the demand was felt (see pp. 407–8). The combined effects of the immigration policies pursued by both Labour and Conservative governments was to make the concept of Commonwealth citizenship virtually meaningless. Britain could hardly claim to be the mother country when she denied admission to so many of her children.

Further strains on the Commonwealth came from the separate foreign policies pursued by the member countries. One striking example we have already noticed. During the Suez crisis, of all the countries of the Commonwealth, only Australia and New Zealand were prepared to defend Britain's actions. The rivalry between India and Pakistan resulted in each country seeking different allies. Pakistan joined first the South East Asia Treaty Organisation in 1954 and then the Baghdad Pact in 1955. India followed a policy of non-alignment until in 1971 she signed a 20-year friendship treaty with the Soviet Union. The Commonwealth played no part in arresting the three wars between India and Pakistan that took place in 1948, 1965 and 1971. In 1973 the Commonwealth was faced with the awkward choice of whether or not to recognise the new State of Bangladesh, previously East Pakistan. It chose to do so, whereupon Pakistan withdrew her membership.

The Commonwealth has also lost whatever economic links it once possessed. Since the floating of the pound by Britain in 1972 the sterling area has lost much of its importance. British membership of the General Agreement of Tariffs and Trade and of the European Economic Community has entailed the ending of imperial preference. Since 1975 the Lomé Convention has instead enabled countries in Africa, the Pacific and the Caribbean to have duty-free access to the EEC for many of their products. The Commonwealth's poorer members are more likely to benefit from their links with Europe than from those with Britain.

The Importance of the Commonwealth

F. S. Northedge, *Descent From Power: British Foreign Policy 1945–1973* (Allen & Unwin, 1974)

The essence of the Commonwealth is that it is a purely voluntary organisation which imposes no obligations upon its members. Of Britain's ex-colonial dependencies 32 have chosen to join it, the important exceptions being Burma, Somaliland, the Sudan and Aden. According to one authority, they did so 'because it was a great international circle of potential mutual helpfulness – provided at practically no cost.' [Northedge, p. 234] The Commonwealth bridges three important divides: that between rich and poor, that between white and coloured, and that between NATO and the non-aligned. In one sense it is precisely this variety of membership that gives the Commonwealth its value. Almost the only function it fulfils today is to be a forum where problems may be discussed and views exchanged in amicable surroundings. But the habit of consultation is not to be despised. At the least it can contribute to improved understanding; at best it can make a positive contribution to warmer relationships between peoples. The British Empire was held together by sentiment. So is the Commonwealth and its importance depends today on the extent to which it can moderate and resolve the inevitable divisions between its members.

Commonwealth Heads of State at a Dinner held in June 1977 to Commemorate the 25th Anniversary of Queen Elizabeth's accession. 'We are not Members of the Commonwealth by accident of colonial history, but by conviction' [Kenneth Kaunda, Prime Minister of Zambia, fourth from the right, front row.]

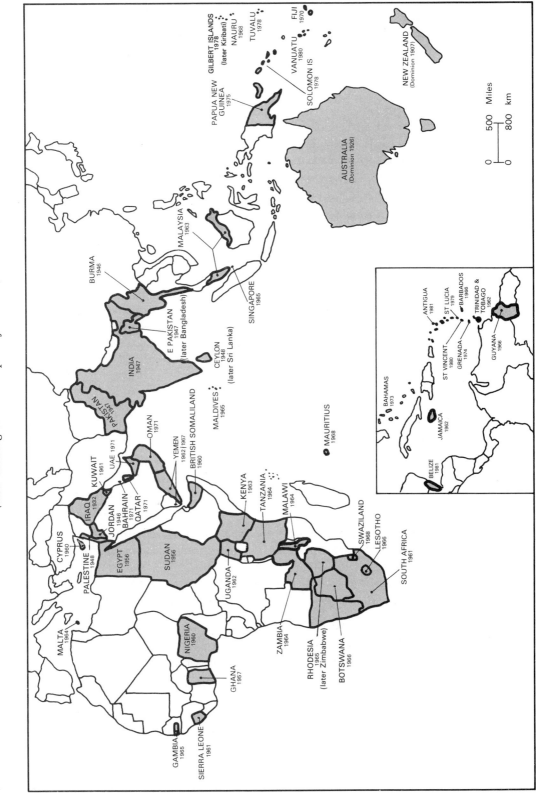

BRITISH OR BRITISH-PROTECTED TERRITORIES, SHOWING DATES OF INDEPENDENCE OR BRITISH DEPARTURE

(inset showing the central part of America)

GILBERT ISLANDS
1978
(later Kiribati)

NAURU
1968

TUVALU
1978

FIJI
1970

PAPUA NEW
GUINEA
1975

VANUATU
1980

SOLOMON IS
1978

NEW ZEALAND
(Dominion 1907)

Miles
km

AUSTRALIA
(Dominion 1926)

500

800

MALAYSIA
1963

BURMA
1946

SINGAPORE
1965

E PAKISTAN
1947
(later Bangladesh)

INDIA
1947

CEYLON
1948
(later Sri Lanka)

PAKISTAN
1947

MALDIVES
1965

MAURITIUS
1968

OMAN
1971

UAE 1971

YEMEN
1962 1967

BRITISH SOMALILAND
1960

KUWAIT
1961

IRAQ
1932

BAHRAIN
1971

QATAR
1971

JORDAN
1946

KENYA
1963

TANZANIA
1964

MALAWI
1964

SWAZILAND
1968

LESOTHO
1966

CYPRUS
1960

PALESTINE
1948

EGYPT
1956

SUDAN
1956

UGANDA
1962

SOUTH AFRICA
1961

MALTA
1964

NIGERIA
1960

ZAMBIA
1964

RHODESIA
1965
(later Zimbabwe)

BOTSWANA
1966

GHANA
1957

GAMBIA
1965

SIERRA LEONE
1961

ANTIGUA
1981

ST LUCIA
1979

BARBADOS
1966

TRINIDAD &
TOBAGO
1962

ST VINCENT
1980

GRENADA
1974

GUYANA
1966

BAHAMAS
1973

JAMAICA
1962

BELIZE
1981

All chronological divisions are arbitrary; 1980 is a convenient stopping place only in that it witnessed the independence of Rhodesia (now Zimbabwe), Britain's last sizeable colony, and the first full year of a Conservative government pledged to reverse the policies of its predecessors. Nonetheless, there is something to be said for taking one's bearings at certain points on the journey, if only to discover how far one has come and in what direction one is going. With this in mind let us return to the themes with which this book began.

In many respects Britain has changed less than the world to which she belongs. The complaints voiced in *The Times* in 1912 about the obsolescence of British industry are still echoed today. British productivity continues to lag behind that of her competitors on the Continent, in Europe and in Japan. The contrast between the dynamic sectors of the economy (computers, chemicals and North Sea oil, for instance) and the declining sectors (iron and steel, shipbuilding, textiles and coal) is as marked as it was in the 1920s and 1930s. The regional imbalance between the prosperous South East, and the North of England, Central Scotland and South Wales is equally evident. The depressed areas are still depressed. These inequalities have been most vividly illustrated in the miners' strike of 1984–85, with the prosperous pits of Nottinghamshire and Leicestershire ranged against the contracting coalfields in Yorkshire and South Wales. The scourge of unemployment, lifted between 1940 and 1974, has returned. In 1976 unemployment rose to 1.3 million, and has risen more or less continuously to its present total (1984) of 3 million.

The gap between rich and poor, so marked in Edwardian England, has certainly narrowed. In 1914, 0.4% of the population owned 65% of the national wealth. In 1981, 5% owned 44% of the national wealth (reduced to 25% when pension rights are taken into account). But it is still the case that the managing director of a large public company can expect to earn roughly 20 times the average industrial wage before tax (£150 000 as against £8000).

The gradualness of change has also been reflected in the slow growth of the Welfare State. Constructed on the foundations laid by Churchill and Lloyd George between 1908 and 1912, the Welfare State has been added to in stages under the guidance of Neville Chamberlain, Beveridge and Bevan, each building on the work of his predecessors. The same continuity can be detected in the growth of the public sector. Nationalisation began in earnest with the Central Electricity Generating Board in 1926. It made rapid progress between 1945 and 1951, but since then changes have been marginal. Iron and steel were re-nationalised in 1967 and the aircraft and shipbuilding industries were added to the list in 1977.

The reversal of the process by the present government has extended so far to the industries just mentioned, and to the telecommunications industry. But the process of privatisation is not likely to go much further. In 1977 nationalised industries contributed 12.7% of the national output, a share they are likely to retain. The mixed economy, whatever its critics on the left or on the right may say, looks here to stay.

The British political system has also proved remarkably resistant to change. Monarchy, Parliament, Cabinet and Prime Minister, and the Civil Service all perform essentially the same roles that they did in 1914. The House of Lords, its powers emasculated by the Parliament Acts of 1911 and 1949, has been re-invigorated by the infusion of new blood in the form of Life Peers. It has recently shown a new willingness to challenge the government of the day. The electoral system has admittedly been widened to include women and all those over 18, but the first-past-the-post system of single-member constituencies has survived all attempts to reform it, whatever anomalies it may have thrown up. Only in Northern Ireland has a British government been prepared to experiment with proportional representation; it was introduced for the Northern Irish Assembly in 1974 and for the direct elections to the European Parliament in 1979.

The electorate sticks firmly to the middle of the road while remaining evenly divided in its allegiance between left and right. No party since 1935 has gained 50% of the electorate's support and when either of the main parties moves away from the middle ground it is likely to lose some of its natural supporters. The election results of 1983 bear this out. The leftward trend in the Labour party resulted in a shift to the Liberals and Social Democrats, now joined in the Alliance, while the Conservative vote also declined, if only slightly. In terms of popular support the results bear an uncanny resemblance to those of 1923:

	Conservative		Labour		Liberal/Social Democratic Alliance	
	% Vote	Seats	% Vote	Seats	% Vote	Seats
1923	38.7	258	30.5	191	29.6	159
1983	42.9	397	27.6	209	25.4	23

It was only the vagaries of the electoral system that allowed a doctrinaire Conservative party to increase its majority in the House of Commons in 1983, while depriving the Alliance parties of their rightful share of seats. Thus, despite the domestic upheavals caused by two world wars and the absolute majorities enjoyed by three Labour governments since 1945, it is finally the continuity of Britain's domestic history that stands out.

The dramatic changes have occurred in Britain's external position. They are most evident in Britain's loss of great-power status, the dissolution of her Empire and her attachment to the EEC. The first two changes were inevitable. Nothing could have halted the rise of the United States and the Soviet Union to the rank of superpower. Britain's retention of her own nuclear deterrent in the form of Polaris missiles give the illusion that Britain still has a seat at the top table. But while one Polaris submarine has greater destructive capability than the whole of the Royal Navy commanded at its height, its deployment in war would almost certainly entail the destruction of Great Britain. Britain's nuclear missiles are at best a makeweight when compared with the nuclear arsenals of the superpowers, and they give her little bargaining power even in arms negotiations. The stationing of Cruise missiles, under American control, on British soil is final proof that Britain's independent nuclear deterrent no longer qualifies her for the status of a great power.

The British Empire was acquired by accident rather than design. Its dissolution was similarly unpremeditated. But equally it could not have been averted as British politicians generally had the sense to recognise. Unlike France or Portugal, Britain fought no debilitating colonial wars and the process of decolonisation was accomplished amicably, except in the cases of Kenya, Cyprus and Rhodesia. An unlooked-for consequence has been the growth in Britain of a plural society enriched by immigrants from the countries of the new Commonwealth in Asia, Africa and the West Indies. It would be foolish to pretend that this has not brought its problems, particularly at times of economic stringency. The British people have had to accept people of different colour and unfamiliar cultures as fellow citizens and neighbours. It is a challenge that has still to be met, and if successfully accomplished will be the best tribute that could be paid to the British Empire.

Britain's entry into the EEC in 1973, while on the surface an equally sharp break with her past, looks less dramatic when seen in perspective. Britain has always been concerned to maintain the balance of power in Europe. Her intervention in both World Wars was undertaken primarily to preserve this balance. But every commitment to Europe has been made with reservations. The Anglo-French *entente* of 1904 and the Treaty of Locarno in 1925 were hedged with limitations. Britain's reluctance to join the EEC and her subsequent refusal to join the European Monetary System reflect the continuing ambivalence of Britain's attitude to European integration and her intention to keep her distance.

Britain in the 1980s has shed most, if not all, of her imperial pretensions. She is a middle-sized European power, rather less prosperous than France or Germany. But to set against this change in status there have been compensating gains. For most of her citizens Britain is a more civilised society than it was in 1914. Women enjoy equal political rights and, in theory at least, equal pay. Free medical treatment, the right to a university education for all who can qualify for it, adequate provision for the disadvantaged groups in society, the right to a dignified old age, all these claims are now at least recognised even where they are not fully met. Britain's greatest asset is something Orwell noticed in 1941: 'The gentleness of English society is perhaps its most marked characteristic. You notice it the moment you set foot on English soil. It is a land where the bus conductors are good tempered and the policemen carry no revolvers.' [Orwell, p. 15]

G. Orwell, *The Lion and the Unicorn* (Secker & Warburg, 1941)

Some policemen do need to carry revolvers and some football team supporters would test the patience of any bus conductor, but Orwell's verdict still stands. Whether it will continue to do so with 3 million out of work is an open question. One can only hope that it will.

POINTS AT ISSUE
POINTS AT ISSUE POINTS AT ISSUE POINTS AT ISSUE
POINTS AT ISSUE

The Suez Crisis, 1956

The Suez Crisis of 1956 is still a matter of great controversy. There are wide disagreements about its causes, its course and its effects. So far as Britain's part in the crisis is concerned argument has tended to focus on four specific issues:

1. The character of Colonel Nasser.
2. The decision to use force.
3. The degree of collusion between France, Britain and Israel.
4. The consequences of Britain's actions.

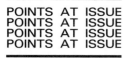

Both of the main British participants in the events leading to the crisis have given their own accounts. The relevant volume of Eden's Memoirs, *Full Circle*, appeared in 1960. Selwyn Lloyd's *Suez 1956, A Personal Account* was published in 1978. Anthony Nutting, Minister of State at the Foreign Office at the time, produced his version of events, *No End of a Lesson, The Story of Suez*, in 1967. There have also been numerous memoirs from French and Israeli participants, including those of Pineau, the French Foreign Minister, and Dayan, a leading figure on the Israeli side. The most recent contribution is to be found in a collection of essays, *Imperialism and Nationalism in the Middle East – The Anglo-Egyptian Experience, 1882–1982*, edited by Keith M. Wilson. The following excerpts have been selected to illustrate from these sources the divisions of opinion at the time on the issues indicated.

The Character of Nasser

Both Eden and Selwyn Lloyd saw real similarities between Nasser and Hitler and between the threat presented by a militant Germany in the 1930s and that presented by a militant Egypt in 1956. In *Full Circle* Eden makes the comparison some 50 times; this passage is typical:

It is important to reduce the stature of the megalomaniacal dictator at an early stage. A check to Hitler when he moved to reoccupy the Rhineland would not have destroyed him, but it would have made him pause .... Nowadays it is considered immoral to recognise an enemy. Some say that Nasser is no Hitler or Mussolini. Allowing for a difference in scale, I am not so sure. He has followed Hitler's pattern, even to concentration camps and the propaganda use of *Mein Kampf* among his officers. [A footnote indicates that a number of copies of this work in an Arabic translation were found by the Israeli army in the possession of Egyptian officers.] He has understood and used the Goebbels pattern of propaganda in all its lying ruthlessness. Egypt's strategic position increases the threat to others from any aggressive militant dictatorship there. [Eden, p. 431]

At a cabinet meeting in March 1956 Lloyd also drew the comparison: 'Above all, I had to be quite certain that, judging by the possession of Czech arms and what had happened since, we were right in assessing Nasser as a potential Hitler who must somehow be checked if British influence was not to be eliminated from the Middle East and West Africa, and all our friends destroyed.' [Lloyd, p. 59] In a later passage Lloyd confirms his earlier judgment:

Others preferred to compare Nasser with Mussolini. I myself thought that the comparison with Hitler was more apt, if only because Nasser's *The Philosophy of Revolution* read like *Mein Kampf* .... Well, we had had our lesson over Hitler. The appetite had grown with eating – the rape of Austria, Munich, the absorption of Czechoslovakia, Poland and the dream of world conquest resulting in 20 million dead.

To sum up, if Nasser was not checked, the prospect in the Middle East was grim: the collapse of pro-Western Governments, Soviet penetration, Nasser's grip on the Canal and on oil supplies for Western Europe, and Israeli desperation which could lead to anything. It was a strong case. [Lloyd, pp. 192–3]

A rather different view of Nasser is presented in Anthony Nutting's biography. Nasser's purchase of arms from Czechoslovakia is defended on the grounds that Britain and the United States refused to supply them in adequate numbers to meet a possible threat from Israel. American and British refusal to finance the Aswan Dam, except on their terms, Nasser described as 'imperialism without soldiers', and the

final refusal of the loan meant that in Arab eyes at least he was fully justified in nationalising the Canal: 'The nationalisation of the Suez Canal Company was hailed as a master-stroke for Arab independence by rulers and populace alike from Morocco to Muscat, save only for Nuri and his followers in Iraq. Nasser was now the unrivalled champion of Arab nationalism and liberation.' [Nutting, *Nasser*, p. 146] Nutting concludes his biography with this assessment:

> Abdel Nasser was a remarkable man. His contribution to Egypt has guaranteed him a place in history. He gave a sense of dignity and national pride to a people who had known little but humiliation and oppression for two and a half thousand years, and his achievement transformed a nation of backward, downtrodden peasants ruled by a corrupt and alien tyrant and occupied by a foreign army, into a community of independent citizens with a stake in their own soil. He planted the seeds of a modern industrial society. [Nutting, *Nasser*, p. 477]

The Use of Force

The decision to use force against Nasser was clearly related to the assessment made of him but it was possible to take a very unfavourable view of Nasser, and yet to insist that any action taken must have the approval of the United Nations. This was the position adopted by Gaitskell. In a speech in the House of Commons on 2 August Gaitskell agreed with a comment made by the French Prime Minister, likening Nasser's speeches to Hitler's, and went on to say: 'It is all very familiar. It is exactly the same that we encountered from Hitler and Mussolini in those years before the war.' But he parted company with Eden on the circumstances in which force might be used, concluding: 'While force cannot be excluded, we must be sure that the circumstances justify it and that it is, if used, consistent with our belief in, and our pledges to, the Charter of the United Nations and not in conflict with them.' [Thomas, pp. 176–83] When Britain vetoed the Security Council Resolution of 30 October, calling for a cease-fire, Gaitskell condemned the veto as 'an act of disastrous folly whose tragic consequences we shall regret for years ....' [Williams, p. 286] Eden and Lloyd justified Britain's actions on the grounds that further delay would have led to an escalation of the conflict:

> The chief danger, especially for us, was that conflict would spread. A localised war between Israel and Egypt, while troublesome, should not be highly dangerous internationally. The same could not be said of a war which had spread to include Syria and Jordan, with Iraq morally compelled to take a hand too. If this were to happen, the Jordan commitment would raise its head again, not in so acute a form, but alarming enough. Two events could be counted on to encourage Jordan and Syria to inaction, swift Israeli military success and the knowledge that British and French forces were on the way and would be used to localise the dispute. If that restraint was to be effective it must be applied at once. Twenty-four hours might well be too late, forty-eight certainly would. [Eden, pp. 526–7]

Lloyd's account is more circumspect. He gives the following reasons for the decision to intervene:

> The United Nations was powerless because of the Russian veto. The negotiations with Egypt were unlikely to achieve anything which would appear other than a success for Nasser. He was skilfully and successfully playing for time.

Eisenhower and Dulles between them had relieved Nasser of any anxiety about strong action by the United States against him. He could go on playing them off against the Russians and vice versa in perfect safety.

Israel was certain sooner or later to break out. I believed what Pineau had told me about the Israeli determination to fight. If we and the French were about, that war was less likely to spread. We would be able to prevent it becoming a general conflagration. Although I had my doubts about toppling Nasser and was horrified by the thought of anything like a reoccupation of the whole of Egypt or having to prop up a pro-Western regime with British troops, the idea of Nasser having the power to interfere at a moment's notice with our shipping and oil supplies was intolerable. I felt that he must be challenged and checked. The restoration of the Canal to international control would be a sufficient defeat for him. [Lloyd, p. 190]

Collusion

In his essay '"Collusion" and the Suez Crisis of 1956' Geoffrey Warner establishes beyond all reasonable doubt the fact that Israeli operations were discussed with the French at the two meetings held in Paris on 16 October and 22 October. According to Nutting, Eden was made privy to French suggestions for a combined operation with Israel at the meeting with Challe and Gazier at Chequers on 14 October. What is still not entirely clear is the degree of support Britain gave to the French suggestion. Lloyd, according to his own account, was discouraging in the meeting that took place on 22 October: 'We had thousands of British subjects in Arab countries with valuable property, and oil installations of great strategic importance. If there was a joint attack, there might be wholesale slaughter of British subjects and destruction of our installations.' [Lloyd, p. 184] It should perhaps also be noted however, that the only thing Lloyd reproached himself for in the Suez crisis was exaggerating possible Arab reaction: 'I do, however, wonder whether I was wise to harbour doubt about co-operation between us and Israel for fear of Arab reaction.' [Lloyd, p. 260] He evidently had no moral scruples about a joint attack on Egypt.

In his memoirs, Eden concealed all suggestions of collusion. He made no mention of the vital meeting that took place at Chequers on 14 October. He cannot be acquitted of telling a downright lie to the House of Commons in the answer he gave to a question that was asked on 20 December. He said:

> I want to say this on the question of foreknowledge, and to say it bluntly, that there was no foreknowledge that Israel would attack Egypt – there was not. But there was something else. There was – we knew it perfectly well – a risk of it, and in the event of the risk of it certain discussions and conversations took place, as I think, was absolutely right and as, I think, anybody would do. [Thomas, p. 212]

The Consequences

Neither Eden nor Lloyd could possibly claim that the Suez operation was a success. But they each maintained that had it not been mounted matters would have been even worse:

> I had seen the chain of failure in the nineteen-thirties from Manchuria to Danzig and had tried in vain to break it. This time we had the opportunity and the responsibility. What we did was only partially effective, but it moved the United Nations to action.

It led later to Anglo-American intervention in the Lebanon and Jordan, after the opposition of the United States to our Suez action had been seen to have brought disaster in Iraq (the ruling dynasty was brutally murdered in 1958). The consequences there may even have taught a little prudence in Cairo. Some of these checks to totalitarian plans may be judged late and feeble, even so they had their impact and their warning message, in revealing contrast to the fatal drift of the nineteen-thirties.

Much of the subsequent controversy over the Suez decision has been about the trees and not about the wood. The main question is whether inertia would have brought better results for the peace of the world than action. I think not. I thought and think the world would have suffered less if Hitler had been opposed on the Rhine, in Austria or in Czechoslovakia, rather than in Poland. This will be for history to determine. [Eden, p. 559]

For Lloyd the debits and credits were more evenly divided. On the debit side he recognised the diplomatic defeat suffered by Britain and France; the failure to establish an international regime for the Canal; the worsening of Israeli-Egyptian relations; and finally 'the psychological wound which it (Suez) inflicted on so many people of British stock, either at home or overseas'. [Lloyd, p. 252] But on the credit side he set the following gains: 'The bubble of Nasser's military might was pricked .... His airforce was eliminated with little or no loss to us.' The Sudan was reassured; collaboration between Egypt and the Soviet Union was exposed; the UNEF was established on the border between Israel and Egypt; the Straits of Tiran were opened to Israeli shipping; shipping companies were encouraged, as a result of the crisis, to find ways of doing without the Canal and were thus much better placed to cope with its closure in 1967–75.

Finally, Lloyd, too, accepts the apparently perverse argument that it was necessary to start a war in order to prevent one:

> Another action on the credit side, too often disregarded, is the fact that our actions, right or wrong, did stop a war which was inevitable. They were the catalyst which precipitated a crisis already imminent. Then followed ten years of uneasy peace between Israel and the Arab states. It may be argued that the Six-Day War (in 1967) ended without foreign military intervention, and so did the Yom Kippur War. It would have been the same, it is said, in 1956. I very much doubt it. Syria and Jordan certainly would have joined in, and it could very easily have escalated. When we and the French announced our intention to intervene, Hakim Amer, Commander-in-Chief of the Egyptian-Syrian-Jordanian military command, ordered the Syrian and Jordanian forces not to become involved. The ten years of uneasy peace is a fact which cannot be denied, and but for Nasser's folly in ordering out the UNEF, this uneasy peace might have lasted much longer. [Lloyd, p. 256]

Nutting could see no compensating benefits:

> To say the least, it was an extraordinary situation. For, in truth, we had achieved none of the objectives, whether pretended or real, with which we had set out upon this sorry adventure. We had not separated the combatants; they had separated themselves. We had not protected the Canal; it was blocked. We had not safeguarded British lives and property, but had subjected them to the gravest hazards. Nor had we achieved our real aim of seizing control of the Canal. Least of all had we toppled Nasser from his throne. [Nutting, *No End of a Lesson*, p. 145]

THE RETREAT FROM EMPIRE

In the long term, perhaps, the results of the Suez crisis were not as far-reaching as they seemed at the time. Good relations with the United States were restored almost immediately; the Commonwealth did not break up; within six months the Canal was re-opened under Egyptian control. But as a turning-point in Britain's imperial history, and as a case study in policy-making, the Suez Crisis remains a significant and dramatic episode.

Books cited

Sir A. Eden, *Full Circle* (Cassell, 1960).
S. Lloyd, *Suez 1956, A Personal Account* (Cape, 1978)
A. Nutting, *Nasser* (Constable, 1972)
A. Nutting, *No End of a Lesson, The Story of Suez* (Constable, 1967)
H. Thomas, *The Suez Affair* (Weidenfeld & Nicolson, 1966)
P. M. Williams, *Hugh Gaitskell* (OUP, 1982)
K. M. Wilson (ed.), *Imperialism and Nationalism in the Middle East — The Anglo-Egyptian Experience* (Mansell, 1983)

BIBLIOGRAPHY BIBLIOGRAPHY BIBLIOGRAPHY BIBLIOGRAPHY BIBLIOGRAPHY BIBLIOGRAPHY
BIBLIOGRAPHY BIBLIOGRAPHY BIBLIOGRAPHY BIBLIOGRAPHY BIBLIOGRAPHY BIBLIOGRAPHY
BIBLIOGRAPHY BIBLIOGRAPHY BIBLIOGRAPHY BIBLIOGRAPHY BIBLIOGRAPHY BIBLIOGRAPHY
BIBLIOGRAPHY BIBLIOGRAPHY BIBLIOGRAPHY BIBLIOGRAPHY BIBLIOGRAPHY BIBLIOGRAPHY
BIBLIOGRAPHY BIBLIOGRAPHY BIBLIOGRAPHY BIBLIOGRAPHY BIBLIOGRAPHY BIBLIOGRAPHY

CHAPTER 14
FURTHER READING

General

As for Chapter Thirteen but see also:

Essential
C. Cross, *The Fall of the British Empire, 1918–1968* (Hodder & Stoughton, 1968)
J. Morris, *Farewell The Trumpets* (Penguin, 1978)
G. Woodcock, *Who Killed the British Empire?* (Cape, 1974)

Recommended
H. Kinder and W. Hilgemann, *The Penguin Atlas of Modern History* (Penguin, 1978)
W. S. Kirkman, *Unscrambling an Empire* (Chatto & Windus, 1966)

India

Essential
M. Brecher, *Nehru* (OUP, 1977)

Recommended
H. V. Hodson, *The Great Divide* (Hutchinson, 1969)
P. Scott, *The Jewel in the Crown* (Heinemann, 1966)

The Middle East

Essential
T. C. Fraser, *The Middle East, 1914–1976* (Arnold, 1981)

Recommended
E. Monroe, *Britain's Moment in the Middle East* (Chatto & Windus, 1966)

Palestine

Essential
A. Bullock, *Ernest Bevin, Foreign Secretary* (Heinemann, 1984)

Recommended
C. Sykes, *Crossroads to Israel* (Collins, 1965)

Egypt

Essential
S. Lloyd, *Suez 1956, A Personal Account* (Cape, 1978)
A. Nutting, *No End of a Lesson, the Story of Suez* (Constable, 1967)
K. M. Wilson (ed.), *Imperialism and Nationalism in the Middle East — The Anglo-Egyptian Experience* (Mansell, 1983)

Recommended
H. Thomas, *The Suez Affair* (Weidenfeld & Nicolson, 1966)

Decolonisation
Essential

Africa
J. Hatch, *Britain in Africa from the Fifteenth Century to the Present* (A. Deutsch, 1969)
R. Blake, *A History of Rhodesia* (Eyre Methuen, 1977)

The Falklands
M. Hastings, *The Falklands War* (Sphere, 1982)
Sunday Times Insight Team, *The Falklands War* (Sphere, 1982)

Northern Ireland
Conor Cruise O'Brien, *States of Ireland* (Hutchinson, 1972)
A. T. Q. Stewart, *The Narrow Ground (Aspects of Ulster, 1609–1969)* (Faber, 1977)

The Commonwealth
N. Mansergh, *The Commonwealth Experience* (Weidenfeld & Nicolson, 1969)

TIME CHART 1945–80

Date	Social and Economic	Political	Foreign Affairs	The Empire and Ireland
1945	*Aug.* Ending of Lend-Lease. *Dec.* American loan agreement.	*Jul.* Labour government formed; Attlee premier.	*Sep.* Foreign Ministers' Conference in London. *Dec.* Foreign Ministers' Conference in Moscow.	*Aug.* Liberation of Burma. *Nov.* Anglo-American Commission on Palestine.
1946	*Mar.* Bank of England nationalised. *Aug.* Civil Aviation nationalised. *Nov.* National Insurance Act passed. *Nov.* National Health Service Act passed. (Both to operate in 1948.) *Dec.* Trades Disputes Act, 1927 repealed. Distribution of Industry Act, New Towns Act.		*5 Mar.* Churchill's Fulton Speech. *Apr.–May* Foreign Ministers' Conference in Paris. *Nov.–Dec.* Foreign Ministers' Conference in New York. Peace treaties signed with Italy, Bulgaria, Hungary, Rumania and Finland.	*Mar.* Gold Coast first colony to have African majority on council. *Sep.* London Conference on Palestine.
1947	*Jan.–Mar.* Coal shortage; 1 million unemployed. *Jan.* Coal industry nationalised. *Jan.* Cable and Wireless nationalised. *Jul.* Sterling made convertible. *Aug.* Convertibility suspended. Town and Country Planning Act passed.	*Nov.* Cripps replaced Dalton as Chancellor.	*Feb.* British withdrawal of troops from Greece announced. *12 Mar.* Truman Doctrine. *Mar.* Treaty of Dunkirk with France. *5 Jun.* Marshall Plan suggested. *29 Jun.–2 Jul.* Talks on Marshall Plan. *Dec.* Last Foreign Ministers' Conference in New York.	*Jan.* Mountbatten made Viceroy of India. *Feb.* Palestine referred to UN. *10–11 May* Partition agreed for India and Pakistan. *15 Aug.* Independence for India and Pakistan; sectional killings follow. *Aug.* UN Plan for partition of Palestine; Britain objected. *Dec.* Burma independent.
1948	*Jan.* Transport nationalised. *Apr.* Marshall Aid begun. Electricity nationalised. *Jul.* National Health Service in operation. Wage restraint successful. National Assistance Act passed.	Representation of People Act (end of plural voting, university seats).	*Mar.* Treaty of Brussels signed. *Apr.* OEEC set up in Paris. *May.* Meeting of European Congress at the Hague. *Jun.–May 1949* Berlin Airlift.	*Jan.* Gandhi assassinated. *Feb.* Ceylon given Dominion status. *Feb.* Riots in Gold Coast. *May* Last British troops left Palestine. Start of Malayan emergency.

Date	Social and Economic	Political	Foreign Affairs	The Empire and Ireland
1949	*Apr.* Gas industry nationalised. *Sep.* The pound devalued from $4.03 – $2.80.	Parliament Act (Lords veto down to one year).	*Mar.* Britain joined NATO. *Apr.* Britain joined Council of Europe.	*Jan.* Britain recognised Israel. *Apr.* New formula for Commonwealth to allow Republics to remain.
1950	Balance of payments surplus of £297 million.	*23 Feb.* General Election; narrow Labour victory. *Oct.* Gaitskell succeeded Cripps as Chancellor.	*May* Britain declined to join ECSC. *Jun.* Outbreak of Korean War. *Sep.* War officially ended between West Powers and West Germany. *Dec.* Attlee visit to Truman. Conscription raised to two years.	
1951	*Feb.* Iron and steel nationalised. Balance of payments deficit of £400 million. Increased re-armament programme.	*Apr.* Bevan, Wilson and Freeman resigned over health charges and defence spending. *25 Oct.* General election; highest Labour vote but Conservative victory. Churchill made premier.	Korean War continued.	*Apr.* Anglo-Iranian Oil Company nationalised. *Oct.* British technicians withdrawn from Abadan. *Oct.* Egypt announced end of 1936 Treaty.
1952	Fall in commodity prices. Ending of economic controls.		*Oct.* First British atomic bomb exploded. Pleven Plan for European Army considered.	
1953	*Mar.* Road transport de-nationalised. *Apr.* Iron and steel de-nationalised.	*Jan.* Coronation of Elizabeth II.	*Jul.* Korean War armistice agreed.	*Jan.* Inauguration of Central African Federation. Start of Mau-Mau emergency in Kenya.

Date	Social and Economic	Political	Foreign Affairs	The Empire and Ireland
1954	*Jul.* All food rationing ended. Commercial Broadcasting introduced.	*Apr.* Bevan resigned from Shadow Cabinet.	*May–Jul.* Geneva Conference on Indo-China. *Oct.* Nine power Defence Conference; Germany and Italy joined Treaty of Brussels; Western European Union. *Oct.* Britain committed to keep troops in Europe.	*Sep.* Britain joined SEATO. *Oct.* Canal Base Agreement with Egypt.
1955	*Dec.* Macmillan made Chancellor. Balance of Payments deficit of £175 million.	*Apr.* Churchill retired; Eden made premier. *26 May* General election; increased Conservative majority. *Dec.* Gaitskell elected leader of Labour party.	*May* Germany admitted to NATO. *Jun.* Messina talks on EEC. *Jul.* Geneva Conference on Germany.	*Apr.* Britain joined Baghdad Pact. *Aug.* London Conference on Cyprus.
1956	Credit squeeze; interest rates to 5½% (highest since 1932).		*Apr.* Visit of Bulganin and Khruschev to Britain. *Jul.–Dec.* Suez Crisis. *29 Oct. – 7 Nov.* Anglo-French invasion of Egypt.	*Mar.* Glubb Pasha dismissed. *Jun.* Last British troops left Canal Base *19 Jul.* Decision not to finance Aswan Dam. *26 Jul.* Nationalisation of Suez Canal.
1957	*Jun.* Premium Bonds introduced. *Aug.* Council on Prices, Productivity and Incomes.	*Jan.* Eden resigned; Macmillan made premier.	*Mar.* Treaty of Rome signed establishing EEC. Maudling negotiations with EEC.	*Mar.* Gold Coast made independent; becomes Ghana. *Mar.* Archbishop Makarios released. *Aug.* Malaya made independent.
1958	*Jan.* Resignations of Thorneycroft, Birch and Powell over public spending. *Feb.* Campaign for Nuclear Disarmament founded.	*Jul.* Life Peerages introduced.	*Nov.* Russian threat to West Berlin.	*Jan.* West Indies Federation in force. *Jul.* Feisal II assassinated in Iraq. *Nov.* Last British troops left Jordan.

Date	Social and Economic	Political	Foreign Affairs	The Empire and Ireland
1959	*Aug.* Publication of Radcliffe Report on Monetary Institutions.	*8 Oct.* General Election; increased Conservative majority. *Oct.* Nationalisation re-affirmed at Labour Party Conference.	*Feb.* Macmillan visited Moscow. *Mar.* Geneva Conference on Germany. *Dec.* Stockholm Convention on European Free Trade Area.	*Jan.* Sean Lemass made premier of Eire. Disturbances in Nyasaland.
1960	National output up 14% on 1955; productivity up 12½% on 1955.	*Oct.* Labour Party Conference voted for unilateral nuclear disarmament. *Nov.* Gaitskell re-elected to Labour leadership.	*Jan.* EFTA in operation. *Apr.* Bluestreak cancelled. *May* U2 shot down. *May* Abortive Geneva Conference.	*Jan.–Feb.* Macmillan's tour of Africa; Wind of Change speech. *Jun.* British Somaliland made independent. *Aug.* Cyprus made independent. *Oct.* South Africa voted to become republic. *Nov.* Monckton Report on Central African Federation. *Dec.* Nigeria made independent.
1961	*Jul.* Pay Pause. National Economic Development Council established. White Paper on Nationalised Industries. Robbins Report on Universities.	*Oct.* Labour Party Conference voted to keep nuclear weapons.	*Jul.* Cabinet agreed to apply for British membership of EEC *Nov.* Formal application. *Aug.* Berlin Wall constructed.	*Mar.* South Africa left Commonwealth. *Dec.* Tanganyika made independent
1962	*Jul.* Maudling made Chancellor. National Incomes Commission set up.	*Mar.* Liberal victory at Orpington by-election. *Jul.* Macmillan dismissed seven members of cabinet.	*Oct.–Nov.* Cuba Missiles crisis. *Dec.* Macmillan talks with de Gaulle. *Dec.* Macmillan talks with Kennedy. *Dec.* Polaris missile agreement.	*Apr.* End of West Indies Federation. *Aug.* Jamaica and Trinidad made independent.

Date	Social and Economic	Political	Foreign Affairs	The Empire and Ireland
1963	Beeching Report recommending closure of many railway lines.	*Jan.* Gaitskell died; Wilson elected leader of Labour party. *Mar.–Apr.* Profumo affair. *Jul.* Peerage Act allowing hereditary peers to resign peerages. *Oct.* Macmillan resigned; Home made premier.	*Jan.* De Gaulle vetoed British entry into EEC. *Aug.* Partial Nuclear Test Ban Treaty signed in Moscow.	*Sep.* Federation of Malaysia formed. *Dec.* Kenya and Zanzibar made independent. *31 Dec.* Central African Federation finally dissolved.
1964	*Oct.* Balance of payments deficit of £700 million. *Oct.* 15% surcharge on tariffs. *Oct.* Ministry of Technology and Department of Economic Affairs set up.	*15 Oct.* General Election; narrow Labour victory; Wilson made premier.	*Nov.* Ban on arms sales to South Africa.	*Aug.* Nyasaland made independent, becomes Malawi. *Sep.* Malta made independent. *Oct.* North Rhodesia made independent, becomes Zambia.
1965	*Feb.* National Board for Prices and Incomes set up. *Sep.* First National Plan announced. Donovan Commission on TU's. Race Relations Act passed. Circular 10/65 advocating comprehensive schools.	*Jul.* Heath replaced Home as Conservative leader. Fulton Commission on Civil Service set up.	*Jul.* Harold Davies sent to Hanoi, to seek solution to Vietnam War.	*Nov.* Unilateral Declaration of independence by Rhodesia.
1966	*Jul.* Prices and Incomes Act; Wages freeze. Iron and Steel re-nationalised. Industrial Reorganisation Corporation set up. Industrial Development Act passed.	*31 Mar.* General Election; Labour increased majority.	*Oct.* Cabinet decided to explore terms of entry to EEC.	*May* British Guiana became independent as Guyana. *Sep.* Bechuanaland became independent as Botswana. *Oct.* Basutoland became independent as Lesotho.

Date	Social and Economic	Political	Foreign Affairs	The Empire and Ireland
1967	*Nov.* Pound devalued from $2.80 to $2.40. White Paper on Nationalised Industries. Sexual Offences Act passed. Abortion Act passed.	*Nov.* Proposals for reform of House of Lords introduced.	*Jan.* Kosygin visited London. *Jan.* Downing Street – Moscow Hot Line agreed. *May* Cabinet approved decision to apply for membership of EEC. Cabinet decision to cut defence spending.	*Nov.* British evacuated Aden. *Dec.* Talks between Wilson and Smith on HMS *Tiger*. 1967–70 Nigerian Civil War; Britain supported Nigerian government.
1968	*Jan.* Public spending cuts. *Mar.* Immigration Act. *Jun.* Donovan Commission Report on Trades Unions. First Balance of Payments surplus since 1963.	*Apr.* Powell dismissed from Shadow Cabinet. *Jun.* Fulton Commission Report.	*Jan.* Defence cuts announced; British withdrawal from East of Suez by 1971. *Nov.* De Gaulle vetoed second application to join EEC.	*Sep.* Swaziland became independent. *Oct.* Talks between Wilson and Smith on HMS *Fearless*. *Oct.–Nov.* Civil Rights marches in Ulster.
1969	*Jun.* *In Place of Strife* proposals on trade unions abandoned. *Dec.* Death penalty permanently abolished. Open University in operation.	*Apr.* House of Lords reform abandoned. *May* Voting age reduced to 18. Crowther Commission on the constitution.	*Dec.* EEC agreed to reopen negociations for British entry.	*Aug.* British troops in Londonderry and Belfast. Split between Official and Provisional IRA.
1970	Equal Pay Act.	*Jan.* Selsdon Park Conference. *18 Jun.* General Election; Conservative majority; Heath made premier.	*Jun.* Arms sales to South Africa renewed. *Jun.* Negotiations under G. Rippon with EEC.	
1971	Collapse of Rolls Royce; taken over by government. Industrial Relations Act passed. Commonwealth Immigration Act passed.	*Oct.* Labour party conference voted against joining EEC.	*May* Heath–Pompidou Talks. *Jul.* Terms of British entry into EEC finally agreed.	*Feb.* First British soldier killed in Ulster. *Aug.* Internment without trial in Ulster. *Dec.* Home opened talks with Smith.

Date	Social and Economic	Political	Foreign Affairs	The Empire and Ireland
1972	*Jan.* Miners' Strike. *Apr.* Reflationary budget. *Jun.* Sterling crisis; pound floated. *Nov.* Pay freeze.	*Apr.* Resignation of Jenkins and others from Labour Shadow Cabinet on EEC referendum decision. *Jul.* European Communities Act passed Third Reading. *Oct.* Kilbrandon Commission on the Constitution recommended Devolution.	*Mar.* Britain and China exchanged ambassadors. *Oct.* Lord Home visited China.	*Jan.* 'Bloody Sunday' in Londonderry. *Mar.* Direct Rule imposed in Ulster. *May* Pearce Commission reported against Home terms in Rhodesia.
1973	*Jan.* Pay Board and Prices Commission set up. *Oct.* Arab/Israeli War caused quadrupling of oil prices. *Nov.* Overtime ban in coal industry. Visible trade deficit reached £2.5 billion.		*1 Jan.* Britain entered EEC.	*Jun.* New Constitution for Ulster. *Dec.* Sunningdale agreement on Power Sharing and Council of Ireland.
1974	*Jan.* Three-day week. *Feb.* Miners' strike v. Pay Policy. Pay Board abolished. Industrial Relations Act Repealed. Social Contract to control wages. Visible trade deficit £5351 billion.	*28 Feb.* General Election; no party with overall majority. *4 Mar.* Wilson became premier.	Terms of entry into EEC renegotiated.	*Jan.* Direct rule of Ulster lifted. *May* Ulster Workers Council Strike; collapse of Power Sharing agreement; direct rule re-imposed.
1975	*Jul.* Limit on pay rises of £6 per week imposed. *Nov.* Industry Act; National Enterprise Board set up. Sex discrimination Act passed. Price inflation reached 25%.	*Feb.* Heath replaced by M. Thatcher as Conservative leader. *Mar.* Labour cabinet split on EEC. *Jun.* Referendum on whether Britain should stay in EEC, 66% in favour. *Nov.* White Paper on Devolution.	*Mar.* Dublin summit; Council of Ministers approved new terms for Britain. *Apr.* Ending of Vietnam War.	Constitutional Convention in Ulster; ended in December.

Date	Social and Economic	Political	Foreign Affairs	The Empire and Ireland
1976	*May* Limit on pay rises of £4 per week. *Dec.* Cuts of £2 500 million in public spending to meet International Monetary Fund (IMF) requirements. Education Act made comprehensive school reorganisation compulsory.	*Mar.* Wilson resigned; Callaghan elected to replace him.	*Jul.* Jenkins made President of European Commission.	*Jul.* Shackleton Report on Falkland Islands.
1977	Shipbuilding and aircraft industries nationalised.	*Feb.* Owen made Foreign Secretary. *Mar.* Liberal–Labour Pact.		*Feb.* Rowlands visited Falkland Islands. *Oct.* British frigates sent to South Atlantic.
1978	*Jul.* 5% limit on pay rises proposed. *Oct.* Labour Party Conference rejected pay limits. *Nov.* TUC rejected pay limits. Strikes in public sector (water workers, hospital employees etc.). Inflation reduced to 8.2%.	*Jan.* Devolution proposed; amendment requiring 40% of total electorate to approve added to bills. *Jul.* Devolution Bills for Wales and Scotland received royal assent. *Oct.* Liberal–Labour Pact ended.	*Dec.* Britain refused to join European Monetary System. End of transitional period for British entry into EEC.	*May* Ban on Nationalist parties in Rhodesia lifted.
1979	Prices Commission abolished. National Enterprise Board abolished. Inflation up to 13.2%. Unemployment up to 1.5 million.	*1 Mar.* Referenda on Devolution; Wales strongly against, Scotland narrowly in favour. *28 Mar.* Government defeat on motion of no confidence. *3 May* General Election; Conservative victory; M. Thatcher made premier.		*Jul.* Ridley visit to Falkland Islands. *Aug.* Commonwealth Conference at Lusaka to prepare way for Rhodesia settlement. *Sep.–Dec.* Lancaster House Conference on Constitution for Rhodesia.
1980			Britain objected to size of her budget contribution to EEC.	*Apr.* Independence granted to new State of Zimbabwe.
(1981)				
(1982)				*(29 Mar. – 14 Jun.* Falklands War.)

Index

A

Abdication Crisis 200, 372
Abdul Habid II, Sultan of Turkey 46
Abdullah, King of Transjordan 196
Abortion Act, 1967 407, 512
Abrial, Admiral, J. 312
Abse, Leo 407
Abyssinia
  1935–36 275–7, 284
  1940–41 315–16, 372
Acheson, Dean 420, 431, 443, 447, 457–8
Acland, Sir Richard 347
Action Française 266
Adamson, W. 221
Adamthwaite, Anthony 167
Addison, Dr. C. (later Lord) 96, 100, 116–17, 221, 416
Addison, P. 342, 347, 354
Adenauer, Konrad 436, 443
Adowa, Battle of 264
Aehrenthal, Baron Lesca von 46
Agadir Crisis, 1911 44, 106
Agriculture 2, 91, 116, 216–17, 246–7, 350–1
Aircraft Production, Ministry of 345, 348, 373
Air Raids 361–2
Airways:
  British European 385
  British Imperial 247
  British Overseas 247
  British South American 385
Aitken, Alexander 99
Alexander, A. V. 221, 465
Alexander, General Sir Harold 321, 324, 333
Algeçiras Conference, 1906 43, 106
Aliens Act (Ireland) 183
Allenby, General Sir Edmund 81, 193
Alliance Parties 499
Allied War Council 144
Amery, L. 24, 123, 299, 342
Amritsar, Massacre 187–8, 191, 204
Amulree, Lord 221
Anderson, Sir John (later Lord Waverley) 216, 293, 297, 343, 345, 354, 430
Angell, Norman 55
Anglo–German Naval Agreement, 1935 275
Anglo–Iranian Oil Company 474–5, 507
Anglo–Japanese Alliance, 1902 41, 164, 169
Anglo–Polish Treaty, 1939 294–5, 373
  confirmed, 296
Anglo–Russian Relations
  1900–14 41–2, 44
  1917–29 155–9
  1929–39 266–7, 294–6

  1939–80 310, 318–21, 423–42
Anschluss 150, 284–5, 373
Anti-Comintern Pact 266
Anti-Semitism in Britain 253
Anzio, Landings at 324, 340
Apartheid 495
Appeasement, Defined 272
  Policies of 272–89
  Ending of 289–99
  Debate on 335–7
Arabs
  in World War I 81–2
  in Palestine 195–8
  after 1945 470–83
Arab League 471
Arcadia Conference, 1942 319
Arcos Affair 159, 205
Ardennes Offensive, 1944–45 331
Arras, Battle of 77
Asquith, H. H. 9, 11, 14, 24, 40, 49, 343, 491
  quoted 12, 171
  and background to World War I 44, 55, 59–61
  and conduct of war 86–9
  and inter-war politics 114, 119–22
Ashetton, Ralph 359
Astor, Lord 270
Aswan Dam 476, 501–2, 509
Atlantic, Battle of 309, 323–4
Atlantic Charter 306, 373, 462
Attlee, C. R. (later Lord) 122
  Leader of Labour Party 249, 252
  Views of Munich Agreement 291
  in War Cabinet 345, 347, 354, 366–7
  as Prime Minister 379–81, 391–5, 398, 412–13, 416
  and Cold War 420–1, 426–35
  and Empire 462, 465–7, 470–5
Aubers Ridge, Battle of 71, 73, 86
Auchinleck, Sir C. 321, 346
Aud 172
Aung Sang 470
Australia 19, 68, 199–200
Axis Pact 384
Azana, Manuel 281

B

Bachelor's Walk Massacre, 1914 22, 28, 107
Baden-Powell, Robert 40
Bad Godesburg Talks 286, 288–9
Badoglio, Marshal P. 322
Bagehot, W. 8, 12
Baghdad Pact 476, 481, 495
Balance of Payments
  before 1914 3
  1919–39 3, 109
  in World War II 353

  1945–80 375–6, 381–3, 400–2, 408, 456
Baldwin, Stanley 16
  and National Debt 109
  and ending of Lloyd George Coalition 119
  Conservative leadership 120–1, 411
  First ministry 127–8
  Second ministry 127–36, 385
  and foreign affairs 153, 159–61
  and 1931 crisis 222–5, 227
  and final ministry 234, 242
  and foreign affairs, 1929–39 271–2, 275–7, 280
Balfour, A. J. 4, 10, 12, 13, 22, 40, 58, 106, 141, 195
  and World War I 84, 87–8
  and Conservative leadership 121
  and Peace Conference 145
  and Commonwealth 182
Balfour Committee on Trade and Industry, 1924–27 112
Balfour Declaration 106, 141, 195
Balfour Education Act, *see* Education
Balfour, Captain H. 367
Balfour Memorandum 182, 199
Balkan League 47
Balkan Wars 47, 107
Banda, Dr. Hastings 484, 487
Bank of England 138, 210–11, 218–26, 382, 384–5, 401, 507
Bank Rate 138, 242
Barlow Commission and Report *see* Environment
Barnes, G. N. 93, 115, 117
Barnett, Corelli 77
Basutoland (Lesotho) 21, 516
Battle of Britain 313–14, 354
Bay of Pigs 439
Beatty, Sir D. 83
Beauchamp, Lord 55
Beaverbrook, Lord 211, 344–5, 356, 365, 367
Bechuanaland (Botswana) 21, 516
Beck, Colonel, J. 294–5
Beeching, Dr. 403
  Report on Railways 403, 516
Beeley, Harold 471
Bell, George, Bishop of Chichester 336–7
Beloff, Max 169
Benes, E. 286–8, 291, 300
Ben Gurion, David 479
Benn, A. Wedgwood 404, 406, 455
Benn, W. Wedgwood 17, 221
Berchtesgaden, Talks at 285–6, 288, 300–1
Berchtold, Count Leopold von 47, 49, 51

Berlin Airlift   433, 436, 507
Berlin Wall   440, 510
Bernal, J. D.   250
Bernhardi, Friedrich von   39
Bethell, N.   198
Bethmann-Hollweg, Theobald   49, 51–5,
    60, 63
Bevan, A.
    expelled from Labour Party   250
    critic of Churchill   347
    opposes 1944 White Paper   359
    Minister of Health   376, 380–1, 388–90
    resignation   394
    further opposition   388–9
    view of Socialism   413, 416
Beveridge Report   347–8, 355, 381,
    383, 388
Beveridge, William (later Lord)   248,
    354–5, 358, 391
Bevin, Ernest
    and 1931 crisis   210–11, 220
    and Labour leadership, 1935   249
    in War Cabinet   344–5, 347, 349,
        354, 363–4
    as Foreign Secretary   380, 394, 414,
        416, 420–2, 426–34, 446–7, 456–9,
        462, 470–3, 483
Bidault, Georges   432
Birell, A.   174
Birkenhead, Lord (F. E. Smith)   118–19,
    127, 130, 136
    and Ireland   177, 202
    and India   188–9
Bismark, Count Otto von   35–7, 41–2,
    58, 101, 162, 165
Bismark   309, 323–4
Black and Tans   177
Black Hand   51
Blake, R.   28
Bletchley Park (Government Code and
    Cipher School)   308, 324
Blitz   3, 14, 336, 354, 356, 358, 361–2
Blitzkrieg   305, 308
Blockade (1914–18)   82, 84–5, 144
Bloody Sunday (N. Ireland)   492
Blue Streak   441, 448, 510
Blum Leon   281, 299, 428, 432
Blunden, Edmund   97, 271
Blunt, Anthony   250
Boer War   21, 86, 185–6
Bolsheviks   114, 142, 152–9, 267
Bomber Command   309, 324–7, 335–7
Bonar Law, Andrew   9–10, 16
    and Ulster   22, 28
    and World War I   86–9, 93, 96
    and Lloyd George Coalition   114–15,
        118–19
    as Prime Minister   120, 123, 153,
        203
Bondfield, Margaret   215, 221
Bonnet, Georges   286, 288, 301
Booth, Charles   6
Boothby, Robert   297

Boscawen   119
Bose, Subhas, Chandra   185, 463
Bottomley, Sir N., Deputy Chief of Air
    Staff   327
Boundary Commissions (Ireland)   177,
    180–1, 201–3
Boundary Commission (India)   467
Boyle, A.   159
Bracken, Brendan   188–9
Bradley, Omar   329
Brecher, M   189, 463–4
Breslau (German cruiser)   78, 82
Brest Litovsk, Treaty of   107, 155, 157
Bretton Woods Agreement   382
Briand, Aristide   152–3, 161, 163, 273
British Airborne Corps   331
British Broadcasting Corporation   136,
    206, 360
British Expeditionary Force
    1914   68, 71–3
    1939   311–12
British Gazette   133
British Medical Association   356, 389–90
British Nationality Act   494
Brittain, Vera   271
Brockway, Fenner   421
Brooke, Sir Alan   321, 330, 345
Brown, George (later Lord George-
    Brown)   399, 402, 420–1, 441,
    450–1, 453
Browning, Frederick   331
Brugha, Cathal   178, 180
Brussels, Treaty of, 1948   432, 436,
    444, 507
Bulganin, Nicolai, R.   437
Bullock, A. (later Lord)   249, 422, 428–9,
    456, 458, 470, 473
Bulow, Prince von   47, 57
Burgess, Guy   250
Burgin, L.   293
Burma   21, 333–4, 374, 470, 507
Burns, John   55, 86
Butler, R. A. (later Lord)   354, 356–7,
    395–6, 400, 487
Butskellism   395
Butt, Isaac   18
Byrnes, James   427–8

C
Cadogan, Sir Alexander   269–70, 295,
    306, 421
Caffery, J. (US Ambassador in
    Paris)   458
Cairo Conference
    1921   194, 205
    1943   319–20
Calais Conference, March 1917   72
Callaghan, James   8, 379
    Chancellor of Exchequer   401–2
    Home Secretary   407
    Prime Minister   411–12
    and EEC   453–5

Calder, A.   355
Cambon, Jules   39, 60
Cambon, Paul   45, 55, 59
Campaign for Nuclear Disarmament
    398–9, 509
Campbell, J. R.   126
Campbell-Bannerman, Sir Henry   11,
    23, 40
Canada   19, 112, 199–200
Cannan, Professor   210
Cannes Conference, 1922   151, 205
Carden, Admiral Sir S. H.   79
Cardwell, Edward   9
Carlton Club Meeting, October 1922
    119, 155, 205
Carson, Sir Edward   28, 87, 89, 175, 190
Casablanca Conference (Symbol),
    January 1943   306, 319–20, 322,
    324, 326, 374
Casement, Sir Roger   171–2
Castle, Barbara   406, 455
Castro, Fidel   439
Catto, Lord   385
Cavell, Edith   95
Cecil, Lord Robert   118, 160
Central African Federation   486–7, 489,
    508, 511–12
Central Electricity Generating Board
    110, 136, 498
Ceylon   21, 470, 507
Challe, M.   478, 503
Chamberlain, Austen   8
    Leader of Conservative Party   119–21
    Foreign Secretary   127, 161–2, 199, 202
Chamberlain, Joseph   16, 23–4, 170,
    243
Chamberlain, Neville   12, 16
    Director of National Service 1917   91
    Hostile view of Lloyd George   118
    Housing Act, 1923   123
    Minister of Health 1924–29   127,
        135–6
    and 1931 crisis   210–11, 221–3
    Chancellor of Exchequer, 1931–37
        241–6
    and Foreign Affairs   269–70, 272,
        274, 277
    Prime Minister, 1937–40   283–302,
        305, 310-11, 341–2
    Fall   342–4, 347
    and Irish Treaty Ports   183–4
Chanak Crisis, 1922   119, 154–5, 199
Channel Tunnel   126
Charteris, Colonel J.   70
Chatfield, Lord   278, 281, 341
Chautemps, C. F.   301
Chelmsford, Lord   122, 185
Cherwell, Lord (Professor
    Lindemann)   278, 325–6, 345, 358
Chester, Lewis (with Stephen Fox,
    Hugo Young)   127
Chiang Kai-Shek   320, 435, 462
Childers, Erskine   40, 130

Chilston, Lord, British Ambassador in Moscow 270
Churchill, Clementine (née Hozier) 317, 347, 368, 396
Churchill, Lady Jenny 317
Churchill, Randolph 346
Churchill, Winston S., quoted 8, 48, 82, 98, 213, 215, 272, 424–5, 428
  First Lord of Admiralty, 1911–15 15, 45, 49, 70, 79–80, 87
  Secretary of State for War and Air, 1919–21 155–7
  Secretary for Colonies, 1921–22:
    Ireland 177, 201
    Middle East 192–7
  in opposition, 1922–24 127
  Chancellor of Exchequer, 1924–29 113, 127, 133, 135, 137
  and Ten Year Rule 162
  in opposition, 1929–39 177, 189–90, 227, 278, 280, 283, 291
  First Lord of Admiralty, 1939–40 310–11
  Prime Minister:
    Passim, (Operations) 311–35
    Passim, (War at Home) 341–68
  in opposition, 1945–51 379, 386
  Prime Minister, 1951–55 11, 396, 400
  and Cold War 419–21, 424–29
  and Europe 443, 446
  and Empire 462, 464
Citrine, Walter 386
Clause Four, Labour Party Constitution 384, 385, 398, 403
Clay, Lucius 433
Clayton, Will 431
Clemenceau, Georges 144–6, 147, 164–7
Clynes, J. R. 93, 122, 126, 213, 221
Coal Industry 1–2, 92, 110, 128–35, 216, 236, 247, 364, 385–6, 410, 507
Coal Mines Act, 1920 117, 205
Collins, Michael 177–80, 201–2
Colombo Plan 463
Colonial Conferences 22
Colonial Development Act, 1929 257
Colonial Development Corporation 463, 484, 493–4
Colonial Office 22–3, 484
Colville, John 318
Colvin, Ian 283, 285, 287, 300–1
Comintern 156, 205, 267
Committee of Imperial Defence 41, 44–5, 126, 161–2
Common Agricultural Policy 445–6, 452–3, 455
Commonwealth 112, 199–200, 420, 446, 448–53, 461–3, 469–70, 481, 483–90, 493–7, 504
Commonwealth Brigade, in Korea 434
Common Wealth Party 347, 374
Communist Information Bureau (Cominform) 432, 507

Congress Party (Indian) 184–91, 463–8
Connolly, James 174–4
Conscientious Objection, in W. War I 91
  in W. War II 349
Conscription, in W. War I 90–1
  in Ireland 175
  between the wars 275, 292–3
  in W. War II 307, 348–9, 360
  post-1945 429, 434, 441
Conservative Party up to 1929 11, 16, 86, 101, 113–14, 118–19, 123–4, 127–8
  1929–45 341–2, 360, 366–8
  1945–80 377–9, 387, 396–8, 409–11, 499
Constantine, S. 240, 245, 259
Convoys, in W. War I 84–5, 92
  in W. War II 307, 309, 313–18, 320, 323–4
Coogan, T. P. 178
Cook, A. J. 122, 131
Cooper, Duff 287, 291, 294, 299
Council of Europe 443, 444, 446
Cosgrave, William 175
Courtney, Leonard 21
Cousins, Frank 404
Cowling, M. 118
Cradock, Admiral Sir P. 83
Craig, Gordon, A 57
Craig, Sir James 179, 201–2, 280, 296
Credit Anstalt, Collapse of 218
Creech-Jones, Arthur 463
Crete, Fall of 308, 316, 338
Crewe, Lord (Ambassador in Paris) 162
Crick, B. 170
Cripps, Sir Stafford, in 1931 crisis 223
  expelled from Labour Party 250
  Leader of House under Churchill 344
  Chancellor of Exchequer, 1947–50 382–3, 393–4, 400
  and nuclear weapons 421, 430
  and Marshall Aid 432
  and India 374, 464
Cromer, Lord 401
Crosland, Anthony 395, 407, 420, 453
Cross, Colin 193, 482
Crossman, R. H. S. 401–2, 405, 412, 441, 450, 482
Crowe, Sir Eyre 41, 53
Crowther-Hunt, Lord 406
Cruise Missiles 441, 499
Ctesiphon, Battle of 71, 81
Cuba Missiles Crisis, 1962 439–40, 510
Cunliffe Committee on Currency and Foreign Exchanges 113, 204
Cunliffe, Lord 148
Cunliffe-Lister (later Lord Swinton) 223
Cunningham, Sir Andrew 316, 345
Curragh Mutiny 22, 107
Curzon, Lord, and the Empire 24–5, 42, 170
  in War Cabinet 84–5

  passed over as Prime Minister 120–2
  Foreign Secretary 155, 158, 195
Curzon Line 158, 425
Cyprus 21–3, 482
Czechoslovakia, Creation of 150
  Czech crisis, 1938–9 285–91, 298–302
  Communist coup, February 1948 432

D

D-Day 323, 329–30
Dahlerus 296
Dail 176–80, 183–4, 202
Daily Mail 86, 131, 136, 252
Daily Mirror 347, 365
Daily Worker 251, 365
Daladier, E. F. 286, 288, 300–1
Dallek, R. 268
Dalton, Hugh 347, 393, 395
  Chancellor of Exchequer, 1945–47 380–2, 416, 421, 430
Dangerfield, George 28–9, 101–2, 202–3
Dardanelles 42, 46, 78–9, 97, 141, 143, 151, 154–5
Dardanelles Committee, Creation of 87
Davenport, Nicholas 385
Davidson, J. C. 121
Davison, Emily 14
Dawes Plan 128, 153
Dawson, Geoffrey (Editor of The Times) 270
Dayan, Moshe 501
Dean, Patrick 479
Declaration of London 84
Defence of the Realm Acts 90
Defence Requirements Committee 270, 272
Deighton, Len. 314
Delbos, Y. 301
Delcassé, T. 48
Denikin, Anton. R. 157
Department of Scientific and Industrial Research 109
Derby, Lord 90
Destroyer Deal, 1940, with USA 317
De Valera, Eamon, and Easter Rising 171, 174
  1917–23 175–9, 201–2
  Irish premier 183–4
Devaluation, 1949 382–3
  1967 401–2, 441
Development (Loan Guarantee and Grants Act) 257
Devolution Proposals for Scotland and Wales 411–12, 514
Devonshire, Duke of 347
Die Hards 118, 201
Dien Bien Phu, Fall of 435
Dieppe, Raid on, 1942 330–7, 339
Dilke, Sir Charles 9
Dill, Sir John 344–5
Dimitrievitch, Colonel 51
Disarmament 162–3, 273–4

Disraeli, B.   4, 16, 19, 231, 289, 366
Doenitz, Admiral Karl G.   308, 324
Dollfuss, E.   284, 372
Donnelly, Desmond   403
Donovan Report on Trades
    Unions   405, 511
Dorman-Smith, Sir R., Governor of Burma
    470
Douglas, Lew, US Ambassador to London
    432
Douhet, Colonel Giulio   309
Dowding, Air Marshal Hugh   314
Dresden Air Raids   306, 326, 340
Driberg, Tom   347
Drummond, Sir Ernest   160
Duffy, G. G.   202
Duke, H. E.   174
Dulles, John Foster   462, 476, 477, 503
Dunkirk, Evacuation from   311–12, 354
Dunkirk, Treaty of   430, 456
Dyarchy   185
Dyer, General R. E. H.   187–8

E
Easter Rising, 1916   87, 171–4
Eastern Front (W. War I)   65, 73
    World War II   318, 419
Eatwell, Roger   415
Economic Advisory Council, 1929
    210, 216, 257
Economic Affairs, Department of   402
Economist   239, 395
Ede, Chuter   357
Eden, Anthony (later Lord Avon)   11,
    273, 275
    Foreign Secretary, 1935–38   269, 270,
        278–80, 283–4, 299
    1940–45   318, 344
    1951–55   420, 422, 435–7
    Prime Minister, 1955–57   396–7, 421
    and Suez crisis   475–81, 500–5
    on Bevin   422
Education
    Balfour Act, 1902   4
    Fisher Act, 1918   96, 100, 107
    Butler Act, 1944   347, 357, 374
    Fleming Report, 1944   357, 374
    Comprehensive schools   391, 407, 410,
        511
    Robbins Report on Higher
        Education   406–7, 509
    Open University, 1969   406–7, 511
Edward VII   9, 10
Edward VIII   9, 200, 254, 305
Edwards, Alfred   387
Edwards, Ebby   386
Egypt   21–2, 71–2, 81–2, 192–3, 315–16,
    321–2, 475–81, 500–5
Eight Hours Act, 1927   134
Eisenhower, Dwight D.   320, 327–30,
    477, 503
El Alamein, Battle of   322, 339, 462
Elections, see General Elections

Electoral Reform   14, 94–5, 102, 217,
    499
Elizabeth II   397, 494, 507
Eliott, Walter   297
Ellis, John   335
Emergency Powers Acts   117, 133, 348
Empire Air Training Plan   200
Employment Act, 1930   215
Enigma (German ciphering machine)
    308, 316, 318, 324
Enosis   482
Entente, Anglo-French   41–4, 59, 106, 500
Entente, Anglo-Russian   44, 106
Environment:
    Barlow Report, 1940   357–8, 373
    Scott Committee   358
    Uthwatt Committee   358, 374
    Town and Country Planning Acts,
        1944, 1947   358
    Distribution of Industry Act, 1946   392
    New Towns Act, 1946   392–3
    National Parks and Access to
        Countryside Act, 1949   392–3
EOKA   482
Equal Pay   363
Erzberger, Mathias   63
European Communities Act   454, 513
European Economic Community
    (Common Market)   395
    Creation of   442–6, 509
    British entry into   446–56, 513
    Effect on Commonwealth   485, 495
European Free Trade Area   401, 448,
    509
European Monetary System   500
European Reconstruction Fund   274
Evacuees   361
Evans, Lincoln   387
Evian Conference on Jewish Problem,
    1938   197
Exchange Equalisation Account   242,
    248, 371
Exchange Rates   113, 137–8, 210–11,
    218–21, 225–6, 376, 382, 401–2, 410
External Relations Act (Ireland)   183,
    372

F
Fabian Society   17, 24, 101, 156, 380
Falkland Islands, Invasion of   490–1, 504
Falkland Islands, Battle of   83, 514
Family Allowances   352, 355, 374
Farouk, King of Egypt   475
Fascism   23, 216, 250, 252–4, 264–6,
    281–2, 372
Faulkner, Brian   492
Fay, S. B.   57
Fearless, HMS, Talks on Rhodesia   489,
    512
Federal Reserve Board (USA)   221
Feetham, Judge   180
Feiling, K.   243, 298–9
Feisal, I., King of Iraq   193–4

Festubert, Battle of   71, 73
Fianna Fail   183
Fighter Command   278, 314
Fischer, F.   57, 60
Fisher, H. A. L.   96
Fisher, J. R.   180
Fisher, Admiral Sir John   39, 56, 86
Fisher, Sir Warren   270
Fitt, Gerry (later Lord Fitt)   492
Five Year Plans, Soviet   267
Flandin, P.   280
Flers, Battle of   69
Foch, Marshal F. F.   72, 77
Foot, Sir Hugh   482
Foot, Michael   394, 405, 411, 413
For Socialism and Peace, 1934   249
Forster, E. M.   170
Four Courts (Dublin)   173, 180
Fourteen Points, Wilson's   142–3, 148,
    166, 306
Franco, General F.   250, 252, 281–2
Franz Ferdinand, Archduke   49, 51–2
Franz Joseph, Emperor   33
Fraser, General D.   293, 311, 317
Fraser, T. G   195
Frederick, III, Emperor   42
Freeman, John   394
Free French   312
Free market economics   4, 112, 410
Free trade   112, 123, 210–12
    Abandonment of   242–4, 248
French, Sir John (later Lord)   45, 72–3,
    86, 97, 174–5
Freyberg, General B.   308, 316
Friedman, Milton   257, 376
Front for the Liberation of South
    Yemen   482
Fuad I, Sultan of Turkey   154, 184, 193
Fuller, J. F. C.   306, 335–6
Fulton Report on Civil Service   406,
    512
Fulton Speech, Churchill's, 1946
    428–9, 507

G
Gaelic League   171
Gaitskell, Hugh, Chancellor of Exchequer
    394–5
    Labour leader   398—9
    Views on socialism   414
    Views on EEC   450
    and Suez crisis   502
Gallagher, William (Communist M.P.)
    250
Gallipoli Campaign   71, 78–80, 86–7,
    97–8, 107, 141, 151, 154
Gandhi, M. K., Career to 1939   170,
    185–91
    1939–48   462–8, 507
Gasperi, Alcide de   443
Gaulle, General Charles de   312, 443,
    449–51
Gazier, A.   478, 503

Geddes, Sir Auckland   91
Geddes, Sir Eric   92, 115–16, 219
Geddes Axe   116, 205
General Elections   14
  Charts   120, 377
  1906   106
  Coupon Election, December
    1918   107, 114–15
  November 1922   120, 205
  December 1923   120, 123, 206
  October 1924   127, 206
  May 1929   207, 212
  October 1931   227–8, 371
  November 1935   242, 250, 372
  July 1945   366–8, 374
  February 1950   393, 508
  October 1951   394–5, 508
  May 1955   396, 509
  October 1959   396, 510
  May 1964   400, 511
  March 1966   400, 511
  June 1970   410, 451, 512
  February 1974   410, 513
  October 1974   411
  April 1979   412, 514
  May 1983   499
General Strike, 1926   112, 128–34, 157,
  159, 205, 216
Geneva Conference on Germany,
  1955   437, 509
Geneva Conference on Indo-China, 1954
  435, 509
Geneva Protocol   161, 205
Genoa, Conference at   153, 204
George V   8–9, 89, 97, 121, 123–4,
  177–8, 199–200, 213, 221–2, 228
George VI   200, 365, 394, 494
Gilbert, M.   195, 270, 299–300
Gladstone, Lord   122
Gladstone, William E.   9, 16, 18, 193
Glubb, Sir John   471, 476, 509
Goering, Hermann   283–4, 308, 313–14
Gokhale, G. K.   185
Gold Coast (Ghana)   21, 461, 483–5
Gold Standard, Defined   3
  Effects of W. War I on   108
  British return to   111–13, 128, 135–8,
    206, 259
  and 1929–31 crisis   218–20
  Britain leaves   225–6
  Effects   242, 244, 248
  International departure from   274
Good Soldier Schweik, The   32
Gordon-Walker, P. C.   420
Gort, Lord   311–12
Gott, R.   270, 299–300
Gough, Brigadier, later General,
  Hubert   22, 77, 98
Government of India Act, 1935
  190–1, 372
Government of Ireland Act, 1920   176,
  180, 205
Graf Spee   309–10, 323

Graham, W.   221
Grandi, D.   275
Graves, Robert,   271
Graziani, Marshal   316
Greenwood, Arthur   217, 221, 297,
  342–3, 346, 354, 421
Greenwood, Walter   234
Gregory, Judge Holman   215
Gregory, Professor   210
Grenfell, Julian   96–7
Grey, Sir Edward   24, 40, 41–56
  passim   59–60, 66, 89, 269
Griffith, Arthur   175–80
Griffiths, James   416
Grivas, Colonel   482
Guest, F. E.   114
Guillebaud Committee on the National
  Health Service   390
Gurney, Ivor   97

H
Hacha, President   291
Haganah   471
Haig, General Sir Douglas   69, 72–7,
  97–9
Hailie Selassie, Emperor   275–7
Hailsham, Lord (formerly Sir D. Hogg)
  242
Hailsham, Lord (formerly Quintin)   398,
  404, 409
Haldane, Lord   24, 44, 68, 87
Halifax, Lord (*see* Lord Irwin), Foreign
  Secretary   269–70, 283–98,
  299–300, 341
  and leadership   342–3
  Ambassador to USA   343
Hamilton, General Sir Ian   78–9
Hankey, Maurice (later Lord)   87–9,
  126–7, 161–2, 228, 270, 341
Hannington, W.   251–2
Harcourt, L.   55
Harcourt, Sir W.   229
Hardie, Keir   17–18
Harding, Warren G. (US President)   163
Hardinge, Sir Arthur   41
Harington, General Sir C.   154
Harmsworth, Lord   86
Harrington, W.   361
Harris, Air Marshal Sir A. T.   309,
  325–7, 336–7, 339
Harris, K.   421
Hart, Captain Liddell   99
Hartington, Marquess of   347
Hartshorn, Vernon   188
Hartwig, Baron   47
Harvey, Sir E.   219, 221–2
Hastings, M.   306, 326–7, 336–7
Hastings, Sir Patrick   123
Hatch, J.   484
Hayes, P.   42, 162
Hazlehurst, C.   45
Healey, Denis   408, 441, 453
Heath, Edward R. G., elected leader   398

Prime Minister   403, 409–11, 441–2
  and EEC   449, 451–4, 489, 492
Heathcote-Amery, Derek   401
Heffer, Eric   455
Heligoland Bight, Battle of   83
Henderson, Arthur   87–8, 93, 114, 126,
  213, 221, 231, 249, 269, 273
Henderson, Sir Neville   270, 283, 287,
  291, 297–8
Henderson, Commander R. C. H.   85
Henlein, K.   285–7, 300
Herriot, E.   153
Herzog, General   200
Hill, C.   250
Hindenburg Line   71, 77
Hipper, Admiral F. von   83
Hirohito, Emperor   263
Hiroshima   306, 334–5, 374
Hitler, Adolf   153, 252, 341, 343
  Foreign policy of   265–6, 273–5,
    278–91, 294–8, 298–302
  and W. War II   304–31, 336
Hoare, Sir Samuel (later Lord
  Templewood)
  and India   190–1
  and 1931 crisis   221, 223
  Foreign Secretary   269–70, 276–7,
    280, 283, 287, 341
Hood, HMS   323
Hoare-Laval Plan   275–7
Hobsbawm, E. J.   250
Hobson, J. A.   24
Hodge, J.   93
Holstein, Friedrich von   36
Holtzendorff, Admiral von   84
Home, Lord (also Sir Alec Douglas-
  Home)   14, 398, 405, 411, 420, 479,
  487, 489
Home Guard   307, 360
Hong Kong   21, 333, 339, 490
Hoover, Herbert (US President)   218–19
Hope-Simpson, Sir J.   197
Hopkinson, Henry   482
Hore-Belisha, Leslie   292, 297, 300,
  341, 373
Hossbach Memorandum   284
'Hotline' agreement   440
Hotzendorff, General Conrad von,   39,
  49, 54
House, Colonel E.   48, 144
Housing   96, 239, 361–2, 390
  Addison's Act, 1919   116
  Chamberlain's Act, 1923   123
  Wheatley's Act, 1924   126
  Greenwood's Act, 1930   217
Howard, A.   402
Howard, Michael   40, 272, 307
Howe, Sir Geoffrey   409
Hume, Allan Octavian (founder of
  Indian Congress Party)   185
Hunter Enquiry (into Amritsar Massacre)
  188
Hurricane, Hawker   314

Hussein, Sherif of Mecca 141, 195–6
Hussein, King of Transjordan 476
Hyndley, Lord 386
Hyndman, H. M. 17

I

Immigration, Control of 407–8, 494–5,
    499–500, 511
Imperial Conferences 22, 182, 200,
    494–6
Imperial Defence League 190
Import Duties Act, 1932 243–4, 248,
    371
Incitement to Disaffection Act,
    1934 252
Income Tax 93, 242, 352–3, 362
Independent Labour Party 17–18, 214,
    249
India 20, 184–91, 333–4, 463–70
India Independence Act, 1947 467–8
Industrial Expansion Act, 1968 404
Industrial Relations Act, 1971 410, 511
Industrial Reorganisation
    Corporation 376, 404
Inflation 93, 108, 153, 227–8, 234, 352,
    362, 375–6, 380, 383, 395, 400–1,
    408–10
Inglis, Dr. Elsie 95
Inskip, Sir T. 278
International Brigades 281–2
Invergordon Mutiny 225, 371
Iran 474–5
Iraq 193–4, 476
Ireland 21–2, 28–9, 171–84, 491–3
Irgun zwei lumi 471
Irish Civil War 178–80
Irish Convention, 1917 107, 175
Irish Nationalist Party 18–19
Irish Nationality and Citizenship Act 183
Irish Republican Army 177–84, 492
Irish Republican Brotherhood 171–2
Irish Treaty, 1921 171, 177–80, 201–3,
    205
Irish Volunteers 22, 28, 171–2, 174, 178
Iron Curtain 428, 507
Iron and Steel Industry 1, 111, 237,
    385, 387, 403
Ironside, Field-Marshal W. E. 344
Irwin, Lord (see Lord Halifax) 188–9, 191
Isaacs, Sir Isaac 199
Ismay, General Sir H. 345
Israel, (see Palestine) 473–4, 477–81,
    500–5, 507
Isvestia, 142
Isvolski, A. 44, 46
Italian Campaign, W. War II 322–3
ITMA 355, 360
Ivanov, Captain 398

J

Jacob, Lt.-General Sir Ian 345
Jagow, Gottlieb von 49, 53–4, 60
Jaksch, Wenzel 300

Jallianwalla Bagh (Amritsar) 187
Jameson Raid 41
Jarrow Crusade 252, 372
Jay, Douglas 382
Jebb, Gladwyn 431
Jellicoe, Admiral of the Fleet Sir
    John 76, 82–5
Jenkins, Roy 402, 407, 450, 453–4
Jennings, Sir Ivor 11
Jerrold, Douglas 387
Jinnah, Mohammed Ali 191, 464–9
Joffre, General J. J. C. 49
Johnson Act, 1934 317
Johnson, Paul 29
Johnston, T. 221
Joint Chiefs of Staff Committee 319
Joint Production Committees 364
Jolly George 158
Jones, Joseph M. 456–9
Jones, Tom 123, 201–3, 210, 228
Jowitt, Sir William 354
Joynson-Hicks, Sir W. 127
Jutland, Battle of 83–4, 87

K

Kahn, R. F. 255
Kaunda, Kenneth 484, 487
Kedourie, Elie 198
Keeler, Christine 397
Kellogg, Frank B. 163
Kellogg-Briand Pact 163, 207, 273
Kemal, Mustafa 154
Kennan, George 431, 457–8
Kennedy, John F. (President of USA)
    439–40, 449
Kennedy, P. M. 40, 160, 167, 419
Kennedy, Robert 440
Kenya 21, 483–6, 508, 511
Kenyatta, Jomo 462, 484, 486
Kerensky, Alexander 71, 155, 281
Kesselring, Albert G. 323
Kettle, Arnold 250
Keyes, Sir Roger 342
Keynes, J. M. on return to gold
    standard 137–8
    on Treaty of Versailles 145, 148,
        164–7
    on unemployment 210–11, 220, 248
    The *General Theory* 254–7, 257–60,
        372
    on war finance 352
    on White Paper, 1944 358–9
    post-1945 economic policy 376, 381,
        383, 408–9, 415
Kilmuir, Lord 479
King, Joseph 86
King, Mackenzie 199–200
Kipling, Rudyard 188
Kitchener, Field-Marshal Lord 23, 66–8,
    72, 74, 86–7, 90, 92, 97
Kitzinger, Uwe 448
Kleist, von 301
Kluck, A. von 73

Kolchak, Admiral A. 157
Kordt, Theo 287
Korean War 382, 394, 434, 508
Kornilov, General L. R. 155
Kruger, President 41
Khruschev, N. 437–40

L

Labouchère, Henry 9
Labour Party, origins 17–18
    in W. War I 86, 93–4, 99–102
    1918–29 114–15, 118, 122, 124–7
    1929–31 209–32
    1931–39 248–50
    in W. War II 341–2, 346–8, 358–60,
        364, 366–7
    1945–80 Domestic Policy 377–395,
            398–400, 401–7, 410–12
        Foreign Policy 428–35,
            441, 450–1, 453–5
Lahore Conference, 1929 189
Land Annuities 183
Land Utilisation Bill, 1931 216
Lansbury, George 213, 221, 228, 249
Lansdowne, Lord 40, 91, 175
Laski, Harold 249, 367, 426
Lausanne Conferences, 1922–23 155,
    205
    1932 273–4, 371
Lausanne, Treaty of 155, 159, 206
Laval, P. 276–7, 280
Lawrence, D. H. 5
Lawrence, T. E. 81
League of Nations 143–4, 147–50,
    160–2, 167, 196, 199, 249, 266–7,
    271–7, 284–5, 425
Leathers, Lord 345
Le Cateau, Battle of 71, 73
Lee, Jennie 394
Lee Kwan Yew 490
Lees-Smith, H. B. 221, 346
Lemass, Sean 491
Lend-Lease 317–18, 353, 381–2, 507
Lenin, V. I. 155–7, 267, 287
Le Quex, W. 40
Lever, Harold 453–4
Lennox-Boyd, Alan 190
Lewin, R. 308, 346
Liberal Party
    before 1914 11, 16–17
    effects of World War I on 86–9,
        101–2
    1918–29 114–15, 118–22
    1929–31 212–14, 217, 221, 224,
        227–8
    1931–45 241–2, 248, 341
    post-1945 337–8, 394–5, 400, 409–12,
        499
Lichnowsky, Prince 45, 49, 53–4, 60
Life Peerages Act, 1958 405
Linlithgow, Lord 191, 295
Litvinov, M. 286, 295

Lloyd, Selwyn 397, 401, 420
and Suez crisis 476–81, 500–5
Lloyd George, David, before 1914 4, 13, 15, 26, 44, 48
in World War I 70, 75–6, 84–5, 87–96, 98–9
Prime Minister, 1918–22 (Home Affairs) 113–19 (Foreign) 144–50, 151–9, 164–7
Empire and Ireland 175–80, 193–5, 199, 201–3
post-1922 122–3, 136, 210–11, 213–14, 217, 228, 248, 269–70, 305, 341–3, 345, 388, 391, 491
Local Government Act, 1929 136, 207
Locarno Conference, 1925 161–2, 206, 372
Locarno, Treaties of 161–3
Lomé Convention, 1975 455, 495
London Agreement with Eire, 1938 183–4
London Conference on Suez Canal, 1956 477–8
London Passenger Transport Board 247, 384
London, Secret Treaty of, 1915 141, 145
Londonderry, Lady 213
Londonderry, Violence in 1972 492, 513
Long, Walter 175
Loos, Battle of 71, 73
Los Alamos 334
Lothian, Lord 271, 280
Lublin Government in Poland 425
Ludendorff, General E. 77, 80, 144
Lusitania 84
Lucknow Pact, 1916 184
Luftwaffe 313–4, 329, 336
Lunn, Arnold 281
Lutz, R. H. 57
Luxemburg Agreement, 1966 446
Lvov, Prince 155
Lynch, Liam 180
Lyons, F. S. L. 178
Lyttleton, Oliver 344–5, 354
Lytton Commission 274, 371

M
MacArthur, General Douglas 434
MacDonald, J. Ramsay 8, 14
and Liberal Party 17
and World War I 56, 86, 93, 122
Party leader and Prime Minister, 1922–29 122–7, 153, 156, 158–9, 160
Prime Minister, 1929–31 212–28, 228–32
1931–35 234, 241–2, 249–50, 269, 273–5, 412, 455
MacDonald, Malcolm 183, 198, 223, 231–2

McKenna, Reginald 93, 112, 120–1
McKenna Duties 112
Mack Smith, Dennis 264
Maclay, Sir John 92
MacLean, Donald 250
MacLean, Sir Donald 221, 242, 244
MacLeod, Ian 390, 398, 486
MacMahon Act (Congress), 1946 429
MacMahon, Sir Henry 141, 195
Macmillan, Harold (later Lord Stockton) 11, 16
and Unemployment 256–7, 259, 372
and Housing 390, 396
Prime Minister, 1957–63 395, 397–8, 401, 404–6
and Cold War 439–41
and EEC 421, 448–51
and Suez 479–80
and Cyprus 482
and Africa 484–9, 495
MacMunn, General 193
MacNeil, Eoin 172–3, 181
MacQuisten Bill 128
Maginot Line 266, 280
Maisky, Ivan 318
Makarios, Archbishop 462, 482, 509
Malan, Dr. D. 200
Malaya, Malay states 21, 333, 489, 509
Malaysia, Federation of 489–90, 511
Malta 21, 315, 483, 511
Manchuria, Invasion of, 1931 274, 371
Margesson, D. R. 342
Marne, Battle of 73
Marquand, D. 124, 220
Marquand, Hilary 394
Marshall Aid, Marshall Plan 382, 431, 443
Russian refusal of 456–9
Marshall, George C. 431, 456–8
Marwick, Arthur 90, 99–103
Marx, Karl 17, 231
Marxism
Influence on intellectuals 250
post-1945 384, 412, 414–15, 423–4, 462
Masterman, Charles 17
Masurian Lakes, Battle of 65
Matapan, Battle of 316, 339
Mau mau rebellion 476, 486
Maude, General F. S. 81
Maudling, Reginald 398, 401
Maurice, General F. D. 89, 114
Maurice Debate 89, 114
Max, Prince of Baden 144
Maxton, James 210, 214
Maxwell, General Sir J. 173–4
May, Sir George, Committee headed by 210, 219–20
Maybury, Sir Henry 216
Mayhew, Christopher 441
Mayne, Richard 446
Mayo, Lord 20
Meade, James 254, 258, 358

Means Test 245–6, 249, 251, 413
Medical Planning Commission 356
Medlicott, W. N. 280
Melba, Nelly 136
Melbourne, Lord 8
Mesopotamian Campaign 71, 81, 193
Messina Conference, 1955 445, 448
Messines, Battle of 71
Metternich, Prince 35
Miall, Leonard 431
Middlebrook, M. 49
Middlemas, K. and Barnes, J. 119, 161
Milner, Lord 23–4, 89, 117–18, 170
Millward, A. S. 108
Miners Federation of Great Britain 128–35
Moggridge, D. E. 137
Mollet, Guy 477–9
Molotov, V. M. 295, 318, 427, 432, 435, 456, 458–9
Molteno, P. A. 86
Moltke, General Helmuth von 38–9, 44, 47, 49, 54
Monckton, Sir Walter 396, 487
Monetarism 257, 376, 401, 416
Monnet, Jean 442, 443, 446
Monopolies and Restrictive Practices Commission 393
Monro, General Sir Charles 79
Mons, Battle of 71, 73
Montagu, C. E. 45
Montagu, Edwin 117, 142, 184–5, 191
Montagu-Chelmsford (Montford) Reforms 106, 184–5, 187–8
Monte Cassino 323
Montgomery, A. E. 154
Montgomery, Field-Marshal Sir B. 321–2, 327–31, 334
Moore v. the Attorney General of the Irish Free State, 1932 199
Moore-Brabazon, J. T. C. 365
Moran, Lord 368, 390
Morel, E. D. 56
Morgan, Lieut.-General F. 327
Morgan, K. O. 115, 117, 379, 415–16
Morgan, M. C. 57
Morley, John (later Viscount) 11, 20, 24, 55, 86
Morley-Minto Reforms 24, 105
Morning Post 181, 188
Moroccan crises, 1905, 1911 42–4, 104
Morrell, Philip 86
Morris, James (later Jan) 19, 25, 464
Morris, William (later Lord Nuffield) 252
Morris Committee 215
Morrison, Herbert, and 1931 crisis 221
and World War II 345, 354
and Labour Governments, 1945–51 380, 384, 386, 393–4, 416, 420–1, 474–5, 484
Morton, Sir Desmond 345
Mosley Memorandum 215–16

Mosley, Sir Oswald 210–11, 213, 215–16, 252–4
Mountbatten, Lord Louis (later Earl) 466–9, 493
Mowat, C. L. 111–12, 235
Mulberry Harbours 328, 345
Munich Agreement, 1938 289, 291, 293–4, 372
Debate on 289–90, 298–302
Munitions Act, 1915 91, 105
Murray, General 81
Murray, Professor Gilbert 160
Muslim League 184, 191, 464–7
Mussadiq, Dr. M. 474–5
Mussolini, Benito 252, 263, 266, 268–9, 281–2, 284, 288, 296–7
and Abyssinia 275–7
and World War II 304, 318, 322

N
Nasser, Colonel G. A. 475–81, 500–5
National Asssistance 388, 391
National Board for Prices and Incomes 403, 511
National Coalition Governments, formation of
1915 86, 106
1916 87–9, 106
1918 106, 114–15
1931 221–4, 228–32, 371
1940 341–3, 373
National Debt, in 1918 93
Effects of 109, 113, 139
Reduction in burden of 219, 243
after World War II 352
National Economic Development Council 376, 404, 509
National Econcomy Bill, 1931 225
National Government, 1931–39, Policies of 241–8
National Electricity Grid 110, 126, 136, 384
National Enterprise Board 410–11, 513
National Health Service, Suggested 249, 355–6, 359
Inauguration of 388–90
National Industrial Conference, 1919 117
National Insurance: Legislation, 1911 5, 96
1920 116
1934 245
1946 388, 391, 507
(see also Beveridge Report, Means Test, Unemployment)
National Liberation Front (Aden) 482
National Savings Movement 352
National Socialist (Nazi) Party 270, 284, 286, 299, 305, 317, 335–6, 423, 463
Nationalisation, Labour commitment to 94, 249, 384
Arguments over 391, 412–16
Progress of 247, 384–7, 403–4, 410–11

Individual industries:
aircraft and shipbuilding 410, 498
cable and wireless 385
civil aviation 247, 385
coal 92, 117, 129, 135, 247, 385–6
electricity 136, 385
gas 387
iron and steel 387, 403
transport 92, 385, 387, 403
Naval Defence Act, 1889 41
Nazi–Soviet Pact, 1939 295–6, 365, 373
Neguib, General M. 475
Nehru, Jawaharlal 185, 188–91, 434, 463–8
Neurath, K. von 284
Neuilly, Treaty of 150, 205
Neutrality Acts (US) 267, 317–18
Neuve Chapelle, Battle of 71, 73
Newall, Air Chief Marshall Sir C. 344–5
Newbolt, Henry 25
New Deal 246
New Party 216, 252
News Chronicle 367
New Zealand 19, 199–200, 452–3
Nicholas I, Tsar 34
Nicholas II, Tsar 47, 53–4, 155
Nicholson, Sir Arthur 41, 44
Nicolson, Harold 124, 143, 164–5, 297, 342
Niemeyer, Sir Otto 137
Nigeria 21, 23, 483, 485, 510
Nivelle, General R. 72, 75
Nkomo, Joshua 484
Nkrumah, Kwame 484, 485
No Independence before Majority African Rule (NIBMAR) 488–9
Norman, Montagu 135
Normandy Landings, see Operation Overlord
North, Admiral Sir, D. 344
North African Campaigns, World War II 308, 315–17, 321–2
North Atlantic Shipping Act 245, 372
North Atlantic Treaty Organisation (NATO) 399, 430
Creation of 432–3
Subsequent developments 434–7, 441
German admission to 436–7
and Cuba crisis 439–40
Northcliffe, Lord 166
Northedge, Professor F. S. 443, 496
Norwegian campaign, 1940 310–11, 338, 341–2
Norwood Committee on examinations 357
Nuclear Test Ban Treaty, 1963 440
Nuclear weapons, Use of in World War II 334, 474
British development of 429–30, 441
Polaris and Cruise Missiles 441, 510
Nuri-es-Said (Iraqi politician) 502
Nutting, A. 476, 500–4
Nye Committee, 1935 (US) 267

Nyasaland (Malawi) 486–7, 511
Nyerere, Julius 484

O
Oath of Allegiance (Ireland) 177–8, 183
O'Brien, William 173
O'Connor, Rory 178, 180
O'Dwyer, Sir Michael 187–8
Offences against the State Bill (Ireland) 184
O'Higgins, Kevin 180
O'Neil, Terence 491
Operation BARBAROSSA 314, 318
Operation BATTLEAXE 316, 320
Operation BOLERO 319
Operation CRUSADER 321
Operation DIADEM 323
Operation GOODWOOD 330
Operation HUSKY 320, 322
Operation MARKET GARDEN 330–1
Operation MENACE 312
Operation OVERLORD 320, 327–30, 340
Operation SEALION 313–14
Operation SICHELSCHNITT 311
Operation TORCH 320, 322, 339
Operation VERITABLE 331, 340
Oran 312, 339
Organisation for European Cooperation and Development, (OECD) 443
Organisation for European Economic Cooperation, (OEEC) 432–3, 448, 507
Orlando, V. 145
Orwell, George 170, 234, 238–9, 246, 281, 365, 500
Ottawa Conference, 1932 242, 244, 371
Ottoman Empire, see Turkey
Owen, David 420
Owen, Wilfred 97, 271
Oxford Union Debate, 1933 271

P
Pact of London, 1914 63
Paget, Sir Arthur 22
Painlevé, Paul F. 76
Paléologue, M. 49, 63
Palestine, in W. War I 71–2, 81, 141–2
1919–39 195–8
post-1945 471–4
Palmer's Shipyard, Jarrow 236
Pankhurst, Mrs. Emmeline 14, 94–5
Paris Peace Conference, 1919 145–50, 164–7, 169, 205
Paris Negotiations over Marshall Aid, 1947 458–9
Paris 'Summit', 1960 438, 448
Parliament Acts, 1911 13, 25
1949 387, 392, 508
Parmoor, Lord 126, 221
Parnell, Charles Stuart 18

Pasic, N., Prime Minister of Serbia 51
Passchendaele, Battle of 69, 71, 76–7, 98–9
Pasternak, Boris 424
Pathet Lao 435
Peace Ballot, 1934–35 271, 372
Pearce, Lord 489, 513
Pearl Harbour 305, 318, 332
Pearse, Padraic 171–4
Pearse, William 174
Peden, G. C. 278
Peel Commission on Palestine, 1937–38 197–8, 372
Peel, Lord 197
Peel, Sir Robert 197
Pelling, Henry 384
Penguin Specials 365
Pensions, Old Age 5
  Widows' and Orphans' 135
  and reparations 148
  Inadequacy of 391
Percival, General A. E. 333
Perth, Lord 270, 288
Pétain, Marshal P. 77, 312
Pethwick-Lawrence, Lord 465
Philby, Kim 250
Phillips, Sir Frederick 256
Picot, Georges 142, 151, 195
Pilgrim Trust 240, 254
Pineau, C. 479, 500–3
Pitt, William (the Younger) 10
Pius XII, Pope 281
Plaid Cymru 378
Pleven Plan for European Army 436, 446, 508
Plowden, Sir Edward 387
Plunkett, Count 174
Plunkett, Joseph 174
PLUTO 328
Poincaré, Raymond 49, 53, 153
Pointblank directive on strategic bombing 326
Polaris, see Nuclear weapons
Poland, after W. War I 143, 147, 150
  War with Russia 157–8
  and Locarno treaties 161
  and causes of W. War II 265, 294–8
  post-war 424–7
Political and Economic Planning 254
Pollard, S. F. 111, 137–8, 235, 248, 254, 257, 350, 382
Pompidou, Georges 451
Ponsonby, Arthur 56, 122
Portal, Sir Charles 326–7, 345
Postgate, R. 26
Potsdam Conference, 1945 334, 367, 374, 419, 425–7, 436
Pound, Admiral of the Fleet Sir Dudley 344–5
Poverty, A Study of Town Life, 6, 240
Powell, Enoch 398, 401, 405, 407–8
Pravda 429, 437
Priestley, J. B. 354, 364

Prince of Wales, HMS 323, 332
Princip, Gabriel 51
Pritt, D. N. 414–15
Privatisation 498
Profumo, John 397–8
Proportional Representation 212, 217, 266, 378, 499
Protection 127, 211, 243–4, 259, 381, 456
Prothero, Sir George 91
Public Assistance Committees 136, 245
Public Expenditure, in W. War I 92–3, 109
  1919–39 113, 116, 211, 214–16, 219–21, 225–6, 242–4
  Keynesian approach to 254–60
  in W. War II 352
  post-1945 375–6, 383, 408–9
Public Order Act, 1936 253, 372
Public Works Unemployment Grants Committee 113
Pugh, Alan 219
Pugh, Arthur 130
Pugh, Martin 160–2, 120
Punch 63

Q

Quebec Agreement, 1943 334, 429
Quebec Conferences: Quadrant, 1943 319–20, 374
  Octagon, 1944 319, 321, 374

R

Race Relations Act, 1965 407
Raczynski, Count E., Polish Ambassador 297
RADAR 293, 307, 314
Radcliffe, Sir Cyril 467
Radcliffe Report, 1959 509
Ramsay, Vice-Admiral B. 312
Rapacki, Adam (Plan) 437
Rapallo, Treaty of, 1922 153, 205
Rationing, in W. War I 92, 106
  in W. War II 352–3, 362–3, 364
  after 1945 383, 400
Read, Herbert 97
Reading, Lord 223, 269
Reconstruction, Plans for in W. War I 96
  in W. War II 354–5
Redmond, John 86, 171, 174–5
Referendums: on EEC, 1975 354–5, 513
  on devolution for Scotland and Wales, 1979 411–12, 514
  on Gibraltar 483
Reinsurance treaty, 1887 36
Reith, Sir John (later Lord) 136, 346, 358
Remilitarisation of Rhineland, 1936 266, 278–80, 372, 501
Rendell, George 198
Reparations, after W. War I 102, 143–50, 151–4, 164–7, 209, 218, 273–4

  after W. War II 424–5, 427
Repington, Colonel C. 86
Representation of the People Acts, 1918 106
  1948 392, 507
Repulse, HMS 332–3
Resistance, German to Hitler 287, 306
Reynaud, Paul 312
Rhodes, Cecil 25, 42, 170
Rhodesia, N. (Zambia) 21, 486–7, 511
Rhodesia, S. (Zimbabwe) 21, 486–9, 511
Rhondda, Lord 92
Ribbentrop, J. von 287, 295–6
Ridley, Nicholas 491
Riga, treaty of, 1921 158
Rippon, G. 453
Ritchie, General Sir N. 321
Ritter, G. 306
Robbins Commission, see Education
Robeck, Admiral Sir J. M. de 79
Roberts, G. H. 115
Roberts, Field Marshal Lord 22
Robertson, General Sir Brian 433
Robertson, Field Marshal Sir W. 97
Rock, W. R. 270, 301–2
Rolls Royce 363, 410
Rome, Treaty of, 1957 443, 445–6, 448, 454, 509
Rommel, General E. 308, 316–17, 321–2, 330
Roosevelt, F. D. (US President) 197
  and pre-war diplomacy 267–8, 274, 284
  and W. War II 306, 317–20, 332, 343
  and Soviet Union 425
  and British Empire 462
Rose, K. 222
Rosebery, Lord 20, 24
Roskill, S. W. 86–7
Ross, William 455
Rossa, O'Donovan 171
Rothermere, Lord 211, 252–3
Round Table Talks (India), 1930–31 189–90
Rowntree, Seebohm 6, 240
Rowlatt Bills (India) 187, 205
Royal Air Force 170, 278, 293, 309, 313–14, 324–7, 335–7, 441
Royal Navy 41–2, 45, 57–8, 82–5, 162–3, 309–11, 316, 323–4
Royal Oak, HMS, Sinking of 310, 341
Ruhr, French occupation of 128, 153
Rumbold, Sir Horace 299
Runciman, W. (later Lord) 242, 286, 287, 300
Runstedt, Field-Marshall G. von 311
Rusk, Dean 411

S

Sackville-West, V. 145
Safeguarding of Industries Act, 1921 112, 205
St. Germain, Treaty of, 1919 150, 205

Salerno, Landings at 322, 338
Salisbury, 3rd Marquess of (1830–1903)
    11, 12, 13, 40–1
Salisbury, 4th Marquess of (1861–1947)
    121, 336
Salonika, in W. War I 71, 80, 97
Samuel Commission, 1925–26 129–30,
    206
Samuel, Herbert (later Lord) 11, 122,
    129–30, 134, 195, 221–3, 227, 242–4
Samuel Memorandum 134
San Remo Conference, 1920 151, 195
Sanctions, against Italy 249, 275–7, 284
    against Japan 332
    against Rhodesia 488–9
Sanders, Liman von 47–8
Sandys, Duncan 354, 368
Sanjurjo, General, J. S. 281
Sankey Commission 117, 205, 385
Sankey, Sir John (later Lord) 117, 221,
    223, 228, 242
Sarajevo 51–2
Sassoon, Siegfried 97, 271
Sazonoff, Sergei 49, 53–4
Scanlon, Hugh (later Lord) 405
Scapa Flow 83, 87, 149
Scheer, Admiral R. 83
Schlieffen, Count A. von 38
Schlieffen Plan 38, 46, 53–5, 64–5, 72–3,
    311
School leaving age, Raising of 215,
    217, 357, 391
    Postponed, 1969 402
Schuman, Robert 442
    Plan 443–4, 447, 456
Schuschnigg, K. von 285
Scott Committee, see Environment
Scott, C. P. 45
Scott, David 490
Scottish National Party 377–8, 411
Selbourne, Lord 41
Selective Employment Tax 376
Severn Barrage, Suggested 126
Sèvres, Treaty of, 1920 150–1, 154,
    205
Seyss-Inquart, A. 285
Shaftesbury, Lord 4, 16
Shaw, G. B. 17, 24
Shaw Commission on Palestine, 1929 197
Shaw, T. 221
Sheriff, R. C. 271
Sherwood, Miss 187
Shinwell, E. (later Lord) 223, 347, 386,
    416, 474
Shipbuilding Industry 2–3, 109–11,
    236–7, 245
Shipping Contol Committee 92
Shore, Peter 402, 455
Sicily, Invasion of 322
Silkin, John 455
Silver Jubilee, 1935 254
Simon, Sir John, and W. War I 55
    and General Strike 133

and foreign affairs 269–70, 273, 275,
    283, 287, 297
Simon Commission on India 188, 206,
    208
Simpson, Mrs 9, 200
Sinclair, Sir Archibald 326, 336, 341
Singapore 126, 263, 333, 339, 374,
    489–90
Sinn Fein 95, 174–80, 201–3
Skidelsky, Robert 209, 258
Skoda Armaments Works 293
Skybolt, see Nuclear weapons
Slim, General Sir William 333–4, 345
Smith, Adam 4
Smith, Herbert 130
Smith, Ian 488–9, 495
Smoot Hawley Tariff, 1930 209
Smuts, Jan Christian 160, 164–5, 169,
    200
Snowden, Philip, Chancellor of
    Exchequer, 1924 113, 126
    1929–31 210–15, 220–3
    and National Government 225–32,
    241–4
Soames, C. 450–1
Social Democratic Federation 17
Socialist League 249–50
Solzhenitsyn, Alexander 424
Somme, Battle of 65, 71–2, 74–5, 87,
    90, 98–9, 171, 309
South Africa 20, 106, 183, 199–200, 495
South Arabian Federation 482
South East Asia Treaty Organisation
    (SEATO) 398, 495, 509
Spa Conference, 1920 151, 205
Spaak, Paul Henry 445, 448
Spanish Civil War 281–2
Spartacist Rising 156
Spear, P. 184–5
Special Areas Acts, 1934, 1937 244–5,
    372
Special Powers Act (N. Ireland), 1922
    180
Spee, Admiral M. von 83
Spinelli, Altiero 446
Spitfire 314
Stack, Austin 178
Stack, Sir Lee 193, 206
Stalin, J. V. 250, 266–7, 295–6, 318–20,
    334, 343, 424–5, 428, 437
Stamfordham, Lord 121
Stanley, Venetia 55, 60–1
Standstill Act, 1935 245, 251
Steel, David 407, 411
Steel-Maitland, Arthur 127, 130
Steiner, Z. 40
Stevenson, Frances 202
Stevenson, J. and Cook, C. 234, 253
Stewart, A. T. Q. 180
Stewart, Sir Malcolm 245
Stewart, Michael 420, 450, 453, 490
Stockholm Convention, 1959 448
Stokes, Richard 336, 474

Stone, N. 39
Stopford, Lieut.-General F. W. 79
Stormont 491–2
Strachan, Hew 309, 336
Strachey, J. 249, 253, 382
Strang, Lord 295
Strategic Air Offensive in W. War
    II 307, 324–7, 335–7
Strauss, G. R. 250, 382
Stresa Conference, 1935 275, 372
Stresemann, G. 153, 161
Sudetenland 150, 161, 265, 285–9,
    299–302
Suez Canal 192–3, 195, 315, 402, 470–1
Suez Crisis 421, 448, 471, 475–81, 500–5
Suffragette Movement 14, 94–5, 101,
    105, 136
Sukhomlinov, General V. 49, 54
Sunday Dispatch 336
Sunday Times Insight Team 491
Sunningdale Agreement, 1973 492, 513
Swales, A. B. 130
Swaziland 512
Swann, Lord 405
Sykes, C. 197–8
Sykes, Sir Mark 142
Sykes–Picot Agreement 142, 195
Syria after W. War I 142, 195–6
Syrian campaign in W. War I 72, 81

T
Taff Vale case, 1901 7
Tanganyika (Tanzania) 486, 509
Tannenburg, Battle of 65
Taranto, Battle of 316, 339
Tawney, R. H. 210
Taylor, A. J. P. 42, 138, 162, 166, 217,
    258–9, 265, 270, 284, 298–9, 316
Teheran Conference, 1943 319–20,
    374, 423
Temple, Archbishop William 365
Templer, General Sir G. 489
Ten Year Rule 162, 207, 278
Terraine, J. 62, 70, 98–9
Thakin Nu 470
Thatcher, Margaret 368, 377, 406,
    411–12, 416
Thomas, A. 479
Thomas, Hugh 281
Thomas, Ivor 387
Thomas, J. H. 126, 130, 134, 210, 213,
    215–16, 221, 223, 228, 242
Thompson, P. 26
Thomson, George 453–4
Thorneycroft, Peter (later Lord) 401
Thorpe, Jeremy 410
Three Emperors' League 36
Tiger, HMS, Talks on Rhodesia 488, 512
Tilak, B. 185
Tillett, B. 8
Times, The 1, 86, 256, 270, 352, 419, 498
Tirpitz, Admiral A. von 40, 42, 57
Tirpitz 309, 324

Tisza, Count 49
Tizard, Sir Henry 326
Todd, Garfield 487
Tomlinson, George 391
Tory Reform Committee 365–6
Tout, H. 240
Townshend, General Sir F. 81
Trade Boards Act, 1909 5
Trade Unions: Before 1914 7–8, 26, 107
  Effects of W. War I on 89–94, 103
  between the wars 117, 128–35, 158, 211–12
  and W. War II 214, 217, 221, 363–4
  post-1945 383–4, 392, 398–400, 402, 404–6, 409–10, 415
  and EEC 453, 455
Trade Union Act, 1913 128
Trade Union Congress 249, 252, 364, 381, 383, 401, 453
Trade Union Congress, General Council of 128–34, 221, 384
Trades Disputes Act, 1927 135, 206
  repealed 392
Trades Disputes Bill, 1931 213, 217
Treaty of Guarantee to Poland, 1939 294
  Confirmed 296
Treaties of Guarantee to Greece, Rumania and Turkey, 1939 294–5
Trenchard, Lord 163, 192–3, 309
Trevelyan, Sir Charles 122, 250
Trianon, Treaty of 150
Tribune 250, 394
Tripartite Agreement, Ireland, 1925 181
Triple Alliance, 1882 36, 53, 141
Triple Alliance (industrial workers) 25–6, 117
Triton Cipher 324
Trotsky, L. D. 2, 157
Truman Doctrine 430–1, 433–5, 457
Truman, Harry S. (US President)
  and nuclear weapons 334
  and end of Lend Lease 381
  and Cold War 425, 428, 430–2, 433–5, 457
  and Palestine 462, 472–3
Tuchman, Barbara 72
Tunku Abdul Raman 489
Turner, L. C. F. 39

U
U-boat campaigns, W. War I 84–5, 141, 142
  W. War II 308–10, 317–18, 320, 324
Ulster 21–2, 28–9, 175–81, 201–2, 491–3
Ulster Volunteer Force 493
Ulster Volunteers 22, 107
Ultra 308, 322
Unconditional Surrender, Decision to require 306
Unemployment, 1919–29: 110–13, 116, 123, 126
  Effects of return to gold on 137–8

1929–39: Effects of Wall Street Crash on 208–9
  Policies for 210–12, 214–16
  and 1931 crisis 219
  Condition of unemployed 234–41
  Policies for 244–6
  Protests against 251–4
  Alternative policies for 254–60
1939–45: Fall of 349
  White Paper, 1944 on 358–60, 374
1945–80: 376–7, 383, 395, 400–1
  Ending of full employment 408–9, 416, 498, 500
Unemployment Acts, 1920 116
  1924 214
  1934 245
  1946 388
Unemployment Assistance Board 245–6, 248, 251
Unemployment Benefit, Cuts in 219–22, 225, 230–1
  Restored 242
  Levels of 240, 245–6
Unemployed Insurance Fund 215, 218–20, 245, 388
Unilateral Declaration of Independence (UDI), Rhodesia 488, 511
Unilateral Nuclear Disarmament 398–9
United Nations Organisation 425, 433–5, 473–4, 478, 480, 482, 485, 488, 502–4
Uthwatt Committee, *see* Environment
Utility Scheme 350, 352

V
V1, V2 336, 340, 361–2
V Bomber Force 441
Vansittart, Sir Robert (later Lord) 270, 299
Varley, Eric 455
Vaughan, R. 444
Venizelos, E. 150, 154
Verdun, Battle of 74
Versailles, Treaty of 147–50, 151, 162, 164–8, 205, 218–19, 265, 273, 275, 278, 291, 299
Verwoerd, H., Premier of S. Africa 495
Vichy government 312
Victoria, Queen 9, 16, 23
Vietminh 435
Vietnam War 450
Viviani, René 49, 53

W
Waite, Air Commodore R. 433
Wall St. crash 207–9, 263, 267, 273
Wallace, Henry 268
Wallas, Graham 55
War Aims, in W. War I 63–4
  in W. War II 305–6
War Aims Committee 354

War Cabinet 89, 341, 343–4
War Guilt 145, 148–9
War Loan 243
Warner, G. 479, 503
Warsaw Pact 437
Washington Conferences, ARCADIA, 1942 319
  TRIDENT, 1943 319, 320
Washington Naval Conference and Agreement (Treaty), 1921–22 163, 170, 205, 263
  subsequent naval conference 1929 273
Watson–Watt, Robert 293
Watt, R. M. 144
Waugh, Evelyn 312
Wavell, Field-Marshall Archibald 316, 321, 346, 464–6
Webb, Beatrice 17, 156, 213, 250–1
Webb, Sydney (later Lord Passfield) 17, 24, 122, 156, 197, 221, 250–1
Weir, I. MacNeill 229–32
Weir, Lord 136
Weizmann, Chaim 142
Welfare State 248, 355, 359, 388–92, 424, 408
Wells, H. G. 17, 96, 156
Western Front in W. War I 68–78, 90, 96–9, 157, 175, 184, 307, 335
West Indian Federation 490, 510
Westminister, Statue of 182, 199, 371, 461, 494
Wheat Act, 1932 245
Wheatley, John 126, 210, 214
Wheeler-Bennett, J. 343
White, Charles 347
White, Stephen 156
Whitelaw, William 492
Whitley, Report, 1917 117
Wigram, Francis 97, 222
Wilhelm II, Kaiser 41, 42, 46–7, 49, 54–84, 115
Wilkinson, Ellen 252, 391
Williams, P. M. 399, 414
Willingdon, Lord 190
Willink, Henry 356
Wilmot, J. 421
Wilson, Field Marshal H. M. 334
Wilson, Harold 378–9
  1945–51 382
  Resignation, 1951 394
  Leadership 399
  Premier, 1964–70 401–7
  1974–76 410–11
  and foreign policy 419–21
  and EEC 450–1, 453–5
  and Rhodesia 488–9
  and Ireland 492
Wilson, Sir Henry 22, 39–40, 44, 180
Wilson, Sir Horace 269, 283–4, 286–8
Wilson, Keith M. 501
Wilson, Trevor 29, 86, 102

Wilson, Woodrow, and W. War I 48,
  142
  and Fourteen Points 142-4
  and peace settlements 144-50, 160,
    164-7
Windhorst, L. 35
Wingate, Orde 345
Wise, Lt.-Colonel A. P. 367
Wolfenden Report 407
Women's Land Army 349, 360
Wood, Kingsley 292, 300, 341-2, 344
Woodcock, George (author) 170, 462
Woodcock, George (TU officer) 364
Woodhead Commission on Palestine 198
Woodward, E. L. 66

Woolworth's 239
Woolf, Leonard 170
Woolton, Lord 345, 353-4, 362
Worker Representation 384
Workers' Weekly 126, 206
World Economic Conference,
  1933 274, 371
World Economic Conference,
  1935 244
Wyatt, Woodrow 403

Y
Yalta Conference, 1945 319, 321, 327,
  419, 424-5
Yeats, W. B. 493

Young, Sir Edward Hilton 242
Young, Michael 343
Young Plan on Reparations 153, 371
Younger, George 119
Younger, Kenneth 416
Ypres, Battles of 71, 73
  see Passchendaele
Yudenitch, General 157

Z
Zimbabwe
  see Rhodesia, S.
Zinoviev Letter 127, 157, 159
Zionism 142, 195-8, 471-4